Beowulf: Scholar's Edition

By Unknown
This Edition Edited by Anthony Uyl

Ingersoll, Ontario, Canada 2025

Beowulf: Scholar's Edition

Beowulf: Scholar's Edition

By Unknown
This Edition Edited by Anthony Uyl

The text of Beowulf: Scholar's Edition is all protected under Copyright ©2025 Devoted Publishing. The covers, background, layout and Devoted Publishing logo are Copyright ©2025 Devoted Publishing. This edition is published by Devoted Publishing a division of 2165467 Ontario Inc.

Contact us at: devotedpub@hotmail.com
X (Formerly Twitter): @AnthonyDevPub

Published in Ingersoll, Ontario, Canada 2025

ISBN: 978-1-77356-535-4

Beowulf: Scholar's Edition

Table of Contents

Editor's Preface 4
BEOWULF 5
  PREFACE 5
    THE STORY 6
    ABBREVIATIONS USED IN THE NOTES 8
    BIBLIOGRAPHY OF TRANSLATIONS 8
    GLOSSARY OF PROPER NAMES 9
    LIST OF WORDS AND PHRASES NOT IN GENERAL USE 13
    BEOWULF 15
    Footnotes: 109
BEOWULF 117
  Footnotes: 185
THE TALE OF BEOWULF 190
  THE MEANING OF SOME WORDS NOT COMMONLY USED NOW 265
  Errors and Inconsistencies 267
BEÓWULF: 268
  APPENDIX 341
  LIST OF NAMES; NOTES; AND GLOSSARY 343
  LIST OF NAMES 343
  ADDITIONAL 350
  Footnotes: 352
  GLOSSARY 372
  GLOSSARY TO FINNSBURH 551
  CORRECTIONS MADE TO THE SOURCE TEXT: 553

Editor's Preface

Beowulf is one of the oldest Old English epic poems that still exists today. Written sometime between the 8th and 11th century, the poem lays the the epic quest of the character Beowulf.

What you will find in this volume is quite extensive work from old editions of the poem. Many attempts have been made at translating the poem from the original Old English and as is true with any translation work, some translators prefer one word to another while another person may feel differently. For those of you with a critical mind, I have included in this book three different modern English translations for your consideration. Read one or all and judge for yourself which translation you prefer.

Lastly is included the original Old English version of the poem. When you first look at it you may think … this is English? The answer is yes. That was what modern English had first started off as and has grown into the language it is today. If anything, glancing over the prose in the original format will give you a good sense of how any language can evolve over 1,000 years.

Anthony Uyl
Editor
President/Owner Devoted Publishing

BEOWULF

AN ANGLO-SAXON EPIC POEM
TRANSLATED FROM THE HEYNE-SOCIN TEXT
BY
JNO: LESSLIE HALL, Ph. D. (J.H.U.)
Professor of English and History in The College of William and Mary
D.C. HEATH & CO., PUBLISHERS
BOSTON NEW YORK CHICAGO

TO My Wife

PREFACE

The present work is a modest effort to reproduce approximately, in modern measures, the venerable epic, Beowulf. _Approximately_, I repeat; for a very close reproduction of Anglo-Saxon verse would, to a large extent, be prose to a modern ear.

The Heyne-Socin text and glossary have been closely followed. Occasionally a deviation has been made, but always for what seemed good and sufficient reason. The translator does not aim to be an editor. Once in a while, however, he has added a conjecture of his own to the emendations quoted from the criticisms of other students of the poem.

This work is addressed to two classes of readers. From both of these alike the translator begs sympathy and co-operation. The Anglo-Saxon scholar he hopes to please by adhering faithfully to the original. The student of English literature he aims to interest by giving him, in modern garb, the most ancient epic of our race. This is a bold and venturesome undertaking; and yet there must be some students of the Teutonic past willing to follow even a daring guide, if they may read in modern phrases of the sorrows of Hrothgar, of the prowess of Beowulf, and of the feelings that stirred the hearts of our forefathers in their primeval homes.

In order to please the larger class of readers, a regular cadence has been used, a measure which, while retaining the essential characteristics of the original, permits the reader to see ahead of him in reading.

Perhaps every Anglo-Saxon scholar has his own theory as to how Beowulf should be translated. Some have given us prose versions of what we believe to be a great poem. Is it any reflection on our honored Kemble and Arnold to say that their translations fail to show a layman that Beowulf is justly called our first _epic_? Of those translators who have used verse, several have written from what would seem a mistaken point of view. Is it proper, for instance, that the grave and solemn speeches of Beowulf and Hrothgar be put in ballad measures, tripping lightly and airily along? Or, again, is it fitting that the rough martial music of Anglo-Saxon verse be interpreted to us in the smooth measures of modern blank verse? Do we hear what has been beautifully called "the clanging tread of a warrior in mail"?

Beowulf: Scholar's Edition

Of all English translations of Beowulf, that of Professor Garnett alone gives any adequate idea of the chief characteristics of this great Teutonic epic.

The measure used in the present translation is believed to be as near a reproduction of the original as modern English affords. The cadences closely resemble those used by Browning in some of his most striking poems. The four stresses of the Anglo-Saxon verse are retained, and as much thesis and anacrusis is allowed as is consistent with a regular cadence. Alliteration has been used to a large extent; but it was thought that modern ears would hardly tolerate it on every line. End-rhyme has been used occasionally; internal rhyme, sporadically. Both have some warrant in Anglo-Saxon poetry. (For end-rhyme, see 1_53, 1_54; for internal rhyme, 2_21, 6_40.)

What Gummere[1] calls the "rime-giver" has been studiously kept; _viz._, the first accented syllable in the second half-verse always carries the alliteration; and the last accented syllable alliterates only sporadically. Alternate alliteration is occasionally used as in the original. (See 7_61, 8_5.)

No two accented syllables have been brought together, except occasionally after a cæsural pause. (See 2_19 and 12_1.) Or, scientifically speaking, Sievers's C type has been avoided as not consonant with the plan of translation. Several of his types, however, constantly occur; _e.g._ A and a variant (/ x | / x) (/ x x | / x); B and a variant (x / | x /) (x x / | x /); a variant of D (/ x | / x x); E (/ x x | /). Anacrusis gives further variety to the types used in the translation.

The parallelisms of the original have been faithfully preserved. (_E.g._, 1_16 and 1_17: "Lord" and "Wielder of Glory"; 1_30, 1_31, 1_32; 2_12 and 2_13; 2_27 and 2_28; 3_5 and 3_6.) Occasionally, some loss has been sustained; but, on the other hand, a gain has here and there been made.

The effort has been made to give a decided flavor of archaism to the translation. All words not in keeping with the spirit of the poem have been avoided. Again, though many archaic words have been used, there are none, it is believed, which are not found in standard modern poetry.

With these preliminary remarks, it will not be amiss to give an outline of the story of the poem.

THE STORY

Hrothgar, king of the Danes, or Scyldings, builds a great mead-hall, or palace, in which he hopes to feast his liegemen and to give them presents. The joy of king and retainers is, however, of short duration. Grendel, the monster, is seized with hateful jealousy. He cannot brook the sounds of joyance that reach him down in his fen-dwelling near the hall. Oft and anon he goes to the joyous building, bent on direful mischief. Thane after thane is ruthlessly carried off and devoured, while no one is found strong enough and bold enough to cope with the monster. For twelve years he persecutes Hrothgar and his vassals.

Over sea, a day's voyage off, Beowulf, of the Geats, nephew of Higelac, king of the Geats, hears of Grendel's doings and of Hrothgar's misery. He resolves to crush the fell monster and relieve the aged king. With fourteen chosen companions, he sets sail for Dane-land. Reaching that country, he soon persuades Hrothgar of his ability to help him. The hours that elapse before night are spent in beer-drinking and conversation. When Hrothgar's bedtime comes he leaves the hall in charge of Beowulf, telling him that never before has he given to another the absolute wardship of his palace. All retire to rest, Beowulf, as it were, sleeping upon his arms.

Grendel comes, the great march-stepper, bearing God's anger. He seizes and kills one of the sleeping warriors. Then he advances towards Beowulf. A fierce and desperate hand-to-hand struggle ensues. No arms are used, both combatants trusting to strength and hand-grip. Beowulf tears Grendel's shoulder from its socket, and the monster retreats to his den, howling and yelling with agony and fury. The wound is fatal.

The next morning, at early dawn, warriors in numbers flock to the hall Heorot, to hear the news. Joy is boundless. Glee runs high. Hrothgar and his retainers are lavish of gratitude and of gifts.

Grendel's mother, however, comes the next night to avenge his death. She is furious and raging. While Beowulf is sleeping in a room somewhat apart from the quarters of the other warriors, she seizes one of Hrothgar's favorite counsellors, and carries him off and devours him. Beowulf is called. Determined to leave Heorot entirely purified, he arms himself, and goes down to look for the female monster. After traveling through the waters many hours, he meets her near the sea-bottom. She drags him to her den. There he sees Grendel lying dead. After a desperate and almost fatal struggle with the woman, he slays her, and swims upward in triumph, taking with him Grendel's head.

Joy is renewed at Heorot. Congratulations crowd upon the victor. Hrothgar literally pours treasures into the lap of Beowulf; and it is agreed among the vassals of the king that Beowulf will be their next liegelord.

Beowulf leaves Dane-land. Hrothgar weeps and laments at his departure.

When the hero arrives in his own land, Higelac treats him as a distinguished guest. He is the hero of the hour.

Beowulf subsequently becomes king of his own people, the Geats. After he has been ruling for fifty years, his own neighborhood is wofully harried by a fire-spewing dragon. Beowulf determines to kill him. In the ensuing struggle both Beowulf and the dragon are slain. The grief of the Geats is inexpressible. They determine, however, to leave nothing undone to honor the memory of their lord. A great funeral-pyre is built, and his body is burnt. Then a memorial-barrow is made, visible from a great distance, that sailors afar may be constantly reminded of the prowess of the national hero of Geatland.

The poem closes with a glowing tribute to his bravery, his gentleness, his goodness of heart, and his generosity.

* * * * *

It is the devout desire of this translator to hasten the day when the story of Beowulf shall be as familiar to English-speaking peoples as that of the Iliad. Beowulf is our first great epic. It is an epitomized history of the life of the Teutonic races. It brings vividly before us our forefathers of pre-Alfredian eras, in their love of war, of sea, and of adventure.

My special thanks are due to Professors Francis A. March and James A. Harrison, for advice, sympathy, and assistance.

J.L. HALL.

ABBREVIATIONS USED IN THE NOTES

B. = Bugge. C. = Cosijn. Gr. = Grein. Grdvtg. = Grundtvig. H. = Heyne. H. and S. = Harrison and Sharp. H.-So. = Heyne-Socin. K.= Kemble. Kl. = Kluge. M.= Müllenhoff. R. = Rieger. S. = Sievers. Sw. = Sweet. t.B. = ten Brink. Th. = Thorpe. W. = Wülcker.

* * * * *

BIBLIOGRAPHY OF TRANSLATIONS

~Arnold, Thomas.~--Beowulf. A heroic poem of the eighth century. London, 1876. With English translation. Prose.

~Botkine, L.~--Beowulf. Epopée Anglo-Saxonne. Havre, 1877. First French translation. Passages occasionally omitted.

~Conybeare, J.J.~--Illustrations of Anglo-Saxon Poetry. London, 1826. Full Latin translation, and some passages translated into English blank-verse.

~Ettmuller, L.~--Beowulf, stabreimend übersetzt. Zürich, 1840.

~Garnett, J.M.~--Beowulf: an Anglo-Saxon Poem, and the Fight at Finnsburg. Boston, 1882. An accurate line-for-line translation, using alliteration occasionally, and sometimes assuming a metrical cadence.

~Grein, C.W.M.~--Dichtungen der Angelsachsen, stabreimend übersetzt. 2 Bde. Göttingen, 1857-59.

~Grion, Giusto.~--Beovulf, poema epico anglo-sassone del VII. secolo, tradotto e illustrato. Lucca, 1883. First Italian translation.

~Grundtvig, N.F.S.~--Bjowulfs Drape. Copenhagen, 1820.

~Heyne, M.~--A translation in iambic measures. Paderborn, 1863.

~Kemble, J.M.~--The Anglo-Saxon Poems of Beowulf, the Traveller's Song, and the Battle of Finnsburg. London, 1833. The second edition contains a prose translation of Beowulf.

~Leo, H.~--Ueber Beowulf. Halle, 1839. Translations of extracts.

~Lumsden, H.W.~--Beowulf, translated into modern rhymes. London, 1881. Ballad measures. Passages occasionally omitted.

~Sandras, G.S.~--De carminibus Cædmoni adjudicatis. Paris, 1859. An extract from Beowulf, with Latin translation.

~Schaldmose, F.~--Beowulf og Scopes Widsith, to Angelsaxiske Digte. Copenhagen, 1847.

~Simrock, K.~--Beowulf. Uebersetzt und erläutert. Stuttgart und Augsburg, 1859. Alliterative measures.

~Thorkelin, G.J.~--De Danorum rebus gestis secul. III. et IV. poema Danicum dialecto Anglosaxonica. Havniæ, 1815. Latin translation.

~Thorpe, B.~--The Anglo-Saxon Poems of Beowulf, the Scôp or Gleeman's Tale, and the Fight at Finnsburg. Oxford, 1855. English translation in short lines, generally containing two stresses.

~Wackerbarth, A.D.~--Beowulf, translated into English verse. London, 1849.

~Wickberg, R.~--Beowulf, en fornengelsk hjeltedikt, öfersatt. Westervik. First Swedish translation.

~von Wolzogen, H.~--Beowulf, in alliterative measures. Leipzig.

~Zinsser, G.~--Der Kampf Beowulfs mit Grendel. Jahresbericht of the Realschule at Forbach, 1881.

GLOSSARY OF PROPER NAMES

[The figures refer to the divisions of the poem in which the respective names occur. The large figures refer to fitts, the small, to lines in the fitts.]

~Ælfhere~.--A kinsman of Wiglaf.--36_3.

~Æschere~.--Confidential friend of King Hrothgar. Elder brother of Yrmenlaf. Killed by Grendel.--21_3; 30_89.

~Beanstan~.--Father of Breca.--9_26.

~Beowulf~.--Son of Scyld, the founder of the dynasty of Scyldings. Father of Healfdene, and grandfather of Hrothgar.--1_18; 2_1.

~Beowulf~.--The hero of the poem. Sprung from the stock of Geats, son of Ecgtheow. Brought up by his maternal grandfather Hrethel, and figuring in manhood as a devoted liegeman of his uncle Higelac. A hero from his youth. Has the strength of thirty men. Engages in a swimming-match with Breca. Goes to the help of Hrothgar against the monster Grendel. Vanquishes Grendel and his mother. Afterwards becomes king of the Geats. Late in life attempts to kill a fire-spewing dragon, and is slain. Is buried with great honors. His memorial mound.--6_26; 7_2; 7_9; 9_3; 9_8; 12_28; 12_43; 23_1, etc.

~Breca~.--Beowulf's opponent in the famous swimming-match.--9_8; 9_19; 9_21; 9_22.

~Brondings~.--A people ruled by Breca.--9_23.

~Brosinga mene~.--A famous collar once owned by the Brosings.--19_7.

~Cain~.--Progenitor of Grendel and other monsters.--2_56; 20_11.

~Dæghrefn~.--A warrior of the Hugs, killed by Beowulf.--35_40.

~Danes~.--Subjects of Scyld and his descendants, and hence often called Scyldings. Other names for them are Victory-Scyldings, Honor-Scyldings, Armor-Danes, Bright-Danes, East-Danes, West-Danes, North-Danes, South-Danes, Ingwins, Hrethmen.--1_1; 2_1; 3_2; 5_14; 7_1, etc.

~Ecglaf~.--Father of Unferth, who taunts Beowulf.--9_1.

~Ecgtheow~.--Father of Beowulf, the hero of the poem. A widely-known Wægmunding warrior. Marries Hrethel's daughter. After slaying Heatholaf, a Wylfing, he flees his country.--7_3; 5_6; 8_4.

~Ecgwela~.--A king of the Danes before Scyld.--25_60.

~Elan~.--Sister of Hrothgar, and probably wife of Ongentheow, king of the Swedes.--2_10.

~Eagle Cape~.--A promontory in Geat-land, under which took place Beowulf's last encounter.--41_87.

~Eadgils~.--Son of Ohthere and brother of Eanmund.--34_2.

~Eanmund~.--Son of Ohthere and brother of Eadgils. The reference to these brothers is vague, and variously understood. Heyne supposes as follows: Raising a revolt against their father, they are obliged to leave Sweden. They go to the land of the Geats; with what intention, is not known, but probably to conquer and plunder. The Geatish king, Heardred, is slain by one of the brothers, probably Eanmund.--36_10; 31_54 to 31_60; 33_66 to 34_6.

~Eofor~.--A Geatish hero who slays Ongentheow in war, and is rewarded by Hygelac with the hand of his only daughter.--41_18; 41_48.

~Eormenric~.--A Gothic king, from whom Hama took away the famous Brosinga mene.--19_9.

~Eomær~.--Son of Offa and Thrytho, king and queen of the Angles.--28_69.

~Finn~.--King of the North-Frisians and the Jutes. Marries Hildeburg. At his court takes place the horrible slaughter in which the Danish general, Hnæf, fell. Later on, Finn himself is slain by Danish warriors.--17_18; 17_30; 17_44; 18_4; 18_23.

~Fin-land~.--The country to which Beowulf was driven by the currents in his swimming-match.--10_22.

~Fitela~.--Son and nephew of King Sigemund, whose praises are sung in XIV.--14_42; 14_53.

~Folcwalda~.--Father of Finn.--17_38.

~Franks~.--Introduced occasionally in referring to the death of Higelac.--19_19; 40_21; 40_24.

~Frisians~.--A part of them are ruled by Finn. Some of them were engaged in the struggle in which Higelac was slain.--17_20; 17_42; 17_52; 40_21.

~Freaware~.--Daughter of King Hrothgar. Married to Ingeld, a Heathobard prince.--29_60; 30_32.

~Froda~.--King of the Heathobards, and father of Ingeld.--29_62.

~Garmund~.--Father of Offa.--28_71.

~Geats, Geatmen~.--The race to which the hero of the poem belongs. Also called Weder-Geats, or Weders, War-Geats, Sea-Geats. They are ruled by Hrethel, Hæthcyn, Higelac, and Beowulf.--4_7; 7_4; 10_45; 11_8; 27_14; 28_8.

~Gepids~.--Named in connection with the Danes and Swedes.--35_34.

~Grendel~.--A monster of the race of Cain. Dwells in the fens and moors. Is furiously envious when he hears sounds of joy in Hrothgar's palace. Causes the king untold agony for years. Is finally conquered by Beowulf, and dies of his wound. His hand and arm are hung up in Hrothgar's hall Heorot. His head is cut off by Beowulf when he goes down to fight with Grendel's mother.--2_50; 3_1; 3_13; 8_19; 11_17; 12_2; 13_27; 15_3.

~Guthlaf~.--A Dane of Hnæf's party.--18_24.

~Half-Danes~.--Branch of the Danes to which Hnæf belonged.--17_19.

~Halga~.--Surnamed the Good. Younger brother of Hrothgar.--2_9.

~Hama~.--Takes the Brosinga mene from Eormenric.--19_7.

~Hæreth~.--Father of Higelac's queen, Hygd.--28_39; 29_18.

~Hæthcyn~.--Son of Hrethel and brother of Higelac. Kills his brother Herebeald accidentally. Is slain at Ravenswood, fighting against Ongentheow.--34_43; 35_23; 40_32.

~Helmings~.--The race to which Queen Wealhtheow belonged.--10_63.

~Heming~.--A kinsman of Garmund, perhaps nephew.--28_54; 28_70.

~Hengest~.--A Danish leader. Takes command on the fall of Hnæf.--17_33; 17_41.

~Herebeald~.--Eldest son of Hrethel, the Geatish king, and brother of Higelac. Killed by his younger brother Hæthcyn.--34_43; 34_47.

~Heremod~.--A Danish king of a dynasty before the Scylding line. Was a source of great sorrow to his people.--14_64; 25_59.

~Hereric~.--Referred to as uncle of Heardred, but otherwise unknown.--31_60.

~Hetwars~.--Another name for the Franks.--33_51.

~Healfdene~.--Grandson of Scyld and father of Hrothgar. Ruled the Danes long and well.--2_5; 4_1; 8_14.

~Heardred~.--Son of Higelac and Hygd, king and queen of the Geats. Succeeds his father, with Beowulf as regent. Is slain by the sons of Ohthere.--31_56; 33_63; 33_75.

~Heathobards~.--Race of Lombards, of which Froda is king. After Froda falls in battle with the Danes, Ingeld, his son, marries Hrothgar's daughter, Freaware, in order to heal the feud.--30_1; 30_6.

~Heatholaf~.--A Wylfing warrior slain by Beowulf's father.--8_5.

~Heathoremes~.--The people on whose shores Breca is cast by the waves during his contest with Beowulf.--9_21.

~Heorogar~.--Elder brother of Hrothgar, and surnamed 'Weoroda Ræswa,' Prince of the Troopers.--2_9; 8_12.

~Hereward~.--Son of the above.--31_17.

~Heort~, ~Heorot~.--The great mead-hall which King Hrothgar builds. It is invaded by Grendel for twelve years. Finally cleansed by Beowulf, the Geat. It is called Heort on account of the hart-antlers which decorate it.--2_25; 3_32; 3_52.

~Hildeburg~.--Wife of Finn, daughter of Hoce, and related to Hnæf,--probably his sister.--17_21; 18_34.

~Hnæf~.--Leader of a branch of the Danes called Half-Danes. Killed in the struggle at Finn's castle.--17_19; 17_61.

~Hondscio~.--One of Beowulf's companions. Killed by Grendel just before Beowulf grappled with that monster.--30_43.

~Hoce~.--Father of Hildeburg and probably of Hnæf.--17_26.

~Hrethel~.--King of the Geats, father of Higelac, and grandfather of Beowulf.--7_4; 34_39.

~Hrethla~.--Once used for Hrethel.--7_82.

~Hrethmen~.--Another name for the Danes.--7_73.

~Hrethric~.--Son of Hrothgar.--18_65; 27_19.

~Hreosna-beorh~.--A promontory in Geat-land, near which Ohthere's sons made plundering raids.--35_18.

~Hrothgar~.--The Danish king who built the hall Heort, but was long unable to enjoy it on account of Grendel's persecutions. Marries Wealhtheow, a Helming lady. Has two sons and a daughter. Is a typical Teutonic king, lavish of gifts. A devoted liegelord, as his lamentations over slain liegemen prove. Also very appreciative of kindness, as is shown by his loving gratitude to Beowulf.--2_9; 2_12; 4_1; 8_10; 15_1; etc., etc.

~Hrothmund~.--Son of Hrothgar.--18_65.

~Hrothulf~.--Probably a son of Halga, younger brother of Hrothgar. Certainly on terms of close intimacy in Hrothgar's palace.--16_26; 18_57.

~Hrunting~.--Unferth's sword, lent to Beowulf.--22_71; 25_9.

~Hugs~.--A race in alliance with the Franks and Frisians at the time of Higelac's fall.--35_41.

~Hun~.--A Frisian warrior, probably general of the Hetwars. Gives Hengest a beautiful sword.--18_19.

~Hunferth~.--Sometimes used for Unferth.

~Hygelac~, ~Higelac~.--King of the Geats, uncle and liegelord of Beowulf, the hero of the poem.--His second wife is the lovely Hygd, daughter of Hæreth. The son of their union is Heardred. Is slain in a war with the Hugs, Franks, and Frisians

11

combined. Beowulf is regent, and afterwards king of the Geats.--4_6; 5_4; 28_34; 29_9; 29_21; 31_56.

~Hygd~.--Wife of Higelac, and daughter of Hæreth. There are some indications that she married Beowulf after she became a widow.--28_37.

~Ingeld~.--Son of the Heathobard king, Froda. Marries Hrothgar's daughter, Freaware, in order to reconcile the two peoples.--29_62; 30_32.

~Ingwins~.--Another name for the Danes.--16_52; 20_69.

~Jutes~.--Name sometimes applied to Finn's people.--17_22; 17_38; 18_17.

~Lafing~.--Name of a famous sword presented to Hengest by Hun.--18_19.

~Merewing~.--A Frankish king, probably engaged in the war in which Higelac was slain.--40_29.

~Nægling~.--Beowulf's sword.--36_76.

~Offa~.--King of the Angles, and son of Garmund. Marries the terrible Thrytho who is so strongly contrasted with Hygd.--28_59; 28_66.

~Ohthere~.--Son of Ongentheow, king of the Swedes. He is father of Eanmund and Eadgils.--40_35; 40_39.

~Onela~.--Brother of Ohthere.--36_15; 40_39.

~Ongentheow~.--King of Sweden, of the Scylfing dynasty. Married, perhaps, Elan, daughter of Healfdene.--35_26; 41_16.

~Oslaf~.--A Dane of Hnæf's party.--18_24.

~Ravenswood~.--The forest near which Hæthcyn was slain.--40_31; 40_41.

~Scefing~.--Applied (1_4) to Scyld, and meaning 'son of Scef.'

~Scyld~.--Founder of the dynasty to which Hrothgar, his father, and grandfather belonged. He dies, and his body is put on a vessel, and set adrift. He goes from Daneland just as he had come to it--in a bark.--1_4; 1_19; 1_27.

~Scyldings~.--The descendants of Scyld. They are also called Honor-Scyldings, Victory-Scyldings, War-Scyldings, etc. (See 'Danes,' above.)--2_1; 7_1; 8_1.

~Scylfings~.--A Swedish royal line to which Wiglaf belonged.--36_2.

~Sigemund~.--Son of Wæls, and uncle and father of Fitela. His struggle with a dragon is related in connection with Beowulf's deeds of prowess.--14_38; 14_47.

~Swerting~.--Grandfather of Higelac, and father of Hrethel.--19_11.

~Swedes~.--People of Sweden, ruled by the Scylfings.--35_13.

~Thrytho~.--Wife of Offa, king of the Angles. Known for her fierce and unwomanly disposition. She is introduced as a contrast to the gentle Hygd, queen of Higelac.--28_42; 28_56.

~Unferth~.--Son of Ecglaf, and seemingly a confidential courtier of Hrothgar. Taunts Beowulf for having taken part in the swimming-match. Lends Beowulf his sword when he goes to look for Grendel's mother. In the MS. sometimes written _Hunferth_.9_1; 18_41.

~Wæls~.--Father of Sigemund.--14_60.

~Wægmunding~.--A name occasionally applied to Wiglaf and Beowulf, and perhaps derived from a common ancestor, Wægmund.--36_6; 38_61.

~Weders~.--Another name for Geats or Wedergeats.

~Wayland~.--A fabulous smith mentioned in this poem and in other old Teutonic literature.--7_83.

~Wendels~.--The people of Wulfgar, Hrothgar's messenger and retainer. (Perhaps = Vandals.)--6_30.

~Wealhtheow~.--Wife of Hrothgar. Her queenly courtesy is well shown in the poem.--10_55.

~Weohstan~, or ~Wihstan~.--A Wægmunding, and father of Wiglaf.--36_1.

~Whale's Ness~.--A prominent promontory, on which Beowulf's mound was built.--38_52; 42_76.

~Wiglaf~.--Son of Wihstan, and related to Beowulf. He remains faithful to Beowulf in the fatal struggle with the fire-drake. Would rather die than leave his lord in his dire emergency.--36_1; 36_3; 36_28.

~Wonred~.--Father of Wulf and Eofor.--41_20; 41_26.

~Wulf~.--Son of Wonred. Engaged in the battle between Higelac's and Ongentheow's forces, and had a hand-to-hand fight with Ongentheow himself. Ongentheow disables him, and is thereupon slain by Eofor.--41_19; 41_29.

~Wulfgar~.--Lord of the Wendels, and retainer of Hrothgar.--6_18; 6_30.

~Wylfings~.--A people to whom belonged Heatholaf, who was slain by Ecgtheow.--8_6; 8_16.

~Yrmenlaf~.--Younger brother of Æschere, the hero whose death grieved Hrothgar so deeply.--21_4.

LIST OF WORDS AND PHRASES NOT IN GENERAL USE

ATHELING.--Prince, nobleman.
BAIRN.--Son, child.
BARROW.--Mound, rounded hill, funeral-mound.
BATTLE-SARK.--Armor.
BEAKER.--Cup, drinking-vessel.
BEGEAR.--Prepare.
BIGHT.--Bay, sea.
BILL.--Sword.
BOSS.--Ornamental projection.
BRACTEATE.--A round ornament on a necklace.
BRAND.--Sword.
BURN.--Stream.
BURNIE.--Armor.
CARLE.--Man, hero.
EARL.--Nobleman, any brave man.
EKE.--Also.
EMPRISE.--Enterprise, undertaking.
ERST.--Formerly.
ERST-WORTHY.--Worthy for a long time past.
FAIN.--Glad.
FERRY.--Bear, carry.
FEY.--Fated, doomed.
FLOAT.--Vessel, ship.
FOIN.--To lunge (Shaks.).
GLORY OF KINGS.--God.
GREWSOME.--Cruel, fierce.
HEFT.--Handle, hilt; used by synecdoche for 'sword.'
HELM.--Helmet, protector.
HENCHMAN.--Retainer, vassal.
HIGHT.--Am (was) named.

HOLM.--Ocean, curved surface of the sea.
HIMSEEMED.--(It) seemed to him.
LIEF.--Dear, valued.
MERE.--Sea; in compounds, 'mere-ways,' 'mere-currents,' etc.
MICKLE.--Much.
NATHLESS.--Nevertheless.
NAZE.--Edge (nose).
NESS.--Edge.
NICKER.--Sea-beast.
QUIT, QUITE.--Requite.
RATHE.--Quickly.
REAVE.--Bereave, deprive.
SAIL-ROAD.--Sea.
SETTLE.--Seat, bench.
SKINKER.--One who pours.
SOOTHLY.--Truly.
SWINGE.--Stroke, blow.
TARGE, TARGET.--Shield.
THROUGHLY.--Thoroughly.
TOLD.--Counted.
UNCANNY.--Ill-featured, grizzly.
UNNETHE.--Difficult.
WAR-SPEED.--Success in war.
WEB.--Tapestry (that which is 'woven').
WEEDED.--Clad (cf. widow's weeds).
WEEN.--Suppose, imagine.
WEIRD.--Fate, Providence.
WHILOM.--At times, formerly, often.
WIELDER.--Ruler. Often used of God; also in compounds, as 'Wielder of Glory,' 'Wielder of Worship.'
WIGHT.--Creature.
WOLD.--Plane, extended surface.
WOT.--Knows.
YOUNKER.--Youth.

BEOWULF

I - THE LIFE AND DEATH OF SCYLD
(The famous race of Spear-Danes.)

Lo! the Spear-Danes' glory through splendid achievements
The folk-kings' former fame we have heard of,
How princes displayed then their prowess-in-battle.

(Scyld, their mighty king, in honor of whom they are often called Scyldings. He is the great-grandfather of Hrothgar, so prominent in the poem.)

Oft Scyld the Scefing from scathers in numbers
From many a people their mead-benches tore.
Since first he found him friendless and wretched,
The earl had had terror: comfort he got for it,
Waxed 'neath the welkin, world-honor gained,
Till all his neighbors o'er sea were compelled to
Bow to his bidding and bring him their tribute:
An excellent atheling! After was borne him

(A son is born to him, who receives the name of Beowulf--a name afterwards made so famous by the hero of the poem.)

A son and heir, young in his dwelling,
Whom God-Father sent to solace the people.
He had marked the misery malice had caused them,
[1]That reaved of their rulers they wretched had erstwhile
Long been afflicted. The Lord, in requital,
Wielder of Glory, with world-honor blessed him.
Famed was Beowulf, far spread the glory
Of Scyld's great son in the lands of the Danemen.[2]

(The ideal Teutonic king lavishes gifts on his vassals.)

So the carle that is young, by kindnesses rendered
The friends of his father, with fees in abundance
Must be able to earn that when age approacheth
Eager companions aid him requitingly,
When war assaults him serve him as liegemen:
By praise-worthy actions must honor be got
'Mong all of the races. At the hour that was fated

(Scyld dies at the hour appointed by Fate.)

Scyld then departed to the All-Father's keeping
Warlike to wend him; away then they bare him
To the flood of the current, his fond-loving comrades,
As himself he had bidden, while the friend of the Scyldings
Word-sway wielded, and the well-lovèd land-prince
Long did rule them.³ The ring-stemmèd vessel,
Bark of the atheling, lay there at anchor,
Icy in glimmer and eager for sailing;

(By his own request, his body is laid on a vessel and wafted seaward.)

The belovèd leader laid they down there,
Giver of rings, on the breast of the vessel,
The famed by the mainmast. A many of jewels,
Of fretted embossings, from far-lands brought over,
Was placed near at hand then; and heard I not ever
That a folk ever furnished a float more superbly
With weapons of warfare, weeds for the battle,
Bills and burnies; on his bosom sparkled
Many a jewel that with him must travel
On the flush of the flood afar on the current.
And favors no fewer they furnished him soothly,
Excellent folk-gems, than others had given him

(He leaves Daneland on the breast of a bark.)

Who when first he was born outward did send him
Lone on the main, the merest of infants:
And a gold-fashioned standard they stretched under heaven
High o'er his head, let the holm-currents bear him,
Seaward consigned him: sad was their spirit,
Their mood very mournful. Men are not able

(No one knows whither the boat drifted.)

Soothly to tell us, they in halls who reside,⁴
Heroes under heaven, to what haven he hied.

II - SCYLD'S SUCCESSORS.--HROTHGAR'S GREAT MEAD-HALL

(Beowulf succeeds his father Scyld)

In the boroughs then Beowulf, bairn of the Scyldings,
Belovèd land-prince, for long-lasting season
Was famed mid the folk (his father departed,
The prince from his dwelling), till afterward sprang
Great-minded Healfdene; the Danes in his lifetime
He graciously governed, grim-mooded, agèd.

(Healfdene's birth.)

Four bairns of his body born in succession
Woke in the world, war-troopers' leader
Heorogar, Hrothgar, and Halga the good;
Heard I that Elan was Ongentheow's consort,

(He has three sons--one of them, Hrothgar--and a daughter named Elan. Hrothgar becomes a mighty king.)

The well-beloved bedmate of the War-Scylfing leader.
Then glory in battle to Hrothgar was given,
Waxing of war-fame, that willingly kinsmen
Obeyed his bidding, till the boys grew to manhood,
A numerous band. It burned in his spirit
To urge his folk to found a great building,
A mead-hall grander than men of the era

(He is eager to build a great hall in which he may feast his retainers)

Ever had heard of, and in it to share
With young and old all of the blessings
The Lord had allowed him, save life and retainers.
Then the work I find afar was assigned
To many races in middle-earth's regions,
To adorn the great folk-hall. In due time it happened
Early 'mong men, that 'twas finished entirely,
The greatest of hall-buildings; Heorot he named it

(The hall is completed, and is called Heort, or Heorot.)

Who wide-reaching word-sway wielded 'mong earlmen.
His promise he brake not, rings he lavished,
Treasure at banquet. Towered the hall up
High and horn-crested, huge between antlers:
It battle-waves bided, the blasting fire-demon;
Ere long then from hottest hatred must sword-wrath
Arise for a woman's husband and father.
Then the mighty war-spirit[1] endured for a season,

(The Monster Grendel is madly envious of the Danemen's joy.)

Bore it bitterly, he who bided in darkness,
That light-hearted laughter loud in the building
Greeted him daily; there was dulcet harp-music,
Clear song of the singer. He said that was able

(The course of the story is interrupted by a short reference to some old account of the creation.)

17

Beowulf: Scholar's Edition

To tell from of old earthmen's beginnings,
That Father Almighty earth had created,
The winsome wold that the water encircleth,
Set exultingly the sun's and the moon's beams
To lavish their lustre on land-folk and races,
And earth He embellished in all her regions
With limbs and leaves; life He bestowed too
On all the kindreds that live under heaven.

(The glee of the warriors is overcast by a horrible dread.)

So blessed with abundance, brimming with joyance,
The warriors abided, till a certain one gan to
Dog them with deeds of direfullest malice,
A foe in the hall-building: this horrible stranger[2]
Was Grendel entitled, the march-stepper famous
Who[3] dwelt in the moor-fens, the marsh and the fastness;
The wan-mooded being abode for a season
In the land of the giants, when the Lord and Creator
Had banned him and branded. For that bitter murder,
The killing of Abel, all-ruling Father

(Cain is referred to as a progenitor of Grendel, and of monsters in general.)

The kindred of Cain crushed with His vengeance;
In the feud He rejoiced not, but far away drove him
From kindred and kind, that crime to atone for,
Meter of Justice. Thence ill-favored creatures,
Elves and giants, monsters of ocean,
Came into being, and the giants that longtime
Grappled with God; He gave them requital.

III - GRENDEL THE MURDERER
(Grendel attacks the sleeping heroes)

When the sun was sunken, he set out to visit
The lofty hall-building, how the Ring-Danes had used it
For beds and benches when the banquet was over.
Then he found there reposing many a noble
Asleep after supper; sorrow the heroes,[1]
Misery knew not. The monster of evil
Greedy and cruel tarried but little,

(He drags off thirty of them, and devours them)

Fell and frantic, and forced from their slumbers
Thirty of thanemen; thence he departed
Leaping and laughing, his lair to return to,
With surfeit of slaughter sallying homeward.

In the dusk of the dawning, as the day was just breaking,
Was Grendel's prowess revealed to the warriors:

(A cry of agony goes up, when Grendel's horrible deed is fully realized.)

Then, his meal-taking finished, a moan was uplifted,
Morning-cry mighty. The man-ruler famous,
The long-worthy atheling, sat very woful,
Suffered great sorrow, sighed for his liegemen,
When they had seen the track of the hateful pursuer,
The spirit accursèd: too crushing that sorrow,

(The monster returns the next night.)

Too loathsome and lasting. Not longer he tarried,
But one night after continued his slaughter
Shameless and shocking, shrinking but little
From malice and murder; they mastered him fully.
He was easy to find then who otherwise looked for
A pleasanter place of repose in the lodges,
A bed in the bowers. Then was brought to his notice
Told him truly by token apparent
The hall-thane's hatred: he held himself after
Further and faster who the foeman did baffle.
[2]So ruled he and strongly strove against justice
Lone against all men, till empty uptowered

(King Hrothgar's agony and suspense last twelve years.)

The choicest of houses. Long was the season:
Twelve-winters' time torture suffered
The friend of the Scyldings, every affliction,
Endless agony; hence it after[3] became
Certainly known to the children of men
Sadly in measures, that long against Hrothgar
Grendel struggled:--his grudges he cherished,
Murderous malice, many a winter,
Strife unremitting, and peacefully wished he
[4]Life-woe to lift from no liegeman at all of
The men of the Dane-folk, for money to settle,
No counsellor needed count for a moment
On handsome amends at the hands of the murderer;

(Grendel is unremitting in his persecutions.)

The monster of evil fiercely did harass,
The ill-planning death-shade, both elder and younger,
Trapping and tricking them. He trod every night then
The mist-covered moor-fens; men do not know where

Witches and wizards wander and ramble.
So the foe of mankind many of evils
Grievous injuries, often accomplished,
Horrible hermit; Heort he frequented,
Gem-bedecked palace, when night-shades had fallen

(God is against the monster.)

Since God did oppose him, not the throne could he touch,[5]
The light-flashing jewel, love of Him knew not).
'Twas a fearful affliction to the friend of the Scyldings

(The king and his council deliberate in vain.)

Soul-crushing sorrow. Not seldom in private
Sat the king in his council; conference held they
What the braves should determine 'gainst terrors unlooked for.

(They invoke the aid of their gods.)

At the shrines of their idols often they promised
Gifts and offerings, earnestly prayed they
The devil from hell would help them to lighten
Their people's oppression. Such practice they used then,
Hope of the heathen; hell they remembered
In innermost spirit, God they knew not,

(The true God they do not know.)

Judge of their actions, All-wielding Ruler,
No praise could they give the Guardian of Heaven,
The Wielder of Glory. Woe will be his who
Through furious hatred his spirit shall drive to
The clutch of the fire, no comfort shall look for,
Wax no wiser; well for the man who,
Living his life-days, his Lord may face
And find defence in his Father's embrace!

IV - BEOWULF GOES TO HROTHGAR'S ASSISTANCE

(Hrothgar sees no way of escape from the persecutions of Grendel.)

So Healfdene's kinsman constantly mused on
His long-lasting sorrow; the battle-thane clever
Was not anywise able evils to 'scape from:
Too crushing the sorrow that came to the people,
Loathsome and lasting the life-grinding torture,

(Beowulf, the Geat, hero of the poem, hears of Hrothgar's sorrow, and resolves to go to his assistance.)

Greatest of night-woes. So Higelac's liegeman,
Good amid Geatmen, of Grendel's achievements
Heard in his home:[1] of heroes then living
He was stoutest and strongest, sturdy and noble.
He bade them prepare him a bark that was trusty;
He said he the war-king would seek o'er the ocean,
The folk-leader noble, since he needed retainers.
For the perilous project prudent companions
Chided him little, though loving him dearly;
They egged the brave atheling, augured him glory.

(With fourteen carefully chosen companions, he sets out for Dane-land.)

The excellent knight from the folk of the Geatmen
Had liegemen selected, likest to prove them
Trustworthy warriors; with fourteen companions
The vessel he looked for; a liegeman then showed them,
A sea-crafty man, the bounds of the country.
Fast the days fleeted; the float was a-water,
The craft by the cliff. Clomb to the prow then
Well-equipped warriors: the wave-currents twisted
The sea on the sand; soldiers then carried
On the breast of the vessel bright-shining jewels,
Handsome war-armor; heroes outshoved then,
Warmen the wood-ship, on its wished-for adventure.

(The vessel sails like a bird)

The foamy-necked floater fanned by the breeze,
Likest a bird, glided the waters,

(In twenty four hours they reach the shores of Hrothgar's dominions)

Till twenty and four hours thereafter
The twist-stemmed vessel had traveled such distance
That the sailing-men saw the sloping embankments,
The sea cliffs gleaming, precipitous mountains,
Nesses enormous: they were nearing the limits
At the end of the ocean.[2] Up thence quickly
The men of the Weders clomb to the mainland,
Fastened their vessel (battle weeds rattled,
War burnies clattered), the Wielder they thanked
That the ways o'er the waters had waxen so gentle.

(They are hailed by the Danish coast guard)

Then well from the cliff edge the guard of the Scyldings
Who the sea-cliffs should see to, saw o'er the gangway
Brave ones bearing beauteous targets,

Armor all ready, anxiously thought he,
Musing and wondering what men were approaching.
High on his horse then Hrothgar's retainer
Turned him to coastward, mightily brandished
His lance in his hands, questioned with boldness.

(His challenge)

"Who are ye men here, mail-covered warriors
Clad in your corslets, come thus a-driving
A high riding ship o'er the shoals of the waters,
[3]And hither 'neath helmets have hied o'er the ocean?
I have been strand-guard, standing as warden,
Lest enemies ever anywise ravage
Danish dominions with army of war-ships.
More boldly never have warriors ventured
Hither to come; of kinsmen's approval,
Word-leave of warriors, I ween that ye surely

(He is struck by Beowulf's appearance.)

Nothing have known. Never a greater one
Of earls o'er the earth have I had a sight of
Than is one of your number, a hero in armor;
No low-ranking fellow[4] adorned with his weapons,
But launching them little, unless looks are deceiving,
And striking appearance. Ere ye pass on your journey
As treacherous spies to the land of the Scyldings
And farther fare, I fully must know now
What race ye belong to. Ye far-away dwellers,
Sea-faring sailors, my simple opinion
Hear ye and hearken: haste is most fitting
Plainly to tell me what place ye are come from."

V - THE GEATS REACH HEOROT
(Beowulf courteously replies.)

The chief of the strangers rendered him answer,
War-troopers' leader, and word-treasure opened:

(We are Geats.)

"We are sprung from the lineage of the people of Geatland,
And Higelac's hearth-friends. To heroes unnumbered

(My father Ecgtheow was well-known in his day.)

My father was known, a noble head-warrior
Ecgtheow titled; many a winter

Beowulf: Scholar's Edition

He lived with the people, ere he passed on his journey,
Old from his dwelling; each of the counsellors
Widely mid world-folk well remembers him.

(Our intentions towards King Hrothgar are of the kindest.)

We, kindly of spirit, the lord of thy people,
The son of King Healfdene, have come here to visit,
Folk-troop's defender: be free in thy counsels!
To the noble one bear we a weighty commission,
The helm of the Danemen; we shall hide, I ween,

(Is it true that a monster is slaying Danish heroes?)

Naught of our message. Thou know'st if it happen,
As we soothly heard say, that some savage despoiler,
Some hidden pursuer, on nights that are murky
By deeds very direful 'mid the Danemen exhibits
Hatred unheard of, horrid destruction
And the falling of dead. From feelings least selfish

(I can help your king to free himself from this horrible creature.)

I am able to render counsel to Hrothgar,
How he, wise and worthy, may worst the destroyer,
If the anguish of sorrow should ever be lessened,[1]
Comfort come to him, and care-waves grow cooler,
Or ever hereafter he agony suffer
And troublous distress, while towereth upward
The handsomest of houses high on the summit."

(The coast-guard reminds Beowulf that it is easier to say than to do.)

Bestriding his stallion, the strand-watchman answered,
The doughty retainer: "The difference surely
'Twixt words and works, the warlike shield-bearer
Who judgeth wisely well shall determine.
This band, I hear, beareth no malice

(I am satisfied of your good intentions, and shall lead you to the palace.)

To the prince of the Scyldings. Pass ye then onward
With weapons and armor. I shall lead you in person;
To my war-trusty vassals command I shall issue
To keep from all injury your excellent vessel,

(Your boat shall be well cared for during your stay here.)

23

Your fresh-tarred craft, 'gainst every opposer
Close by the sea-shore, till the curved-neckèd bark shall
Waft back again the well-beloved hero
O'er the way of the water to Weder dominions.

(He again compliments Beowulf.)

To warrior so great 'twill be granted sure
In the storm of strife to stand secure."
Onward they fared then (the vessel lay quiet,
The broad-bosomed bark was bound by its cable,
Firmly at anchor); the boar-signs glistened[2]
Bright on the visors vivid with gilding,
Blaze-hardened, brilliant; the boar acted warden.
The heroes hastened, hurried the liegemen,

(The land is perhaps rolling.)

Descended together, till they saw the great palace,
The well-fashioned wassail-hall wondrous and gleaming:

(Heorot flashes on their view.)

'Mid world-folk and kindreds that was widest reputed
Of halls under heaven which the hero abode in;
Its lustre enlightened lands without number.
Then the battle-brave hero showed them the glittering
Court of the bold ones, that they easily thither
Might fare on their journey; the aforementioned warrior
Turning his courser, quoth as he left them:

(The coast-guard, having discharged his duty, bids them God-speed.)

"'Tis time I were faring; Father Almighty
Grant you His grace, and give you to journey
Safe on your mission! To the sea I will get me
'Gainst hostile warriors as warden to stand."

VI - BEOWULF INTRODUCES HIMSELF AT THE PALACE

The highway glistened with many-hued pebble,
A by-path led the liegemen together.
[1]Firm and hand-locked the war-burnie glistened,
The ring-sword radiant rang 'mid the armor
As the party was approaching the palace together

(They set their arms and armor against the wall.)

In warlike equipments. 'Gainst the wall of the building
Their wide-fashioned war-shields they weary did set then,
Battle-shields sturdy; benchward they turned then;
Their battle-sarks rattled, the gear of the heroes;
The lances stood up then, all in a cluster,
The arms of the seamen, ashen-shafts mounted
With edges of iron: the armor-clad troopers

(A Danish hero asks them whence and why they are come.)

Were decked with weapons. Then a proud-mooded hero
Asked of the champions questions of lineage:
"From what borders bear ye your battle-shields plated,
Gilded and gleaming, your gray-colored burnies,
Helmets with visors and heap of war-lances?--
To Hrothgar the king I am servant and liegeman.
'Mong folk from far-lands found I have never

(He expresses no little admiration for the strangers.)

Men so many of mien more courageous.
I ween that from valor, nowise as outlaws,
But from greatness of soul ye sought for King Hrothgar."

(Beowulf replies.)

Then the strength-famous earlman answer rendered,
The proud-mooded Wederchief replied to his question,

(We are Higelac's table-companions, and bear an important commission to your prince.)

Hardy 'neath helmet: "Higelac's mates are we;
Beowulf hight I. To the bairn of Healfdene,
The famous folk-leader, I freely will tell
To thy prince my commission, if pleasantly hearing
He'll grant we may greet him so gracious to all men."
Wulfgar replied then (he was prince of the Wendels,
His boldness of spirit was known unto many,
His prowess and prudence): "The prince of the Scyldings,

(Wulfgar, the thane, says that he will go and ask Hrothgar whether he will see the strangers.)

The friend-lord of Danemen, I will ask of thy journey,
The giver of rings, as thou urgest me do it,
The folk-chief famous, and inform thee early
What answer the good one mindeth to render me."
He turned then hurriedly where Hrothgar was sitting,

²Old and hoary, his earlmen attending him;
The strength-famous went till he stood at the shoulder
Of the lord of the Danemen, of courteous thanemen
The custom he minded. Wulfgar addressed then
His friendly liegelord: "Folk of the Geatmen

(He thereupon urges his liegelord to receive the visitors courteously.)

O'er the way of the waters are wafted hither,
Faring from far-lands: the foremost in rank
The battle-champions Beowulf title.
They make this petition: with thee, O my chieftain,
To be granted a conference; O gracious King Hrothgar,
Friendly answer refuse not to give them!

(Hrothgar, too, is struck with Beowulf's appearance.)

In war-trappings weeded worthy they seem
Of earls to be honored; sure the atheling is doughty
Who headed the heroes hitherward coming."

VII - HROTHGAR AND BEOWULF
(Hrothgar remembers Beowulf as a youth, and also remembers his father.)

Hrothgar answered, helm of the Scyldings:
"I remember this man as the merest of striplings.
His father long dead now was Ecgtheow titled,
Him Hrethel the Geatman granted at home his
One only daughter; his battle-brave son
Is come but now, sought a trustworthy friend.
Seafaring sailors asserted it then,

(Beowulf is reported to have the strength of thirty men.)

Who valuable gift-gems of the Geatmen[1] carried
As peace-offering thither, that he thirty men's grapple
Has in his hand, the hero-in-battle.

(God hath sent him to our rescue.)

The holy Creator usward sent him,
To West-Dane warriors, I ween, for to render
'Gainst Grendel's grimness gracious assistance:
I shall give to the good one gift-gems for courage.
Hasten to bid them hither to speed them,[2]
To see assembled this circle of kinsmen;
Tell them expressly they're welcome in sooth to
The men of the Danes." To the door of the building

(Wulfgar invites the strangers in.)

Wulfgar went then, this word-message shouted:
"My victorious liegelord bade me to tell you,
The East-Danes' atheling, that your origin knows he,
And o'er wave-billows wafted ye welcome are hither,
Valiant of spirit. Ye straightway may enter
Clad in corslets, cased in your helmets,
To see King Hrothgar. Here let your battle-boards,
Wood-spears and war-shafts, await your conferring."
The mighty one rose then, with many a liegeman,
An excellent thane-group; some there did await them,
And as bid of the brave one the battle-gear guarded.
Together they hied them, while the hero did guide them,
'Neath Heorot's roof; the high-minded went then
Sturdy 'neath helmet till he stood in the building.
Beowulf spake (his burnie did glisten,
His armor seamed over by the art of the craftsman):

(Beowulf salutes Hrothgar, and then proceeds to boast of his youthful achievements.)

"Hail thou, Hrothgar! I am Higelac's kinsman
And vassal forsooth; many a wonder
I dared as a stripling. The doings of Grendel,
In far-off fatherland I fully did know of:
Sea-farers tell us, this hall-building standeth,
Excellent edifice, empty and useless
To all the earlmen after evenlight's glimmer
'Neath heaven's bright hues hath hidden its glory.
This my earls then urged me, the most excellent of them,
Carles very clever, to come and assist thee,
Folk-leader Hrothgar; fully they knew of

(His fight with the nickers.)

The strength of my body. Themselves they beheld me
When I came from the contest, when covered with gore
Foes I escaped from, where five[3] I had bound,
The giant-race wasted, in the waters destroying
The nickers by night, bore numberless sorrows,
The Weders avenged (woes had they suffered)
Enemies ravaged; alone now with Grendel

(He intends to fight Grendel unaided.)

I shall manage the matter, with the monster of evil,
The giant, decide it. Thee I would therefore
Beg of thy bounty, Bright-Danish chieftain,

Beowulf: Scholar's Edition

Lord of the Scyldings, this single petition:
Not to refuse me, defender of warriors,
Friend-lord of folks, so far have I sought thee,
That I may unaided, my earlmen assisting me,
This brave-mooded war-band, purify Heorot.
I have heard on inquiry, the horrible creature

(Since the monster uses no weapons,)

From veriest rashness recks not for weapons;
I this do scorn then, so be Higelac gracious,
My liegelord belovèd, lenient of spirit,
To bear a blade or a broad-fashioned target,
A shield to the onset; only with hand-grip

(I, too, shall disdain to use any.)

The foe I must grapple, fight for my life then,
Foeman with foeman; he fain must rely on
The doom of the Lord whom death layeth hold of.

(Should he crush me, he will eat my companions as he has eaten thy thanes.)

I ween he will wish, if he win in the struggle,
To eat in the war-hall earls of the Geat-folk,
Boldly to swallow[4] them, as of yore he did often
The best of the Hrethmen! Thou needest not trouble
A head-watch to give me;[5] he will have me dripping

(In case of my defeat, thou wilt not have the trouble of burying me.)

And dreary with gore, if death overtake me,[6]
Will bear me off bleeding, biting and mouthing me,
The hermit will eat me, heedless of pity,
Marking the moor-fens; no more wilt thou need then

(Should I fall, send my armor to my lord, King Higelac.)

Find me my food.[7] If I fall in the battle,
Send to Higelac the armor that serveth
To shield my bosom, the best of equipments,
Richest of ring-mails; 'tis the relic of Hrethla,

(Weird is supreme)

The work of Wayland. Goes Weird as she must go!"

VIII - HROTHGAR AND BEOWULF--Continued
(Hrothgar responds.)

Hrothgar discoursed, helm of the Scyldings:
"To defend our folk and to furnish assistance,[1]
Thou soughtest us hither, good friend Beowulf.

(Reminiscences of Beowulf's father, Ecgtheow.)

The fiercest of feuds thy father engaged in,
Heatholaf killed he in hand-to-hand conflict
'Mid Wilfingish warriors; then the Wederish people
For fear of a feud were forced to disown him.
Thence flying he fled to the folk of the South-Danes,
The race of the Scyldings, o'er the roll of the waters;
I had lately begun then to govern the Danemen,
The hoard-seat of heroes held in my youth,
Rich in its jewels: dead was Heregar,
My kinsman and elder had earth-joys forsaken,
Healfdene his bairn. He was better than I am!
That feud thereafter for a fee I compounded;
O'er the weltering waters to the Wilfings I sent
Ornaments old; oaths did he swear me.

(Hrothgar recounts to Beowulf the horrors of Grendel's persecutions.)

It pains me in spirit to any to tell it,
What grief in Heorot Grendel hath caused me,
What horror unlooked-for, by hatred unceasing.
Waned is my war-band, wasted my hall-troop;
Weird hath offcast them to the clutches of Grendel.
God can easily hinder the scather
From deeds so direful. Oft drunken with beer

(My thanes have made many boasts, but have not executed them.)

O'er the ale-vessel promised warriors in armor
They would willingly wait on the wassailing-benches
A grapple with Grendel, with grimmest of edges.
Then this mead-hall at morning with murder was reeking,
The building was bloody at breaking of daylight,
The bench-deals all flooded, dripping and bloodied,
The folk-hall was gory: I had fewer retainers,
Dear-beloved warriors, whom death had laid hold of.

(Sit down to the feast, and give us comfort.)

Sit at the feast now, thy intents unto heroes,[2]
Thy victor-fame show, as thy spirit doth urge thee!"

Beowulf: Scholar's Edition
(A bench is made ready for Beowulf and his party.)

For the men of the Geats then together assembled,
In the beer-hall blithesome a bench was made ready;
There warlike in spirit they went to be seated,
Proud and exultant. A liegeman did service,
Who a beaker embellished bore with decorum,

(The gleeman sings)

And gleaming-drink poured. The gleeman sang whilom

(The heroes all rejoice together.)

Hearty in Heorot; there was heroes' rejoicing,
A numerous war-band of Weders and Danemen.

IX - UNFERTH TAUNTS BEOWULF
(Unferth, a thane of Hrothgar, is jealous of Beowulf, and undertakes to twit him.)

Unferth spoke up, Ecglaf his son,
Who sat at the feet of the lord of the Scyldings,
Opened the jousting (the journey[1] of Beowulf,
Sea-farer doughty, gave sorrow to Unferth
And greatest chagrin, too, for granted he never
That any man else on earth should attain to,
Gain under heaven, more glory than he):

(Did you take part in a swimming-match with Breca?)

"Art thou that Beowulf with Breca did struggle,
On the wide sea-currents at swimming contended,
Where to humor your pride the ocean ye tried,

('Twas mere folly that actuated you both to risk your lives on the ocean.)

From vainest vaunting adventured your bodies
In care of the waters? And no one was able
Nor lief nor loth one, in the least to dissuade you
Your difficult voyage; then ye ventured a-swimming,
Where your arms outstretching the streams ye did cover,
The mere-ways measured, mixing and stirring them,
Glided the ocean; angry the waves were,
With the weltering of winter. In the water's possession,
Ye toiled for a seven-night; he at swimming outdid thee,
In strength excelled thee. Then early at morning
On the Heathoremes' shore the holm-currents tossed him,
Sought he thenceward the home of his fathers,
Beloved of his liegemen, the land of the Brondings,

Beowulf: Scholar's Edition

The peace-castle pleasant, where a people he wielded,
Had borough and jewels. The pledge that he made thee

(Breca outdid you entirely.)

The son of Beanstan hath soothly accomplished.
Then I ween thou wilt find thee less fortunate issue,

(Much more will Grendel outdo you, if you vie with him in prowess.)

Though ever triumphant in onset of battle,
A grim grappling, if Grendel thou darest
For the space of a night near-by to wait for!"

(Beowulf retaliates.)

Beowulf answered, offspring of Ecgtheow:
"My good friend Unferth, sure freely and wildly,

(O friend Unferth, you are fuddled with beer, and cannot talk coherently.)

Thou fuddled with beer of Breca hast spoken,
Hast told of his journey! A fact I allege it,
That greater strength in the waters I had then,
Ills in the ocean, than any man else had.
We made agreement as the merest of striplings
Promised each other (both of us then were

(We simply kept an engagement made in early life.)

Younkers in years) that we yet would adventure
Out on the ocean; it all we accomplished.
While swimming the sea-floods, sword-blade unscabbarded
Boldly we brandished, our bodies expected
To shield from the sharks. He sure was unable

(He could not excel me, and I would not excel him.)

To swim on the waters further than I could,
More swift on the waves, nor would I from him go.
Then we two companions stayed in the ocean

(After five days the currents separated us.)

Five nights together, till the currents did part us,
The weltering waters, weathers the bleakest,
And nethermost night, and the north-wind whistled
Fierce in our faces; fell were the billows.
The mere fishes' mood was mightily ruffled:

And there against foemen my firm-knotted corslet,
Hand-jointed, hardy, help did afford me;
My battle-sark braided, brilliantly gilded,

(A horrible sea-beast attacked me, but I slew him.)

Lay on my bosom. To the bottom then dragged me,
A hateful fiend-scather, seized me and held me,
Grim in his grapple: 'twas granted me, nathless,
To pierce the monster with the point of my weapon,
My obedient blade; battle offcarried
The mighty mere-creature by means of my hand-blow.

X - BEOWULF SILENCES UNFERTH--GLEE IS HIGH

"So ill-meaning enemies often did cause me
Sorrow the sorest. I served them, in quittance,

(My dear sword always served me faithfully.)

With my dear-lovèd sword, as in sooth it was fitting;
They missed the pleasure of feasting abundantly,
Ill-doers evil, of eating my body,
Of surrounding the banquet deep in the ocean;
But wounded with edges early at morning
They were stretched a-high on the strand of the ocean,

(I put a stop to the outrages of the sea-monsters.)

Put to sleep with the sword, that sea-going travelers
No longer thereafter were hindered from sailing
The foam-dashing currents. Came a light from the east,
God's beautiful beacon; the billows subsided,
That well I could see the nesses projecting,

(Fortune helps the brave earl.)

The blustering crags. Weird often saveth
The undoomed hero if doughty his valor!
But me did it fortune[1] to fell with my weapon
Nine of the nickers. Of night-struggle harder
'Neath dome of the heaven heard I but rarely,
Nor of wight more woful in the waves of the ocean;
Yet I 'scaped with my life the grip of the monsters,

(After that escape I drifted to Finland.)

Weary from travel. Then the waters bare me
To the land of the Finns, the flood with the current,

(I have never heard of your doing any such bold deeds.)

The weltering waves. Not a word hath been told me
Of deeds so daring done by thee, Unferth,
And of sword-terror none; never hath Breca
At the play of the battle, nor either of you two,
Feat so fearless performèd with weapons
Glinting and gleaming . . . .
. . . . I utter no boasting;

(You are a slayer of brothers, and will suffer damnation, wise as you may be.)

Though with cold-blooded cruelty thou killedst thy brothers,
Thy nearest of kin; thou needs must in hell get
Direful damnation, though doughty thy wisdom.
I tell thee in earnest, offspring of Ecglaf,
Never had Grendel such numberless horrors,
The direful demon, done to thy liegelord,
Harrying in Heorot, if thy heart were as sturdy,

(Had your acts been as brave as your words, Grendel had not ravaged your land so long.)

Thy mood as ferocious as thou dost describe them.
He hath found out fully that the fierce-burning hatred,
The edge-battle eager, of all of your kindred,
Of the Victory-Scyldings, need little dismay him:
Oaths he exacteth, not any he spares

(The monster is not afraid of the Danes,)

Of the folk of the Danemen, but fighteth with pleasure,
Killeth and feasteth, no contest expecteth

(but he will soon learn to dread the Geats.)

From Spear-Danish people. But the prowess and valor
Of the earls of the Geatmen early shall venture
To give him a grapple. He shall go who is able
Bravely to banquet, when the bright-light of morning

(On the second day, any warrior may go unmolested to the mead-banquet.)

Which the second day bringeth, the sun in its ether-robes,
O'er children of men shines from the southward!"
Then the gray-haired, war-famed giver of treasure

(Hrothgar's spirits are revived.)

Was blithesome and joyous, the Bright-Danish ruler
Expected assistance; the people's protector

(The old king trusts Beowulf. The heroes are joyful.)

Heard from Beowulf his bold resolution.
There was laughter of heroes; loud was the clatter,
The words were winsome. Wealhtheow advanced then,

(Queen Wealhtheow plays the hostess.)

Consort of Hrothgar, of courtesy mindful,
Gold-decked saluted the men in the building,
And the freeborn woman the beaker presented

(She offers the cup to her husband first.)

To the lord of the kingdom, first of the East-Danes,
Bade him be blithesome when beer was a-flowing,
Lief to his liegemen; he lustily tasted
Of banquet and beaker, battle-famed ruler.
The Helmingish lady then graciously circled
'Mid all the liegemen lesser and greater:

(She gives presents to the heroes.)

Treasure-cups tendered, till time was afforded
That the decorous-mooded, diademed folk-queen

(Then she offers the cup to Beowulf, thanking God that aid has come.)

Might bear to Beowulf the bumper o'errunning;
She greeted the Geat-prince, God she did thank,
Most wise in her words, that her wish was accomplished,
That in any of earlmen she ever should look for
Solace in sorrow. He accepted the beaker,
Battle-bold warrior, at Wealhtheow's giving,

(Beowulf states to the queen the object of his visit.)

Then equipped for combat quoth he in measures,
Beowulf spake, offspring of Ecgtheow:
"I purposed in spirit when I mounted the ocean,

(I determined to do or die.)

When I boarded my boat with a band of my liegemen,
I would work to the fullest the will of your people
Or in foe's-clutches fastened fall in the battle.
Deeds I shall do of daring and prowess,

Or the last of my life-days live in this mead-hall."
These words to the lady were welcome and pleasing,
The boast of the Geatman; with gold trappings broidered
Went the freeborn folk-queen her fond-lord to sit by.

(Glee is high.)

Then again as of yore was heard in the building
Courtly discussion, conquerors' shouting,
Heroes were happy, till Healfdene's son would
Go to his slumber to seek for refreshing;
For the horrid hell-monster in the hall-building knew he
A fight was determined,[2] since the light of the sun they
No longer could see, and lowering darkness
O'er all had descended, and dark under heaven
Shadowy shapes came shying around them.

(Hrothgar retires, leaving Beowulf in charge of the hall.)

The liegemen all rose then. One saluted the other,
Hrothgar Beowulf, in rhythmical measures,
Wishing him well, and, the wassail-hall giving
To his care and keeping, quoth he departing:
"Not to any one else have I ever entrusted,
But thee and thee only, the hall of the Danemen,
Since high I could heave my hand and my buckler.
Take thou in charge now the noblest of houses;
Be mindful of honor, exhibiting prowess,
Watch 'gainst the foeman! Thou shalt want no enjoyments,
Survive thou safely adventure so glorious!"

XI - ALL SLEEP SAVE ONE
(Hrothgar retires.)

Then Hrothgar departed, his earl-throng attending him,
Folk-lord of Scyldings, forth from the building;
The war-chieftain wished then Wealhtheow to look for,
The queen for a bedmate. To keep away Grendel

(God has provided a watch for the hall.)

The Glory of Kings had given a hall-watch,
As men heard recounted: for the king of the Danemen
He did special service, gave the giant a watcher:
And the prince of the Geatmen implicitly trusted

(Beowulf is self-confident)

Beowulf: Scholar's Edition
His warlike strength and the Wielder's protection.

(He prepares for rest.)

His armor of iron off him he did then,
His helmet from his head, to his henchman committed
His chased-handled chain-sword, choicest of weapons,
And bade him bide with his battle-equipments.
The good one then uttered words of defiance,
Beowulf Geatman, ere his bed he upmounted:

(Beowulf boasts of his ability to cope with Grendel.)

"I hold me no meaner in matters of prowess,
In warlike achievements, than Grendel does himself;
Hence I seek not with sword-edge to sooth him to slumber,
Of life to bereave him, though well I am able.

(We will fight with nature's weapons only.)

No battle-skill[1] has he, that blows he should strike me,
To shatter my shield, though sure he is mighty
In strife and destruction; but struggling by night we
Shall do without edges, dare he to look for
Weaponless warfare, and wise-mooded Father
The glory apportion, God ever-holy,

(God may decide who shall conquer)

On which hand soever to him seemeth proper."
Then the brave-mooded hero bent to his slumber,
The pillow received the cheek of the noble;

(The Geatish warriors lie down.)

And many a martial mere-thane attending
Sank to his slumber. Seemed it unlikely

(They thought it very unlikely that they should ever see their homes again.)

That ever thereafter any should hope to
Be happy at home, hero-friends visit
Or the lordly troop-castle where he lived from his childhood;
They had heard how slaughter had snatched from the wine-hall,
Had recently ravished, of the race of the Scyldings

(But God raised up a deliverer.)

Too many by far. But the Lord to them granted
The weaving of war-speed, to Wederish heroes

Aid and comfort, that every opponent
By one man's war-might they worsted and vanquished,

(God rules the world.)

By the might of himself; the truth is established
That God Almighty hath governed for ages
Kindreds and nations. A night very lurid

(Grendel comes to Heorot.)

The trav'ler-at-twilight came tramping and striding.
The warriors were sleeping who should watch the horned-building,

(Only one warrior is awake.)

One only excepted. 'Mid earthmen 'twas 'stablished,
Th' implacable foeman was powerless to hurl them
To the land of shadows, if the Lord were unwilling;
But serving as warder, in terror to foemen,
He angrily bided the issue of battle.[2]

XII - GRENDEL AND BEOWULF
(Grendel comes from the fens.)

'Neath the cloudy cliffs came from the moor then
Grendel going, God's anger bare he.
The monster intended some one of earthmen
In the hall-building grand to entrap and make way with:

(He goes towards the joyous building.)

He went under welkin where well he knew of
The wine-joyous building, brilliant with plating,
Gold-hall of earthmen. Not the earliest occasion

(This was not his first visit there.)

He the home and manor of Hrothgar had sought:
Ne'er found he in life-days later nor earlier
Hardier hero, hall-thanes[1] more sturdy!
Then came to the building the warrior marching,

(His horrid fingers tear the door open.)

Bereft of his joyance. The door quickly opened
On fire-hinges fastened, when his fingers had touched it;
The fell one had flung then--his fury so bitter--
Open the entrance. Early thereafter

The foeman trod the shining hall-pavement,

(He strides furiously into the hall.)

Strode he angrily; from the eyes of him glimmered
A lustre unlovely likest to fire.
He beheld in the hall the heroes in numbers,
A circle of kinsmen sleeping together,

(He exults over his supposed prey.)

A throng of thanemen: then his thoughts were exultant,
He minded to sunder from each of the thanemen
The life from his body, horrible demon,
Ere morning came, since fate had allowed him

(Fate has decreed that he shall devour no more heroes. Beowulf suffers from suspense.)

The prospect of plenty. Providence willed not
To permit him any more of men under heaven
To eat in the night-time. Higelac's kinsman
Great sorrow endured how the dire-mooded creature
In unlooked-for assaults were likely to bear him.
No thought had the monster of deferring the matter,

(Grendel immediately seizes a sleeping warrior, and devours him.)

But on earliest occasion he quickly laid hold of
A soldier asleep, suddenly tore him,
Bit his bone-prison, the blood drank in currents,
Swallowed in mouthfuls: he soon had the dead man's
Feet and hands, too, eaten entirely.
Nearer he strode then, the stout-hearted warrior

(Beowulf and Grendel grapple.)

Snatched as he slumbered, seizing with hand-grip,
Forward the foeman foined with his hand;
Caught he quickly the cunning deviser,
On his elbow he rested. This early discovered
The master of malice, that in middle-earth's regions,
'Neath the whole of the heavens, no hand-grapple greater

(The monster is amazed at Beowulf's strength.)

In any man else had he ever encountered:
Fearful in spirit, faint-mooded waxed he,
Not off could betake him; death he was pondering,

(He is anxious to flee.)

Would fly to his covert, seek the devils' assembly:
His calling no more was the same he had followed
Long in his lifetime. The liege-kinsman worthy

(Beowulf recalls his boast of the evening, and determines to fulfil it.)

Of Higelac minded his speech of the evening,
Stood he up straight and stoutly did seize him.
His fingers crackled; the giant was outward,
The earl stepped farther. The famous one minded
To flee away farther, if he found an occasion,
And off and away, avoiding delay,
To fly to the fen-moors; he fully was ware of
The strength of his grapple in the grip of the foeman.

('Twas a luckless day for Grendel.)

'Twas an ill-taken journey that the injury-bringing,
Harrying harmer to Heorot wandered:

(The hall groans.)

The palace re-echoed; to all of the Danemen,
Dwellers in castles, to each of the bold ones,
Earlmen, was terror. Angry they both were,
Archwarders raging.[2] Rattled the building;
'Twas a marvellous wonder that the wine-hall withstood then
The bold-in-battle, bent not to earthward,
Excellent earth-hall; but within and without it
Was fastened so firmly in fetters of iron,
By the art of the armorer. Off from the sill there
Bent mead-benches many, as men have informed me,
Adorned with gold-work, where the grim ones did struggle.
The Scylding wise men weened ne'er before
That by might and main-strength a man under heaven
Might break it in pieces, bone-decked, resplendent,
Crush it by cunning, unless clutch of the fire
In smoke should consume it. The sound mounted upward

(Grendel's cries terrify the Danes.)

Novel enough; on the North Danes fastened
A terror of anguish, on all of the men there
Who heard from the wall the weeping and plaining,
The song of defeat from the foeman of heaven,
Heard him hymns of horror howl, and his sorrow
Hell-bound bewailing. He held him too firmly

Who was strongest of main-strength of men of that era.

XIII - GRENDEL IS VANQUISHED
(Beowulf has no idea of letting Grendel live.)

For no cause whatever would the earlmen's defender
Leave in life-joys the loathsome newcomer,
He deemed his existence utterly useless
To men under heaven. Many a noble
Of Beowulf brandished his battle-sword old,
Would guard the life of his lord and protector,
The far-famed chieftain, if able to do so;
While waging the warfare, this wist they but little,
Brave battle-thanes, while his body intending

(No weapon would harm Grendel; he bore a charmed life.)

To slit into slivers, and seeking his spirit:
That the relentless foeman nor finest of weapons
Of all on the earth, nor any of war-bills
Was willing to injure; but weapons of victory
Swords and suchlike he had sworn to dispense with.
His death at that time must prove to be wretched,
And the far-away spirit widely should journey
Into enemies' power. This plainly he saw then
Who with mirth[1] of mood malice no little
Had wrought in the past on the race of the earthmen
(To God he was hostile), that his body would fail him,
But Higelac's hardy henchman and kinsman
Held him by the hand; hateful to other

(Grendel is sorely wounded.)

Was each one if living. A body-wound suffered
The direful demon, damage incurable

(His body bursts.)

Was seen on his shoulder, his sinews were shivered,
His body did burst. To Beowulf was given
Glory in battle; Grendel thenceward
Must flee and hide him in the fen-cliffs and marshes,
Sick unto death, his dwelling must look for
Unwinsome and woful; he wist the more fully

(The monster flees away to hide in the moors.)

The end of his earthly existence was nearing,
His life-days' limits. At last for the Danemen,

When the slaughter was over, their wish was accomplished.
The comer-from-far-land had cleansed then of evil,
Wise and valiant, the war-hall of Hrothgar,
Saved it from violence. He joyed in the night-work,
In repute for prowess; the prince of the Geatmen
For the East-Danish people his boast had accomplished,
Bettered their burdensome bale-sorrows fully,
The craft-begot evil they erstwhile had suffered
And were forced to endure from crushing oppression,
Their manifold misery. 'Twas a manifest token,

(Beowulf suspends Grendel's hand and arm in Heorot.)

When the hero-in-battle the hand suspended,
The arm and the shoulder (there was all of the claw
Of Grendel together) 'neath great-stretching hall-roof.

XIV - REJOICING OF THE DANES
(At early dawn, warriors from far and near come together to hear of the night's adventures.)

In the mist of the morning many a warrior
Stood round the gift-hall, as the story is told me:
Folk-princes fared then from far and from near
Through long-stretching journeys to look at the wonder,
The footprints of the foeman. Few of the warriors

(Few warriors lamented Grendel's destruction.)

Who gazed on the foot-tracks of the inglorious creature
His parting from life pained very deeply,
How, weary in spirit, off from those regions
In combats conquered he carried his traces,
Fated and flying, to the flood of the nickers.

(Grendel's blood dyes the waters.)

There in bloody billows bubbled the currents,
The angry eddy was everywhere mingled
And seething with gore, welling with sword-blood;[1]
He death-doomed had hid him, when reaved of his joyance
He laid down his life in the lair he had fled to,
His heathenish spirit, where hell did receive him.
Thence the friends from of old backward turned them,
And many a younker from merry adventure,
Striding their stallions, stout from the seaward,
Heroes on horses. There were heard very often

(Beowulf is the hero of the hour.)

Beowulf: Scholar's Edition

Beowulf's praises; many often asserted
That neither south nor north, in the circuit of waters,

(He is regarded as a probable successor to Hrothgar.)

O'er outstretching earth-plain, none other was better
'Mid bearers of war-shields, more worthy to govern,
'Neath the arch of the ether. Not any, however,
'Gainst the friend-lord muttered, mocking-words uttered

(But no word is uttered to derogate from the old king)

Of Hrothgar the gracious (a good king he).
Oft the famed ones permitted their fallow-skinned horses
To run in rivalry, racing and chasing,
Where the fieldways appeared to them fair and inviting,
Known for their excellence; oft a thane of the folk-lord,[2]

(The gleeman sings the deeds of heroes.)

[3]A man of celebrity, mindful of rhythms,
Who ancient traditions treasured in memory,
New word-groups found properly bound:
The bard after 'gan then Beowulf's venture

(He sings in alliterative measures of Beowulf's prowess.)

Wisely to tell of, and words that were clever
To utter skilfully, earnestly speaking,
Everything told he that he heard as to Sigmund's

(Also of Sigemund, who has slain a great fire-dragon.)

Mighty achievements, many things hidden,
The strife of the Wælsing, the wide-going ventures
The children of men knew of but little,
The feud and the fury, but Fitela with him,
When suchlike matters he minded to speak of,
Uncle to nephew, as in every contention
Each to other was ever devoted:
A numerous host of the race of the scathers
They had slain with the sword-edge. To Sigmund accrued then
No little of glory, when his life-days were over,
Since he sturdy in struggle had destroyed the great dragon,
The hoard-treasure's keeper; 'neath the hoar-grayish stone he,
The son of the atheling, unaided adventured
The perilous project; not present was Fitela,
Yet the fortune befell him of forcing his weapon
Through the marvellous dragon, that it stood in the wall,
Well-honored weapon; the worm was slaughtered.

The great one had gained then by his glorious achievement
To reap from the ring-hoard richest enjoyment,
As best it did please him: his vessel he loaded,
Shining ornaments on the ship's bosom carried,
Kinsman of Wæls: the drake in heat melted.

(Sigemund was widely famed.)

He was farthest famed of fugitive pilgrims,
Mid wide-scattered world-folk, for works of great prowess,
War-troopers' shelter: hence waxed he in honor.[4]

(Heremod, an unfortunate Danish king, is introduced by way of contrast.)

Afterward Heremod's hero-strength failed him,
His vigor and valor. 'Mid venomous haters
To the hands of foemen he was foully delivered,
Offdriven early. Agony-billows

(Unlike Sigemund and Beowulf, Heremod was a burden to his people.)

Oppressed him too long, to his people he became then,
To all the athelings, an ever-great burden;
And the daring one's journey in days of yore
Many wise men were wont to deplore,
Such as hoped he would bring them help in their sorrow,
That the son of their ruler should rise into power,
Holding the headship held by his fathers,
Should govern the people, the gold-hoard and borough,
The kingdom of heroes, the realm of the Scyldings.

(Beowulf is an honor to his race.)

He to all men became then far more beloved,
Higelac's kinsman, to kindreds and races,
To his friends much dearer; him malice assaulted.--

(The story is resumed.)

Oft running and racing on roadsters they measured
The dun-colored highways. Then the light of the morning
Was hurried and hastened. Went henchmen in numbers
To the beautiful building, bold ones in spirit,
To look at the wonder; the liegelord himself then
From his wife-bower wending, warden of treasures,
Glorious trod with troopers unnumbered,
Famed for his virtues, and with him the queen-wife
Measured the mead-ways, with maidens attending.

XV - HROTHGAR'S GRATITUDE

Hrothgar discoursed (to the hall-building went he,
He stood by the pillar,[1] saw the steep-rising hall-roof
Gleaming with gold-gems, and Grendel his hand there):

(Hrothgar gives thanks for the overthrow of the monster.)

"For the sight we behold now, thanks to the Wielder
Early be offered! Much evil I bided,
Snaring from Grendel:[2] God can e'er 'complish
Wonder on wonder, Wielder of Glory!

(I had given up all hope, when this brave liegeman came to our aid.)

But lately I reckoned ne'er under heaven
Comfort to gain me for any of sorrows,
While the handsomest of houses horrid with bloodstain
Gory uptowered; grief had offfrightened[3]
Each of the wise ones who weened not that ever
The folk-troop's defences 'gainst foes they should strengthen,
'Gainst sprites and monsters. Through the might of the Wielder
A doughty retainer hath a deed now accomplished
Which erstwhile we all with our excellent wisdom

(If his mother yet liveth, well may she thank God for this son.)

Failed to perform. May affirm very truly
What woman soever in all of the nations
Gave birth to the child, if yet she surviveth,
That the long-ruling Lord was lavish to herward
In the birth of the bairn. Now, Beowulf dear,

(Hereafter, Beowulf, thou shalt be my son.)

Most excellent hero, I'll love thee in spirit
As bairn of my body; bear well henceforward
The relationship new. No lack shall befall thee
Of earth-joys any I ever can give thee.
Full often for lesser service I've given
Hero less hardy hoard-treasure precious,

(Thou hast won immortal distinction.)

To a weaker in war-strife. By works of distinction
Thou hast gained for thyself now that thy glory shall flourish
Forever and ever. The All-Ruler quite thee
With good from His hand as He hitherto did thee!"

(Beowulf replies: I was most happy to render thee this service.)

Beowulf answered, Ecgtheow's offspring:
"That labor of glory most gladly achieved we,
The combat accomplished, unquailing we ventured
The enemy's grapple; I would grant it much rather
Thou wert able to look at the creature in person,
Faint unto falling, the foe in his trappings!
On murder-bed quickly I minded to bind him,
With firm-holding fetters, that forced by my grapple
Low he should lie in life-and-death struggle
'Less his body escape; I was wholly unable,

(I could not keep the monster from escaping, as God did not will that I should.)

Since God did not will it, to keep him from going,
Not held him that firmly, hated opposer;
Too swift was the foeman. Yet safety regarding
He suffered his hand behind him to linger,
His arm and shoulder, to act as watcher;

(He left his hand and arm behind.)

No shadow of solace the woe-begone creature
Found him there nathless: the hated destroyer
Liveth no longer, lashed for his evils,
But sorrow hath seized him, in snare-meshes hath him
Close in its clutches, keepeth him writhing
In baleful bonds: there banished for evil
The man shall wait for the mighty tribunal,

(God will give him his deserts.)

How the God of glory shall give him his earnings."
Then the soldier kept silent, son of old Ecglaf,

(Unferth has nothing more to say, for Beowulf's actions speak louder than words.)

From boasting and bragging of battle-achievements,
Since the princes beheld there the hand that depended
'Neath the lofty hall-timbers by the might of the nobleman,
Each one before him, the enemy's fingers;
Each finger-nail strong steel most resembled,
The heathen one's hand-spur, the hero-in-battle's
Claw most uncanny; quoth they agreeing,

(No sword will harm the monster.)

That not any excellent edges of brave ones

Was willing to touch him, the terrible creature's
Battle-hand bloody to bear away from him.

XVI - HROTHGAR LAVISHES GIFTS UPON HIS DELIVERER
(Heorot is adorned with hands.)

Then straight was ordered that Heorot inside[1]
With hands be embellished: a host of them gathered,
Of men and women, who the wassailing-building
The guest-hall begeared. Gold-flashing sparkled
Webs on the walls then, of wonders a many
To each of the heroes that look on such objects.

(The hall is defaced, however.)

The beautiful building was broken to pieces
Which all within with irons was fastened,
Its hinges torn off: only the roof was
Whole and uninjured when the horrible creature
Outlawed for evil off had betaken him,
Hopeless of living. 'Tis hard to avoid it

([A vague passage of five verses.])

(Whoever will do it!); but he doubtless must come to[2]
The place awaiting, as Wyrd hath appointed,
Soul-bearers, earth-dwellers, earls under heaven,
Where bound on its bed his body shall slumber

(Hrothgar goes to the banquet.)

When feasting is finished. Full was the time then
That the son of Healfdene went to the building;
The excellent atheling would eat of the banquet.
Ne'er heard I that people with hero-band larger
Bare them better tow'rds their bracelet-bestower.
The laden-with-glory stooped to the bench then
(Their kinsmen-companions in plenty were joyful,
Many a cupful quaffing complaisantly),
Doughty of spirit in the high-tow'ring palace,

(Hrothgar's nephew, Hrothulf, is present.)

Hrothgar and Hrothulf. Heorot then inside
Was filled with friendly ones; falsehood and treachery
The Folk-Scyldings now nowise did practise.

(Hrothgar lavishes gifts upon Beowulf.)

Then the offspring of Healfdene offered to Beowulf
A golden standard, as reward for the victory,
A banner embossed, burnie and helmet;
Many men saw then a song-famous weapon
Borne 'fore the hero. Beowulf drank of
The cup in the building; that treasure-bestowing
He needed not blush for in battle-men's presence.

(Four handsomer gifts were never presented.)

Ne'er heard I that many men on the ale-bench
In friendlier fashion to their fellows presented
Four bright jewels with gold-work embellished.
'Round the roof of the helmet a head-guarder outside
Braided with wires, with bosses was furnished,
That swords-for-the-battle fight-hardened might fail
Boldly to harm him, when the hero proceeded

(Hrothgar commands that eight finely caparisoned steeds be brought to Beowulf.)

Forth against foemen. The defender of earls then
Commanded that eight steeds with bridles
Gold-plated, gleaming, be guided to hallward,
Inside the building; on one of them stood then
An art-broidered saddle embellished with jewels;
'Twas the sovereign's seat, when the son of King Healfdene
Was pleased to take part in the play of the edges;
The famous one's valor ne'er failed at the front when
Slain ones were bowing. And to Beowulf granted
The prince of the Ingwins, power over both,
O'er war-steeds and weapons; bade him well to enjoy them.
In so manly a manner the mighty-famed chieftain,
Hoard-ward of heroes, with horses and jewels
War-storms requited, that none e'er condemneth
Who willeth to tell truth with full justice.

XVII - BANQUET (continued)--THE SCOP'S SONG OF FINN AND HNÆF

(Each of Beowulf's companions receives a costly gift.)

And the atheling of earlmen to each of the heroes
Who the ways of the waters went with Beowulf,
A costly gift-token gave on the mead-bench,
Offered an heirloom, and ordered that that man

(The warrior killed by Grendel is to be paid for in gold.)

Beowulf: Scholar's Edition

With gold should be paid for, whom Grendel had erstwhile
Wickedly slaughtered, as he more of them had done
Had far-seeing God and the mood of the hero
The fate not averted: the Father then governed
All of the earth-dwellers, as He ever is doing;
Hence insight for all men is everywhere fittest,
Forethought of spirit! much he shall suffer
Of lief and of loathsome who long in this present
Useth the world in this woful existence.
There was music and merriment mingling together

(Hrothgar's scop recalls events in the reign of his lord's father.)

Touching Healfdene's leader; the joy-wood was fingered,
Measures recited, when the singer of Hrothgar
On mead-bench should mention the merry hall-joyance
Of the kinsmen of Finn, when onset surprised them:

(Hnæf, the Danish general, is treacherously attacked while staying at Finn's castle.)

"The Half-Danish hero, Hnæf of the Scyldings,
On the field of the Frisians was fated to perish.
Sure Hildeburg needed not mention approving
The faith of the Jutemen: though blameless entirely,

(Queen Hildeburg is not only wife of Finn, but a kinswoman of the murdered Hnæf.)

When shields were shivered she was shorn of her darlings,
Of bairns and brothers: they bent to their fate
With war-spear wounded; woe was that woman.
Not causeless lamented the daughter of Hoce
The decree of the Wielder when morning-light came and
She was able 'neath heaven to behold the destruction
Of brothers and bairns, where the brightest of earth-joys

(Finn's force is almost exterminated.)

She had hitherto had: all the henchmen of Finn
War had offtaken, save a handful remaining,
That he nowise was able to offer resistance[1]

(Hengest succeeds Hnæf as Danish general.)

To the onset of Hengest in the parley of battle,
Nor the wretched remnant to rescue in war from
The earl of the atheling; but they offered conditions,

(Compact between the Frisians and the Danes.)

Another great building to fully make ready,
A hall and a high-seat, that half they might rule with
The sons of the Jutemen, and that Folcwalda's son would
Day after day the Danemen honor
When gifts were giving, and grant of his ring-store
To Hengest's earl-troop ever so freely,
Of his gold-plated jewels, as he encouraged the Frisians

(Equality of gifts agreed on.)

On the bench of the beer-hall. On both sides they swore then
A fast-binding compact; Finn unto Hengest
With no thought of revoking vowed then most solemnly
The woe-begone remnant well to take charge of,
His Witan advising; the agreement should no one
By words or works weaken and shatter,
By artifice ever injure its value,
Though reaved of their ruler their ring-giver's slayer
They followed as vassals, Fate so requiring:

(No one shall refer to old grudges.)

Then if one of the Frisians the quarrel should speak of
In tones that were taunting, terrible edges
Should cut in requital. Accomplished the oath was,
And treasure of gold from the hoard was uplifted.

(Danish warriors are burned on a funeral-pyre.)

The best of the Scylding braves was then fully
Prepared for the pile; at the pyre was seen clearly
The blood-gory burnie, the boar with his gilding,
The iron-hard swine, athelings many
Fatally wounded; no few had been slaughtered.
Hildeburg bade then, at the burning of Hnæf,

(Queen Hildeburg has her son burnt along with Hnæf.)

The bairn of her bosom to bear to the fire,
That his body be burned and borne to the pyre.
The woe-stricken woman wept on his shoulder,[2]
In measures lamented; upmounted the hero.[3]
The greatest of dead-fires curled to the welkin,
On the hill's-front crackled; heads were a-melting,
Wound-doors bursting, while the blood was a-coursing
From body-bite fierce. The fire devoured them,
Greediest of spirits, whom war had offcarried
From both of the peoples; their bravest were fallen.

XVIII - THE FINN EPISODE (continued)--THE BANQUET CONTINUES
(The survivors go to Friesland, the home of Finn.)

"Then the warriors departed to go to their dwellings,
Reaved of their friends, Friesland to visit,
Their homes and high-city. Hengest continued

(Hengest remains there all winter, unable to get away.)

Biding with Finn the blood-tainted winter,
Wholly unsundered;[1] of fatherland thought he
Though unable to drive the ring-stemmèd vessel
O'er the ways of the waters; the wave-deeps were tossing,
Fought with the wind; winter in ice-bonds
Closed up the currents, till there came to the dwelling
A year in its course, as yet it revolveth,
If season propitious one alway regardeth,
World-cheering weathers. Then winter was gone,
Earth's bosom was lovely; the exile would get him,

(He devises schemes of vengeance.)

The guest from the palace; on grewsomest vengeance
He brooded more eager than on oversea journeys,
Whe'r onset-of-anger he were able to 'complish,
The bairns of the Jutemen therein to remember.
Nowise refused he the duties of liegeman
When Hun of the Frisians the battle-sword Láfing,
Fairest of falchions, friendly did give him:
Its edges were famous in folk-talk of Jutland.
And savage sword-fury seized in its clutches
Bold-mooded Finn where he bode in his palace,

(Guthlaf and Oslaf revenge Hnæf's slaughter.)

When the grewsome grapple Guthlaf and Oslaf
Had mournfully mentioned, the mere-journey over,
For sorrows half-blamed him; the flickering spirit
Could not bide in his bosom. Then the building was covered[2]

(Finn is slain.)

With corpses of foemen, and Finn too was slaughtered,
The king with his comrades, and the queen made a prisoner.

(The jewels of Finn, and his queen are carried away by the Danes.)

The troops of the Scyldings bore to their vessels
All that the land-king had in his palace,
Such trinkets and treasures they took as, on searching,
At Finn's they could find. They ferried to Daneland
The excellent woman on oversea journey,

(The lay is concluded, and the main story is resumed.)

Led her to their land-folk." The lay was concluded,
The gleeman's recital. Shouts again rose then,
Bench-glee resounded, bearers then offered

(Skinkers carry round the beaker.)

Wine from wonder-vats. Wealhtheo advanced then
Going 'neath gold-crown, where the good ones were seated

(Queen Wealhtheow greets Hrothgar, as he sits beside Hrothulf, his nephew.)

Uncle and nephew; their peace was yet mutual,
True each to the other. And Unferth the spokesman
Sat at the feet of the lord of the Scyldings:
Each trusted his spirit that his mood was courageous,
Though at fight he had failed in faith to his kinsmen.
Said the queen of the Scyldings: "My lord and protector,
Treasure-bestower, take thou this beaker;
Joyance attend thee, gold-friend of heroes,

(Be generous to the Geats.)

And greet thou the Geatmen with gracious responses!
So ought one to do. Be kind to the Geatmen,
In gifts not niggardly; anear and afar now
Peace thou enjoyest. Report hath informed me
Thou'lt have for a bairn the battle-brave hero.
Now is Heorot cleansèd, ring-palace gleaming;

(Have as much joy as possible in thy hall, once more purified.)

Give while thou mayest many rewards,
And bequeath to thy kinsmen kingdom and people,
On wending thy way to the Wielder's splendor.
I know good Hrothulf, that the noble young troopers

(I know that Hrothulf will prove faithful if he survive thee.)

He'll care for and honor, lord of the Scyldings,
If earth-joys thou endest earlier than he doth;
I reckon that recompense he'll render with kindness

Our offspring and issue, if that all he remember,
What favors of yore, when he yet was an infant,
We awarded to him for his worship and pleasure."
Then she turned by the bench where her sons were carousing,
Hrethric and Hrothmund, and the heroes' offspring,

(Beowulf is sitting by the two royal sons.)

The war-youth together; there the good one was sitting
'Twixt the brothers twain, Beowulf Geatman.

XIX - BEOWULF RECEIVES FURTHER HONOR
(More gifts are offered Beowulf.)

A beaker was borne him, and bidding to quaff it
Graciously given, and gold that was twisted
Pleasantly proffered, a pair of arm-jewels,
Rings and corslet, of collars the greatest
I've heard of 'neath heaven. Of heroes not any
More splendid from jewels have I heard 'neath the welkin,

(A famous necklace is referred to, in comparison with the gems presented to Beowulf.)

Since Hama off bore the Brosingmen's necklace,
The bracteates and jewels, from the bright-shining city,[1]
Eormenric's cunning craftiness fled from,
Chose gain everlasting. Geatish Higelac,
Grandson of Swerting, last had this jewel
When tramping 'neath banner the treasure he guarded,
The field-spoil defended; Fate offcarried him
When for deeds of daring he endured tribulation,
Hate from the Frisians; the ornaments bare he
O'er the cup of the currents, costly gem-treasures,
Mighty folk-leader, he fell 'neath his target;
The[2] corpse of the king then came into charge of
The race of the Frankmen, the mail-shirt and collar:
Warmen less noble plundered the fallen,
When the fight was finished; the folk of the Geatmen
The field of the dead held in possession.
The choicest of mead-halls with cheering resounded.
Wealhtheo discoursed, the war-troop addressed she:

(Queen Wealhtheow magnifies Beowulf's achievements.)

"This collar enjoy thou, Beowulf worthy,
Young man, in safety, and use thou this armor,
Gems of the people, and prosper thou fully,
Show thyself sturdy and be to these liegemen

Mild with instruction! I'll mind thy requital.
Thou hast brought it to pass that far and near
Forever and ever earthmen shall honor thee,
Even so widely as ocean surroundeth
The blustering bluffs. Be, while thou livest,
A wealth-blessèd atheling. I wish thee most truly

(May gifts never fail thee.)

Jewels and treasure. Be kind to my son, thou
Living in joyance! Here each of the nobles
Is true unto other, gentle in spirit,
Loyal to leader. The liegemen are peaceful,
The war-troops ready: well-drunken heroes,[3]
Do as I bid ye." Then she went to the settle.
There was choicest of banquets, wine drank the heroes:

(They little know of the sorrow in store for them.)

Weird they knew not, destiny cruel,
As to many an earlman early it happened,
When evening had come and Hrothgar had parted
Off to his manor, the mighty to slumber.
Warriors unnumbered warded the building
As erst they did often: the ale-settle bared they,
'Twas covered all over with beds and pillows.

(A doomed thane is there with them.)

Doomed unto death, down to his slumber
Bowed then a beer-thane. Their battle-shields placed they,
Bright-shining targets, up by their heads then;
O'er the atheling on ale-bench 'twas easy to see there
Battle-high helmet, burnie of ring-mail,

(They were always ready for battle.)

And mighty war-spear. 'Twas the wont of that people
To constantly keep them equipped for the battle,[4]
At home or marching--in either condition--
At seasons just such as necessity ordered
As best for their ruler; that people was worthy.

XX - THE MOTHER OF GRENDEL

They sank then to slumber. With sorrow one paid for
His evening repose, as often betid them
While Grendel was holding[1] the gold-bedecked palace,
Ill-deeds performing, till his end overtook him,

Death for his sins. 'Twas seen very clearly,

(Grendel's mother is known to be thirsting for revenge.)

Known unto earth-folk, that still an avenger
Outlived the loathed one, long since the sorrow
Caused by the struggle; the mother of Grendel,
Devil-shaped woman, her woe ever minded,
Who was held to inhabit the horrible waters,

([Grendel's progenitor, Cain, is again referred to.])

The cold-flowing currents, after Cain had become a
Slayer-with-edges to his one only brother,
The son of his sire; he set out then banished,
Marked as a murderer, man-joys avoiding,
Lived in the desert. Thence demons unnumbered

(The poet again magnifies Beowulf's valor.)

Fate-sent awoke; one of them Grendel,
Sword-cursèd, hateful, who at Heorot met with
A man that was watching, waiting the struggle,
Where a horrid one held him with hand-grapple sturdy;
Nathless he minded the might of his body,
The glorious gift God had allowed him,
And folk-ruling Father's favor relied on,
His help and His comfort: so he conquered the foeman,
The hell-spirit humbled: he unhappy departed then,
Reaved of his joyance, journeying to death-haunts,
Foeman of man. His mother moreover

(Grendel's mother comes to avenge her son.)

Eager and gloomy was anxious to go on
Her mournful mission, mindful of vengeance
For the death of her son. She came then to Heorot
Where the Armor-Dane earlmen all through the building
Were lying in slumber. Soon there became then
Return[2] to the nobles, when the mother of Grendel
Entered the folk-hall; the fear was less grievous
By even so much as the vigor of maidens,
War-strength of women, by warrior is reckoned,
When well-carved weapon, worked with the hammer,
Blade very bloody, brave with its edges,
Strikes down the boar-sign that stands on the helmet.
Then the hard-edgèd weapon was heaved in the building,[3]
The brand o'er the benches, broad-lindens many
Hand-fast were lifted; for helmet he recked not,
For armor-net broad, whom terror laid hold of.

Beowulf: Scholar's Edition

She went then hastily, outward would get her
Her life for to save, when some one did spy her;

(She seizes a favorite liegemen of Hrothgar's.)

Soon she had grappled one of the athelings
Fast and firmly, when fenward she hied her;
That one to Hrothgar was liefest of heroes
In rank of retainer where waters encircle,
A mighty shield-warrior, whom she murdered at slumber,
50 A broadly-famed battle-knight. Beowulf was absent,

(Beowulf was asleep in another part of the palace.)

But another apartment was erstwhile devoted
To the glory-decked Geatman when gold was distributed.
There was hubbub in Heorot. The hand that was famous
She grasped in its gore;[4] grief was renewed then
In homes and houses: 'twas no happy arrangement
In both of the quarters to barter and purchase
With lives of their friends. Then the well-agèd ruler,
The gray-headed war-thane, was woful in spirit,
When his long-trusted liegeman lifeless he knew of,

(Beowulf is sent for.)

His dearest one gone. Quick from a room was
Beowulf brought, brave and triumphant.
As day was dawning in the dusk of the morning,

(He comes at Hrothgar's summons.)

Went then that earlman, champion noble,
Came with comrades, where the clever one bided
Whether God all gracious would grant him a respite
After the woe he had suffered. The war-worthy hero
With a troop of retainers trod then the pavement
(The hall-building groaned), till he greeted the wise one,

(Beowulf inquires how Hrothgar had enjoyed his night's rest.)

The earl of the Ingwins;[5] asked if the night had
Fully refreshed him, as fain he would have it.

Beowulf: Scholar's Edition
XXI - HROTHGAR'S ACCOUNT OF THE MONSTERS
(Hrothgar laments the death of Æschere, his shoulder-companion.)

Hrothgar rejoined, helm of the Scyldings:
"Ask not of joyance! Grief is renewed to
The folk of the Danemen. Dead is Æschere,
Yrmenlaf's brother, older than he,
My true-hearted counsellor, trusty adviser,
Shoulder-companion, when fighting in battle
Our heads we protected, when troopers were clashing,

(He was my ideal hero.)

And heroes were dashing; such an earl should be ever,
An erst-worthy atheling, as Æschere proved him.
The flickering death-spirit became in Heorot
His hand-to-hand murderer; I can not tell whither
The cruel one turned in the carcass exulting,

(This horrible creature came to avenge Grendel's death.)

By cramming discovered.[1] The quarrel she wreaked then,
That last night igone Grendel thou killedst
In grewsomest manner, with grim-holding clutches,
Since too long he had lessened my liege-troop and wasted
My folk-men so foully. He fell in the battle
With forfeit of life, and another has followed,
A mighty crime-worker, her kinsman avenging,
And henceforth hath 'stablished her hatred unyielding,[2]
As it well may appear to many a liegeman,
Who mourneth in spirit the treasure-bestower,
Her heavy heart-sorrow; the hand is now lifeless
Which[3] availed you in every wish that you cherished.

(I have heard my vassals speak of these two uncanny monsters who lived in the moors.)

Land-people heard I, liegemen, this saying,
Dwellers in halls, they had seen very often
A pair of such mighty march-striding creatures,
Far-dwelling spirits, holding the moorlands:
One of them wore, as well they might notice,
The image of woman, the other one wretched
In guise of a man wandered in exile,
Except he was huger than any of earthmen;
Earth-dwelling people entitled him Grendel
In days of yore: they know not their father,
Whe'r ill-going spirits any were borne him

(The inhabit the most desolate and horrible places.)

Ever before. They guard the wolf-coverts,
Lands inaccessible, wind-beaten nesses,
Fearfullest fen-deeps, where a flood from the mountains
'Neath mists of the nesses netherward rattles,
The stream under earth: not far is it henceward
Measured by mile-lengths that the mere-water standeth,
Which forests hang over, with frost-whiting covered,[4]
A firm-rooted forest, the floods overshadow.
There ever at night one an ill-meaning portent
A fire-flood may see; 'mong children of men
None liveth so wise that wot of the bottom;
Though harassed by hounds the heath-stepper seek for,

(Even the hounded deer will not seek refuge in these uncanny regions.)

Fly to the forest, firm-antlered he-deer,
Spurred from afar, his spirit he yieldeth,
His life on the shore, ere in he will venture
To cover his head. Uncanny the place is:
Thence upward ascendeth the surging of waters,
Wan to the welkin, when the wind is stirring
The weathers unpleasing, till the air groweth gloomy,

(To thee only can I look for assistance.)

And the heavens lower. Now is help to be gotten
From thee and thee only! The abode thou know'st not,
The dangerous place where thou'rt able to meet with
The sin-laden hero: seek if thou darest!
For the feud I will fully fee thee with money,
With old-time treasure, as erstwhile I did thee,
With well-twisted jewels, if away thou shalt get thee."

XXII - BEOWULF SEEKS GRENDEL'S MOTHER

Beowulf answered, Ecgtheow's son:

(Beowulf exhorts the old king to arouse himself for action.)

"Grieve not, O wise one! for each it is better,
His friend to avenge than with vehemence wail him;
Each of us must the end-day abide of
His earthly existence; who is able accomplish
Glory ere death! To battle-thane noble
Lifeless lying, 'tis at last most fitting.
Arise, O king, quick let us hasten
To look at the footprint of the kinsman of Grendel!

Beowulf: Scholar's Edition
I promise thee this now: to his place he'll escape not,
To embrace of the earth, nor to mountainous forest,
Nor to depths of the ocean, wherever he wanders.
Practice thou now patient endurance
Of each of thy sorrows, as I hope for thee soothly!"

(Hrothgar rouses himself. His horse is brought.)

Then up sprang the old one, the All-Wielder thanked he,
Ruler Almighty, that the man had outspoken.
Then for Hrothgar a war-horse was decked with a bridle,
Curly-maned courser. The clever folk-leader

(They start on the track of the female monster.)

Stately proceeded: stepped then an earl-troop
Of linden-wood bearers. Her footprints were seen then
Widely in wood-paths, her way o'er the bottoms,
Where she faraway fared o'er fen-country murky,
Bore away breathless the best of retainers
Who pondered with Hrothgar the welfare of country.
The son of the athelings then went o'er the stony,
Declivitous cliffs, the close-covered passes,
Narrow passages, paths unfrequented,
Nesses abrupt, nicker-haunts many;
One of a few of wise-mooded heroes,
He onward advanced to view the surroundings,
Till he found unawares woods of the mountain
O'er hoar-stones hanging, holt-wood unjoyful;
The water stood under, welling and gory.
'Twas irksome in spirit to all of the Danemen,
Friends of the Scyldings, to many a liegeman

(The sight of Æschere's head causes them great sorrow.)

Sad to be suffered, a sorrow unlittle
To each of the earlmen, when to Æschere's head they
Came on the cliff. The current was seething
With blood and with gore (the troopers gazed on it).
The horn anon sang the battle-song ready.
The troop were all seated; they saw 'long the water then

(The water is filled with serpents and sea-dragons.)

Many a serpent, mere-dragons wondrous
Trying the waters, nickers a-lying
On the cliffs of the nesses, which at noonday full often
Go on the sea-deeps their sorrowful journey,
Wild-beasts and wormkind; away then they hastened

Beowulf: Scholar's Edition

(One of them is killed by Beowulf.)

Hot-mooded, hateful, they heard the great clamor,
The war-trumpet winding. One did the Geat-prince
Sunder from earth-joys, with arrow from bowstring,
From his sea-struggle tore him, that the trusty war-missile

(The dead beast is a poor swimmer)

Pierced to his vitals; he proved in the currents
Less doughty at swimming whom death had offcarried.
Soon in the waters the wonderful swimmer
Was straitened most sorely with sword-pointed boar-spears,
Pressed in the battle and pulled to the cliff-edge;
The liegemen then looked on the loath-fashioned stranger.

(Beowulf prepares for a struggle with the monster.)

Beowulf donned then his battle-equipments,
Cared little for life; inlaid and most ample,
The hand-woven corslet which could cover his body,
Must the wave-deeps explore, that war might be powerless
To harm the great hero, and the hating one's grasp might
Not peril his safety; his head was protected
By the light-flashing helmet that should mix with the bottoms,
Trying the eddies, treasure-emblazoned,
Encircled with jewels, as in seasons long past
The weapon-smith worked it, wondrously made it,
With swine-bodies fashioned it, that thenceforward no longer
Brand might bite it, and battle-sword hurt it.
And that was not least of helpers in prowess

(He has Unferth's sword in his hand.)

That Hrothgar's spokesman had lent him when straitened;
And the hilted hand-sword was Hrunting entitled,
Old and most excellent 'mong all of the treasures;
Its blade was of iron, blotted with poison,
Hardened with gore; it failed not in battle
Any hero under heaven in hand who it brandished,
Who ventured to take the terrible journeys,
The battle-field sought; not the earliest occasion
That deeds of daring 'twas destined to 'complish.

(Unferth has little use for swords.)

Ecglaf's kinsman minded not soothly,
Exulting in strength, what erst he had spoken
Drunken with wine, when the weapon he lent to

A sword-hero bolder; himself did not venture
'Neath the strife of the currents his life to endanger,
To fame-deeds perform; there he forfeited glory,
Repute for his strength. Not so with the other
When he clad in his corslet had equipped him for battle.

XXIII - BEOWULF'S FIGHT WITH GRENDEL'S MOTHER
(Beowulf makes a parting speech to Hrothgar.)

Beowulf spake, Ecgtheow's son:
"Recall now, oh, famous kinsman of Healfdene,
Prince very prudent, now to part I am ready,
Gold-friend of earlmen, what erst we agreed on,

(If I fail, act as a kind liegelord to my thanes,)

Should I lay down my life in lending thee assistance,
When my earth-joys were over, thou wouldst evermore serve me
In stead of a father; my faithful thanemen,
My trusty retainers, protect thou and care for,
Fall I in battle: and, Hrothgar belovèd,

(and send Higelac the jewels thou hast given me)

Send unto Higelac the high-valued jewels
Thou to me hast allotted. The lord of the Geatmen
May perceive from the gold, the Hrethling may see it

(I should like my king to know how generous a lord I found thee to be.)

When he looks on the jewels, that a gem-giver found I
Good over-measure, enjoyed him while able.
And the ancient heirloom Unferth permit thou,
The famed one to have, the heavy-sword splendid[1]
The hard-edgèd weapon; with Hrunting to aid me,
I shall gain me glory, or grim-death shall take me."

(Beowulf is eager for the fray.)

The atheling of Geatmen uttered these words and
Heroic did hasten, not any rejoinder
Was willing to wait for; the wave-current swallowed

(He is a whole day reaching the bottom of the sea.)

The doughty-in-battle. Then a day's-length elapsed ere
He was able to see the sea at its bottom.
Early she found then who fifty of winters
The course of the currents kept in her fury,

Grisly and greedy, that the grim one's dominion

(Grendel's mother knows that some one has reached her domains.)

Some one of men from above was exploring.
Forth did she grab them, grappled the warrior
With horrible clutches; yet no sooner she injured
His body unscathèd: the burnie out-guarded,
That she proved but powerless to pierce through the armor,
The limb-mail locked, with loath-grabbing fingers.
The sea-wolf bare then, when bottomward came she,

(She grabs him, and bears him to her den.)

The ring-prince homeward, that he after was powerless
(He had daring to do it) to deal with his weapons,
But many a mere-beast tormented him swimming,

(Sea-monsters bite and strike him.)

Flood-beasts no few with fierce-biting tusks did
Break through his burnie, the brave one pursued they.
The earl then discovered he was down in some cavern
Where no water whatever anywise harmed him,
And the clutch of the current could come not anear him,
Since the roofed-hall prevented; brightness a-gleaming
Fire-light he saw, flashing resplendent.
The good one saw then the sea-bottom's monster,

(Beowulf attacks the mother of Grendel.)

The mighty mere-woman; he made a great onset
With weapon-of-battle, his hand not desisted
From striking, that war-blade struck on her head then
A battle-song greedy. The stranger perceived then

(The sword will not bite.)

The sword would not bite, her life would not injure,
But the falchion failed the folk-prince when straitened:
Erst had it often onsets encountered,
Oft cloven the helmet, the fated one's armor:
'Twas the first time that ever the excellent jewel
Had failed of its fame. Firm-mooded after,
Not heedless of valor, but mindful of glory,
Was Higelac's kinsman; the hero-chief angry
Cast then his carved-sword covered with jewels
That it lay on the earth, hard and steel-pointed;

Beowulf: Scholar's Edition

(The hero throws down all weapons, and again trusts to his hand-grip.)

He hoped in his strength, his hand-grapple sturdy.
So any must act whenever he thinketh
To gain him in battle glory unending,
And is reckless of living. The lord of the War-Geats
(He shrank not from battle) seized by the shoulder[2]
The mother of Grendel; then mighty in struggle
Swung he his enemy, since his anger was kindled,
That she fell to the floor. With furious grapple

(Beowulf falls.)

She gave him requital[3] early thereafter,
And stretched out to grab him; the strongest of warriors
Faint-mooded stumbled, till he fell in his traces,

(The monster sits on him with drawn sword.)

Foot-going champion. Then she sat on the hall-guest
And wielded her war-knife wide-bladed, flashing,
For her son would take vengeance, her one only bairn.

(His armor saves his life.)

His breast-armor woven bode on his shoulder;
It guarded his life, the entrance defended
'Gainst sword-point and edges. Ecgtheow's son there
Had fatally journeyed, champion of Geatmen,
In the arms of the ocean, had the armor not given,
Close-woven corslet, comfort and succor,

(God arranged for his escape.)

And had God most holy not awarded the victory,
All-knowing Lord; easily did heaven's
Ruler most righteous arrange it with justice;[4]
Uprose he erect ready for battle.

XXIV - BEOWULF IS DOUBLE-CONQUEROR
(Beowulf grasps a giant-sword,)

Then he saw mid the war-gems a weapon of victory,
An ancient giant-sword, of edges a-doughty,
Glory of warriors: of weapons 'twas choicest,
Only 'twas larger than any man else was
Able to bear to the battle-encounter,
The good and splendid work of the giants.
He grasped then the sword-hilt, knight of the Scyldings,

Bold and battle-grim, brandished his ring-sword,
Hopeless of living, hotly he smote her,
That the fiend-woman's neck firmly it grappled,

(and fells the female monster.)

Broke through her bone-joints, the bill fully pierced her
Fate-cursèd body, she fell to the ground then:
The hand-sword was bloody, the hero exulted.
The brand was brilliant, brightly it glimmered,
Just as from heaven gemlike shineth
The torch of the firmament. He glanced 'long the building,
And turned by the wall then, Higelac's vassal
Raging and wrathful raised his battle-sword
Strong by the handle. The edge was not useless
To the hero-in-battle, but he speedily wished to
Give Grendel requital for the many assaults he
Had worked on the West-Danes not once, but often,
When he slew in slumber the subjects of Hrothgar,
Swallowed down fifteen sleeping retainers
Of the folk of the Danemen, and fully as many
Carried away, a horrible prey.
He gave him requital, grim-raging champion,

(Beowulf sees the body of Grendel, and cuts off his head.)

When he saw on his rest-place weary of conflict
Grendel lying, of life-joys bereavèd,
As the battle at Heorot erstwhile had scathed him;
His body far bounded, a blow when he suffered,
Death having seized him, sword-smiting heavy,
And he cut off his head then. Early this noticed
The clever carles who as comrades of Hrothgar

(The waters are gory.)

Gazed on the sea-deeps, that the surging wave-currents
Were mightily mingled, the mere-flood was gory:
Of the good one the gray-haired together held converse,

(Beowulf is given up for dead.)

The hoary of head, that they hoped not to see again
The atheling ever, that exulting in victory
He'd return there to visit the distinguished folk-ruler:
Then many concluded the mere-wolf had killed him.[1]
The ninth hour came then. From the ness-edge departed
The bold-mooded Scyldings; the gold-friend of heroes
Homeward betook him. The strangers sat down then

Soul-sick, sorrowful, the sea-waves regarding:
They wished and yet weened not their well-loved friend-lord

(The giant-sword melts.)

To see any more. The sword-blade began then,
The blood having touched it, contracting and shriveling
With battle-icicles; 'twas a wonderful marvel
That it melted entirely, likest to ice when
The Father unbindeth the bond of the frost and
Unwindeth the wave-bands, He who wieldeth dominion
Of times and of tides: a truth-firm Creator.
Nor took he of jewels more in the dwelling,
Lord of the Weders, though they lay all around him,
Than the head and the handle handsome with jewels;
The brand early melted, burnt was the weapon:[2]
So hot was the blood, the strange-spirit poisonous

(The hero swims back to the realms of day.)

That in it did perish. He early swam off then
Who had bided in combat the carnage of haters,
Went up through the ocean; the eddies were cleansèd,
The spacious expanses, when the spirit from farland
His life put aside and this short-lived existence.
The seamen's defender came swimming to land then
Doughty of spirit, rejoiced in his sea-gift,
The bulky burden which he bore in his keeping.
The excellent vassals advanced then to meet him,
To God they were grateful, were glad in their chieftain,
That to see him safe and sound was granted them.
From the high-minded hero, then, helmet and burnie
Were speedily loosened: the ocean was putrid,
The water 'neath welkin weltered with gore.
Forth did they fare, then, their footsteps retracing,
Merry and mirthful, measured the earth-way,
The highway familiar: men very daring[3]
Bare then the head from the sea-cliff, burdening
Each of the earlmen, excellent-valiant.

(It takes four men to carry Grendel's head on a spear.)

Four of them had to carry with labor
The head of Grendel to the high towering gold-hall
Upstuck on the spear, till fourteen most-valiant
And battle-brave Geatmen came there going
Straight to the palace: the prince of the people
Measured the mead-ways, their mood-brave companion.
The atheling of earlmen entered the building,
Deed-valiant man, adorned with distinction,

Doughty shield-warrior, to address King Hrothgar:
Then hung by the hair, the head of Grendel
Was borne to the building, where beer-thanes were drinking,
Loth before earlmen and eke 'fore the lady:
The warriors beheld then a wonderful sight.

XXV - BEOWULF BRINGS HIS TROPHIES--HROTHGAR'S GRATITUDE

(Beowulf relates his last exploit.)

Beowulf spake, offspring of Ecgtheow:
"Lo! we blithely have brought thee, bairn of Healfdene,
Prince of the Scyldings, these presents from ocean
Which thine eye looketh on, for an emblem of glory.
I came off alive from this, narrowly 'scaping:
In war 'neath the water the work with great pains I
Performed, and the fight had been finished quite nearly,
Had God not defended me. I failed in the battle
Aught to accomplish, aided by Hrunting,
Though that weapon was worthy, but the Wielder of earth-folk

(God was fighting with me.)

Gave me willingly to see on the wall a
Heavy old hand-sword hanging in splendor
(He guided most often the lorn and the friendless),
That I swung as a weapon. The wards of the house then
I killed in the conflict (when occasion was given me).
Then the battle-sword burned, the brand that was lifted,[1]
As the blood-current sprang, hottest of war-sweats;
Seizing the hilt, from my foes I offbore it;
I avenged as I ought to their acts of malignity,
The murder of Danemen. I then make thee this promise,

(Heorot is freed from monsters.)

Thou'lt be able in Heorot careless to slumber
With thy throng of heroes and the thanes of thy people
Every and each, of greater and lesser,
And thou needest not fear for them from the selfsame direction
As thou formerly fearedst, oh, folk-lord of Scyldings,
End-day for earlmen." To the age-hoary man then,

(The famous sword is presented to Hrothgar.)

The gray-haired chieftain, the gold-fashioned sword-hilt,
Old-work of giants, was thereupon given;
Since the fall of the fiends, it fell to the keeping

Beowulf: Scholar's Edition
Of the wielder of Danemen, the wonder-smith's labor,
And the bad-mooded being abandoned this world then,
Opponent of God, victim of murder,
And also his mother; it went to the keeping
Of the best of the world-kings, where waters encircle,
Who the scot divided in Scylding dominion.

(Hrothgar looks closely at the old sword.)

Hrothgar discoursed, the hilt he regarded,
The ancient heirloom where an old-time contention's
Beginning was graven: the gurgling currents,
The flood slew thereafter the race of the giants,
They had proved themselves daring: that people was loth to

(It had belonged to a race hateful to God.)

The Lord everlasting, through lash of the billows
The Father gave them final requital.
So in letters of rune on the clasp of the handle
Gleaming and golden, 'twas graven exactly,
Set forth and said, whom that sword had been made for,
Finest of irons, who first it was wrought for,
Wreathed at its handle and gleaming with serpents.
The wise one then said (silent they all were)

(Hrothgar praises Beowulf.)

Son of old Healfdene: "He may say unrefuted
Who performs 'mid the folk-men fairness and truth
(The hoary old ruler remembers the past),
That better by birth is this bairn of the nobles!
Thy fame is extended through far-away countries,
Good friend Beowulf, o'er all of the races,
Thou holdest all firmly, hero-like strength with
Prudence of spirit. I'll prove myself grateful
As before we agreed on; thou granted for long shalt
Become a great comfort to kinsmen and comrades,

(Heremod's career is again contrasted with Beowulf's.)

A help unto heroes. Heremod became not
Such to the Scyldings, successors of Ecgwela;
He grew not to please them, but grievous destruction,
And diresome death-woes to Danemen attracted;
He slew in anger his table-companions,
Trustworthy counsellors, till he turned off lonely
From world-joys away, wide-famous ruler:
Though high-ruling heaven in hero-strength raised him,
In might exalted him, o'er men of all nations

Made him supreme, yet a murderous spirit
Grew in his bosom: he gave then no ring-gems

(A wretched failure of a king, to give no jewels to his retainers.)

To the Danes after custom; endured he unjoyful
Standing the straits from strife that was raging,
Longsome folk-sorrow. Learn then from this,
Lay hold of virtue! Though laden with winters,
I have sung thee these measures. 'Tis a marvel to tell it,

(Hrothgar moralizes.)

How all-ruling God from greatness of spirit
Giveth wisdom to children of men,
Manor and earlship: all things He ruleth.
He often permitteth the mood-thought of man of
The illustrious lineage to lean to possessions,
Allows him earthly delights at his manor,
A high-burg of heroes to hold in his keeping,
Maketh portions of earth-folk hear him,
And a wide-reaching kingdom so that, wisdom failing him,
He himself is unable to reckon its boundaries;
He liveth in luxury, little debars him,
Nor sickness nor age, no treachery-sorrow
 Becloudeth his spirit, conflict nowhere,
No sword-hate, appeareth, but all of the world doth
Wend as he wisheth; the worse he knoweth not,
Till arrant arrogance inward pervading,
Waxeth and springeth, when the warder is sleeping,
The guard of the soul: with sorrows encompassed,
Too sound is his slumber, the slayer is near him,
Who with bow and arrow aimeth in malice.

XXVI - HROTHGAR MORALIZES--REST AFTER LABOR
(A wounded spirit.)

"Then bruised in his bosom he with bitter-toothed missile
Is hurt 'neath his helmet: from harmful pollution
He is powerless to shield him by the wonderful mandates
Of the loath-cursèd spirit; what too long he hath holden
Him seemeth too small, savage he hoardeth,
Nor boastfully giveth gold-plated rings,[1]
The fate of the future flouts and forgetteth
Since God had erst given him greatness no little,
Wielder of Glory. His end-day anear,
It afterward happens that the bodily-dwelling
Fleetingly fadeth, falls into ruins;
Another lays hold who doleth the ornaments,

Beowulf: Scholar's Edition

The nobleman's jewels, nothing lamenting,
Heedeth no terror. Oh, Beowulf dear,
Best of the heroes, from bale-strife defend thee,
And choose thee the better, counsels eternal;

(Be not over proud: life is fleeting, and its strength soon wasteth away.)

Beware of arrogance, world-famous champion!
But a little-while lasts thy life-vigor's fulness;
'Twill after hap early, that illness or sword-edge
Shall part thee from strength, or the grasp of the fire,
Or the wave of the current, or clutch of the edges,
Or flight of the war-spear, or age with its horrors,
Or thine eyes' bright flashing shall fade into darkness:
'Twill happen full early, excellent hero,

(Hrothgar gives an account of his reign.)

That death shall subdue thee. So the Danes a half-century
I held under heaven, helped them in struggles
'Gainst many a race in middle-earth's regions,
With ash-wood and edges, that enemies none
On earth molested me. Lo! offsetting change, now,

(Sorrow after joy.)

Came to my manor, grief after joyance,
When Grendel became my constant visitor,
Inveterate hater: I from that malice
Continually travailed with trouble no little.
Thanks be to God that I gained in my lifetime,
To the Lord everlasting, to look on the gory
Head with mine eyes, after long-lasting sorrow!
Go to the bench now, battle-adornèd
Joy in the feasting: of jewels in common
We'll meet with many when morning appeareth."
The Geatman was gladsome, ganged he immediately
To go to the bench, as the clever one bade him.
Then again as before were the famous-for-prowess,
Hall-inhabiters, handsomely banqueted,
Feasted anew. The night-veil fell then
Dark o'er the warriors. The courtiers rose then;
The gray-haired was anxious to go to his slumbers,
The hoary old Scylding. Hankered the Geatman,

(Beowulf is fagged, and seeks rest.)

The champion doughty, greatly, to rest him:
An earlman early outward did lead him,
Fagged from his faring, from far-country springing,

Who for etiquette's sake all of a liegeman's
Needs regarded, such as seamen at that time
Were bounden to feel. The big-hearted rested;
The building uptowered, spacious and gilded,
The guest within slumbered, till the sable-clad raven
Blithely foreboded the beacon of heaven.
Then the bright-shining sun o'er the bottoms came going;[2]
The warriors hastened, the heads of the peoples
Were ready to go again to their peoples,

(The Geats prepare to leave Dane-land.)

The high-mooded farer would faraway thenceward
Look for his vessel. The valiant one bade then,[3]

(Unferth asks Beowulf to accept his sword as a gift. Beowulf thanks him.)

Offspring of Ecglaf, off to bear Hrunting,
To take his weapon, his well-beloved iron;
He him thanked for the gift, saying good he accounted
The war-friend and mighty, nor chid he with words then
The blade of the brand: 'twas a brave-mooded hero.
When the warriors were ready, arrayed in their trappings,
The atheling dear to the Danemen advanced then
On to the dais, where the other was sitting,
Grim-mooded hero, greeted King Hrothgar.

XXVII - SORROW AT PARTING
(Beowulf's farewell.)

Beowulf spake, Ecgtheow's offspring:
"We men of the water wish to declare now
Fared from far-lands, we're firmly determined
To seek King Higelac. Here have we fitly
Been welcomed and feasted, as heart would desire it;
Good was the greeting. If greater affection
I am anywise able ever on earth to
Gain at thy hands, ruler of heroes,
Than yet I have done, I shall quickly be ready

(I shall be ever ready to aid thee.)

For combat and conflict. O'er the course of the waters
Learn I that neighbors alarm thee with terror,
As haters did whilom, I hither will bring thee
For help unto heroes henchmen by thousands.

(My liegelord will encourage me in aiding thee.)

Beowulf: Scholar's Edition
I know as to Higelac, the lord of the Geatmen,
Though young in years, he yet will permit me,
By words and by works, ward of the people,
Fully to furnish thee forces and bear thee
My lance to relieve thee, if liegemen shall fail thee,
And help of my hand-strength; if Hrethric be treating,
Bairn of the king, at the court of the Geatmen,
He thereat may find him friends in abundance:
Faraway countries he were better to seek for
Who trusts in himself." Hrothgar discoursed then,
Making rejoinder: "These words thou hast uttered
All-knowing God hath given thy spirit!

(O Beowulf, thou art wise beyond thy years.)

Ne'er heard I an earlman thus early in life
More clever in speaking: thou'rt cautious of spirit,
Mighty of muscle, in mouth-answers prudent.
I count on the hope that, happen it ever
That missile shall rob thee of Hrethel's descendant,
Edge-horrid battle, and illness or weapon
Deprive thee of prince, of people's protector,

(Should Higelac die, the Geats could find no better successor than thou wouldst make.)

And life thou yet holdest, the Sea-Geats will never
Find a more fitting folk-lord to choose them,
Gem-ward of heroes, than _thou_ mightest prove thee,
If the kingdom of kinsmen thou carest to govern.
Thy mood-spirit likes me the longer the better,
Beowulf dear: thou hast brought it to pass that
To both these peoples peace shall be common,

(Thou hast healed the ancient breach between our races.)

To Geat-folk and Danemen, the strife be suspended,
The secret assailings they suffered in yore-days;
And also that jewels be shared while I govern
The wide-stretching kingdom, and that many shall visit
Others o'er the ocean with excellent gift-gems:
The ring-adorned bark shall bring o'er the currents
Presents and love-gifts. This people I know
Tow'rd foeman and friend firmly established,[1]
After ancient etiquette everywise blameless."
Then the warden of earlmen gave him still farther,

(Parting gifts)

Kinsman of Healfdene, a dozen of jewels,
Bade him safely seek with the presents
His well-beloved people, early returning.

(Hrothgar kisses Beowulf, and weeps.)

Then the noble-born king kissed the distinguished,
Dear-lovèd liegeman, the Dane-prince saluted him,
And claspèd his neck; tears from him fell,
From the gray-headed man: he two things expected,
Agèd and reverend, but rather the second,
[2]That bold in council they'd meet thereafter.
The man was so dear that he failed to suppress the
Emotions that moved him, but in mood-fetters fastened

(The old king is deeply grieved to part with his benefactor.)

The long-famous hero longeth in secret
Deep in his spirit for the dear-beloved man
Though not a blood-kinsman. Beowulf thenceward,
Gold-splendid warrior, walked o'er the meadows
Exulting in treasure: the sea-going vessel
Riding at anchor awaited its owner.
As they pressed on their way then, the present of Hrothgar

(Giving liberally is the true proof of kingship.)

Was frequently referred to: a folk-king indeed that
Everyway blameless, till age did debar him
The joys of his might, which hath many oft injured.

XXVIII - THE HOMEWARD JOURNEY--THE TWO QUEENS

Then the band of very valiant retainers
Came to the current; they were clad all in armor,

(The coast-guard again.)

In link-woven burnies. The land-warder noticed
The return of the earlmen, as he erstwhile had seen them;
Nowise with insult he greeted the strangers
From the naze of the cliff, but rode on to meet them;
Said the bright-armored visitors[1] vesselward traveled
Welcome to Weders. The wide-bosomed craft then
Lay on the sand, laden with armor,
With horses and jewels, the ring-stemmèd sailer:
The mast uptowered o'er the treasure of Hrothgar.

(Beowulf gives the guard a handsome sword.)

Beowulf: Scholar's Edition

To the boat-ward a gold-bound brand he presented,
That he was afterwards honored on the ale-bench more highly
As the heirloom's owner.² Set he out on his vessel,
To drive on the deep, Dane-country left he.
Along by the mast then a sea-garment fluttered,
A rope-fastened sail. The sea-boat resounded,
The wind o'er the waters the wave-floater nowise
Kept from its journey; the sea-goer traveled,
The foamy-necked floated forth o'er the currents,
The well-fashioned vessel o'er the ways of the ocean,

(The Geats see their own land again.)

Till they came within sight of the cliffs of the Geatmen,
The well-known headlands. The wave-goer hastened
Driven by breezes, stood on the shore.

(The port-warden is anxiously looking for them.)

Prompt at the ocean, the port-ward was ready,
Who long in the past outlooked in the distance,³
At water's-edge waiting well-lovèd heroes;
He bound to the bank then the broad-bosomed vessel
Fast in its fetters, lest the force of the waters
Should be able to injure the ocean-wood winsome.
Bade he up then take the treasure of princes,
Plate-gold and fretwork; not far was it thence
To go off in search of the giver of jewels:
Hrethel's son Higelac at home there remaineth,⁴
Himself with his comrades close to the sea-coast.
The building was splendid, the king heroic,
Great in his hall, Hygd very young was,

(Hygd, the noble queen of Higelac, lavish of gifts.)

Fine-mooded, clever, though few were the winters
That the daughter of Hæreth had dwelt in the borough;
But she nowise was cringing nor niggard of presents,
Of ornaments rare, to the race of the Geatmen.

(Offa's consort, Thrytho, is contrasted with Hygd.)

Thrytho nursed anger, excellent⁵ folk-queen,
Hot-burning hatred: no hero whatever
'Mong household companions, her husband excepted

(She is a terror to all save her husband.)

Dared to adventure to look at the woman
With eyes in the daytime;⁶ but he knew that death-chains

Hand-wreathed were wrought him: early thereafter,
When the hand-strife was over, edges were ready,
That fierce-raging sword-point had to force a decision,
Murder-bale show. Such no womanly custom
For a lady to practise, though lovely her person,
That a weaver-of-peace, on pretence of anger
A belovèd liegeman of life should deprive.
Soothly this hindered Heming's kinsman;
Other ale-drinking earlmen asserted
That fearful folk-sorrows fewer she wrought them,
Treacherous doings, since first she was given
Adorned with gold to the war-hero youthful,
For her origin honored, when Offa's great palace
O'er the fallow flood by her father's instructions
She sought on her journey, where she afterwards fully,
Famed for her virtue, her fate on the king's-seat
Enjoyed in her lifetime, love did she hold with
The ruler of heroes, the best, it is told me,
Of all of the earthmen that oceans encompass,
Of earl-kindreds endless; hence Offa was famous
Far and widely, by gifts and by battles,
Spear-valiant hero; the home of his fathers
He governed with wisdom, whence Eomær did issue
For help unto heroes, Heming's kinsman,
Grandson of Garmund, great in encounters.

XXIX - BEOWULF AND HIGELAC

Then the brave one departed, his band along with him,

(Beowulf and his party seek Higelac.)

Seeking the sea-shore, the sea-marches treading,
The wide-stretching shores. The world-candle glimmered,
The sun from the southward; they proceeded then onward,
Early arriving where they heard that the troop-lord,
Ongentheow's slayer, excellent, youthful
Folk-prince and warrior was distributing jewels,
Close in his castle. The coming of Beowulf
Was announced in a message quickly to Higelac,
That the folk-troop's defender forth to the palace
The linden-companion alive was advancing,
Secure from the combat courtward a-going.
The building was early inward made ready
For the foot-going guests as the good one had ordered.

(Beowulf sits by his liegelord.)

He sat by the man then who had lived through the struggle,
Kinsman by kinsman, when the king of the people
Had in lordly language saluted the dear one,

(Queen Hygd receives the heroes.)

In words that were formal. The daughter of Hæreth
Coursed through the building, carrying mead-cups:[1]
She loved the retainers, tendered the beakers
To the high-minded Geatmen. Higelac 'gan then

(Higelac is greatly interested in Beowulf's adventures.)

Pleasantly plying his companion with questions
In the high-towering palace. A curious interest
Tormented his spirit, what meaning to see in
The Sea-Geats' adventures: "Beowulf worthy,

(Give an account of thy adventures, Beowulf dear.)

How throve your journeying, when thou thoughtest suddenly
Far o'er the salt-streams to seek an encounter,
A battle at Heorot? Hast bettered for Hrothgar,
The famous folk-leader, his far-published sorrows
Any at all? In agony-billows

(My suspense has been great.)

I mused upon torture, distrusted the journey
Of the belovèd liegeman; I long time did pray thee
By no means to seek out the murderous spirit,
To suffer the South-Danes themselves to decide on[2]
Grappling with Grendel. To God I am thankful
To be suffered to see thee safe from thy journey."

(Beowulf narrates his adventures.)

Beowulf answered, bairn of old Ecgtheow:
"'Tis hidden by no means, Higelac chieftain,
From many of men, the meeting so famous,
What mournful moments of me and of Grendel
Were passed in the place where he pressing affliction
On the Victory-Scyldings scathefully brought,
Anguish forever; that all I avengèd,
So that any under heaven of the kinsmen of Grendel

(Grendel's kindred have no cause to boast.)

Needeth not boast of that cry-in-the-morning,
Who longest liveth of the loth-going kindred,[3]

Encompassed by moorland. I came in my journey
To the royal ring-hall, Hrothgar to greet there:

(Hrothgar received me very cordially.)

Soon did the famous scion of Healfdene,
When he understood fully the spirit that led me,
Assign me a seat with the son of his bosom.
The troop was in joyance; mead-glee greater
'Neath arch of the ether not ever beheld I

(The queen also showed up no little honor.)

'Mid hall-building holders. The highly-famed queen,
Peace-tie of peoples, oft passed through the building,
Cheered the young troopers; she oft tendered a hero
A beautiful ring-band, ere she went to her sitting.

(Hrothgar's lovely daughter.)

Oft the daughter of Hrothgar in view of the courtiers
To the earls at the end the ale-vessel carried,
Whom Freaware I heard then hall-sitters title,
When nail-adorned jewels she gave to the heroes:

(She is betrothed to Ingeld, in order to unite the Danes and Heathobards.)

Gold-bedecked, youthful, to the glad son of Froda
Her faith has been plighted; the friend of the Scyldings,
The guard of the kingdom, hath given his sanction,[4]
And counts it a vantage, for a part of the quarrels,
A portion of hatred, to pay with the woman.
[5]Somewhere not rarely, when the ruler has fallen,
The life-taking lance relaxeth its fury
For a brief breathing-spell, though the bride be charming!

XXX - BEOWULF NARRATES HIS ADVENTURES TO HIGELAC

"It well may discomfit the prince of the Heathobards
And each of the thanemen of earls that attend him,
When he goes to the building escorting the woman,
That a noble-born Daneman the knights should be feasting:
There gleam on his person the leavings of elders
Hard and ring-bright, Heathobards' treasure,
While they wielded their arms, till they misled to the battle
Their own dear lives and belovèd companions.
He saith at the banquet who the collar beholdeth,

Beowulf: Scholar's Edition

An ancient ash-warrior who earlmen's destruction
Clearly recalleth (cruel his spirit),
Sadly beginneth sounding the youthful
Thane-champion's spirit through the thoughts of his bosom,
War-grief to waken, and this word-answer speaketh:

(Ingeld is stirred up to break the truce.)

'Art thou able, my friend, to know when thou seest it
The brand which thy father bare to the conflict
In his latest adventure, 'neath visor of helmet,
The dearly-loved iron, where Danemen did slay him,
And brave-mooded Scyldings, on the fall of the heroes,
(When vengeance was sleeping) the slaughter-place wielded?
E'en now some man of the murderer's progeny
Exulting in ornaments enters the building,
Boasts of his blood-shedding, offbeareth the jewel
Which thou shouldst wholly hold in possession!'
So he urgeth and mindeth on every occasion
With woe-bringing words, till waxeth the season
When the woman's thane for the works of his father,
The bill having bitten, blood-gory sleepeth,
Fated to perish; the other one thenceward
'Scapeth alive, the land knoweth thoroughly.[1]
Then the oaths of the earlmen on each side are broken,
When rancors unresting are raging in Ingeld
And his wife-love waxeth less warm after sorrow.
So the Heathobards' favor not faithful I reckon,
Their part in the treaty not true to the Danemen,
Their friendship not fast. I further shall tell thee

(Having made these preliminary statements, I will now tell thee of Grendel, the monster.)

More about Grendel, that thou fully mayst hear,
Ornament-giver, what afterward came from
The hand-rush of heroes. When heaven's bright jewel
O'er earthfields had glided, the stranger came raging,
The horrible night-fiend, us for to visit,
Where wholly unharmed the hall we were guarding.

(Hondscio fell first)

To Hondscio happened a hopeless contention,
Death to the doomed one, dead he fell foremost,
Girded war-champion; to him Grendel became then,
To the vassal distinguished, a tooth-weaponed murderer,
The well-beloved henchman's body all swallowed.
Not the earlier off empty of hand did
The bloody-toothed murderer, mindful of evils,

Beowulf: Scholar's Edition

Wish to escape from the gold-giver's palace,
But sturdy of strength he strove to outdo me,
Hand-ready grappled. A glove was suspended
Spacious and wondrous, in art-fetters fastened,
Which was fashioned entirely by touch of the craftman
From the dragon's skin by the devil's devices:
He down in its depths would do me unsadly
One among many, deed-doer raging,
Though sinless he saw me; not so could it happen
When I in my anger upright did stand.
'Tis too long to recount how requital I furnished
For every evil to the earlmen's destroyer;

(I reflected honor upon my people.)

'Twas there, my prince, that I proudly distinguished
Thy land with my labors. He left and retreated,
He lived his life a little while longer:
Yet his right-hand guarded his footstep in Heorot,
And sad-mooded thence to the sea-bottom fell he,
Mournful in mind. For the might-rush of battle

(King Hrothgar lavished gifts upon me.)

The friend of the Scyldings, with gold that was plated,
With ornaments many, much requited me,
When daylight had dawned, and down to the banquet
We had sat us together. There was chanting and joyance:
The age-stricken Scylding asked many questions
And of old-times related; oft light-ringing harp-strings,
Joy-telling wood, were touched by the brave one;
Now he uttered measures, mourning and truthful,
Then the large-hearted land-king a legend of wonder
Truthfully told us. Now troubled with years

(The old king is sad over the loss of his youthful vigor.)

The age-hoary warrior afterward began to
Mourn for the might that marked him in youth-days;
His breast within boiled, when burdened with winters
Much he remembered. From morning till night then
We joyed us therein as etiquette suffered,
Till the second night season came unto earth-folk.
Then early thereafter, the mother of Grendel

(Grendel's mother.)

Was ready for vengeance, wretched she journeyed;
Her son had death ravished, the wrath of the Geatmen.

The horrible woman avengèd her offspring,
And with mighty mainstrength murdered a hero.

(Æschere falls a prey to her vengeance.)

There the spirit of Æschere, agèd adviser,
Was ready to vanish; nor when morn had lightened
Were they anywise suffered to consume him with fire,
Folk of the Danemen, the death-weakened hero,
Nor the belovèd liegeman to lay on the pyre;

(She suffered not his body to be burned, but ate it.)

She the corpse had offcarried in the clutch of the foeman[2]
'Neath mountain-brook's flood. To Hrothgar 'twas saddest
Of pains that ever had preyed on the chieftain;
By the life of thee the land-prince then me[3]
Besought very sadly, in sea-currents' eddies
To display my prowess, to peril my safety,
Might-deeds accomplish; much did he promise.

(I sought the creature in her den,)

I found then the famous flood-current's cruel,
Horrible depth-warder. A while unto us two
Hand was in common; the currents were seething
With gore that was clotted, and Grendel's fierce mother's

(and hewed her head off.)

Head I offhacked in the hall at the bottom
With huge-reaching sword-edge, hardly I wrested
My life from her clutches; not doomed was I then,

(Jewels were freely bestowed upon me.)

But the warden of earlmen afterward gave me
Jewels in quantity, kinsman of Healfdene.

XXXI - GIFT-GIVING IS MUTUAL

"So the belovèd land-prince lived in decorum;
I had missed no rewards, no meeds of my prowess,
But he gave me jewels, regarding my wishes,
Healfdene his bairn; I'll bring them to thee, then,

(All my gifts I lay at thy feet.)

Atheling of earlmen, offer them gladly.
And still unto thee is all my affection:[1]
But few of my folk-kin find I surviving
But thee, dear Higelac!" Bade he in then to carry[2]
The boar-image, banner, battle-high helmet,
Iron-gray armor, the excellent weapon,

(This armor I have belonged of yore to Heregar.)

In song-measures said: "This suit-for-the-battle
Hrothgar presented me, bade me expressly,
Wise-mooded atheling, thereafter to tell thee[3]
The whole of its history, said King Heregar owned it,
Dane-prince for long: yet he wished not to give then
The mail to his son, though dearly he loved him,
Hereward the hardy. Hold all in joyance!"
I heard that there followed hard on the jewels
Two braces of stallions of striking resemblance,
Dappled and yellow; he granted him usance
Of horses and treasures. So a kinsman should bear him,
No web of treachery weave for another,
Nor by cunning craftiness cause the destruction

(Higelac loves his nephew Beowulf.)

Of trusty companion. Most precious to Higelac,
The bold one in battle, was the bairn of his sister,
And each unto other mindful of favors.

(Beowulf gives Hygd the necklace that Wealhtheow had given him.)

I am told that to Hygd he proffered the necklace,
Wonder-gem rare that Wealhtheow gave him,
The troop-leader's daughter, a trio of horses
Slender and saddle-bright; soon did the jewel
Embellish her bosom, when the beer-feast was over.
So Ecgtheow's bairn brave did prove him,

(Beowulf is famous.)

War-famous man, by deeds that were valiant,
He lived in honor, belovèd companions
Slew not carousing; his mood was not cruel,
But by hand-strength hugest of heroes then living
The brave one retained the bountiful gift that
The Lord had allowed him. Long was he wretched,
So that sons of the Geatmen accounted him worthless,
And the lord of the liegemen loth was to do him
Mickle of honor, when mead-cups were passing;

They fully believed him idle and sluggish,

(He is requited for the slights suffered in earlier days.)

An indolent atheling: to the honor-blest man there
Came requital for the cuts he had suffered.
The folk-troop's defender bade fetch to the building
The heirloom of Hrethel, embellished with gold,

(Higelac overwhelms the conqueror with gifts.)

So the brave one enjoined it; there was jewel no richer
In the form of a weapon 'mong Geats of that era;
In Beowulf's keeping he placed it and gave him
Seven of thousands, manor and lordship.
Common to both was land 'mong the people,
Estate and inherited rights and possessions,
To the second one specially spacious dominions,
To the one who was better. It afterward happened
In days that followed, befell the battle-thanes,

(After Heardred's death, Beowulf becomes king.)

After Higelac's death, and when Heardred was murdered
With weapons of warfare 'neath well-covered targets,
When valiant battlemen in victor-band sought him,
War-Scylfing heroes harassed the nephew
Of Hereric in battle. To Beowulf's keeping
 Turned there in time extensive dominions:

(He rules the Geats fifty years.)

He fittingly ruled them a fifty of winters
(He a man-ruler wise was, manor-ward old) till
A certain one 'gan, on gloom-darkening nights, a

(The fire-drake.)

Dragon, to govern, who guarded a treasure,
A high-rising stone-cliff, on heath that was grayish:
A path 'neath it lay, unknown unto mortals.
Some one of earthmen entered the mountain,
The heathenish hoard laid hold of with ardor;
…

XXXII - THE HOARD AND THE DRAGON

He sought of himself who sorely did harm him,
But, for need very pressing, the servant of one of

The sons of the heroes hate-blows evaded,
Seeking for shelter and the sin-driven warrior
Took refuge within there. He early looked in it,
...
... when the onset surprised him,

(The hoard.)

He a gem-vessel saw there: many of suchlike
Ancient ornaments in the earth-cave were lying,
As in days of yore some one of men of
Illustrious lineage, as a legacy monstrous,
There had secreted them, careful and thoughtful,
Dear-valued jewels. Death had offsnatched them,
In the days of the past, and the one man moreover
Of the flower of the folk who fared there the longest,
Was fain to defer it, friend-mourning warder,
A little longer to be left in enjoyment
Of long-lasting treasure.[1] A barrow all-ready
Stood on the plain the stream-currents nigh to,
New by the ness-edge, unnethe of approaching:
The keeper of rings carried within a
[2]Ponderous deal of the treasure of nobles,
Of gold that was beaten, briefly he spake then:[3]

(The ring-giver bewails the loss of retainers.)

"Hold thou, O Earth, now heroes no more may,
The earnings of earlmen. Lo! erst in thy bosom
Worthy men won them; war-death hath ravished,
Perilous life-bale, all my warriors,
Liegemen belovèd, who this life have forsaken,
Who hall-pleasures saw. No sword-bearer have I,
And no one to burnish the gold-plated vessel,
The high-valued beaker: my heroes are vanished.
The hardy helmet behung with gilding
Shall be reaved of its riches: the ring-cleansers slumber
Who were charged to have ready visors-for-battle,
And the burnie that bided in battle-encounter
O'er breaking of war-shields the bite of the edges
Moulds with the hero. The ring-twisted armor,
Its lord being lifeless, no longer may journey
Hanging by heroes; harp-joy is vanished,
The rapture of glee-wood, no excellent falcon
Swoops through the building, no swift-footed charger
Grindeth the gravel. A grievous destruction
No few of the world-folk widely hath scattered!"
So, woful of spirit one after all
Lamented mournfully, moaning in sadness

By day and by night, till death with its billows

(The fire-dragon)

Dashed on his spirit. Then the ancient dusk-scather
Found the great treasure standing all open,
He who flaming and fiery flies to the barrows,
Naked war-dragon, nightly escapeth
Encompassed with fire; men under heaven
Widely beheld him. 'Tis said that he looks for[4]
The hoard in the earth, where old he is guarding
The heathenish treasure; he'll be nowise the better.

(The dragon meets his match.)

So three-hundred winters the waster of peoples
Held upon earth that excellent hoard-hall,
Till the forementioned earlman angered him bitterly:
The beat-plated beaker he bare to his chieftain
And fullest remission for all his remissness
Begged of his liegelord. Then the hoard[5] was discovered,
The treasure was taken, his petition was granted

(The hero plunders the dragon's den)

The lorn-mooded liegeman. His lord regarded
The old-work of earth-folk--'twas the earliest occasion.
When the dragon awoke, the strife was renewed there;
 He snuffed 'long the stone then, stout-hearted found he
The footprint of foeman; too far had he gone
With cunning craftiness close to the head of
The fire-spewing dragon. So undoomed he may 'scape from
Anguish and exile with ease who possesseth
The favor of Heaven. The hoard-warden eagerly
Searched o'er the ground then, would meet with the person
That caused him sorrow while in slumber reclining:
Gleaming and wild he oft went round the cavern,
All of it outward; not any of earthmen
Was seen in that desert.[6] Yet he joyed in the battle,
Rejoiced in the conflict: oft he turned to the barrow,
Sought for the gem-cup;[7] this he soon perceived then

(The dragon perceives that some one has disturbed his treasure.)

That some man or other had discovered the gold,
The famous folk-treasure. Not fain did the hoard-ward
Wait until evening; then the ward of the barrow
Was angry in spirit, the loathèd one wished to
Pay for the dear-valued drink-cup with fire.
Then the day was done as the dragon would have it,

He no longer would wait on the wall, but departed

(The dragon is infuriated.)

Fire-impelled, flaming. Fearful the start was
To earls in the land, as it early thereafter
To their giver-of-gold was grievously ended.

XXXIII - BRAVE THOUGH AGED--REMINISCENCES
(The dragon spits fire.)

The stranger began then to vomit forth fire,
To burn the great manor; the blaze then glimmered
For anguish to earlmen, not anything living
Was the hateful air-goer willing to leave there.
The war of the worm widely was noticed,
The feud of the foeman afar and anear,
How the enemy injured the earls of the Geatmen,
Harried with hatred: back he hied to the treasure,
To the well-hidden cavern ere the coming of daylight.
He had circled with fire the folk of those regions,
With brand and burning; in the barrow he trusted,
In the wall and his war-might: the weening deceived him.

(Beowulf hears of the havoc wrought by the dragon.)

Then straight was the horror to Beowulf published,
Early forsooth, that his own native homestead,[1]
The best of buildings, was burning and melting,
Gift-seat of Geatmen. 'Twas a grief to the spirit
Of the good-mooded hero, the greatest of sorrows:

(He fears that Heaven is punishing him for some crime.)

The wise one weened then that wielding his kingdom
'Gainst the ancient commandments, he had bitterly angered
The Lord everlasting: with lorn meditations
His bosom welled inward, as was nowise his custom.
The fire-spewing dragon fully had wasted
The fastness of warriors, the water-land outward,
The manor with fire. The folk-ruling hero,
Prince of the Weders, was planning to wreak him.
The warmen's defender bade them to make him,
Earlmen's atheling, an excellent war-shield

(He orders an iron shield to be made from him, wood is useless.)

Wholly of iron: fully he knew then
That wood from the forest was helpless to aid him,

Shield against fire. The long-worthy ruler
Must live the last of his limited earth-days,
Of life in the world and the worm along with him,
Though he long had been holding hoard-wealth in plenty.

(He determines to fight alone.)

Then the ring-prince disdained to seek with a war-band,
With army extensive, the air-going ranger;
He felt no fear of the foeman's assaults and
He counted for little the might of the dragon,
His power and prowess: for previously dared he

(Beowulf's early triumphs referred to)

A heap of hostility, hazarded dangers,
War-thane, when Hrothgar's palace he cleansèd,
Conquering combatant, clutched in the battle
The kinsmen of Grendel, of kindred detested.[2]

(Higelac's death recalled.)

'Twas of hand-fights not least where Higelac was slaughtered,
When the king of the Geatmen with clashings of battle,
Friend-lord of folks in Frisian dominions,
Offspring of Hrethrel perished through sword-drink,
With battle-swords beaten; thence Beowulf came then
On self-help relying, swam through the waters;
He bare on his arm, lone-going, thirty
Outfits of armor, when the ocean he mounted.
The Hetwars by no means had need to be boastful
Of their fighting afoot, who forward to meet him
Carried their war-shields: not many returned from
The brave-mooded battle-knight back to their homesteads.
Ecgtheow's bairn o'er the bight-courses swam then,
Lone-goer lorn to his land-folk returning,
Where Hygd to him tendered treasure and kingdom,

(Heardred's lack of capacity to rule.)

Rings and dominion: her son she not trusted,
To be able to keep the kingdom devised him
'Gainst alien races, on the death of King Higelac.

(Beowulf's tact and delicacy recalled.)

Yet the sad ones succeeded not in persuading the atheling
In any way ever, to act as a suzerain
To Heardred, or promise to govern the kingdom;
Yet with friendly counsel in the folk he sustained him,

Gracious, with honor, till he grew to be older,

(Reference is here made to a visit which Beowulf receives from Eanmund and Eadgils, why they come is not known.)

Wielded the Weders. Wide-fleeing outlaws,
Ohthere's sons, sought him o'er the waters:
They had stirred a revolt 'gainst the helm of the Scylfings,
The best of the sea-kings, who in Swedish dominions
Distributed treasure, distinguished folk-leader.
'Twas the end of his earth-days; injury fatal³
By swing of the sword he received as a greeting,
Offspring of Higelac; Ongentheow's bairn
Later departed to visit his homestead,
When Heardred was dead; let Beowulf rule them,
Govern the Geatmen: good was that folk-king.

XXXIV - BEOWULF SEEKS THE DRAGON--BEOWULF'S REMINISCENCES

He planned requital for the folk-leader's ruin
In days thereafter, to Eadgils the wretched
Becoming an enemy. Ohthere's son then
Went with a war-troop o'er the wide-stretching currents
With warriors and weapons: with woe-journeys cold he
After avenged him, the king's life he took.

(Beowulf has been preserved through many perils.)

So he came off uninjured from all of his battles,
Perilous fights, offspring of Ecgtheow,
From his deeds of daring, till that day most momentous
When he fate-driven fared to fight with the dragon.

(With eleven comrades, he seeks the dragon.)

With eleven companions the prince of the Geatmen
Went lowering with fury to look at the fire-drake:
Inquiring he'd found how the feud had arisen,
Hate to his heroes; the highly-famed gem-vessel
Was brought to his keeping through the hand of th' informer.

(A guide leads the way, but)

That in the throng was thirteenth of heroes,
That caused the beginning of conflict so bitter,
Captive and wretched, must sad-mooded thenceward

Beowulf: Scholar's Edition
(very reluctantly.)

Point out the place: he passed then unwillingly
To the spot where he knew of the notable cavern,
The cave under earth, not far from the ocean,
The anger of eddies, which inward was full of
Jewels and wires: a warden uncanny,
Warrior weaponed, wardered the treasure,
Old under earth; no easy possession
For any of earth-folk access to get to.
Then the battle-brave atheling sat on the naze-edge,
While the gold-friend of Geatmen gracious saluted
His fireside-companions: woe was his spirit,
Death-boding, wav'ring; Weird very near him,
Who must seize the old hero, his soul-treasure look for,
Dragging aloof his life from his body:
Not flesh-hidden long was the folk-leader's spirit.
Beowulf spake, Ecgtheow's son:

(Beowulf's retrospect.)

"I survived in my youth-days many a conflict,
Hours of onset: that all I remember.
I was seven-winters old when the jewel-prince took me,
High-lord of heroes, at the hands of my father,
Hrethel the hero-king had me in keeping,

(Hrethel took me when I was seven.)

Gave me treasure and feasting, our kinship remembered;
Not ever was I any less dear to him

(He treated me as a son.)

Knight in the boroughs, than the bairns of his household,
Herebald and Hæthcyn and Higelac mine.
To the eldest unjustly by acts of a kinsman
Was murder-bed strewn, since him Hæthcyn from horn-bow

(One of the brothers accidentally kills another.)

His sheltering chieftain shot with an arrow,
Erred in his aim and injured his kinsman,
One brother the other, with blood-sprinkled spear:

(No fee could compound for such a calamity.)

'Twas a feeless fight, finished in malice,
Sad to his spirit; the folk-prince however
Had to part from existence with vengeance untaken.

([A parallel case is supposed.])

So to hoar-headed hero 'tis heavily crushing[1]
To live to see his son as he rideth
Young on the gallows: then measures he chanteth,
A song of sorrow, when his son is hanging
For the raven's delight, and aged and hoary
He is unable to offer any assistance.
Every morning his offspring's departure
Is constant recalled: he cares not to wait for
The birth of an heir in his borough-enclosures,
Since that one through death-pain the deeds hath experienced.
He heart-grieved beholds in the house of his son the
Wine-building wasted, the wind-lodging places
Reaved of their roaring; the riders are sleeping,
The knights in the grave; there's no sound of the harp-wood,
Joy in the yards, as of yore were familiar.

XXXV - REMINISCENCES (continued)--BEOWULF'S LAST BATTLE

"He seeks then his chamber, singeth a woe-song
One for the other; all too extensive
Seemed homesteads and plains. So the helm of the Weders

(Hrethel grieves for Herebald.)

Mindful of Herebald heart-sorrow carried,
Stirred with emotion, nowise was able
To wreak his ruin on the ruthless destroyer:
He was unable to follow the warrior with hatred,
With deeds that were direful, though dear he not held him.
Then pressed by the pang this pain occasioned him,
He gave up glee, God-light elected;
He left to his sons, as the man that is rich does,
His land and fortress, when from life he departed.

(Strife between Swedes and Geats.)

Then was crime and hostility 'twixt Swedes and Geatmen,
O'er wide-stretching water warring was mutual,
Burdensome hatred, when Hrethel had perished,
And Ongentheow's offspring were active and valiant,
Wished not to hold to peace oversea, but
Round Hreosna-beorh often accomplished
Cruelest massacre. This my kinsman avengèd,
The feud and fury, as 'tis found on inquiry,

Though one of them paid it with forfeit of life-joys,

(Hæthcyn's fall at Ravenswood.)

With price that was hard: the struggle became then
Fatal to Hæthcyn, lord of the Geatmen.
Then I heard that at morning one brother the other
With edges of irons egged on to murder,
Where Ongentheow maketh onset on Eofor:
The helmet crashed, the hoary-haired Scylfing
Sword-smitten fell, his hand then remembered
Feud-hate sufficient, refused not the death-blow.

(I requited him for the jewels he gave me.)

The gems that he gave me, with jewel-bright sword I
'Quited in contest, as occasion was offered:
Land he allowed me, life-joy at homestead,
Manor to live on. Little he needed
From Gepids or Danes or in Sweden to look for
Trooper less true, with treasure to buy him;
'Mong foot-soldiers ever in front I would hie me,
Alone in the vanguard, and evermore gladly
Warfare shall wage, while this weapon endureth
That late and early often did serve me

(Beowulf refers to his having slain Dæghrefn.)

When I proved before heroes the slayer of Dæghrefn,
Knight of the Hugmen: he by no means was suffered
To the king of the Frisians to carry the jewels,
The breast-decoration; but the banner-possessor
Bowed in the battle, brave-mooded atheling.
No weapon was slayer, but war-grapple broke then
The surge of his spirit, his body destroying.
Now shall weapon's edge make war for the treasure,
And hand and firm-sword." Beowulf spake then,
Boast-words uttered--the latest occasion:

(He boasts of his youthful prowess, and declares himself still fearless.)

"I braved in my youth-days battles unnumbered;
Still am I willing the struggle to look for,
Fame-deeds perform, folk-warden prudent,
If the hateful despoiler forth from his cavern
Seeketh me out!" Each of the heroes,
Helm-bearers sturdy, he thereupon greeted

(His last salutations.)

Belovèd co-liegemen--his last salutation:
"No brand would I bear, no blade for the dragon,
Wist I a way my word-boast to 'complish[1]
Else with the monster, as with Grendel I did it;
But fire in the battle hot I expect there,
Furious flame-burning: so I fixed on my body
Target and war-mail. The ward of the barrow[2]
I'll not flee from a foot-length, the foeman uncanny.
At the wall 'twill befall us as Fate decreeth,

(Let Fate decide between us.)

Each one's Creator. I am eager in spirit,
With the wingèd war-hero to away with all boasting.
Bide on the barrow with burnies protected,

(Wait ye here till the battle is over.)

Earls in armor, which of us two may better
Bear his disaster, when the battle is over.
'Tis no matter of yours, and man cannot do it,
But me and me only, to measure his strength with
The monster of malice, might-deeds to 'complish.
I with prowess shall gain the gold, or the battle,
Direful death-woe will drag off your ruler!"
The mighty champion rose by his shield then,
Brave under helmet, in battle-mail went he
'Neath steep-rising stone-cliffs, the strength he relied on
Of one man alone: no work for a coward.
Then he saw by the wall who a great many battles
Had lived through, most worthy, when foot-troops collided,

(The place of strife is described.)

Stone-arches standing, stout-hearted champion,
Saw a brook from the barrow bubbling out thenceward:
The flood of the fountain was fuming with war-flame:
Not nigh to the hoard, for season the briefest
Could he brave, without burning, the abyss that was yawning,
The drake was so fiery. The prince of the Weders
Caused then that words came from his bosom,
So fierce was his fury; the firm-hearted shouted:
His battle-clear voice came in resounding
'Neath the gray-colored stone. Stirred was his hatred,

(Beowulf calls out under the stone arches.)

The hoard-ward distinguished the speech of a man;
Time was no longer to look out for friendship.

Beowulf: Scholar's Edition
The breath of the monster issued forth first,
Vapory war-sweat, out of the stone-cave:

(The terrible encounter.)

The earth re-echoed. The earl 'neath the barrow
Lifted his shield, lord of the Geatmen,
Tow'rd the terrible stranger: the ring-twisted creature's
Heart was then ready to seek for a struggle.

(Beowulf brandishes his sword,)

The excellent battle-king first brandished his weapon,
The ancient heirloom, of edges unblunted,[3]
To the death-planners twain was terror from other.

(and stands against his shield.)

The lord of the troopers intrepidly stood then
'Gainst his high-rising shield, when the dragon coiled him

(The dragon coils himself.)

Quickly together: in corslet he bided.
He went then in blazes, bended and striding,
Hasting him forward. His life and body
The targe well protected, for time-period shorter
Than wish demanded for the well-renowned leader,
Where he then for the first day was forced to be victor,
Famous in battle, as Fate had not willed it.
The lord of the Geatmen uplifted his hand then,
Smiting the fire-drake with sword that was precious,
That bright on the bone the blade-edge did weaken,
Bit more feebly than his folk-leader needed,
Burdened with bale-griefs. Then the barrow-protector,

(The dragon rages)

When the sword-blow had fallen, was fierce in his spirit,
Flinging his fires, flamings of battle
Gleamed then afar: the gold-friend of Weders

(Beowulf's sword fails him.)

Boasted no conquests, his battle-sword failed him
Naked in conflict, as by no means it ought to,
Long-trusty weapon. 'Twas no slight undertaking
That Ecgtheow's famous offspring would leave
The drake-cavern's bottom; he must live in some region
Other than this, by the will of the dragon,

As each one of earthmen existence must forfeit.
'Twas early thereafter the excellent warriors

(The combat is renewed.)

Met with each other. Anew and afresh
The hoard-ward took heart (gasps heaved then his bosom):

(The great hero is reduced to extremities.)

Sorrow he suffered encircled with fire
Who the people erst governed. His companions by no means
Were banded about him, bairns of the princes,

(His comrades flee!)

With valorous spirit, but they sped to the forest,
Seeking for safety. The soul-deeps of one were

(Blood is thicker than water.)

Ruffled by care: kin-love can never
Aught in him waver who well doth consider.

XXXVI - WIGLAF THE TRUSTY--BEOWULF IS DESERTED BY FRIENDS AND BY SWORD
(Wiglaf remains true--the ideal Teutonic liegeman.)

The son of Weohstan was Wiglaf entitled,
Shield-warrior precious, prince of the Scylfings,
Ælfhere's kinsman: he saw his dear liegelord
Enduring the heat 'neath helmet and visor.
Then he minded the holding that erst he had given him,

(Wiglaf recalls Beowulf's generosity.)

The Wægmunding warriors' wealth-blessèd homestead,
Each of the folk-rights his father had wielded;
He was hot for the battle, his hand seized the target,
The yellow-bark shield, he unsheathed his old weapon,
Which was known among earthmen as the relic of Eanmund,
Ohthere's offspring, whom, exiled and friendless,
Weohstan did slay with sword-edge in battle,
And carried his kinsman the clear-shining helmet,
The ring-made burnie, the old giant-weapon
That Onela gave him, his boon-fellow's armor,
Ready war-trappings: he the feud did not mention,
Though he'd fatally smitten the son of his brother.

Beowulf: Scholar's Edition

Many a half-year held he the treasures,
The bill and the burnie, till his bairn became able,
Like his father before him, fame-deeds to 'complish;
Then he gave him 'mong Geatmen a goodly array of
Weeds for his warfare; he went from life then
Old on his journey. 'Twas the earliest time then

(This is Wiglaf's first battle as liegeman of Beowulf.)

That the youthful champion might charge in the battle
Aiding his liegelord; his spirit was dauntless.
Nor did kinsman's bequest quail at the battle:
This the dragon discovered on their coming together.
Wiglaf uttered many a right-saying,
Said to his fellows, sad was his spirit:

(Wiglaf appeals to the pride of the cowards.)

"I remember the time when, tasting the mead-cup,
We promised in the hall the lord of us all
Who gave us these ring-treasures, that this battle-equipment,
Swords and helmets, we'd certainly quite him,
Should need of such aid ever befall him:

(How we have forfeited our liegelord's confidence!)

In the war-band he chose us for this journey spontaneously,
Stirred us to glory and gave me these jewels,
Since he held and esteemed us trust-worthy spearmen,
Hardy helm-bearers, though this hero-achievement
Our lord intended alone to accomplish,
Ward of his people, for most of achievements,
Doings audacious, he did among earth-folk.

(Our lord is in sore need of us.)

The day is now come when the ruler of earthmen
Needeth the vigor of valiant heroes:
Let us wend us towards him, the war-prince to succor,
While the heat yet rageth, horrible fire-fight.

(I would rather die than go home with out my suzerain.)

God wot in me, 'tis mickle the liefer
The blaze should embrace my body and eat it
With my treasure-bestower. Meseemeth not proper
To bear our battle-shields back to our country,
'Less first we are able to fell and destroy the
Long-hating foeman, to defend the life of

(Surely he does not deserve to die alone.)

The prince of the Weders. Well do I know 'tisn't
Earned by his exploits, he only of Geatmen
Sorrow should suffer, sink in the battle:
Brand and helmet to us both shall be common,
¹Shield-cover, burnie." Through the bale-smoke he stalked then,
Went under helmet to the help of his chieftain,

(Wiglaf reminds Beowulf of his youthful boasts.)

Briefly discoursing: "Beowulf dear,
Perform thou all fully, as thou formerly saidst,
In thy youthful years, that while yet thou livedst
Thou wouldst let thine honor not ever be lessened.
Thy life thou shalt save, mighty in actions,
Atheling undaunted, with all of thy vigor;

(The monster advances on them.)

I'll give thee assistance." The dragon came raging,
Wild-mooded stranger, when these words had been uttered
('Twas the second occasion), seeking his enemies,
Men that were hated, with hot-gleaming fire-waves;
With blaze-billows burned the board to its edges:
The fight-armor failed then to furnish assistance
To the youthful spear-hero: but the young-agèd stripling
Quickly advanced 'neath his kinsman's war-target,
Since his own had been ground in the grip of the fire.

(Beowulf strikes at the dragon.)

Then the warrior-king was careful of glory,
He soundly smote with sword-for-the-battle,
That it stood in the head by hatred driven;
Nægling was shivered, the old and iron-made

(His sword fails him.)

Brand of Beowulf in battle deceived him.
'Twas denied him that edges of irons were able
To help in the battle; the hand was too mighty
²Which every weapon, as I heard on inquiry,
Outstruck in its stroke, when to struggle he carried
The wonderful war-sword: it waxed him no better.

(The dragon advances on Beowulf again.)

Beowulf: Scholar's Edition

Then the people-despoiler--third of his onsets--
Fierce-raging fire-drake, of feud-hate was mindful,
Charged on the strong one, when chance was afforded,
Heated and war-grim, seized on his neck
With teeth that were bitter; he bloody did wax with
Soul-gore seething; sword-blood in waves boiled.

XXXVII - THE FATAL STRUGGLE--BEOWULF'S LAST MOMENTS

(Wiglaf defends Beowulf.)

Then I heard that at need of the king of the people
The upstanding earlman exhibited prowess,
Vigor and courage, as suited his nature;
[1]He his head did not guard, but the high-minded liegeman's
Hand was consumed, when he succored his kinsman,
So he struck the strife-bringing strange-comer lower,
Earl-thane in armor, that in went the weapon
Gleaming and plated, that 'gan then the fire[2]

(Beowulf draws his knife,)

Later to lessen. The liegelord himself then
Retained his consciousness, brandished his war-knife,
Battle-sharp, bitter, that he bare on his armor:

(and cuts the dragon.)

The Weder-lord cut the worm in the middle.
They had felled the enemy (life drove out then[3]
Puissant prowess), the pair had destroyed him,
Land-chiefs related: so a liegeman should prove him,
A thaneman when needed. To the prince 'twas the last of
His era of conquest by his own great achievements,

(Beowulf's wound swells and burns.)

The latest of world-deeds. The wound then began
Which the earth-dwelling dragon erstwhile had wrought him
To burn and to swell. He soon then discovered
That bitterest bale-woe in his bosom was raging,
Poison within. The atheling advanced then,

(He sits down exhausted.)

That along by the wall, he prudent of spirit
Might sit on a settle; he saw the giant-work,
How arches of stone strengthened with pillars
The earth-hall eternal inward supported.

Then the long-worthy liegeman laved with his hand the

(Wiglaf bathes his lord's head.)

Far-famed chieftain, gory from sword-edge,
Refreshing the face of his friend-lord and ruler,
Sated with battle, unbinding his helmet.
Beowulf answered, of his injury spake he,
His wound that was fatal (he was fully aware
He had lived his allotted life-days enjoying
The pleasures of earth; then past was entirely
His measure of days, death very near):

(Beowulf regrets that he has no son.)

"My son I would give now my battle-equipments,
Had any of heirs been after me granted,
Along of my body. This people I governed
Fifty of winters: no king 'mong my neighbors
Dared to encounter me with comrades-in-battle,
Try me with terror. The time to me ordered
I bided at home, mine own kept fitly,
Sought me no snares, swore me not many

(I can rejoice in a well-spent life.)

Oaths in injustice. Joy over all this
I'm able to have, though ill with my death-wounds;
Hence the Ruler of Earthmen need not charge me
With the killing of kinsmen, when cometh my life out
Forth from my body. Fare thou with haste now

(Bring me the hoard, Wiglaf, that my dying eyes may be refreshed by a sight of it.)

To behold the hoard 'neath the hoar-grayish stone,
Well-lovèd Wiglaf, now the worm is a-lying,
Sore-wounded sleepeth, disseized of his treasure.
Go thou in haste that treasures of old I,
Gold-wealth may gaze on, together see lying
The ether-bright jewels, be easier able,
Having the heap of hoard-gems, to yield my
Life and the land-folk whom long I have governed."

Beowulf: Scholar's Edition

XXXVIII - WIGLAF PLUNDERS THE DRAGON'S DEN-- BEOWULF'S DEATH

(Wiglaf fulfils his lord's behest.)

Then heard I that Wihstan's son very quickly,
These words being uttered, heeded his liegelord
Wounded and war-sick, went in his armor,
His well-woven ring-mail, 'neath the roof of the barrow.
Then the trusty retainer treasure-gems many

(The dragon's den.)

Victorious saw, when the seat he came near to,
Gold-treasure sparkling spread on the bottom,
Wonder on the wall, and the worm-creature's cavern,
The ancient dawn-flier's, vessels a-standing,
Cups of the ancients of cleansers bereavèd,
Robbed of their ornaments: there were helmets in numbers,
Old and rust-eaten, arm-bracelets many,
Artfully woven. Wealth can easily,
Gold on the sea-bottom, turn into vanity[1]
Each one of earthmen, arm him who pleaseth!
And he saw there lying an all-golden banner
High o'er the hoard, of hand-wonders greatest,
Linkèd with lacets: a light from it sparkled,
That the floor of the cavern he was able to look on,

(The dragon is not there.)

To examine the jewels. Sight of the dragon
Not any was offered, but edge offcarried him.

(Wiglaf bears the hoard away.)

Then I heard that the hero the hoard-treasure plundered,
The giant-work ancient reaved in the cavern,
Bare on his bosom the beakers and platters,
As himself would fain have it, and took off the standard,
The brightest of beacons;[2] the bill had erst injured
(Its edge was of iron), the old-ruler's weapon,
Him who long had watched as ward of the jewels,
Who fire-terror carried hot for the treasure,
Rolling in battle, in middlemost darkness,
Till murdered he perished. The messenger hastened,
Not loth to return, hurried by jewels:
Curiosity urged him if, excellent-mooded,
Alive he should find the lord of the Weders
Mortally wounded, at the place where he left him.
'Mid the jewels he found then the famous old chieftain,

His liegelord belovèd, at his life's-end gory:
He thereupon 'gan to lave him with water,
Till the point of his word piercèd his breast-hoard.
Beowulf spake (the gold-gems he noticed),

(Beowulf is rejoiced to see the jewels.)

The old one in sorrow: "For the jewels I look on
Thanks do I utter for all to the Ruler,
Wielder of Worship, with words of devotion,
The Lord everlasting, that He let me such treasures
Gain for my people ere death overtook me.
Since I've bartered the agèd life to me granted
For treasure of jewels, attend ye henceforward

(He desires to be held in memory by his people.)

The wants of the war-thanes; I can wait here no longer.
The battle-famed bid ye to build them a grave-hill,
Bright when I'm burned, at the brim-current's limit;
As a memory-mark to the men I have governed,
Aloft it shall tower on Whale's-Ness uprising,
That earls of the ocean hereafter may call it
Beowulf's barrow, those who barks ever-dashing
From a distance shall drive o'er the darkness of waters."

(The hero's last gift)

The bold-mooded troop-lord took from his neck then
The ring that was golden, gave to his liegeman,
The youthful war-hero, his gold-flashing helmet,
His collar and war-mail, bade him well to enjoy them:

(and last words.)

"Thou art latest left of the line of our kindred,
Of Wægmunding people: Weird hath offcarried
All of my kinsmen to the Creator's glory,
Earls in their vigor: I shall after them fare."
'Twas the aged liegelord's last-spoken word in
His musings of spirit, ere he mounted the fire,
The battle-waves burning: from his bosom departed
His soul to seek the sainted ones' glory.

Beowulf: Scholar's Edition

XXXIX - THE DEAD FOES--WIGLAF'S BITTER TAUNTS

(Wiglaf is sorely grieved to see his lord look so un-warlike.)

It had wofully chanced then the youthful retainer
To behold on earth the most ardent-belovèd
At his life-days' limit, lying there helpless.
The slayer too lay there, of life all bereavèd,
Horrible earth-drake, harassed with sorrow:

(The dragon has plundered his last hoard.)

The round-twisted monster was permitted no longer
To govern the ring-hoards, but edges of war-swords
Mightily seized him, battle-sharp, sturdy
Leavings of hammers, that still from his wounds
The flier-from-farland fell to the earth
Hard by his hoard-house, hopped he at midnight
Not e'er through the air, nor exulting in jewels
Suffered them to see him: but he sank then to earthward
Through the hero-chief's handwork. I heard sure it throve then

(Few warriors dared to face the monster.)

But few in the land of liegemen of valor,
Though of every achievement bold he had proved him,
To run 'gainst the breath of the venomous scather,
Or the hall of the treasure to trouble with hand-blows,
If he watching had found the ward of the hoard-hall
On the barrow abiding. Beowulf's part of
The treasure of jewels was paid for with death;
Each of the twain had attained to the end of
Life so unlasting. Not long was the time till

(The cowardly thanes come out of the thicket.)

The tardy-at-battle returned from the thicket,
The timid truce-breakers ten all together,
Who durst not before play with the lances
In the prince of the people's pressing emergency;

(They are ashamed of their desertion.)

But blushing with shame, with shields they betook them,
With arms and armor where the old one was lying:
They gazed upon Wiglaf. He was sitting exhausted,
Foot-going fighter, not far from the shoulders
Of the lord of the people, would rouse him with water;
No whit did it help him; though he hoped for it keenly,
He was able on earth not at all in the leader

Life to retain, and nowise to alter
The will of the Wielder; the World-Ruler's power[1]
Would govern the actions of each one of heroes,

(Wiglaf is ready to excoriate them.)

As yet He is doing. From the young one forthwith then
Could grim-worded greeting be got for him quickly
Whose courage had failed him. Wiglaf discoursed then,
Weohstan his son, sad-mooded hero,

(He begins to taunt them.)

Looked on the hated: "He who soothness will utter
Can say that the liegelord who gave you the jewels,
The ornament-armor wherein ye are standing,
When on ale-bench often he offered to hall-men
Helmet and burnie, the prince to his liegemen,
As best upon earth he was able to find him,--

(Surely our lord wasted his armor on poltroons.)

That he wildly wasted his war-gear undoubtedly
When battle o'ertook him.[2] The troop-king no need had
To glory in comrades; yet God permitted him,

(He, however, got along without you)

Victory-Wielder, with weapon unaided
Himself to avenge, when vigor was needed.
I life-protection but little was able
To give him in battle, and I 'gan, notwithstanding,

(With some aid, I could have saved our liegelord)

Helping my kinsman (my strength overtaxing):
He waxed the weaker when with weapon I smote on
My mortal opponent, the fire less strongly
Flamed from his bosom. Too few of protectors
Came round the king at the critical moment.

(Gift-giving is over with your people: the ring-lord is dead.)

Now must ornament-taking and weapon-bestowing,
Home-joyance all, cease for your kindred,
Food for the people; each of your warriors
Must needs be bereavèd of rights that he holdeth
In landed possessions, when faraway nobles
Shall learn of your leaving your lord so basely,

Beowulf: Scholar's Edition
(What is life without honor?)

The dastardly deed. Death is more pleasant
To every earlman than infamous life is!"

XL - THE MESSENGER OF DEATH
(Wiglaf sends the news of Beowulf's death to liegemen near by.)

Then he charged that the battle be announced at the hedge
Up o'er the cliff-edge, where the earl-troopers bided
The whole of the morning, mood-wretched sat them,
Bearers of battle-shields, both things expecting,
The end of his lifetime and the coming again of
The liegelord belovèd. Little reserved he
Of news that was known, who the ness-cliff did travel,
But he truly discoursed to all that could hear him:

(The messenger speaks.)

"Now the free-giving friend-lord of the folk of the Weders,
The folk-prince of Geatmen, is fast in his death-bed,
By the deeds of the dragon in death-bed abideth;
Along with him lieth his life-taking foeman
Slain with knife-wounds: he was wholly unable
To injure at all the ill-planning monster

(Wiglaf sits by our dead lord.)

With bite of his sword-edge. Wiglaf is sitting,
Offspring of Wihstan, up over Beowulf,
Earl o'er another whose end-day hath reached him,
Head-watch holdeth o'er heroes unliving,[1]

(Our lord's death will lead to attacks from our old foes.)

For friend and for foeman. The folk now expecteth
A season of strife when the death of the folk-king
To Frankmen and Frisians in far-lands is published.
The war-hatred waxed warm 'gainst the Hugmen,

(Higelac's death recalled.)

When Higelac came with an army of vessels
Faring to Friesland, where the Frankmen in battle
Humbled him and bravely with overmight 'complished
That the mail-clad warrior must sink in the battle,
Fell 'mid his folk-troop: no fret-gems presented
The atheling to earlmen; aye was denied us
Merewing's mercy. The men of the Swedelands

For truce or for truth trust I but little;
But widely 'twas known that near Ravenswood Ongentheow

(Hæthcyn's fall referred to.)

Sundered Hæthcyn the Hrethling from life-joys,
When for pride overweening the War-Scylfings first did
Seek the Geatmen with savage intentions.
Early did Ohthere's age-laden father,
Old and terrible, give blow in requital,
Killing the sea-king, the queen-mother rescued,
The old one his consort deprived of her gold,
Onela's mother and Ohthere's also,
And then followed the feud-nursing foemen till hardly,
Reaved of their ruler, they Ravenswood entered.
Then with vast-numbered forces he assaulted the remnant,
Weary with wounds, woe often promised
The livelong night to the sad-hearted war-troop:
Said he at morning would kill them with edges of weapons,
Some on the gallows for glee to the fowls.
Aid came after to the anxious-in-spirit
At dawn of the day, after Higelac's bugle
And trumpet-sound heard they, when the good one proceeded
And faring followed the flower of the troopers.

XLI - THE MESSENGER'S RETROSPECT
(The messenger continues, and refers to the feuds of Swedes and Geats.)

"The blood-stainèd trace of Swedes and Geatmen,
The death-rush of warmen, widely was noticed,
How the folks with each other feud did awaken.
The worthy one went then[1] with well-beloved comrades,
Old and dejected to go to the fastness,
Ongentheo earl upward then turned him;
Of Higelac's battle he'd heard on inquiry,
The exultant one's prowess, despaired of resistance,
With earls of the ocean to be able to struggle,
'Gainst sea-going sailors to save the hoard-treasure,
His wife and his children; he fled after thenceward
Old 'neath the earth-wall. Then was offered pursuance
To the braves of the Swedemen, the banner[2] to Higelac.
They fared then forth o'er the field-of-protection,
When the Hrethling heroes hedgeward had thronged them.
Then with edges of irons was Ongentheow driven,
The gray-haired to tarry, that the troop-ruler had to
Suffer the power solely of Eofor:

(Wulf wounds Ongentheow.)

Beowulf: Scholar's Edition

Wulf then wildly with weapon assaulted him,
Wonred his son, that for swinge of the edges
The blood from his body burst out in currents,
Forth 'neath his hair. He feared not however,
Gray-headed Scylfing, but speedily quited

(Ongentheow gives a stout blow in return.)

The wasting wound-stroke with worse exchange,
When the king of the thane-troop thither did turn him:
The wise-mooded son of Wonred was powerless
To give a return-blow to the age-hoary man,
But his head-shielding helmet first hewed he to pieces,
That flecked with gore perforce he did totter,
Fell to the earth; not fey was he yet then,
But up did he spring though an edge-wound had reached him.

(Eofor smites Ongentheow fiercely.)

Then Higelac's vassal, valiant and dauntless,
When his brother lay dead, made his broad-bladed weapon,
Giant-sword ancient, defence of the giants,
Bound o'er the shield-wall; the folk-prince succumbed then,

(Ongentheow is slain.)

Shepherd of people, was pierced to the vitals.
There were many attendants who bound up his kinsman,
Carried him quickly when occasion was granted
That the place of the slain they were suffered to manage.
This pending, one hero plundered the other,
His armor of iron from Ongentheow ravished,
His hard-sword hilted and helmet together;

(Eofor takes the old king's war-gear to Higelac.)

The old one's equipments he carried to Higelac.
He the jewels received, and rewards 'mid the troopers
Graciously promised, and so did accomplish:
The king of the Weders requited the war-rush,
Hrethel's descendant, when home he repaired him,

(Higelac rewards the brothers.)

To Eofor and Wulf with wide-lavished treasures,
To each of them granted a hundred of thousands
In land and rings wrought out of wire:

(His gifts were beyond cavil.)

None upon mid-earth needed to twit him³
With the gifts he gave them, when glory they conquered;

(To Eofor he also gives his only daughter in marriage.)

And to Eofor then gave he his one only daughter,
The honor of home, as an earnest of favor.
That's the feud and hatred--as ween I 'twill happen--
The anger of earthmen, that earls of the Swedemen
Will visit on us, when they hear that our leader
Lifeless is lying, he who longtime protected
His hoard and kingdom 'gainst hating assailers,
Who on the fall of the heroes defended of yore
The deed-mighty Scyldings,⁴ did for the troopers
What best did avail them, and further moreover

(It is time for us to pay the last marks of respect to our lord.)

Hero-deeds 'complished. Now is haste most fitting,
That the lord of liegemen we look upon yonder,
And that one carry on journey to death-pyre
Who ring-presents gave us. Not aught of it all
Shall melt with the brave one--there's a mass of bright jewels,
Gold beyond measure, grewsomely purchased
And ending it all ornament-rings too
Bought with his life; these fire shall devour,
Flame shall cover, no earlman shall wear
A jewel-memento, nor beautiful virgin
Have on her neck rings to adorn her,
But wretched in spirit bereavèd of gold-gems
She shall oft with others be exiled and banished,
Since the leader of liegemen hath laughter forsaken,
Mirth and merriment. Hence many a war-spear
Cold from the morning shall be clutched in the fingers,
Heaved in the hand, no harp-music's sound shall
Waken the warriors, but the wan-coated raven
Fain over fey ones freely shall gabble,
Shall say to the eagle how he sped in the eating,
When, the wolf his companion, he plundered the slain."
So the high-minded hero was rehearsing these stories
Loathsome to hear; he lied as to few of

(The warriors go sadly to look at Beowulf's lifeless body.)

Weirds and of words. All the war-troop arose then,
'Neath the Eagle's Cape sadly betook them,
Weeping and woful, the wonder to look at.
They saw on the sand then soulless a-lying,
His slaughter-bed holding, him who rings had given them

In days that were done; then the death-bringing moment
Was come to the good one, that the king very warlike,
Wielder of Weders, with wonder-death perished.
First they beheld there a creature more wondrous,

(They also see the dragon.)

The worm on the field, in front of them lying,
The foeman before them: the fire-spewing dragon,
Ghostly and grisly guest in his terrors,
Was scorched in the fire; as he lay there he measured
Fifty of feet; came forth in the night-time[5]
To rejoice in the air, thereafter departing
To visit his den; he in death was then fastened,
He would joy in no other earth-hollowed caverns.
There stood round about him beakers and vessels,
Dishes were lying and dear-valued weapons,
With iron-rust eaten, as in earth's mighty bosom
A thousand of winters there they had rested:

(The hoard was under a magic spell.)

That mighty bequest then with magic was guarded,
Gold of the ancients, that earlman not any
The ring-hall could touch, save Ruling-God only,
Sooth-king of Vict'ries gave whom He wished to

(God alone could give access to it.)

[6](He is earth-folk's protector) to open the treasure,
E'en to such among mortals as seemed to Him proper.

XLII - WIGLAF'S SAD STORY--THE HOARD CARRIED OFF

Then 'twas seen that the journey prospered him little
Who wrongly within had the ornaments hidden[1]
Down 'neath the wall. The warden erst slaughtered
Some few of the folk-troop: the feud then thereafter
Was hotly avengèd. 'Tis a wonder where,[2]
When the strength-famous trooper has attained to the end of
Life-days allotted, then no longer the man may
Remain with his kinsmen where mead-cups are flowing.
So to Beowulf happened when the ward of the barrow,
Assaults, he sought for: himself had no knowledge
How his leaving this life was likely to happen.
So to doomsday, famous folk-leaders down did
Call it with curses--who 'complished it there--
That that man should be ever of ill-deeds convicted,
Confined in foul-places, fastened in hell-bonds,

Punished with plagues, who this place should e'er ravage.³
He cared not for gold: rather the Wielder's
Favor preferred he first to get sight of.⁴

(Wiglaf addresses his comrades.)

Wiglaf discoursed then, Wihstan his son:
"Oft many an earlman on one man's account must
Sorrow endure, as to us it hath happened.
The liegelord belovèd we could little prevail on,
Kingdom's keeper, counsel to follow,
Not to go to the guardian of the gold-hoard, but let him
Lie where he long was, live in his dwelling
Till the end of the world. Met we a destiny
Hard to endure: the hoard has been looked at,
Been gained very grimly; too grievous the fate that⁵
The prince of the people pricked to come thither.
I was therein and all of it looked at,
The building's equipments, since access was given me,
Not kindly at all entrance permitted

(He tells them of Beowulf's last moments.)

Within under earth-wall. Hastily seized I
And held in my hands a huge-weighing burden
Of hoard-treasures costly, hither out bare them
To my liegelord belovèd: life was yet in him,
And consciousness also; the old one discoursed then
Much and mournfully, commanded to greet you,

(Beowulf's dying request.)

Bade that remembering the deeds of your friend-lord
Ye build on the fire-hill of corpses a lofty
Burial-barrow, broad and far-famous,
As 'mid world-dwelling warriors he was widely most honored
While he reveled in riches. Let us rouse us and hasten
Again to see and seek for the treasure,
The wonder 'neath wall. The way I will show you,
That close ye may look at ring-gems sufficient
And gold in abundance. Let the bier with promptness
Fully be fashioned, when forth we shall come,
And lift we our lord, then, where long he shall tarry,
Well-belovèd warrior, 'neath the Wielder's protection."

(Wiglaf charges them to build a funeral-pyre.)

Then the son of Wihstan bade orders be given,
Mood-valiant man, to many of heroes,

Holders of homesteads, that they hither from far,
⁶Leaders of liegemen, should look for the good one
With wood for his pyre: "The flame shall now swallow
(The wan fire shall wax⁷) the warriors' leader
Who the rain of the iron often abided,
When, sturdily hurled, the storm of the arrows
Leapt o'er linden-wall, the lance rendered service,
Furnished with feathers followed the arrow."
Now the wise-mooded son of Wihstan did summon
The best of the braves from the band of the ruler

(He takes seven thanes, and enters the den.)

Seven together; 'neath the enemy's roof he
Went with the seven; one of the heroes
Who fared at the front, a fire-blazing torch-light
Bare in his hand. No lot then decided
Who that hoard should havoc, when hero-earls saw it
Lying in the cavern uncared-for entirely,
Rusting to ruin: they rued then but little
That they hastily hence hauled out the treasure,

(They push the dragon over the wall.)

The dear-valued jewels; the dragon eke pushed they,
The worm o'er the wall, let the wave-currents take him,
The waters enwind the ward of the treasures.

(The hoard is laid on a wain.)

There wounden gold on a wain was uploaded,
A mass unmeasured, the men-leader off then,
The hero hoary, to Whale's-Ness was carried.

XLIII - THE BURNING OF BEOWULF
(Beowulf's pyre.)

The folk of the Geatmen got him then ready
A pile on the earth strong for the burning,
Behung with helmets, hero-knights' targets,
And bright-shining burnies, as he begged they should have them;
Then wailing war-heroes their world-famous chieftain,
Their liegelord beloved, laid in the middle.

(The funeral-flame.)

Soldiers began then to make on the barrow
The largest of dead-fires: dark o'er the vapor
The smoke-cloud ascended, the sad-roaring fire,

Mingled with weeping (the wind-roar subsided)
Till the building of bone it had broken to pieces,
Hot in the heart. Heavy in spirit
They mood-sad lamented the men-leader's ruin;
And mournful measures the much-grieving widow
   ...

(The Weders carry out their lord's last request.)

The men of the Weders made accordingly
A hill on the height, high and extensive,
Of sea-going sailors to be seen from a distance,
And the brave one's beacon built where the fire was,
In ten-days' space, with a wall surrounded it,
As wisest of world-folk could most worthily plan it.
They placed in the barrow rings and jewels,

(Rings and gems are laid in the barrow.)

All such ornaments as erst in the treasure
War-mooded men had won in possession:
The earnings of earlmen to earth they entrusted,
The gold to the dust, where yet it remaineth
As useless to mortals as in foregoing eras.
'Round the dead-mound rode then the doughty-in-battle,
Bairns of all twelve of the chiefs of the people,

(They mourn for their lord, and sing his praises.)

More would they mourn, lament for their ruler,
Speak in measure, mention him with pleasure,
Weighed his worth, and his warlike achievements
Mightily commended, as 'tis meet one praise his
Liegelord in words and love him in spirit,
When forth from his body he fares to destruction.
So lamented mourning the men of the Geats,
Fond-loving vassals, the fall of their lord,

(An ideal king.)

Said he was kindest of kings under heaven,
Gentlest of men, most winning of manner,
Friendliest to folk-troops and fondest of honor.

ADDENDA

Several discrepancies and other oversights have been noticed in the H.-So. glossary. Of these a good part were avoided by Harrison and Sharp, the American editors of Beowulf, in their last edition, 1888. The rest will, I hope, be noticed in their fourth edition. As, however, this book may fall into the hands of some who have no copy of the American edition, it seems best to notice all the principal oversights of the German editors.

~From hám~ (194).--Notes and glossary conflict; the latter not having been altered to suit the conclusions accepted in the former.

~Þær gelýfan sceal dryhtnes dóme~ (440).--Under 'dóm' H. says 'the might of the Lord'; while under 'gelýfan' he says 'the judgment of the Lord.'

~Eal bencþelu~ (486).--Under 'benc-þelu' H. says nom. plu.; while under 'eal' he says nom. sing.

~Heatho-ræmas~ (519).--Under 'ætberan' H. translates 'to the Heathoremes'; while under 'Heatho-ræmas' he says 'Heathoræmas reaches Breca in the swimming-match with Beowulf.' Harrison and Sharp (3d edition, 1888) avoid the discrepancy.

~Fáh féond-scaða~ (554).--Under 'féond-scaða' H. says 'a gleaming sea-monster'; under 'fáh' he says 'hostile.'

~Onfeng hraðe inwit-þancum~ (749).--Under 'onfón' H. says 'he received the maliciously-disposed one'; under 'inwit-þanc' he says 'he grasped,' etc.

~Níð-wundor séon~ (1366).--Under 'níð-wundor' H. calls this word itself nom. sing.; under 'séon' he translates it as accus. sing., understanding 'man' as subject of 'séon.' H. and S. (3d edition) make the correction.

~Forgeaf hilde-bille~ (1521).--H., under the second word, calls it instr. dat.; while under 'forgifan' he makes it the dat. of indir. obj. H. and S. (3d edition) make the change.

~Brád~ and ~brún-ecg~ (1547).--Under 'brád' H. says 'das breite Hüftmesser mit bronzener Klinge'; under 'brún-ecg' he says 'ihr breites Hüftmesser mit blitzender Klinge.'

~Yðelíce~ (1557).--Under this word H. makes it modify 'ástód.' If this be right, the punctuation of the fifth edition is wrong. See H. and S., appendix.

~Sélran gesóhte~ (1840).--Under 'sél' and 'gesécan' H. calls these two words accus. plu.; but this is clearly an error, as both are nom. plu., pred. nom. H. and S. correct under 'sél.'

~Wið sylfne~ (1978).--Under 'wið' and 'gesittan' H. says 'wið = near, by'; under 'self' he says 'opposite.'

~þéow~ (2225) is omitted from the glossary.

~For duguðum~ (2502).--Under 'duguð' H. translates this phrase, 'in Tüchtigkeit'; under 'for,' by 'vor der edlen Kriegerschaar.'

~þær~ (2574).--Under 'wealdan' H. translates _þær_ by 'wo'; under 'mótan,' by 'da.' H. and S. suggest 'if' in both passages.

~Wunde~ (2726).--Under 'wund' H. says 'dative,' and under 'wæl-bléate' he says 'accus.' It is without doubt accus., parallel with 'benne.'

~Strengum gebæded~ (3118).--Under 'strengo' H. says 'Strengum' = mit Macht; under 'gebæded' he translates 'von den Sehnen.' H. and S. correct this discrepancy by rejecting the second reading.

~Bronda be láfe~ (3162).--A recent emendation. The fourth edition had 'bronda betost.' In the fifth edition the editor neglects to change the glossary to suit the new emendation. See 'bewyrcan.'

Footnotes:

Footnotes I

1. For the 'Þæt' of verse 15, Sievers suggests 'Þá' (= which). If this be accepted, the sentence 'He had ... afflicted' will read: He (i.e. God) had perceived the malice-caused sorrow which they, lordless, had formerly long endured_.

2. For 'aldor-léase' (15) Gr. suggested 'aldor-ceare': He perceived their distress, that they formerly had suffered life-sorrow a long while.

3. A very difficult passage. 'Áhte' (31) has no object. H. supplies 'geweald' from the context; and our translation is based upon this assumption, though it is far from satisfactory. Kl. suggests 'lændagas' for 'lange': _And the beloved land-prince enjoyed (had) his transitory days (i.e. lived). B. suggests a dislocation; but this is a dangerous doctrine, pushed rather far by that eminent scholar.

4. The reading of the H.-So. text has been quite closely followed; but some eminent scholars read 'séle-rædenne' for 'sele-rædende.' If that be adopted, the passage will read: _Men cannot tell us, indeed, the order of Fate, etc._ 'Sele-rædenne' has two things to support it: (1) v. 1347; (2) it affords a parallel to 'men' in v. 50.

Footnotes II

1. R. and t. B. prefer 'ellor-gæst' to 'ellen-gæst' (86): _Then the stranger from afar endured, etc._

2. Some authorities would translate 'demon' instead of 'stranger.'

3. Some authorities arrange differently, and render: Who dwelt in the moor-fens, the marsh and the fastness, the land of the giant-race.

Footnotes III

1. The translation is based on 'weras,' adopted by H.-So.--K. and Th. read 'wera' and, arranging differently, render 119(2)-120: They knew not sorrow, the wretchedness of man, aught of misfortune.—For 'unhælo' (120) R. suggests 'unfælo': The uncanny creature, greedy and cruel, etc_.

2. S. rearranges and translates: So he ruled and struggled unjustly, one against all, till the noblest of buildings stood useless (it was a long while) twelve years' time: the friend of the Scyldings suffered distress, every woe, great sorrows, etc.

3. For 'syððan,' B. suggests 'sárcwidum': Hence in mournful words it became well known, etc. Various other words beginning with 's' have been conjectured.

4. The H.-So. glossary is very inconsistent in referring to this passage.--'Sibbe' (154), which H.-So. regards as an instr., B. takes as accus., obj. of 'wolde.' Putting a comma after Deniga, he renders: He did not desire peace with any of the Danes, nor did he wish to remove their life-woe, nor to settle for money.

5. Of this difficult passage the following interpretations among others are given: (1) Though Grendel has frequented Heorot as a demon, he could not become ruler of the Danes, on account of his hostility to God. (2) Hrothgar was much grieved that Grendel had not appeared before his throne to receive presents. (3) He was not permitted to devastate the hall, on account of the Creator; i.e. God wished to make his visit fatal to him.--Ne ... wisse (169) W. renders: Nor had he any desire to do so; 'his' being obj. gen. = danach.

Footnotes IV

1 'From hám' (194) is much disputed. One rendering is: Beowulf, being away from home, heard of Hrothgar's troubles, etc. Another, that adopted by S. and endorsed in the H.-So. notes, is: B. heard from his neighborhood (neighbors), i.e. in his home, etc. A third is: B., being at home, heard this as occurring away from home. The H.-So. glossary and notes conflict.

2. 'Eoletes' (224) is marked with a (?) by H.-So.; our rendering simply follows his conjecture.--Other conjectures as to 'eolet' are: (1) voyage, (2) toil, labor, (3) hasty journey.

3. The lacuna of the MS at this point has been supplied by various conjectures. The reading adopted by H.-So. has been rendered in the above translation. W., like H.-So., makes 'ic' the beginning of a new sentence, but, for 'helmas bæron,' he reads 'hringed stefnan.' This has the advantage of giving a parallel to 'brontne ceol' instead of a kenning for 'go.'--B puts the (?) after 'holmas', and begins a new sentence at the middle of the line. Translate: What warriors are ye, clad in

Beowulf: Scholar's Edition

armor, who have thus come bringing the foaming vessel over the water way, hither over the seas? For some time on the wall I have been coast guard, etc. S. endorses most of what B. says, but leaves out 'on the wall' in the last sentence. If W.'s 'hringed stefnan' be accepted, change line 51 above to, A ring-stemmed vessel hither o'ersea.

4. 'Seld-guma' (249) is variously rendered: (1) housecarle; (2) home-stayer; (3) common man. Dr. H. Wood suggests a man-at-arms in another's house.

Footnotes V

1. 'Edwendan' (280) B. takes to be the subs. 'edwenden' (cf. 1775); and 'bisigu' he takes as gen. sing., limiting 'edwenden': If reparation for sorrows is ever to come. This is supported by t.B.

2. Combining the emendations of B. and t.B., we may read: The boar-images glistened ... brilliant, protected the life of the war-mooded man. They read 'ferh-wearde' (305) and 'gúðmódgum men' (306).

Footnotes VI

1. Instead of the punctuation given by H.-So., S. proposed to insert a comma after 'scír' (322), and to take 'hring-íren' as meaning 'ring-mail' and as parallel with 'gúð-byrne.' The passage would then read: The firm and hand-locked war-burnie shone, bright ring-mail, rang 'mid the armor, etc.

2. Gr. and others translate 'unhár' by 'bald'; old and bald.

Footnotes VII

1. Some render 'gif-sceattas' by 'tribute.'--'Géata' B. and Th. emended to 'Géatum.' If this be accepted, change 'of the Geatmen' to 'to the Geatmen.'

2. If t.B.'s emendation of vv. 386, 387 be accepted, the two lines, 'Hasten ... kinsmen' will read: Hasten thou, bid the throng of kinsmen go into the hall together.

3. For 420 (b) and 421 (a), B. suggests: Þær ic (on) fifelgeban ýðde eotena cyn = _where I in the ocean destroyed the eoten-race_.--t.B. accepts B.'s "brilliant" 'fifelgeban,' omits 'on,' emends 'cyn' to 'hám,' arranging: Þær ic fifelgeban ýðde, eotena hám = where I desolated the ocean, the home of the eotens.--This would be better but for changing 'cyn' to 'hám.'--I suggest: Þær ic fifelgeband (cf. nhd. Bande) ýðde, eotena cyn = where I conquered the monster band, the race of the eotens. This makes no change except to read 'fifel' for 'fife.'

4. 'Unforhte' (444) is much disputed.--H.-So. wavers between adj. and adv. Gr. and B. take it as an adv. modifying etan: Will eat the Geats fearlessly.--Kl. considers this reading absurd, and proposes 'anforhte' = timid.--Understanding 'unforhte' as an adj. has this advantage, viz. that it gives a parallel to 'Geátena leóde': but to take it as an adv. is more natural. Furthermore, to call the Geats 'brave' might, at this point, seem like an implied thrust at the Danes, so long helpless; while to call his own men 'timid' would be befouling his own nest.

5. For 'head-watch,' cf. H.-So. notes and cf. v. 2910.--Th. translates: Thou wilt not need my head to hide (i.e., thou wilt have no occasion to bury me, as Grendel will devour me whole).--Simrock imagines a kind of dead-watch.--Dr. H. Wood suggests: Thou wilt not have to bury so much as my head (for Grendel will be a thorough undertaker),--grim humor.

6. S. proposes a colon after 'nimeð' (l. 447). This would make no essential change in the translation.

7. Owing to the vagueness of 'feorme' (451), this passage is variously translated. In our translation, H.-So.'s glossary has been quite closely followed. This agrees substantially with B.'s translation (P. and B. XII. 87). R. translates: Thou needst not take care longer as to the consumption of my dead body. 'Líc' is also a crux here, as it may mean living body or dead body.

Footnotes VIII

1. B. and S. reject the reading given in H.-So., and suggested by Grtvg. B. suggests for 457-458: wáere-ryhtum Þú, wine mín Beówulf, and for ár-stafum úsic sóhtest.

This means: From the obligations of clientage, my friend Beowulf, and for assistance thou hast sought us.--This gives coherence to Hrothgar's opening remarks in VIII., and also introduces a new motive for Beowulf's coming to Hrothgar's aid.

2. Sit now at the feast, and disclose thy purposes to the victorious heroes, as thy spirit urges.--Kl. reaches the above translation by erasing the comma after 'meoto' and reading 'sige-hreðsecgum.'--There are other and bolder emendations and suggestions. Of these the boldest is to regard 'meoto' as a verb (imperative), and read 'on sæl': Think upon gayety, etc.--All the renderings are unsatisfactory, the one given in our translation involving a zeugma.

Footnotes IX

1. It has been plausibly suggested that 'síð' (in 501 and in 353) means 'arrival.' If so, translate the bracket: (the arrival of Beowulf, the brave seafarer, was a source of great chagrin to Unferth,etc.).

Footnotes X

1. The repetition of 'hwæðere' (574 and 578) is regarded by some scholars as a defect. B. suggests 'swá Þær' for the first: So there it befell me, etc. Another suggestion is to change the second 'hwæðere' into 'swá Þær': So there I escaped with my life, etc.

2. Kl. suggests a period after 'determined.' This would give the passage as follows: Since they no longer could see the light of the sun, and lowering darkness was down over all, dire under the heavens shadowy beings came going around them.

Footnotes XI

1. Gr. understood 'gódra' as meaning 'advantages in battle.' This rendering H.-So. rejects. The latter takes the passage as meaning that Grendel, though mighty and formidable, has no skill in the art of war.

2. B. in his masterly articles on Beowulf (P. and B. XII.) rejects the division usually made at this point, 'Þá.' (711), usually rendered 'then,' he translates 'when,' and connects its clause with the foregoing sentence. These changes he makes to reduce the number of 'cóm's as principal verbs. (Cf. 703, 711, 721.) With all deference to this acute scholar, I must say that it seems to me that the poet is exhausting his resources to bring out clearly the supreme event on which the whole subsequent action turns. First, he (Grendel) came in the wan night; second, he came from the moor; third, he came to the hall. Time, place from which, place to which, are all given.

Footnotes XII

1. B. and t.B. emend so as to make lines 9 and 10 read: Never in his life, earlier or later, had he, the hell-thane, found a braver hero.--They argue that Beowulf's companions had done nothing to merit such encomiums as the usual readings allow them.

2. For 'réðe rén-weardas' (771), t.B. suggests 'réðe, rénhearde.' Translate: They were both angry, raging and mighty.

Footnotes XIII

1. It has been proposed to translate 'myrðe' by with sorrow; but there seems no authority for such a rendering. To the present translator, the phrase 'módes myrðe' seems a mere padding for gladly; i.e., he who gladly harassed mankind.

Footnotes XIV

1. S. emends, suggesting 'déop' for 'déog,' and removing semicolon after 'wéol.' The two half-lines 'welling ... hid him' would then read: The bloody deep welled with sword-gore. B. accepts 'déop' for 'déog,' but reads 'déað-fæges': The deep boiled with the sword-gore of the death-doomed one.

2. Another and quite different rendering of this passage is as follows: Oft a liegeman of the king, a fame-covered man mindful of songs, who very many ancient traditions remembered (he found other word-groups accurately bound together) began afterward to tell of Beowulf's adventure, skilfully to narrate it, etc.

3. Might 'guma gilp-hladen' mean 'a man laden with boasts of the deeds of others'?

4. t.B. accepts B.'s 'hé þæs áron þáh' as given by H.-So., but puts a comma after 'þáh,' and takes 'siððan' as introducing a dependent clause: He throve in honor since Heremod's strength ... had decreased.

Footnotes XV

1. B. and t.B. read 'staþole,' and translate stood on the floor.

2. For 'snaring from Grendel,' 'sorrows at Grendel's hands' has been suggested. This gives a parallel to 'láðes.' 'Grynna' may well be gen. pl. of 'gyrn,' by a scribal slip.

3. The H.-So punctuation has been followed; but B. has been followed in understanding 'gehwylcne' as object of 'wíd-scofen (hæfde).' Gr. construes 'wéa' as nom abs.

Footnotes XVI

1. Kl. suggests 'hroden' for 'háten,' and renders: Then quickly was Heorot adorned within, with hands bedecked.--B. suggests 'gefrætwon' instead of 'gefrætwod,' and renders: Then was it commanded to adorn Heorot within quickly with hands.--The former has the advantage of affording a parallel to 'gefrætwod': both have the disadvantage of altering the text.

2. The passage 1005-1009 seems to be hopeless. One difficult point is to find a subject for 'gesacan.' Some say 'he'; others supply 'each,' i.e., every soul-bearer ... must gain the inevitable place. The genitives in this case are partitive.--If 'he' be subj., the genitives are dependent on 'gearwe' (= prepared).--The 'he' itself is disputed, some referring it to Grendel; but B. takes it as involved in the parenthesis.

Footnotes XVII

1. For 1084, R. suggests 'wiht Hengeste wið gefeohtan.'--K. suggests 'wið Hengeste wiht gefeohtan.' Neither emendation would make any essential change in the translation.

2. The separation of adjective and noun by a phrase (cf. v. 1118) being very unusual, some scholars have put 'earme on eaxle' with

the foregoing lines, inserting a semicolon after 'eaxle.' In this case 'on eaxe' (i.e., on the ashes, cinders) is sometimes read, and this affords a parallel to 'on bæl.' Let us hope that a satisfactory rendering shall yet be reached without resorting to any tampering with the text, such as Lichtenheld proposed: 'earme ides on eaxle gnornode.'

3. For 'gúð-rinc,' 'gúð-réc,' battle-smoke, has been suggested.

Footnotes XVIII

1. For 1130 (1) R. and Gr. suggest 'elne unflitme' as 1098 (1) reads. The latter verse is undisputed; and, for the former, 'elne' would be as possible as 'ealles,' and 'unflitme' is well supported. Accepting 'elne unflitme' for both, I would suggest 'very peaceably' for both places: (1) Finn to Hengest very peaceably vowed with oaths, etc. (2) Hengest then still the slaughter-stained winter remained there with Finn very peaceably. The two passages become thus correlatives, the second a sequel of the first. 'Elne,' in the sense of very (swíðe), needs no argument; and 'unflitme' (from 'flítan') can, it seems to me, be more plausibly rendered 'peaceful,' 'peaceable,' than 'contestable,' or 'conquerable.'

2. Some scholars have proposed 'roden'; the line would then read: Then the building was reddened, etc., instead of 'covered.' The 'h' may have been carried over from the three alliterating 'h's.'

Footnotes XIX

1. C. suggests a semicolon after 'city,' with 'he' as supplied subject of 'fled' and 'chose.'

2. For 'feorh' S. suggests 'feoh': 'corpse' in the translation would then be changed to 'possessions,' 'belongings.' This is a better reading than one joining, in such intimate syntactical relations, things so unlike as 'corpse' and 'jewels.'

3. S. suggests 'wine-joyous heroes,' 'warriors elated with wine.'

4. I believe this translation brings out the meaning of the poet, without departing seriously from the H.-So. text. 'Oft' frequently means 'constantly,' 'continually,' not always 'often.'--Why 'an (on) wíg gearwe' should be written 'ánwíg-gearwe' (= ready for single combat), I cannot see. 'Gearwe' occurs quite frequently with 'on'; cf. B. 1110 (ready for the pyre), El. 222 (ready for the glad journey). Moreover, what has the idea of single combat to do with B. 1247 ff.? The poet is giving an inventory of the arms and armor which they lay aside on retiring, and he closes his narration by saying that they were always prepared for battle both at home and on the march.

Footnotes XX

1. Several eminent authorities either read or emend the MS. so as to make this verse read, While Grendel was wasting the gold-bedecked palace. So 20_15 below: ravaged the desert.

2. For 'sóna' (1281), t.B. suggests 'sára,' limiting 'edhwyrft.' Read then: Return of sorrows to the nobles, etc. This emendation supplies the syntactical gap after 'edhwyrft.'

3. Some authorities follow Grein's lexicon in treating 'heard ecg' as an adj. limiting 'sweord': H.-So. renders it as a subst. (So v. 1491.) The sense of the translation would be the same.

4. B. suggests 'under hróf genam' (v. 1303). This emendation, as well as an emendation with (?) to v. 739, he offers, because 'under' baffles him in both passages. All we need is to take 'under' in its secondary meaning of 'in,' which, though not given by Grein, occurs in the literature. Cf. Chron. 876 (March's A.-S. Gram. § 355) and Oro. Amaz. I. 10, where 'under' = in the midst of. Cf. modern Eng. 'in such circumstances,' which interchanges in good usage with 'under such circumstances.'

5. For 'néod-laðu' (1321) C. suggests 'néad-láðum,' and translates: asked whether the night had been pleasant to him after crushing-hostility.

Footnotes XXI

1. For 'gefrægnod' (1334), K. and t.B. suggest 'gefægnod,' rendering 'rejoicing in her fill.' This gives a parallel to 'æse wlanc' (1333).

2. The line 'And ... yielding,' B. renders: And she has performed a deed of blood-vengeance whose effect is far-reaching.

3. 'Sé Þe' (1345) is an instance of masc. rel. with fem. antecedent. So v. 1888, where 'sé Þe' refers to 'yldo.'

4. For 'hrímge' in the H.-So. edition, Gr. and others read 'hrínde' (=hrínende), and translate: which rustling forests overhang.

Footnotes XXIII

1. Kl. emends 'wæl-sweord.' The half-line would then read, 'the battle-sword splendid.'--For 'heard-ecg' in next half-verse, see note to 20_39 above.

2. Sw., R., and t.B. suggest 'feaxe' for 'eaxle' (1538) and render: Seized by the hair.

3. If 'hand-léan' be accepted (as the MS. has it), the line will read: She hand-reward gave him early thereafter.

4. Sw. and S. change H.-So.'s semicolon (v. 1557) to a comma, and translate: The

Ruler of Heaven arranged it in justice easily, after he arose again.

Footnotes XXIV

1. 'Þæs monige gewearð' (1599) and 'hafað þæs geworden' (2027).--In a paper published some years ago in one of the Johns Hopkins University circulars, I tried to throw upon these two long-doubtful passages some light derived from a study of like passages in Alfred's prose.--The impersonal verb 'geweorðan,' with an accus. of the person, and a þæt-clause is used several times with the meaning 'agree.' See Orosius (Sweet's ed.) 178_7; 204_34; 208_28; 210_15; 280_20. In the two Beowulf passages, the þæt-clause is anticipated by 'þæs,' which is clearly a gen. of the thing agreed on.

The first passage (v. 1599 (b)-1600) I translate literally: Then many agreed upon this (namely), that the sea-wolf had killed him.

The second passage (v. 2025 (b)-2027): She is promised ...; to this the friend of the Scyldings has agreed, etc. By emending 'is' instead of 'wæs' (2025), the tenses will be brought into perfect harmony.

In v. 1997 ff. this same idiom occurs, and was noticed in B.'s great article on Beowulf, which appeared about the time I published my reading of 1599 and 2027. Translate 1997 then: Wouldst let the South-Danes themselves decide about their struggle with Grendel. Here 'Súð-Dene' is accus. of person, and 'gúðe' is gen. of thing agreed on.

With such collateral support as that afforded by B. (P. and B. XII. 97), I have no hesitation in departing from H.-So., my usual guide.

The idiom above treated runs through A.-S., Old Saxon, and other Teutonic languages, and should be noticed in the lexicons.

2. 'Bróden-mæl' is regarded by most scholars as meaning a damaskeened sword. Translate: The damaskeened sword burned up. Cf. 25_16 and note.

3. 'Cyning-balde' (1635) is the much-disputed reading of K. and Th. To render this, "nobly bold," "excellently bold," have been suggested. B. would read 'cyning-holde' (cf. 290), and render: Men well-disposed towards the king carried the head, etc. 'Cynebealde,' says t.B., endorsing Gr.

Footnotes XXV

1. Or rather, perhaps, 'the inlaid, or damaskeened weapon.' Cf. 24_57 and note.

Footnotes XXVI

1. K. says 'proudly giveth.'--Gr. says, 'And gives no gold-plated rings, in order to incite the recipient to boastfulness.'--B. suggests 'gyld' for 'gylp,' and renders: And gives no beaten rings for reward.

2. If S.'s emendation be accepted, v. 57 will read: Then came the light, going bright after darkness: the warriors, etc.

3. As the passage stands in H.-So., Unferth presents Beowulf with the sword Hrunting, and B. thanks him for the gift. If, however, the suggestions of Grdtvg. and M. be accepted, the passage will read: Then the brave one (_i.e._ Beowulf) commanded that Hrunting be borne to the son of Ecglaf (Unferth), bade him take his sword, his dear weapon; he (B.) thanked him (U.) for the loan, etc.

Footnotes XXVII

1. For 'geworhte,' the crux of this passage, B. proposes 'geþóhte,' rendering: I know this people with firm thought every way blameless towards foe and friends.

2. S. and B. emend so as to negative the verb 'meet.' "Why should Hrothgar weep if he expects to meet Beowulf again?" both these scholars ask. But the weeping is mentioned before the 'expectations': the tears may have been due to many emotions, especially gratitude, struggling for expression.

Footnotes XXVIII

1. For 'scawan' (1896), 'scaðan' has been proposed. Accepting this, we may render: He said the bright-armored warriors were going to their vessel, welcome, etc. (Cf. 1804.)

2. R. suggests, 'Gewát him on naca,' and renders: The vessel set out, to drive on the sea, the Dane-country left. 'On' bears the alliteration; cf. 'on hafu' (2524). This has some advantages over the H.-So. reading; viz. (1) It adds nothing to the text; (2) it makes 'naca' the subject, and thus brings the passage into keeping with the context, where the poet has exhausted his vocabulary in detailing the actions of the vessel.--B.'s emendation (cf. P. and B. XII. 97) is violent.

3. B. translates: Who for a long time, ready at the coast, had looked out into the distance eagerly for the dear men. This changes the syntax of 'léofra manna.'

4. For 'wunað' (v. 1924) several eminent critics suggest 'wunade' (=remained). This makes the passage much clearer.

5. Why should such a woman be described as an 'excellent' queen? C. suggests 'frécnu' = dangerous, bold.

6. For 'an dæges' various readings have been offered. If 'and-éges' be accepted, the sentence will read: No hero ... dared look upon her, eye to eye. If 'án-dæges' be

adopted, translate: Dared look upon her the whole day.

Footnotes XXIX

1. 'Meodu-scencum' (1981) some would render 'with mead-pourers.' Translate then: The daughter of Hæreth went through the building accompanied by mead-pourers.

2. See my note to 1599, supra, and B. in P. and B. XII. 97.

3. For 'fenne,' supplied by Grdtvg., B. suggests 'fácne' (cf. Jul. 350). Accepting this, translate: Who longest lives of the hated race, steeped in treachery.

4. See note to v. 1599 above.

5. This is perhaps the least understood sentence in the poem, almost very word being open to dispute. (1) The 'nó' of our text is an emendation, and is rejected by many scholars. (2) 'Seldan' is by some taken as an adv. (= seldom), and by others as a noun (= page, companion). (3) 'Léod-hryre,' some render 'fall of the people'; others, 'fall of the prince.' (4) 'Búgeð,' most scholars regard as the intrans. verb meaning 'bend,' 'rest'; but one great scholar has translated it 'shall kill.' (5) 'Hwær,' Very recently, has been attacked, 'wære' being suggested. (6) As a corollary to the above, the same critic proposes to drop 'oft' out of the text.--t.B. suggests: Oft seldan wære after léodhryre: lýtle hwíle bongár búgeð, þeáh seó brýd duge = often has a treaty been (thus) struck, after a prince had fallen: (but only) a short time is the spear (then) wont to rest, however excellent the bride may be.

Footnotes XXX

1. For 'lifigende' (2063), a mere conjecture, 'wígende' has been suggested. The line would then read: Escapeth by fighting, knows the land thoroughly.

2. For 'fæðmum,' Gr.'s conjecture, B. proposes 'færunga.' These three half-verses would then read: She bore off the corpse of her foe suddenly under the mountain-torrent.

3. The phrase 'þíne lýfe' (2132) was long rendered 'with thy (presupposed) permission.' The verse would read: The land-prince then sadly besought me, with thy (presupposed) permission, etc.

Footnotes XXXI

1. This verse B. renders, 'Now serve I again thee alone as my gracious king.'

2. For 'eafor' (2153), Kl. suggests 'ealdor.' Translate then: Bade the prince then to bear in the banner, battle-high helmet, etc. On the other hand, W. takes 'eaforhéafodsegn' as a compound, meaning 'helmet': He bade them bear in the helmet, battle-high helm, gray armor, etc.

3. The H.-So. rendering (ærest = history, origin; 'eft' for 'est'), though liable to objection, is perhaps the best offered. 'That I should very early tell thee of his favor, kindness' sounds well; but 'his' is badly placed to limit 'ést.'--Perhaps, 'eft' with verbs of saying may have the force of Lat. prefix 're,' and the H.-So. reading mean, 'that I should its origin rehearse to thee.'

Footnotes XXXII

1. For 'long-gestréona,' B. suggests 'láengestréona,' and renders, Of fleeting treasures. S. accepts H.'s 'long-gestréona,' but renders, The treasure long in accumulating.

2. For 'hard-fyrdne' (2246), B. first suggested 'hard-fyndne,' rendering: A heap of treasures ... so great that its equal would be hard to find. The same scholar suggests later 'hord-wynne dæl' = A deal of treasure-joy.

3. Some read 'fec-word' (2247), and render: Banning words uttered.

4. An earlier reading of H.'s gave the following meaning to this passage: He is said to inhabit a mound under the earth, where he, etc. The translation in the text is more authentic.

5. The repetition of 'hord' in this passage has led some scholars to suggest new readings to avoid the second 'hord.' This, however, is not under the main stress, and, it seems to me, might easily be accepted.

6. The reading of H.-So. is well defended in the notes to that volume. B. emends and renders: Nor was there any man in that desert who rejoiced in conflict, in battle-work. That is, the hoard-ward could not find any one who had disturbed his slumbers, for no warrior was there, t.B.'s emendation would give substantially the same translation.

7. 'Sinc-fæt' (2301): this word both here and in v. 2232, t.B. renders 'treasure.'

Footnotes XXXIII

1. 'Hám' (2326), the suggestion of B. is accepted by t.B. and other scholars.

2. For 'láðan cynnes' (2355), t.B. suggests 'láðan cynne,' apposition to 'mægum.' From syntactical and other considerations, this is a most excellent emendation.

3. Gr. read 'on feorme' (2386), rendering: He there at the banquet a fatal wound received by blows of the sword.

Footnotes XXXIV

1. 'Gomelum ceorle' (2445).--H. takes these words as referring to Hrethel; but the translator here departs from his editor by understanding the poet to refer to a hypothetical old man, introduced as an illustration of a father's sorrow.

Hrethrel had certainly never seen a son of his ride on the gallows to feed the crows.

The passage beginning 'swá bið géomorlic' seems to be an effort to reach a full simile, 'as ... so.' 'As it is mournful for an old man, etc. ... so the defence of the Weders (2463) bore heart-sorrow, etc.' The verses 2451 to 2463-1/2 would be parenthetical, the poet's feelings being so strong as to interrupt the simile. The punctuation of the fourth edition would be better--a comma after 'galgan' (2447). The translation may be indicated as follows: (Just) as it is sad for an old man to see his son ride young on the gallows when he himself is uttering mournful measures, a sorrowful song, while his son hangs for a comfort to the raven, and he, old and infirm, cannot render him any kelp--(he is constantly reminded, etc., 2451-2463)--so the defence of the Weders, etc.

Footnotes XXXV
1. The clause 2520(2)-2522(1), rendered by 'Wist I ... monster,' Gr., followed by S., translates substantially as follows: If I knew how else I might combat the boastful defiance of the monster.--The translation turns upon 'wiðgrípan,' a word not understood.

2. B. emends and translates: I will not flee the space of a foot from the guard of the barrow, but there shall be to us a fight at the wall, as fate decrees, each one's Creator.

3. The translation of this passage is based on 'unsláw' (2565), accepted by H.-So., in lieu of the long-standing 'ungléaw.' The former is taken as an adj. limiting 'sweord'; the latter as an adj. c. 'gúð-cyning': The good war-king, rash with edges, brandished his sword, his old relic. The latter gives a more rhetorical Anglo-Saxon (poetical) sentence.

Footnotes XXXVI
1. The passage 'Brand ... burnie,' is much disputed. In the first place, some eminent critics assume a gap of at least two half-verses.--'Úrum' (2660), being a peculiar form, has been much discussed. 'Byrdu-scrúd' is also a crux. B. suggests 'býwdu-scrúd' = splendid vestments. Nor is 'bám' accepted by all, 'béon' being suggested. Whatever the individual words, the passage must mean, "I intend to share with him my equipments of defence."

2. B. would render: Which, as I heard, excelled in stroke every sword that he carried to the strife, even the strongest (sword). For 'Þonne' he reads 'Þone,' rel. pr.

Footnotes XXXVII
1. B. renders: He (W.) did not regard his (the dragon's) head (since Beowulf had struck it without effect), but struck the dragon a little lower down.-- One crux is to find out whose head is meant; another is to bring out the antithesis between 'head' and 'hand.'

2. 'Þæt Þæt fýr' (2702), S. emends to 'Þá Þæt fýr' = when the fire began to grow less intense afterward. This emendation relieves the passage of a plethora of conjunctive Þæt's.

3. For 'gefyldan' (2707), S. proposes 'gefylde.' The passage would read: He felled the foe (life drove out strength), and they then both had destroyed him, chieftains related. This gives Beowulf the credit of having felled the dragon; then they combine to annihilate him.--For 'ellen' (2707), Kl. suggests 'e(a)llne.'--The reading 'life drove out strength' is very unsatisfactory and very peculiar. I would suggest as follows: Adopt S.'s emendation, remove H.'s parenthesis, read 'ferh-ellen wræc,' and translate: He felled the foe, drove out his life-strength (that is, made him hors de combat), and then they both, etc.

Footnotes XXXVIII
1. The word 'oferhígian' (2767) being vague and little understood, two quite distinct translations of this passage have arisen. One takes 'oferhígian' as meaning 'to exceed,' and, inserting 'hord' after 'gehwone,' renders: The treasure may easily, the gold in the ground, exceed in value every hoard of man, hide it who will. The other takes 'oferhígian' as meaning 'to render arrogant,' and, giving the sentence a moralizing tone, renders substantially as in the body of this work. (Cf. 28_13 et seq.)

2. The passage beginning here is very much disputed. 'The bill of the old lord' is by some regarded as Beowulf's sword; by others, as that of the ancient possessor of the hoard. 'Ær gescód' (2778), translated in this work as verb and adverb, is by some regarded as a compound participial adj. = sheathed in brass.

Footnotes XXXIX
1. For 'dædum rædan' (2859) B. suggests 'déað árædan,' and renders: The might (or judgment) of God would determine death for every man, as he still does.

2. Some critics, H. himself in earlier editions, put the clause, 'When ... him' (A.-S. 'Þá ... beget') with the following sentence; that is, they make it dependent upon 'Þorfte' (2875) instead of upon 'forwurpe' (2873).

Footnotes XL
1. 'Hige-méðum' (2910) is glossed by H. as dat. plu. (= for the dead). S. proposes 'hige-méðe,' nom. sing. limiting Wigláf; i.e. W., mood-weary, holds head-watch o'er friend

and foe.--B. suggests taking the word as dat. inst. plu. of an abstract noun in -'u.' The translation would be substantially the same as S.'s.

Footnotes XLI

1. For 'góda,' which seems a surprising epithet for a Geat to apply to the "terrible" Ongentheow, B. suggests 'gomela.' The passage would then stand: 'The old one went then,' etc.

2. For 'segn Higeláce,' K., Th., and B. propose 'segn Higeláces,' meaning: Higelac's banner followed the Swedes (in pursuit). --S. suggests 'sæcc Higeláces,' and renders: Higelac's pursuit. --The H.-So. reading, as translated in our text, means that the banner of the enemy was captured and brought to Higelac as a trophy.

3. The rendering given in this translation represents the king as being generous beyond the possibility of reproach; but some authorities construe 'him' (2996) as plu., and understand the passage to mean that no one reproached the two brothers with having received more reward than they were entitled to.

4. The name 'Scyldingas' here (3006) has caused much discussion, and given rise to several theories, the most important of which are as follows: (1) After the downfall of Hrothgar's family, Beowulf was king of the Danes, or Scyldings. (2) For 'Scyldingas' read 'Scylfingas'--that is, after killing Eadgils, the Scylfing prince, Beowulf conquered his land, and held it in subjection. (3) M. considers 3006 a thoughtless repetition of 2053. (Cf. H.-So.)

5. B. takes 'nihtes' and 'hwílum' (3045) as separate adverbial cases, and renders: Joy in the air had he of yore by night, etc. He thinks that the idea of vanished time ought to be expressed.

6. The parenthesis is by some emended so as to read: (1) (He (i.e. God) is the hope of men); (2) (he is the hope of heroes). Gr.'s reading has no parenthesis, but says: ... could touch, unless God himself, true king of victories, gave to whom he would to open the treasure, the secret place of enchanters, etc. The last is rejected on many grounds.

Footnotes XLII

1. For 'gehýdde,' B. suggests 'gehýðde': the passage would stand as above except the change of 'hidden' (v. 2) to 'plundered.' The reference, however, would be to the thief, not to the dragon.

2. The passage 'Wundur ... búan' (3063-3066), M. took to be a question asking whether it was strange that a man should die when his appointed time had come.--B. sees a corruption, and makes emendations introducing the idea that a brave man should not die from sickness or from old age, but should find death in the performance of some deed of daring.--S. sees an indirect question introduced by 'hwár' and dependent upon 'wundur': _A secret is it when the hero is to die, etc.--Why may the two clauses not be parallel, and the whole passage an Old English cry of '_How wonderful is death!'? --S.'s is the best yet offered, if 'wundor' means 'mystery.'

3. For 'strude' in H.-So., S. suggests 'stride.' This would require 'ravage' (v. 16) to be changed to 'tread.'

4. 'He cared ... sight of' (17, 18), S. emends so as to read as follows: He (Beowulf) had not before seen the favor of the avaricious possessor.

5. B. renders: That which drew the king thither (i.e. the treasure) was granted us, but in such a way that it overcomes us.

6. 'Folc-ágende' (3114) B. takes as dat. sing. with 'gódum,' and refers it to Beowulf; that is, Should bring fire-wood to the place where the good folk-ruler lay.

7. C. proposes to take 'weaxan' = L. 'vescor,' and translate devour. This gives a parallel to 'fretan' above. The parenthesis would be discarded and the passage read: Now shall the fire consume, the wan-flame devour, the prince of warriors, etc.

BEOWULF

By Anonymous
Translated by Gummere

PRELUDE OF THE FOUNDER OF THE DANISH HOUSE

LO, praise of the prowess of people-kings
of spear-armed Danes, in days long sped,
we have heard, and what honor the athelings won!
Oft Scyld the Scefing from squadroned foes,
from many a tribe, the mead-bench tore,
awing the earls. Since erst he lay
friendless, a foundling, fate repaid him:
for he waxed under welkin, in wealth he throve,
till before him the folk, both far and near,
who house by the whale-path, heard his mandate,
gave him gifts: a good king he!
To him an heir was afterward born,
a son in his halls, whom heaven sent
to favor the folk, feeling their woe
that erst they had lacked an earl for leader
so long a while; the Lord endowed him,
the Wielder of Wonder, with world's renown.
Famed was this Beowulf:[1] far flew the boast of him,
son of Scyld, in the Scandian lands.
So becomes it a youth to quit him well
with his father's friends, by fee and gift,
that to aid him, aged, in after days,
come warriors willing, should war draw nigh,
liegemen loyal: by lauded deeds
shall an earl have honor in every clan.

Forth he fared at the fated moment,
sturdy Scyld to the shelter of God.
Then they bore him over to ocean's billow,
loving clansmen, as late he charged them,
while wielded words the winsome Scyld,
the leader beloved who long had ruled....
In the roadstead rocked a ring-dight vessel,
ice-flecked, outbound, atheling's barge:
there laid they down their darling lord
on the breast of the boat, the breaker-of-rings,[2]
by the mast the mighty one. Many a treasure

fetched from far was freighted with him.
No ship have I known so nobly dight
with weapons of war and weeds of battle,
with breastplate and blade: on his bosom lay
a heaped hoard that hence should go
far o'er the flood with him floating away.
No less these loaded the lordly gifts,
thanes' huge treasure, than those had done
who in former time forth had sent him
sole on the seas, a suckling child.
High o'er his head they hoist the standard,
a gold-wove banner; let billows take him,
gave him to ocean. Grave were their spirits,
mournful their mood. No man is able
to say in sooth, no son of the halls,
no hero 'neath heaven, -- who harbored that freight!

I

Now Beowulf bode in the burg of the Scyldings,
leader beloved, and long he ruled
in fame with all folk, since his father had gone
away from the world, till awoke an heir,
haughty Healfdene, who held through life,
sage and sturdy, the Scyldings glad.
Then, one after one, there woke to him,
to the chieftain of clansmen, children four:
Heorogar, then Hrothgar, then Halga brave;
and I heard that -- was -- 's queen,
the Heathoscylfing's helpmate dear.
To Hrothgar was given such glory of war,
such honor of combat, that all his kin
obeyed him gladly till great grew his band
of youthful comrades. It came in his mind
to bid his henchmen a hall uprear,
a master mead-house, mightier far
than ever was seen by the sons of earth,
and within it, then, to old and young
he would all allot that the Lord had sent him,
save only the land and the lives of his men.
Wide, I heard, was the work commanded,
for many a tribe this mid-earth round,
to fashion the folkstead. It fell, as he ordered,
in rapid achievement that ready it stood there,
of halls the noblest: Heorot[1] he named it
whose message had might in many a land.
Not reckless of promise, the rings he dealt,
treasure at banquet: there towered the hall,
high, gabled wide, the hot surge waiting
of furious flame.[2] Nor far was that day

when father and son-in-law stood in feud
for warfare and hatred that woke again.[3]
With envy and anger an evil spirit
endured the dole in his dark abode,
that he heard each day the din of revel
high in the hall: there harps rang out,
clear song of the singer. He sang who knew[4]
tales of the early time of man,
how the Almighty made the earth,
fairest fields enfolded by water,
set, triumphant, sun and moon
for a light to lighten the land-dwellers,
and braided bright the breast of earth
with limbs and leaves, made life for all
of mortal beings that breathe and move.
So lived the clansmen in cheer and revel
a winsome life, till one began
to fashion evils, that field of hell.
Grendel this monster grim was called,
march-riever[5] mighty, in moorland living,
in fen and fastness; fief of the giants
the hapless wight a while had kept
since the Creator his exile doomed.
On kin of Cain was the killing avenged
by sovran God for slaughtered Abel.
Ill fared his feud,[6] and far was he driven,
for the slaughter's sake, from sight of men.
Of Cain awoke all that woful breed,
Etins[7] and elves and evil-spirits,
as well as the giants that warred with God
weary while: but their wage was paid them!

II

WENT he forth to find at fall of night
that haughty house, and heed wherever
the Ring-Danes, outrevelled, to rest had gone.
Found within it the atheling band
asleep after feasting and fearless of sorrow,
of human hardship. Unhallowed wight,
grim and greedy, he grasped betimes,
wrathful, reckless, from resting-places,
thirty of the thanes, and thence he rushed
fain of his fell spoil, faring homeward,
laden with slaughter, his lair to seek.
Then at the dawning, as day was breaking,
the might of Grendel to men was known;
then after wassail was wail uplifted,
loud moan in the morn. The mighty chief,
atheling excellent, unblithe sat,

labored in woe for the loss of his thanes,
when once had been traced the trail of the fiend,
spirit accurst: too cruel that sorrow,
too long, too loathsome. Not late the respite;
with night returning, anew began
ruthless murder; he recked no whit,
firm in his guilt, of the feud and crime.
They were easy to find who elsewhere sought
in room remote their rest at night,
bed in the bowers,[1] when that bale was shown,
was seen in sooth, with surest token, --
the hall-thane's[2] hate. Such held themselves
far and fast who the fiend outran!
Thus ruled unrighteous and raged his fill
one against all; until empty stood
that lordly building, and long it bode so.
Twelve years' tide the trouble he bore,
sovran of Scyldings, sorrows in plenty,
boundless cares. There came unhidden
tidings true to the tribes of men,
in sorrowful songs, how ceaselessly Grendel
harassed Hrothgar, what hate he bore him,
what murder and massacre, many a year,
feud unfading, -- refused consent
to deal with any of Daneland's earls,
make pact of peace, or compound for gold:
still less did the wise men ween to get
great fee for the feud from his fiendish hands.
But the evil one ambushed old and young
death-shadow dark, and dogged them still,
lured, or lurked in the livelong night
of misty moorlands: men may say not
where the haunts of these Hell-Runes[3] be.
Such heaping of horrors the hater of men,
lonely roamer, wrought unceasing,
harassings heavy. O'er Heorot he lorded,
gold-bright hall, in gloomy nights;
and ne'er could the prince[4] approach his throne,
-- 'twas judgment of God, -- or have joy in his hall.
Sore was the sorrow to Scyldings'-friend,
heart-rending misery. Many nobles
sat assembled, and searched out counsel
how it were best for bold-hearted men
against harassing terror to try their hand.
Whiles they vowed in their heathen fanes
altar-offerings, asked with words[5]
that the slayer-of-souls would succor give them
for the pain of their people. Their practice this,
their heathen hope; 'twas Hell they thought of
in mood of their mind. Almighty they knew not,

Doomsman of Deeds and dreadful Lord,
nor Heaven's-Helmet heeded they ever,
Wielder-of-Wonder. -- Woe for that man
who in harm and hatred hales his soul
to fiery embraces; -- nor favor nor change
awaits he ever. But well for him
that after death-day may draw to his Lord,
and friendship find in the Father's arms!

III

THUS seethed unceasing the son of Healfdene
with the woe of these days; not wisest men
assuaged his sorrow; too sore the anguish,
loathly and long, that lay on his folk,
most baneful of burdens and bales of the night.

This heard in his home Hygelac's thane,
great among Geats, of Grendel's doings.
He was the mightiest man of valor
in that same day of this our life,
stalwart and stately. A stout wave-walker
he bade make ready. Yon battle-king, said he,
far o'er the swan-road he fain would seek,
the noble monarch who needed men!
The prince's journey by prudent folk
was little blamed, though they loved him dear;
they whetted the hero, and hailed good omens.
And now the bold one from bands of Geats
comrades chose, the keenest of warriors
e'er he could find; with fourteen men
the sea-wood[1] he sought, and, sailor proved,
led them on to the land's confines.
Time had now flown;[2] afloat was the ship,
boat under bluff. On board they climbed,
warriors ready; waves were churning
sea with sand; the sailors bore
on the breast of the bark their bright array,
their mail and weapons: the men pushed off,
on its willing way, the well-braced craft.
Then moved o'er the waters by might of the wind
that bark like a bird with breast of foam,
till in season due, on the second day,
the curved prow such course had run
that sailors now could see the land,
sea-cliffs shining, steep high hills,
headlands broad. Their haven was found,
their journey ended. Up then quickly
the Weders'[3] clansmen climbed ashore,
anchored their sea-wood, with armor clashing

and gear of battle: God they thanked
or passing in peace o'er the paths of the sea.
Now saw from the cliff a Scylding clansman,
a warden that watched the water-side,
how they bore o'er the gangway glittering shields,
war-gear in readiness; wonder seized him
to know what manner of men they were.
Straight to the strand his steed he rode,
Hrothgar's henchman; with hand of might
he shook his spear, and spake in parley.
"Who are ye, then, ye armed men,
mailed folk, that yon mighty vessel
have urged thus over the ocean ways,
here o'er the waters? A warden I,
sentinel set o'er the sea-march here,
lest any foe to the folk of Danes
with harrying fleet should harm the land.
No aliens ever at ease thus bore them,
linden-wielders:[4] yet word-of-leave
clearly ye lack from clansmen here,
my folk's agreement. -- A greater ne'er saw I
of warriors in world than is one of you, --
yon hero in harness! No henchman he
worthied by weapons, if witness his features,
his peerless presence! I pray you, though, tell
your folk and home, lest hence ye fare
suspect to wander your way as spies
in Danish land. Now, dwellers afar,
ocean-travellers, take from me
simple advice: the sooner the better
I hear of the country whence ye came."

IV

To him the stateliest spake in answer;
the warriors' leader his word-hoard unlocked: --
"We are by kin of the clan of Geats,
and Hygelac's own hearth-fellows we.
To folk afar was my father known,
noble atheling, Ecgtheow named.
Full of winters, he fared away
aged from earth; he is honored still
through width of the world by wise men all.
To thy lord and liege in loyal mood
we hasten hither, to Healfdene's son,
people-protector: be pleased to advise us!
To that mighty-one come we on mickle errand,
to the lord of the Danes; nor deem I right
that aught be hidden. We hear -- thou knowest
if sooth it is -- the saying of men,

that amid the Scyldings a scathing monster,
dark ill-doer, in dusky nights
shows terrific his rage unmatched,
hatred and murder. To Hrothgar I
in greatness of soul would succor bring,
so the Wise-and-Brave[1] may worst his foes, --
if ever the end of ills is fated,
of cruel contest, if cure shall follow,
and the boiling care-waves cooler grow;
else ever afterward anguish-days
he shall suffer in sorrow while stands in place
high on its hill that house unpeered!"
Astride his steed, the strand-ward answered,
clansman unquailing: "The keen-souled thane
must be skilled to sever and sunder duly
words and works, if he well intends.
I gather, this band is graciously bent
to the Scyldings' master. March, then, bearing
weapons and weeds the way I show you.
I will bid my men your boat meanwhile
to guard for fear lest foemen come, --
your new-tarred ship by shore of ocean
faithfully watching till once again
it waft o'er the waters those well-loved thanes,
-- winding-neck'd wood, -- to Weders' bounds,
heroes such as the hest of fate
shall succor and save from the shock of war."
They bent them to march, -- the boat lay still,
fettered by cable and fast at anchor,
broad-bosomed ship. Then shone the boars[2]
over the cheek-guard; chased with gold,
keen and gleaming, guard it kept
o'er the man of war, as marched along
heroes in haste, till the hall they saw,
broad of gable and bright with gold:
that was the fairest, 'mid folk of earth,
of houses 'neath heaven, where Hrothgar lived,
and the gleam of it lightened o'er lands afar.
The sturdy shieldsman showed that bright
burg-of-the-boldest; bade them go
straightway thither; his steed then turned,
hardy hero, and hailed them thus: --
"'Tis time that I fare from you. Father Almighty
in grace and mercy guard you well,
safe in your seekings. Seaward I go,
'gainst hostile warriors hold my watch."

Beowulf: Scholar's Edition

V

STONE-BRIGHT the street:[1] it showed the way
to the crowd of clansmen. Corselets glistened
hand-forged, hard; on their harness bright
the steel ring sang, as they strode along
in mail of battle, and marched to the hall.
There, weary of ocean, the wall along
they set their bucklers, their broad shields, down,
and bowed them to bench: the breastplates clanged,
war-gear of men; their weapons stacked,
spears of the seafarers stood together,
gray-tipped ash: that iron band
was worthily weaponed! -- A warrior proud
asked of the heroes their home and kin.
"Whence, now, bear ye burnished shields,
harness gray and helmets grim,
spears in multitude? Messenger, I,
Hrothgar's herald! Heroes so many
ne'er met I as strangers of mood so strong.
'Tis plain that for prowess, not plunged into exile,
for high-hearted valor, Hrothgar ye seek!"
Him the sturdy-in-war bespake with words,
proud earl of the Weders answer made,
hardy 'neath helmet: -- "Hygelac's, we,
fellows at board; I am Beowulf named.
I am seeking to say to the son of Healfdene
this mission of mine, to thy master-lord,
the doughty prince, if he deign at all
grace that we greet him, the good one, now."
Wulfgar spake, the Wendles' chieftain,
whose might of mind to many was known,
his courage and counsel: "The king of Danes,
the Scyldings' friend, I fain will tell,
the Breaker-of-Rings, as the boon thou askest,
the famed prince, of thy faring hither,
and, swiftly after, such answer bring
as the doughty monarch may deign to give."
Hied then in haste to where Hrothgar sat
white-haired and old, his earls about him,
till the stout thane stood at the shoulder there
of the Danish king: good courtier he!
Wulfgar spake to his winsome lord: --
"Hither have fared to thee far-come men
o'er the paths of ocean, people of Geatland;
and the stateliest there by his sturdy band
is Beowulf named. This boon they seek,
that they, my master, may with thee
have speech at will: nor spurn their prayer
to give them hearing, gracious Hrothgar!

In weeds of the warrior worthy they,
methinks, of our liking; their leader most surely,
a hero that hither his henchmen has led."

VI

HROTHGAR answered, helmet of Scyldings: --
"I knew him of yore in his youthful days;
his aged father was Ecgtheow named,
to whom, at home, gave Hrethel the Geat
his only daughter. Their offspring bold
fares hither to seek the steadfast friend.
And seamen, too, have said me this, --
who carried my gifts to the Geatish court,
thither for thanks, -- he has thirty men's
heft of grasp in the gripe of his hand,
the bold-in-battle. Blessed God
out of his mercy this man hath sent
to Danes of the West, as I ween indeed,
against horror of Grendel. I hope to give
the good youth gold for his gallant thought.
Be thou in haste, and bid them hither,
clan of kinsmen, to come before me;
and add this word, -- they are welcome guests
to folk of the Danes."
[To the door of the hall
Wulfgar went] and the word declared: --
"To you this message my master sends,
East-Danes' king, that your kin he knows,
hardy heroes, and hails you all
welcome hither o'er waves of the sea!
Ye may wend your way in war-attire,
and under helmets Hrothgar greet;
but let here the battle-shields bide your parley,
and wooden war-shafts wait its end."
Uprose the mighty one, ringed with his men,
brave band of thanes: some bode without,
battle-gear guarding, as bade the chief.
Then hied that troop where the herald led them,
under Heorot's roof: [the hero strode,]
hardy 'neath helm, till the hearth he neared.
Beowulf spake, -- his breastplate gleamed,
war-net woven by wit of the smith: --
"Thou Hrothgar, hail! Hygelac's I,
kinsman and follower. Fame a plenty
have I gained in youth! These Grendel-deeds
I heard in my home-land heralded clear.
Seafarers say how stands this hall,
of buildings best, for your band of thanes
empty and idle, when evening sun

Beowulf: Scholar's Edition

in the harbor of heaven is hidden away.
So my vassals advised me well, --
brave and wise, the best of men, --
O sovran Hrothgar, to seek thee here,
for my nerve and my might they knew full well.
Themselves had seen me from slaughter come
blood-flecked from foes, where five I bound,
and that wild brood worsted. I' the waves I slew
nicors[1] by night, in need and peril
avenging the Weders,[2] whose woe they sought, --
crushing the grim ones. Grendel now,
monster cruel, be mine to quell
in single battle! So, from thee,
thou sovran of the Shining-Danes,
Scyldings'-bulwark, a boon I seek, --
and, Friend-of-the-folk, refuse it not,
O Warriors'-shield, now I've wandered far, --
that I alone with my liegemen here,
this hardy band, may Heorot purge!
More I hear, that the monster dire,
in his wanton mood, of weapons recks not;
hence shall I scorn -- so Hygelac stay,
king of my kindred, kind to me! --
brand or buckler to bear in the fight,
gold-colored targe: but with gripe alone
must I front the fiend and fight for life,
foe against foe. Then faith be his
in the doom of the Lord whom death shall take.
Fain, I ween, if the fight he win,
in this hall of gold my Geatish band
will he fearless eat, -- as oft before, --
my noblest thanes. Nor need'st thou then
to hide my head;[3] for his shall I be,
dyed in gore, if death must take me;
and my blood-covered body he'll bear as prey,
ruthless devour it, the roamer-lonely,
with my life-blood redden his lair in the fen:
no further for me need'st food prepare!
To Hygelac send, if Hild[4] should take me,
best of war-weeds, warding my breast,
armor excellent, heirloom of Hrethel
and work of Wayland.[5] Fares Wyrd[6] as she must."

VII

HROTHGAR spake, the Scyldings'-helmet: --
"For fight defensive, Friend my Beowulf,
to succor and save, thou hast sought us here.
Thy father's combat[1] a feud enkindled
when Heatholaf with hand he slew

among the Wylfings; his Weder kin
for horror of fighting feared to hold him.
Fleeing, he sought our South-Dane folk,
over surge of ocean the Honor-Scyldings,
when first I was ruling the folk of Danes,
wielded, youthful, this widespread realm,
this hoard-hold of heroes. Heorogar was dead,
my elder brother, had breathed his last,
Healfdene's bairn: he was better than I!
Straightway the feud with fee[2] I settled,
to the Wylfings sent, o'er watery ridges,
treasures olden: oaths he[3] swore me.
Sore is my soul to say to any
of the race of man what ruth for me
in Heorot Grendel with hate hath wrought,
what sudden harryings. Hall-folk fail me,
my warriors wane; for Wyrd hath swept them
into Grendel's grasp. But God is able
this deadly foe from his deeds to turn!
Boasted full oft, as my beer they drank,
earls o'er the ale-cup, armed men,
that they would bide in the beer-hall here,
Grendel's attack with terror of blades.
Then was this mead-house at morning tide
dyed with gore, when the daylight broke,
all the boards of the benches blood-besprinkled,
gory the hall: I had heroes the less,
doughty dear-ones that death had reft.
-- But sit to the banquet, unbind thy words,
hardy hero, as heart shall prompt thee."

Gathered together, the Geatish men
in the banquet-hall on bench assigned,
sturdy-spirited, sat them down,
hardy-hearted. A henchman attended,
carried the carven cup in hand,
served the clear mead. Oft minstrels sang
blithe in Heorot. Heroes revelled,
no dearth of warriors, Weder and Dane.

VIII

UNFERTH spake, the son of Ecglaf,
who sat at the feet of the Scyldings' lord,
unbound the battle-runes.[1] -- Beowulf's quest,
sturdy seafarer's, sorely galled him;
ever he envied that other men
should more achieve in middle-earth
of fame under heaven than he himself. --
"Art thou that Beowulf, Breca's rival,

who emulous swam on the open sea,
when for pride the pair of you proved the floods,
and wantonly dared in waters deep
to risk your lives? No living man,
or lief or loath, from your labor dire
could you dissuade, from swimming the main.
Ocean-tides with your arms ye covered,
with strenuous hands the sea-streets measured,
swam o'er the waters. Winter's storm
rolled the rough waves. In realm of sea
a sennight strove ye. In swimming he topped thee,
had more of main! Him at morning-tide
billows bore to the Battling Reamas,
whence he hied to his home so dear
beloved of his liegemen, to land of Brondings,
fastness fair, where his folk he ruled,
town and treasure. In triumph o'er thee
Beanstan's bairn[2] his boast achieved.
So ween I for thee a worse adventure
-- though in buffet of battle thou brave hast been,
in struggle grim, -- if Grendel's approach
thou darst await through the watch of night!"

Beowulf spake, bairn of Ecgtheow: --
"What a deal hast uttered, dear my Unferth,
drunken with beer, of Breca now,
told of his triumph! Truth I claim it,
that I had more of might in the sea
than any man else, more ocean-endurance.
We twain had talked, in time of youth,
and made our boast, -- we were merely boys,
striplings still, -- to stake our lives
far at sea: and so we performed it.
Naked swords, as we swam along,
we held in hand, with hope to guard us
against the whales. Not a whit from me
could he float afar o'er the flood of waves,
haste o'er the billows; nor him I abandoned.
Together we twain on the tides abode
five nights full till the flood divided us,
churning waves and chillest weather,
darkling night, and the northern wind
ruthless rushed on us: rough was the surge.
Now the wrath of the sea-fish rose apace;
yet me 'gainst the monsters my mailed coat,
hard and hand-linked, help afforded, --
battle-sark braided my breast to ward,
garnished with gold. There grasped me firm
and haled me to bottom the hated foe,
with grimmest gripe. 'Twas granted me, though,

to pierce the monster with point of sword,
with blade of battle: huge beast of the sea
was whelmed by the hurly through hand of mine.

IX

ME thus often the evil monsters
thronging threatened. With thrust of my sword,
the darling, I dealt them due return!
Nowise had they bliss from their booty then
to devour their victim, vengeful creatures,
seated to banquet at bottom of sea;
but at break of day, by my brand sore hurt,
on the edge of ocean up they lay,
put to sleep by the sword. And since, by them
on the fathomless sea-ways sailor-folk
are never molested. -- Light from east,
came bright God's beacon; the billows sank,
so that I saw the sea-cliffs high,
windy walls. For Wyrd oft saveth
earl undoomed if he doughty be!
And so it came that I killed with my sword
nine of the nicors. Of night-fought battles
ne'er heard I a harder 'neath heaven's dome,
nor adrift on the deep a more desolate man!
Yet I came unharmed from that hostile clutch,
though spent with swimming. The sea upbore me,
flood of the tide, on Finnish land,
the welling waters. No wise of thee
have I heard men tell such terror of falchions,
bitter battle. Breca ne'er yet,
not one of you pair, in the play of war
such daring deed has done at all
with bloody brand, -- I boast not of it! --
though thou wast the bane[1] of thy brethren dear,
thy closest kin, whence curse of hell
awaits thee, well as thy wit may serve!
For I say in sooth, thou son of Ecglaf,
never had Grendel these grim deeds wrought,
monster dire, on thy master dear,
in Heorot such havoc, if heart of thine
were as battle-bold as thy boast is loud!
But he has found no feud will happen;
from sword-clash dread of your Danish clan
he vaunts him safe, from the Victor-Scyldings.
He forces pledges, favors none
of the land of Danes, but lustily murders,
fights and feasts, nor feud he dreads
from Spear-Dane men. But speedily now
shall I prove him the prowess and pride of the Geats,

shall bid him battle. Blithe to mead
go he that listeth, when light of dawn
this morrow morning o'er men of earth,
ether-robed sun from the south shall beam!"
Joyous then was the Jewel-giver,
hoar-haired, war-brave; help awaited
the Bright-Danes' prince, from Beowulf hearing,
folk's good shepherd, such firm resolve.
Then was laughter of liegemen loud resounding
with winsome words. Came Wealhtheow forth,
queen of Hrothgar, heedful of courtesy,
gold-decked, greeting the guests in hall;
and the high-born lady handed the cup
first to the East-Danes' heir and warden,
bade him be blithe at the beer-carouse,
the land's beloved one. Lustily took he
banquet and beaker, battle-famed king.

Through the hall then went the Helmings' Lady,
to younger and older everywhere
carried the cup, till come the moment
when the ring-graced queen, the royal-hearted,
to Beowulf bore the beaker of mead.
She greeted the Geats' lord, God she thanked,
in wisdom's words, that her will was granted,
that at last on a hero her hope could lean
for comfort in terrors. The cup he took,
hardy-in-war, from Wealhtheow's hand,
and answer uttered the eager-for-combat.
Beowulf spake, bairn of Ecgtheow: --
"This was my thought, when my thanes and I
bent to the ocean and entered our boat,
that I would work the will of your people
fully, or fighting fall in death,
in fiend's gripe fast. I am firm to do
an earl's brave deed, or end the days
of this life of mine in the mead-hall here."
Well these words to the woman seemed,
Beowulf's battle-boast. -- Bright with gold
the stately dame by her spouse sat down.
Again, as erst, began in hall
warriors' wassail and words of power,
the proud-band's revel, till presently
the son of Healfdene hastened to seek
rest for the night; he knew there waited
fight for the fiend in that festal hall,
when the sheen of the sun they saw no more,
and dusk of night sank darkling nigh,
and shadowy shapes came striding on,
wan under welkin. The warriors rose.

Man to man, he made harangue,
Hrothgar to Beowulf, bade him hail,
let him wield the wine hall: a word he added: --
"Never to any man erst I trusted,
since I could heave up hand and shield,
this noble Dane-Hall, till now to thee.
Have now and hold this house unpeered;
remember thy glory; thy might declare;
watch for the foe! No wish shall fail thee
if thou bidest the battle with bold-won life."

X

THEN Hrothgar went with his hero-train,
defence-of-Scyldings, forth from hall;
fain would the war-lord Wealhtheow seek,
couch of his queen. The King-of-Glory
against this Grendel a guard had set,
so heroes heard, a hall-defender,
who warded the monarch and watched for the monster.
In truth, the Geats' prince gladly trusted
his mettle, his might, the mercy of God!
Cast off then his corselet of iron,
helmet from head; to his henchman gave, --
choicest of weapons, -- the well-chased sword,
bidding him guard the gear of battle.
Spake then his Vaunt the valiant man,
Beowulf Geat, ere the bed be sought: --
"Of force in fight no feebler I count me,
in grim war-deeds, than Grendel deems him.
Not with the sword, then, to sleep of death
his life will I give, though it lie in my power.
No skill is his to strike against me,
my shield to hew though he hardy be,
bold in battle; we both, this night,
shall spurn the sword, if he seek me here,
unweaponed, for war. Let wisest God,
sacred Lord, on which side soever
doom decree as he deemeth right."
Reclined then the chieftain, and cheek-pillows held
the head of the earl, while all about him
seamen hardy on hall-beds sank.
None of them thought that thence their steps
to the folk and fastness that fostered them,
to the land they loved, would lead them back!
Full well they wist that on warriors many
battle-death seized, in the banquet-hall,
of Danish clan. But comfort and help,
war-weal weaving, to Weder folk
the Master gave, that, by might of one,

over their enemy all prevailed,
by single strength. In sooth 'tis told
that highest God o'er human kind
hath wielded ever! -- Thro' wan night striding,
came the walker-in-shadow. Warriors slept
whose hest was to guard the gabled hall, --
all save one. 'Twas widely known
that against God's will the ghostly ravager
him[1] could not hurl to haunts of darkness;
wakeful, ready, with warrior's wrath,
bold he bided the battle's issue.

XI

THEN from the moorland, by misty crags,
with God's wrath laden, Grendel came.
The monster was minded of mankind now
sundry to seize in the stately house.
Under welkin he walked, till the wine-palace there,
gold-hall of men, he gladly discerned,
flashing with fretwork. Not first time, this,
that he the home of Hrothgar sought, --
yet ne'er in his life-day, late or early,
such hardy heroes, such hall-thanes, found!
To the house the warrior walked apace,
parted from peace;[1] the portal opended,
though with forged bolts fast, when his fists had struck it,
and baleful he burst in his blatant rage,
the house's mouth. All hastily, then,
o'er fair-paved floor the fiend trod on,
ireful he strode; there streamed from his eyes
fearful flashes, like flame to see.

He spied in hall the hero-band,
kin and clansmen clustered asleep,
hardy liegemen. Then laughed his heart;
for the monster was minded, ere morn should dawn,
savage, to sever the soul of each,
life from body, since lusty banquet
waited his will! But Wyrd forbade him
to seize any more of men on earth
after that evening. Eagerly watched
Hygelac's kinsman his cursed foe,
how he would fare in fell attack.
Not that the monster was minded to pause!
Straightway he seized a sleeping warrior
for the first, and tore him fiercely asunder,
the bone-frame bit, drank blood in streams,
swallowed him piecemeal: swiftly thus
the lifeless corse was clear devoured,

e'en feet and hands. Then farther he hied;
for the hardy hero with hand he grasped,
felt for the foe with fiendish claw,
for the hero reclining, -- who clutched it boldly,
prompt to answer, propped on his arm.
Soon then saw that shepherd-of-evils
that never he met in this middle-world,
in the ways of earth, another wight
with heavier hand-gripe; at heart he feared,
sorrowed in soul, -- none the sooner escaped!
Fain would he flee, his fastness seek,
the den of devils: no doings now
such as oft he had done in days of old!
Then bethought him the hardy Hygelac-thane
of his boast at evening: up he bounded,
grasped firm his foe, whose fingers cracked.
The fiend made off, but the earl close followed.
The monster meant -- if he might at all --
to fling himself free, and far away
fly to the fens, -- knew his fingers' power
in the gripe of the grim one. Gruesome march
to Heorot this monster of harm had made!
Din filled the room; the Danes were bereft,
castle-dwellers and clansmen all,
earls, of their ale. Angry were both
those savage hall-guards: the house resounded.
Wonder it was the wine-hall firm
in the strain of their struggle stood, to earth
the fair house fell not; too fast it was
within and without by its iron bands
craftily clamped; though there crashed from sill
many a mead-bench -- men have told me --
gay with gold, where the grim foes wrestled.
So well had weened the wisest Scyldings
that not ever at all might any man
that bone-decked, brave house break asunder,
crush by craft, -- unless clasp of fire
in smoke engulfed it. -- Again uprose
din redoubled. Danes of the North
with fear and frenzy were filled, each one,
who from the wall that wailing heard,
God's foe sounding his grisly song,
cry of the conquered, clamorous pain
from captive of hell. Too closely held him
he who of men in might was strongest
in that same day of this our life.

XII

NOT in any wise would the earls'-defence[1]
suffer that slaughterous stranger to live,
useless deeming his days and years
to men on earth. Now many an earl
of Beowulf brandished blade ancestral,
fain the life of their lord to shield,
their praised prince, if power were theirs;
never they knew, -- as they neared the foe,
hardy-hearted heroes of war,
aiming their swords on every side
the accursed to kill, -- no keenest blade,
no farest of falchions fashioned on earth,
could harm or hurt that hideous fiend!
He was safe, by his spells, from sword of battle,
from edge of iron. Yet his end and parting
on that same day of this our life
woful should be, and his wandering soul
far off flit to the fiends' domain.
Soon he found, who in former days,
harmful in heart and hated of God,
on many a man such murder wrought,
that the frame of his body failed him now.
For him the keen-souled kinsman of Hygelac
held in hand; hateful alive
was each to other. The outlaw dire
took mortal hurt; a mighty wound
showed on his shoulder, and sinews cracked,
and the bone-frame burst. To Beowulf now
the glory was given, and Grendel thence
death-sick his den in the dark moor sought,
noisome abode: he knew too well
that here was the last of life, an end
of his days on earth. -- To all the Danes
by that bloody battle the boon had come.
From ravage had rescued the roving stranger
Hrothgar's hall; the hardy and wise one
had purged it anew. His night-work pleased him,
his deed and its honor. To Eastern Danes
had the valiant Geat his vaunt made good,
all their sorrow and ills assuaged,
their bale of battle borne so long,
and all the dole they erst endured
pain a-plenty. -- 'Twas proof of this,
when the hardy-in-fight a hand laid down,
arm and shoulder, -- all, indeed,
of Grendel's gripe, -- 'neath the gabled roof.

XIII

MANY at morning, as men have told me,
warriors gathered the gift-hall round,
folk-leaders faring from far and near,
o'er wide-stretched ways, the wonder to view,
trace of the traitor. Not troublous seemed
the enemy's end to any man
who saw by the gait of the graceless foe
how the weary-hearted, away from thence,
baffled in battle and banned, his steps
death-marked dragged to the devils' mere.
Bloody the billows were boiling there,
turbid the tide of tumbling waves
horribly seething, with sword-blood hot,
by that doomed one dyed, who in den of the moor
laid forlorn his life adown,
his heathen soul, and hell received it.
Home then rode the hoary clansmen
from that merry journey, and many a youth,
on horses white, the hardy warriors,
back from the mere. Then Beowulf's glory
eager they echoed, and all averred
that from sea to sea, or south or north,
there was no other in earth's domain,
under vault of heaven, more valiant found,
of warriors none more worthy to rule!
(On their lord beloved they laid no slight,
gracious Hrothgar: a good king he!)
From time to time, the tried-in-battle
their gray steeds set to gallop amain,
and ran a race when the road seemed fair.
From time to time, a thane of the king,
who had made many vaunts, and was mindful of verses,
stored with sagas and songs of old,
bound word to word in well-knit rime,
welded his lay; this warrior soon
of Beowulf's quest right cleverly sang,
and artfully added an excellent tale,
in well-ranged words, of the warlike deeds
he had heard in saga of Sigemund.
Strange the story: he said it all, --
the Waelsing's wanderings wide, his struggles,
which never were told to tribes of men,
the feuds and the frauds, save to Fitela only,
when of these doings he deigned to speak,
uncle to nephew; as ever the twain
stood side by side in stress of war,
and multitude of the monster kind
they had felled with their swords. Of Sigemund grew,

when he passed from life, no little praise;
for the doughty-in-combat a dragon killed
that herded the hoard:[1] under hoary rock
the atheling dared the deed alone
fearful quest, nor was Fitela there.
Yet so it befell, his falchion pierced
that wondrous worm, -- on the wall it struck,
best blade; the dragon died in its blood.
Thus had the dread-one by daring achieved
over the ring-hoard to rule at will,
himself to pleasure; a sea-boat he loaded,
and bore on its bosom the beaming gold,
son of Waels; the worm was consumed.
He had of all heroes the highest renown
among races of men, this refuge-of-warriors,
for deeds of daring that decked his name
since the hand and heart of Heremod
grew slack in battle. He, swiftly banished
to mingle with monsters at mercy of foes,
to death was betrayed; for torrents of sorrow
had lamed him too long; a load of care
to earls and athelings all he proved.
Oft indeed, in earlier days,
for the warrior's wayfaring wise men mourned,
who had hoped of him help from harm and bale,
and had thought their sovran's son would thrive,
follow his father, his folk protect,
the hoard and the stronghold, heroes' land,
home of Scyldings. -- But here, thanes said,
the kinsman of Hygelac kinder seemed
to all: the other[2] was urged to crime!
And afresh to the race,[3] the fallow roads
by swift steeds measured! The morning sun
was climbing higher. Clansmen hastened
to the high-built hall, those hardy-minded,
the wonder to witness. Warden of treasure,
crowned with glory, the king himself,
with stately band from the bride-bower strode;
and with him the queen and her crowd of maidens
measured the path to the mead-house fair.

XIV

HROTHGAR spake, -- to the hall he went,
stood by the steps, the steep roof saw,
garnished with gold, and Grendel's hand: --
"For the sight I see to the Sovran Ruler
be speedy thanks! A throng of sorrows
I have borne from Grendel; but God still works
wonder on wonder, the Warden-of-Glory.

It was but now that I never more
for woes that weighed on me waited help
long as I lived, when, laved in blood,
stood sword-gore-stained this stateliest house, --
widespread woe for wise men all,
who had no hope to hinder ever
foes infernal and fiendish sprites
from havoc in hall. This hero now,
by the Wielder's might, a work has done
that not all of us erst could ever do
by wile and wisdom. Lo, well can she say
whoso of women this warrior bore
among sons of men, if still she liveth,
that the God of the ages was good to her
in the birth of her bairn. Now, Beowulf, thee,
of heroes best, I shall heartily love
as mine own, my son; preserve thou ever
this kinship new: thou shalt never lack
wealth of the world that I wield as mine!
Full oft for less have I largess showered,
my precious hoard, on a punier man,
less stout in struggle. Thyself hast now
fulfilled such deeds, that thy fame shall endure
through all the ages. As ever he did,
well may the Wielder reward thee still!"
Beowulf spake, bairn of Ecgtheow: --
"This work of war most willingly
we have fought, this fight, and fearlessly dared
force of the foe. Fain, too, were I
hadst thou but seen himself, what time
the fiend in his trappings tottered to fall!
Swiftly, I thought, in strongest gripe
on his bed of death to bind him down,
that he in the hent of this hand of mine
should breathe his last: but he broke away.
Him I might not -- the Maker willed not --
hinder from flight, and firm enough hold
the life-destroyer: too sturdy was he,
the ruthless, in running! For rescue, however,
he left behind him his hand in pledge,
arm and shoulder; nor aught of help
could the cursed one thus procure at all.
None the longer liveth he, loathsome fiend,
sunk in his sins, but sorrow holds him
tightly grasped in gripe of anguish,
in baleful bonds, where bide he must,
evil outlaw, such awful doom
as the Mighty Maker shall mete him out."

More silent seemed the son of Ecglaf[1]
in boastful speech of his battle-deeds,
since athelings all, through the earl's great prowess,
beheld that hand, on the high roof gazing,
foeman's fingers, -- the forepart of each
of the sturdy nails to steel was likest, --
heathen's "hand-spear," hostile warrior's
claw uncanny. 'Twas clear, they said,
that him no blade of the brave could touch,
how keen soever, or cut away
that battle-hand bloody from baneful foe.

XV

THERE was hurry and hest in Heorot now
for hands to bedeck it, and dense was the throng
of men and women the wine-hall to cleanse,
the guest-room to garnish. Gold-gay shone the hangings
that were wove on the wall, and wonders many
to delight each mortal that looks upon them.
Though braced within by iron bands,
that building bright was broken sorely;[1]
rent were its hinges; the roof alone
held safe and sound, when, seared with crime,
the fiendish foe his flight essayed,
of life despairing. -- No light thing that,
the flight for safety, -- essay it who will!
Forced of fate, he shall find his way
to the refuge ready for race of man,
for soul-possessors, and sons of earth;
and there his body on bed of death shall rest after revel.
Arrived was the hour
when to hall proceeded Healfdene's son:
the king himself would sit to banquet.
Ne'er heard I of host in haughtier throng
more graciously gathered round giver-of-rings!
Bowed then to bench those bearers-of-glory,
fain of the feasting. Featly received
many a mead-cup the mighty-in-spirit,
kinsmen who sat in the sumptuous hall,
Hrothgar and Hrothulf. Heorot now
was filled with friends; the folk of Scyldings
ne'er yet had tried the traitor's deed.
To Beowulf gave the bairn of Healfdene
a gold-wove banner, guerdon of triumph,
broidered battle-flag, breastplate and helmet;
and a splendid sword was seen of many
borne to the brave one. Beowulf took
cup in hall:[2] for such costly gifts
he suffered no shame in that soldier throng.

For I heard of few heroes, in heartier mood,
with four such gifts, so fashioned with gold,
on the ale-bench honoring others thus!
O'er the roof of the helmet high, a ridge,
wound with wires, kept ward o'er the head,
lest the relict-of-files[3] should fierce invade,
sharp in the strife, when that shielded hero
should go to grapple against his foes.
Then the earls'-defence[4] on the floor[5] bade lead
coursers eight, with carven head-gear,
adown the hall: one horse was decked
with a saddle all shining and set in jewels;
'twas the battle-seat of the best of kings,
when to play of swords the son of Healfdene
was fain to fare. Ne'er failed his valor
in the crush of combat when corpses fell.
To Beowulf over them both then gave
the refuge-of-Ingwines right and power,
o'er war-steeds and weapons: wished him joy of them.
Manfully thus the mighty prince,
hoard-guard for heroes, that hard fight repaid
with steeds and treasures contemned by none
who is willing to say the sooth aright.

XVI

AND the lord of earls, to each that came
with Beowulf over the briny ways,
an heirloom there at the ale-bench gave,
precious gift; and the price[1] bade pay
in gold for him whom Grendel erst
murdered, -- and fain of them more had killed,
had not wisest God their Wyrd averted,
and the man's[2] brave mood. The Maker then
ruled human kind, as here and now.
Therefore is insight always best,
and forethought of mind. How much awaits him
of lief and of loath, who long time here,
through days of warfare this world endures!

Then song and music mingled sounds
in the presence of Healfdene's head-of-armies[3]
and harping was heard with the hero-lay
as Hrothgar's singer the hall-joy woke
along the mead-seats, making his song
of that sudden raid on the sons of Finn.[4]
Healfdene's hero, Hnaef the Scylding,
was fated to fall in the Frisian slaughter.[5]
Hildeburh needed not hold in value
her enemies' honor![6] Innocent both

were the loved ones she lost at the linden-play,
bairn and brother, they bowed to fate,
stricken by spears; 'twas a sorrowful woman!
None doubted why the daughter of Hoc
bewailed her doom when dawning came,
and under the sky she saw them lying,
kinsmen murdered, where most she had kenned
of the sweets of the world! By war were swept, too,
Finn's own liegemen, and few were left;
in the parleying-place[7] he could ply no longer
weapon, nor war could he wage on Hengest,
and rescue his remnant by right of arms
from the prince's thane. A pact he offered:
another dwelling the Danes should have,
hall and high-seat, and half the power
should fall to them in Frisian land;
and at the fee-gifts, Folcwald's son
day by day the Danes should honor,
the folk of Hengest favor with rings,
even as truly, with treasure and jewels,
with fretted gold, as his Frisian kin
he meant to honor in ale-hall there.
Pact of peace they plighted further
on both sides firmly. Finn to Hengest
with oath, upon honor, openly promised
that woful remnant, with wise-men's aid,
nobly to govern, so none of the guests
by word or work should warp the treaty,[8]
or with malice of mind bemoan themselves
as forced to follow their fee-giver's slayer,
lordless men, as their lot ordained.
Should Frisian, moreover, with foeman's taunt,
that murderous hatred to mind recall,
then edge of the sword must seal his doom.

Oaths were given, and ancient gold
heaped from hoard. -- The hardy Scylding,
battle-thane best,[9] on his balefire lay.
All on the pyre were plain to see
the gory sark, the gilded swine-crest,
boar of hard iron, and athelings many
slain by the sword: at the slaughter they fell.
It was Hildeburh's hest, at Hnaef's own pyre
the bairn of her body on brands to lay,
his bones to burn, on the balefire placed,
at his uncle's side. In sorrowful dirges
bewept them the woman: great wailing ascended.
Then wound up to welkin the wildest of death-fires,
roared o'er the hillock:[10] heads all were melted,
gashes burst, and blood gushed out

from bites[11] of the body. Balefire devoured,
greediest spirit, those spared not by war
out of either folk: their flower was gone.

XVII

THEN hastened those heroes their home to see,
friendless, to find the Frisian land,
houses and high burg. Hengest still
through the death-dyed winter dwelt with Finn,
holding pact, yet of home he minded,
though powerless his ring-decked prow to drive
over the waters, now waves rolled fierce
lashed by the winds, or winter locked them
in icy fetters. Then fared another
year to men's dwellings, as yet they do,
the sunbright skies, that their season ever
duly await. Far off winter was driven;
fair lay earth's breast; and fain was the rover,
the guest, to depart, though more gladly he pondered
on wreaking his vengeance than roaming the deep,
and how to hasten the hot encounter
where sons of the Frisians were sure to be.
So he escaped not the common doom,
when Hun with "Lafing," the light-of-battle,
best of blades, his bosom pierced:
its edge was famed with the Frisian earls.
On fierce-heart Finn there fell likewise,
on himself at home, the horrid sword-death;
for Guthlaf and Oslaf of grim attack
had sorrowing told, from sea-ways landed,
mourning their woes.[1] Finn's wavering spirit
bode not in breast. The burg was reddened
with blood of foemen, and Finn was slain,
king amid clansmen; the queen was taken.
To their ship the Scylding warriors bore
all the chattels the chieftain owned,
whatever they found in Finn's domain
of gems and jewels. The gentle wife
o'er paths of the deep to the Danes they bore, led to her land.
The lay was finished,
the gleeman's song. Then glad rose the revel;
bench-joy brightened. Bearers draw
from their "wonder-vats" wine. Comes Wealhtheow forth,
under gold-crown goes where the good pair sit,
uncle and nephew, true each to the other one,
kindred in amity. Unferth the spokesman
at the Scylding lord's feet sat: men had faith in his spirit,
his keenness of courage, though kinsmen had found him
unsure at the sword-play. The Scylding queen spoke:

"Quaff of this cup, my king and lord,
breaker of rings, and blithe be thou,
gold-friend of men; to the Geats here speak
such words of mildness as man should use.
Be glad with thy Geats; of those gifts be mindful,
or near or far, which now thou hast.

Men say to me, as son thou wishest
yon hero to hold. Thy Heorot purged,
jewel-hall brightest, enjoy while thou canst,
with many a largess; and leave to thy kin
folk and realm when forth thou goest
to greet thy doom. For gracious I deem
my Hrothulf,[2] willing to hold and rule
nobly our youths, if thou yield up first,
prince of Scyldings, thy part in the world.
I ween with good he will well requite
offspring of ours, when all he minds
that for him we did in his helpless days
of gift and grace to gain him honor!"
Then she turned to the seat where her sons wereplaced,
Hrethric and Hrothmund, with heroes' bairns,
young men together: the Geat, too, sat there,
Beowulf brave, the brothers between.

XVIII

A CUP she gave him, with kindly greeting
and winsome words. Of wounden gold,
she offered, to honor him, arm-jewels twain,
corselet and rings, and of collars the noblest
that ever I knew the earth around.
Ne'er heard I so mighty, 'neath heaven's dome,
a hoard-gem of heroes, since Hama bore
to his bright-built burg the Brisings' necklace,
jewel and gem casket. -- Jealousy fled he,
Eormenric's hate: chose help eternal.
Hygelac Geat, grandson of Swerting,
on the last of his raids this ring bore with him,
under his banner the booty defending,
the war-spoil warding; but Wyrd o'erwhelmed him
what time, in his daring, dangers he sought,
feud with Frisians. Fairest of gems
he bore with him over the beaker-of-waves,
sovran strong: under shield he died.
Fell the corpse of the king into keeping of Franks,
gear of the breast, and that gorgeous ring;
weaker warriors won the spoil,
after gripe of battle, from Geatland's lord,
and held the death-field.

Din rose in hall.
Wealhtheow spake amid warriors, and said: --
"This jewel enjoy in thy jocund youth,
Beowulf lov'd, these battle-weeds wear,
a royal treasure, and richly thrive!
Preserve thy strength, and these striplings here
counsel in kindness: requital be mine.
Hast done such deeds, that for days to come
thou art famed among folk both far and near,
so wide as washeth the wave of Ocean
his windy walls. Through the ways of life
prosper, O prince! I pray for thee
rich possessions. To son of mine
be helpful in deed and uphold his joys!
Here every earl to the other is true,
mild of mood, to the master loyal!
Thanes are friendly, the throng obedient,
liegemen are revelling: list and obey!"
Went then to her place. -- That was proudest of feasts;
flowed wine for the warriors. Wyrd they knew not,
destiny dire, and the doom to be seen
by many an earl when eve should come,
and Hrothgar homeward hasten away,
royal, to rest. The room was guarded
by an army of earls, as erst was done.
They bared the bench-boards; abroad they spread
beds and bolsters. -- One beer-carouser
in danger of doom lay down in the hall. --

At their heads they set their shields of war,
bucklers bright; on the bench were there
over each atheling, easy to see,
the high battle-helmet, the haughty spear,
the corselet of rings. 'Twas their custom so
ever to be for battle prepared,
at home, or harrying, which it were,
even as oft as evil threatened
their sovran king. -- They were clansmen good.

XIX

THEN sank they to sleep. With sorrow one bought
his rest of the evening, -- as ofttime had happened
when Grendel guarded that golden hall,
evil wrought, till his end drew nigh,
slaughter for sins. 'Twas seen and told
how an avenger survived the fiend,
as was learned afar. The livelong time
after that grim fight, Grendel's mother,
monster of women, mourned her woe.

Beowulf: Scholar's Edition

She was doomed to dwell in the dreary waters,
cold sea-courses, since Cain cut down
with edge of the sword his only brother,
his father's offspring: outlawed he fled,
marked with murder, from men's delights
warded the wilds. -- There woke from him
such fate-sent ghosts as Grendel, who,
war-wolf horrid, at Heorot found
a warrior watching and waiting the fray,
with whom the grisly one grappled amain.
But the man remembered his mighty power,
the glorious gift that God had sent him,
in his Maker's mercy put his trust
for comfort and help: so he conquered the foe,
felled the fiend, who fled abject,
reft of joy, to the realms of death,
mankind's foe. And his mother now,
gloomy and grim, would go that quest
of sorrow, the death of her son to avenge.
To Heorot came she, where helmeted Danes
slept in the hall. Too soon came back
old ills of the earls, when in she burst,
the mother of Grendel. Less grim, though, that terror,
e'en as terror of woman in war is less,
might of maid, than of men in arms
when, hammer-forged, the falchion hard,
sword gore-stained, through swine of the helm,
crested, with keen blade carves amain.
Then was in hall the hard-edge drawn,
the swords on the settles,[1] and shields a-many
firm held in hand: nor helmet minded
nor harness of mail, whom that horror seized.
Haste was hers; she would hie afar
and save her life when the liegemen saw her.
Yet a single atheling up she seized
fast and firm, as she fled to the moor.
He was for Hrothgar of heroes the dearest,
of trusty vassals betwixt the seas,
whom she killed on his couch, a clansman famous,
in battle brave. -- Nor was Beowulf there;
another house had been held apart,
after giving of gold, for the Geat renowned. --
Uproar filled Heorot; the hand all had viewed,
blood-flecked, she bore with her; bale was returned,
dole in the dwellings: 'twas dire exchange
where Dane and Geat were doomed to give
the lives of loved ones. Long-tried king,
the hoary hero, at heart was sad
when he knew his noble no more lived,
and dead indeed was his dearest thane.

To his bower was Beowulf brought in haste,
dauntless victor. As daylight broke,
along with his earls the atheling lord,
with his clansmen, came where the king abode
waiting to see if the Wielder-of-All
would turn this tale of trouble and woe.
Strode o'er floor the famed-in-strife,
with his hand-companions, -- the hall resounded, --
wishing to greet the wise old king,
Ingwines' lord; he asked if the night
had passed in peace to the prince's mind.

XX

HROTHGAR spake, helmet-of-Scyldings: --
"Ask not of pleasure! Pain is renewed
to Danish folk. Dead is Aeschere,
of Yrmenlaf the elder brother,
my sage adviser and stay in council,
shoulder-comrade in stress of fight
when warriors clashed and we warded our heads,
hewed the helm-boars; hero famed
should be every earl as Aeschere was!
But here in Heorot a hand hath slain him
of wandering death-sprite. I wot not whither,[1]
proud of the prey, her path she took,
fain of her fill. The feud she avenged
that yesternight, unyieldingly,
Grendel in grimmest grasp thou killedst, --
seeing how long these liegemen mine
he ruined and ravaged. Reft of life,
in arms he fell. Now another comes,
keen and cruel, her kin to avenge,
faring far in feud of blood:
so that many a thane shall think, who e'er
sorrows in soul for that sharer of rings,
this is hardest of heart-bales. The hand lies low
that once was willing each wish to please.
Land-dwellers here[2] and liegemen mine,
who house by those parts, I have heard relate
that such a pair they have sometimes seen,
march-stalkers mighty the moorland haunting,
wandering spirits: one of them seemed,
so far as my folk could fairly judge,
of womankind; and one, accursed,
in man's guise trod the misery-track
of exile, though huger than human bulk.
Grendel in days long gone they named him,
folk of the land; his father they knew not,
nor any brood that was born to him

of treacherous spirits. Untrod is their home;
by wolf-cliffs haunt they and windy headlands,
fenways fearful, where flows the stream
from mountains gliding to gloom of the rocks,
underground flood. Not far is it hence
in measure of miles that the mere expands,
and o'er it the frost-bound forest hanging,
sturdily rooted, shadows the wave.
By night is a wonder weird to see,
fire on the waters. So wise lived none
of the sons of men, to search those depths!
Nay, though the heath-rover, harried by dogs,
the horn-proud hart, this holt should seek,
long distance driven, his dear life first
on the brink he yields ere he brave the plunge
to hide his head: 'tis no happy place!
Thence the welter of waters washes up
wan to welkin when winds bestir
evil storms, and air grows dusk,
and the heavens weep. Now is help once more
with thee alone! The land thou knowst not,
place of fear, where thou findest out
that sin-flecked being. Seek if thou dare!
I will reward thee, for waging this fight,
with ancient treasure, as erst I did,
with winding gold, if thou winnest back."

XXI

BEOWULF spake, bairn of Ecgtheow:
"Sorrow not, sage! It beseems us better
friends to avenge than fruitlessly mourn them.
Each of us all must his end abide
in the ways of the world; so win who may
glory ere death! When his days are told,
that is the warrior's worthiest doom.
Rise, O realm-warder! Ride we anon,
and mark the trail of the mother of Grendel.
No harbor shall hide her -- heed my promise! --
enfolding of field or forested mountain
or floor of the flood, let her flee where she will!
But thou this day endure in patience,
as I ween thou wilt, thy woes each one."
Leaped up the graybeard: God he thanked,
mighty Lord, for the man's brave words.
For Hrothgar soon a horse was saddled
wave-maned steed. The sovran wise
stately rode on; his shield-armed men
followed in force. The footprints led
along the woodland, widely seen,

a path o'er the plain, where she passed, and trod
the murky moor; of men-at-arms
she bore the bravest and best one, dead,
him who with Hrothgar the homestead ruled.
On then went the atheling-born
o'er stone-cliffs steep and strait defiles,
narrow passes and unknown ways,
headlands sheer, and the haunts of the Nicors.
Foremost he[1] fared, a few at his side
of the wiser men, the ways to scan,
till he found in a flash the forested hill
hanging over the hoary rock,
a woful wood: the waves below
were dyed in blood. The Danish men
had sorrow of soul, and for Scyldings all,
for many a hero, 'twas hard to bear,
ill for earls, when Aeschere's head
they found by the flood on the foreland there.
Waves were welling, the warriors saw,
hot with blood; but the horn sang oft
battle-song bold. The band sat down,
and watched on the water worm-like things,
sea-dragons strange that sounded the deep,
and nicors that lay on the ledge of the ness --
such as oft essay at hour of morn
on the road-of-sails their ruthless quest, --
and sea-snakes and monsters. These started away,
swollen and savage that song to hear,
that war-horn's blast. The warden of Geats,
with bolt from bow, then balked of life,
of wave-work, one monster, amid its heart
went the keen war-shaft; in water it seemed
less doughty in swimming whom death had seized.
Swift on the billows, with boar-spears well
hooked and barbed, it was hard beset,
done to death and dragged on the headland,
wave-roamer wondrous. Warriors viewed the grisly guest.
Then girt him Beowulf
in martial mail, nor mourned for his life.
His breastplate broad and bright of hues,
woven by hand, should the waters try;
well could it ward the warrior's body
that battle should break on his breast in vain
nor harm his heart by the hand of a foe.
And the helmet white that his head protected
was destined to dare the deeps of the flood,
through wave-whirl win: 'twas wound with chains,
decked with gold, as in days of yore
the weapon-smith worked it wondrously,

with swine-forms set it, that swords nowise,
brandished in battle, could bite that helm.
Nor was that the meanest of mighty helps
which Hrothgar's orator offered at need:
"Hrunting" they named the hilted sword,
of old-time heirlooms easily first;
iron was its edge, all etched with poison,
with battle-blood hardened, nor blenched it at fight
in hero's hand who held it ever,
on paths of peril prepared to go
to folkstead[2] of foes. Not first time this
it was destined to do a daring task.
For he bore not in mind, the bairn of Ecglaf
sturdy and strong, that speech he had made,
drunk with wine, now this weapon he lent
to a stouter swordsman. Himself, though, durst not
under welter of waters wager his life
as loyal liegeman. So lost he his glory,
honor of earls. With the other not so,
who girded him now for the grim encounter.

XXII

BEOWULF spake, bairn of Ecgtheow: --
"Have mind, thou honored offspring of Healfdene
gold-friend of men, now I go on this quest,
sovran wise, what once was said:
if in thy cause it came that I
should lose my life, thou wouldst loyal bide
to me, though fallen, in father's place!
Be guardian, thou, to this group of my thanes,
my warrior-friends, if War should seize me;
and the goodly gifts thou gavest me,
Hrothgar beloved, to Hygelac send!
Geatland's king may ken by the gold,
Hrethel's son see, when he stares at the treasure,
that I got me a friend for goodness famed,
and joyed while I could in my jewel-bestower.
And let Unferth wield this wondrous sword,
earl far-honored, this heirloom precious,
hard of edge: with Hrunting I
seek doom of glory, or Death shall take me."

After these words the Weder-Geat lord
boldly hastened, biding never
answer at all: the ocean floods
closed o'er the hero. Long while of the day
fled ere he felt the floor of the sea.

Soon found the fiend who the flood-domain
sword-hungry held these hundred winters,
greedy and grim, that some guest from above,
some man, was raiding her monster-realm.
She grasped out for him with grisly claws,
and the warrior seized; yet scathed she not
his body hale; the breastplate hindered,
as she strove to shatter the sark of war,
the linked harness, with loathsome hand.
Then bore this brine-wolf, when bottom she touched,
the lord of rings to the lair she haunted
whiles vainly he strove, though his valor held,
weapon to wield against wondrous monsters
that sore beset him; sea-beasts many
tried with fierce tusks to tear his mail,
and swarmed on the stranger. But soon he marked
he was now in some hall, he knew not which,
where water never could work him harm,
nor through the roof could reach him ever
fangs of the flood. Firelight he saw,
beams of a blaze that brightly shone.
Then the warrior was ware of that wolf-of-the-deep,
mere-wife monstrous. For mighty stroke
he swung his blade, and the blow withheld not.
Then sang on her head that seemly blade
its war-song wild. But the warrior found
the light-of-battle[1] was loath to bite,
to harm the heart: its hard edge failed
the noble at need, yet had known of old
strife hand to hand, and had helmets cloven,
doomed men's fighting-gear. First time, this,
for the gleaming blade that its glory fell.
Firm still stood, nor failed in valor,
heedful of high deeds, Hygelac's kinsman;
flung away fretted sword, featly jewelled,
the angry earl; on earth it lay
steel-edged and stiff. His strength he trusted,
hand-gripe of might. So man shall do
whenever in war he weens to earn him
lasting fame, nor fears for his life!
Seized then by shoulder, shrank not from combat,
the Geatish war-prince Grendel's mother.
Flung then the fierce one, filled with wrath,
his deadly foe, that she fell to ground.
Swift on her part she paid him back
with grisly grasp, and grappled with him.
Spent with struggle, stumbled the warrior,
fiercest of fighting-men, fell adown.
On the hall-guest she hurled herself, hent her short sword,

broad and brown-edged,² the bairn to avenge,
the sole-born son. -- On his shoulder lay
braided breast-mail, barring death,
withstanding entrance of edge or blade.
Life would have ended for Ecgtheow's son,
under wide earth for that earl of Geats,
had his armor of war not aided him,
battle-net hard, and holy God
wielded the victory, wisest Maker.
The Lord of Heaven allowed his cause;
and easily rose the earl erect.

XXIII

'MID the battle-gear saw he a blade triumphant,
old-sword of Eotens, with edge of proof,
warriors' heirloom, weapon unmatched,
-- save only 'twas more than other men
to bandy-of-battle could bear at all --
as the giants had wrought it, ready and keen.
Seized then its chain-hilt the Scyldings' chieftain,
bold and battle-grim, brandished the sword,
reckless of life, and so wrathfully smote
that it gripped her neck and grasped her hard,
her bone-rings breaking: the blade pierced through
that fated-one's flesh: to floor she sank.
Bloody the blade: he was blithe of his deed.
Then blazed forth light. 'Twas bright within
as when from the sky there shines unclouded
heaven's candle. The hall he scanned.
By the wall then went he; his weapon raised
high by its hilts the Hygelac-thane,
angry and eager. That edge was not useless
to the warrior now. He wished with speed
Grendel to guerdon for grim raids many,
for the war he waged on Western-Danes
oftener far than an only time,
when of Hrothgar's hearth-companions
he slew in slumber, in sleep devoured,
fifteen men of the folk of Danes,
and as many others outward bore,
his horrible prey. Well paid for that
the wrathful prince! For now prone he saw
Grendel stretched there, spent with war,
spoiled of life, so scathed had left him
Heorot's battle. The body sprang far
when after death it endured the blow,
sword-stroke savage, that severed its head.
Soon,¹ then, saw the sage companions
who waited with Hrothgar, watching the flood,

that the tossing waters turbid grew,
blood-stained the mere. Old men together,
hoary-haired, of the hero spake;
the warrior would not, they weened, again,
proud of conquest, come to seek
their mighty master. To many it seemed
the wolf-of-the-waves had won his life.
The ninth hour came. The noble Scyldings
left the headland; homeward went
the gold-friend of men.[2] But the guests sat on,
stared at the surges, sick in heart,
and wished, yet weened not, their winsome lord again to see.

Now that sword began,
from blood of the fight, in battle-droppings,[3]
war-blade, to wane: 'twas a wondrous thing
that all of it melted as ice is wont
when frosty fetters the Father loosens,
unwinds the wave-bonds, wielding all
seasons and times: the true God he!
Nor took from that dwelling the duke of the Geats
save only the head and that hilt withal
blazoned with jewels: the blade had melted,
burned was the bright sword, her blood was so hot,
so poisoned the hell-sprite who perished within there.
Soon he was swimming who safe saw in combat
downfall of demons; up-dove through the flood.
The clashing waters were cleansed now,
waste of waves, where the wandering fiend
her life-days left and this lapsing world.
Swam then to strand the sailors'-refuge,
sturdy-in-spirit, of sea-booty glad,
of burden brave he bore with him.
Went then to greet him, and God they thanked,
the thane-band choice of their chieftain blithe,
that safe and sound they could see him again.
Soon from the hardy one helmet and armor
deftly they doffed: now drowsed the mere,
water 'neath welkin, with war-blood stained.
Forth they fared by the footpaths thence,
merry at heart the highways measured,
well-known roads. Courageous men
carried the head from the cliff by the sea,
an arduous task for all the band,
the firm in fight, since four were needed
on the shaft-of-slaughter[4] strenuously
to bear to the gold-hall Grendel's head.
So presently to the palace there
foemen fearless, fourteen Geats,

marching came. Their master-of-clan
mighty amid them the meadow-ways trod.
Strode then within the sovran thane
fearless in fight, of fame renowned,
hardy hero, Hrothgar to greet.
And next by the hair into hall was borne
Grendel's head, where the henchmen were drinking,
an awe to clan and queen alike,
a monster of marvel: the men looked on.

XXIV

BEOWULF spake, bairn of Ecgtheow: --
"Lo, now, this sea-booty, son of Healfdene,
Lord of Scyldings, we've lustily brought thee,
sign of glory; thou seest it here.
Not lightly did I with my life escape!
In war under water this work I essayed
with endless effort; and even so
my strength had been lost had the Lord not shielded me.
Not a whit could I with Hrunting do
in work of war, though the weapon is good;
yet a sword the Sovran of Men vouchsafed me
to spy on the wall there, in splendor hanging,
old, gigantic, -- how oft He guides
the friendless wight! -- and I fought with that brand,
felling in fight, since fate was with me,
the house's wardens. That war-sword then
all burned, bright blade, when the blood gushed o'er it,
battle-sweat hot; but the hilt I brought back
from my foes. So avenged I their fiendish deeds
death-fall of Danes, as was due and right.
And this is my hest, that in Heorot now
safe thou canst sleep with thy soldier band,
and every thane of all thy folk
both old and young; no evil fear,
Scyldings' lord, from that side again,
aught ill for thy earls, as erst thou must!"
Then the golden hilt, for that gray-haired leader,
hoary hero, in hand was laid,
giant-wrought, old. So owned and enjoyed it
after downfall of devils, the Danish lord,
wonder-smiths' work, since the world was rid
of that grim-souled fiend, the foe of God,
murder-marked, and his mother as well.
Now it passed into power of the people's king,
best of all that the oceans bound
who have scattered their gold o'er Scandia's isle.
Hrothgar spake -- the hilt he viewed,
heirloom old, where was etched the rise

of that far-off fight when the floods o'erwhelmed,
raging waves, the race of giants
(fearful their fate!), a folk estranged
from God Eternal: whence guerdon due
in that waste of waters the Wielder paid them.
So on the guard of shining gold
in runic staves it was rightly said
for whom the serpent-traced sword was wrought,
best of blades, in bygone days,
and the hilt well wound. -- The wise-one spake,
son of Healfdene; silent were all: --
"Lo, so may he say who sooth and right
follows 'mid folk, of far times mindful,
a land-warden old,[1] that this earl belongs
to the better breed! So, borne aloft,
thy fame must fly, O friend my Beowulf,
far and wide o'er folksteads many. Firmly thou
shalt all maintain,
mighty strength with mood of wisdom. Love of
mine will I assure thee,
as, awhile ago, I promised; thou shalt prove a stay in future,
in far-off years, to folk of thine,
to the heroes a help. Was not Heremod thus
to offspring of Ecgwela, Honor-Scyldings,
nor grew for their grace, but for grisly slaughter,
for doom of death to the Danishmen.

He slew, wrath-swollen, his shoulder-comrades,
companions at board! So he passed alone,
chieftain haughty, from human cheer.
Though him the Maker with might endowed,
delights of power, and uplifted high
above all men, yet blood-fierce his mind,
his breast-hoard, grew, no bracelets gave he
to Danes as was due; he endured all joyless
strain of struggle and stress of woe,
long feud with his folk. Here find thy lesson!
Of virtue advise thee! This verse I have said for thee,
wise from lapsed winters. Wondrous seems
how to sons of men Almighty God
in the strength of His spirit sendeth wisdom,
estate, high station: He swayeth all things.
Whiles He letteth right lustily fare
the heart of the hero of high-born race, --
in seat ancestral assigns him bliss,
his folk's sure fortress in fee to hold,
puts in his power great parts of the earth,
empire so ample, that end of it
this wanter-of-wisdom weeneth none.

So he waxes in wealth, nowise can harm him
illness or age; no evil cares
shadow his spirit; no sword-hate threatens
from ever an enemy: all the world
wends at his will, no worse he knoweth,
till all within him obstinate pride
waxes and wakes while the warden slumbers,
the spirit's sentry; sleep is too fast
which masters his might, and the murderer nears,
stealthily shooting the shafts from his bow!

XXV

"UNDER harness his heart then is hit indeed
by sharpest shafts; and no shelter avails
from foul behest of the hellish fiend.[1]
Him seems too little what long he possessed.
Greedy and grim, no golden rings
he gives for his pride; the promised future
forgets he and spurns, with all God has sent him,
Wonder-Wielder, of wealth and fame.
Yet in the end it ever comes
that the frame of the body fragile yields,
fated falls; and there follows another
who joyously the jewels divides,
the royal riches, nor recks of his forebear.
Ban, then, such baleful thoughts, Beowulf dearest,
best of men, and the better part choose,
profit eternal; and temper thy pride,
warrior famous! The flower of thy might
lasts now a while: but erelong it shall be
that sickness or sword thy strength shall minish,
or fang of fire, or flooding billow,
or bite of blade, or brandished spear,
or odious age; or the eyes' clear beam
wax dull and darken: Death even thee
in haste shall o'erwhelm, thou hero of war!
So the Ring-Danes these half-years a hundred I ruled,
wielded 'neath welkin, and warded them bravely
from mighty-ones many o'er middle-earth,
from spear and sword, till it seemed for me
no foe could be found under fold of the sky.
Lo, sudden the shift! To me seated secure
came grief for joy when Grendel began
to harry my home, the hellish foe;
for those ruthless raids, unresting I suffered
heart-sorrow heavy. Heaven be thanked,
Lord Eternal, for life extended
that I on this head all hewn and bloody,
after long evil, with eyes may gaze!

-- Go to the bench now! Be glad at banquet,
warrior worthy! A wealth of treasure
at dawn of day, be dealt between us!"
Glad was the Geats' lord, going betimes
to seek his seat, as the Sage commanded.
Afresh, as before, for the famed-in-battle,
for the band of the hall, was a banquet dight
nobly anew. The Night-Helm darkened
dusk o'er the drinkers.
The doughty ones rose:
for the hoary-headed would hasten to rest,
aged Scylding; and eager the Geat,
shield-fighter sturdy, for sleeping yearned.
Him wander-weary, warrior-guest
from far, a hall-thane heralded forth,
who by custom courtly cared for all
needs of a thane as in those old days
warrior-wanderers wont to have.
So slumbered the stout-heart. Stately the hall
rose gabled and gilt where the guest slept on
till a raven black the rapture-of-heaven[2]
blithe-heart boded. Bright came flying
shine after shadow. The swordsmen hastened,
athelings all were eager homeward
forth to fare; and far from thence
the great-hearted guest would guide his keel.
Bade then the hardy-one Hrunting be brought
to the son of Ecglaf, the sword bade him take,
excellent iron, and uttered his thanks for it,
quoth that he counted it keen in battle,
"war-friend" winsome: with words he slandered not
edge of the blade: 'twas a big-hearted man!
Now eager for parting and armed at point
warriors waited, while went to his host
that Darling of Danes. The doughty atheling
to high-seat hastened and Hrothgar greeted.

XXVI

BEOWULF spake, bairn of Ecgtheow: --
"Lo, we seafarers say our will,
far-come men, that we fain would seek
Hygelac now. We here have found
hosts to our heart: thou hast harbored us well.
If ever on earth I am able to win me
more of thy love, O lord of men,
aught anew, than I now have done,
for work of war I am willing still!
If it come to me ever across the seas
that neighbor foemen annoy and fright thee, --

as they that hate thee erewhile have used, --
thousands then of thanes I shall bring,
heroes to help thee. Of Hygelac I know,
ward of his folk, that, though few his years,
the lord of the Geats will give me aid
by word and by work, that well I may serve thee,
wielding the war-wood to win thy triumph
and lending thee might when thou lackest men.
If thy Hrethric should come to court of Geats,
a sovran's son, he will surely there
find his friends. A far-off land
each man should visit who vaunts him brave."
Him then answering, Hrothgar spake: --
"These words of thine the wisest God
sent to thy soul! No sager counsel
from so young in years e'er yet have I heard.
Thou art strong of main and in mind art wary,
art wise in words! I ween indeed
if ever it hap that Hrethel's heir
by spear be seized, by sword-grim battle,
by illness or iron, thine elder and lord,
people's leader, -- and life be thine, --
no seemlier man will the Sea-Geats find
at all to choose for their chief and king,
for hoard-guard of heroes, if hold thou wilt
thy kinsman's kingdom! Thy keen mind pleases me
the longer the better, Beowulf loved!

Thou hast brought it about that both our peoples,
sons of the Geat and Spear-Dane folk,
shall have mutual peace, and from murderous strife,
such as once they waged, from war refrain.
Long as I rule this realm so wide,
let our hoards be common, let heroes with gold
each other greet o'er the gannet's-bath,
and the ringed-prow bear o'er rolling waves
tokens of love. I trow my landfolk
towards friend and foe are firmly joined,
and honor they keep in the olden way."
To him in the hall, then, Healfdene's son
gave treasures twelve, and the trust-of-earls
bade him fare with the gifts to his folk beloved,
hale to his home, and in haste return.
Then kissed the king of kin renowned,
Scyldings' chieftain, that choicest thane,
and fell on his neck. Fast flowed the tears
of the hoary-headed. Heavy with winters,
he had chances twain, but he clung to this,[1] --
that each should look on the other again,
and hear him in hall. Was this hero so dear to him.

his breast's wild billows he banned in vain;
safe in his soul a secret longing,
locked in his mind, for that loved man
burned in his blood. Then Beowulf strode,
glad of his gold-gifts, the grass-plot o'er,
warrior blithe. The wave-roamer bode
riding at anchor, its owner awaiting.
As they hastened onward, Hrothgar's gift
they lauded at length. -- 'Twas a lord unpeered,
every way blameless, till age had broken
-- it spareth no mortal -- his splendid might.

XXVII

CAME now to ocean the ever-courageous
hardy henchmen, their harness bearing,
woven war-sarks. The warden marked,
trusty as ever, the earl's return.
From the height of the hill no hostile words
reached the guests as he rode to greet them;
but "Welcome!" he called to that Weder clan
as the sheen-mailed spoilers to ship marched on.
Then on the strand, with steeds and treasure
and armor their roomy and ring-dight ship
was heavily laden: high its mast
rose over Hrothgar's hoarded gems.
A sword to the boat-guard Beowulf gave,
mounted with gold; on the mead-bench since
he was better esteemed, that blade possessing,
heirloom old. -- Their ocean-keel boarding,
they drove through the deep, and Daneland left.
A sea-cloth was set, a sail with ropes,
firm to the mast; the flood-timbers moaned;[1]
nor did wind over billows that wave-swimmer blow
across from her course. The craft sped on,
foam-necked it floated forth o'er the waves,
keel firm-bound over briny currents,
till they got them sight of the Geatish cliffs,
home-known headlands. High the boat,
stirred by winds, on the strand updrove.
Helpful at haven the harbor-guard stood,
who long already for loved companions
by the water had waited and watched afar.
He bound to the beach the broad-bosomed ship
with anchor-bands, lest ocean-billows
that trusty timber should tear away.
Then Beowulf bade them bear the treasure,
gold and jewels; no journey far
was it thence to go to the giver of rings,
Hygelac Hrethling: at home he dwelt

by the sea-wall close, himself and clan.
Haughty that house, a hero the king,
high the hall, and Hygd² right young,
wise and wary, though winters few
in those fortress walls she had found a home,
Haereth's daughter. Nor humble her ways,
nor grudged she gifts to the Geatish men,
of precious treasure. Not Thryth's pride showed she,
folk-queen famed, or that fell deceit.
Was none so daring that durst make bold
(save her lord alone) of the liegemen dear
that lady full in the face to look,
but forged fetters he found his lot,
bonds of death! And brief the respite;
soon as they seized him, his sword-doom was spoken,
and the burnished blade a baleful murder
proclaimed and closed. No queenly way
for woman to practise, though peerless she,
that the weaver-of-peace³ from warrior dear
by wrath and lying his life should reave!
But Hemming's kinsman hindered this. --
For over their ale men also told
that of these folk-horrors fewer she wrought,
onslaughts of evil, after she went,
gold-decked bride, to the brave young prince,
atheling haughty, and Offa's hall
o'er the fallow flood at her father's bidding
safely sought, where since she prospered,
royal, throned, rich in goods,
fain of the fair life fate had sent her,
and leal in love to the lord of warriors.
He, of all heroes I heard of ever
from sea to sea, of the sons of earth,
most excellent seemed. Hence Offa was praised
for his fighting and feeing by far-off men,
the spear-bold warrior; wisely he ruled
over his empire. Eomer woke to him,
help of heroes, Hemming's kinsman,
Grandson of Garmund, grim in war.

XXVIII

HASTENED the hardy one, henchmen with him,
sandy strand of the sea to tread
and widespread ways. The world's great candle,
sun shone from south. They strode along
with sturdy steps to the spot they knew
where the battle-king young, his burg within,
slayer of Ongentheow, shared the rings,
shelter-of-heroes. To Hygelac

Beowulf's coming was quickly told, --
that there in the court the clansmen's refuge,
the shield-companion sound and alive,
hale from the hero-play homeward strode.
With haste in the hall, by highest order,
room for the rovers was readily made.
By his sovran he sat, come safe from battle,
kinsman by kinsman. His kindly lord
he first had greeted in gracious form,
with manly words. The mead dispensing,
came through the high hall Haereth's daughter,
winsome to warriors, wine-cup bore
to the hands of the heroes. Hygelac then
his comrade fairly with question plied
in the lofty hall, sore longing to know
what manner of sojourn the Sea-Geats made.
"What came of thy quest, my kinsman Beowulf,
when thy yearnings suddenly swept thee yonder
battle to seek o'er the briny sea,
combat in Heorot? Hrothgar couldst thou
aid at all, the honored chief,
in his wide-known woes? With waves of care
my sad heart seethed; I sore mistrusted
my loved one's venture: long I begged thee
by no means to seek that slaughtering monster,
but suffer the South-Danes to settle their feud
themselves with Grendel. Now God be thanked
that safe and sound I can see thee now!"
Beowulf spake, the bairn of Ecgtheow: --
"'Tis known and unhidden, Hygelac Lord,
to many men, that meeting of ours,
struggle grim between Grendel and me,
which we fought on the field where full too many
sorrows he wrought for the Scylding-Victors,
evils unending. These all I avenged.
No boast can be from breed of Grendel,
any on earth, for that uproar at dawn,
from the longest-lived of the loathsome race
in fleshly fold! -- But first I went
Hrothgar to greet in the hall of gifts,
where Healfdene's kinsman high-renowned,
soon as my purpose was plain to him,
assigned me a seat by his son and heir.
The liegemen were lusty; my life-days never
such merry men over mead in hall
have I heard under heaven! The high-born queen,
people's peace-bringer, passed through the hall,
cheered the young clansmen, clasps of gold,
ere she sought her seat, to sundry gave.

Beowulf: Scholar's Edition

Oft to the heroes Hrothgar's daughter,
to earls in turn, the ale-cup tendered, --
she whom I heard these hall-companions
Freawaru name, when fretted gold
she proffered the warriors. Promised is she,
gold-decked maid, to the glad son of Froda.
Sage this seems to the Scylding's-friend,
kingdom's-keeper: he counts it wise
the woman to wed so and ward off feud,
store of slaughter. But seldom ever
when men are slain, does the murder-spear sink
but briefest while, though the bride be fair![1]
"Nor haply will like it the Heathobard lord,
and as little each of his liegemen all,
when a thane of the Danes, in that doughty throng,
goes with the lady along their hall,
and on him the old-time heirlooms glisten
hard and ring-decked, Heathobard's treasure,
weapons that once they wielded fair
until they lost at the linden-play[2]
liegeman leal and their lives as well.
Then, over the ale, on this heirloom gazing,
some ash-wielder old who has all in mind
that spear-death of men,[3] -- he is stern of mood,
heavy at heart, -- in the hero young
tests the temper and tries the soul
and war-hate wakens, with words like these: --
Canst thou not, comrade, ken that sword
which to the fray thy father carried
in his final feud, 'neath the fighting-mask,
dearest of blades, when the Danish slew him
and wielded the war-place on Withergild's fall,
after havoc of heroes, those hardy Scyldings?
Now, the son of a certain slaughtering Dane,
proud of his treasure, paces this hall,
joys in the killing, and carries the jewel[4]
that rightfully ought to be owned by thee!_
Thus he urges and eggs him all the time
with keenest words, till occasion offers
that Freawaru's thane, for his father's deed,
after bite of brand in his blood must slumber,
losing his life; but that liegeman flies
living away, for the land he kens.
And thus be broken on both their sides
oaths of the earls, when Ingeld's breast
wells with war-hate, and wife-love now
after the care-billows cooler grows.
"So[5] I hold not high the Heathobards' faith
due to the Danes, or their during love
and pact of peace. -- But I pass from that,

turning to Grendel, O giver-of-treasure,
and saying in full how the fight resulted,
hand-fray of heroes. When heaven's jewel
had fled o'er far fields, that fierce sprite came,
night-foe savage, to seek us out
where safe and sound we sentried the hall.
To Hondscio then was that harassing deadly,
his fall there was fated. He first was slain,
girded warrior. Grendel on him
turned murderous mouth, on our mighty kinsman,
and all of the brave man's body devoured.
Yet none the earlier, empty-handed,
would the bloody-toothed murderer, mindful of bale,
outward go from the gold-decked hall:
but me he attacked in his terror of might,
with greedy hand grasped me. A glove hung by him[6]
wide and wondrous, wound with bands;
and in artful wise it all was wrought,
by devilish craft, of dragon-skins.
Me therein, an innocent man,
the fiendish foe was fain to thrust
with many another. He might not so,
when I all angrily upright stood.
'Twere long to relate how that land-destroyer
I paid in kind for his cruel deeds;
yet there, my prince, this people of thine
got fame by my fighting. He fled away,
and a little space his life preserved;
but there staid behind him his stronger hand
left in Heorot; heartsick thence
on the floor of the ocean that outcast fell.
Me for this struggle the Scyldings'-friend
paid in plenty with plates of gold,
with many a treasure, when morn had come
and we all at the banquet-board sat down.
Then was song and glee. The gray-haired Scylding,
much tested, told of the times of yore.
Whiles the hero his harp bestirred,
wood-of-delight; now lays he chanted
of sooth and sadness, or said aright
legends of wonder, the wide-hearted king;
or for years of his youth he would yearn at times,
for strength of old struggles, now stricken with age,
hoary hero: his heart surged full
when, wise with winters, he wailed their flight.
Thus in the hall the whole of that day
at ease we feasted, till fell o'er earth
another night. Anon full ready
in greed of vengeance, Grendel's mother

set forth all doleful. Dead was her son
through war-hate of Weders; now, woman monstrous
with fury fell a foeman she slew,
avenged her offspring. From Aeschere old,
loyal councillor, life was gone;
nor might they e'en, when morning broke,
those Danish people, their death-done comrade
burn with brands, on balefire lay
the man they mourned. Under mountain stream
she had carried the corpse with cruel hands.
For Hrothgar that was the heaviest sorrow
of all that had laden the lord of his folk.
The leader then, by thy life, besought me
(sad was his soul) in the sea-waves' coil
to play the hero and hazard my being
for glory of prowess: my guerdon he pledged.
I then in the waters -- 'tis widely known --
that sea-floor-guardian savage found.
Hand-to-hand there a while we struggled;
billows welled blood; in the briny hall
her head I hewed with a hardy blade
from Grendel's mother, -- and gained my life,
though not without danger. My doom was not yet.
Then the haven-of-heroes, Healfdene's son,
gave me in guerdon great gifts of price.

XXIX

"So held this king to the customs old,
that I wanted for nought in the wage I gained,
the meed of my might; he made me gifts,
Healfdene's heir, for my own disposal.
Now to thee, my prince, I proffer them all,
gladly give them. Thy grace alone
can find me favor. Few indeed
have I of kinsmen, save, Hygelac, thee!"
Then he bade them bear him the boar-head standard,
the battle-helm high, and breastplate gray,
the splendid sword; then spake in form: --
"Me this war-gear the wise old prince,
Hrothgar, gave, and his hest he added,
that its story be straightway said to thee. --
A while it was held by Heorogar king,
for long time lord of the land of Scyldings;
yet not to his son the sovran left it,
to daring Heoroweard, -- dear as he was to him,
his harness of battle. -- Well hold thou it all!"
And I heard that soon passed o'er the path of this treasure,
all apple-fallow, four good steeds,
each like the others, arms and horses

he gave to the king. So should kinsmen be,
not weave one another the net of wiles,
or with deep-hid treachery death contrive
for neighbor and comrade. His nephew was ever
by hardy Hygelac held full dear,
and each kept watch o'er the other's weal.
I heard, too, the necklace to Hygd he presented,
wonder-wrought treasure, which Wealhtheow gave him
sovran's daughter: three steeds he added,
slender and saddle-gay. Since such gift
the gem gleamed bright on the breast of the queen.
Thus showed his strain the son of Ecgtheow
as a man remarked for mighty deeds
and acts of honor. At ale he slew not
comrade or kin; nor cruel his mood,
though of sons of earth his strength was greatest,
a glorious gift that God had sent
the splendid leader. Long was he spurned,
and worthless by Geatish warriors held;
him at mead the master-of-clans
failed full oft to favor at all.
Slack and shiftless the strong men deemed him,
profitless prince; but payment came,
to the warrior honored, for all his woes. --
Then the bulwark-of-earls[1] bade bring within,
hardy chieftain, Hrethel's heirloom
garnished with gold: no Geat e'er knew
in shape of a sword a statelier prize.
The brand he laid in Beowulf's lap;
and of hides assigned him seven thousand,[2]
with house and high-seat. They held in common
land alike by their line of birth,
inheritance, home: but higher the king
because of his rule o'er the realm itself.

Now further it fell with the flight of years,
with harryings horrid, that Hygelac perished,[3]
and Heardred, too, by hewing of swords
under the shield-wall slaughtered lay,
when him at the van of his victor-folk
sought hardy heroes, Heatho-Scilfings,
in arms o'erwhelming Hereric's nephew.
Then Beowulf came as king this broad
realm to wield; and he ruled it well
fifty winters,[4] a wise old prince,
warding his land, until One began
in the dark of night, a Dragon, to rage.
In the grave on the hill a hoard it guarded,
in the stone-barrow steep. A strait path reached it,

unknown to mortals. Some man, however,
came by chance that cave within
to the heathen hoard.⁵ In hand he took
a golden goblet, nor gave he it back,
stole with it away, while the watcher slept,
by thievish wiles: for the warden's wrath
prince and people must pay betimes!

XXX

THAT way he went with no will of his own,
in danger of life, to the dragon's hoard,
but for pressure of peril, some prince's thane.
He fled in fear the fatal scourge,
seeking shelter, a sinful man,
and entered in. At the awful sight
tottered that guest, and terror seized him;
yet the wretched fugitive rallied anon
from fright and fear ere he fled away,
and took the cup from that treasure-hoard.
Of such besides there was store enough,
heirlooms old, the earth below,
which some earl forgotten, in ancient years,
left the last of his lofty race,
heedfully there had hidden away,
dearest treasure. For death of yore
had hurried all hence; and he alone
left to live, the last of the clan,
weeping his friends, yet wished to bide
warding the treasure, his one delight,
though brief his respite. The barrow, new-ready,
to strand and sea-waves stood anear,
hard by the headland, hidden and closed;
there laid within it his lordly heirlooms
and heaped hoard of heavy gold
that warden of rings. Few words he spake:
"Now hold thou, earth, since heroes may not,
what earls have owned! Lo, erst from thee
brave men brought it! But battle-death seized
and cruel killing my clansmen all,
robbed them of life and a liegeman's joys.
None have I left to lift the sword,
or to cleanse the carven cup of price,
beaker bright. My brave are gone.
And the helmet hard, all haughty with gold,
shall part from its plating. Polishers sleep
who could brighten and burnish the battle-mask;
and those weeds of war that were wont to brave
over bicker of shields the bite of steel
rust with their bearer. The ringed mail

fares not far with famous chieftain,
at side of hero! No harp's delight,
no glee-wood's gladness! No good hawk now
flies through the hall! Nor horses fleet
stamp in the burgstead! Battle and death
the flower of my race have reft away."
Mournful of mood, thus he moaned his woe,
alone, for them all, and unblithe wept
by day and by night, till death's fell wave
o'erwhelmed his heart. His hoard-of-bliss
that old ill-doer open found,
who, blazing at twilight the barrows haunteth,
naked foe-dragon flying by night
folded in fire: the folk of earth
dread him sore. 'Tis his doom to seek
hoard in the graves, and heathen gold
to watch, many-wintered: nor wins he thereby!
Powerful this plague-of-the-people thus
held the house of the hoard in earth
three hundred winters; till One aroused
wrath in his breast, to the ruler bearing
that costly cup, and the king implored
for bond of peace. So the barrow was plundered,
borne off was booty. His boon was granted
that wretched man; and his ruler saw
first time what was fashioned in far-off days.
When the dragon awoke, new woe was kindled.
O'er the stone he snuffed. The stark-heart found
footprint of foe who so far had gone
in his hidden craft by the creature's head. --
So may the undoomed easily flee
evils and exile, if only he gain
the grace of The Wielder! -- That warden of gold
o'er the ground went seeking, greedy to find
the man who wrought him such wrong in sleep.
Savage and burning, the barrow he circled
all without; nor was any there,
none in the waste.... Yet war he desired,
was eager for battle. The barrow he entered,
sought the cup, and discovered soon
that some one of mortals had searched his treasure,
his lordly gold. The guardian waited
ill-enduring till evening came;
boiling with wrath was the barrow's keeper,
and fain with flame the foe to pay
for the dear cup's loss. -- Now day was fled
as the worm had wished. By its wall no more
was it glad to bide, but burning flew
folded in flame: a fearful beginning

for sons of the soil; and soon it came,
in the doom of their lord, to a dreadful end.

XXXI

THEN the baleful fiend its fire belched out,
and bright homes burned. The blaze stood high
all landsfolk frighting. No living thing
would that loathly one leave as aloft it flew.
Wide was the dragon's warring seen,
its fiendish fury far and near,
as the grim destroyer those Geatish people
hated and hounded. To hidden lair,
to its hoard it hastened at hint of dawn.
Folk of the land it had lapped in flame,
with bale and brand. In its barrow it trusted,
its battling and bulwarks: that boast was vain!

To Beowulf then the bale was told
quickly and truly: the king's own home,
of buildings the best, in brand-waves melted,
that gift-throne of Geats. To the good old man
sad in heart, 'twas heaviest sorrow.
The sage assumed that his sovran God
he had angered, breaking ancient law,
and embittered the Lord. His breast within
with black thoughts welled, as his wont was never.
The folk's own fastness that fiery dragon
with flame had destroyed, and the stronghold all
washed by waves; but the warlike king,
prince of the Weders, plotted vengeance.
Warriors'-bulwark, he bade them work
all of iron -- the earl's commander --
a war-shield wondrous: well he knew
that forest-wood against fire were worthless,
linden could aid not. -- Atheling brave,
he was fated to finish this fleeting life,[1]
his days on earth, and the dragon with him,
though long it had watched o'er the wealth of the hoard! --
Shame he reckoned it, sharer-of-rings,
to follow the flyer-afar with a host,
a broad-flung band; nor the battle feared he,
nor deemed he dreadful the dragon's warring,
its vigor and valor: ventures desperate
he had passed a-plenty, and perils of war,
contest-crash, since, conqueror proud,
Hrothgar's hall he had wholly purged,
and in grapple had killed the kin of Grendel,
loathsome breed! Not least was that
of hand-to-hand fights where Hygelac fell,

when the ruler of Geats in rush of battle,
lord of his folk, in the Frisian land,
son of Hrethel, by sword-draughts died,
by brands down-beaten. Thence Beowulf fled
through strength of himself and his swimming power,
though alone, and his arms were laden with thirty
coats of mail, when he came to the sea!
Nor yet might Hetwaras[2] haughtily boast
their craft of contest, who carried against him
shields to the fight: but few escaped
from strife with the hero to seek their homes!
Then swam over ocean Ecgtheow's son
lonely and sorrowful, seeking his land,
where Hygd made him offer of hoard and realm,
rings and royal-seat, reckoning naught
the strength of her son to save their kingdom
from hostile hordes, after Hygelac's death.
No sooner for this could the stricken ones
in any wise move that atheling's mind
over young Heardred's head as lord
and ruler of all the realm to be:
yet the hero upheld him with helpful words,
aided in honor, till, older grown,
he wielded the Weder-Geats. -- Wandering exiles
sought him o'er seas, the sons of Ohtere,
who had spurned the sway of the Scylfings'-helmet,
the bravest and best that broke the rings,
in Swedish land, of the sea-kings' line,
haughty hero.[3] Hence Heardred's end.
For shelter he gave them, sword-death came,
the blade's fell blow, to bairn of Hygelac;
but the son of Ongentheow sought again
house and home when Heardred fell,
leaving Beowulf lord of Geats
and gift-seat's master. -- A good king he!

XXXII

THE fall of his lord he was fain to requite
in after days; and to Eadgils he proved
friend to the friendless, and forces sent
over the sea to the son of Ohtere,
weapons and warriors: well repaid he
those care-paths cold when the king he slew.[1]
Thus safe through struggles the son of Ecgtheow
had passed a plenty, through perils dire,
with daring deeds, till this day was come
that doomed him now with the dragon to strive.
With comrades eleven the lord of Geats
swollen in rage went seeking the dragon.

Beowulf: Scholar's Edition
He had heard whence all the harm arose
and the killing of clansmen; that cup of price
on the lap of the lord had been laid by the finder.
In the throng was this one thirteenth man,
starter of all the strife and ill,
care-laden captive; cringing thence
forced and reluctant, he led them on
till he came in ken of that cavern-hall,
the barrow delved near billowy surges,
flood of ocean. Within 'twas full
of wire-gold and jewels; a jealous warden,
warrior trusty, the treasures held,
lurked in his lair. Not light the task
of entrance for any of earth-born men!
Sat on the headland the hero king,
spake words of hail to his hearth-companions,
gold-friend of Geats. All gloomy his soul,
wavering, death-bound. Wyrd full nigh
stood ready to greet the gray-haired man,
to seize his soul-hoard, sunder apart
life and body. Not long would be
the warrior's spirit enwound with flesh.
Beowulf spake, the bairn of Ecgtheow: --
"Through store of struggles I strove in youth,
mighty feuds; I mind them all.
I was seven years old when the sovran of rings,
friend-of-his-folk, from my father took me,
had me, and held me, Hrethel the king,
with food and fee, faithful in kinship.
Ne'er, while I lived there, he loathlier found me,
bairn in the burg, than his birthright sons,
Herebeald and Haethcyn and Hygelac mine.
For the eldest of these, by unmeet chance,
by kinsman's deed, was the death-bed strewn,
when Haethcyn killed him with horny bow,
his own dear liege laid low with an arrow,
missed the mark and his mate shot down,
one brother the other, with bloody shaft.
A feeless fight,[2] and a fearful sin,
horror to Hrethel; yet, hard as it was,
unavenged must the atheling die!
Too awful it is for an aged man
to bide and bear, that his bairn so young
rides on the gallows. A rime he makes,
sorrow-song for his son there hanging
as rapture of ravens; no rescue now
can come from the old, disabled man!
Still is he minded, as morning breaks,
of the heir gone elsewhere;[3] another he hopes not
he will bide to see his burg within

as ward for his wealth, now the one has found
doom of death that the deed incurred.
Forlorn he looks on the lodge of his son,
wine-hall waste and wind-swept chambers
reft of revel. The rider sleepeth,
the hero, far-hidden;[4] no harp resounds,
in the courts no wassail, as once was heard.

XXXIII

"THEN he goes to his chamber, a grief-song chants
alone for his lost. Too large all seems,
homestead and house. So the helmet-of-Weders
hid in his heart for Herebeald
waves of woe. No way could he take
to avenge on the slayer slaughter so foul;
nor e'en could he harass that hero at all
with loathing deed, though he loved him not.
And so for the sorrow his soul endured,
men's gladness he gave up and God's light chose.
Lands and cities he left his sons
(as the wealthy do) when he went from earth.
There was strife and struggle 'twixt Swede and Geat
o'er the width of waters; war arose,
hard battle-horror, when Hrethel died,
and Ongentheow's offspring grew
strife-keen, bold, nor brooked o'er the seas
pact of peace, but pushed their hosts
to harass in hatred by Hreosnabeorh.
Men of my folk for that feud had vengeance,
for woful war ('tis widely known),
though one of them bought it with blood of his heart,
a bargain hard: for Haethcyn proved
fatal that fray, for the first-of-Geats.
At morn, I heard, was the murderer killed
by kinsman for kinsman,[1] with clash of sword,
when Ongentheow met Eofor there.
Wide split the war-helm: wan he fell,
hoary Scylfing; the hand that smote him
of feud was mindful, nor flinched from the death-blow.
-- "For all that he[2] gave me, my gleaming sword
repaid him at war, -- such power I wielded, --
for lordly treasure: with land he entrusted me,
homestead and house. He had no need
from Swedish realm, or from Spear-Dane folk,
or from men of the Gifths, to get him help, --
some warrior worse for wage to buy!
Ever I fought in the front of all,
sole to the fore; and so shall I fight
while I bide in life and this blade shall last

that early and late hath loyal proved
since for my doughtiness Daeghrefn fell,
slain by my hand, the Hugas' champion.
Nor fared he thence to the Frisian king
with the booty back, and breast-adornments;
but, slain in struggle, that standard-bearer
fell, atheling brave. Not with blade was he slain,
but his bones were broken by brawny gripe,
his heart-waves stilled. -- The sword-edge now,
hard blade and my hand, for the hoard shall strive."
Beowulf spake, and a battle-vow made
his last of all: "I have lived through many
wars in my youth; now once again,
old folk-defender, feud will I seek,
do doughty deeds, if the dark destroyer
forth from his cavern come to fight me!"
Then hailed he the helmeted heroes all,
for the last time greeting his liegemen dear,
comrades of war: "I should carry no weapon,
no sword to the serpent, if sure I knew
how, with such enemy, else my vows
I could gain as I did in Grendel's day.
But fire in this fight I must fear me now,
and poisonous breath; so I bring with me
breastplate and board.[3] From the barrow's keeper
no footbreadth flee I. One fight shall end
our war by the wall, as Wyrd allots,
all mankind's master. My mood is bold
but forbears to boast o'er this battling-flyer.
-- Now abide by the barrow, ye breastplate-mailed,
ye heroes in harness, which of us twain
better from battle-rush bear his wounds.
Wait ye the finish. The fight is not yours,
nor meet for any but me alone
to measure might with this monster here
and play the hero. Hardily I
shall win that wealth, or war shall seize,
cruel killing, your king and lord!"
Up stood then with shield the sturdy champion,
stayed by the strength of his single manhood,
and hardy 'neath helmet his harness bore
under cleft of the cliffs: no coward's path!
Soon spied by the wall that warrior chief,
survivor of many a victory-field
where foemen fought with furious clashings,
an arch of stone; and within, a stream
that broke from the barrow. The brooklet's wave
was hot with fire. The hoard that way
he never could hope unharmed to near,
or endure those deeps,[4] for the dragon's flame.

Then let from his breast, for he burst with rage,
the Weder-Geat prince a word outgo;
stormed the stark-heart; stern went ringing
and clear his cry 'neath the cliff-rocks gray.
The hoard-guard heard a human voice;
his rage was enkindled. No respite now
for pact of peace! The poison-breath
of that foul worm first came forth from the cave,
hot reek-of-fight: the rocks resounded.
Stout by the stone-way his shield he raised,
lord of the Geats, against the loathed-one;
while with courage keen that coiled foe
came seeking strife. The sturdy king
had drawn his sword, not dull of edge,
heirloom old; and each of the two
felt fear of his foe, though fierce their mood.
Stoutly stood with his shield high-raised
the warrior king, as the worm now coiled
together amain: the mailed-one waited.
Now, spire by spire, fast sped and glided
that blazing serpent. The shield protected,
soul and body a shorter while
for the hero-king than his heart desired,
could his will have wielded the welcome respite
but once in his life! But Wyrd denied it,
and victory's honors. -- His arm he lifted
lord of the Geats, the grim foe smote
with atheling's heirloom. Its edge was turned
brown blade, on the bone, and bit more feebly
than its noble master had need of then
in his baleful stress. -- Then the barrow's keeper
waxed full wild for that weighty blow,
cast deadly flames; wide drove and far
those vicious fires. No victor's glory
the Geats' lord boasted; his brand had failed,
naked in battle, as never it should,
excellent iron! -- 'Twas no easy path
that Ecgtheow's honored heir must tread
over the plain to the place of the foe;
for against his will he must win a home
elsewhere far, as must all men, leaving
this lapsing life! -- Not long it was
ere those champions grimly closed again.
The hoard-guard was heartened; high heaved his breast
once more; and by peril was pressed again,
enfolded in flames, the folk-commander!
Nor yet about him his band of comrades,
sons of athelings, armed stood
with warlike front: to the woods they bent them,

their lives to save. But the soul of one
with care was cumbered. Kinship true
can never be marred in a noble mind!

XXXIV

WIGLAF his name was, Weohstan's son,
linden-thane loved, the lord of Scylfings,
Aelfhere's kinsman. His king he now saw
with heat under helmet hard oppressed.
He minded the prizes his prince had given him,
wealthy seat of the Waegmunding line,
and folk-rights that his father owned
Not long he lingered. The linden yellow,
his shield, he seized; the old sword he drew: --
as heirloom of Eanmund earth-dwellers knew it,
who was slain by the sword-edge, son of Ohtere,
friendless exile, erst in fray
killed by Weohstan, who won for his kin
brown-bright helmet, breastplate ringed,
old sword of Eotens, Onela's gift,
weeds of war of the warrior-thane,
battle-gear brave: though a brother's child
had been felled, the feud was unfelt by Onela.[1]
For winters this war-gear Weohstan kept,
breastplate and board, till his bairn had grown
earlship to earn as the old sire did:
then he gave him, mid Geats, the gear of battle,
portion huge, when he passed from life,
fared aged forth. For the first time now
with his leader-lord the liegeman young
was bidden to share the shock of battle.
Neither softened his soul, nor the sire's bequest
weakened in war.[2] So the worm found out
when once in fight the foes had met!
Wiglaf spake, -- and his words were sage;
sad in spirit, he said to his comrades: --
"I remember the time, when mead we took,
what promise we made to this prince of ours
in the banquet-hall, to our breaker-of-rings,
for gear of combat to give him requital,
for hard-sword and helmet, if hap should bring
stress of this sort! Himself who chose us
from all his army to aid him now,
urged us to glory, and gave these treasures,
because he counted us keen with the spear
and hardy 'neath helm, though this hero-work
our leader hoped unhelped and alone
to finish for us, -- folk-defender
who hath got him glory greater than all men

for daring deeds! Now the day is come
that our noble master has need of the might
of warriors stout. Let us stride along
the hero to help while the heat is about him
glowing and grim! For God is my witness
I am far more fain the fire should seize
along with my lord these limbs of mine![3]
Unsuiting it seems our shields to bear
homeward hence, save here we essay
to fell the foe and defend the life
of the Weders' lord. I wot 'twere shame
on the law of our land if alone the king
out of Geatish warriors woe endured
and sank in the struggle! My sword and helmet,
breastplate and board, for us both shall serve!"
Through slaughter-reek strode he to succor his chieftain,
his battle-helm bore, and brief words spake: --
"Beowulf dearest, do all bravely,
as in youthful days of yore thou vowedst
that while life should last thou wouldst let no wise
thy glory droop! Now, great in deeds,
atheling steadfast, with all thy strength
shield thy life! I will stand to help thee."
At the words the worm came once again,
murderous monster mad with rage,
with fire-billows flaming, its foes to seek,
the hated men. In heat-waves burned
that board[4] to the boss, and the breastplate failed
to shelter at all the spear-thane young.
Yet quickly under his kinsman's shield
went eager the earl, since his own was now
all burned by the blaze. The bold king again
had mind of his glory: with might his glaive
was driven into the dragon's head, --
blow nerved by hate. But Naegling[5] was shivered,
broken in battle was Beowulf's sword,
old and gray. 'Twas granted him not
that ever the edge of iron at all
could help him at strife: too strong was his hand,
so the tale is told, and he tried too far
with strength of stroke all swords he wielded,
though sturdy their steel: they steaded him nought.
Then for the third time thought on its feud
that folk-destroyer, fire-dread dragon,
and rushed on the hero, where room allowed,
battle-grim, burning; its bitter teeth
closed on his neck, and covered him
with waves of blood from his breast that welled.

Beowulf: Scholar's Edition
XXXV
'TWAS now, men say, in his sovran's need
that the earl made known his noble strain,
craft and keenness and courage enduring.
Heedless of harm, though his hand was burned,
hardy-hearted, he helped his kinsman.
A little lower the loathsome beast
he smote with sword; his steel drove in
bright and burnished; that blaze began
to lose and lessen. At last the king
wielded his wits again, war-knife drew,
a biting blade by his breastplate hanging,
and the Weders'-helm smote that worm asunder,
felled the foe, flung forth its life.
So had they killed it, kinsmen both,
athelings twain: thus an earl should be
in danger's day! -- Of deeds of valor
this conqueror's-hour of the king was last,
of his work in the world. The wound began,
which that dragon-of-earth had erst inflicted,
to swell and smart; and soon he found
in his breast was boiling, baleful and deep,
pain of poison. The prince walked on,
wise in his thought, to the wall of rock;
then sat, and stared at the structure of giants,
where arch of stone and steadfast column
upheld forever that hall in earth.
Yet here must the hand of the henchman peerless
lave with water his winsome lord,
the king and conqueror covered with blood,
with struggle spent, and unspan his helmet.
Beowulf spake in spite of his hurt,
his mortal wound; full well he knew
his portion now was past and gone
of earthly bliss, and all had fled
of his file of days, and death was near:
"I would fain bestow on son of mine
this gear of war, were given me now
that any heir should after me come
of my proper blood. This people I ruled
fifty winters. No folk-king was there,
none at all, of the neighboring clans
who war would wage me with 'warriors'-friends'[1]
and threat me with horrors. At home I bided
what fate might come, and I cared for mine own;
feuds I sought not, nor falsely swore
ever on oath. For all these things,
though fatally wounded, fain am I!
From the Ruler-of-Man no wrath shall seize me,

when life from my frame must flee away,
for killing of kinsmen! Now quickly go
and gaze on that hoard 'neath the hoary rock,
Wiglaf loved, now the worm lies low,
sleeps, heart-sore, of his spoil bereaved.
And fare in haste. I would fain behold
the gorgeous heirlooms, golden store,
have joy in the jewels and gems, lay down
softlier for sight of this splendid hoard
my life and the lordship I long have held."

XXXVI

I HAVE heard that swiftly the son of Weohstan
at wish and word of his wounded king, --
war-sick warrior, -- woven mail-coat,
battle-sark, bore 'neath the barrow's roof.
Then the clansman keen, of conquest proud,
passing the seat,[1] saw store of jewels
and glistening gold the ground along;
by the wall were marvels, and many a vessel
in the den of the dragon, the dawn-flier old:
unburnished bowls of bygone men
reft of richness; rusty helms
of the olden age; and arm-rings many
wondrously woven. -- Such wealth of gold,
booty from barrow, can burden with pride
each human wight: let him hide it who will! --
His glance too fell on a gold-wove banner
high o'er the hoard, of handiwork noblest,
brilliantly broidered; so bright its gleam,
all the earth-floor he easily saw
and viewed all these vessels. No vestige now
was seen of the serpent: the sword had ta'en him.
Then, I heard, the hill of its hoard was reft,
old work of giants, by one alone;
he burdened his bosom with beakers and plate
at his own good will, and the ensign took,
brightest of beacons. -- The blade of his lord
-- its edge was iron -- had injured deep
one that guarded the golden hoard
many a year and its murder-fire
spread hot round the barrow in horror-billows
at midnight hour, till it met its doom.
Hasted the herald, the hoard so spurred him
his track to retrace; he was troubled by doubt,
high-souled hero, if haply he'd find
alive, where he left him, the lord of Weders,
weakening fast by the wall of the cave.
So he carried the load. His lord and king

he found all bleeding, famous chief
at the lapse of life. The liegeman again
plashed him with water, till point of word
broke through the breast-hoard. Beowulf spake,
sage and sad, as he stared at the gold. --
"For the gold and treasure, to God my thanks,
to the Wielder-of-Wonders, with words I say,
for what I behold, to Heaven's Lord,
for the grace that I give such gifts to my folk
or ever the day of my death be run!
Now I've bartered here for booty of treasure
the last of my life, so look ye well
to the needs of my land! No longer I tarry.
A barrow bid ye the battle-fanned raise
for my ashes. 'Twill shine by the shore of the flood,
to folk of mine memorial fair
on Hrones Headland high uplifted,
that ocean-wanderers oft may hail
Beowulf's Barrow, as back from far
they drive their keels o'er the darkling wave."
From his neck he unclasped the collar of gold,
valorous king, to his vassal gave it
with bright-gold helmet, breastplate, and ring,
to the youthful thane: bade him use them in joy.
"Thou art end and remnant of all our race
the Waegmunding name. For Wyrd hath swept them,
all my line, to the land of doom,
earls in their glory: I after them go."
This word was the last which the wise old man
harbored in heart ere hot death-waves
of balefire he chose. From his bosom fled
his soul to seek the saints' reward.

XXXVII

IT was heavy hap for that hero young
on his lord beloved to look and find him
lying on earth with life at end,
sorrowful sight. But the slayer too,
awful earth-dragon, empty of breath,
lay felled in fight, nor, fain of its treasure,
could the writhing monster rule it more.
For edges of iron had ended its days,
hard and battle-sharp, hammers' leaving;[1]
and that flier-afar had fallen to ground
hushed by its hurt, its hoard all near,
no longer lusty aloft to whirl
at midnight, making its merriment seen,
proud of its prizes: prone it sank
by the handiwork of the hero-king.

Forsooth among folk but few achieve,
-- though sturdy and strong, as stories tell me,
and never so daring in deed of valor, --
the perilous breath of a poison-foe
to brave, and to rush on the ring-board hall,
whenever his watch the warden keeps
bold in the barrow. Beowulf paid
the price of death for that precious hoard;
and each of the foes had found the end of this fleeting life.
Befell erelong
that the laggards in war the wood had left,
trothbreakers, cowards, ten together,
fearing before to flourish a spear
in the sore distress of their sovran lord.
Now in their shame their shields they carried,
armor of fight, where the old man lay;
and they gazed on Wiglaf. Wearied he sat
at his sovran's shoulder, shieldsman good,
to wake him with water.[2] Nowise it availed.
Though well he wished it, in world no more
could he barrier life for that leader-of-battles
nor baffle the will of all-wielding God.
Doom of the Lord was law o'er the deeds
of every man, as it is to-day.
Grim was the answer, easy to get,
from the youth for those that had yielded to fear!
Wiglaf spake, the son of Weohstan, --
mournful he looked on those men unloved: --
"Who sooth will speak, can say indeed
that the ruler who gave you golden rings
and the harness of war in which ye stand
-- for he at ale-bench often-times
bestowed on hall-folk helm and breastplate,
lord to liegemen, the likeliest gear
which near of far he could find to give, --
threw away and wasted these weeds of battle,
on men who failed when the foemen came!
Not at all could the king of his comrades-in-arms
venture to vaunt, though the Victory-Wielder,
God, gave him grace that he got revenge
sole with his sword in stress and need.
To rescue his life, 'twas little that I
could serve him in struggle; yet shift I made
(hopeless it seemed) to help my kinsman.
Its strength ever waned, when with weapon I struck
that fatal foe, and the fire less strongly
flowed from its head. -- Too few the heroes
in throe of contest that thronged to our king!
Now gift of treasure and girding of sword,

joy of the house and home-delight
shall fail your folk; his freehold-land
every clansman within your kin
shall lose and leave, when lords high-born
hear afar of that flight of yours,
a fameless deed. Yea, death is better
for liegemen all than a life of shame!"

XXXVIII

THAT battle-toil bade he at burg to announce,
at the fort on the cliff, where, full of sorrow,
all the morning earls had sat,
daring shieldsmen, in doubt of twain:
would they wail as dead, or welcome home,
their lord beloved? Little[1] kept back
of the tidings new, but told them all,
the herald that up the headland rode. --
"Now the willing-giver to Weder folk
in death-bed lies; the Lord of Geats
on the slaughter-bed sleeps by the serpent's deed!
And beside him is stretched that slayer-of-men
with knife-wounds sick:[2] no sword availed
on the awesome thing in any wise
to work a wound. There Wiglaf sitteth,
Weohstan's bairn, by Beowulf's side,
the living earl by the other dead,
and heavy of heart a head-watch[3] keeps
o'er friend and foe. -- Now our folk may look
for waging of war when once unhidden
to Frisian and Frank the fall of the king
is spread afar. -- The strife began
when hot on the Hugas[4] Hygelac fell
and fared with his fleet to the Frisian land.
Him there the Hetwaras humbled in war,
plied with such prowess their power o'erwhelming
that the bold-in-battle bowed beneath it
and fell in fight. To his friends no wise
could that earl give treasure! And ever since
the Merowings' favor has failed us wholly.
Nor aught expect I of peace and faith
from Swedish folk. 'Twas spread afar
how Ongentheow reft at Ravenswood
Haethcyn Hrethling of hope and life,
when the folk of Geats for the first time sought
in wanton pride the Warlike-Scylfings.
Soon the sage old sire[5] of Ohtere,
ancient and awful, gave answering blow;
the sea-king[6] he slew, and his spouse redeemed,
his good wife rescued, though robbed of her gold,

mother of Ohtere and Onela.
Then he followed his foes, who fled before him
sore beset and stole their way,
bereft of a ruler, to Ravenswood.

With his host he besieged there what swords had left,
the weary and wounded; woes he threatened
the whole night through to that hard-pressed throng:
some with the morrow his sword should kill,
some should go to the gallows-tree
for rapture of ravens. But rescue came
with dawn of day for those desperate men
when they heard the horn of Hygelac sound,
tones of his trumpet; the trusty king
had followed their trail with faithful band.

XXXIX

"THE bloody swath of Swedes and Geats
and the storm of their strife, were seen afar,
how folk against folk the fight had wakened.
The ancient king with his atheling band
sought his citadel, sorrowing much:
Ongentheow earl went up to his burg.
He had tested Hygelac's hardihood,
the proud one's prowess, would prove it no longer,
defied no more those fighting-wanderers
nor hoped from the seamen to save his hoard,
his bairn and his bride: so he bent him again,
old, to his earth-walls. Yet after him came
with slaughter for Swedes the standards of Hygelac
o'er peaceful plains in pride advancing,
till Hrethelings fought in the fenced town.[1]
Then Ongentheow with edge of sword,
the hoary-bearded, was held at bay,
and the folk-king there was forced to suffer
Eofor's anger. In ire, at the king
Wulf Wonreding with weapon struck;
and the chieftain's blood, for that blow, in streams
flowed 'neath his hair. No fear felt he,
stout old Scylfing, but straightway repaid
in better bargain that bitter stroke
and faced his foe with fell intent.
Nor swift enough was the son of Wonred
answer to render the aged chief;
too soon on his head the helm was cloven;
blood-bedecked he bowed to earth,
and fell adown; not doomed was he yet,
and well he waxed, though the wound was sore.
Then the hardy Hygelac-thane,[2]

when his brother fell, with broad brand smote,
giants' sword crashing through giants'-helm
across the shield-wall: sank the king,
his folk's old herdsman, fatally hurt.
There were many to bind the brother's wounds
and lift him, fast as fate allowed
his people to wield the place-of-war.
But Eofor took from Ongentheow,
earl from other, the iron-breastplate,
hard sword hilted, and helmet too,
and the hoar-chief's harness to Hygelac carried,
who took the trappings, and truly promised
rich fee 'mid folk, -- and fulfilled it so.
For that grim strife gave the Geatish lord,
Hrethel's offspring, when home he came,
to Eofor and Wulf a wealth of treasure,
Each of them had a hundred thousand[3]
in land and linked rings; nor at less price reckoned
mid-earth men such mighty deeds!
And to Eofor he gave his only daughter
in pledge of grace, the pride of his home.

"Such is the feud, the foeman's rage,
death-hate of men: so I deem it sure
that the Swedish folk will seek us home
for this fall of their friends, the fighting-Scylfings,
when once they learn that our warrior leader
lifeless lies, who land and hoard
ever defended from all his foes,
furthered his folk's weal, finished his course
a hardy hero. -- Now haste is best,
that we go to gaze on our Geatish lord,
and bear the bountiful breaker-of-rings
to the funeral pyre. No fragments merely
shall burn with the warrior. Wealth of jewels,
gold untold and gained in terror,
treasure at last with his life obtained,
all of that booty the brands shall take,
fire shall eat it. No earl must carry
memorial jewel. No maiden fair
shall wreathe her neck with noble ring:
nay, sad in spirit and shorn of her gold,
oft shall she pass o'er paths of exile
now our lord all laughter has laid aside,
all mirth and revel. Many a spear
morning-cold shall be clasped amain,
lifted aloft; nor shall lilt of harp
those warriors wake; but the wan-hued raven,
fain o'er the fallen, his feast shall praise
and boast to the eagle how bravely he ate

when he and the wolf were wasting the slain."

So he told his sorrowful tidings,
and little[4] he lied, the loyal man
of word or of work. The warriors rose;
sad, they climbed to the Cliff-of-Eagles,
went, welling with tears, the wonder to view.
Found on the sand there, stretched at rest,
their lifeless lord, who had lavished rings
of old upon them. Ending-day
had dawned on the doughty-one; death had seized
in woful slaughter the Weders' king.
There saw they, besides, the strangest being,
loathsome, lying their leader near,
prone on the field. The fiery dragon,
fearful fiend, with flame was scorched.
Reckoned by feet, it was fifty measures
in length as it lay. Aloft erewhile
it had revelled by night, and anon come back,
seeking its den; now in death's sure clutch
it had come to the end of its earth-hall joys.
By it there stood the stoups and jars;
dishes lay there, and dear-decked swords
eaten with rust, as, on earth's lap resting,
a thousand winters they waited there.
For all that heritage huge, that gold
of bygone men, was bound by a spell,[5]
so the treasure-hall could be touched by none
of human kind, -- save that Heaven's King,
God himself, might give whom he would,
Helper of Heroes, the hoard to open, --
even such a man as seemed to him meet.

XL

A PERILOUS path, it proved, he[1] trod
who heinously hid, that hall within,
wealth under wall! Its watcher had killed
one of a few,[2] and the feud was avenged
in woful fashion. Wondrous seems it,
what manner a man of might and valor
oft ends his life, when the earl no longer
in mead-hall may live with loving friends.
So Beowulf, when that barrow's warden
he sought, and the struggle; himself knew not
in what wise he should wend from the world at last.
For[3] princes potent, who placed the gold,
with a curse to doomsday covered it deep,
so that marked with sin the man should be,
hedged with horrors, in hell-bonds fast,

racked with plagues, who should rob their hoard.
Yet no greed for gold, but the grace of heaven,
ever the king had kept in view.[4]
Wiglaf spake, the son of Weohstan: --
"At the mandate of one, oft warriors many
sorrow must suffer; and so must we.
The people's-shepherd showed not aught
of care for our counsel, king beloved!
That guardian of gold he should grapple not, urged we,
but let him lie where he long had been
in his earth-hall waiting the end of the world,
the hest of heaven. -- This hoard is ours
but grievously gotten; too grim the fate
which thither carried our king and lord.
I was within there, and all I viewed,
the chambered treasure, when chance allowed me
(and my path was made in no pleasant wise)
under the earth-wall. Eager, I seized
such heap from the hoard as hands could bear
and hurriedly carried it hither back
to my liege and lord. Alive was he still,
still wielding his wits. The wise old man
spake much in his sorrow, and sent you greetings
and bade that ye build, when he breathed no more,
on the place of his balefire a barrow high,
memorial mighty. Of men was he
worthiest warrior wide earth o'er
the while he had joy of his jewels and burg.
Let us set out in haste now, the second time
to see and search this store of treasure,
these wall-hid wonders, -- the way I show you, --
where, gathered near, ye may gaze your fill
at broad-gold and rings. Let the bier, soon made,
be all in order when out we come,
our king and captain to carry thither
-- man beloved -- where long he shall bide
safe in the shelter of sovran God."
Then the bairn of Weohstan bade command,
hardy chief, to heroes many
that owned their homesteads, hither to bring
firewood from far -- o'er the folk they ruled --
for the famed-one's funeral. "Fire shall devour
and wan flames feed on the fearless warrior
who oft stood stout in the iron-shower,
when, sped from the string, a storm of arrows
shot o'er the shield-wall: the shaft held firm,
featly feathered, followed the barb."
And now the sage young son of Weohstan
seven chose of the chieftain's thanes,
the best he found that band within,

and went with these warriors, one of eight,
under hostile roof. In hand one bore
a lighted torch and led the way.
No lots they cast for keeping the hoard
when once the warriors saw it in hall,
altogether without a guardian,
lying there lost. And little they mourned
when they had hastily haled it out,
dear-bought treasure! The dragon they cast,
the worm, o'er the wall for the wave to take,
and surges swallowed that shepherd of gems.
Then the woven gold on a wain was laden --
countless quite! -- and the king was borne,
hoary hero, to Hrones-Ness.

XLI

THEN fashioned for him the folk of Geats
firm on the earth a funeral-pile,
and hung it with helmets and harness of war
and breastplates bright, as the boon he asked;
and they laid amid it the mighty chieftain,
heroes mourning their master dear.
Then on the hill that hugest of balefires
the warriors wakened. Wood-smoke rose
black over blaze, and blent was the roar
of flame with weeping (the wind was still),
till the fire had broken the frame of bones,
hot at the heart. In heavy mood
their misery moaned they, their master's death.
Wailing her woe, the widow[1] old,
her hair upbound, for Beowulf's death
sung in her sorrow, and said full oft
she dreaded the doleful days to come,
deaths enow, and doom of battle,
and shame. -- The smoke by the sky was devoured.
The folk of the Weders fashioned there
on the headland a barrow broad and high,
by ocean-farers far descried:
in ten days' time their toil had raised it,
the battle-brave's beacon. Round brands of the pyre
a wall they built, the worthiest ever
that wit could prompt in their wisest men.
They placed in the barrow that precious booty,
the rounds and the rings they had reft erewhile,
hardy heroes, from hoard in cave, --
trusting the ground with treasure of earls,
gold in the earth, where ever it lies
useless to men as of yore it was.
Then about that barrow the battle-keen rode,

atheling-born, a band of twelve,
lament to make, to mourn their king,
chant their dirge, and their chieftain honor.
They praised his earlship, his acts of prowess
worthily witnessed: and well it is
that men their master-friend mightily laud,
heartily love, when hence he goes
from life in the body forlorn away.

Thus made their mourning the men of Geatland,
for their hero's passing his hearth-companions:
quoth that of all the kings of earth,
of men he was mildest and most beloved,
to his kin the kindest, keenest for praise.

Footnotes:

Preface Footnotes
　1. Not, of course, Beowulf the Great, hero of the epic.
　2. Kenning for king or chieftain of a comitatus: he breaks off gold from the spiral rings -- often worn on the arm -- and so rewards his followers.

Footnotes I
　1. That is, "The Hart," or "Stag," so called from decorations in the gables that resembled the antlers of a deer. This hall has been carefully described in a pamphlet by Heyne. The building was rectangular, with opposite doors -- mainly west and east -- and a hearth in the middle of th single room. A row of pillars down each side, at some distance from the walls, made a space which was raised a little above the main floor, and was furnished with two rows of seats. On one side, usually south, was the high-seat midway between the doors. Opposite this, on the other raised space, was another seat of honor. At the banquet soon to be described, Hrothgar sat in the south or chief high-seat, and Beowulf opposite to him. The scene for a flying (see below, v.499) was thus very effectively set. Planks on trestles -- the "board" of later English literature -- formed the tables just in front of the long rows of seats, and were taken away after banquets, when the retainers were ready to stretch themselves out for sleep on the benches.
　2. Fire was the usual end of these halls. See v. 781 below. One thinks of the splendid scene at the end of the Nibelungen, of the Nialssaga, of Saxo's story of Amlethus, and many a less famous instance.
　3. It is to be supposed that all hearers of this poem knew how Hrothgar's hall was burnt, -- perhaps in the unsuccessful attack made on him by his son-in-law Ingeld.
　4. A skilled minstrel. The Danes are heathens, as one is told presently; but this lay of beginnings is taken from Genesis.
　5. A disturber of the border, one who sallies from his haunt in the fen and roams over the country near by. This probably pagan nuisance is now furnished with biblical credentials as a fiend or devil in good standing, so that all Christian Englishmen might read about him. "Grendel" may mean one who grinds and crushes.
　6. Cain's.
　7. Giants.

Footnotes II
　1. The smaller buildings within the main enclosure but separate from the hall.
　2. Grendel.
　　3. "Sorcerers-of-hell."
　　4. Hrothgar, who is the "Scyldings'-friend" of 170.
　　5. That is, in formal or prescribed phrase.

Footnotes III
　1. Ship.
　2. That is, since Beowulf selected his ship and led his men to the harbor.
　　3. One of the auxiliary names of the Geats.
　　4. Or: Not thus openly ever came warriors hither; yet...

Footnotes IV
　1. Hrothgar.
　2. Beowulf's helmet has several boar-images on it; he is the "man of war"; and the boar-helmet guards him as typical representative of the marching party as a whole. The boar was sacred to Freyr, who was the favorite god of the Germanic tribes about the North Sea and the Baltic. Rude representations of warriors show the boar on the helmet quite as large as the helmet itself.

Footnotes V
　1. Either merely paved, the strata via of the Romans, or else thought of as a sort of mosaic, an extravagant touch like the reckless waste of gold on the walls and roofs of a hall.

Footnotes VI
　1. The nicor, says Bugge, is a hippopotamus; a walrus, says Ten Brink. But that water-goblin who covers the space from Old Nick of jest to the Neckan and Nix of poetry and tale, is all one needs, and Nicor is a good name for him.
　2. His own people, the Geats.
　　3. That is, cover it as with a face-cloth. "There will be no need of funeral rites."
　　4. Personification of Battle.
　　5. The Germanic Vulcan.

6. This mighty power, whom the Christian poet can still revere, has here the general force of "Destiny."

Footnotes VII
1. There is no irrelevance here. Hrothgar sees in Beowulf's mission a heritage of duty, a return of the good offices which the Danish king rendered to Beowulf's father in time of dire need.
2. Money, for wergild, or man-price.
3. Ecgtheow, Beowulf's sire.

Footnotes VIII
1. "Began the fight."
2. Breca.

Footnotes IX
1. Murder.

Footnotes X
1. Beowulf, -- the "one."

Footnotes XI
1. That is, he was a "lost soul," doomed to hell.

Footnotes XII
1. Kenning for Beowulf.

Footnotes XIII
1. "Guarded the treasure."
2. Sc. Heremod.
3. The singer has sung his lays, and the epic resumes its story. The time-relations are not altogether good in this long passage which describes the rejoicings of "the day after"; but the present shift from the riders on the road to the folk at the hall is not very violent, and is of a piece with the general style.

Footnotes XIV
1. Unferth, Beowulf's sometime opponent in the flyting.

Footnotes XV
1. There is no horrible inconsistency here such as the critics strive and cry about. In spite of the ruin that Grendel and Beowulf had made within the hall, the framework and roof held firm, and swift repairs made the interior habitable. Tapestries were hung on the walls, and willing hands prepared the banquet.
2. From its formal use in other places, this phrase, to take cup in hall, or "on the floor," would seem to mean that Beowulf stood up to receive his gifts, drink to the donor, and say thanks.
3. Kenning for sword.
4. Hrothgar. He is also the "refuge of the friends of Ing," below. Ing belongs to myth.
5. Horses are frequently led or ridden into the hall where folk sit at banquet: so in Chaucer's Squire's tale, in the ballad of King Estmere, and in the romances.

Footnotes XVI
1. Man-price, wergild.
2. Beowulf's.
3. Hrothgar.
4. There is no need to assume a gap in the Ms. As before about Sigemund and Heremod, so now, though at greater length, about Finn and his feud, a lay is chanted or recited; and the epic poet, counting on his readers' familiarity with the story, -- a fragment of it still exists, -- simply gives the headings.
5. The exact story to which this episode refers in summary is not to be determined, but the following account of it is reasonable and has good support among scholars. Finn, a Frisian chieftain, who nevertheless has a "castle" outside the Frisian border, marries Hildeburh, a Danish princess; and her brother, Hnaef, with many other Danes, pays Finn a visit. Relations between the two peoples have been strained before. Something starts the old feud anew; and the visitors are attacked in their quarters. Hnaef is killed; so is a son of Hildeburh. Many fall on both sides. Peace is patched up; a stately funeral is held; and the surviving visitors become in a way vassals or liegemen of Finn, going back with him to Frisia. So matters rest a while. Hengest is now leader of the Danes; but he is set upon revenge for his former lord, Hnaef. Probably he is killed in feud; but his clansmen, Guthlaf and Oslaf, gather at their home a force of sturdy Danes, come back to Frisia, storm Finn's stronghold, kill him, and carry back their kinswoman Hildeburh.
6. The "enemies" must be the Frisians.
7. Battlefield. -- Hengest is the "prince's thane," companion of Hnaef. "Folcwald's son" is Finn.
8. That is, Finn would govern in all honor the few Danish warriors who were left, provided, of course, that none of them tried to renew the quarrel or avenge Hnaef their fallen lord. If, again, one of Finn's Frisians began a quarrel, he should die by the sword.
9. Hnaef.
10. The high place chosen for the funeral: see description of Beowulf's funeral-pile at the end of the poem.
11. Wounds.

Footnotes XVII
1. That is, these two Danes, escaping home, had told the story of the attack on Hnaef, the slaying of Hengest, and all the

Danish woes. Collecting a force, they return to Frisia and kill Finn in his home.

2. Nephew to Hrothgar, with whom he subsequently quarrels, and elder cousin to the two young sons of Hrothgar and Wealhtheow, -- their natural guardian in the event of the king's death. There is something finely feminine in this speech of Wealhtheow's, apart from its somewhat irregular and irrelevant sequence of topics. Both she and her lord probably distrust Hrothulf; but she bids the king to be of good cheer, and, turning to the suspect, heaps affectionate assurances on his probity. "My own Hrothulf" will surely not forget these favors and benefits of the past, but will repay them to the orphaned boy.

Footnotes XIX

1. They had laid their arms on the benches near where they slept.

Footnotes XX

1. He surmises presently where she is.
2. The connection is not difficult. The words of mourning, of acute grief, are said; and according to Germanic sequence of thought, inexorable here, the next and only topic is revenge. But is it possible? Hrothgar leads up to his appeal and promise with a skillful and often effective description of the horrors which surround the monster's home and await the attempt of an avenging foe.

Footnotes XXI

1. Hrothgar is probably meant.
2. Meeting place.

Footnotes XXII

1. Kenning for "sword." Hrunting is bewitched, laid under a spell of uselessness, along with all other swords.
2. This brown of swords, evidently meaning burnished, bright, continues to be a favorite adjective in the popular ballads.

Footnotes XXIII

1. After the killing of the monster and Grendel's decapitation.
2. Hrothgar.
3. The blade slowly dissolves in blood-stained drops like icicles.
4. Spear.

Footnotes XXIV

1. That is, "whoever has as wide authority as I have and can remember so far back so many instances of heroism, may well say, as I say, that no better hero ever lived than Beowulf."

Footnotes XXV

1. That is, he is now undefended by conscience from the temptations (shafts) of the devil.
2. Kenning for the sun. -- This is a strange role for the raven. He is the warrior's bird of battle, exults in slaughter and carnage; his joy here is a compliment to the sunrise.

Footnotes XXVI

1. That is, he might or might not see Beowulf again. Old as he was, the latter chance was likely; but he clung to the former, hoping to see his young friend again "and exchange brave words in the hall."

Footnotes XXVII

1. With the speed of the boat.
2. Queen to Hygelac. She is praised by contrast with the antitype, Thryth, just as Beowulf was praised by contrast with Heremod.
3. Kenning for "wife."

Footnotes XXVIII

1. Beowulf gives his uncle the king not mere gossip of his journey, but a statesmanlike forecast of the outcome of certain policies at the Danish court. Talk of interpolation here is absurd. As both Beowulf and Hygelac know, -- and the folk for whom the Beowulf was put together also knew, -- Froda was king of the Heathobards (probably the Langobards, once near neighbors of Angle and Saxon tribes on the continent), and had fallen in fight with the Danes. Hrothgar will set aside this feud by giving his daughter as "peace-weaver" and wife to the young king Ingeld, son of the slain Froda. But Beowulf, on general principles and from his observation of the particular case, foretells trouble. Note:

2. Play of shields, battle. A Danish warrior cuts down Froda in the fight, and takes his sword and armor, leaving them to a son. This son is selected to accompany his mistress, the young princess Freawaru, to her new home when she is Ingeld's queen. Heedlessly he wears the sword of Froda in hall. An old warrior points it out to Ingeld, and eggs him on to vengeance. At his instigation the Dane is killed; but the murderer, afraid of results, and knowing the land, escapes. So the old feud must break out again.

3. That is, their disastrous battle and the slaying of their king.
4. The sword.
5. Beowulf returns to his forecast. Things might well go somewhat as follows, he says; sketches a little tragic story; and with this

prophecy by illustration returns to the tale of his adventure.

    6. Not an actual glove, but a sort of bag.

Footnotes XXIX
    1. Hygelac.
    2. This is generally assumed to mean hides, though the text simply says "seven thousand." A hide in England meant about 120 acres, though "the size of the acre varied."
    3. On the historical raid into Frankish territory between 512 and 520 A.D. The subsequent course of events, as gathered from hints of this epic, is partly told in Scandinavian legend.
    4. The chronology of this epic, as scholars have worked it out, would make Beowulf well over ninety years of age when he fights the dragon. But the fifty years of his reign need not be taken as historical fact.
    5. The text is here hopelessly illegible, and only the general drift of the meaning can be rescued. For one thing, we have the old myth of a dragon who guards hidden treasure. But with this runs the story of some noble, last of his race, who hides all his wealth within this barrow and there chants his farewell to life's glories. After his death the dragon takes possession of the hoard and watches over it. A condemned or banished man, desperate, hides in the barrow, discovers the treasure, and while the dragon sleeps, makes off with a golden beaker or the like, and carries it for propitiation to his master. The dragon discovers the loss and exacts fearful penalty from the people round about.

Footnotes XXXI
    1. Literally "loan-days," days loaned to man.
    2. Chattuarii, a tribe that dwelt along the Rhine, and took part in repelling the raid of (Hygelac) Chocilaicus.
    3. Onla, son of Ongentheow, who pursues his two nephews Eanmund and Eadgils to Heardred's court, where they have taken refuge after their unsuccessful rebellion. In the fighting Heardred is killed.

Footnotes XXXII
    1. That is, Beowulf supports Eadgils against Onela, who is slain by Eadgils in revenge for the "care-paths" of exile into which Onela forced him.
    2. That is, the king could claim no wergild, or man-price, from one son for the killing of the other.
    3. Usual euphemism for death
    4. Sc. in the grave.

Footnotes XXXIII
    1. Eofor for Wulf. -- The immediate provocation for Eofor in killing "the hoary Scylfing," Ongentheow, is that the latter has just struck Wulf down; but the king, Haethcyn, is also avenged by the blow. See the detailed description below.
    2. Hygelac.
    3. Shield.
    4. The hollow passage.

Footnotes XXXIV
    1. That is, although Eanmund was brother's son to Onela, the slaying of the former by Weohstan is not felt as cause of feud, and is rewarded by gift of the slain man's weapons.
    2. Both Wiglaf and the sword did their duty. -- The following is one of the classic passages for illustrating the comitatus as the most conspicuous Germanic institution, and its underlying sense of duty, based partly on the idea of loyalty and partly on the practical basis of benefits received and repaid.
    3. Sc. "than to bide safely here," -- a common figure of incomplete comparison.
    4. Wiglaf's wooden shield.
    5. Gering would translate "kinsman of the nail," as both are made of iron.

Footnotes XXXV
    1. That is, swords.

Footnotes XXXVI
    1. Where Beowulf lay.

Footnotes XXXVII
    1. What had been left or made by the hammer; well-forged.
    2. Trying to revive him.

Footnotes XXXVIII
    1. Nothing.
    2. Dead.
    3. Death-watch, guard of honor, "lyke-wake."
    4. A name for the Franks.
    5. Ongentheow.
    6. Haethcyn.

Footnotes XXXIX
    1. The line may mean: till Hrethelings stormed on the hedged shields, -- i.e. the shield-wall or hedge of defensive war -- Hrethelings, of course, are Geats.
    2. Eofor, brother to Wulf Wonreding.
    3. Sc. "value in" hides and the weight of the gold.
    4. Not at all.
    5. Laid on it when it was put in the barrow. This spell, or in our days the "curse,"

either prevented discovery or brought dire ills on the finder and taker.

Footnotes XL

1. Probably the fugitive is meant who discovered the hoard. Ten Brink and Gering assume that the dragon is meant. "Hid" may well mean here "took while in hiding."

2. That is "one and a few others." But Beowulf seems to be indicated.

3. Ten Brink points out the strongly heathen character of this part of the epic. Beowulf's end came, so the old tradition ran, from his unwitting interference with spell-bound treasure.

4. A hard saying, variously interpreted. In any case, it is the somewhat clumsy effort of the Christian poet to tone down the heathenism of his material by an edifying observation.

Footnotes XLI

1. Nothing is said of Beowulf's wife in the poem, but Bugge surmises that Beowulf finally accepted Hygd's offer of kingdom and hoard, and, as was usual, took her into the bargain.

THE TALE OF BEOWULF
Sometime King of the Folk of the Weder Geats
Translated by WILLIAM MORRIS and A. J. WYATT

ARGUMENT

Hrothgar, king of the Danes, lives happily and peacefully, and bethinks him to build a glorious hall called Hart. But a little after, one Grendel, of the kindred of the evil wights that are come of Cain, hears the merry noise of Hart and cannot abide it; so he enters thereinto by night, and slays and carries off and devours thirty of Hrothgar's thanes. Thereby he makes Hart waste for twelve years, and the tidings of this mishap are borne wide about lands. Then comes to the helping of Hrothgar Beowulf, the son of Ecgtheow, a thane of King Hygelac of the Geats, with fourteen fellows. They are met on the shore by the land-warder, and by him shown to Hart and the stead of Hrothgar, who receives them gladly, and to whom Beowulf tells his errand, that he will help him against Grendel. They feast in the hall, and one Unferth, son of Ecglaf, taunts Beowulf through jealousy that he was outdone by Breca in swimming. Beowulf tells the true tale thereof. And a little after, at nightfall, Hrothgar and his folk leave the hall Hart, and it is given in charge to Beowulf, who with his Geats abides there the coming of Grendel.

Soon comes Grendel to the hall, and slays a man of the Geats, hight Handshoe, and then grapples with Beowulf, who will use no weapon against him: Grendel feels himself over-mastered and makes for the door, and gets out, but leaves his hand and arm behind him with Beowulf: men on the wall hear the great noise of this battle and the wailing of Grendel. In the morning the Danes rejoice, and follow the bloody slot of Grendel, and return to Hart racing and telling old tales, as of Sigemund and the Worm. Then come the king and his thanes to look on the token of victory, Grendel's hand and arm, which Beowulf has let fasten: to the hall-gable.

The king praises Beowulf and rewards him, and they feast in Hart, and the tale of Finn and Hengest is told. Then Hrothgar leaves Hart, and so does Beowulf also with his Geats, but the Danes keep guard there.

In the night comes in Grendel's Mother, and catches up Aeschere, a thane of Hrothgar, and carries him off to her lair. In the morning is Beowulf fetched to Hrothgar, who tells him of this new grief and craves his help.

Then they follow up the slot and come to a great water-side, and find thereby Aeschere's head, and the place is known for the lair of those two: monsters are playing in the deep, and Beowulf shoots one of them to death. Then Beowulf dights him and leaps into the water, and is a day's while reaching the bottom. There he is straightway caught hold of by Grendel's Mother, who bears him into her hall. When he gets free he falls on her, but the edge of the sword Hrunting (lent to him by Unferth) fails him, and she casts him to the ground and draws her sax to slay him; but he rises up, and sees an old sword of the giants hanging on the wall; he takes it and smites off her head therewith. He sees Grendel lying dead, and his head also he strikes off; but the blade of the sword is molten in his venomous blood. Then Beowulf strikes upward, taking with him the head of Grendel and the hilts of the sword. When he comes to the shore he finds his Geats there alone; for the Danes fled when they saw the blood floating in the water.

They go up to Hrothgar's stead, and four men must needs bear the head. They come to Hrothgar, and Beowulf gives him the hilts and tells him what he has done. Much praise is given to Beowulf; and they feast together.

On the morrow Beowulf bids farewell to Hrothgar, more gifts are given, and messages are sent to Hygelac: Beowulf departs with the full love of Hrothgar. The Geats come to their ship and reward the ship-warder, and put off and sail to their own land. Beowulf comes to Hygelac's house. Hygelac is told of, and his wife Hygd, and her good conditions, against whom is set as a warning the evil Queen Thrytho.

Beowulf tells all the tale of his doings in full to Hygelac, and gives him his gifts, and the precious-gemmed collar to Hygd. Here is told of Beowulf, and how he was contemned in his youth, and is now grown so renowned.

Time wears; Hygelac is slain in battle; Heardred, his son, reigns in his stead, he is slain by the Swedes, and Beowulf is made king. When he is grown old, and has been king for fifty years, come new tidings. A great dragon finds on the sea-shore a mound wherein is stored the treasure of ancient folk departed. The said dragon abides there, and broods the gold for 300 years.

Now a certain thrall, who had misdone against his lord and was fleeing from his wrath, haps on the said treasure and takes a cup thence, which he brings to his lord to appease his wrath. The Worm waketh, and findeth his treasure lessened, but can find no man who hath done the deed. Therefore he turns on the folk, and wars on them, and burns Beowulf's house.

Now Beowulf will go and meet the Worm. He has an iron shield made, and sets forth with eleven men and the thrall the thirteenth. He comes to the ness, and speaks to his men, telling them of his past days, and gives them his last greeting: then he cries out a challenge to the Worm, who comes forth, and the battle begins: Beowulf's sword will not bite on the Worm. Wiglaf eggs on the others to come to Beowulf's help, and goes himself straightway, and offers himself to Beowulf; the Worm comes on again, and Beowulf breaks his sword Nægling on him, and the Worm wounds Beowulf. Wiglaf smites the Worm in the belly; Beowulf draws his ax, and between them they slay the Worm.

Beowulf now feels his wounds, and knows that he is hurt deadly; he sits down by the wall, and Wiglaf bathes his wounds. Beowulf speaks, tells how he would give his armour to his son if he had one; thanks God that he has not sworn falsely or done guilefully; and prays Wiglaf to bear out the treasure that he may see it before he dies.

Wiglaf fetches out the treasure, and again bathes Beowulf's wounds; Beowulf speaks again, rejoices over the sight of the treasure; gives to Wiglaf his ring and his armour, and bids the manner of his bale-fire. With that he passes away. Now the dastards come thereto and find Wiglaf vainly bathing his dead lord. He casteth shame upon them with great wrath. Thence he sends a messenger to the barriers of the town, who comes to the host, and tells them of the death of Beowulf. He tells withal of the old feud betwixt the Geats and the Swedes, and how these, when they hear of the death of the king, will be upon them. The warriors go to look on Beowulf, and find him and the Worm lying dead together. Wiglaf chooses out seven of them to go void the treasure-house, after having bidden them gather wood for the bale-fire. They shove the Worm over the cliff into the sea, and bear off the treasure in wains. Then they bring Beowulf's corpse to bale, and they kindle it; a woman called the wife of aforetime, it may be Hygd, widow of Hygelac, bemoans him: and twelve children of the athelings ride round the bale, and bemoan Beowulf and praise him: and thus ends the poem.

THE STORY OF BEOWULF

I - AND FIRST OF THE KINDRED OF HROTHGAR

What! we of the Spear-Danes of yore days, so was it
That we learn'd of the fair fame of kings of the folks
And the athelings a-faring in framing of valour.
Oft then Scyld the Sheaf-son from the hosts of the scathers,
From kindreds a many the mead-settles tore;
It was then the earl fear'd them, sithence was he first
Found bare and all-lacking; so solace he bided,
Wax'd under the welkin in worship to thrive,
Until it was so that the round-about sitters
All over the whale-road must hearken his will
And yield him the tribute. A good king was that,
By whom then thereafter a son was begotten,
A youngling in garth, whom the great God sent thither
To foster the folk; and their crime-need he felt
The load that lay on them while lordless they lived
For a long while and long. He therefore, the Life-lord,
The Wielder of glory, world's worship he gave him:
Brim Beowulf waxed, and wide the weal upsprang
Of the offspring of Scyld in the parts of the Scede-lands.
Such wise shall a youngling with wealth be a-working
With goodly fee-gifts toward the friends of his father,
That after in eld-days shall ever bide with him,
Fair fellows well-willing when wendeth the war-tide,
Their lief lord a-serving. By praise-deeds it shall be
That in each and all kindreds a man shall have thriving.
Then went his ways Scyld when the shapen while was,
All hardy to wend him to the lord and his warding:
Out then did they bear him to the side of the sea-flood,
The dear fellows of him, as he himself pray'd them
While yet his word wielded the friend of the Scyldings,
The dear lord of the land; a long while had he own'd it.
With stem all be-ringed at the hythe stood the ship,
All icy and out-fain, the Atheling's ferry.
There then did they lay him, the lord well beloved,
The gold-rings' bestower, within the ship's barm,
The mighty by mast. Much there was the treasure,
From far ways forsooth had the fret-work been led:
Never heard I of keel that was comelier dighted
With weapons of war, and with weed of the battle,
With bills and with byrnies. There lay in his barm

Much wealth of the treasure that with him should be,
And he into the flood's might afar to depart.
No lesser a whit were the wealth-goods they dight him
Of the goods of the folk, than did they who aforetime,
When was the beginning, first sent him away
Alone o'er the billows, and he but a youngling.
Moreover they set him up there a sign golden
High up overhead, and let the holm bear him,
Gave all to the Spearman. Sad mind they had in them,
And mourning their mood was. Now never knew men,
For sooth how to say it, rede-masters in hall,
Or heroes 'neath heaven, to whose hands came the lading.

II - CONCERNING HROTHGAR, AND HOW HE BUILT THE HOUSE CALLED HART. ALSO GRENDEL IS TOLD OF

In the burgs then was biding Beowulf the Scylding,
Dear King of the people, for long was he dwelling
Far-famed of folks (his father turn'd elsewhere,
From his stead the Chief wended) till awoke to him after
Healfdene the high, and long while he held it,
Ancient and war-eager, o'er the glad Scyldings:
Of his body four bairns are forth to him rimed;
Into the world woke the leader of war-hosts
Heorogar; eke Hrothgar, and Halga the good;
Heard I that Elan queen was she of Ongentheow,
That Scylding of battle, the bed-mate behalsed.
Then was unto Hrothgar the war-speed given,
Such worship of war that his kin and well-willers
Well hearken'd his will till the younglings were waxen,
A kin-host a many. Then into his mind ran
That he would be building for him now a hall-house,
That men should be making a mead-hall more mighty
Than the children of ages had ever heard tell of:
And there within eke should he be out-dealing
To young and to old all things God had given,
Save the share of the folk and the life-days of men.
Then heard I that widely the work was a-banning
To kindreds a many the Middle-garth over
To fret o'er that folk-stead. So befell to him timely
Right soon among men that made was it yarely
The most of hall-houses, and Hart its name shap'd he,
Who wielded his word full widely around.
His behest he belied not; it was he dealt the rings,
The wealth at the high-tide. Then up rose the hall-house,
High up and horn-gabled. Hot surges it bided
Of fire-flame the loathly, nor long was it thenceforth
Ere sorely the edge-hate 'twixt Son and Wife's Father
After the slaughter-strife there should awaken.

Then the ghost heavy-strong bore with it hardly
E'en for a while of time, bider in darkness,
That there on each day of days heard he the mirth-tide
Loud in the hall-house. There was the harp's voice,
And clear song of shaper. Said he who could it
To tell the first fashion of men from aforetime;
Quoth how the Almighty One made the Earth's fashion,
The fair field and bright midst the bow of the Waters,
And with victory beglory'd set Sun and Moon,
Bright beams to enlighten the biders on land:
And how he adorned all parts of the earth
With limbs and with leaves; and life withal shaped
For the kindred of each thing that quick on earth wendeth.
So liv'd on all happy the host of the kinsmen
In game and in glee, until one wight began,
A fiend out of hell-pit, the framing of evil,
And Grendel forsooth the grim guest was hight,
The mighty mark-strider, the holder of moorland,
The fen and the fastness. The stead of the fifel
That wight all unhappy a while of time warded,
Sithence that the Shaper him had for-written.
On the kindred of Cain the Lord living ever
Awreaked the murder of the slaying of Abel.
In that feud he rejoic'd not, but afar him He banish'd,
The Maker, from mankind for the crime he had wrought.
But offspring uncouth thence were they awoken
Eotens and elf-wights, and ogres of ocean,
And therewith the Giants, who won war against God
A long while; but He gave them their wages therefor.

III - HOW GRENDEL FELL UPON HART AND WASTED IT

Now went he a-spying, when come was the night-tide,
The house on high builded, and how there the Ring-Danes
Their beer-drinking over had boune them to bed;
And therein he found them, the atheling fellows,
Asleep after feasting. Then sorrow they knew not
Nor the woe of mankind: but the wight of wealth's waning,
The grim and the greedy, soon yare was he gotten,
All furious and fierce, and he raught up from resting
A thirty of thanes, and thence aback got him
Right fain of his gettings, and homeward to fare,
Fulfilled of slaughter his stead to go look on.
Thereafter at dawning, when day was yet early,
The war-craft of Grendel to men grew unhidden,
And after his meal was the weeping uphoven,
Mickle voice of the morning-tide: there the Prince mighty,
The Atheling exceeding good, unblithe he sat,
Tholing the heavy woe; thane-sorrow dreed he
Since the slot of the loathly wight there they had look'd on,

The ghost all accursed. O'er grisly the strife was,
So loathly and longsome. No longer the frist was
But after the wearing of one night; then fram'd he
Murder-bales more yet, and nowise he mourned
The feud and the crime; over fast therein was he.
Then easy to find was the man who would elsewhere
Seek out for himself a rest was more roomsome,
Beds end-long the bowers, when beacon'd to him was,
And soothly out told by manifest token,
The hate of the hell-thane. He held himself sithence
Further and faster who from the fiend gat him.
In such wise he rul'd it and wrought against right,
But one against all, until idle was standing
The best of hall-houses; and mickle the while was,
Twelve winter-tides' wearing; and trouble he tholed,
That friend of the Scyldings, of woes every one
And wide-spreading sorrows: for sithence it fell
That unto men's children unbidden 'twas known
Full sadly in singing, that Grendel won war
'Gainst Hrothgar a while of time, hate-envy waging,
And crime-guilts and feud for seasons no few,
And strife without stinting. For the sake of no kindness
Unto any of men of the main-host of Dane-folk
Would he thrust off the life-bale, or by fee-gild allay it,
Nor was there a wise man that needed to ween
The bright boot to have at the hand of the slayer.
The monster the fell one afflicted them sorely,
That death-shadow darksome the doughty and youthful
Enfettered, ensnared; night by night was he faring
The moorlands the misty. But never know men
Of spell-workers of Hell to and fro where they wander.
So crime-guilts a many the foeman of mankind,
The fell alone-farer, fram'd oft and full often,
Cruel hard shames and wrongful, and Hart he abode in,
The treasure-stain'd hall, in the dark of the night-tide;
But never the gift-stool therein might he greet,
The treasure before the Creator he trow'd not.
Mickle wrack was it soothly for the friend of the Scyldings,
Yea heart and mood breaking. Now sat there a many
Of the mighty in rune, and won them the rede
Of what thing for the strong-soul'd were best of all things
Which yet they might frame 'gainst the fear and the horror.
And whiles they behight them at the shrines of the heathen
To worship the idols; and pray'd they in words,
That he, the ghost-slayer, would frame for them helping
'Gainst the folk-threats and evil So far'd they their wont,
The hope of the heathen; nor hell they remember'd
In mood and in mind. And the Maker they knew not,
The Doomer of deeds: nor of God the Lord wist they,

Nor the Helm of the Heavens knew aught how to hery,
The Wielder of Glory. Woe worth unto that man
Who through hatred the baneful his soul shall shove into
The fire's embrace; nought of fostering weens he,
Nor of changing one whit. But well is he soothly
That after the death-day shall seek to the Lord,
In the breast of the Father all peace ever craving.

IV - NOW COMES BEOWULF ECGTHEOW'S SON TO THE LAND OF THE DANES, AND THE WALL-WARDEN SPEAKETH WITH HIM

So care that was time-long the kinsman of Healfdene
Still seeth'd without ceasing, nor might the wise warrior
Wend otherwhere woe, for o'er strong was the strife
All loathly so longsome late laid on the people,
Need-wrack and grim nithing, of night-bales the greatest.
Now that from his home heard the Hygelac's thane,
Good midst of the Geat-folk; of Grendel's deeds heard he.
But he was of mankind of might and main mightiest
In the day that we tell of, the day of this life,
All noble, strong-waxen. He bade a wave-wearer
Right good to be gear'd him, and quoth he that the war-king
Over the swan-road he would be seeking,
The folk-lord far-famed, since lack of men had he.
Forsooth of that faring the carles wiser-fashion'd
Laid little blame on him, though lief to them was he;
The heart-hardy whetted they, heeded the omen.
There had the good one, e'en he of the Geat-folk,
Champions out-chosen of them that he keenest
Might find for his needs; and he then the fifteenth,
Sought to the sound-wood. A swain thereon show'd him,
A sea-crafty man, all the make of the land-marks.
Wore then a while, on the waves was the floater,
The boat under the berg, and yare then the warriors
Strode up on the stem; the streams were a-winding
The sea 'gainst the sands. Upbore the swains then
Up into the bark's barm the bright-fretted weapons,
The war-array stately; then out the lads shov'd her,
The folk on the welcome way shov'd out the wood-bound.
Then by the wind driven out o'er the wave-holm
Far'd the foamy-neck'd floater most like to a fowl,
Till when was the same tide of the second day's wearing
The wound-about-stemm'd one had waded her way,
So that then they that sail'd her had sight of the land,
Bleak shine of the sea-cliffs, bergs steep up above,
Sea-nesses wide reaching; the sound was won over,
The sea-way was ended: then up ashore swiftly
The band of the Weder-folk up on earth wended;
They bound up the sea-wood, their sarks on them rattled,

Their weed of the battle, and God there they thanked
For that easy the wave-ways were waxen unto them.
But now from the wall saw the Scylding-folks' warder,
E'en he whom the holm-cliffs should ever be holding,
Men bear o'er the gangway the bright shields a-shining,
Folk-host gear all ready. Then mind-longing wore him,
And stirr'd up his mood to wot who were the men-folk.
So shoreward down far'd he his fair steed a-riding,
Hrothgar's Thane, and full strongly then set he a-quaking
The stark wood in his hands, and in council-speech speer'd he:
What men be ye then of them that have war-gear,
With byrnies bewarded, who the keel high up-builded
Over the Lake-street thus have come leading.
Hither o'er holm-ways hieing in ring-stem?
End-sitter was I, a-holding the sea-ward,
That the land of the Dane-folk none of the loathly
Faring with ship-horde ever might scathe it.
None yet have been seeking more openly hither
Of shield-havers than ye, and ye of the leave-word
Of the framers of war naught at all wotting,
Or the manners of kinsmen. But no man of earls greater
Saw I ever on earth than one of you yonder,
The warrior in war-gear: no hall-man, so ween I,
Is that weapon-beworthy'd, but his visage belie him,
The sight seen once only. Now I must be wotting
The spring of your kindred ere further ye cast ye,
And let loose your false spies in the Dane-land a-faring
Yet further afield. So now, ye far-dwellers,
Ye wenders o'er sea-flood, this word do ye hearken
Of my one-folded thought: and haste is the handiest
To do me to wit of whence is your coming.

V - HERE BEOWULF MAKES ANSWER TO THE LAND-WARDEN, WHO SHOWETH HIM THE WAY TO THE KING'S ABODE

He then that was chiefest in thus wise he answer'd,
The war-fellows' leader unlock'd he the word-hoard:
We be a people of the Weder-Geats' man-kin
And of Hygelac be we the hearth-fellows soothly.
My father before me of folks was well-famed
Van-leader and atheling, Ecgtheow he hight.
Many winters abode he, and on the way wended
An old man from the garths, and him well remembers
Every wise man well nigh wide yond o'er the earth.
Through our lief mood and friendly the lord that is thine,
Even Healfdene's son, are we now come a-seeking,
Thy warder of folk. Learn us well with thy leading,
For we have to the mighty an errand full mickle,

Beowulf: Scholar's Edition

To the lord of the Dane-folk: naught dark shall it be,
That ween I full surely. If it be so thou wottest,
As soothly for our parts we now have heard say,
That one midst of the Scyldings, who of scathers I wot not,
A deed-hater secret, in the dark of the night-tide
Setteth forth through the terror the malice untold of,
The shame-wrong and slaughter. I therefore to Hrothgar
Through my mind fashion'd roomsome the rede may now learn him,
How he, old-wise and good, may get the fiend under,
If once more from him awayward may turn
The business of bales, and the boot come again,
And the weltering of care wax cooler once more;
Or for ever sithence time of stress he shall thole,
The need and the wronging, the while yet there abideth
On the high stead aloft the best of all houses.
Then spake out the warden on steed there a-sitting,
The servant all un-fear'd: It shall be of either
That the shield-warrior sharp the sundering wotteth,
Of words and of works, if he think thereof well.
I hear it thus said that this host here is friendly
To the lord of the Scyldings; forth fare ye then, bearing
Your weed and your weapons, of the way will I wise you;
Likewise mine own kinsmen I will now be bidding
Against every foeman your floater before us,
Your craft but new-tarred, the keel on the sand,
With honour to hold, until back shall be bearing
Over the lake-streams this one, the lief man,
The wood of the wounden-neck back unto Wedermark.
Unto such shall be granted amongst the good-doers
To win the way out all whole from the war-race.
Then boun they to faring, the bark biding quiet;
Hung upon hawser the wide-fathom'd ship
Fast at her anchor. Forth shone the boar-shapes
Over the check-guards golden adorned,
Fair-shifting, fire-hard; ward held the farrow.
Snorted the war-moody, hasten'd the warriors
And trod down together until the hall timbered,
Stately and gold-bestain'd, gat they to look on,
That was the all-mightiest unto earth's dwellers
Of halls 'neath the heavens, wherein bode the mighty;
Glisten'd the gleam thereof o'er lands a many.
Unto them then the war-deer the court of the proud one
Full clearly betaught it, that they therewithal
Might wend their ways thither. Then he of the warriors
Round wended his steed, and spake a word backward:
Time now for my faring; but the Father All-wielder
May He with all helping henceforward so hold you
All whole in your wayfaring. Will I to sea-side
Against the wroth folk to hold warding ever.

VI - BEOWULF AND THE GEATS COME INTO HART

Stone-diverse the street was, straight uplong the path led
The warriors together. There shone the war-byrny
The hard and the hand-lock'd; the ring-iron sheer
Sang over their war-gear, when they to the hall first
In their gear the all-fearful had gat them to ganging.
So then the sea-weary their wide shields set down,
Their war-rounds the mighty, against the hall's wall.
Then bow'd they to bench, and rang there the byrnies,
The war-weed of warriors, and up-stood the spears,
The war-gear of the sea-folk all gather'd together.
The ash-holt grey-headed; that host of the iron
With weapons was worshipful. There then a proud chief
Of those lads of the battle speer'd after their line:
Whence ferry ye then the shields golden-faced,
The grey sarks therewith, and the helms all bevisor'd,
And a heap of the war-shafts? Now am I of Hrothgar
The man and the messenger: ne'er saw I of aliens
So many of men more might-like of mood.
I ween that for pride-sake, no wise for wrack-wending
But for high might of mind, ye to Hrothgar have sought.
Unto him then the heart-hardy answer'd and spake,
The proud earl of the Weders the word gave aback,
The hardy neath helm: Now of Hygelac are we
The board-fellows; Beowulf e'en is my name,
And word will I say unto Healfdene's son,
To the mighty, the folk-lord, what errand is mine,
Yea unto thy lord, if to us he will grant it
That him, who so good is, anon we may greet.
Spake Wulfgar the word, a lord of the Wendels,
And the mood of his heart of a many was kenned,
His war and his wisdom: I therefore the Danes' friend
Will lightly be asking, of the lord of the Scyldings,
The dealer of rings, since the boon thou art bidding,
The mighty folk-lord, concerning thine errand,
And swiftly the answer shall do thee to wit
Which the good one to give thee aback may deem meetest.
Then turn'd he in haste to where Hrothgar was sitting
Right old and all hoary mid the host of his earl-folk:
Went the valour-stark; stood he the shoulders before
Of the Dane-lord: well could he the doughty ones' custom.
So Wulfgar spake forth to his lord the well-friendly:
Hither are ferry'd now, come from afar off
O'er the field of the ocean, a folk of the Geats;
These men of the battle e'en Beowulf name they
Their elder and chiefest, and to thee are they bidding
That they, O dear lord, with thee may be dealing
In word against word. Now win them no naysay
Of thy speech again-given, O Hrothgar the glad-man:

For they in their war-gear, methinketh, be worthy
Of good deeming of earls; and forsooth naught but doughty
Is he who hath led o'er the warriors hither.

VII - BEOWULF SPEAKETH WITH HROTHGAR, AND TELLETH HOW HE WILL MEET GRENDEL

Word then gave out Hrothgar the helm of the Scyldings:
I knew him in sooth when he was but a youngling,
And his father, the old man, was Ecgtheow hight;
Unto whom at his home gave Hrethel the Geat-lord
His one only daughter; and now hath his offspring
All hardy come hither a lief lord to seek him.
For that word they spake then, the sea-faring men,
E'en they who the gift-seat for the Geat-folk had ferry'd,
Brought thither for thanks, that of thirty of menfolk
The craft of might hath he within his own handgrip,
That war-strong of men. Now him holy God
For kind help hath sent off here even to us,
We men of the West Danes, as now I have weening,
'Gainst the terror of Grendel. So I to that good one
For his mighty mood-daring shall the dear treasure bid.
Haste now and be speedy, and bid them in straightway,
The kindred-band gather'd together, to see us,
And in words say thou eke that they be well comen
To the folk of the Danes. To the door of the hall then
Went Wulfgar, and words withinward he flitted:
He bade me to say you, my lord of fair battle,
The elder of East-Danes, that he your blood knoweth,
And that unto him are ye the sea-surges over,
Ye lads hardy-hearted, well come to land hither;
And now may ye wend you all in war-raiment
Under the battle-mask Hrothgar to see.
But here let your battle-boards yet be abiding,
With your war-weed and slaughter-shafts, issue of words.
Then rose up the rich one, much warriors around him,
Chosen heap of the thanes, but there some abided
The war-gear to hold, as the wight one was bidding.
Swift went they together, as the warrior there led them,
Under Hart's roof: went the stout-hearted,
The hardy neath helm, till he stood by the high-seat.
Then Beowulf spake out, on him shone the byrny,
His war-net besown by the wiles of the smith:
Hail to thee, Hrothgar! I am of Hygelac
Kinsman and folk-thane; fair deeds have I many
Begun in my youth-tide, and this matter of Grendel
On the turf of mine own land undarkly I knew.
'Tis the seafarers' say that standeth this hall,
The best house forsooth, for each one of warriors
All idle and useless, after the even-light

Under the heaven-loft hidden becometh.
Then lightly they learn'd me, my people, this lore,
E'en the best that there be of the wise of the churls,
O Hrothgar the kingly, that thee should I seek to,
Whereas of the might of my craft were they cunning;
For they saw me when came I from out of my wargear,
Blood-stain'd from the foe whenas five had I bounden,
Quell'd the kin of the eotens, and in the wave slain
The nicors by night-tide: strait need then I bore,
Wreak'd the grief of the Weders, the woe they had gotten;
I ground down the wrathful; and now against Grendel
I here with the dread one alone shall be dooming,
In Thing with the giant. I now then with thee,
O lord of the bright Danes, will fall to my bidding,
O berg of Scyldings, and bid thee one boon,
Which, O refuge of warriors, gainsay me not now,
Since, O free friend of folks, from afar have I come,
That I alone, I and my band of the earls,
This hard heap of men, may cleanse Hart of ill.
This eke have I heard say, that he, the fell monster,
In his wan-heed recks nothing of weapons of war;
Forgo I this therefore (if so be that Hygelac
Will still be my man-lord, and he blithe of mood)
To bear the sword with me, or bear the broad shield,
Yellow-round to the battle; but with naught save the hand-grip
With the foe shall I grapple, and grope for the life
The loathly with loathly. There he shall believe
In the doom of the Lord whom death then shall take.
Now ween I that he, if he may wield matters,
E'en there in the war-hall the folk of the Geats
Shall eat up unafear'd, as oft he hath done it
With the might of the Hrethmen: no need for thee therefore
My head to be hiding; for me will he have
With gore all bestain'd, if the death of men get me;
He will bear off my bloody corpse minded to taste it;
Unmournfully then will the Lone-goer eat it,
Will blood-mark the moor-ways; for the meat of my body
Naught needest thou henceforth in any wise grieve thee.
But send thou to Hygelac, if the war have me,
The best of all war-shrouds that now my breast wardeth,
The goodliest of railings, the good gift of Hrethel,
The hand-work of Weland. Weird wends as she willeth.

VIII - HROTHGAR ANSWERETH BEOWULF AND BIDDETH HIM SIT TO THE FEAST

Spake out then Hrothgar the helm of the Scyldings:
Thou Beowulf, friend mine, for battle that wardeth
And for help that is kindly hast sought to us hither.

Beowulf: Scholar's Edition

Fought down thy father the most of all feuds;
To Heatholaf was he forsooth for a hand-bane
Amidst of the Wylfings. The folk of the Weders
Him for the war-dread that while might not hold.
So thence did he seek to the folk of the South-Danes
O'er the waves' wallow, to the Scyldings be-worshipped.
Then first was I wielding the weal of the Dane-folk,
That time was I holding in youth-tide the gem-rich
Hoard-burg of the heroes. Dead then was Heorogar,
Mine elder of brethren; unliving was he,
The Healfdene's bairn that was better than I.
That feud then thereafter with fee did I settle;
I sent to the Wylfing folk over the waters' back
Treasures of old time; he swore the oaths to me.
Sorrow is in my mind that needs must I say it
To any of grooms, of Grendel what hath he
Of shaming in Hart, and he with his hate-wiles
Of sudden harms framed; the host of my hall-floor,
The war-heap, is waned; Weird swept them away
Into horror of Grendel. It is God now that may lightly
The scather the doltish from deeds thrust aside.
Full oft have they boasted with beer well bedrunken,
My men of the battle all over the ale-stoup,
That they in the beer-hall would yet be abiding
The onset of Grendel with the terror of edges.
But then was this mead-hall in the tide of the morning,
This warrior-hall, gore-stain'd when day at last gleamed,
All the boards of the benches with blood besteam'd over,
The hall laid with sword-gore: of lieges less had I
Of dear and of doughty, for them death had gotten.
Now sit thou to feast and unbind thy mood freely,
Thy war-fame unto men as the mind of thee whetteth.
Then was for the Geat-folk and them all together
There in the beer-hall a bench bedight roomsome,
There the stout-hearted hied them to sitting
Proud in their might: a thane minded the service,
Who in hand upbare an ale-stoup adorned,
Skinked the sheer mead; whiles sang the shaper
Clear out in Hart-hall; joy was of warriors,
Men doughty no little of Danes and of Weders.

IX - UNFERTH CONTENDETH IN WORDS WITH BEOWULF

Spake out then Unferth that bairn was of Ecglaf,
And he sat at the feet of the lord of the Scyldings,
He unbound the battle-rune; was Beowulf's faring,
Of him the proud mere-farer, mickle unliking,
Whereas he begrudg'd it of any man other
That he glories more mighty the middle-garth over
Should hold under heaven than he himself held:

Art thou that Beowulf who won strife with Breca
On the wide sea contending in swimming,
When ye two for pride's sake search'd out the floods
And for a dolt's cry into deep water
Thrust both your life-days? No man the twain of you,
Lief or loth were he, might lay wyte to stay you
Your sorrowful journey, when on the sea row'd ye;
Then when the ocean-stream ye with your arms deck'd,
Meted the mere-streets, there your hands brandish'd!
O'er the Spearman ye glided; the sea with waves welter'd,
The surge of the winter. Ye twain in the waves' might
For a seven nights swink'd. He outdid thee in swimming,
And the more was his might; but him in the morn-tide
To the Heatho-Remes' land the holm bore ashore.
And thence away sought he to his dear land and lovely,
The lief to his people sought the land of the Brondings,
The fair burg peace-warding, where he the folk owned,
The burg and the gold rings. What to theeward he boasted,
Beanstan's son, for thee soothly he brought it about.
Now ween I for thee things worser than erewhile,
Though thou in the war-race wert everywhere doughty,
In the grim war, if thou herein Grendel darest
Night-long for a while of time nigh to abide.
Then Beowulf spake out, the Ecgtheow's bairn:
What! thou no few of things, O Unferth my friend,
And thou drunken with beer, about Breca hast spoken,
Saidest out of his journey; so the sooth now I tell:
To wit, that the more might ever I owned,
Hard wearing on wave more than any man else.
We twain then, we quoth it, while yet we were younglings,
And we boasted between us, the twain of us being yet
In our youth-days, that we out onto the Spearman
Our lives would adventure; and e'en so we wrought It.
We had a sword naked, when on the sound row'd we,
Hard in hand, as we twain against the whale-fishes
Had mind to be warding us. No whit from me
In the waves of the sea-flood afar might he float
The hastier in holm, nor would I from him hie me.
Then we two together, we were in the sea
For a five nights, till us twain the flood drave asunder,
The weltering of waves. Then the coldest of weathers
In the dusking of night and the wind from the northward
Battle-grim turn'd against us, rough grown were the billows.
Of the mere-fishes then was the mood all up-stirred;
There me 'gainst the loathly the body-sark mine,
The hard and the hand-lock'd, was framing me help,
My battle-rail braided, it lay on my breast
Gear'd graithly with gold. But me to the ground tugg'd
A foe and fiend-scather; fast he had me In hold

That grim one in grip: yet to me was it given.
That the wretch there, the monster, with point might I reach,
With my bill of the battle, and the war-race off bore
The mighty mere-beast through the hand that was mine.

X - BEOWULF MAKES AN END OF HIS TALE OF THE SWIMMING. WEALHTHEOW, HROTHGAR'S QUEEN, GREETS HIM; AND HROTHGAR DELIVERS TO HIM THE WARDING OF THE HALL

Thus oft and oft over the doers of evil
They threatened me hard; thane-service I did them
With the dear sword of mine, as forsooth it was meet,
That nowise of their fill did they win them the joy
The evil fordoers in swallowing me down,
Sitting round at the feast nigh the ground of the sea.
Yea rather, a morning-tide, mangled by sword-edge
Along the waves' leaving up there did they lie
Lull'd asleep with the sword, so that never sithence
About the deep floods for the farers o'er ocean
The way have they letted. Came the light from the eastward,
The bright beacon of God, and grew the seas calm,
So that the sea-nesses now might I look on,
The windy walls. Thuswise Weird oft will be saving
The earl that is unfey, when his valour availeth.
Whatever, it happ'd me that I with the sword slew
Nicors nine. Never heard I of fighting a night-tide
'Neath the vault of the heavens was harder than that,
Nor yet on the sea-streams of woefuller wight.
Whatever, forth won I with life from the foes' clutch
All of wayfaring weary. But me the sea upbore,
The flood downlong the tide with the weltering of waters,
All onto the Finnland. No whit of thee ever
Mid such strife of the battle-gear have I heard say,
Such terrors of bills. Nor never yet Breca
In the play of the battle, nor both you, nor either,
So dearly the deeds have framed forsooth
With the bright flashing swords; though of this naught I boast me.
But thou of thy brethren the banesman becamest,
Yea thine head-kin forsooth, for which in hell shalt thou
Dree weird of damnation, though doughty thy wit be;
For unto thee say I forsooth, son of Ecglaf,
That so many deeds never Grendel had done,
That monster the loathly, against thine own lord,
The shaming in Hart-hall, if suchwise thy mind were,
And thy soul e'en as battle-fierce, such as thou sayest.
But he, he hath fram'd it that the feud he may heed not,
The fearful edge-onset that is of thy folk,
Nor sore need be fearful of the Victory-Scyldings.
The need-pledges taketh he, no man he spareth

Of the folk of the Danes, driveth war as he lusteth,
Slayeth and feasteth unweening of strife
With them of the Spear-Danes. But I, I shall show it,
The Geats' wightness and might ere the time weareth old,
Shall bide him in war-tide. Then let him go who may go
High-hearted to mead, sithence when the morn-light
O'er the children of men of the second day hence,
The sun clad in heaven's air, shines from the southward.
Then merry of heart was the meter of treasures,
The hoary-man'd war-renown'd, help now he trow'd in;
The lord of the Bright-Danes on Beowulf hearken'd,
The folk-shepherd knew him, his fast-ready mind.
There was laughter of heroes, and high the din rang
And winsome the words were. Went Wealhtheow forth,
The Queen she of Hrothgar, of courtesies mindful,
The gold-array'd greeted the grooms in the hall,
The free and frank woman the beaker there wended,
And first to the East-Dane-folk's fatherland's warder,
And bade him be blithe at the drinking of beer,
To his people beloved, and lustily took he
The feast and the hall-cup, that victory-fam'd King.
Then round about went she, the Dame of the Helmings,
And to doughty and youngsome, each deal of the folk there,
Gave cups of the treasure, till now it betid
That to Beowulf duly the Queen the ring-dighted,
Of mind high uplifted, the mead-beaker bare.
Then she greeted the Geat-lord, and gave God the thank,
She, the wisefast In words, that the will had wax'd in her
In one man of the earls to have trusting and troth
For comfort from crimes. But the cup then he took,
The slaughter-fierce warrior, from Wealhtheow the Queen.
And then rim'd he the word, making ready for war,
And Beowulf spake forth, the Ecgtheow's bairn:
E'en that in mind had I when up on holm strode I,
And in sea-boat sat down with a band of my men,
That for once and for all the will of your people
Would I set me to work, or on slaughter-field cringe
Fast in grip of the fiend; yea and now shall I frame
The valour of earl-folk, or else be abiding
The day of mine end, here down in the mead-hall.
To the wife those his words well liking they were,
The big word of the Geat; and the gold-adorn'd wended,
The frank and free Queen to sit by her lord.
And thereafter within the high hall was as erst
The proud word outspoken and bliss on the people,
Was the sound of the victory-folk, till on a sudden
The Healfdene's son would now be a-seeking
His rest of the even: wotted he for the Evil
Within the high hall was the Hild-play bedight,

Sithence that the sun-light no more should they see,
When night should be darkening, and down over all
The shapes of the shadow-helms should be a-striding
Wan under the welkin. Uprose then all war-folk;
Then greeted the glad-minded one man the other,
Hrothgar to Beowulf, bidding him hail,
And the wine-hall to wield, and withal quoth the word:
Never to any man erst have I given,
Since the hand and the shield's round aloft might I heave,
This high hall of the Dane-folk, save now unto thee.
Have now and hold the best of all houses,
Mind thee of fame, show the might of thy valour!
Wake the wroth one: no lack shall there be to thy willing
If that wight work thou win and life therewithal.

XI - NOW IS BEOWULF LEFT IN THE HALL ALONE WITH HIS MEN

Then wended him Hrothgar with the band of his warriors,
The high-ward of the Scyldings from out of the hall,
For then would the war-lord go seek unto Wealhtheow
The Queen for a bed-mate. The glory of king-folk
Against Grendel had set, as men have heard say,
A hall-ward who held him a service apart
In the house of the Dane-lord, for eoten-ward held he.
Forsooth he, the Geat-lord, full gladly he trowed
In the might of his mood and the grace of the Maker.
Therewith he did off him his byrny of iron
And the helm from his head, and his dighted sword gave,
The best of all irons, to the thane that abode him,
And bade him to hold that harness of battle.
Bespake then the good one, a big word he gave out,
Beowulf the Geat, ere on the bed strode he:
Nowise in war I deem me more lowly
In the works of the battle than Grendel, I ween;
So not with the sword shall I lull him to slumber,
Or take his life thuswise, though to me were it easy;
Of that good wise he wots not, to get the stroke on me,
To hew on my shield, for as stark as he shall be
In the works of the foeman. So we twain a night-tide
Shall forgo the sword, if he dare yet to seek
The war without weapons. Sithence the wise God,
The Lord that is holy, on which hand soever
The glory may doom as due to him seemeth.
Bowed down then the war-deer, the cheek-bolster took
The face of the earl; and about him a many
Of sea-warriors bold to their hall-slumber bow'd them;
No one of them thought that thence away should he
Seek ever again to his home the beloved,
His folk or his free burg, where erst he was fed;

For of men had they learn'd that o'er mickle a many
In that wine-hall aforetime the fell death had gotten
Of the folk of the Danes; but the Lord to them gave it,
To the folk of the Weders, the web of war-speeding,
Help fair and good comfort, e'en so that their foeman
Through the craft of one man all they overcame,
By the self-might of one. So is manifest truth
That God the Almighty the kindred of men
Hath wielded wide ever. Now by wan night there came,
There strode in the shade-goer; slept there the shooters,
They who that horn-house should be a-holding,
All men but one man: to men was that known,
That them indeed might not, since will'd not the Maker,
The scather unceasing drag off 'neath the shadow;
But he ever watching in wrath 'gainst the wroth one
Mood-swollen abided the battle-mote ever.

XII - GRENDEL COMETH INTO HART: OF THE STRIFE BETWIXT HIM AND BEOWULF

Came then from the moor-land, all under the mist-bents,
Grendel a-going there, bearing God's anger.
The scather the ill one was minded of mankind
To have one in his toils from the high hall aloft.
'Neath the welkin he waded, to the place whence the wine-house,
The gold-hall of men, most yarely he wist
With gold-plates fair coloured; nor was it the first time
That he unto Hrothgar's high home had betook him.
Never he in his life-days, either erst or thereafter,
Of warriors more hardy or hall-thanes had found.
Came then to the house the wight on his ways,
Of all joys bereft; and soon sprang the door open,
With fire-bands made fast, when with hand he had touch'd it;
Brake the bale-heedy, he with wrath bollen,
The mouth of the house there, and early thereafter
On the shiny-fleck'd floor thereof trod forth the fiend;
On went he then mood-wroth, and out from his eyes stood
Likest to fire-flame light full unfair.
In the high house beheld he a many of warriors,
A host of men sib all sleeping together,
Of man-warriors a heap; then laugh'd out his mood;
In mind deem'd he to sunder, or ever came day,
The monster, the fell one, from each of the men there
The life from the body; for befell him a boding
Of fulfilment of feeding: but weird now it was not
That he any more of mankind thenceforward
Should eat, that night over. Huge evil beheld then
The Hygelac's kinsman, and how the foul scather
All with his fear-grips would fare there before him;

Beowulf: Scholar's Edition
How never the monster was minded to tarry,
For speedily gat he, and at the first stour,
A warrior a-sleeping, and unaware slit him,
Bit his bone-coffer, drank blood a-streaming,
Great gobbets swallow'd in; thenceforth soon had he
Of the unliving one every whit eaten
To hands and feet even: then forth strode he nigher,
And took hold with his hand upon him the highhearted.
The warrior a-resting; reach'd out to himwards
The fiend with his hand, gat fast on him rathely
With thought of all evil, and besat him his arm.
Then swiftly was finding the herdsman of fouldeeds
That forsooth he had met not in Middle-garth ever,
In the parts of the earth, in any man else
A hand-grip more mighty; then wax'd he of mood
Heart-fearful, but none the more outward might he;
Hence-eager his heart was to the darkness to hie him,
And the devil-dray seek: not there was his service
E'en such as he found in his life-days before.
Then to heart laid the good one, the Hygelac's kinsman,
His speech of the even-tide; uplong he stood
And fast with him grappled, till bursted his fingers.
The eoten was out-fain, but on strode the earl.
The mighty fiend minded was, whereso he might,
To wind him about more widely away thence,
And flee fenwards; he found then the might of his fingers
In the grip of the fierce one; sorry faring was that
Which he, the harm-scather, had taken to Hart.
The warrior-hall dinn'd now; unto all Danes there waxed,
To the castle-abiders, to each of the keen ones,
To all earls, as an ale-dearth. Now angry were both
Of the fierce mighty warriors, far rang out the hall-house;
Then mickle the wonder it was that the wine-hall
Withstood the two war-deer, nor welter'd to earth
The fair earthly dwelling; but all fast was it builded
Within and without with the banding of iron
By crafty thought smithy'd. But there from the sill bow'd
Fell many a mead-bench, by hearsay of mine,
With gold well adorned, where strove they the wrothful.
Hereof never ween'd they, the wise of the Scyldings,
That ever with might should any of men
The excellent, bone-dight, break into pieces,
Or unlock with cunning, save the light fire's embracing
In smoke should it swallow. So uprose the roar
New and enough; now fell on the North-Danes
Ill fear and the terror, on each and on all men,
Of them who from wall-top hearken'd the weeping,
Even God's foeman singing the fear-lay,
The triumphless song, and the wound-bewailing
Of the thrall of the Hell; for there now fast held him

He who of men of main was the mightiest
In that day which is told of, the day of this life.

XIII - BEOWULF HATH THE VICTORY: GRENDEL IS HURT DEADLY AND LEAVETH HAND AND ARM IN THE HALL

Naught would the earls' help for anything thenceforth
That murder-comer yet quick let loose of,
Nor his life-days forsooth to any of folk
Told he for useful. Out then drew full many
Of Beowult's earls the heir-loom of old days,
For their lord and their master's fair life would hey ward,
That mighty of princes, if so might they do it.
For this did they know not when they the strife dreed,
Those hardy-minded men of the battle,
And on every half there thought to be hewing,
And search out his soul, that the ceaseless scather
Not any on earth of the choice of all irons,
Not one of the war-bills, would greet home for ever.
For he had forsworn him from victory-weapons,
And each one of edges. But his sundering of soul
In the days that we tell of, the day of this life,
Should be weary and woeful, the ghost wending elsewhere
To the wielding of fiends to wend him afar.
Then found he out this, he who mickle erst made
Out of mirth of his mood unto children of men
And had fram'd many crimes, he the foeman of God,
That the body of him would not bide to avail him,
But the hardy of mood, even Hygelac's kinsman,
Had him fast by the hand: now was each to the other
All loathly while living: his body-sore bided
The monster: was manifest now on his shoulder
The unceasing wound, sprang the sinews asunder,
The bone-lockers bursted. To Beowulf now
Was the battle-fame given; should Grendel thenceforth
Flee life-sick awayward and under the fen-bents
Seek his unmerry stead: now wist he more surely
That ended his life was, and gone over for ever,
His day-tale told out. But was for all Dane-folk
After that slaughter-race all their will done.
Then had he cleans'd for them, he the far-comer,
Wise and stout-hearted, the high hall of Hrothgar,
And say'd it from war. So the night-work he joy'd in
And his doughty deed done. Yea, but he for the East-Danes
That lord of the Geat-folk his boast's end had gotten,
Withal their woes bygone all had he booted,
And the sorrow hate-fashion'd that afore they had dreed,
And the hard need and bitter that erst they must bear,
The sorrow unlittle. Sithence was clear token

When the deer of the battle laid down there the hand
The arm and the shoulder, and all there together
Of the grip of that Grendel 'neath the great roof upbuilded.

XIV - THE DANES REJOICE; THEY GO TO LOOK ON THE SLOT OF GRENDEL, AND COME BACK TO HART, AND ON THE WAY MAKE MERRY WITH RACING AND THE TELLING OF TALES

There was then on the morning, as I have heard tell it,
Round the gift-hall a many of men of the warriors:
Were faring folk-leaders from far and from near
O'er the wide-away roads the wonder to look on,
The track of the loathly: his life-sundering nowise
Was deem'd for a sorrow to any of men there
Who gaz'd on the track of the gloryless wight;
How he all a-weary of mood thence awayward,
Brought to naught in the battle, to the mere of the nicors,
Now fey and forth-fleeing, his life-steps had flitted.
There all in the blood was the sea-brim a-welling,
The dread swing of the waves was washing all mingled
With hot blood; with the gore of the sword was it welling;
The death-doom'd had dyed it, sithence he unmerry
In his fen-hold had laid down the last of his life,
His soul of the heathen, and hell gat hold on him.
Thence back again far'd they those fellows of old,
With many a young one, from their wayfaring merry,
Full proud from the mere-side on mares there a-riding
The warriors on white steeds. There then was of Beowulf
Set forth the might mighty; oft quoth it a many
That nor northward nor southward beside the twin sea-floods,
Over all the huge earth's face now never another,
Never under the heaven's breadth, was there a better,
Nor of wielders of war-shields a worthier of kingship;
But neither their friendly lord blam'd they one whit,
Hrothgar the glad, for good of kings was he.
There whiles the warriors far-famed let leap
Their fair fallow horses and fare into flyting
Where unto them the earth-ways for fair-fashion'd seemed,
Through their choiceness well kenned; and whiles a king's thane,
A warrior vaunt-laden, of lays grown bemindful,
E'en he who all many of tales of the old days
A multitude minded, found other words also
Sooth-bounden, and boldly the man thus began
E'en Beowulf's wayfare well wisely to stir,
With good speed to set forth the spells well areded
And to shift about words. And well of all told he
That he of Sigemund erst had heard say,
Of the deeds of his might; and many things uncouth:
Of the strife of the Wælsing and his wide wayfarings,

Of those that men's children not well yet they wist,
The feud and the crimes, save Fitela with him;
Somewhat of such things yet would he say,
The eme to the nephew; e'en as they aye were
In all strife soever fellows full needful;
And full many had they of the kin of the eotens
Laid low with the sword. And to Sigemund upsprang
After his death-day fair doom unlittle
Sithence that the war-hard the Worm there had quelled,
The herd of the hoard; he under the hoar stone,
The bairn of the Atheling, all alone dar'd it,
That wight deed of deeds; with him Fitela was not.
But howe'er, his hap was that the sword so through-waded
The Worm the all-wondrous, that in the wall stood
The iron dear-wrought: and the drake died the murder.
There had the warrior so won by wightness,
That he of the ring-hoard the use might be having
All at his own will. The sea-boat he loaded,
And into the ship's barm bore the bright fretwork
Wæls' son. In the hotness the Worm was to-molten.
Now he of all wanderers was widely the greatest
Through the peoples of man-kind, the warder of warriors,
By mighty deeds; erst then and early he throve.
Now sithence the warfare of Heremod waned,
His might and his valour, amidst of the eotens
To the wielding of foemen straight was he betrayed,
And speedily sent forth: by the surges of sorrow
O'er-long was he lam'd, became he to his lieges,
To all of the athelings, a life-care thenceforward.
Withal oft bemoaned in times that were older
The ways of that stout heart many a carle of the wisest,
Who trow'd in him boldly for booting of bales,
And had look'd that the king's bairn should ever be thriving,
His father's own lordship should take, hold the folk,
The hoard and the ward-burg, and realm of the heroes,
The own land of the Scyldings. To all men was Beowulf,
The Hygelac's kinsman to the kindred of menfolk,
More fair unto friends; but on Heremod crime fell.
So whiles the men flyting the fallow street there
With their mares were they meting. There then was the morn-light
Thrust forth and hasten'd; went many a warrior
All hardy of heart to the high hall aloft
The rare wonder to see; and the King's self withal
From the bride-bower wended, the warder of ring-hoards,
All glorious he trod and a mickle troop had he,
He for choice ways beknown; and his Queen therewithal
Meted the mead-path with a meyny of maidens.

XV - KING HROTHGAR AND HIS THANES LOOK ON THE ARM OF GRENDEL. CONVERSE BETWIXT HROTHGAR AND BEOWULF CONCERNING THE BATTLE

Out then spake Hrothgar; for he to the hall went,
By the staple a-standing the steep roof he saw
Shining fair with the gold, and the hand there of Grendel:
For this sight that I see to the All-wielder thanks
Befall now forthwith, for foul evil I bided,
All griefs from this Grendel; but God, glory's Herder,
Wonder on wonder ever can work.
Unyore was it then when I for myself
Might ween never more, wide all through my life-days,
Of the booting of woes; when all blood-besprinkled
The best of all houses stood sword-gory here;
Wide then had the woe thrust off each of the wise
Of them that were looking that never life-long
That land-work of the folk they might ward from the loathly,
From ill wights and devils. But now hath a warrior
Through the might of the Lord a deed made thereunto
Which we, and all we together, in nowise
By wisdom might work. What! well might be saying
That maid whosoever this son brought to birth
According to man's kind, if yet she be living,
That the Maker of old time to her was all-gracious
In the bearing of bairns. O Beowulf, I now
Thee best of all men as a son unto me
Will love in my heart, and hold thou henceforward
Our kinship new-made now; nor to thee shall be lacking
As to longings of world-goods whereof I have wielding;
Full oft I for lesser things guerdon have given,
The worship of hoards, to a warrior was weaker,
A worser in strife. Now thyself for thyself
By deeds hast thou fram'd it that liveth thy fair fame
For ever and ever. So may the All-wielder
With good pay thee ever, as erst he hath done it.
Then Beowulf spake out, the Ecgtheow's bairn:
That work of much might with mickle of love
We framed with fighting, and frowardly ventur'd
The might of the uncouth; now I would that rather
Thou mightest have look'd on the very man there,
The foe in his fret-gear all worn unto falling.
There him in all haste with hard griping did I
On the slaughter-bed deem it to bind him indeed,
That he for my hand-grip should have to be lying
All busy for life: but his body fled off.
Him then, I might not (since would not the Maker)
From his wayfaring sunder, nor naught so well sought I
The life-foe; o'er-mickle of might was he yet,
The foeman afoot: but his hand has he left us,

A life-ward, a-warding the ways of his wending,
His arm and his shoulder therewith. Yet in nowise
That wretch of the grooms any solace hath got him,
Nor longer will live the loathly deed-doer,
Beswinked with sins; for the sore hath him now
In the grip of need grievous, in strait hold togather'd
With bonds that be baleful: there shall he abide,
That wight dyed with all evil-deeds, the doom mickle,
For what wise to him the bright Maker will write it.
Then a silenter man was the son there of Ecglaf
In the speech of the boasting of works of the battle,
After when every atheling by craft of the earl
Over the high roof had look'd on the hand there,
Yea, the fiend's fingers before his own eyen,
Each one of the nail-steads most like unto steel,
Hand-spur of the heathen one; yea, the own claw
Uncouth of the war-wight. But each one there quoth it,
That no iron of the best, of the hardy of folk,
Would touch him at all, which e'er of the monster
The battle-hand bloody might bear away thence.

XVI - HROTHGAR GIVETH GIFTS TO BEOWULF

Then was speedily bidden that Hart be withinward
By hand of man well adorn'd; was there a many
Of warriors and wives, who straightway that wine-house
The guest-house, bedight them: there gold-shotten shone
The webs over the walls, many wonders to look on
For men every one who on such things will stare.
Was that building the bright all broken about
All withinward, though fast in the bands of the iron;
Asunder the hinges rent, only the roof there
Was saved all sound, when the monster of evil
The guilty of crime-deeds had gat him to flight
Never hoping for life. Nay, lightly now may not
That matter be fled from, frame it whoso may frame it.
But by strife man shall win of the bearers of souls,
Of the children of men, compelled by need,
The abiders on earth, the place made all ready,
The stead where his body laid fast on his death-bed
Shall sleep after feast. Now time and place was it
When unto the hall went that Healfdene's son,
And the King himself therein the feast should be sharing;
Never heard I of men-folk in fellowship more
About their wealth-giver so well themselves bearing.
Then bow'd unto bench there the abounders in riches
And were fain of their fill. Full fairly there took
A many of mead-cups the kin of those men,
The sturdy of heart in the hall high aloft,
Hrothgar and Hrothulf. Hart there withinward

Of friends was fulfilled; naught there that was guilesome
The folk of the Scyldings for yet awhile framed.
Gave then to Beowulf Healfdene's bairn
A golden war-ensign, the victory's guerdon,
A staff-banner fair-dight, a helm and a byrny:
The great jewel-sword a many men saw them
Bear forth to the hero. Then Beowulf took
The cup on the floor, and nowise of that fee-gift
Before the shaft-shooters the shame need he have.
Never heard I how friendlier four of the treasures,
All gear'd with the gold about, many men erewhile
On the ale-bench have given to others of men.
Round the roof of the helm, the burg of the head,
A wale wound with wires held ward from without-ward,
So that the file-leavings might not over fiercely,
Were they never so shower-hard, scathe the shield-bold,
When he 'gainst the angry in anger should get him.
Therewith bade the earls' burg that eight of the horses
With cheek-plates adorned be led down the floor
In under the fences; on one thereof stood
A saddle all craft-bedeck'd, seemly with treasure.
That same was the war-seat of the high King full surely
Whenas that the sword-play that Healfdene's son
Would work; never failed in front of the war
The wide-kenn'd one's war-might, whereas fell the slain.
So to Beowulf thereon of either of both
The Ingwines' high warder gave wielding to have,
Both the war-steeds and weapons, and bade him well brook them.
Thuswise and so manly the mighty of princes,
Hoard-warden of heroes, the battle-race paid
With mares and with gems, so as no man shall blame them,
E'en he who will say sooth aright as it is.

XVII - THEY FEAST IN HART. THE GLEEMAN SINGS OF FINN AND HENGEST

Then the lord of the earl-folk to every and each one
Of them who with Beowulf the sea-ways had worn
Then and there on the mead-bench did handsel them treasure,
An heir-loom to wit; for him also he bade it
That a were-gild be paid, whom Grendel aforetime
By wickedness quell'd, as far more of them would he,
Save from them God all-witting the weird away wended,
And that man's mood withal. But the Maker all wielded
Of the kindred of mankind, as yet now he doeth.
Therefore through-witting will be the best everywhere
And the forethought of mind. Many things must abide
Of lief and of loth, he who here a long while
In these days of the strife with the world shall be dealing.
There song was and sound all gather'd together

Of that Healfdene's warrior and wielder of battle,
The wood of glee greeted, the lay wreaked often,
Whenas the hall-game the minstrel of Hrothgar
All down by the mead-bench tale must be making:
By Finn's sons aforetime, when the fear gat them,
The hero of Half-Danes, Hnaef of the Scyldings,
On the slaughter-field Frisian needs must he fall.
Forsooth never Hildeburh needed to hery
The troth of the Eotens; she all unsinning
Was lorne of her lief ones in that play of the linden,
Her bairns and her brethren, by fate there they fell
Spear-wounded. That was the all-woeful of women.
Not unduly without cause the daughter of Hoc
Mourn'd the Maker's own shaping, sithence came the morn
When she under the heavens that tide came to see,
Murder-bale of her kinsmen, where most had she erewhile?
Of world's bliss. The war-tide took all men away
Of Finn's thanes that were, save only a few;
E'en so that he might not on the field of the meeting
Hold Hengest a war-tide, or fight any whit,
Nor yet snatch away thence by war the woe-leavings
From the thane of the King; but terms now they bade him
That for them other stead all for all should make room,
A hall and high settle, whereof the half-wielding
They with the Eotens' bairns henceforth might hold,
And with fee-gifts moreover the son of Folkwalda
Each day of the days the Danes should beworthy;
The war-heap of Hengest with rings should he honour
Even so greatly with treasure of treasures,
Of gold all beplated, as he the kin Frisian
Down in the beer-hall duly should dight.
Troth then they struck there each of the two halves,
A peace-troth full fast. There Finn unto Hengest
Strongly, unstrifeful, with oath-swearing swore,
That he the woe-leaving by the doom of the wise ones
Should hold in ail honour, that never man henceforth
With word or with work the troth should be breaking,
Nor through craft of the guileful should undo it ever,
Though their ring-giver's bane they must follow in rank
All lordless, e'en so need is it to be:
But if any of Frisians by over-bold speaking
The murderful hatred should call unto mind,
Then naught but the edge of the sword should avenge it.
Then done was the oath there, and gold of the golden
Heav'd up from the hoard. Of the bold Here-Scyldings
All yare on the bale was the best battle-warrior;
On the death-howe beholden was easily there
The sark stain'd with war-sweat, the all-golden swine,
The iron-hard boar; there was many an atheling

With wounds all outworn; some on slaughter-field welter'd.
But Hildeburh therewith on Hnæf's bale she bade them
The own son of herself to set fast in the flame,
His bone-vats to burn up and lay on the bale there:
On his shoulder all woeful the woman lamented,
Sang songs of bewailing, as the warrior strode upward,
Wound up to the welkin that most of death-fires,
Before the howe howled; there molten the heads were,
The wound-gates burst open, there blood was out-springing
From foe-bites of the body; the flame swallow'd all,
The greediest of ghosts, of them that war gat him
Of either of folks; shaken off was their life-breath.

XVIII - THE ENDING OF THE TALE OF FINN

Departed the warriors their wicks to visit
All forlorn of their friends now, Friesland to look on,
Their homes and their high burg. Hengest a while yet
Through the slaughter-dyed winter bode dwelling with Finn
And all without strife: he remember'd his homeland,
Though never he might o'er the mere be a-driving
The high prow be-ringed: with storm the holm welter'd,
Won war 'gainst the winds; winter locked the waves
With bondage of ice, till again came another
Of years into the garth, as yet it is ever,
And the days which the season to watch never cease,
The glory-bright weather; then gone was the winter,
And fair was the earth's barm. Now hastened the exile.
The guest from the garths; he on getting of vengeance
Of harms thought more greatly than of the sea's highway,
If he but a wrath-mote might yet be a-wending
Where the bairns of the Eotens might he still remember.
The ways of the world forwent he in nowise
Then, whenas Hunlafing the light of the battle,
The best of all bills, did into his breast,
Whereof mid the Eotens were the edges well knowen.
Withal to the bold-hearted Finn befell after
Sword-bales the deadly at his very own dwelling,
When the grim grip of war Guthlaf and Oslaf
After the sea-fare lamented with sorrow
And wyted him deal of their woes; nor then might he
In his breast hold his wavering heart. Was the hall dight
With the lives of slain foemen, and slain eke was Finn
The King 'midst of his court-men; and there the Queen, taken,
The shooters of the Scyldings ferry'd down to the sea-ships,
And the house-wares and chattels the earth-king had had,
E'en such as at Finn's home there might they find,
Of collars and cunning gems. They on the sea-path
The all-lordly wife to the Danes straightly wended,
Led her home to their people. So sung was the lay,

The song of the gleeman; then again arose game,
The bench-voice wax'd brighter, gave forth the birlers
Wine of the wonder-vats. Then came forth Wealhtheow
Under gold ring a-going to where sat the two good ones,
The uncle and nephew, yet of kindred unsunder'd,
Each true to the other. Eke Unferth the spokesman
Sat at feet of the Scyldings' lord; each of his heart trow'd
That of mickle mood was he, though he to his kinsmen
Were un-upright in edge-play. Spake the dame of the Scyldings:
Now take thou this cup, my lord of the kingly,
Bestower of treasures! Be thou in thy joyance,
Thou gold-friend of men! and speak to these Geat-folk
In mild words, as duly behoveth to do;
Be glad toward the Geat-folk, and mindful of gifts;
From anigh and from far peace hast thou as now.
To me one hath said it, that thou for a son wouldst
This warrior be holding. Lo! Hart now is cleansed,
The ring-hall bright-beaming. Have joy while thou mayest
In many a meed, and unto thy kinsmen
Leave folk and dominion, when forth thou must fare
To look on the Maker's own making. I know now
My Hrothulf the gladsome, that he this young man
Will hold in all honour if thou now before him,
O friend of the Scyldings, shall fare from the world;
I ween that good-will yet this man will be yielding
To our offspring that after us be, if he mind him
Of all that which we two, for good-will and for worship,
Unto him erst a child yet have framed of kindness.
Then along by the bench did she turn, where her boys were,
Hrethric and Hrothmund, and the bairns of high warriors,
The young ones together; and there sat the good one,
Beowulf the Geat, betwixt the two brethren.

XIX - MORE GIFTS ARE GIVEN TO BEOWULF. THE BRISING COLLAR TOLD OF

Borne to him then the cup was, and therewith friendly bidding
In words was put forth; and gold about wounden
All blithely they bade him bear; arm-gearings twain,
Rail and rings, the most greatest of fashion of neck-rings
Of them that on earth I have ever heard tell of:
Not one under heaven wrought better was heard of
Midst the hoard-gems of heroes, since bore away Hama
To the bright burg and brave the neck-gear of the Brisings,
The gem and the gem-chest: from the foeman's guile fled he
Of Eormenric then, and chose rede everlasting.
That ring Hygelac had, e'en he of the Geat-folk,
The grandson of Swerting, the last time of all times
When he under the war-sign his treasure defended,

Beowulf: Scholar's Edition

The slaughter-prey warded. Him weird bore away
Sithence he for pride-sake the war-woe abided,
The feud with the Frisians; the fretwork he flitted,
The gem-stones much worthy, all over the waves' cup.
The King the full mighty cring'd under the shield;
Into grasp of the Franks the King's life was gotten
With the gear of the breast and the ring altogether;
It was worser war-wolves then reft gear from the slain
After the war-shearing; there the Geats' war-folk
Held the house of the dead men. The Hall took the voices;
Spake out then Wealhtheow; before the host said she:
Brook thou this roundel, lief Beowulf, henceforth,
Dear youth, with all hail, and this rail be thou using,
These gems of folk-treasures, and thrive thou well ever;
Thy might then make manifest! Be to these lads here
Kind of lore, and for that will I look to thy guerdon.
Thou hast won by thy faring, that far and near henceforth,
Through wide time to come, men will give thee the worship,
As widely as ever the sea winds about
The windy land-walls. Be the while thou art living
An atheling wealthy, and well do I will thee
Of good of the treasures; be thou to my son
In deed ever friendly, and uphold thy joyance!
Lo! each of the earls here to the other is trusty,
And mild of his mood and to man-lord full faithful,
Kind friends all the thanes are, the folk ever yare.
Ye well drunk of folk-grooms, now do ye my biddings.
To her settle then far'd she; was the feast of the choicest,
The men drank the wine nothing wotting of weird,
The grim shaping of old, e'en as forth it had gone
To a many of earls; sithence came the even,
And Hrothgar departed to his chamber on high,
The rich to his rest; and aright the house warded
Earls untold of number, as oft did they erewhile.
The bench-boards they bar'd them, and there they spread over
With beds and with bolsters. Of the beer-skinkers one
Who fain was and fey bow'd adown to his floor-rest.
At their heads then they rested their rounds of the battle,
Their board-woods bright-shining. There on the bench was,
Over the atheling, easy to look on
The battle-steep war-helm, the byrny be-ringed,
The wood of the onset, all-glorious. Their wont was
That oft and oft were they all yare for the war-tide,
Both at home and in hosting, were it one were it either,
And for every such tide as their liege lord unto
The need were befallen: right good was that folk.

XX - GRENDEL'S DAM BREAKS INTO HART AND BEARS OFF AESCHERE

So sank they to slumber; but one paid full sorely
For his rest of the even, as to them fell full often
Sithence that the gold-hall Grendel had guarded,
And won deed of unright, until that the end came
And death after sinning: but clear was it shown now,
Wide wotted of men, that e'en yet was a wreaker
Living after the loathly, a long while of time
After the battle-care, Grendel's own mother;
The woman, the monster-wife, minded her woe,
She who needs must in horror of waters be wonning,
The streams all a-cold, sithence Cain was become
For an edge-bane forsooth to his very own brother,
The own son of his father. Forth bann'd then he fared,
All marked by murder, from man's joy to flee,
And dwelt in the waste-land. Thence woke there a many
Ghosts shapen of old time, of whom one was Grendel,
The fierce wolf, the hateful, who found him at Hart
A man there a-watching, abiding the war-tide;
Where to him the fell ogre to hand-grips befell;
Howe'er he him minded of the strength of his might,
The great gift set fast in him given of God,
And trowed in grace by the All-wielder given,
His fostering, his staying; so the fiend he o'ercame
And bow'd down the Hell's ghost, that all humble he wended
Fordone of all mirth death's house to go look on,
That fiend of all mankind. But yet was his mother,
The greedy, the glum-moody, fain to be going
A sorrowful journey her son's death to wreak.
So came she to Hart whereas now the Ring-Danes
Were sleeping adown the hall; soon there befell
Change of days to the earl-folk, when in she came thrusting,
Grendel's mother: and soothly was minish'd the terror
By even so much as the craft-work of maidens,
The war-terror of wife, is beside the man weapon'd,
When the sword all hard bounden, by hammers to-beaten,
The sword all sweat-stain'd, through the swine o'er the war-helm
With edges full doughty down rightly sheareth.
But therewith in the hall was tugg'd out the hard edge,
The sword o'er the settles, and wide shields a many
Heaved fast in the hand: no one the helm heeded,
Nor the byrny wide-wrought, when the wild fear fell on them.
In haste was she then, and out would she thenceforth
For the saving her life, whenas she should be found there.
But one of the athelings she speedily handled
And caught up full fast, and fenward so fared.
But he was unto Hrothgar the liefest of heroes

Of the sort of the fellows; betwixt the two sea-floods
A mighty shield-warrior, whom she at rest brake up,
A war-wight well famed. There Beowulf was not;
Another house soothly had erewhile been dighted
After gift of that treasure to that great one of Geats.
Uprose cry then in Hart, all 'mid gore had she taken
The hand, the well-known, and now care wrought anew
In the wicks was arisen. Naught well was the bargain
That on both halves they needs must be buying that tide
With the life-days of friends. Then the lord king, the wise,
The hoary of war-folk, was harmed of mood
When his elder of thanes and he now unliving,
The dearest of all, he knew to be dead.
To the bower full swiftly was Beowulf brought now,
The man victory-dower'd; together with day-dawn
Went he, one of the earls, that champion beworthy'd,
Himself with his fellows, where the wise was abiding
To wot if the All-wielder ever will to him
After the tale of woe happy change work.
Then went down the floor he the war-worthy
With the host of his hand, while high dinn'd the hall-wood,
Till he there the wise one with words had well greeted,
The lord of the Ingwines, and ask'd had the night been.
Since sore he was summon'd, a night of sweet easement.

XXI - HROTHGAR LAMENTS THE SLAYING OF AESCHERE, AND TELLS OF GRENDEL'S MOTHER AND HER DEN

Spake out then Hrothgar the helm of the Scyldings:
Ask no more after bliss; for new-made now is sorrow
For the folk of the Danes; for Aeschere is dead,
He who was Yrmenlaf's elder of brethren,
My wise man of runes, my bearer of redes,
Mine own shoulder-fellow, when we in the war-tide
Warded our heads and the host on the host fell,
And the boars were a-crashing; e'en such should an earl be,
An atheling exceeding good, e'en as was Aeschere.
Now in Hart hath befallen for a hand-bane unto him
A slaughter-ghost wandering; naught wot I whither
The fell one, the carrion-proud, far'd hath her back-fare,
By her fill made all famous. That feud hath she wreaked
Wherein yesternight gone by Grendel thou quelledst
Through thy hardihood fierce with grips hard enow.
For that he over-long the lief people of me
Made to wane and undid. In the war then he cringed,
Being forfeit of life. But now came another,
An ill-scather mighty, her son to awreak;
And further hath she now the feud set on foot,
As may well be deemed of many a thane,
Who after the wealth-giver weepeth in mind,

A hard bale of heart. Now the hand lieth low
Which well-nigh for every joy once did avail you.
The dwellers in land here, my people indeed,
The wise-of-rede hall-folk, have I heard say e'en this:
That they have set eyes on two such-like erewhile,
Two mickle mark-striders the moorland a-holding,
Ghosts come from elsewhere, but of them one there was,
As full certainly might they then know it to be,
In the likeness of woman; and the other shap'd loathly
All after man's image trod the tracks of the exile,
Save that more was he shapen than any man other;
And in days gone away now they named him Grendel,
The dwellers in fold; they wot not if a father
Unto him was born ever in the days of erewhile
Of dark ghosts. They dwell in a dim hidden land,
The wolf-bents they bide in, on the nesses the windy,
The perilous fen-paths where the stream of the fell-side
Midst the mists of the nesses wends netherward ever,
The flood under earth. Naught far away hence,
But a mile-mark forsooth, there standeth the mere,
And over it ever hang groves all berimed,
The wood fast by the roots over-helmeth the water.
But each night may one a dread wonder there see,
A fire in the flood. But none liveth so wise
Of the bairns of mankind, that the bottom may know.
Although the heath-stepper beswinked by hounds,
The hart strong of horns, that holt-wood should seek to
Driven fleeing from far, he shall sooner leave life,
Leave life-breath on the bank, or ever will he
Therein hide his head. No hallow'd stead is it:
Thence the blending of water-waves ever upriseth
Wan up to the welkin, whenso the wind stirreth
Weather-storms loathly, until the lift darkens
And weepeth the heavens. Now along the rede wendeth
Of thee again only. Of that earth yet thou know'st not,
The fearful of steads, wherein thou mayst find
That much-sinning wight; seek then if thou dare,
And thee for that feud will I guerdon with fee,
The treasures of old time, as erst did I do,
With the gold all-bewounden, if away thence thou get thee.

XXII - THEY FOLLOW GRENDEL'S DAM TO HER LAIR

Spake out then Beowulf the Ecgtheow's bairn:
O wise of men, mourn not; for to each man 'tis better
That his friend he awreak than weep overmuch.
Lo! each of us soothly abideth the ending
Of the life of the world. Then let him work who work may
High deeds ere the death: to the doughty of war-lads
When he is unliving shall it best be hereafter.

Beowulf: Scholar's Edition

Rise up, warder of kingdom! and swiftly now wend we
The Grendel Kinswoman's late goings to look on;
And this I behote thee, that to holm shall she flee not,
Nor into earth's fathom, nor into the fell-holt,
Nor the grounds of the ocean, go whereas she will go.
For this one of days patience dree thou a while then
Of each one of thy woes, as I ween it of thee.
Then leapt up the old man, and lightly gave God thank,
That mighty of Lords, for the word which the man spake.
And for Hrothgar straightway then was bitted a horse,
A wave-maned steed: and the wise of the princes
Went stately his ways; and stepp'd out the man-troop,
The linden-board bearers. Now lightly the tracks were
All through the woodland ways wide to be seen there,
Her goings o'er ground; she had gotten her forthright
Over the mirk-moor: bore she of kindred thanes
The best that there was, all bare of his soul,
Of them that with Hrothgar heeded the home.
Overwent then that bairn of the athelings
Steep bents of the stones, and stridings full narrow,
Strait paths nothing pass'd over, ways all uncouth,
Sheer nesses to wit, many houses of nicors.
He one of the few was going before
Of the wise of the men the meadow to look on,
Until suddenly there the trees of the mountains
Over the hoar-stone found he a-leaning,
A wood without gladness: the water stood under
Dreary and troubled. Unto all the Danes was it,
To the friends of the Scyldings, most grievous in mood
To many of thanes such a thing to be tholing,
Sore evil to each one of earls, for of Aeschere
The head did they find e'en there on the holm-cliff;
The flood with gore welled (the folk looking on it),
With hot blood. But whiles then the horn fell to singing
A song of war eager. There sat down the band;
They saw down the water a many of worm-kind,
Sea-drakes seldom seen a-kenning the sound;
Likewise on the ness-bents nicors a-lying,
Who oft on the undern-tide wont are to hold them
A course full of sorrow all over the sail-road.
Now the worms and the wild-deer away did they speed
Bitter and wrath-swollen all as they heard it,
The war-horn a-wailing: but one the Geats' warden
With his bow of the shafts from his life-days there sunder'd,
From his strife of the waves; so that stood in his life-parts
The hard arrow of war; and he in the holm was
The slower in swimming as death away swept him.
So swiftly in sea-waves with boar-spears forsooth
Sharp-hook'd and hard-press'd was he thereupon,
Set on with fierce battle, and on to the ness tugg'd,

The wondrous wave-bearer; and men were beholding
The grisly guest, Beowulf therewith he gear'd him
With weed of the earls: nowise of life reck'd he:
Needs must his war-byrny, braided by hands,
Wide, many-colour'd by cunning, the sound seek,
E'en that which his bone-coffer knew how to ward,
So that the war-grip his heart ne'er a while,
The foe-snatch of the wrathful his life ne'er should scathe;
Therewith the white war-helm warded his head,
E'en that which should mingle with ground of the mere,
And seek the sound-welter, with treasure beworthy'd
All girt with the lordly chains, as in days gone by
The weapon-smith wrought it most wondrously done,
Beset with the swine-shapes, so that sithence
The brand or the battle-blades never might bite it.
Nor forsooth was that littlest of all of his mainstays,
Which to him in his need lent the spokesman of Hrothgar,
E'en the battle-sword hafted that had to name Hrunting,
That in fore days was one of the treasures of old,
The edges of iron with the poison twigs o'er-stain'd,
With battle-sweat harden'd; in the brunt never fail'd he
Any one of the warriors whose hand wound about him,
Who in grisly wayfarings durst ever to wend him
To the folk-stead of foemen. Not the first of times was it
That battle-work doughty it had to be doing.
Forsooth naught remember'd that son there of Ecglaf,
The crafty in mighty deeds, what ere he quoth
All drunken with wine, when the weapon he lent
To a doughtier sword-wolf: himself naught he durst it
Under war of the waves there his life to adventure
And warrior-ship work. So forwent he the glory,
The fair fame of valour. Naught far'd so the other
Syth he to the war-tide had gear'd him to wend.

XXIII - BEOWULF REACHETH THE MERE-BOTTOM IN A DAY'S WHILE, AND CONTENDS WITH GRENDEL'S DAM

Out then spake Beowulf, Ecgtheow's bairn:
Forsooth be thou mindful, O great son of Healfdene,
O praise of the princes, now way-fain am I,
O gold-friend of men, what we twain spake aforetime:
If to me for thy need it might so befall
That I cease from my life-days, thou shouldest be ever
To me, forth away wended, in the stead of a father.
Do thou then bear in hand these thanes of my kindred,
My hand-fellows, if so be battle shall have me;
Those same treasures withal, which thou gavest me erst,
O Hrothgar the lief, unto Hygelac send thou;
By that gold then shall wot the lord of the Geat-folk,

Shall Hrethel's son see, when he stares on the treasure,
That I in fair man-deeds a good one have found me,
A ring-giver; while I might, joy made I thereof.
And let thou then Unferth the ancient loom have,
The wave-sword adorned, that man kenned widely,
The blade of hard edges; for I now with Hrunting
Will work me the glory, or else shall death get me.
So after these words the Weder-Geats' chieftain
With might of heart hasten'd; nor for answer then would he
Aught tarry; the sea-welter straightway took hold on
The warrior of men: wore the while of a daytide
Or ever the ground-plain might he set eyes on.
Soon did she find, she who the flood-ring
Sword-ravening had held for an hundred of seasons,
Greedy and grim, that there one man of grooms
The abode of the alien-wights sought from above;
Then toward him she grasp'd and gat hold on the warrior
With fell clutch, but no sooner she scathed withinward
The hale body; rings from without-ward it warded,
That she could in no wise the war-skin clutch through,
The fast locked limb-sark, with fingers all loathly.
So bare then that sea-wolf when she came unto bottom
The king of the rings to the court-hall adown
In such wise that he might not, though hard-moody was he,
Be wielding of weapons. But a many of wonders
In sea-swimming swink'd him, and many a sea-deer
With his war-tusks was breaking his sark of the battle;
The fell wights him follow'd. 'Twas then the earl found it
That in foe-hall there was he, I wot not of which,
Where never the water might scathe him a whit,
Nor because of the roof-hall might reach to him there
The fear-grip of the flood. Now fire-light he saw,
The bleak beam forsooth all brightly a-shining.
Then the good one, he saw the wolf of the ground,
The mere-wife the mighty, and main onset made he
With his battle-bill; never his hand withheld sword-swing
So that there on her head sang the ring-sword forsooth
The song of war greedy. But then found the guest
That the beam of the battle would bite not therewith,
Or scathe life at all, but there failed the edge
The king in his need. It had ere thol'd a many
Of meetings of hand; oft it sheared the helm,
The host-rail of the fey one; and then was the first time
For that treasure dear lov'd that its might lay a-low.
But therewithal steadfast, naught sluggish of valour,
All mindful of high deeds was Hygelac's kinsman.
Cast then the wounden blade bound with the gem-stones
The warrior all angry, that it lay on the earth there,
Stiff-wrought and steel-edged. In strength now he trusted,
The hard hand-grip of might and main; so shall a man do

When he in the war-tide yet looketh to winning
The praise that is longsome, nor aught for life careth.
Then fast by the shoulder, of the feud nothing recking,
The lord of the War-Geats clutch'd Grendel's mother,
Cast down the battle-hard, bollen with anger,
That foe of the life, till she bow'd to the floor;
But swiftly to him gave she back the hand-guerdon
With hand-graspings grim, and griped against him;
Then mood-weary stumbled the strongest of warriors,
The foot-kemp, until that adown there he fell.
Then she sat on the hall-guest and tugg'd out her sax,
The broad and brown-edged, to wreak her her son,
Her offspring her own. But lay yet on his shoulder
The breast-net well braided, the berg of his life,
That 'gainst point and 'gainst edge the entrance withstood.
Gone amiss then forsooth had been Ecgtheow's son
Underneath the wide ground there, the kemp of the Geats,
Save to him his war-byrny had fram'd him a help,
The hard host-net; and save that the Lord God the Holy
Had wielded the war-gain, the Lord the All-wise;
Save that the skies' Ruler had rightwisely doom'd it
All easily. Sithence he stood up again.

XXIV - BEOWULF SLAYETH GRENDEL'S DAM, SMITETH OFF GRENDEL'S HEAD, AND COMETH BACK WITH HIS THANES TO HART

Midst the war-gear he saw then a bill victory-wealthy,
An old sword of eotens full doughty of edges,
The worship of warriors. That was choice of all weapons,
Save that more was it made than any man other
In the battle-play ever might bear it afield,
So goodly, all glorious, the work of the giants.
Then the girdled hilt seiz'd he, the Wolf of the Scyldings,
The rough and the sword-grim, and drew forth the ring-sword,
Naught weening of life, and wrathful he smote then
So that there on her halse the hard edge begripped,
And brake through the bone-rings: the bill all through-waded
Her flesh-sheathing fey; cring'd she down on the floor;
The sword was war-sweaty, the man in his work joy'd.
The bright beam shone forth, the light stood withinward,
E'en as down from the heavens' clear high aloft shineth
The sky's candle. He all along the house scanned;
Then turn'd by the wall along, heav'd up his weapon
Hard by the hilts the Hygelac's thane there,
Ireful one-reded; naught worthless the edge was
Unto the warrior; but rathely now would he
To Grendel make payment of many war-onsets,
Of them that he wrought on the folk of the West Danes

Beowulf: Scholar's Edition

Oftener by mickle than one time alone,
Whenas he the hearthfellows of Hrothgar the King
Slew in their slumber and fretted them sleeping,
Men fifteen to wit of the folk of the Danes,
And e'en such another deal ferry'd off outward,
Loathly prey. Now he paid him his guerdon therefor,
The fierce champion; so well, that abed there he saw
Where Grendel war-weary was lying adown
Forlorn of his life, as him ere had scathed
The battle at Hart; sprang wide the body,
Sithence after death he suffer'd the stroke,
The hard swing of sword. Then he smote the head off him.
Now soon were they seeing, those sage of the carles,
E'en they who with Hrothgar gaz'd down on the holm,
That the surge of the billows was blended about,
The sea stain'd with blood. Therewith the hoar-blended,
The old men, of the good one gat talking together
That they of the Atheling ween'd never eft-soon
That he, glad in his war-gain, should wend him a-seeking
The mighty king, since unto many it seemed
That him the mere-she-wolf had sunder'd and broken.
Came then nones of the day, and the ness there they gave up,
The Scyldings the brisk; and then busk'd him home thence-ward
The gold-friend of men. But the guests, there they sat
All sick of their mood, and star'd on the mere;
They wist not, they ween'd not if him their own friend-lord
Himself they should see.
Now that sword began
Because of the war-sweat into icicles war-made,
The war-bill, to wane: that was one of the wonders
That it melted away most like unto ice
When the bond of the frost the Father lets loosen,
Unwindeth the wave-ropes, e'en he that hath wielding
Of times and of seasons, who is the sooth Shaper.
In those wicks there he took not, the Weder-Geats' champion,
Of treasure-wealth more, though he saw there a many,
Than the off-smitten head and the sword-hilts together
With treasure made shifting; for the sword-blade was molten,
The sword broider'd was burn'd up, so hot was that blood,
So poisonous the alien ghost there that had died.
Now soon was a-swimming he who erst in the strife bode
The war-onset of wrath ones; he div'd up through the water;
And now were the wave-welters cleansed full well,
Yea the dwellings full wide, where the ghost of elsewhither
Let go of his life-days and the waning of living.
Came then unto land the helm of the ship-lads
Swimming stout-hearted, glad of his sea-spoil,
The burden so mighty of that which he bore there.
Yode then against him and gave thanks to God
That fair heap of thanes, and were fain of their lord,

O high lord of Scyldings, on that behalf soothly
Life-bale for the earls as erst thou hast done.
Then was the hilt golden to the ancient of warriors,
The hoary of host-leaders, into hand given,
The old work of giants; it turn'd to the owning,
After fall of the Devils, of the lord of the Danes,
That work of the wonder-smith, syth gave up the world
The fierce-hearted groom, the foeman of God,
The murder-beguilted, and there eke his mother;
Unto the wielding of world-kings it turned,
The best that there be betwixt of the sea-floods
Of them that in Scaney dealt out the scat.
Now spake out Hrothgar, as he look'd on the hilts there,
The old heir-loom whereon was writ the beginning
Of the strife of the old time, whenas the flood slew,
The ocean a-gushing, that kin of the giants
As fiercely they fared. That was a folk alien
To the Lord everlasting; so to them a last guerdon
Through the welling of waters the Wielder did give.
So was on the sword-guards all of the sheer gold
By dint of the rune-staves rightly bemarked,
Set down and said for whom first was that sword wrought,
And the choice of all irons erst had been done,
Wreath-hilted and worm-adorn'd. Then spake the wise one,
Healfdene's son, and all were gone silent:
Lo that may he say, who the right and the soothfast
Amid the folk frameth, and far back all remembers,
The old country's warden, that as for this earl here
Born better was he. Uprear'd is the fame-blast
Through wide ways far yonder, O Beowulf, friend mine,
Of thee o'er all peoples. Thou hold'st all with patience,
Thy might with mood-wisdom; I shall make thee my love good,
As we twain at first spake it. For a comfort thou shalt be
Granted long while and long unto thy people,
For a help unto heroes. Naught such became Heremod
To Ecgwela's offspring, the honourful Scyldings;
For their welfare naught wax'd he, but for felling in slaughter,
For the quelling of death to the folk of the Danes.
Mood-swollen he brake there his board-fellows soothly,
His shoulder-friends, until he sunder'd him lonely,
That mighty of princes, from the mirth of all men-folk.
Though him God the mighty in the joyance of might,
In main strength, exalted high over all-men,
And framed him forth, yet fast in his heart grew
A breast-hoard blood-fierce; none of fair rings he gave
To the Danes as due doom would. Unmerry he dured
So that yet of that strife the trouble he suffer'd.
A folk-bale so longsome. By such do thou learn thee,
Get thee hold of man-valour: this tale for thy teaching
Old in winters I tell thee. 'Tis wonder to say it,

For that hale and sound now they might see him with eyen;
Then was from the bold one the helm and the byrny
All speedily loosen'd. The lake now was laid,
The water 'neath welkin with war-gore bestained.
Forth then they far'd them alongst of the foot-tracks,
Men fain of heart all, as they meted the earth-way,
The street the well known; then those king-bold of men
Away from the holm-cliff the head there they bore
Uneasily ever to each one that bore it,
The full stout-heart of men: it was four of them needs must
On the stake of the slaughter with strong toil there ferry
Unto the gold-hall the head of that Grendel;
Until forthright in haste came into that hall,
Fierce, keen in the hosting, a fourteen of men
Of the Geat-folk a-ganging; and with them their lord,
The moody amidst of the throng, trod the mead-plains;
Came then in a-wending the foreman of thanes,
The man keen of his deeds all beworshipp'd of doom,
The hero, the battle-deer, Hrothgar to greet.
Then was by the fell borne in onto the floor
Grendel's head, whereas men were a-drinking in hall,
Aweful before the earls, yea and the woman.
The sight wondrous to see the warriors there look'd on.

XXV - CONVERSE OF HROTHGAR WITH BEOWULF

Spake out then Beowulf, Ecgtheow's bairn:
What! we the sea-spoils here to thee, son of Healfdene,
High lord of the Scyldings, with lust have brought hither
For a token of glory, e'en these thou beholdest.
Now I all unsoftly with life I escaped,
In war under the water dar'd I the work
Full hard to be worked, and well-nigh there was
The sundering of strife, save that me God had shielded.
So it is that in battle naught might I with Hrunting
One whit do the work, though the weapon be doughty;
But to me then he granted, the Wielder of men,
That on wall I beheld there all beauteous hanging
An ancient sword, might-endow'd (often he leadeth right
The friendless of men); so forth drew I that weapon.
In that onset I slew there, as hap then appaid me,
The herd of the house; then that bill of the host,
The broider'd sword, burn'd up, and that blood sprang forth
The hottest of battle-sweats; but the hilts thereof thenceforth
From the foemen I ferry'd. I wreaked the foul deeds,
The death-quelling of Danes, e'en as duly behoved.
Now this I behote thee, that here in Hart mayst thou
Sleep sorrowless henceforth with the host of thy men
And the thanes every one that are of thy people
Of doughty and young; that for them need thou dread not,

How the high God almighty to the kindred of mankind
Through his mind the wide-fashion'd deals wisdom about,
Home and earlship; he owneth the wielding of all.
At whiles unto love he letteth to turn
The mood-thought of a man that Is mighty of kindred,
And in his land giveth him joyance of earth,
And to have and to hold the high ward-burg of men,
And sets so 'neath his wielding the deals of the world,
Dominion wide reaching, that he himself may not
In all his unwisdom of the ending bethink him.
He wonneth well-faring, nothing him wasteth
Sickness nor eld, nor the foe-sorrow to him
Dark in mind waxeth, nor strife any where,
The edge-hate, appeareth; but all the world for him
Wends as he willeth, and the worse naught he wotteth.

XXVI - MORE CONVERSE OF HROTHGAR AND BEOWULF: THE GEATS MAKE THEM READY FOR DEPARTURE

Until that within him a deal of o'erthink-ing
Waxeth and groweth while sleepeth the warder,
The soul's herdsman; that slumber too fast is forsooth,
Fast bounden by troubles, the banesman all nigh,
E'en he that from arrow-bow evilly shooteth.
Then he in his heart under helm is besmitten
With a bitter shaft; not a whit then may he ward him
From the wry wonder-biddings of the ghost the all-wicked.
Too little he deems that which long he hath hold.
Wrath-greedy he covets; nor e'en for boast-sake gives
The rings fair beplated; and the forth-coming doom
Forgetteth, forheedeth, for that God gave him erewhile,
The Wielder of glory, a deal of the worship.
At the ending-stave then it after befalleth
That the shell of his body sinks fleeting away,
And falleth all fey; and another one fetcheth,
E'en one that undolefully dealeth the treasure,
The earl's gains of aforetime, and fear never heedeth.
From the bale-envy ward thee, lief Beowulf, therefore,
Thou best of all men, and choose thee the better,
The redes everlasting; to o'erthinkirig turn not,
O mighty of champions! for now thy might breatheth
For a short while of time; but eft-soon it shall be
That sickness or edges from thy strength thee shall sunder,
Or the hold of the fire, or the welling of floods,
Or the grip of the sword-blade, or flight of the spear,
Or eld the all-evil: or the beaming of eyen
Shall fail and shall dim: then shall it be forthright
That thee, lordly man, the death over-masters.
E'en so I the Ring-Danes for an hundred of seasons

Did wield under the welkin and lock'd them by war
From many a kindred the Middle-Garth over
With ash-spears and edges, in such wise that not ever
Under the sky's run of my foemen I reckoned.
What! to me in my land came a shifting of that,
Came grief after game, sithence Grendel befell,
My foeman of old, mine ingoer soothly.
I from that onfall bore ever unceasing
Mickle mood-care; herefor be thanks to the Maker,
To the Lord everlasting, that in life I abided,
Yea, that I on that head all sword-gory there,
Now the old strife is over, with eyen should stare.
Go fare thou to settle, the feast-joyance dree thou,
O war-worshipp'd! unto us twain yet there will be
Mickle treasure in common when come is the morning.
Glad of mood then the Geat was, and speedy he gat him
To go see the settle, as the sage one commanded.
Then was after as erst, that they of the might-fame,
The floor-sitters, fairly the feasting bedight them
All newly. The helm of the night loured over
Dark over the host-men. Uprose all the doughty,
For he, the hoar-blended, would wend to his bed,
That old man of the Scyldings. The Geat without measure,
The mighty shield-warrior, now willed him rest.
And soon now the hall-thane him of way-faring weary,
From far away come, forth show'd him the road,
E'en he who for courtesy cared for all things
Of the needs of the thane, e'en such as on that day
The farers o'er ocean would fainly have had.
Rested then the wide-hearted; high up the house tower'd
Wide-gaping all gold-dight; within slept the guest;
Until the black raven, the blithe-hearted, boded
The heavens' joy: then was come thither a-hastening
The bright sun o'er the plains, and hastened the scathers,
The athelings once more aback to their people
All fain to be faring; and far away thence
Would the comer high-hearted go visit his keel.
Bade then the hard one Hrunting to bear,
The Ecglaf's son bade to take him his sword,
The iron well-lov'd; gave him thanks for the lending,
Quoth he that the war-friend for worthy he told,
Full of craft in the war; nor with word he aught
The edge of the sword. Hah! the high-hearted warrior.
So whenas all way-forward, yare in their war-gear,
Were the warriors, the dear one then went to the Danes,
To the high seat went the Atheling, whereas was the other;
The battle-bold warrior gave greeting to Hrothgar.

XXVII - BEOWULF BIDS HROTHGAR FAREWELL: THE GEATS FARE TO SHIP

Out then spake Beowulf, Ecgtheow's bairn:
As now we sea-farers have will to be saying,
We from afar come, that now are we fainest
Of seeking to Hygelac. Here well erst were we
Serv'd as our wills would, and well thine avail was.
If I on the earth then, be it e'en but a little,
Of the love of thy mood may yet more be an-earning,
O lord of the men-folk, than heretofore might I,
Of the works of the battle yare then soon shall I be.
If I should be learning, I over the flood's run,
That the sitters about thee beset thee with dread,
Even thee hating as otherwhile did they;
Then thousands to theeward of thanes shall I bring
For the helping of heroes. Of Hygelac wot I,
The lord of the Geat-folk, though he be but a youngling,
That shepherd of folk, that me will he further
By words and by works, that well may I ward thee,
And unto thine helping the spear-holt may bear,
A main-staying mighty, whenas men thou art needing.
And if therewith Hrethric in the courts of the Geat-house,
The King's bairn, take hosting, then may he a many
Of friends find him soothly: far countries shall be
Better sought to by him who for himself is doughty.
Out then spake Hrothgar in answer to himward:
Thy word-saying soothly the Lord of all wisdom
Hath sent into thy mind; never heard I more sagely
In a life that so young was a man word be laying;
Strong of might and main art thou and sage of thy mood,
Wise the words of thy framing. Tell I this for a weening,
If it so come to pass that the spear yet shall take,
Or the battle all sword-grim, the son of that Hrethel,
Or sickness or iron thine Alderman have,
Thy shepherd of folk, and thou fast to life hold thee,
Then no better than thee may the Sea-Geats be having
To choose for themselves, no one of the kings,
Hoard-warden of heroes, if then thou wilt hold
Thy kinsman's own kingdom. Me liketh thy mood-heart,
The longer the better, O Beowulf the lief;
In such wise hast thou fared, that unto the folks now,
The folk of the Geats and the Gar-Danes withal,
In common shall peace be, and strife rest appeased
And the hatreds the doleful which erst they have dreed;
Shall become, whiles I wield it, this wide realm of ours,
Treasures common to either folk: many a one other
With good things shall greet o'er the bath of the gannet;
And the ring'd bark withal over sea shall be bringing

The gifts and love-tokens. The twain folks I know
Toward foeman toward friend fast-fashion'd together,
In every way blameless as in the old wise.
Then the refuge of warriors, he gave him withal,
Gave Healfdene's son of treasures yet twelve;
And he bade him with those gifts to go his own people
To seek in all soundness, and swiftly come back.
Then kissed the king, he of noble kin gotten,
The lord of the Scyldings, that best of the thanes,
By the halse then he took him; from him fell the tears
From the blended of hoar hair. Of both things was there hoping
To the old, the old wise one; yet most of the other,
To wit, that they sithence each each might be seeing,
The high-heart in council. To him so lief was he
That he his breast-welling might nowise forbear,
But there in his bosom, bound fast in his heart-bonds,
After that dear man a longing dim-hidden
Burn'd against blood-tie. So Beowulf thenceforth,
The gold-proud of warriors, trod the mould grassy,
Exulting in gold-store. The sea-ganger bided
Its owning-lord whereas at anchor it rode.
Then was there in going the gift of King Hrothgar
Oft highly accounted; yea, that was a king
In every wise blameless, till eld took from him eftsoon
The joyance of might, as it oft scathes a many.

XXVIII - BEOWULF COMES BACK TO HIS LAND. OF THE TALE OF THRYTHO

Came a many to flood then all mighty of mood,
Of the bachelors were they, and ring-nets they bore,
The limb-sarks belocked. The land-warden noted
The earls' aback-faring, as erst he beheld them;
Then nowise with harm from the nose of the cliff
The guests there he greeted, but rode unto themward,
And quoth that full welcome to the folk of the Weders
The bright-coated warriors were wending to ship.
Then was on the sand there the bark the wide-sided
With war-weed beladen, the ring-stemm'd as she lay there
With mares and with treasure; uptower'd the mast
High over Hrothgar's wealth of the hoards.
He then to the boat-warden handsel'd a gold-bounden
Sword, so that sithence was he on mead-bench
Worthy'd the more for that very same wealth,
The heirloom. Sithence in the ship he departed
To stir the deep water; the Dane-land he left.
Then was by the mast there one of the sea-rails,
A sail, with rope made fast; thunder'd the sound-wood.
Not there the wave-floater did the wind o'er the billows
Waft off from its ways; the sea-wender fared,

Floated the foamy-neck'd forth o'er the waves,
The bounden-stemm'd over the streams of the sea;
Till the cliffs of the Geats there they gat them to wit,
The nesses well kenned. Throng'd up the keel then
Driven hard by the lift, and stood on the land.
Then speedy at holm was the hythe-warden yare,
E'en he who a long while after the lief men
Eager at stream's side far off had looked.
To the sand thereon bound he the wide-fathom'd ship
With anchor-bands fast, lest from them the waves' might
The wood that was winsome should drive thence awayward.
Thereon bade he upbear the athelings' treasures,
The fretwork and wrought gold. Not far from them thenceforth
To seek to the giver of treasures it was,
E'en Hygelac, Hrethel's son, where at home wonneth
Himself and his fellows hard by the sea-wall.
Brave was the builded house, bold king the lord was,
High were the walls, Hygd very young,
Wise and well-thriven, though few of winters
Under the burg-locks had she abided,
The daughter of Hæreth; naught was she dastard;
Nowise niggard of gifts to the folk of the Geats,
Of wealth of the treasures. But wrath Thrytho bore,
The folk-queen the fierce, wrought the crime-deed full fearful.
No one there durst it, the bold one, to dare,
Of the comrades beloved, save only her lord,
That on her by day with eyen he stare,
But if to him death-bonds predestin'd he count on,
Hand-wreathed; thereafter all rathely it was
After the hand-grip the sword-blade appointed,
That the cunning-wrought sword should show forth the deed,
Make known the murder-bale. Naught is such queenlike
For a woman to handle, though peerless she be,
That a weaver of peace the life should waylay,
For a shame that was lying, of a lief man of men;
But the kinsman of Hemming, he hinder'd it surely.
Yet the drinkers of ale otherwise said they;
That folk-bales, which were lesser, she framed forsooth,
Lesser enmity-malice, since thence erst she was
Given gold-deck'd to the young one of champions,
She the dear of her lineage, since Offa's floor
Over the fallow flood by the lore of her father
She sought in her wayfaring. Well was she sithence
There on the man-throne mighty with good;
Her shaping of life well brooked she living;
High love she held toward the lord of the heroes;
Of all kindred of men by the hearsay of me
The best of all was he the twain seas beside,
Of the measureless kindred; thereof Offa was

For gifts and for war, the spear-keen of men,
Full widely beworthy'd, with wisdom he held
The land of his heritage. Thence awoke Eomær
For a help unto heroes, the kinsman of Hemming,
The grandson of Garmund, the crafty in war-strife.

XXIX - BEOWULF TELLS HYGELAC OF HROTHGAR: ALSO OF FREAWARU HIS DAUGHTER

Went his ways then the hard one, and he with his hand-shoal,
Himself over the sand the sea-plain a-treading,
The warths wide away; shone the world's candle,
The sun slop'd from the southward; so dreed they their journey,
And went their ways stoutly unto where the earls' refuge,
The banesman of Ongentheow all in his burgs there,
The young king of war, the good, as they heard it.
Was dealing the rings. Aright unto Hygelac
Was Beowulf's speeding made knowen full swiftly,
That there into the house-place that hedge of the warriors,
His mate of the linden-board, living was come,
Hale from the battle-play home to him houseward.
Then rathe was beroomed, as the rich one was bidding,
For the guests a-foot going the floor all withinward.
Then sat in the face of him he from the fight sav'd,
Kinsman by kinsman, whenas his man-lord
In fair-sounding speech had greeted the faithful
With mightyful words. With mead-skinking turned
Through the high house adown the daughter of Hæreth:
The people she loved: the wine-bucket bare she
To the hands of the men. But now fell to Hygelac
His very house-fellow in that hall the high
To question full fairly, for wit-lust to-brake him,
Of what like were the journeys the Sea-Geats had wended:
How befell you the sea-lode, O Beowulf lief,
When thou on a sudden bethoughtst thee afar
Over the salt water the strife to be seeking,
The battle in Hart? or for Hrothgar forsooth
The wide-kenned woe some whit didst thou mend,
For that mighty of lords? I therefore the mood-care
In woe-wellings seethed; trow'd not in the wending
Of thee the lief man. A long while did I pray thee
That thou the death-guest there should greet not a whit;
Wouldst let those same South-Danes their own selves to settle
The war-tide with Grendel. Now to God say I thank
That thee, and thee sound, now may I see.
Out then spake Beowulf, Ecgtheow's bairn:
All undark it is, O Hygelac lord,
That meeting the mighty, to a many of men;
Of what like was the meeting of Grendel and me
On that field of the deed, where he many a deal

For the Victory-Scyldings of sorrow had framed,
And misery for ever; but all that I awreaked,
So that needeth not boast any kinsman of Grendel
Any one upon earth of that uproar of dawn-dusk,
Nay not who lives longest of that kindred the loathly
Encompass'd of fenland. Thither first did I come
Unto that ring-hall Hrothgar to greet;
Soon unto me the great Healfdene's son,
So soon as my heart he was wotting forsooth.
Right against his own son a settle there showed.
All that throng was in joy, nor life-long saw I ever
Under vault of the heavens amidst any hall-sitters
More mirth of the mead. There the mighty Queen whiles,
Peace-sib of the folk, went all over the floor,
To the young sons bade heart up; oft she there the ring-wreath
Gave unto a man ere to settle she wended.
At whiles fore the doughty the daughter of Hrothgar
To the earls at the end the ale-bucket bore;
E'en she whom Freawaru the floor-sitters thereat
Heard I to name; where she the nail'd treasure
Gave to the warriors. She was behight then
Youngling and gold-dight to the glad son of Froda.
This hath seemed fair to the friend of the Scyldings,
The herd of the realm, and good rede he accounts it,
That he with that wife of death-feuds a deal
And of strifes should allay. Oft unseldom eachwhere
After a lord's fall e'en but for a little
Bows down the bane-spear, though doughty the bride be.

XXX - BEOWULF FOREBODES ILL FROM THE WEDDING OF FREAWARU: HE TELLS OF GRENDEL AND HIS DAM

Ill-liking this may be to the lord of the Heathobards,
And to each of the thanes of that same people.
When he with fair bride on the floor of hall wendeth,
That the Dane's noble bairn his doughty should wait on,
As on him glisten there the heirlooms of the aged,
Hard and with rings bedight, Heathobards' treasure,
Whileas the weapons yet they might wield;
Till astray did they lead there at the lind-play
Their own fellows belov'd and their very own lives.
For then saith at the beer, he who seeth the ring,
An ancient ash-warrior who mindeth of all
The spear-death of men; grim is he of mind;
Sad of mood he beginneth to tell the young champion.
Through the thought of his heart his mind there to try,
The war-bale to waken, and sayeth this word:
Mayest thou, friend mine, wot of the war-sword,
That which thy father bore in the fight

Beowulf: Scholar's Edition

Under the war-mask e'en on the last time,
That the dear iron, whereas the Danes slew him,
Wielded the death-field, since Withergyld lay,
After fall of the heroes, the keen-hearted Scyldings?
Now here of those banesmen the son, whoseso he be,
All merry in fretwork forth on floor fareth;
Of the murder he boasteth, and that jewel he beareth,
E'en that which of right thou shouldest arede.
Thus he mindeth and maketh word every of times,
With sore words he telleth, until the time cometh
That the thane of the fair bride for the deeds of his father
After bite of the bill sleepeth all blood-stain'd,
All forfeit of life; but thenceforth the other
Escapeth alive; the land well he kenneth;
Then will be broken on both sides forsooth
The oath-swearing of earls, whenas unto Ingeld
Well up the death-hatreds, and the wife-loves of him
Because of the care-wellings cooler become.
Therefore the Heathobards' faith I account not,
Their deal of the folk-peace, unguileful to Danes,
Their fast-bounden friendship. Henceforth must I speak on
Again about Grendel, that thou get well to know it,
O treasure-out-dealer, how sithence betided
The hand-race of heroes: sithence heaven's gem
All over the grounds glided, came the wroth guest,
The dire night-angry one us to go look on,
Whereas we all sound were warding the hall.
There then for Handshoe was battle abiding,
Life-bale to the fey; he first lay alow,
The war-champion girded; unto him became Grendel,
To the great thane of kindreds, a banesman of mouth,
Of the man well-beloved the body he swallow'd;
Nor the sooner therefor out empty-handed
The bloody-tooth'd banesman, of bales all bemindful,
Out from that gold-hall yet would he get him;
But he, mighty of main, made trial of me,
And gripp'd ready-handed. His glove hung aloft,
Wondrous and wide, in wily bands fast,
With cunning wiles was it begeared forsooth,
With crafts of the devils and fells of the dragons;
He me withinwards there, me the unsinning,
The doer of big deeds would do me to be
As one of the many; but naught so it might be,
Sithence in mine anger upright I stood.
'Tis over-long telling how I to the folkscather
For each one of evils out paid the hand-gild.
There I, O my lord king, them thy leal people
Worthy'd with works: but away he gat loosed
Out thence for a little while, brooked yet life-joys;
But his right hand held ward of his track howsoever,

High upon Hart-hall, and thence away humble
He sad of his mood to the mere-ground fell downward.
Me for that slaughter-race the friend of the Scyldings
With gold that beplated was mickle deal paid,
With a many of treasures, sithence came the morning,
And we to the feast-tide had sat us adown;
Song was and glee there; the elder of Scyldings,
Asking of many things, told of things o'erpast;
Whiles hath the battle-deer there the harp's joy,
The wood of mirth greeted; whiles the lay said he
Soothfast and sorrowful; whiles a spell seldom told
Told he by right, the king roomy-hearted;
Whiles began afterward he by eld bounden,
The aged hoar warrior, of his youth to bewail him,
Its might of the battle; his breast well'd within him,
When he, wont in winters, of many now minded.
So we there withinward the livelong day's wearing
Took pleasure amongst us, till came upon men
Another of nights; then eftsoons again
Was yare for the harm-wreak the mother of Grendel:
All sorry she wended, for her son death had taken,
The war-hate of the Weders: that monster of women
Awreaked her bairn, and quelled a warrior
In manner all mighty. Then was there from Aeschere,
The wise man of old, life waning away;
Nor him might they even when come was the morning,
That death-weary wight, the folk of the Danes
Burn up with the brand, nor lade on the bale
The man well-belov'd, for his body she bare off
In her fathom the fiendly all under the fell-stream.
That was unto Hrothgar of sorrows the heaviest
Of them which the folk-chieftain long had befallen.
Then me did the lord king, and e'en by thy life,
Mood-heavy beseech me that I in the holm-throng
Should do after earlship, my life to adventure,
And frame me main-greatness, and meed he behight me.
Then I of the welling flood, which is well kenned,
The grim and the grisly ground-herder did find.
There to us for a while was the blending of hands;
The holm welled with gore, and the head I becarved
In that hall of the ground from the Mother of Grendel
With the all-eked edges; unsoftly out thence
My life forth I ferry'd, for not yet was I fey.
But the earls' burg to me was giving thereafter
Much sort of the treasures, e'en Healfdene's son.

XXXI - BEOWULF GIVES HROTHGAR'S GIFTS TO HYGELAC, AND BY HIM IS REWARDED. OF THE DEATH OF HYGELAC AND OF HEARDRED HIS SON, AND HOW BEOWULF IS KING OF THE GEATS: THE WORM IS FIRST TOLD OF

So therewith the folk-king far'd, living full seemly;
By those wages forsooth ne'er a whit had I lost,
By the meed of my main, but to me treasure gave he,
The Healfdene's son, to the doom of myself;
Which to thee, king of bold ones, will I be a-bringing,
And gladly will give thee; for of thee is all gotten
Of favours along, and but little have I
Of head-kinsmen forsooth, saving, Hygelac, thee.
Then he bade them bear in the boar-shape, the head-sign,
The battle-steep war-helm, the byrny all hoary,
The sword stately-good, and spell after he said:
This raiment of war Hrothgar gave to my hand,
The wise of the kings, and therewithal bade me,
That I first of all of his favour should flit thee;
He quoth that first had it King Heorogar of old,
The king of the Scyldings, a long while of time;
But no sooner would he give it unto his son,
Heoroward the well-whet, though kind to him were he,
This weed of the breast. Do thou brook it full well.
On these fretworks, so heard I, four horses therewith,
All alike, close followed after the track,
Steeds apple-fallow. Fair grace he gave him
Of horses and treasures. E'en thus shall do kinsman,
And nowise a wile-net shall weave for another
With craft of the darkness, or do unto death
His very hand-fellow. But now unto Hygelac
The bold in the battle was his nephew full faithful,
And either to other of good deeds was mindful.
I heard that the neck-ring to Hygd did he give,
E'en the wonder-gem well-wrought, that Wealh-theow gave him,
The king's daughter; gave he three steeds therewithal
Slender, and saddle-bright; sithence to her was,
After the ring-gift, the breast well beworthy'd.
Thus boldly he bore him, the Ecgtheow's bairn,
The groom kenned in battle, in good deeds a-doing;
After due doom he did, and ne'er slew he the drunken
Hearth-fellows of him: naught rough was his heart;
But of all men of mankind with the greatest of might
The gift fully and fast set, which had God to him given,
That war-deer did hold. Long was he contemned,
While the bairns of the Geats naught told him for good,
Nor him on the mead-bench worthy of mickle
The lord of the war-hosts would be a-making.
Weened they strongly that he were but slack then,

An atheling unkeen; then came about change
To the fame-happy man for every foul harm.
Bade then the earls' burg in to be bringing,
The king battle-famed, the leaving of Hrethel,
All geared with gold; was not 'mid the Geats then
A treasure-gem better of them of the sword-kind,
That which then on Beowulf's harm there he laid;
And gave to him there seven thousand in gift,
A built house and king-stool; to both them together
Was in that folkship land that was kindly,
Father-right, home; to the other one rather
A wide realm, to him who was there the better.
But thereafter it went so in days later worn
Through the din of the battle, sithence Hygelac lay low
And unto Heardred swords of the battle
Under the war-board were for a bane;
When fell on him midst of this victory-folk
The hard battle-wolves, the Scyldings of war,
And by war overwhelmed the nephew of Hereric;
That sithence unto Beowulf turned the broad realm
All into his hand. Well then did he hold it
For a fifty of winters; then was he an old king,
An old fatherland's warder; until one began
Through the dark of the night-tide, a drake, to hold sway.
In a howe high aloft watched over an hoard,
A stone-burg full steep; thereunder a path sty'd
Unknown unto men, and therewithin wended
Who of men do I know not; for his lust there took he,
From the hoard of the heathen his hand took away
A hall-bowl gem-flecked, nowise back did he give it
Though the herd of the hoard him sleeping beguil'd he
With thief-craft; and this then found out the king,
The best of folk-heroes, that wrath-bollen was he.

XXXII - HOW THE WORM CAME TO THE HOWE, AND HOW HE WAS ROBBED OF A CUP; AND HOW HE FELL ON THE FOLK

Not at all with self-wielding the craft of the worm-hoards
He sought of his own will, who sore himself harmed;
But for threat of oppression a thrall, of I wot not
Which bairn of mankind, from blows wrathful fled,
House-needy forsooth, and hied him therein,
A man by guilt troubled. Then soon it betided
That therein to the guest there stood grisly terror;
However the wretched, of every hope waning
…
The ill-shapen wight, whenas the fear gat him,
The treasure-vat saw; of such there was a many

Beowulf: Scholar's Edition
Up in that earth-house of treasures of old,
As them in the yore-days, though what man I know not,
The huge leavings and loom of a kindred of high ones,
Well thinking of thoughts there had hidden away.
Dear treasures. But all them had death borne away
In the times of erewhile; and the one at the last
Of the doughty of that folk that there longest lived,
There waxed he friend-sad, yet ween'd he to tarry,
That he for a little those treasures the longsome
Might brook for himself. But a burg now all ready
Wonn'd on the plain nigh the waves of the water,
New by a ness, by narrow-crafts fasten'd;
Within there then bare of the treasures of earls
That herd of the rings a deal hard to carry,
Of gold fair beplated, and few words he quoth:
Hold thou, O earth, now, since heroes may hold not,
The owning of earls. What! it erst within thee
Good men did get to them; now war-death hath gotten,
Life-bale the fearful, each man and every
Of my folk; e'en of them who forwent the life:
The hall-joy had they seen. No man to wear sword
I own, none to brighten the beaker beplated,
The dear drink-vat; the doughty have sought to else-whither.
Now shall the hard war-helm bedight with the gold
Be bereft of its plating; its polishers sleep,
They that the battle-mask erewhile should burnish:
Likewise the war-byrny, which abode in the battle
O'er break of the war-boards the bite of the irons,
Crumbles after the warrior; nor may the ring'd byrny
After the war-leader fare wide afield
On behalf of the heroes: nor joy of the harp is,
No game of the glee-wood; no goodly hawk now
Through the hall swingeth; no more the swift horse
Beateth the burg-stead. Now hath bale-quelling
A many of life-kin forth away sent.
Suchwise sad-moody moaned in sorrow
One after all, unblithely bemoaning
By day and by night, till the welling of death
Touch'd at his heart. The old twilight-scather
Found the hoard's joyance standing all open,
E'en he that, burning, seeketh to burgs,
The evil drake, naked, that flieth a night-tide,
With fire encompass'd; of him the earth-dwellers
Are strongly adrad; wont is he to seek to
The hoard in the earth, where he the gold heathen
Winter-old wardeth; nor a whit him it betters.
So then the folk-scather for three hundred winters
Held in the earth a one of hoard-houses
All-eked of craft, until him there anger'd
A man in his mood, who bare to his man-lord

A beaker beplated, and bade him peace-warding
Of his lord: then was lightly the hoard searched over,
And the ring-hoard off borne; and the boon it was granted
To that wretched-wrought man. There then the lord saw
That work of men foregone the first time of times.
Then awaken'd the Worm, and anew the strife was;
Along the stone stank he, the stout-hearted found
The foot-track of the foe; he had stept forth o'er-far
With dark craft, over-nigh to the head of the drake.
So may the man unfey full easily outlive
The woe and the wrack-journey, he whom the Wielder's
Own grace is holding. Now sought the hoard-warden
Eager over the ground; for the groom he would find
Who unto him sleeping had wrought out the sore:
Hot and rough-moody oft he turn'd round the howe
All on the outward; but never was any man
On the waste; but however in war he rejoiced,
In battle-work. Whiles he turn'd back to his howe
And sought to his treasure-vat; soon he found this,
That one of the grooms had proven the gold,
The high treasures; then the hoard-warden abided,
But hardly forsooth, until come was the even,
And all anger-bollen was then the burg-warden,
And full much would the loath one with the fire-flame pay back
For his drink-vat the dear. Then day was departed
E'en at will to the Worm, and within wall no longer
Would he bide, but awayward with burning he fared,
All dight with the fire: it was fearful beginning
To the folk in the land, and all swiftly it fell
On their giver of treasure full grievously ended.

XXXIII - THE WORM BURNS BEOWULF'S HOUSE, AND BEOWULF GETS READY TO GO AGAINST HIM. BEOWULF'S EARLY DEEDS IN BATTLE WITH THE HETWARE TOLD OF

Began then the guest to spew forth of gleeds,
The bright dwellings to burn; stood the beam of the burning
For a mischief to menfolk; now nothing that quick was
The loathly lift-flier would leave there forsooth;
The war of the Worm was wide to be seen there,
The narrowing foe's hatred anigh and afar,
How he, the fight-scather, the folk of the Geats
Hated and harm'd; shot he back to the hoard,
His dark lordly hall, ere yet was the day's while;
The land-dwellers had he in the light low encompass'd
With bale and with brand; in his burg yet he trusted,
His war-might and his wall: but his weening bewray'd him.
Then Beowulf was done to wit of the terror
Full swiftly forsooth, that the house of himself,

Beowulf: Scholar's Edition

Best of buildings, was molten in wellings of fire,
The gift-stool of the Geats. To the good one was that
A grief unto heart; of mind-sorrows the greatest.
Weened the wise one, that Him, e'en the Wielder,
The Lord everlasting, against the old rights
He had bitterly anger'd; the breast boil'd within him
With dark thoughts, that to him were naught duly wonted.
Now had the fire-drake the own fastness of folk,
The water-land outward, that ward of the earth,
With gleeds to ground wasted; so therefore the war-king,
The lord of the Weder-folk, learned him vengeance.
Then he bade be work'd for him, that fence of the warriors,
And that all of iron, the lord of the earls,
A war-board all glorious, for wissed he yarely
That the holt-wood hereto might help him no whit,
The linden 'gainst fire-flame. Of fleeting days now
The Atheling exceeding good end should abide,
The end of the world's life, and the Worm with him also,
Though long he had holden the weal of the hoard.
Forsooth scorned then the lord of the rings
That he that wide-flier with war-band should seek,
With a wide host; he fear'd not that war for himself,
Nor for himself the Worm's war accounted one whit,
His might and his valour, for that he erst a many
Strait-daring of battles had bided, and liv'd,
Clashings huge of the battle, sithence he of Hrothgar,
He, the man victory-happy, had cleansed the hall,
And in war-tide had gripped the kindred of Grendel,
The loathly of kindreds; nor was that the least
Of hand-meetings, wherein erst was Hygelac slain,
Sithence the Geats' king in the onrush of battle,
The lord-friend of the folks, down away in the Frieslands,
The offspring of Hrethel, died, drunken of sword-drinks,
All beaten of bill. Thence Beowulf came forth
By his own craft forsooth, dreed the work of the swimming;
He had on his arm, he all alone, thirty
Of war-gears, when he to the holm went adown.
Then nowise the Hetware needed to joy them
Over the foot-war, wherein forth against him
They bore the war-linden: few went back again
From that wolf of the battle to wend to their homes.
O'erswam then the waters' round Ecgtheow's son,
Came all wretched and byrd-alone back to his people,
Whereas offer'd him Hygd then the kingdom and hoard,
The rings and the king-stool: trowed naught in the child,
That he 'gainst folks outland the fatherland-seats
Might can how to hold, now was Hygelac dead:
Yet no sooner therefor might the poor folk prevail
To gain from the Atheling in any of ways
That he unto Heardred would be for a lord,

Or eke that that kingdom henceforward should choose;
Yet him midst of the folk with friend-lore he held,
All kindly with honour till older he waxed
And wielded the Weder-Geats. To him men-waifs thereafter
Sought from over the sea, the sons they of Ohthere,
For they erst had withstood the helm of the Scylfings,
E'en him that was best of the kings of the sea,
Of them that in Swede-realm dealt out the treasure,
The mighty of princes. Unto him 'twas a life-mark;
To him without food there was fated the life-wound,
That Hygelac's son, by the swinging of swords;
And him back departed Ongentheow's bairn,
To go seek to his house, sithence Heardred lay dead,
And let Beowulf hold the high seat of the king
And wield there the Geats. Yea, good was that king.

XXXIV - BEOWULF GOES AGAINST THE WORM. HE TELLS OF HEREBEALD AND HÆTHCYN

Of that fall of the folk-king he minded the payment
In days that came after: unto Eadgils he was
A friend to him wretched; with folk he upheld him
Over the wide sea, that same son of Ohthere,
With warriors and weapons. Sithence had he wreaking
With cold journeys of care: from the king took he life.
Now each one of hates thus had he outlived,
And of perilous slaughters, that Ecgtheow's son,
All works that be doughty, until that one day
When he with the Worm should wend him to deal.
So twelvesome he set forth all swollen with anger,
The lord of the Geats, the drake to go look on.
Aright had he learnt then whence risen the feud was,
The bale-hate against men-folk: to his barm then had come
The treasure-vat famous by the hand of the finder;
He was in that troop of men the thirteenth
Who the first of that battle had set upon foot,
The thrall, the sad-minded; in shame must he thenceforth
Wise the way to the plain; and against his will went he
Thereunto, where the earth-hall the one there he wist,
The howe under earth anigh the holm's welling,
The wave-strife: there was it now full all within
With gems and with wires; the monster, the warden,
The yare war-wolf, he held him therein the hoard golden,
The old under the earth: it was no easy cheaping
To go and to gain for any of grooms.
Sat then on the ness there the strife-hardy king
While farewell he bade to his fellows of hearth,
The gold-friend of the Geats; sad was gotten his soul,
Wavering, death-minded; weird nigh beyond measure,

Which him old of years gotten now needs must be greeting,
Must seek his soul's hoard and asunder must deal
His life from his body: no long while now was
The life of the Atheling in flesh all bewounden.
Now spake out Beowulf, Ecgtheow's bairn:
Many a one in my youth of war-onsets I outliv'd,
And the whiles of the battle: all that I remember.
Seven winters had I when the wielder of treasures,
The lord-friend of folk, from my father me took,
Held me and had me Hrethel the king,
Gave me treasure and feast, and remember'd the friendship.
For life thence I was not to him a whit loather,
A berne in his burgs than his bairns were, or each one,
Herebeald, or Hæthcyn, or Hygelac mine.
For the eldest there was in unseemly wise
By the mere deed of kinsman a murder-bed strawen,
Whenas him did Hæthcyn from out of his horn-bow,
His lord and his friend, with shaft lay alow:
His mark he miss'd shooting, and shot down his kinsman,
One brother another with shaft all bebloody'd;
That was fight feeless by fearful crime sinned,
Soul-weary to heart, yet natheless then had
The atheling from life all unwreak'd to be ceasing.
So sad-like it is for a carle that is aged
To be biding the while that his boy shall be riding
Yet young on the gallows; then a lay should he utter,
A sorrowful song whenas hangeth his son
A gain unto ravens, and naught good of avail
May he, old and exceeding old, anywise frame.
Ever will he be minded on every each morning
Of his son's faring otherwhere; nothing he heedeth
Of abiding another withinward his burgs,
An heritage-warder, then whenas the one
By the very death's need hath found out the ill.
Sorrow-careful he seeth within his son's bower
The waste wine-hall, the resting-place now of the winds,
All bereft of the revel; the riders are sleeping,
The heroes in grave, and no voice of the harp is,
No game in the garths such as erewhile was gotten.

XXXV - BEOWULF TELLS OF PAST FEUDS, AND BIDS FAREWELL TO HIS FELLOWS: HE FALLS ON THE WORM, AND THE BATTLE OF THEM BEGINS

Then to sleeping-stead wendeth he, singeth he sorrow,
The one for the other; o'er-roomy all seem'd him
The meads and the wick-stead. So the helm of the Weders
For Herebeald's sake the sorrow of heart
All welling yet bore, and in nowise might he
On the banesman of that life the feud be a-booting;

Nor ever the sooner that warrior might hate
With deeds loathly, though he to him nothing was lief.
He then with the sorrow wherewith that sore beset him
Man's joy-tide gave up, and chose him God's light.
To his offspring he left, e'en as wealthy man doeth,
His land and his folk-burgs when he from life wended.
Then sin was and striving of Swedes and of Geats,
Over the wide water war-tide in common,
The hard horde-hate to wit sithence Hrethel perish'd;
And to them ever were the Ongentheow's sons
Doughty and host-whetting, nowise then would friendship
Hold over the waters; but round about Hreosnaburgh
The fierce fray of foeman was oftentimes fram'd.
Kin of friends that mine were, there they awreaked
The feud and the evil deed, e'en as was famed;
Although he, the other, with his own life he bought it,
A cheaping full hard: unto Hæthcyn it was,
To the lord of the Geat-folk, a life-fateful war.
Learned I that the morrow one brother the other
With the bills' edges wreaked the death on the banesman,
Whereas Ongentheow is a-seeking of Eofor:
Glode the war-helm asunder, the aged of Scylfings
Fell, sword-bleak; e'en so remember'd the hand
Feud enough; nor e'en then did the life-stroke withhold.
I to him for the treasure which erewhile he gave me
Repaid it in warring, as was to me granted,
With my light-gleaming sword. To me gave he land,
The hearth and the home-bliss: unto him was no need
That unto the Gifthas or unto the Spear-Danes
Or into the Swede-realm he needs must go seeking
A worse wolf of war for a worth to be cheaping;
For in the host ever would I be before him
Alone in the fore-front, and so life-long shall I
Be a-framing of strife, whileas tholeth the sword,
Which early and late hath bestead me full often,
Sithence was I by doughtiness unto Day-raven
The hand-bane erst waxen, to the champion of Hug-folk;
He nowise the fretwork to the king of the Frisians,
The breast-worship to wit, might bring any more,
But cringed in battle that herd of the banner,
The Atheling in might: the edge naught was his bane,
But for him did the war-grip the heart-wellings of him
Break, the house of the bones. Now shall the bill's edge,
The hand and hard sword, about the hoard battle.
So word uttered Beowulf, spake out the boast word
For the last while as now: Many wars dared I
In the days of my youth, and now will I yet,
The old warder of folk, seek to the feud,
Full gloriously frame, if the scather of foul-deed

Beowulf: Scholar's Edition

From the hall of the earth me out shall be seeking.
Greeted he then each one of the grooms,
The keen wearers of helms, for the last while of whiles,
His own fellows the dear: No sword would I fare with,
No weapon against the Worm, wist I but how
'Gainst the monster of evil in otherwise might I
Uphold me my boast, as erst did I with Grendel;
But there fire of the war-tide full hot do I ween me,
And the breath, and the venom; I shall bear on me therefore
Both the board and the byrny; nor the burg's warden shall I
Overflee for a foot's-breadth, but unto us twain
It shall be at the wall as to us twain Weird willeth,
The Maker of each man. Of mood am I eager;
So that 'gainst that war-flier from boast I withhold me.
Abide ye upon burg with your byrnies bewarded,
Ye men in your battle-gear, which may the better
After the slaughter-race save us from wounding
Of the twain of us. Naught is it yours to take over,
Nor the measure of any man save alone me,
That he on the monster should mete out his might,
Or work out the earlship: but I with my main might
Shall gain me the gold, or else gets me the battle,
The perilous life-bale, e'en me your own lord.
Arose then by war-round the warrior renowned
Hard under helm, and the sword-sark he bare
Under the stone-cliffs: in the strength then he trowed
Of one man alone; no dastard's way such is.
Then he saw by the wall (e'en he, who so many,
The good of man-bounties, of battles had out-liv'd,
Of crashes of battle whenas hosts were blended)
A stone-bow a-standing, and from out thence a stream
Breaking forth from the burg; was that burn's outwelling
All hot with the war-fire; and none nigh to the hoard then
Might ever unburning any while bide,
Live out through the deep for the flame of the drake.
Out then from his breast, for as bollen as was he,
Let the Weder-Geats' chief the words be out faring;
The stout-hearted storm'd and the stave of him enter'd
Battle-bright sounding in under the hoar stone.
Then uproused was hate, and the hoard-warden wotted
The speech of man's word, and no more while there was
Friendship to fetch. Then forth came there first
The breath of the evil beast out from the stone,
The hot sweat of battle, and dinn'd then the earth.
The warrior beneath the burg swung up his war-round
Against that grisly guest, the lord of the Geats;
Then the heart of the ring-bow'd grew eager therewith
To seek to the strife. His sword ere had he drawn,
That good lord of the battle, the leaving of old,
The undull of edges: there was unto either

Of the bale-minded ones the fear of the other.
All steadfast of mind stood against his steep shield
The lord of the friends, when the Worm was a-bowing
Together all swiftly, in war-gear he bided;
Then boune was the burning one, bow'd in his going,
To the fate of him faring. The shield was well warding
The life and the lyke of the mighty lord king
For a lesser of whiles than his will would have had it,
If he at that frist on the first of the day
Was to wield him, as weird for him never will'd it,
The high-day of battle. His hand he up braided,
The lord of the Geats, and the grisly-fleck'd smote he
With the leaving of Ing, in such wise that the edge fail'd,
The brown blade on the bone, and less mightily bit
Than the king of the nation had need in that stour,
With troubles beset. But then the burg-warden
After the war-swing all wood of his mood
Cast forth the slaughter-flame, sprung thereon widely
The battle-gleams: nowise of victory he boasted,
The gold-friend of the Geats; his war-bill had falter'd,
All naked in war, in such wise as it should not,
The iron exceeding good. Naught was it easy
For him there, the mighty-great offspring of Ecgtheow,
That he now that earth-plain should give up for ever;
But against his will needs must he dwell in the wick
Of the otherwhere country; as ever must each man
Let go of his loan-days. Not long was it thenceforth
Ere the fell ones of fight fell together again.
The hoard-warden up-hearten'd him, welled his breast
With breathing anew. Then narrow need bore he,
Encompass'd with fire, who erst the folk wielded;
Nowise in a heap his hand-fellows there,
The bairns of the athelings, stood all about him
In valour of battle; but they to holt bow'd them;
Their dear life they warded; but in one of them welled
His soul with all sorrow. So sib-ship may never
Turn aside any whit to the one that well thinketh

XXXVI - WIGLAF SON OF WEOHSTAN GOES TO THE HELP OF BEOWULF: NÆGLING, BEOWULF'S SWORD, IS BROKEN ON THE WORM

Wiglaf so hight he, the son of Weohstan,
Lief linden-warrior, and lord of Scylfings,
The kinsman of Aelfhere: and he saw his man-lord
Under his host-mask tholing the heat;
He had mind of the honour that to him gave he erewhile.
The wick-stead the wealthy of them, the Wægmundings,
And the folk-rights each one which his father had owned.

Beowulf: Scholar's Edition

Then he might not withhold him, his hand gripp'd the round,
Yellow linden; he tugg'd out withal the old sword,
That was known among men for the heirloom of Eanmund,
Ohthere's son, unto whom in the strife did become,
To the exile unfriended, Weohstan for the bane
With the sword-edge, and unto his kinsmen bare off
The helm the brown-brindled, the byrny beringed,
And the old eoten-sword that erst Onela gave him;
Were they his kinsman's weed of the war,
Host-fight-gear all ready. Of the feud nothing spake he.
Though he of his brother the bairn had o'er-thrown.
But the host-gear befretted he held many seasons,
The bill and the byrny, until his own boy might
Do him the earlship as did his ere-father.
Amidst of the Geats then he gave him the war-weed
Of all kinds unnumber'd, whenas he from life wended
Old on the forth-way. Then was the first time
For that champion the young that he the war-race
With his high lord the famed e'er he should frame:
Naught melted his mood, naught the loom of his kinsman
Weaken'd in war-tide; that found out the Worm
When they two together had gotten to come.
Now spake out Wiglaf many words rightwise,
And said to his fellows: all sad was his soul:
I remember that while when we gat us the mead,
And whenas we behight to the high lord of us
In the beer-hall, e'en he who gave us these rings,
That we for the war-gear one while would pay,
If unto him thislike need e'er should befall,
For these helms and hard swords. So he chose us from host
To this faring of war by his very own will,
Of glories he minded us, and gave me these gems here,
Whereas us of gar-warriors he counted for good,
And bold bearers of helms. Though our lord e'en for us
This work of all might was of mind all alone
Himself to be framing, the herd of the folk,
Whereas most of all men he hath mightiness framed.
Of deeds of all daring, yet now is the day come
Whereon to our man-lord behoveth the main
Of good battle-warriors; so thereunto wend we,
And help we the host-chief, whiles that the heat be,
The gleed-terror grim. Now of me wotteth God
That to me is much liefer that that, my lyke-body,
With my giver of gold the gleed should engrip.
Unmeet it methinketh that we shields should bear
Back unto our own home, unless we may erst
The foe fell adown and the life-days defend
Of the king of the Weders. Well wot I hereof
That his old deserts naught such were, that he only
Of all doughty of Geats the grief should be bearing.

Sink at strife. Unto us shall one sword be, one helm,
One byrny and shield, to both of us common.
Through the slaughter-reek waded he then, bare his war-helm
To the finding his lord, and few words he quoth:
O Beowulf the dear, now do thee all well,
As thou in thy youthful life quothest of yore,
That naught wouldst thou let, while still thou wert living,
Thy glory fade out. Now shalt thou of deeds famed,
The atheling of single heart, with all thy main deal
For the warding thy life, and to stay thee I will.
Then after these words all wroth came the Worm,
The dire guest foesome, that second of whiles
With fire-wellings flecked, his foes to go look on,
The loath men. With flame was lightly then burnt up
The board to the boss, and might not the byrny
To the warrior the young frame any help yet.
But so the young man under shield of his kinsman
Went onward with valour, whenas his own was
All undone with gleeds; then again the war-king
Remember'd his glories, and smote with mainmight
With his battle-bill, so that it stood in the head
Need-driven by war-hate. Then asunder burst Nægling,
Waxed weak in the war-tide, e'en Beowulf's sword,
The old and grey-marked; to him was not given
That to him any whit might the edges of irons
Be helpful in battle; over-strong was the hand
Which every of swords, by the hearsay of me,
With its swing over-wrought, when he bare unto strife
A wondrous hard weapon; naught it was to him better.
Then was the folk-scather for the third of times yet,
The fierce fire-drake, all mindful of feud;
He rac'd on that strong one, when was room to him given,
Hot and battle-grim; he all the halse of him gripped
With bitter-keen bones; all bebloody'd he waxed
With the gore of his soul. Well'd in waves then the war-sweat.

XXXVII - THEY TWO SLAY THE WORM. BEOWULF IS WOUNDED DEADLY: HE BIDDETH WIGLAF BEAR OUT THE TREASURE

Then heard I that at need of the high king of folk
The upright earl made well manifest might,
His craft and his keenness as kind was to him;
The head there he heeded not (but the hand burned
Of that man of high mood when he helped his kinsman),
Whereas he now the hate-guest smote yet a deal nether,
That warrior in war-gear, whereby the sword dived,
The plated, of fair hue, and thereby fell the flame
To minish thereafter, and once more the king's self

Beowulf: Scholar's Edition

Wielded his wit, and his slaying-sax drew out,
The bitter and battle-sharp, borne on his byrny;
Asunder the Weder's helm smote the Worm midmost;
They felled the fiend, and force drave the life out,
And they twain together had gotten him ending,
Those athelings sib. E'en such should a man be,
A thane good at need. Now that to the king was
The last victory-while, by the deeds of himself,
Of his work of the world. Sithence fell the wound,
That the earth-drake to him had wrought but erewhile,
To swell and to sweal; and this soon he found out,
That down in the breast of him bale-evil welled,
The venom withinward; then the Atheling wended,
So that he by the wall, bethinking him wisdom.
Sat on seat there and saw on the works of the giants,
How that the stone-bows fast stood on pillars,
The earth-house everlasting upheld withinward.
Then with his hand him the sword-gory,
That great king his thane, the good beyond measure,
His friend-lord with water washed full well,
The sated of battle, and unspanned his war-helm.
Forth then spake Beowulf, and over his wound said,
His wound piteous deadly; wist he full well,
That now of his day-whiles all had he dreed,
Of the joy of the earth; all was shaken asunder
The tale of his days; death without measure nigh:
Unto my son now should I be giving
My gear of the battle, if to me it were granted
Any ward of the heritage after my days
To my body belonging. This folk have I holden
Fifty winters; forsooth was never a folk-king
Of the sitters around, no one of them soothly,
Who me with the war-friends durst wend him to greet
And bear down with the terror. In home have I abided
The shapings of whiles, and held mine own well.
No wily hates sought I; for myself swore not many
Of oaths in unright. For all this may I,
Sick with the life-wounds, soothly have joy.
Therefore naught need wyte me the Wielder of men
With kin murder-bale, when breaketh asunder
My life from my lyke. And now lightly go thou
To look on the hoard under the hoar stone,
Wiglaf mine lief, now that lieth the Worm
And sleepeth sore wounded, beshorn of his treasure;
And be hasty that I now the wealth of old time,
The gold-having may look on, and yarely behold
The bright cunning gems, that the softlier may I
After the treasure-weal let go away
My life, and the folk-ship that long I have held.

XXXVIII - BEOWULF BEHOLDETH THE TREASURE AND PASSETH AWAY

Then heard I that swiftly the son of that Weohstan
After this word-say his lord the sore wounded,
Battle-sick, there obeyed, and bare forth his ring-net,
His battle-sark woven, in under the burg-roof;
Saw then victory-glad as by the seat went he,
The kindred-thane moody, sun-jewels a many,
Much glistering gold lying down on the ground,
Many wonders on wall, and the den of the Worm,
The old twilight-flier; there were flagons a-standing,
The vats of men bygone, of brighteners bereft,
And maim'd of adornment; was many an helm
Rusty and old, and of arm-rings a many
Full cunningly twined. All lightly may treasure,
The gold in the ground, every one of mankind
Befool with o'erweening, hide it who will.
Likewise he saw standing a sign there all-golden
High over the hoard, the most of hand-wonders,
With limb-craft belocked, whence light a ray gleamed.
Whereby the den's ground-plain gat he to look on,
The fair works scan throughly. Not of the Worm there
Was aught to be seen now, but the edge had undone him.
Heard I then that in howe of the hoard was bereaving,
The old work of the giants, but one man alone,
Into his barm laded beakers and dishes
At his very own doom; and the sign eke he took,
The brightest of beacons. But the bill of the old lord
(The edge was of iron) erewhile it scathed
Him who of that treasure hand-bearer was
A long while, and fared a-bearing the flame-dread
Before the hoard hot, and welling of fierceness
In the midnights, until that by murder he died.
In haste was the messenger, eager of back-fare,
Further'd with fretted gems. Him longing fordid
To wot whether the bold man he quick there shall meet
In that mead-stead, e'en he the king of the Weders,
All sick of his might, whereas he erst ltft him.
He fetching the treasure then found the king mighty,
His own lord, yet there, and him ever all gory
At end of his life; and he yet once again
Fell the water to warp o'er him, till the word's point
Brake through the breast-hoard, and Beowulf spake out.
The aged, in grief as he gaz'd on the gold:
Now I for these fretworks to the Lord of all thanking,
To the King of all glory, in words am yet saying,
To the Lord ever living, for that which I look on;
Whereas such I might for the people of mine,

Ere ever my death-day, get me to own.
Now that for the treasure-hoard here have I sold
My life and laid down the same, frame still then ever
The folk-need, for here never longer I may be.
So bid ye the war-mighty work me a howe
Bright after the bale-fire at the sea's nose,
Which for a remembrance to the people of me
Aloft shall uplift him at Whale-ness for ever,
That it the sea-goers sithence may hote
Beowulf's Howe, e'en they that the high-ships
Over the flood-mists drive from afar.
Did off from his halse then a ring was all golden,
The king the great-hearted, and gave to his thane,
To the spear-warrior young his war-helm gold-brindled,
The ring and the byrny, and bade him well brook them:
Thou art the end-leaving of all of our kindred,
The Wægmundings; Weird now hath swept all away
Of my kinsmen, and unto the doom of the Maker
The earls in their might; now after them shall I.
That was to the aged lord youngest of words
Of his breast-thoughts, ere ever he chose him the bale,
The hot battle-wellings; from his heart now departed
His soul, to seek out the doom of the soothfast.

XXXIX - WIGLAF CASTETH SHAME ON THOSE FLEERS

But gone was it then with the unaged man
Full hard that there he beheld on the earth
The liefest of friends at the ending of life,
Of bearing most piteous. And likewise lay his bane
The Earth-drake, the loathly fear, reft of his life,
By bale laid undone: the ring-hoards no longer
The Worm, the crook-bowed, ever might wield;
For soothly the edges of the irons him bare off,
The hard battle-sharded leavings of hammers,
So that the wide-flier stilled with wounding
Fell onto earth anigh to his hoard-hall,
Nor along the lift ever more playing he turned
At middle-nights, proud of the owning of treasure,
Show'd the face of him forth, but to earth there he fell
Because of the host-leader's work of the hand.
This forsooth on the land hath thriven to few,
Of men might and main bearing, by hearsay of mine,
Though in each of all deeds full daring he were,
That against venom-scather's fell breathing he set on,
Or the hall of his rings with hand be a-stirring,
If so be that he waking the warder had found
Abiding in burg. By Beowulf was
His deal of the king-treasure paid for by death;
There either had they fared on to the end

Of this loaned life. Long it was not until
Those laggards of battle the holt were a-leaving,
Unwarlike troth-liars, the ten there together,
Who durst not e'en now with darts to be playing
E'en in their man-lord's most mickle need.
But shamefully now their shields were they bearing,
Their weed of the battle, there where lay the aged;
They gazed on Wiglaf where weary'd he sat,
The foot-champion, hard by his very lord's shoulder,
And wak'd him with water: but no whit it sped him;
Never might he on earth howsoe'er well he will'd it
In that leader of spears hold the life any more,
Nor the will of the Wielder change ever a whit;
But still should God's doom of deeds rule the rede
For each man of men, as yet ever it doth.
Then from out of the youngling an answer full grim
Easy got was for him who had lost heart erewhile,
And word gave out Wiglaf, Weohstan's son
The sorrowful-soul'd man: on those unlief he saw:
Lo that may he say who sooth would be saying,
That the man-lord who dealt you the gift of those dear things,
The gear of the war-host wherein there ye stand,
Whereas he on the ale-bench full oft was a-giving
Unto the hall-sitters war-helm and byrny,
The king to his thanes, e'en such as he choicest
Anywhere, far or near, ever might find:
That he utterly wrongsome those weeds of the war
Had cast away, then when the war overtook him.
Surely never the folk-king of his fellows in battle
Had need to be boastful; howsoever God gave him,
The Victory-wielder, that he himself wreaked him
Alone with the edge, when to him need of might was.
Unto him of life-warding but little might I
Give there in the war-tide; and yet I began
Above measure of my might my kinsman to help;
Ever worse was the Worm then when I with sword
Smote the life-foe, and ever the fire less strongly
Welled out from his wit. Of warders o'er little
Throng'd about the king when him the battle befell.
Now shall taking of treasures and giving of swords
And all joy of your country-home fail from your kindred,
All hope wane away; of the land-right moreover
May each of the men of that kinsman's burg ever
Roam lacking; sithence that the athelings eft-soons
From afar shall have heard of your faring in flight,
Your gloryless deed. Yea, death shall be better
For each of the earls than a life ever ill-fam'd.

Beowulf: Scholar's Edition

XL - WIGLAF SENDETH TIDING TO THE HOST: THE WORDS OF THE MESSENGER

Then he bade them that war-work give out at the barriers
Up over the sea-cliff, whereas then the earl-host
The morning-long day sat sad of their mood,
The bearers of war-boards, in weening of both things,
Either the end-day, or else the back-coming
Of the lief man. Forsooth he little was silent
Of the new-fallen tidings who over the ness rode,
But soothly he said over all there a-sitting:
Now is the will-giver of the folk of the Weders,
The lord of the Geats, fast laid in the death-bed,
In the slaughter-rest wonneth he by the Worm's doings.
And beside him yet lieth his very life-winner
All sick with the sax-wounds; with sword might he never
On the monster, the fell one, in any of manners
Work wounding at all. There yet sitteth Wiglaf,
Weohstan's own boy, over Beowulf king,
One earl over the other, over him the unliving;
With heart-honours holdeth he head-ward withal
Over lief, over loath. But to folk is a weening
Of war-tide as now, so soon as unhidden
To Franks and to Frisians the fall of the king
Is become over widely. Once was the strife shapen
Hard 'gainst the Hugs, sithence Hygelac came
Faring with float-host to Frisian land,
Whereas him the Hetware vanquish'd in war,
With might gat the gain, with o'er-mickle main;
The warrior bebyrny'd he needs must bow down:
He fell in the host, and no fretted war-gear
Gave that lord to the doughty, but to us was aye sithence
The mercy ungranted that was of the Merwing.
Nor do I from the Swede folk of peace or good faith
Ween ever a whit. For widely 'twas wotted
That Ongentheow erst had undone the life
Of Hæthcyn the Hrethel's son hard by the Raven-wood,
Then when in their pride the Scylfings of war
Erst gat them to seek to the folk of the Geats.
Unto him soon the old one, the father of Ohthere,
The ancient and fearful gave back the hand-stroke,
Brake up the sea-wise one, rescued his bride.
The aged his spouse erst, bereft of the gold,
Mother of Onela, yea and of Ohthere;
And follow'd up thereon his foemen the deadly,
Until they betook them and sorrowfully therewith
Unto the Raven-holt, reft of their lord.
With huge host then beset he the leaving of swords
All weary with wounds, and woe he behight them,
That lot of the wretched, the livelong night through;

Quoth he that the morrow's morn with the swords' edges
He would do them to death, hang some on the gallows
For a game unto fowl. But again befell comfort
To the sorry of mood with the morrow-day early;
Whereas they of Hygelac's war-horn and trumpet
The voice wotted, whenas the good king his ways came
Faring on in the track of his folk's doughty men.

XLI - MORE WORDS OF THE MESSENGER. HOW HE FEARS THE SWEDES WHEN THEY WOT OF BEOWULF DEAD

Was the track of the war-sweat of Swedes and of Geats,
The men's slaughter-race, right wide to be seen,
How those folks amongst them were waking the feud.
Departed that good one, and went with his fellows,
Old and exceeding sad, fastness to seek;
The earl Ongentheow upward returned;
Of Hygelac's battle-might oft had he heard,
The war-craft of the proud one; in withstanding he trow'd not,
That he to the sea-folk in fight might debate,
Or against the sea-farers defend him his hoard,
His bairns and his bride. He bow'd him aback thence,
The old under the earth-wall. Then was the chase bidden
To the Swede-folk, and Hygelac's sign was upreared,
And the plain of the peace forth on o'er-pass'd they,
After the Hrethlings onto the hedge throng'd.
There then was Ongentheow by the swords' edges,
The blent-hair'd, the hoary one, driven to biding,
So that the folk-king fain must he take
Sole doom of Eofor. Him in his wrath then
Wulf the Wonreding reach'd with his weapon,
So that from the stroke sprang the war-sweat in streams
Forth from under his hair; yet naught fearsome was he,
The aged, the Scylfing, but paid aback rathely
With chaffer that worse was that war-crash of slaughter,
Sithence the folk-king turned him thither;
And nowise might the brisk one that son was of Wonred
Unto the old carle give back the hand-slaying,
For that he on Wulf's head the helm erst had sheared,
So that all with the blood stained needs must he bow,
And fell on the field; but not yet was he fey,
But he warp'd himself up, though the wound had touch'd nigh.
But thereon the hard Hygelac's thane there,
Whenas down lay his brother, let the broad blade,
The old sword of eotens, that helm giant-fashion'd
Break over the board-wall, and down the king bowed,
The herd of the folk unto fair life was smitten.
There were many about there who bound up his kinsman,
Upraised him swiftly when room there was made them,

That the slaughter-stead there at the stour they might wield,
That while when was reaving one warrior the other:
From Ongentheow took he the iron-wrought byrny,
The hard-hilted sword, with his helm all together:
The hoary one's harness to Hygelac bare he;
The fret war-gear then took he, and fairly behight him
Before the folk due gifts, and even so did it;
Gild he gave for that war-race, the lord of the Geats,
The own son of Hrethel, when home was he come,
To Eofor and Wulf gave he over-much treasure,
To them either he gave an hundred of thousands,
Land and lock'd rings. Of the gift none needed to wyte him
Of mid earth, since the glory they gained by battle.
Then to Eofor he gave his one only daughter,
An home-worship soothly, for pledge of his good will.
That is the feud and the foeship full soothly,
The dead-hate of men, e'en as I have a weening,
Wherefor the Swede people against us shall seek,
Sithence they have learned that lieth our lord
All lifeless; e'en he that erewhile hath held
Against all the haters the hoard and the realm;
Who after the heroes' fall held the fierce Scylfings,
Framed the folk-rede, and further thereto
Did earlship-deeds. Now is haste best of all
That we now the folk-king should fare to be seeing,
And then that we bring him who gave us the rings
On his way to the bale: nor shall somewhat alone
With the moody be molten; but manifold hoard is,
Gold untold of by tale that grimly is cheapened,
And now at the last by this one's own life
Are rings bought, and all these the brand now shall fret,
The flame thatch them over: no earl shall bear off
One gem in remembrance; nor any fair maiden
Shall have on her halse a ring-honour thereof,
But in grief of mood henceforth, bereaved of gold,
Shall oft, and not once alone, alien earth tread,
Now that the host-learn'd hath laid aside laughter,
The game and the glee-joy. Therefore shall the spear,
Full many a morn-cold, of hands be bewounden,
Uphoven in hand; and no swough of the harp
Shall waken the warriors; but the wan raven rather
Fain over the fey many tales shall tell forth,
And say to the erne how it sped him at eating,
While he with the wolf was a-spoiling the slain.
So was the keen-whetted a-saying this while
Spells of speech loathly; he lied not much
Of weirds or of words. Then uprose all the war-band,
And unblithe they wended under the Ernes-ness,
All welling of tears, the wonder to look on.
Found they then on the sand, now lacking of soul,

Holding his bed, him that gave them the rings
In time erewhile gone by. But then was the end-day
Gone for the good one; since the king of the battle,
The lord of the Weders, in wonder-death died.
But erst there they saw a more seldom-seen sight,
The Worm on the lea-land over against him
Down lying there loathly; there was the fire-drake,
The grim of the terrors, with gleeds all beswealed.
He was of fifty feet of his measure
Long of his lying. Lift-joyance held he
In the whiles of the night, but down again wended
To visit his den. Now fast was he in death,
He had of the earth-dens the last end enjoyed.
There by him now stood the beakers and bowls,
There lay the dishes and dearly-wrought swords,
Rusty, through-eaten they, as in earth's bosom
A thousand of winters there they had wonned.
For that heritage there was, all craftily eked,
Gold of the yore men, in wizardry wounden;
So that that ring-hall might none reach thereto,
Not any of mankind but if God his own self,
Sooth king of victories, gave unto whom he would
(He is holder of men) to open that hoard,
E'en to whichso of mankind should seem to him meet.

XLII - THEY GO TO LOOK ON THE FIELD OF DEED
Then it was to be seen that throve not the way
To him that unrightly had hidden within there
The fair gear 'neath the wall. The warder erst slew
Some few of folk, and the feud then became
Wrothfully wreaked. A wonder whenas
A valour-strong earl may reach on the ending
Of the fashion of life, when he longer in nowise
One man with his kinsmen may dwell in the mead-hall!
So to Beowulf was it when the burg's ward he sought.
For the hate of the weapons: he himself knew not
Wherethrough forsooth his world's sundering should be.
So until Doomsday they cursed it deeply,
Those princes the dread, who erst there had done it,
That that man should be of sins never sackless,
A-hoppled in shrines, in hell-bonds fast set,
With plague-spots be punish'd, who that plain should plunder.
But naught gold-greedy was he, more gladly had he
The grace of the Owner erst gotten to see.
Now spake out Wiglaf, that son was of Weohstan:
Oft shall many an earl for the will but of one
Dree the wrack, as to us even now is befallen:
Nowise might we learn the lief lord of us,
The herd of the realm, any of rede,

That he should not go greet that warder of gold,
But let him live yet, whereas long he was lying,
And wonne in his wicks until the world's ending;
But he held to high weird and the hoard hath been seen,
Grimly gotten: o'er hard forsooth was that giving,
That the king of the folk e'en thither enticed.
Lo! I was therein, and I look'd it all over,
The gear of the house, when for me room was gotten,
But I lightly in nowise had leave for the passage
In under the earth-wall; in haste I gat hold
Forsooth with my hands of a mickle main burden
Of hoard-treasures, and hither then out did I bear them,
Out unto my king, and then quick was he yet,
Wise, and wit-holding: a many things spake he,
That aged in grief-care, and bade me to greet you,
And prayed ye would do e'en after your friend's deeds
Aloft in the bale-stead a howe builded high,
Most mickle and mighty, as he amongst men was
The worthfullest warrior wide over the world,
While he the burg-weal erewhile might brook.
Then so let us hasten this second of whiles
To see and to seek the throng of things strange,
The wonder 'neath wall; I shall wise you the way,
So that ye from a-near may look on enough
Of rings and broad gold; and be the bier swiftly
All yare thereunto, whenas out we shall fare.
Then let us so ferry the lord that was ours,
The lief man of men, to where long shall he
In the All-Wielder's keeping full patiently wait.
Bade then to bid the bairn of that Weohstan,
The deer of the battle, to a many of warriors,
The house-owning wights, that the wood of the bale
They should ferry from far, e'en the folk-owning men,
Toward the good one. And now shall the gleed fret away,
The wan flame a-waxing, the strong one of warriors,
Him who oft-times abided the shower of iron
When the storm of the shafts driven on by the strings
Shook over the shield-wall, and the shaft held its service,
And eager with feather-gear follow'd the barb.
Now then the wise one, that son was of Weohstan,
Forth from the throng then call'd of the king's thanes
A seven together, the best to be gotten,
And himself went the eighth in under the foe-roof;
One man of the battlers in hand there he bare
A gleam of the fire, of the first went he inward.
It was nowise allotted who that hoard should despoil,
Sithence without warden some deal that there was
The men now beheld in the hall there a-wonning,
Lying there fleeting; little mourn'd any,
That they in all haste outward should ferry

The dear treasures. But forthwith the drake did they shove,
The Worm, o'er the cliff-wall, and let the wave take him,
The flood fathom about the fretted works' herd.
There then was wounden gold on the wain laden
Untold of each kind, and the Atheling borne,
The hoary of warriors, out on to Whale-ness.

XLIII - OF THE BURIAL OF BEOWULF

For him then they geared, the folk of the Geats,
A pile on the earth all unweaklike that was,
With war-helms behung, and with boards of the battle,
And bright byrnies, e'en after the boon that he bade.
Laid down then amidmost their king mighty-famous
The warriors lamenting, the lief lord of them.
Began on the burg of bale-fires the biggest
The warriors to waken: the wood-reek went up
Swart over the smoky glow, sound of the flame
Bewound with the weeping (the wind-blending stilled),
Until it at last the bone-house had broken
Hot at the heart. All unglad of mind
With mood-care they mourned their own liege lord's quelling.
Likewise a sad lay the wife of aforetime
For Beowulf the king, with her hair all upbounden,
Sang sorrow-careful; said oft and over
That harm-days for herself in hard wise she dreaded,
The slaughter-falls many, much fear of the warrior,
The shaming and bondage. Heaven swallow'd the reek.
Wrought there and fashion'd the folk of the Weders
A howe on the lithe, that high was and broad.
Unto the wave-farers wide to be seen:
Then it they betimber'd in time of ten days,
The battle-strong's beacon; the brands' very-leavings
They bewrought with a wall in the worthiest of ways,
That men of all wisdom might find how to work.
Into burg then they did the rings and bright sun-gems,
And all such adornments as in the hoard there
The war-minded men had taken e'en now;
The earls' treasures let they the earth to be holding,
Gold in the grit, wherein yet it liveth,
As useless to men-folk as ever it erst was.
Then round the howe rode the deer of the battle,
The bairns of the athelings, twelve were they in all.
Their care would they mourn, and bemoan them their king,
The word-lay would they utter and over the man speak:
They accounted his earlship and mighty deeds done,
And doughtily deem'd them; as due as it is
That each one his friend-lord with words should belaud,
And love in his heart, whenas forth shall he
Away from the body be fleeting at last.

Beowulf: Scholar's Edition

In such wise they grieved, the folk of the Geats,
For the fall of their lord, e'en they his hearth-fellows;
Quoth they that he was a world-king forsooth,
The mildest of all men, unto men kindest,
To his folk the most gentlest, most yearning of fame.

PERSONS AND PLACES

BEANSTAN, father of Breca.

Beowulf the Dane (not Beowulf the Geat, the hero of the poem) was the grandfather of Hrothgar.

Beowulf the Geat. _See_ the Argument.

Breca, who contended with Beowulf in swimming, was a chief of the Brondings.

Brisings' neck-gear. "This necklace is the Brisinga-men, the costly necklace of Freyja, which she won from the dwarfs and which was stolen from her by Loki, as is told in the Edda" (Kemble). In our poem, it is said that Hama carried off this necklace when he fled from Eormenric, king of the Ostrogoths.

DAYRAVEN, a brave warrior of the Hugs, and probably the slayer of Hygelac, whom, in that case, Beowulf avenged.

EADGILS, Eanmund, "sons of Ohthere," and nephews of the Swedish King Onela, by whom they were banished from their native land for rebellion. They took refuge at the court of the Geat King Heardred, and Onela, "Ongentheow's bairn," enraged at their finding an asylum with his hereditary foes, invaded Geatland, and slew Heardred. At a later time Beowulf, when king of the Geats, balanced the feud by supporting Eadgils in an invasion of Sweden, in which King Onela was slain.

Eanmund, while in exile at the court of the Geats, was slain by Weohstan, father of Wiglaf, and stripped of the armour given him by his uncle, the Swedish King Onela. Weohstan "spake not about the feud, although he had slain Onela's brother's son," probably because he was not proud of having slain an "exile unfriended" in a private quarrel.

Ecglaf, father of Unferth, Hrothgar's spokesman.

Ecgtheow, father of Beowulf the Geat, by the only daughter of Hrethel, king of the Geats. Having slain Heatholaf, a warrior of the Wylfings, Ecgtheow sought protection at the court of the Danish King Hrothgar, who accepted his fealty and settled the feud by a money-payment. Hence the heartiness of Beowulf's welcome at Hrothgar's hands.

Ecgwela. The Scyldings or Danes are once called "Ecgwela's offspring". He may have been the founder of the older dynasty of Danish kings which ended with Heremod.

Eofor, a Geat warrior, brother of Wulf. He came to the aid of his brother in his single combat with the Swedish King Ongentheow, and slew the king, being rewarded by Hygelac with the hand of his only daughter.

Eotens are the people of Finn, king of Friesland. In other passages, it is merely a name for a race of monsters.

FINN. The somewhat obscure Finn episode in Beowulf appears to be part of a Finn epic, of which only the merest fragment, called the Fight at Finnsburg, is extant. The following conjectured outline of the whole story is based on this fragment and on the Beowulf episode; Finn, king of the Frisians, had carried off Hildeburh, daughter of Hoc, probably with her consent. Her father, Hoc, seems to have pursued the fugitives, and to have been slain in the fight which ensued on his overtaking them. After the lapse of some twenty years Hoc's sons, Hnæf and Hengest, are old enough to undertake the duty of avenging their father's death. They make an inroad into Finn's country, and a battle takes place in which many warriors, among them Hnæf and a son of Finn, are killed. Peace is then solemnly concluded, and the slain warriors are burnt. As the year is too far advanced for

Hengest to return home, he and those of his men who survive remain for the winter in the Frisian country with Finn. But Hengest's thoughts dwell constantly on the death of his brother Hnæf, and he would gladly welcome any excuse to break the peace which had been sworn by both parties. His ill-concealed desire for revenge is noticed by the Frisians, who anticipate it by themselves attacking Hengest and his men whilst they are sleeping in the hall. This is the night attack described in the Fight at Finnsburg. It would seem that after a brave and desperate resistance Hengest himself falls in this fight at the hands of the son of Hunlaf, but two of his retainers, Guthlaf and Oslaf, succeed in cutting their way through their enemies and in escaping to their own land. They return with fresh troops, attack and slay Finn, and carry his queen Hildeburh back to the Daneland.

    Folkwalda, father of Finn.

    Franks. Hygelac, king of the Geats, was defeated and slain early in the sixth century, in his historical invasion of the Netherlands, by a combined army of Frisians, Franks, and Hugs.

    Freawaru, daughter of Hrothgar and Wealhtheow. Beowulf tells Hygelac that her father has betrothed her to Ingeld, prince of the Heathobards, in the hope of settling the feud between the two peoples. But he prophesies that the hope will prove vain: for an old Heathobard warrior, seeing a Danish chieftain accompany Freawaru to their court laden with Heathobard spoils, will incite the son of the former owner of the plundered treasure to revenge, until blood is shed, and the feud is renewed. That this was what afterwards befell, we learn from the Old English poem Widsith.

    Friesland, the land of the North Frisians.

    Frieslands, Frisian land, the home of the West Frisians.

    Frisians. Two tribes are to be distinguished: 1. The North Frisians, the people of Finn. 2. The West Frisians, who combined with the Franks and Hugs and defeated Hygelac, between 512 and 520 A.D.

    Froda, father of Ingeld. See Freawaru.

    GUTHLAF and Oslaf. See Finn.

    HÆRETH, father of Hygd, wife of Hygelac.

    Hæthcyn, second son of Hrethel, king of the Geats, and thus elder brother of Hygelac. He accidentally killed his elder brother Herebeald with a bow-shot, to the inconsolable grief of Hrethel. He succeeded to the throne at his father's death, but fell in battle at Ravenwood by the hand of the Swedish King Ongentheow.

    Half-Danes, the tribe to which Hnæf belongs. See Finn.

    Hama. See Brisings.

    Healfdene, king of the Danes, son of Beowulf the Scylding, and father of Hrothgar, "Healfdene's son".

    Heardred, son of Hygelac and Hygd. While still under age he succeeds his father as king of the Geats, Beowulf, who has refused the throne himself, being his counsellor and protector. He is slain by "Ongentheow's bairn", Onela, king of the Swedes.

    Heathobards, Lombards, the tribe of Ingeld, the betrothed of Freawaru, Hrothgar's daughter.

    Heatholaf. See Ecgtheow.

    Helmings. "The Dame of the Helmings" is Hrothgar's queen, Wealhtheow.

    Hemming. "The Kinsman of Hemming" is a name for Offa and for his son Eomær.

    Hengest. See Finn.

Heorogar, elder brother of Hrothgar, did not leave his armour to his son Heoroward; but Hrothgar gives it to Beowulf, and Beowulf gives it to Hygelac.

Herebeald, eldest son of the Geat King Hrethel, was accidentally shot dead with an arrow by his brother Hæthcyn.

Heremod is twice spoken of as a bad and cruel Danish king. In the end he is betrayed into the hands of his foes.

Hereric may have been brother of Hygd, Hygelac's queen, for their son Heardred is spoken of as "the nephew of Hereric".

Here-Scyldings, Army-Scyldings, a name of the Danes.

Hetware, the Hattuarii of the Historia Francorum of Gregory of Tours and of the Gesta Regum Francorum, were the tribe against which Hygelac was raiding when he was defeated and slain by an army of Frisians, Franks, and Hugs.

Hildeburh. See Finn.

Hnæf. See Finn.

Hoc. See Finn.

Hrethel, a former king of the Geats; son of Swerting, father of Hygelac and grandfather of Beowulf, to whom he left his coat of mail. He died of grief at the loss of his eldest son Herebeald, who was accidentally slain by his brother Hæthcyn.

Hrethlings, the people of Hrethel, the Geats.

Hrethmen, Triumph-men, the Danes.

Hrethric, elder son of Hrothgar and Wealhtheow.

Hrothgar. See the Argument.

Hrothulf, probably the son of Hrothgar's younger brother Halga. He lives at the Danish court. Wealhtheow hopes that, if he survives Hrothgar, he will be good to their children in return for their kindness to him. It would seem that this hope was not to be fulfilled ("yet of kindred unsunder'd,".

Hygd, daughter of Hæreth, wife of Hygelac, the king of the Geats, and mother of Heardred. She may well be "the wife of aforetime".

Hygelac, third son of Hrethel and uncle to Beowulf, is the reigning king of the Geats during the greater part of the action of the poem. When his brother Hæthcyn was defeated and slain by Ongentheow at Ravenwood, Hygelac quickly went in pursuit and put Ongentheow to flight; but although, as leader of the attack, he is called "the banesman of Ongentheow", the actual slayer was Eofor, whom Hygelac rewarded with the hand of his only daughter. Hygelac came by his death between 512 and 520 A.D., in his historical invasion of the Netherlands, which is referred to in the poem four times.

ING. See Ingwines.

Ingeld. See Freawaru.

Ingwines, "friends of Ing," the Danes. Ing, according to the Old English Rune-Poem, "was first seen by men amid the East Danes"; he has been identified with Frea.

MERWING, The, the Merovingian king of the Franks.

OFFA. See Thrytho.

Ohthere, son of the Swedish King Ongentheow, and father of Eanmund and Eadgils (q.v.).

Onela, "Ongentheow's bairn" and elder brother of Ohthere, is king of Sweden ("the helm of the Scylfings," at the time of the rebellion of Eanmund and Eadgils. He invades the land of the Geats, which has harboured the rebels, slays Heardred, son of Hygelac, and then retreats before Beowulf. At a later time Beowulf avenges the death of Heardred by supporting Eadgils, "son of Ohthere", in an invasion of Sweden, in which Onela is slain. See also Eadgils; and compare the slaying of Ali by Athils on the ice of Lake Wener in the Icelandic "Heimskringla."

Ongentheow, father of Onela and Ohthere, was a former king of the Swedes. The earlier strife between the Swedes and the Geats, in which he is the chief figure, is fully related by the messenger who brings the tidings of Beowulf's death. In retaliation for the marauding invasions of Onela and Ohthere, Hæthcyn invaded Sweden, and took Ongentheow's queen prisoner. Ongentheow in return invaded the land of her captor, whom he slew, and rescued his wife; but in his hour of triumph he was attacked in his turn by Hygelac near Ravenwood, and fell by the hand of Eofor.

SCANEY, Scede-lands, the most southern portion of the Scandinavian peninsula, belonging to the Danes; used in our poem for the whole Danish kingdom.

Scyld, son of Sheaf, was the mythical founder of the royal Danish dynasty of Scyldings.

Scyldings, descendants of Scyld, properly the name of the reigning Danish dynasty, is commonly extended to include the Danish people.

Scylfing: "the Scylfing", "the aged of Scylfings", is Ongentheow.

Scylfings, the name of the reigning Swedish dynasty, was extended to the Swedish people in the same way as "Scyldings" to the Danes. Beowulf's kinsman Wiglaf is called "lord of Scylfings", and in another passage the name is apparently applied to the Geats; this seems to point to a common ancestry of Swedes and Geats, or it may be that Beowulf's father Ecgtheow was a "Scylfing."

THRYTHO, wife of the Angle King Offa and mother of Eomær, is mentioned in contrast to Hygd, just as Heremod is a foil to Beowulf. She is at first the type of a cruel, unwomanly queen. But by her marriage with Offa, who seems to be her second husband, she is subdued and changed until her fame even adds glory to his.

UNFERTH, son of Ecglaf, is the spokesman of Hrothgar, at whose feet he sits. He is of a jealous disposition, and is twice spoken of as the murderer of his own brothers. Taunting Beowulf with defeat in his swimming-match with Breca, he is silenced by the hero's reply, and more effectually still by the issue of the struggle with Grendel. Afterwards, however, he lends his sword Hrunting for Beowulf's encounter with Grendel's mother.

WÆGMUNDINGS, the family to which both Beowulf and Wiglaf belong. Their fathers, Ecgtheow and Weohstan, may have been sons of Wægmund.

Wedermark, the land of the Weder-Geats, i.e. the Geats.

Weders, Weder-Geats, Geats.

Weland, the Völund of the Edda, the famous smith of Teutonic legend, was the maker of Beowulf's coat of mail. See the figured casket in the British Museum; and compare "Wayland Smith's Cave" near the White Horse, in Berkshire.

Weohstan was the father of Beowulf's kinsman and faithful henchman Wiglaf, and the slayer of Eanmund.

Wonred, father of "Wulf the Wonreding", and of Eofor.

Wulf. See Eofor.

Wulfgar, "a lord of the Wendels", is an official of Hrothgar's court, where he is the first to greet Beowulf and his Geats, and introduces them to Hrothgar.

Wythergyld is a warrior of the Heathobards.

THE MEANING OF SOME WORDS NOT COMMONLY USED NOW

A-banning, the work was, orders for the work were given.
Arede, possess.
Atheling, prince, noble, noble warrior.
Barm, lap, bosom.
Behalsed, embraced by the neck.
Berne, man, warrior, hero.
Bestead, served.
Beswealed, scorched, burnt.
Beswinked, sweated.
Birlers, cup-bearers.
Board, shield.
Bode, announce.
Bollen, swollen, angry.
Boot, compensation.
Boun, made ready.
Braided, drew, lifted.
Brim, sea.
Brook, use, enjoy.
Burg, fortified place, stronghold, mount, barrow; protection; protector; family.
Byrny, coat of mail.
Devil-dray, nest of devils. Cf. squirrel's-dray, common in Berks; used by Cowper.
Dreary, bloody.
Dree, do, accomplish, suffer, enjoy, spend.
Ealdor, chief, lord.
Eme, uncle.
Eoten, giant, monster, enemy.
Fathom, embrace.
Feeless, not to be atoned for with money.
Ferry, bring, carry.
Fifel, monster.
Flyting, contending, scolding.
Fold, the earth.
Forheed, disregard.
Forwritten, proscribed.
Frist, space of time, delay.
Gar, spear.
Graithly, readily, well.
Halse, neck.
Hand-shoal, band of warriors.
Hery, praise.
Hild-play, battle.

Holm, ocean, sea.
Holm-throng, eddy of the sea.
Holt, wood.
Hote, call.
Howe, mound, burial-mound.
Hythe, ferry, haven.
Kemp, champion, fighter.
Lithe, slope.
Loom, heirloom.
Low, flame.
Lyke, body.
Moody, brave, proud.
Nicors, sea-monsters.
Nithing, spite, malice.
O'erthinking, overweening, arrogance.
Rail, railings, coat, armour.
Rimed, counted, reckoned.
Sea-lode, sea-voyage.
Sin, malice, hatred, hostility.
Skinked, poured out.
Slot, track.
Staple, threshold.
Stone-bow, arch of stone.
Sty, stride, ascend, descend.
Sweal, burn.
Through-witting, understanding.
Undern, from 9 o'clock till 12 o'clock; "at undren and at middai," O.E. Miscellany.
Warths, shores, still in use at Wick St. Lawrence, in Somerset.
Wick, dwelling.
Wick-stead, dwelling-place.
Wise, direct, show.
Wit-lust, curiosity.
Worth, shall be.
Wreak, utter.
Wyte, blame, charge with.
Yare, ready.
Yode, went.

Errors and Inconsistencies

List of Names
    Dayraven, Ravenwood
    Freawaru, text reads "Ereawaru"
    Hrethel ... at the loss of his eldest son Herebeald
    Wythergyld, name spelled "Withergyld" in body text

BEÓWULF:

AN ANGLO-SAXON POEM. & THE FIGHT AT FINNSBURH:
A FRAGMENT.
WITH TEXT AND GLOSSARY ON THE BASIS OF M. HEYNE.
EDITED, CORRECTED, AND ENLARGED, BY
JAMES A. HARRISON, LL.D., LITT. D.,
PROFESSOR OF ENGLISH AND MODERN LANGUAGES, WASHINGTON AND LEE UNIVERSITY,
AND
ROBERT SHARP (PH.D. LIPS.),
PROFESSOR OF GREEK AND ENGLISH, TULANE UNIVERSITY OF LOUISIANA.

PREFACE

The favor with which the successive editions of "Beówulf" have been received during the past thirteen years emboldens the editors to continue the work of revision in a fourth issue, the most noticeable feature of which is a considerable body of explanatory Notes, now for the first time added. These Notes mainly concern themselves with new textual readings, with here and there grammatical, geographical, and archæological points that seemed worthy of explanation. Parallelisms and parallel passages are constantly compared, with the view of making the poem illustrate and explain itself. A few emendations and textual changes are suggested by the editors with all possible diffidence; numerous corrections have been made in the Glossary and List of Names; and the valuable parts of former Appendices have been embodied in the Notes.

For the Notes, the editors are much indebted to the various German periodicals mentioned on page 116, to the recent publications of Professors Earle and J. L. Hall, to Mr. S. A. Brooke, and to the Heyne-Socin edition of "Beówulf." No change has been made in the system of accentuation, though a few errors in quantity have been corrected. The editors are looking forward to an eventual fifth edition, in which an entirely new text will be presented.

October, 1893.

This third edition of the American issue of Beówulf will, the editors hope, be found more accurate and useful than either of the preceding editions. Further corrections in text and glossary have been made, and some additional new readings and suggestions will be found in two brief appendices at the back of the book. Students of the metrical system of Beówulf will find ample material for their studies in Sievers' exhaustive essay on that subject (Beiträge, X. 209-314).

Socin's edition of Heyne's Beówulf (called the fifth edition) has been utilized to some extent in this edition, though it unfortunately came too late to be freely used. While it repeats many of the omissions and inaccuracies of Heyne's fourth edition, it contains much that is valuable to the student, particularly in the notes and commentary. Students of the poem, which has been subjected to much searching criticism during the last decade, will also derive especial help from the contributions of Sievers and Kluge on difficult questions appertaining to it. Wülker's new edition (in the Grein Bibliothek) is of the highest value, however one may dissent from particular textual views laid down in the 'Berichtigter Text.' Paul and Braune's Beiträge contain a varied miscellany of hints, corrections, and suggestions principally embodying the views of Kluge, Cosijn, Sievers, and Bugge, some of the more important of which are found in the appendices to the present and the preceding edition. Holder and Zupitza, Sarrazin and Hermann Möller (Kiel, 1883), Heinzel (Anzeiger f.d. Alterthum, X.), Gering (Zacher's Zeitschrift, XII.), Brenner (Eng. Studien, IX.), and the contributors to Anglia, have assisted materially in the textual and metrical interpretation of the poem.

The subject of Anglo-Saxon quantity has been discussed in several able essays by Sievers, Sweet, Ten Brink (Anzeiger, f.d. Alterthum, V.), Kluge (Beiträge, XI.), and others; but so much is uncertain in this field that the editors have left undisturbed the marking of vowels found in the text of their original edition, while indicating in the appendices the now accepted views of scholars on the quantity of the personal pronouns (mê, wê, þû, þê, gê, hê); the adverb nû, etc. Perhaps it would be best to banish absolutely all attempts at marking quantities except in cases where the Ms. has them marked.

An approximately complete Bibliography of Beówulf literature will be found in Wülker's Grundriss and in Garnett's translation of the poem.

JAMES A. HARRISON,
ROBERT SHARP.
WASHINGTON AND LEE UNIVERSITY,
LEXINGTON, VA., May, 1888.

The editors feel so encouraged at the kind reception accorded their edition of Beówulf (1883), that, in spite of its many shortcomings, they have determined to prepare a second revised edition of the book, and thus endeavor to extend its sphere of usefulness. About twenty errors had, notwithstanding a vigilant proof-reading, crept into the text,--errors in single letters, accents, and punctuation. These have been corrected, and it is hoped that the text has been rendered generally accurate and trustworthy. In the List of Names one or two corrections have been made, and in the Glossary numerous mistakes in gender, classification, and translation, apparently unavoidable in a first edition, have been rectified. Wherever these mistakes concern single letters, or occupy very small space, they have been corrected in the plates; where they are longer, and the expense of correcting them in the plates would have been very great, the editors have thought it best to include them in an Appendix of Corrections and Additions, which will be found at the back of the book. Students are accordingly referred to this Appendix for important longer corrections and additions. It is believed that the value of the book has been much enhanced by an Appendix of Recent Readings, based on late criticisms and essays from the pens of Sievers, Kluge, Cosijn, Holder, Wülker, and Sweet. A perplexed student, in turning to these suggested readings, will often find great help in unravelling obscure or corrupt passages.

The objectionable ä and æ, for the short and the long diphthong, have been retained in the revised edition, owing to the impossibility of removing them without entirely recasting the plates.

In conclusion, the editors would acknowledge their great indebtedness to the friends and critics whose remarks and criticisms have materially aided in the correction of the text,--particularly to Profs. C.P.G. Scott, Baskervill, Price, and J.M. Hart; to Prof. J.W. Bright; and to the authorities of Cornell University, for the loan of periodicals necessary to the completeness of the revision. While the second revised edition still contains much that might be improved, the editors cannot but hope that it is an advance on its predecessor, and that it will continue its work of extending the study of Old English throughout the land.

JUNE, 1885.

NOTE I

The present work, carefully edited from Heyne's fourth edition, (Paderborn, 1879), is designed primarily for college classes in Anglo-Saxon, rather than for independent investigators or for seekers after a restored or ideal text. The need of an American edition of "Beówulf" has long been felt, as, hitherto, students have had either to send to Germany for a text, or secure, with great trouble, one of the scarce and expensive English editions. Heyne's first edition came out in 1863, and was followed in 1867 and 1873 by a second and a third edition, all three having essentially the same text.

So many important contributions to the "Beówulf" literature were, however, made between 1873 and 1879 that Heyne found it necessary to put forth a new edition (1879). In this new, last edition, the text was subjected to a careful revision, and was fortified by the views, contributions, and criticisms of other zealous scholars. In it the collation of the unique "Beówulf" Ms. (Vitellius A. 15: Cottonian Mss. of the British Museum), as made by E. Kölbing in Herrig's Archiv (Bd. 56; 1876), was followed wherever the present condition of the Ms. had to be discussed; and the researches of Bugge, Bieger, and others, on single passages, were made use of. The discussion of the metrical structure of the poem, as occurring in the second and third editions, was omitted in the fourth, owing to the many controversies in which the subject is still involved. The present editor has thought it best to do the same, though, happily, the subject of Old English Metrik is undergoing a steady illumination through the labors of Schipper and others.

Some errors and misplaced accents in Heyne's text have been corrected in the present edition, in which, as in the general revision of the text, the editor has been most kindly aided by Prof. J.M. Garnett, late Principal of St. John's College, Maryland.

In the preparation of the present school edition it has been thought best to omit Heyne's notes, as they concern themselves principally with conjectural emendations, substitutions of one reading for another, and discussions of the condition of the Ms. Until Wülker's text and the photographic fac-simile of the original Ms. are in the hands of all scholars, it will be better not to introduce such matters in the school room, where they would puzzle without instructing.

For convenience of reference, the editor has added a head-line to each "fit" of the poem, with a view to facilitate a knowledge of its episodes.

WASHINGTON AND LEE UNIVERSITY,
LEXINGTON, VA., June, 1882.

NOTE II

The editors now have the pleasure of presenting to the public a complete text and a tolerably complete glossary of "Beówulf." The edition is the first published in America, and the first of its special kind presented to the English public, and it is the initial volume of a "Library of Anglo-Saxon Poetry," to be edited under the same auspices and with the coöperation of distinguished scholars in this country. Among these scholars may be mentioned Professors F.A. March of Lafayette College, T.K. Price of Columbia College, and W.M. Baskervill of Vanderbilt University.

In the preparation of the Glossary the editors found it necessary to abandon a literal and exact translation of Heyne for several reasons, and among others from the fact that Heyne seems to be wrong in the translation of some of his illustrative quotations, and even translates the same passage in two or three different ways under different headings. The orthography of his glossary differs considerably from the orthography of his text. He fails to discriminate with due nicety the meanings of many of the words in his vocabulary, while criticism more recent than his latest edition (1879) has illustrated or overthrown several of his renderings. The references were found to be incorrect in innumerable instances, and had to be verified in every individual case so far as this was possible, a few only, which resisted all efforts at verification, having to be indicated by an interrogation point (?). The references are exceedingly numerous, and the labor of verifying them was naturally great. To many passages in the Glossary, where Heyne's translation could not be trusted with entire certainty, the editors have added other translations of phrases and sentences or of special words; and in this they have been aided by a careful study of the text and a comparison and utilization of the views of Kemble and Professor J.M. Garnett (who takes Grein for his foundation). Many new references have been added; and the various passages in which Heyne fails to indicate whether a given verb is weak or strong, or fails to point out the number, etc., of the illustrative form, have been corrected and made to harmonize with the general plan of the work. Numerous misprints in the glossary have also been corrected, and a brief glossary to the Finnsburh-fragment, prepared by Dr. Wm. Hand Browne, and supplemented and adapted by the editor-in-chief, has been added.

The editors think that they may without immodesty put forth for themselves something more than the claim of being re-translators of a translation: the present edition is, so far as they were able to make it so, an adaptation, correction, and extension of the work of the great German scholar to whose loving appreciation of the Anglo-Saxon epic all students of Old English owe a debt of gratitude. While following his usually sure and cautious guidance, and in the main appropriating his results, they have thought it best to deviate from him in the manner above indicated, whenever it seemed that he was wrong. The careful reader will notice at once the marks of interrogation which point out these deviations, or which introduce a point of view illustrative of, or supplementary to, the one given by the German editor. No doubt the editors are wrong themselves in many places,-- "Beówulf" is a most difficult poem,--but their view may at least be defended by a reference to the original text, which they have faithfully and constantly consulted.

Beowulf: Scholar's Edition

A good many cognate Modern English words have been introduced here and there in the Glossary with a view to illustration, and other addenda will be found between brackets and parenthetical marks.

It is hoped that the present edition of the most famous of Old English poems will do something to promote a valuable and interesting study.

JAMES A. HARRISON,
Washington and Lee University, Lexington, Va.

ROBERT SHARP,
University of Louisiana, New Orleans.
April, 1883.

The responsibility of the editors is as follows: H. is responsible for the Text, and for the Glossary from hrînan on; S. for the List of Names, and for the Glossary as far as hrînan.

ARGUMENT

The only national [Anglo-Saxon] epic which has been preserved entire is Beówulf. Its argument is briefly as follows:--The poem opens with a few verses in praise of the Danish Kings, especially Scild, the son of Sceaf. His death is related, and his descendants briefly traced down to Hroðgar. Hroðgar, elated with his prosperity and success in war, builds a magnificent hall, which he calls Heorot. In this hall Hroðgar and his retainers live in joy and festivity, until a malignant fiend, called Grendel, jealous of their happiness, carries off by night thirty of Hroðgar's men, and devours them in his moorland retreat. These ravages go on for twelve years. Beówulf, a thane of Hygelac, King of the Goths, hearing of Hroðgar's calamities, sails from Sweden with fourteen warriors--to help him. They reach the Danish coast in safety; and, after an animated parley with Hroðgar's coastguard, who at first takes them for pirates, they are allowed to proceed to the royal hall, where they are well received by Hroðgar. A banquet ensues, during which Beówulf is taunted by the envious Hunferhð about his swimming-match with Breca, King of the Brondings. Beówulf gives the true account of the contest, and silences Hunferhð. At night-fall the King departs, leaving Beówulf in charge of the hall. Grendel soon breaks in, seizes and devours one of Beówulf's companions; is attacked by Beówulf, and, after losing an arm, which is torn off by Beówulf, escapes to the fens. The joy of Hroðgar and the Danes, and their festivities, are described, various episodes are introduced, and Beówulf and his companions receive splendid gifts. The next night Grendel's mother revenges her son by carrying off Æschere, the friend and councillor of Hroðgar, during the absence of Beówulf. Hroðgar appeals to Beówulf for vengeance, and describes the haunts of Grendel and his mother. They all proceed thither; the scenery of the lake, and the monsters that dwell in it, are described. Beówulf plunges into the water, and attacks Grendel's mother in her dwelling at the bottom of the lake. He at length overcomes her, and cuts off her head, together with that of Grendel, and brings the heads to Hroðgar. He then takes leave of Hroðgar, sails back to Sweden, and relates his adventures to Hygelac. Here the first half of the poem ends. The second begins with the accession of Beówulf to the throne, after the fall of Hygelac and his son Heardred. He rules prosperously for fifty years, till a dragon, brooding over a hidden treasure, begins to ravage the country, and destroys Beówulf's palace with fire. Beówulf sets out in quest of its hiding-place, with twelve men. Having a presentiment of his approaching end, he pauses and recalls to mind his past life and exploits. He then takes leave of his followers, one by one, and advances alone to attack the dragon. Unable, from the heat, to enter the cavern, he shouts aloud, and the dragon comes forth. The dragon's scaly hide is proof against Beówulf's sword, and he is reduced to great straits. Then Wiglaf, one of his followers, advances to help him. Wiglaf's shield is consumed by the dragon's fiery breath, and he is compelled to seek shelter under Beówulf's shield of iron. Beówulf's sword snaps asunder, and he is seized by the dragon. Wiglaf stabs the dragon from underneath, and Beówulf cuts it in two with his dagger. Feeling that his end is near, he bids Wiglaf bring out the treasures from the cavern, that he may see them before he dies. Wiglaf enters the dragon's den, which is described, returns to Beówulf, and receives his last commands. Beówulf dies, and Wiglaf bitterly reproaches his companions for their cowardice. The disastrous consequences of Beówulf's death are then foretold, and the poem ends with his funeral.--H. Sweet, in Warton's History of English Poetry, Vol. II. (ed. 1871). Cf. also Ten Brink's History of English Literature.

BEÓWULF

I - THE PASSING OF SCYLD

Hwät! we Gâr-Dena   in geâr-dagum
þeód-cyninga   þrym gefrunon,
hû þâ äðelingas   ellen fremedon.
Oft Scyld Scêfing   sceaðena þreátum,
monegum mægðum   meodo-setla ofteáh.
Egsode eorl,   syððan ærest wearð
feá-sceaft funden: he þäs frôfre gebâd,
weôx under wolcnum,   weorð-myndum ðâh,
ôð þät him æghwylc   þâra ymb-sittendra
ofer hron-râde   hýran scolde,
gomban gyldan: þät wäs gôd cyning!
þäm eafera wäs   äfter cenned
geong in geardum,   þone god sende
folce tô frôfre;   fyren-þearfe ongeat,
þät hie ær drugon   aldor-leáse
lange hwîle.   Him þäs lîf-freá,
wuldres wealdend,   worold-âre forgeaf;
Beówulf wäs breme   (blæd wîde sprang),
Scyldes eafera   Scede-landum in.
Swâ sceal geong guma,   gôde gewyrcean,
fromum feoh-giftum   on fäder wine,
þät hine on ylde   eft gewunigen
wil-gesîðas,   þonne wîg cume,
leóde gelæsten: lof-dædum sceal
in mægða gehwære   man geþeón.
Him þâ Scyld gewât   tô gescäp-hwîle
fela-hrôr fêran   on freán wære;

hi hyne þâ ätbæron   tô brimes faroðe.
swæse gesîðas,   swâ he selfa bäd,
þenden wordum weóld   wine Scyldinga,
leóf land-fruma   lange âhte.
Þær ät hýðe stôd   hringed-stefna,
îsig and ûtfûs,   äðelinges fär;
â-lêdon þâ   leófne þeóden,
beága bryttan   on bearm scipes,
mærne be mäste.   Þær wäs mâdma fela,
of feor-wegum   frätwa gelæded:
ne hýrde ic cymlîcor   ceól gegyrwan
hilde-wæpnum   and heaðo-wædum,
billum and byrnum;   him on bearme läg
mâdma mänigo,   þâ him mid scoldon
on flôdes æht   feor gewîtan.
Nalas hi hine lässan   lâcum teódan,
þeód-gestreónum,   þonne þâ dydon,
þe hine ät frumsceafte   forð onsendon
ænne ofer ýðe   umbor wesende:
þâ gyt hie him âsetton   segen gyldenne
heáh ofer heáfod,   lêton holm beran,
geâfon on gâr-secg: him wäs geômor sefa,
murnende môd.   Men ne cunnon
secgan tô soðe   sele-rædende,
häleð under heofenum,   hwâ þäm hläste onfêng.

II - THE HALL HEOROT

Þâ wäs on burgum   Beówulf Scyldinga,
leóf leód-cyning,   longe þrage
folcum gefræge   (fäder ellor hwearf,
aldor of earde),   ôð þät him eft onwôc
heáh Healfdene;   heóld þenden lifde,
gamol and gûð-reów,   gläde Scyldingas.
Þäm feówer bearn   forð-gerîmed
in worold wôcun,   weoroda ræswan,
Heorogâr and Hrôðgâr   and Hâlga til;
hýrde ic, þat Elan cwên   Ongenþeówes wäs
Heaðoscilfinges   heals-gebedde.
Þâ wäs Hrôðgâre   here-spêd gyfen,
wîges weorð-mynd,   þät him his wine-mâgas
georne hýrdon,   ôð þät seó geogoð geweôx,
mago-driht micel.   Him on môd bearn,
þät heal-reced   hâtan wolde,
medo-ärn micel   men gewyrcean,
þone yldo bearn   æfre gefrunon,
and þær on innan   eall gedælan
geongum and ealdum,   swylc him god sealde,
bûton folc-scare   and feorum gumena.
Þâ ic wîde gefrägn   weorc gebannan

manigre mægðe   geond þisne middan-geard,
folc-stede frätwan.   Him on fyrste gelomp
ädre mid yldum,   þät hit wearð eal gearo,
heal-ärna mæst;   scôp him Heort naman,
se þe his wordes geweald   wîde häfde.
He beót ne âlêh,   beágas dælde,
sinc ät symle.   Sele hlifade
heáh and horn-geáp: heaðo-wylma bâd,
lâðan lîges;   ne wäs hit lenge þâ gen
þät se ecg-hete   âðum-swerian
äfter wäl-nîðe   wäcnan scolde.
Þâ se ellen-gæst   earfoðlîce
þrage geþolode,   se þe in þýstrum bâd,
þät he dôgora gehwâm   dreám gehýrde
hlûdne in healle;   þær wäs hearpan swêg,
swutol sang scôpes.   Sägde se þe cûðe
frum-sceaft fira   feorran reccan,
cwäð þät se älmihtiga   eorðan worhte,
wlite-beorhtne wang,   swâ wäter bebûgeð,
gesette sige-hrêðig   sunnan and mônan
leóman tô leóhte   land-bûendum,
and gefrätwade   foldan sceátas
leomum and leáfum;   lîf eác gesceôp
cynna gehwylcum,   þâra þe cwice hwyrfað.
Swâ þâ driht-guman   dreámum lifdon
eádiglîce,   ôð þät ân ongan
fyrene fremman,   feónd on helle:
wäs se grimma gäst   Grendel hâten,
mære mearc-stapa,   se þe môras heóld,
fen and fästen;   fîfel-cynncs card
won-sælig wer   weardode hwîle,
siððan him scyppend   forscrifen häfde.
In Caines cynne   þone cwealm gewräc,
êce drihten,   þäs þe he Abel slôg;
ne gefeah he þære fæhðe,   ac he hine feor forwräc,
metod for þý mâne   man-cynne fram.
Þanon untydras   ealle onwôcon,
eotenas and ylfe   and orcnêas,
swylce gigantas,   þâ wið gode wunnon
lange þrage;   he him þäs leán forgeald.

III - GRENDEL'S VISITS

Gewât þâ neósian,   syððan niht becom,
heán hûses,   hû hit Hring-Dene
äfter beór-þege   gebûn häfdon.
Fand þâ þær inne   äðelinga gedriht
swefan äfter symble;   sorge ne cûðon,
won-sceaft wera.   Wiht unhælo
grim and grædig   gearo sôna wäs,

reóc and rêðe,   and on räste genam
þritig þegna: þanon eft gewât
hûðe hrêmig   tô hâm faran,
mid þære wäl-fylle   wîca neósan.
Þâ wäs on uhtan   mid ær-däge
Grendles gûð-cräft   gumum undyrne:
þâ wäs äfter wiste   wôp up âhafen,
micel morgen-swêg.   Mære þeóden,
äðeling ær-gôd,   unblîðe sät,
þolode þrýð-swýð,   þegn-sorge dreáh,
syððan hie þäs lâðan   lâst sceáwedon,
wergan gâstes;   wäs þät gewin tô strang,
lâð and longsum.   Näs hit lengra fyrst,
ac ymb âne niht   eft gefremede
morð-beala mâre   and nô mearn fore
fæhðe and fyrene;   wäs tô fäst on þâm.
Þâ wäs eáð-fynde,   þe him elles hwær
gerûmlîcor   räste sôhte,
bed äfter bûrum,   þâ him gebeácnod wäs,
gesägd sôðlîce   sweotolan tâcne
heal-þegnes hete;   heóld hine syððan
fyr and fästor,   se þäm feónde ätwand.
Swâ rîxode   and wið rihte wan
âna wið eallum,   ôð þät îdel stôd
hûsa sêlest.   Wäs seó hwîl micel:
twelf wintra tîd   torn geþolode
wine Scyldinga,   weána gehwelcne,
sîdra sorga;   forþam syððan wearð
ylda bearnum   undyrne cûð,
gyddum geômore,   þätte Grendel wan,
hwîle wið Hrôðgâr;--   hete-nîðas wäg,
fyrene and fæhðe   fela missera,
singale säce,   sibbe ne wolde
wið manna hwone   mägenes Deniga
feorh-bealo feorran,   feó þingian,
ne þær nænig witena   wênan þorfte
beorhtre bôte   tô banan folmum;
atol äglæca   êhtende wäs,
deorc deáð-scûa   duguðe and geogoðe
seomade and syrede.   Sin-nihte heóld
mistige môras;   men ne cunnon,
hwyder hel-rûnan   hwyrftum scrîðað.
Swâ fela fyrena   feónd man-cynnes,
atol ân-gengea,   oft gefremede
heardra hýnða;   Heorot eardode,
sinc-fâge sel   sweartum nihtum
(nô he þone gif-stôl   grêtan môste,
mâððum for metode,   ne his myne wisse);
þät wäs wræc micel   wine Scyldinga,
môdes brecða.   Monig-oft gesät

rîce tô rûne;   ræd eahtedon,
hwät swîð-ferhðum   sêlest wære
wið fær-gryrum   tô gefremmanne.
Hwîlum hie gehêton   ät härg-trafum
wig-weorðunga,   wordum bædon,
þät him gâst-bona   geóce gefremede
wið þeód-þreáum.   Swylc wäs þeáw hyra,
hæðenra hyht;   helle gemundon
in môd-sefan,   metod hie ne cûðon,
dæda dêmend,   ne wiston hie drihten god,
ne hie hûru heofena helm   hêrian ne cûðon,
wuldres waldend.   Wâ bið þäm þe sceal
þurh slîðne nîð   sâwle bescûfan
in fýres fäðm,   frôfre ne wênan,
wihte gewendan;   wel bið þäm þe môt
äfter deáð-däge   drihten sêcean
and tô fäder fäðmum   freoðo wilnian.

IV - HYGELAC'S THANE

Swâ þâ mæl-ceare   maga Healfdenes
singala seáð;   ne mihte snotor häleð
weán onwendan: wäs þät gewin tô swýð,
lâð and longsum,   þe on þâ leóde becom,
nýd-wracu nîð-grim,   niht-bealwa mæst.
Þät fram hâm gefrägn   Higelâces þegn,
gôd mid Geátum,   Grendles dæda:
se wäs mon-cynnes   mägenes strengest
on þäm däge   þysses lîfes,
äðele and eácen.   Hêt him ýð-lidan
gôdne gegyrwan;   cwäð he gûð-cyning
ofer swan-râde   sêcean wolde,
mærne þeóden,   þâ him wäs manna þearf.
Þone sîð-fät him   snotere ceorlas
lyt-hwôn lôgon,   þeáh he him leóf wære;
hwetton higerôfne,   hæl sceáwedon.
Häfde se gôda   Geáta leóda
cempan gecorone,   þâra þe he cênoste
findan mihte;   fîftena sum
sund-wudu sôhte;   secg wîsade,
lagu-cräftig mon,   land-gemyrcu.
Fyrst forð gewât: flota wäs on ýðum,
bât under beorge.   Beornas gearwe
on stefn stigon;   streámas wundon
sund wið sande;   secgas bæron
on bearm nacan   beorhte frätwe,
gûð-searo geatolîc;   guman ût scufon,
weras on wil-sîð   wudu bundenne.
Gewât þâ ofer wæg-holm   winde gefýsed
flota fâmig-heals   fugle gelîcost,

ôð þät ymb ân-tîd   ôðres dôgores
wunden-stefna   gewaden häfde,
þät þâ lîðende   land gesâwon,
brim-clifu blîcan,   beorgas steápe,
sîde sæ-nässas: þâ wäs sund liden,
eoletes ät ende.   Þanon up hraðe
Wedera leóde   on wang stigon,
sæ-wudu sældon   (syrcan hrysedon,
gûð-gewædo);   gode þancedon,
þäs þe him ýð-lâde   eáðe wurdon.
Þâ of wealle geseah   weard Scildinga,
se þe holm-clifu   healdan scolde,
beran ofer bolcan   beorhte randas,
fyrd-searu fûslîcu;   hine fyrwyt bräc
môd-gehygdum,   hwät þâ men wæron.
Gewât him þâ tô waroðe   wicge rîdan
þegn Hrôðgâres,   þrymmum cwehte
mägen-wudu mundum,   meðel-wordum frägn:
"Hwät syndon ge   searo-häbbendra
"byrnum werede,   þe þus brontne ceól
"ofer lagu-stræte   lædan cwômon,
"hider ofer holmas   helmas bæron?
"Ic wäs ende-sæta,   æg-wearde heóld,
"þät on land Dena   lâðra nænig
"mid scip-herge   sceððan ne meahte.
"Nô her cûðlîcor   cuman ongunnon
"lind-häbbende;   ne ge leáfnes-word
"gûð-fremmendra   gearwe ne wisson,
"mâga gemêdu.   Næfre ic mâran geseah
"eorla ofer eorðan,   þonne is eówer sum,
"secg on searwum;   nis þät seld-guma
"wæpnum geweorðad,   näfne him his wlite leóge,
"ænlîc an-sýn.   Nu ic eówer sceal
"frum-cyn witan,   ær ge fyr heonan
"leáse sceáweras   on land Dena
"furður fêran.   Nu ge feor-bûend,
"mere-lîðende,   mînne gehýrað
"ân-fealdne geþôht: ôfost is sêlest
"tô gecýðanne,   hwanan eówre cyme syndon."

V - THE ERRAND

Him se yldesta   andswarode,
werodes wîsa,   word-hord onleác:
"We synt gum-cynnes   Geáta leóde
"and Higelâces   heorð-geneátas.
"Wäs mîn fäder   folcum gecýðed,
"äðele ord-fruma   Ecgþeów hâten;
"gebâd wintra worn,   ær he on weg hwurfe,
"gamol of geardum;   hine gearwe geman

"witena wel-hwylc   wîde geond eorðan.--
"We þurh holdne hige   hlâford þinne,
"sunu Healfdenes,   sêcean cwômon,
"leód-gebyrgean: wes þu ûs lârena gôd!
"Habbað we tô þäm mæran   micel ærende
"Deniga freán;   ne sceal þær dyrne sum
"wesan, þäs ic wêne.   Þu wâst, gif hit is,
"swâ we sôðlice   secgan hýrdon,
"þät mid Scyldingum   sceaða ic nât hwylc,
"deógol dæd-hata,   deorcum nihtum
"eáweð þurh egsan   uncûðne nîð,
"hýnðu and hrâ-fyl.   Ic þäs Hrôðgâr mäg
"þurh rûmne sefan   ræd gelæran,
"hû he frôd and gôd   feónd oferswýðeð,
"gyf him ed-wendan   æfre scolde
"bealuwa bisigu,   bôt eft cuman
"and þâ cear-wylmas   côlran wurðað;
"oððe â syððan   earfoð-þrage,
"þreá-nýd þolað,   þenden þær wunað
"on heáh-stede   hûsa sêlest."
Weard maðelode,   þær on wicge sät
ombeht unforht: "Æghwäðres sceal
"scearp scyld-wîga   gescâd witan,
"worda and worca,   se þe wel þenceð.
"Ic þät gehýre,   þät þis is hold weorod
"freán Scyldinga.   Gewîtað forð beran
"wæpen and gewædu,   ic eów wîsige:
"swylce ic magu-þegnas   mîne hâte
"wið feónda gehwone   flotan eówerne,
"niw-tyrwedne   nacan on sande
"ârum healdan,   ôð þät eft byreð
"ofer lagu-streámas   leófne mannan
"wudu wunden-hals   tô Weder-mearce.
"Gûð-fremmendra   swylcum gifeðe bið,
"þät þone hilde-ræs   hâl gedîgeð."
Gewiton him þâ fêran   (flota stille bâd,
seomode on sâle   sîd-fäðmed scyp,
on ancre fäst);   eofor-lîc scionon
ofer hleór-beran   gehroden golde
fâh and fýr-heard,   ferh wearde heóld.
Gûðmôde grummon,   guman onetton,
sigon ätsomne,   ôð þät hy säl timbred
geatolîc and gold-fâh   ongytan mihton;
þät wäs fore-mærost   fold-bûendum
receda under roderum,   on þäm se rîca bâd;
lixte se leóma   ofer landa fela.
Him þâ hilde-deór   hof môdigra
torht getæhte,   þät hie him tô mihton
gegnum gangan;   gûð-beorna sum

wicg gewende,   word äfter cwäð:
"Mæl is me tô fêran;   fäder alwalda
"mid âr-stafum   eówic gehealde
"sîða gesunde!   ic tô sæ wille,
"wið wrâð werod   wearde healdan."

VI - BEÓWULF'S SPEECH

Stræt wäs stân-fâh,   stîg wîsode
gumum ätgädere.   Gûð-byrne scân
heard hond-locen,   hring-îren scîr
song in searwum,   þâ hie tô sele furðum
in hyra gryre-geatwum   gangan cwômon.
Setton sæ-mêðe   sîde scyldas,
rondas regn-hearde   wið þäs recedes weal,
bugon þâ tô bence;   byrnan hringdon,
gûð-searo gumena;   gâras stôdon,
sæ-manna searo,   samod ätgädere,
äsc-holt ufan græg;   wäs se îren-þreát
wæpnum gewurðad.   Þâ þær wlonc häleð
oret-mecgas   äfter äðelum frägn:
"Hwanon ferigeað ge   fätte scyldas,
"græge syrcan   and grîm-helmas,
"here-sceafta heáp?--   Ic eom Hrôðgâres
"âr and ombiht.   Ne seah ic el-þeódige
"þus manige men   môdiglîcran.
"Wên' ic þät ge for wlenco,   nalles for wräc-sîðum,
"ac for hige-þrymmum   Hrôðgâr sôhton."
Him þâ ellen-rôf   andswarode,
wlanc Wedera leód   word äfter spräc,
heard under helme: "We synt Higelâces
"beód-geneátas;   Beówulf is mîn nama.
"Wille ic âsecgan   suna Healfdenes,
"mærum þeódne   mîn ærende,
"aldre þînum,   gif he ûs geunnan wile,
"þät we hine swâ gôdne   grêtan môton."
Wulfgâr maðelode   (þät wäs Wendla leód,
wäs his môd-sefa   manegum gecýðed,
wîg and wîs-dôm):   "ic þäs wine Deniga,
"freán Scildinga   frinan wille,
"beága bryttan,   swâ þu bêna eart,
"þeóden mærne   ymb þînne sîð ;
"and þe þâ andsware   ädre gecýðan,
"þe me se gôda   âgifan þenceð."
Hwearf þâ hrädlîce,   þær Hrôðgâr sät,
eald and unhâr   mid his eorla gedriht;
eode ellen-rôf,   þät he for eaxlum gestôd
Deniga freán,   cûðe he duguðe þeáw.
Wulfgâr maðelode   tô his wine-drihtne:
"Her syndon geferede   feorran cumene

"ofer geofenes begang   Geáta leóde:
"þone yldestan   oret-mecgas
"Beówulf nemnað.   Hy bênan synt,
"þät hie, þeóden mîn,   wið þe môton
"wordum wrixlan;   nô þu him wearne geteóh,
"þînra gegn-cwida   glädnian, Hrôðgâr!
"Hy on wîg-geatwum   wyrðe þinceað
"eorla geæhtlan;   hûru se aldor deáh,
"se þæm heaðo-rincum   hider wîsade."

VII - HROTHGAR'S WELCOME

Hrôðgâr maðelode,   helm Scyldinga:
"Ic hine cûðe   cniht-wesende.
"Wäs his eald-fäder   Ecgþeó hâten,
"þäm tô hâm forgeaf   Hrêðel Geáta
"ângan dôhtor;   is his eafora nu
"heard her cumen,   sôhte holdne wine.
"þonne sägdon þät   sæ-lîðende,
"þâ þe gif-sceattas   Geáta fyredon
"þyder tô þance,   þät he þrittiges
"manna mägen-cräft   on his mund-grîpe
"heaðo-rôf häbbe.   Hine hâlig god
"for âr-stafum   us onsende,
"tô West-Denum,   þäs ic wên häbbe,
"wið Grendles gryre: ic þäm gôdan sceal
"for his môd-þräce   mâdmas beódan.
"Beó þu on ôfeste,   hât hig in gân,
"seón sibbe-gedriht   samod ätgädere;
"gesaga him eác wordum,   þät hie sint wil-cuman
"Deniga leódum."   Þâ wið duru healle
Wulfgâr eode,   word inne âbeád:
"Eów hêt secgan   sige-drihten mîn,
"aldor Eást-Dena,   þät he eówer äðelu can
"and ge him syndon   ofer sæ-wylmas,
"heard-hicgende,   hider wil-cuman.
"Nu ge môton gangan   in eówrum guð-geatawum,
"under here-grîman,   Hrôðgâr geseón;
"lætað hilde-bord   her onbidian,
"wudu wäl-sceaftas,   worda geþinges."
Ârâs þâ se rîca,   ymb hine rinc manig,
þryðlîc þegna heáp;   sume þær bidon,
heaðo-reáf heóldon,   swâ him se hearda bebeád.
Snyredon ätsomne,   þâ secg wîsode
under Heorotes hrôf;   hyge-rôf eode,
heard under helme,   þät he on heoðe gestôd.
Beówulf maðelode   (on him byrne scân,
searo-net seówed   smiðes or-þancum):
"Wes þu Hrôðgâr hâl!   ic eom Higelâces
"mæg and mago-þegn;   häbbe ic mærða fela

"ongunnen on geogoðe.   Me wearð Grendles þing
"on mînre êðel-tyrf   undyrne cûð:
"secgað sæ-lîðend,   þät þes sele stande,
"reced sêlesta,   rinca gehwylcum
"îdel and unnyt,   siððan æfen-leóht
"under heofenes hâdor   beholen weorðeð.
"Þâ me þät gelærdon   leóde mîne,
"þâ sêlestan,   snotere ceorlas,
"þeóden Hrôðgâr,   þät ic þe sôhte;
"forþan hie mägenes cräft   mînne cûðon:
"selfe ofersâwon,   þâ ic of searwum cwom,
"fâh from feóndum,   þær ic fîfe geband,
"ýðde eotena cyn,   and on ýðum slôg
"niceras nihtes,   nearo-þearfe dreáh,
"wräc Wedera nîð   (weán âhsodon)
"forgrand gramum;   and nu wið Grendel sceal,
"wið þam aglæcan,   âna gehegan
"þing wið þyrse.   Ic þe nu þâ,
"brego Beorht-Dena,   biddan wille,
"eodor Scyldinga,   ânre bêne;
"þät þu me ne forwyrne,   wîgendra hleó,
"freó-wine folca,   nu ic þus feorran com,
"þät ic môte âna   and mînra eorla gedryht,
"þes hearda heáp,   Heorot fælsian.
"Häbbe ic eác geâhsod,   þät se äglæca
"for his won-hýdum   wæpna ne rêceð;
"ic þät þonne forhicge,   swâ me Higelâc sîe,
"mîn mon-drihten,   môdes blîðe,
"þät ic sweord bere   oððe sîdne scyld
"geolo-rand tô gûðe;   ac ic mid grâpe sceal
"fôn wið feónde   and ymb feorh sacan,
"lâð wið lâðum;   þær gelýfan sceal
"dryhtnes dôme   se þe hine deáð nimeð.
"Wên' ic þät he wille,   gif he wealdan môt,
"in þäm gûð-sele   Geátena leóde
"etan unforhte,   swâ he oft dyde
"mägen Hrêðmanna.   Nâ þu mînne þearft
"hafalan hýdan,   ac he me habban wile
"dreóre fâhne,   gif mec deáð nimeð;
"byreð blôdig wäl,   byrgean þenceð,
"eteð ân-genga   unmurnlîce,
"mearcað môr-hopu: nô þu ymb mînes ne þearft
"lîces feorme   leng sorgian.
"Onsend Higelâce,   gif mec hild nime,
"beadu-scrûda betst,   þät mîne breóst wereð,
"hrägla sêlest;   þät is Hrêðlan lâf,
"Wêlandes geweorc.   Gæð â Wyrd swâ hió scel!"

VIII - HROTHGAR TELLS OF GRENDEL

Hrôðgâr maðelode,   helm Scyldinga:
"for were-fyhtum þu,   wine mîn Beówulf,
"and for âr-stafum   ûsic sôhtest.
"Geslôh þin fäder   fæhðe mæste,
"wearð he Heaðolâfe   tô hand-bonan
"mid Wilfingum;   þâ hine Wedera cyn
"for here-brôgan   habban ne mihte.
"Þanon he gesôhte   Sûð-Dena folc
"ofer ýða gewealc,   Âr-Scyldinga;
"þâ ic furðum weóld   folce Deninga,
"and on geogoðe heóld   gimme-rîce
"hord-burh häleða: þâ wäs Heregâr deád,
"mîn yldra mæg   unlifigende,
"bearn Healfdenes.   Se wäs betera þonne ic!
"Siððan þâ fæhðe   feó þingode;
"sende ic Wylfingum   ofer wäteres hrycg
"ealde mâdmas: he me âðas swôr.
"Sorh is me tô secganne   on sefan mînum
"gumena ængum,   hwät me Grendel hafað
"hýnðo on Heorote   mid his hete-þancum,
"fær-nîða gefremed.   Is mîn flet-werod,
"wîg-heáp gewanod;   hie Wyrd forsweóp
"on Grendles gryre.   God eáðe mäg
"þone dol-scaðan   dæda getwæfan!
"Ful oft gebeótedon   beóre druncne
"ofer ealo-wæge   oret-mecgas,
"þät hie in beór-sele   bîdan woldon
"Grendles gûðe   mid gryrum ecga.
"Þonne wäs þeós medo-heal   on morgen-tîd,
"driht-sele dreór-fâh,   þonne däg lixte,
"eal benc-þelu   blôde bestýmed,
"heall heoru-dreóre: âhte ic holdra þý läs,
"deórre duguðe,   þe þâ deáð fornam.
"Site nu tô symle   and onsæl meoto,
"sige-hrêð secgum,   swâ þîn sefa hwette!"
Þâ wäs Geát-mäcgum   geador ätsomne
on beór-sele   benc gerýmed;
þær swîð-ferhðe   sittan eodon
þryðum dealle.   Þegn nytte beheóld,
se þe on handa bär   hroden ealo-wæge,
scencte scîr wered.   Scôp hwîlum sang
hâdor on Heorote;   þær wäs häleða dreám,
duguð unlytel   Dena and Wedera.

IX - HUNFERTH OBJECTS TO BEÓWULF

Ûnferð maðelode,   Ecglâfes bearn,
þe ät fôtum sät   freán Scyldinga;
onband beadu-rûne   (wäs him Beówulfes sîð,
môdges mere-faran,   micel äf-þunca,
forþon þe he ne ûðe,   þät ænig ôðer man
æfre mærða þon mâ   middan-geardes
gehêdde under heofenum   þonne he sylfa):
"Eart þu se Beówulf,   se þe wið Brecan wunne,
"on sîdne sæ   ymb sund flite,
"þær git for wlence   wada cunnedon
"and for dol-gilpe   on deóp wäter
"aldrum nêðdon?   Ne inc ænig mon,
"ne leóf ne lâð,   beleán mihte
"sorh-fullne sîð;   þâ git on sund reón,
"þær git eágor-streám   earmum þehton,
"mæton mere-stræta,   mundum brugdon,
"glidon ofer gâr-secg;   geofon ýðum weól,
"wintres wylme.   Git on wäteres æht
"seofon niht swuncon;   he þe ät sunde oferflât,
"häfde mâre mägen.   Þâ hine on morgen-tîd
"on Heaðo-ræmas   holm up ätbär,
"þonon he gesôhte   swæsne êðel
"leóf his leódum   lond Brondinga,
"freoðo-burh fägere,   þær he folc âhte,
"burg and beágas.   Beót eal wið þe
"sunu Beánstânes   sôðe gelæste.
"Þonne wêne ic tô þe   wyrsan geþinges,
"þeáh þu heaðo-ræsa   gehwær dohte,
"grimre gûðe,   gif þu Grendles dearst
"niht-longne fyrst   neán bîdan!"
Beówulf maðelode,   bearn Ecgþeówes:
"Hwät þu worn fela,   wine mîn Ûnferð,
"beóre druncen   ymb Brecan spræce,
"sägdest from his sîðe!   Sôð ic talige,
"þät ic mere-strengo   mâran âhte,
"earfeðo on ýðum,   þonne ænig ôðer man.
"Wit þät gecwædon   cniht-wesende
"and gebeótedon   (wæron begen þâ git
"on geogoð-feore)   þät wit on gâr-secg ût
"aldrum nêðdon;   and þät geäfndon swâ.
"Häfdon swurd nacod,   þâ wit on sund reón,
"heard on handa,   wit unc wið hron-fixas
"werian þôhton.   Nô he wiht fram me
"flôd-ýðum feor   fleótan meahte,
"hraðor on holme,   nô ic fram him wolde.
"Þâ wit ätsomne   on sæ wæron
"fîf nihta fyrst,   ôð þät unc flôd tôdrâf,
"wado weallende,   wedera cealdost,

"nîpende niht   and norðan wind
"heaðo-grim andhwearf;   hreó wæron ýða,
"Wäs mere-fixa   môd onhrêred:
"þær me wið lâðum   lîc-syrce mîn,
"heard hond-locen,   helpe gefremede;
"beado-hrägl broden   on breóstum läg,
"golde gegyrwed.   Me tô grunde teáh
"fâh feónd-scaða,   fäste häfde
"grim on grâpe: hwäðre me gyfeðe wearð,
"þät ic aglæcan   orde geræhte,
"hilde-bille;   heaðo-ræs fornam
"mihtig mere-deór   þurh mîne hand.

X - BEÓWULF'S CONTEST WITH BRECA--THE FEAST

"Swâ mec gelôme   lâð-geteónan
"þreátedon þearle.   Ic him þênode
"deóran sweorde,   swâ hit gedêfe wäs;
"näs hie þære fylle   gefeán häfdon,
"mân-fordædlan,   þät hie me þêgon,
"symbel ymb-sæton   sæ-grunde neáh,
"ac on mergenne   mêcum wunde
"be ýð-lâfe   uppe lægon,
"sweordum âswefede,   þät syððan nâ
"ymb brontne ford   brim-lîðende
"lâde ne letton.   Leóht eástan com,
"beorht beácen godes;   brimu swaðredon,
"þät ic sæ-nässas   geseón mihte,
"windige weallas.   Wyrd oft nereð
"unfægne eorl,   ðonne his ellen deáh!
"Hwäðcre me gesælde,   þät ic mid sweorde ofslôh
"niceras nigene.   Nô ic on niht gefrägn
"under heofones hwealf   heardran feohtan,
"ne on êg-streámum   earmran mannan;
"hwäðere ic fâra feng   feore gedîgde,
"siðes wêrig.   Þâ mec sæ ôðbär,
"flôd äfter faroðe,   on Finna land,
"wadu weallendu.   Nô ic wiht fram þe
"swylcra searo-nîða   secgan hýrde,
"billa brôgan: Breca næfre git
"ät heaðo-lâce,   ne gehwäðer incer
"swâ deórlîce   dæd gefremede
"fâgum sweordum   . . . .
". . . . . . .   nô ic þäs gylpe;
"þeáh þu þînum brôðrum   tô banan wurde,
"heáfod-mægum;   þäs þu in helle scealt
"werhðo dreógan,   þeáh þîn wit duge,
"Secge ic þe tô sôðe,   sunu Ecglâfes,
"þät næfre Grendel swâ fela   gryra gefremede,
"atol äglæca   ealdre þînum,

"hýnðo on Heorote,   gif þîn hige wære,
"sefa swâ searo-grim,   swâ þu self talast.
"Ac he hafað onfunden,   þät he þâ fæhðe ne þearf,
"atole ecg-þräce   eówer leóde
"swîðe onsittan,   Sige-Scyldinga;
"nymeð nýd-bâde,   nænegum ârað
"leóde Deniga,   ac he on lust wîgeð,
"swefeð ond sendeð,   secce ne wêneð
"tô Gâr-Denum.   Ac him Geáta sceal
"eafoð and ellen   ungeâra nu
"gûðe gebeódan.   Gæð eft se þe môt
"tô medo môdig,   siððan morgen-leóht
"ofer ylda bearn   ôðres dôgores,
"sunne swegl-wered   sûðan scîneð!"
Þâ wäs on sâlum   sinces brytta
gamol-feax and gûð-rôf,   geóce gelýfde
brego Beorht-Dena;   gehýrde on Beówulfe
folces hyrde   fäst-rædne geþôht.
Þær wäs häleða hleahtor;   hlyn swynsode,
word wæron wynsume.   Eode Wealhþeów forð,
cwên Hrôðgâres,   cynna gemyndig,
grêtte gold-hroden   guman on healle,
and þâ freólîc wîf   ful gesealde
ærest Eást-Dena   êðel-wearde,
bäd hine blîðne   ät þære beór-þege,
leódum leófne;   he on lust geþeah
symbel and sele-ful,   sige-rôf kyning.
Ymb-eode þâ   ides Helminga
duguðe and geogoðe   dæl æghwylcne;
sinc-fato sealde,   ôð þät sæl âlamp,
þät hió Beówulfe,   beág-hroden cwên,
môde geþungen,   medo-ful ätbär;
grêtte Geáta leód,   gode þancode
wîs-fäst wordum,   þäs þe hire se willa gelamp,
þät heó on ænigne   eorl gelýfde
fyrena frôfre.   He þät ful geþeah,
wäl-reów wîga   ät Wealhþeón,
and þâ gyddode   gûðe gefýsed,
Beówulf maðelode,   bearn Ecgþeówes:
"Ic þät hogode,   þâ ic on holm gestâh,
"sæ-bât gesät   mid mînra secga gedriht,
"þät ic ânunga   eówra leóda
"willan geworhte,   oððe on wäl crunge,
"feónd-grâpum fäst.   Ic gefremman sceal
"eorlîc ellen,   oððe ende-däg
"on þisse meodu-healle   mînne gebîdan."
Þam wîfe þâ word   wel lîcodon,
gilp-cwide Geátes;   eode gold-hroden
freólîcu folc-cwên   tô hire freán sittan.
Þâ wäs eft swâ ær   inne on healle

þryð-word sprecen,   þeód on sælum,
sige-folca swêg,   ôð þät semninga
sunu Healfdenes   sêcean wolde
æfen-räste;   wiste ät þäm ahlæcan
tô þäm heáh-sele   hilde geþinged,
siððan hie sunnan leóht   geseón ne meahton,
oððe nîpende   niht ofer ealle,
scadu-helma gesceapu   scrîðan cwôman,
wan under wolcnum.   Werod eall ârâs.
Grêtte þâ giddum   guma ôðerne,
Hrôðgâr Beówulf,   and him hæl âbeád,
wîn-ärnes geweald   and þät word âcwäð:
"Næfre ic ænegum men   ær âlýfde,
"siððan ic hond and rond   hebban mihte,
"þryð-ärn Dena   bûton þe nu þâ.
"Hafa nu and geheald   hûsa sêlest;
"gemyne mærðo,   mägen-ellen cýð,
"waca wið wrâðum!   Ne bið þe wilna gâd,
"gif þu þät ellen-weorc   aldre gedîgest."

XI - THE WATCH FOR GRENDEL

Þâ him Hrôðgâr gewât   mid his häleða gedryht,
eodur Scyldinga   ût of healle;
wolde wîg-fruma   Wealhþeó sêcan,
cwên tô gebeddan   Häfde kyninga wuldor
Grendle tô-geánes,   swâ guman gefrungon,
sele-weard âseted,   sundor-nytte beheóld
ymb aldor Dena,   eoton weard âbeád;
hûru Geáta leód   georne trûwode
môdgan mägnes,   metodes hyldo.
Þâ he him of dyde   îsern-byrnan,
helm of hafelan,   sealde his hyrsted sweord,
îrena cyst   ombiht-þegne,
and gehealdan hêt   hilde-geatwe.
Gespräc þâ se gôda   gylp-worda sum
Beówulf Geáta,   ær he on bed stige:
"Nô ic me an here-wæsmum   hnâgran talige
"gûð-geweorca,   þonne Grendel hine;
"forþan ic hine sweorde   swebban nelle,
"aldre beneótan,   þeáh ic eal mæge.
"Nât he þâra gôda,   þät he me on-geán sleá,
"rand geheáwe,   þeáh þe he rôf sîe
"nîð-geweorca;   ac wit on niht sculon
"secge ofersittan,   gif he gesêcean dear
"wîg ofer wæpen,   and siððan witig god
"on swâ hwäðere hond   hâlig dryhten
"mærðo dême,   swâ him gemet þince."
Hylde hine þâ heaðo-deór,   hleór-bolster onfêng
eorles andwlitan;   and hine ymb monig

snellîc sæ-rinc   sele-reste gebeáh.
Nænig heora þôhte   þät he þanon scolde
eft eard-lufan   æfre gesêcean,
folc oððe freó-burh,   þær he âfêded wäs,
ac hie häfdon gefrunen,   þät hie ær tô fela micles
in þäm wîn-sele   wäl-deáð fornam,
Denigea leóde.   Ac him dryhten forgeaf
wîg-spêda gewiofu,   Wedera leódum
frôfor and fultum,   þät hie feónd heora
þurh ânes cräft   ealle ofercômon,
selfes mihtum: sôð is gecýðed,
þät mihtig god   manna cynnes
weóld wîde-ferhð.   Com on wanre niht
scrîðan sceadu-genga.   Sceótend swæfon,
þâ þät horn-reced   healdan scoldon,
ealle bûton ânum.   Þät wäs yldum cûð,
þät hie ne môste,   þâ metod nolde,
se syn-scaða   under sceadu bregdan;
ac he wäccende   wrâðum on andan
bâd bolgen-môd   beadwa geþinges.

XII - GRENDEL'S RAID

Ðâ com of môre   under mist-hleoðum
Grendel gongan,   godes yrre bär.
Mynte se mân-scaða   manna cynnes
sumne besyrwan   in sele þam heán;
wôd under wolcnum,   tô þäs þe he wîn-reced,
gold-sele gumena,   gearwost wisse
fättum fâhne.   Ne wäs þät forma sîð,
þät he Hrôðgâres   hâm gesôhte:
næfre he on aldor-dagum   ær ne siððan
heardran häle,   heal-þegnas fand!
Com þâ tô recede   rinc sîðian
dreámum bedæled.   Duru sôna onarn
fýr-bendum fäst,   syðð[a]n he hire folmum hrân;
onbräd þâ bealo-hydig,   þâ he âbolgen wäs,
recedes mûðan.   Raðe äfter þon
on fâgne flôr   feónd treddode,
eode yrre-môd;   him of eágum stôd
lîge gelîcost   leóht unfäger.
Geseah he in recede   rinca manige,
swefan sibbe-gedriht   samod ätgädere,
mago-rinca heáp: þâ his môd âhlôg,
mynte þät he gedælde,   ær þon däg cwôme,
atol aglæca,   ânra gehwylces
lîf wið lîce,   þâ him âlumpen wäs
wist-fylle wên.   Ne wäs þät wyrd þâ gen,
þät he mâ môste   manna cynnes
þicgean ofer þâ niht.   Þrýð-swýð beheóld

Beowulf: Scholar's Edition

mæg Higelâces,   hû se mân-scaða
under fær-gripum   gefaran wolde.
Ne þät se aglæca   yldan þôhte,
ac he gefêng hraðe   forman siðe
slæpendne rinc,   slât unwearnum,
bât bân-locan,   blôd êdrum dranc,
syn-snædum swealh: sôna häfde
unlyfigendes   eal gefeormod
fêt and folma.   Forð neár ätstôp,
nam þâ mid handa   hige-þihtigne
rinc on räste;   ræhte ongeán
feónd mid folme,   he onfêng hraðe
inwit-þancum   and wið earm gesät.
Sôna þät onfunde   fyrena hyrde,
þät he ne mêtte   middan-geardes
eorðan sceáta   on elran men
mund-gripe mâran: he on môde wearð
forht on ferhðe,   nô þý ær fram meahte;
hyge wäs him hin-fûs,   wolde on heolster fleón,
sêcan deófla gedräg: ne wäs his drohtoð þær,
swylce he on ealder-dagum   ær gemêtte.
Gemunde þâ se gôda   mæg Higelâces
æfen-spræce,   up-lang âstôd
and him fäste wiðfêng.   Fingras burston;
eoten wäs ût-weard,   eorl furður stôp.
Mynte se mæra,   þær he meahte swâ,
wîdre gewindan   and on weg þanon
fleón on fen-hopu;   wiste his fingra geweald
on grames grâpum.   Þät wäs geócor sîð,
þät se hearm-scaða   tô Heorute âteáh:
dryht-sele dynede,   Denum eallum wearð,
ceaster-bûendum,   cênra gehwylcum,
eorlum ealu-scerwen.   Yrre wæron begen,
rêðe rên-weardas.   Reced hlynsode;
þâ wäs wundor micel,   þät se wîn-sele
wiðhäfde heaðo-deórum,   þät he on hrusan ne feól,
fäger fold-bold;   ac he þäs fäste wäs
innan and ûtan   îren-bendum
searo-þoncum besmiðod.   Þær fram sylle âbeág
medu-benc monig   mîne gefræge,
golde geregnad,   þær þâ graman wunnon;
þäs ne wêndon ær   witan Scyldinga,
þät hit â mid gemete   manna ænig
bètlîc and bân-fâg   tôbrecan meahte,
listum tôlûcan,   nymðe lîges fäðm
swulge on swaðule.   Swêg up âstâg
niwe geneahhe;   Norð-Denum stôd
atelîc egesa   ânra gehwylcum
þâra þe of wealle   wôp gehýrdon,

gryre-leóð galan   godes andsacan,
sige-leásne sang,   sâr wânigean
helle häftan.   Heóld hine tô fäste
se þe manna wäs   mägene strengest
on þäm däge   þysses lîfes.

XIII - BEÓWULF TEARS OFF GRENDEL'S ARM

Nolde eorla hleó   ænige þinga
þone cwealm-cuman   cwicne forlætan,
ne his lîf-dagas   leóda ænigum
nytte tealde.   Þær genehost brägd
eorl Beówulfes   ealde lâfe,
wolde freá-drihtnes   feorh ealgian
mæres þeódnes,   þær hie meahton swâ;
hie þät ne wiston,   þâ hie gewin drugon,
heard-hicgende   hilde-mecgas,
and on healfa gehwone   heáwan þôhton,
sâwle sêcan,   þät þone syn-scaðan
ænig ofer eorðan   îrenna cyst,
gûð-billa nân   grêtan nolde;
ac he sige-wæpnum   forsworen häfde,
ecga gehwylcre.   Scolde his aldor-gedâl
on þäm däge   þysses lîfes
earmlîc wurðan   and se ellor-gâst
on feónda geweald   feor sîðian.
Þâ þät onfunde   se þe fela æror
môdes myrðe   manna cynne
fyrene gefremede   (he wäs fâg wið god)
þät him se lîc-homa   læstan nolde,
ac hine se môdega   mæg Hygelâces
häfde be honda;   wäs gehwäðer ôðrum
lifigende lâð.   Lîc-sâr gebâd
atol äglæca,   him on eaxle wearð
syn-dolh sweotol,   seonowe onsprungon
burston bân-locan.   Beówulfe wearð
gûð-hrêð gyfeðe;   scolde Grendel þonan
feorh-seóc fleón   under fen-hleoðu,
sêcean wyn-leás wîc;   wiste þê geornor,
þät his aldres wäs   ende gegongen,
dôgera däg-rîm.   Denum eallum wearð
äfter þam wäl-ræse   willa gelumpen.
Häfde þâ gefælsod,   se þe ær feorran com,
snotor and swýð-ferhð   sele Hrôðgâres,
genered wið nîðe.   Niht-weorce gefeh,
ellen-mærðum;   häfde Eást-Denum
Geát-mecga leód   gilp gelæsted,
swylce oncýðde   ealle gebêtte,
inwid-sorge,   þe hie ær drugon
and for þreá-nýdum   þolian scoldon,

torn unlytel.   Þät wäs tâcen sweotol,
syððan hilde-deór   hond âlegde,
earm and eaxle   (þær wäs eal geador
Grendles grâpe)   under geápne hrôf.

XIV - THE JOY AT HEOROT

Þâ wäs on morgen   mîne gefræge
ymb þâ gif-healle   gûð-rinc monig:
fêrdon folc-togan   feorran and neán
geond wîd-wegas   wundor sceáwian,
lâðes lâstas.   Nô his lîf-gedâl
sârlîc þûhte   secga ænegum,
þâra þe tîr-leáses   trode sceáwode,
hû he wêrig-môd   on weg þanon,
nîða ofercumen,   on nicera mere
fæge and geflýmed   feorh-lâstas bär.
Þær wäs on blôde   brim weallende,
atol ýða geswing   eal gemenged
hâtan heolfre,   heoro-dreóre weól;
deáð-fæge deóg,   siððan dreáma leás
in fen-freoðo   feorh âlegde
hæðene sâwle,   þær him hel onfêng.
Þanon eft gewiton   eald-gesîðas,
swylce geong manig   of gomen-wâðe,
fram mere môdge,   mearum rîdan,
beornas on blancum.   Þær wäs Beówulfes
mærðo mæned;   monig oft gecwäð,
þätte sûð ne norð   be sæm tweonum
ofer eormen-grund   ôðer nænig
under swegles begong   sêlra nære
rond-häbbendra,   rîces wyrðra.
Ne hie hûru wine-drihten   wiht ne lôgon,
glädne Hrôðgâr,   ac þät wäs gôd cyning.
Hwîlum heaðo-rôfe   hleápan lêton,
on geflît faran   fealwe mearas,
þær him fold-wegas   fägere þûhton,
cystum cûðe;   hwîlum cyninges þegn,
guma gilp-hläden   gidda gemyndig,
se þe eal-fela   eald-gesegena
worn gemunde,   word ôðer fand
sôðe gebunden: secg eft ongan
sîð Beówulfes   snyttrum styrian
and on spêd wrecan   spel gerâde,
wordum wrixlan,   wel-hwylc gecwäð,
þät he fram Sigemunde   secgan hýrde,
ellen-dædum,   uncûðes fela,
Wälsinges gewin,   wîde sîðas,
þâra þe gumena bearn   gearwe ne wiston,
fæhðe and fyrene,   bûton Fitela mid hine,

Beowulf: Scholar's Edition

þonne he swylces hwät   secgan wolde
eám his nefan,   swâ hie â wæron
ät nîða gehwâm   nýd-gesteallan:
häfdon eal-fela   eotena cynnes
sweordum gesæged.   Sigemunde gesprong
äfter deáð-däge   dôm unlýtel,
syððan wîges heard   wyrm âcwealde,
hordes hyrde;   he under hârne stân,
äðelinges bearn,   âna genêðde
frêcne dæde;   ne wäs him Fitela mid.
Hwäðre him gesælde,   þät þät swurd þurhwôd
wrätlîcne wyrm,   þät hit on wealle ätstôd,
dryhtlîc îren;   draca morðre swealt.
Häfde aglæca   elne gegongen,
þät he beáh-hordes   brûcan môste
selfes dôme: sæ-bât gehlôd,
bär on bearm scipes   beorhte frätwa,
Wälses eafera;   wyrm hât gemealt.
Se wäs wreccena   wîde mærost
ofer wer-þeóde,   wîgendra hleó
ellen-dædum: he þäs âron þâh.
Siððan Heremôdes   hild sweðrode
eafoð and ellen.   He mid eotenum wearð
on feónda geweald   forð forlâcen,
snûde forsended.   Hine sorh-wylmas
lemede tô lange,   he his leódum wearð,
eallum äðelingum   tô aldor-ceare;
swylce oft bemearn   ærran mælum
swîð-ferhðes sîð   snotor ceorl monig,
se þe him bealwa tô   bôte gelýfde,
þät þät þeódnes bearn   geþeón scolde,
fäder-äðelum onfôn,   folc gehealdan,
hord and hleó-burh,   häleða rîce,
êðel Scyldinga.   He þær eallum wearð,
mæg Higelâces   manna cynne,
freóndum gefägra;   hine fyren onwôd.

Hwîlum flîtende   fealwe stræte
mearum mæton.   Þâ wäs morgen-leóht
scofen and scynded.   Eode scealc monig
swîð-hicgende   tô sele þam heán,
searo-wundor seón,   swylce self cyning,
of brýd-bûre   beáh-horda weard,
tryddode tîr-fäst   getrume micle,
cystum gecýðed,   and his cwên mid him
medo-stîg gemät   mägða hôse.

XV - HROTHGAR'S GRATULATION

Hrôðgâr maðelode   (he tô healle geóng,
stôd on stapole,   geseah steápne hrôf
golde fâhne   and Grendles hond):
"þisse ansýne   al-wealdan þanc
"lungre gelimpe!   Fela ic lâðes gebâd,
"grynna ät Grendle: â mäg god wyrcan
"wunder äfter wundre,   wuldres hyrde!
"Þät wäs ungeâra,   þät ic änigra me
"weána ne wênde   tô wîdan feore
"bôte gebîdan   þonne blôde fâh
"hûsa sêlest   heoro-dreórig stôd;
"weá wîd-scofen   witena gehwylcne
"þâra þe ne wêndon,   þät hie wîde-ferhð
"leóda land-geweorc   lâðum beweredon
"scuccum and scinnum.   Nu scealc hafað
"þurh drihtnes miht   däd gefremede,
"þe we ealle   är ne meahton
"snyttrum besyrwan.   Hwät! þät secgan mäg
"efne swâ hwylc mägða,   swâ þone magan cende
"äfter gum-cynnum,   gyf heó gyt lyfað,
"þät hyre eald-metod   êste wäre
"bearn-gebyrdo.   Nu ic Beówulf
"þec, secg betsta,   me for sunu wylle
"freógan on ferhðe;   heald forð tela
"niwe sibbe.   Ne bið þe nänigra gâd
"worolde wilna,   þe ic geweald häbbe.
"Ful-oft ic for lässan   leán teohhode
"hord-weorðunge   hnâhran rince,
"sämran ät säcce.   Þu þe self hafast
"dädum gefremed,   þät þîn dôm lyfað
"âwâ tô aldre.   Alwalda þec
"gôde forgylde,   swâ he nu gyt dyde!"
Beówulf maðelode,   bearn Ecgþeówes:
"We þät ellen-weorc   êstum miclum,
"feohtan fremedon,   frêcne genêðdon
"eafoð uncûðes;   ûðe ic swîðor,
"þät þu hinc selfne   geseón môste,
"feónd on frätewum   fyl-wêrigne!
"Ic hine hrädlîce   heardan clammum
"on wäl-bedde   wrîðan þôhte,
"þät he for mund-gripe   mînum scolde
"licgean lîf-bysig,   bûtan his lîc swice;
"ic hine ne mihte,   þâ metod nolde,
"ganges getwäman,   nô ic him þäs georne ätfealh,
"feorh-genîðlan;   wäs tô fore-mihtig
"feónd on fêðe.   Hwäðere he his folme forlêt
"tô lîf-wraðe   lâst weardian,
"earm and eaxle;   nô þär änige swâ þeáh

"feá-sceaft guma   frôfre gebohte:
"nô þý leng leofað   lâð-geteóna
"synnum geswenced,   ac hyne sâr hafað
"in nýd-gripe   nearwe befongen,
"balwon bendum: þær âbîdan sceal
"maga mâne fâh   miclan dômes,
"hû him scîr metod   scrîfan wille."
Þâ wäs swîgra secg,   sunu Ecglâfes,
on gylp-spræce   gûð-geweorca,
siððan äðelingas   eorles cräfte
ofer heáhne hrôf   hand sceáwedon,
feóndes fingras,   foran æghwylc;
wäs stêde nägla gehwylc,   stýle gelîcost,
hæðenes hand-sporu   hilde-rinces
egle unheóru;   æg-hwylc gecwäð,
þät him heardra nân   hrînan wolde
îren ær-gôd,   þät þäs ahlæcan
blôdge beadu-folme   onberan wolde.

XVI - THE BANQUET AND THE GIFTS
Þâ wäs hâten hreðe   Heort innan-weard
folmum gefrätwod: fela þæra wäs
wera and wîfa,   þe þät wîn-reced,
gest-sele gyredon.   Gold-fâg scinon
web äfter wagum,   wundor-sióna fela
secga gehwylcum   þâra þe on swylc staráð
Wäs þät beorhte bold   tôbrocen swîðe
eal inne-weard   îren-bendum fäst,
heorras tôhlidene;   hrôf âna genäs
ealles ansund,   þâ se aglæca
fyren-dædum fâg   on fleám gewand,
aldres or-wêna.   Nô þät ýðe byð
tô befleónne   (fremme se þe wille!)
ac gesacan sceal   sâwl-berendra
nýde genýdde   niðða bearna
grund-bûendra   gearwe stôwe,
þær his lîc-homa   leger-bedde fäst
swefeð äfter symle.   Þâ wäs sæl and mæl,
þät tô healle gang   Healfdenes sunu;
wolde self cyning   symbel þicgan.
Ne gefrägen ic þâ mægðe   mâran weorode
ymb hyra sinc-gyfan   sêl gebæran.
Bugon þâ tô bence   blæd-âgende,
fylle gefægon.   Fägere geþægon
medo-ful manig   mâgas + þâra
swîð-hicgende   on sele þam heán,
Hrôðgâr and Hrôðulf.   Heorot innan wäs
freóndum âfylled;   nalles fâcen-stafas
Þeód-Scyldingas   þenden fremedon.

Beowulf: Scholar's Edition

Forgeaf þâ Beówulfe   bearn Healfdenes
segen gyldenne   sigores tô leáne,
hroden hilte-cumbor,   helm and byrnan;
mære mâððum-sweord   manige gesâwon
beforan beorn beran.   Beówulf geþah
ful on flette;   nô he þære feoh-gyfte
for sceótendum   scamigan þorfte,
ne gefrägn ic freóndlîcor   feówer mâdmas
golde gegyrede   gum-manna fela
in ealo-bence   ôðrum gesellan.
Ymb þäs helmes hrôf   heáfod-beorge
wîrum bewunden   walan ûtan heóld,
þät him fêla lâfe   frêcne ne meahton
scûr-heard sceððan,   þonne scyld-freca
ongeán gramum   gangan scolde.
Hêht þâ eorla hleó   eahta mearas,
fäted-hleóre,   on flet teón
in under eoderas;   þâra ânum stôd
sadol searwum fâh   since gewurðad,
þät wäs hilde-setl   heáh-cyninges,
þonne sweorda gelâc   sunu Healfdenes
efnan wolde;   næfre on ôre läg
wîd-cûðes wîg,   þonne walu feóllon.
And þâ Beówulfe   bega gehwäðres
eodor Ingwina   onweald geteáh,
wicga and wæpna;   hêt hine wel brûcan.
Swâ manlîce   mære þeóden,
hord-weard häleða   heaðo-ræsas geald
mearum and mâdmum,   swâ hý næfre man lyhð,
se þe secgan wile   sôð äfter rihte.

XVII - SONG OF HROTHGAR'S POET--THE LAY OF HNAEF AND HENGEST

Þâ gyt æghwylcum   eorla drihten
þâra þe mid Beówulfe   brim-lâde teáh,
on þære medu-bence   mâððum gesealde,
yrfe-lâfe,   and þone ænne hêht
golde forgyldan,   þone þe Grendel ær
mâne âcwealde,   swâ he hyra mâ wolde,
nefne him witig god   wyrd forstôde
and þäs mannes môd: metod eallum weóld
gumena cynnes,   swâ he nu git dêð;
forþan bið andgit   æghwær sêlest,
ferhðes fore-þanc!   fela sceal gebîdan
leófes and lâðes,   se þe longe her
on þyssum win-dagum   worolde brûceð.
Þær wäs sang and swêg   samod ätgädere
fore Healfdenes   hilde-wîsan,

Beowulf: Scholar's Edition

gomen-wudu grêted,   gid oft wrecen,
þonne heal-gamen   Hrôðgâres scôp
äfter medo-bence   mænan scolde
Finnes eaferum,   þâ hie se fær begeat:
"Häleð Healfdenes,   Hnäf Scyldinga,
"in Fr..es wäle   feallan scolde.
"Ne hûru Hildeburh   hêrian þorfte
"Eotena treówe: unsynnum wearð
"beloren leófum   ät þam lind-plegan
"bearnum and brôðrum;   hie on gebyrd hruron
"gâre wunde;   þät wäs geômuru ides.
"Nalles hôlinga   Hôces dôhtor
"meotod-sceaft bemearn,   syððan morgen com,
"þâ heó under swegle   geseón meahte
"morðor-bealo mâga,   þær heó ær mæste heóld
"worolde wynne: wîg ealle fornam
"Finnes þegnas,   nemne feáum ânum,
"þät he ne mehte   on þäm meðel-stede
"wîg Hengeste   wiht gefeohtan,
"ne þâ weá-lâfe   wîge forþringan
"þeódnes þegne;   ac hig him geþingo budon,
"þät hie him ôðer flet   eal gerýmdon,
"healle and heáh-setl,   þät hie healfre geweald
"wið Eotena bearn   âgan môston,
"and ät feoh-gyftum   Folcwaldan sunu
"dôgra gehwylce   Dene weorðode,
"Hengestes heáp   hringum wenede,
"efne swâ swîðe   sinc-gestreónum
"fättan goldes,   swâ he Fresena cyn
"on beór-sele   byldan wolde.
"Þâ hie getrûwedon   on twâ healfa
"fäste frioðu-wære;   Fin Hengeste
"elne unflitme   âðum benemde,
"þät he þâ weá-lâfe   weotena dôme
"ârum heolde,   þät þær ænig mon
"wordum ne worcum   wære ne bræce,
"ne þurh inwit-searo   æfre gemænden,
"þeáh hie hira beág-gyfan   banan folgedon
"þeóden-leáse,   þâ him swâ geþearfod wäs:
"gyf þonne Frysna hwylc   frêcnan spræce
"þäs morðor-hetes   myndgiend wære,
"þonne hit sweordes ecg   syððan scolde.
"Âð wäs geäfned   and icge gold
"âhäfen of horde.   Here-Scyldinga
"betst beado-rinca   wäs on bæl gearu;
"ät þäm âde wäs   êð-gesýne
"swât-fâh syrce,   swýn eal-gylden,
"eofer îren-heard,   äðeling manig
"wundum âwyrded;   sume on wäle crungon.
"Hêt þâ Hildeburh   ät Hnäfes âde

"hire selfre sunu   sweoloðe befästan,
"bân-fatu bärnan   and on bæl dôn.
"Earme on eaxle   ides gnornode,
"geômrode giddum;   gûð-rinc âstâh.
"Wand tô wolcnum   wäl-fýra mæst,
"hlynode for hlâwe;   hafelan multon,
"ben-geato burston,   þonne blôd ätspranc
"lâð-bite lîces.   Lîg ealle forswealg,
"gæsta gîfrost,   þâra þe þær gûð fornam
"bega folces;   wäs hira blæd scacen.

XVIII - THE GLEEMAN'S TALE IS ENDED

"Gewiton him þâ wîgend   wîca neósian,
"freóndum befeallen   Frysland geseón,
"hâmas and heá-burh.   Hengest þâ gyt
"wäl-fâgne winter   wunode mid Finne
"ealles unhlitme;   eard gemunde,
"þeáh þe he ne meahte   on mere drîfan
"hringed-stefnan;   holm storme weól,
"won wið winde;   winter ýðe beleác
"îs-gebinde   ôð þät ôðer com
"geâr in geardas,   swâ nu gyt dêð,
"þâ þe syngales   sêle bewitiað,
"wuldor-torhtan weder.   Þâ wäs winter scacen,
"fäger foldan bearm;   fundode wrecca,
"gist of geardum;   he tô gyrn-wräce
"swîðor þôhte,   þonne tô sæ-lâde,
"gif he torn-gemôt   þurhteón mihte,
"þät he Eotena bearn   inne gemunde.
"Swâ he ne forwyrnde   worold-rædenne,
"þonne him Hûnlâfing   hilde-leóman,
"billa sêlest,   on bearm dyde:
"þäs wæron mid Eotenum   ecge cûðe.
"Swylce ferhð-frecan   Fin eft begeat
"sweord-bealo slîðen   ät his selfes hâm,
"siððan grimne gripe   Gûðlaf ond Ôslâf
"äfter sæ-siðe   sorge mændon,
"ätwiton weána dæl;   ne meahte wäfre môd
"forhabban in hreðre.   Þâ wäs heal hroden
"feónda feorum,   swilce Fin slägen,
"cyning on corðre,   and seó cwên numen.
"Sceótend Scyldinga   tô scypum feredon
"eal in-gesteald   eorð-cyninges,
"swylce hie ät Finnes hâm   findan meahton
"sigla searo-gimma.   Hie on sæ-lâde
"drihtlîce wîf   tô Denum feredon,
"læddon tô leódum."   Leóð wäs âsungen,
gleó-mannes gyd.   Gamen eft âstâh,
beorhtode benc-swêg,   byrelas sealdon

wîn of wunder-fatum.   Þâ cwom Wealhþeó forð
gân under gyldnum beáge,   þær þâ gôdan twegen
sæton suhter-gefäderan;   þâ gyt wäs hiera sib ätgädere
æghwylc ôðrum trýwe.   Swylce þær Ûnferð þyle
ät fôtum sät freán Scyldinga: gehwylc hiora his ferhðe treówde,
þät he häfde môd micel,   þeáh þe he his mâgum nære
ârfäst ät ecga gelâcum.   Spräc þâ ides Scyldinga:
"Onfôh þissum fulle,   freó-drihten mîn,
"sinces brytta;   þu on sælum wes,
"gold-wine gumena,   and tô Geátum sprec
"mildum wordum!   Swâ sceal man dôn.
"Beó wið Geátas gläd,   geofena gemyndig;
"neán and feorran   þu nu friðu hafast.
"Me man sägde,   þät þu þe for sunu wolde
"here-rinc habban.   Heorot is gefælsod,
"beáh-sele beorhta;   brûc þenden þu môte
"manigra mêda   and þînum mâgum læf
"folc and rîce,   þonne þu forð scyle
"metod-sceaft seón.   Ic mînne can
"glädne Hrôðulf,   þät he þâ geogoðe wile
"ârum healdan,   gyf þu ær þonne he,
"wine Scildinga,   worold oflætest;
"wêne ic, þät he mid gôde   gyldan wille
"uncran eaferan,   gif he þät eal gemon,
"hwät wit tô willan   and tô worð-myndum
"umbor wesendum ær   ârna gefremedon."
Hwearf þâ bî bence,   þær hyre byre wæron,
Hrêðrîc and Hrôðmund,   and häleða bearn,
giogoð ätgädere;   þær se gôda sät
Beówulf Geáta   be þæm gebrôðrum twæm.

XIX - BEÓWULF'S JEWELLED COLLAR. THE HEROES REST

Him wäs ful boren   and freónd-laðu
wordum bewägned   and wunden gold
êstum geeáwed,   earm-hreáde twâ,
hrägl and hringas,   heals-beága mæst
þâra þe ic on foldan   gefrägen häbbe.
Nænigne ic under swegle   sêlran hýrde
hord-mâððum häleða,   syððan Hâma ätwäg
tô þære byrhtan byrig   Brosinga mene,
sigle and sinc-fät,   searo-nîðas fealh
Eormenrîces,   geceás êcne ræd.
Þone hring häfde   Higelâc Geáta,
nefa Swertinges,   nýhstan sîðe,
siððan he under segne   sinc ealgode,
wäl-reáf werede;   hyne Wyrd fornam,
syððan he for wlenco   weán âhsode,
fæhðe tô Frysum;   he þâ frätwe wäg,
eorclan-stânas   ofer ýða ful,

rîce þeóden,   he under rande gecranc;
gehwearf þâ in Francna fäðm   feorh cyninges,
breóst-gewædu   and se beáh somod:
wyrsan wîg-frecan   wäl reáfedon
äfter gûð-sceare,   Geáta leóde
hreâ-wîc heóldon.   Heal swêge onfêng.
Wealhþeó maðelode,   heó fore þäm werede spräc:
"Brûc þisses beáges,   Beówulf, leófa
"hyse, mid hæle,   and þisses hrägles neót
"þeód-gestreóna,   and geþeóh tela,
"cen þec mid cräfte   and þyssum cnyhtum wes
"lâra lîðe!   ic þe þäs leán geman.
"Hafast þu gefêred,   þät þe feor and neáh
"ealne wîde-ferhð   weras ehtigað,
"efne swâ sîde   swâ sæ bebûgeð
"windige weallas.   Wes, þenden þu lifige,
"äðeling eádig!   ic þe an tela
"sinc-gestreóna.   Beó þu suna mînum
"dædum gedêfe   dreám healdende!
"Her is æghwylc eorl   ôðrum getrýwe,
"môdes milde,   man-drihtne hold,
"þegnas syndon geþwære,   þeód eal gearo:
"druncne dryht-guman,   dôð swâ ic bidde!"
Eode þâ tô setle.   Þær wäs symbla cyst,
druncon wîn weras: wyrd ne cûðon,
geó-sceaft grimme,   swâ hit âgangen wearð
eorla manegum,   syððan æfen cwom
and him Hrôðgâr gewât   tô hofe sînum,
rîce tô räste.   Reced weardode
unrîm eorla,   swâ hie oft ær dydon:
benc-þelu beredon,   hit geond-bræded wearð
beddum and bolstrum.   Beór-scealca sum
fûs and fæge   flet-räste gebeág.
Setton him tô heáfdum   hilde-randas,
bord-wudu beorhtan;   þær on bence wäs
ofer äðelinge   ýð-gesêne
heaðo-steápa helm,   hringed byrne
þrec-wudu þrymlîc.   Wäs þeáw hyra,
þät hie oft wæron   an wîg gearwe,
ge ät hâm ge on herge,   ge gehwäðer þâra
efne swylce mæla,   swylce hira man-dryhtne
þearf gesælde;   wäs seó þeód tilu.

XX - GRENDEL'S MOTHER ATTACKS THE RING-DANES

Sigon þâ tô slæpe.   Sum sâre angeald
æfen-räste,   swâ him ful-oft gelamp,
siððan gold-sele   Grendel warode,
unriht äfnde,   ôð þät ende becwom,
swylt äfter synnum.   Þät gesýne wearð,

wîd-cûð werum,   þätte wrecend þâ gyt
lifde äfter lâðum,   lange þrage
äfter gûð-ceare;   Grendles môdor,
ides aglæc-wîf   yrmðe gemunde,
se þe wäter-egesan   wunian scolde,
cealde streámas,   siððan Cain wearð
tô ecg-banan   ângan brêðer,
fäderen-mæge;   he þâ fâg gewât,
morðre gemearcod   man-dreám fleón,
wêsten warode.   Þanon wôc fela
geósceaft-gâsta;   wäs þæra Grendel sum,
heoro-wearh hetelîc,   se ät Heorote fand
wäccendne wer   wîges bîdan,
þær him aglæca   ät-græpe wearð;
hwäðre he gemunde   mägenes strenge,
gim-fäste gife,   þe him god sealde,
and him tô anwaldan   âre gelýfde,
frôfre and fultum: þý he þone feónd ofercwom,
gehnægde helle gâst: þâ he heán gewât,
dreáme bedæled   deáð-wîc seón,
man-cynnes feónd.   And his môdor þâ gyt
gîfre and galg-môd   gegân wolde
sorh-fulne sîð,   suna deáð wrecan.
Com þâ tô Heorote,   þær Hring-Dene
geond þät säld swæfun.   Þâ þær sôna wearð
ed-hwyrft eorlum,   siððan inne fealh
Grendles môdor;   wäs se gryre lässa
efne swâ micle,   swâ bið mägða cräft,
wîg-gryre wîfes   be wæpned-men,
þonne heoru bunden,   hamere geþuren,
sweord swâte fâh   swîn ofer helme,
ecgum dyhtig   andweard scireð.
Þâ wäs on healle   heard-ecg togen,
sweord ofer setlum,   sîd-rand manig
hafen handa fäst;   helm ne gemunde,
byrnan sîde,   þe hine se brôga angeat.
Heó wäs on ôfste,   wolde ût þanon
feore beorgan,   þâ heó onfunden wäs;
hraðe heó äðelinga   ânne häfde
fäste befangen,   þâ heó tô fenne gang.
se wäs Hrôðgâre   häleða leófost
on gesîðes hâd   be sæm tweonum,
rîce rand-wîga,   þone þe heó on räste âbreát,
blæd-fästne beorn.   Näs Beówulf þær,
ac wäs ôðer in   ær geteohhod
äfter mâððum-gife   mærum Geáte.
Hreám wearð on Heorote.   Heó under heolfre genam
cûðe folme;   cearu wäs geniwod
geworden in wîcum: ne wäs þät gewrixle til,
þät hie on bâ healfa   bicgan scoldon

freónda feorum.   Þâ wäs frôd cyning,
hâr hilde-rinc,   on hreón môde,
syððan he aldor-þegn   unlyfigendne,
þone deórestan   deádne wisse.
Hraðe wäs tô bûre   Beówulf fetod,
sigor-eádig secg.   Samod ær-däge
eode eorla sum,   äðele cempa
self mid gesîðum,   þær se snottra bâd,
hwäðre him al-walda   æfre wille
äfter weá-spelle   wyrpe gefremman.
Gang þâ äfter flôre   fyrd-wyrðe man
mid his hand-scale   (heal-wudu dynede)
þät he þone wîsan   wordum hnægde
freán Ingwina;   frägn gif him wære
äfter neód-laðu   niht getæse.

XXI - SORROW AT HEOROT: ÆSCHERE'S DEATH
Hrôðgâr maðelode,   helm Scildinga:
"Ne frin þu äfter sælum!   Sorh is geniwod
"Denigea leódum.   Deád is Äsc-here,
"Yrmenlâfes   yldra brôðor,
"mîn rûn-wita   and mîn ræd-bora,
"eaxl-gestealla,   þonne we on orlege
"hafelan weredon,   þonne hniton fêðan,
"eoferas cnysedan;   swylc scolde eorl wesan
"äðeling ær-gôd,   swylc Äsc-here wäs.
"Wearð him on Heorote   tô hand-banan
"wäl-gæst wäfre;   ic ne wât hwäder
"atol æse wlanc   eft-sîðas teáh,
"fylle gefrægnod.   Heó þâ fæhðe wräc,
"þe þu gystran niht   Grendel cwealdest
"þurh hæstne hâd   heardum clammum,
"forþan he tô lange   leóde mîne
"wanode and wyrde.   He ät wîge gecrang
"ealdres scyldig,   and nu ôðer cwom
"mihtig mân-scaða,   wolde hyre mæg wrecan,
"ge feor hafað   fæhðe gestæled,
"þäs þe þincean mäg   þegne monegum,
"se þe äfter sinc-gyfan   on sefan greóteð,
"hreðer-bealo hearde;   nu seó hand ligeð,
"se þe eów wel-hwylcra   wilna dohte.
"Ic þät lond-bûend   leóde mîne
"sele-rædende   secgan hýrde,
"þät hie gesâwon   swylce twegen
"micle mearc-stapan   môras healdan,
"ellor-gæstas: þæra ôðer wäs,
"þäs þe hie gewislîcost   gewitan meahton,
"idese onlîcnes,   ôðer earm-sceapen
"on weres wästmum   wräc-lâstas träd,

"näfne he wäs mâra   þonne ænig man ôðer,
"þone on geâr-dagum   Grendel nemdon
"fold-bûende: nô hie fäder cunnon,
"hwäðer him ænig wäs   ær âcenned
"dyrnra gâsta.   Hie dýgel lond
"warigeað, wulf-hleoðu,   windige nässas,
"frêcne fen-gelâd,   þær fyrgen-streám
"under nässa genipu   niðer gewîteð,
"flôd under foldan;   nis þät feor heonon
"mîl-gemearces,   þät se mere standeð,
"ofer þäm hongiað   hrîmge bearwas,
"wudu wyrtum fäst,   wäter oferhelmað.
"Þær mäg nihta gehwæm   nîð-wundor seón,
"fýr on flôde;   nô þäs frôd leofað
"gumena bearna,   þät þone grund wite;
"þeáh þe hæð-stapa   hundum geswenced,
"heorot hornum trum   holt-wudu sêce,
"feorran geflýmed,   ær he feorh seleð,
"aldor on ôfre,   ær he in wille,
"hafelan hýdan.   Nis þät heóru stôw:
"þonon ýð-geblond   up âstîgeð
"won tô wolcnum,   þonne wind styreð
"lâð gewidru,   ôð þät lyft drysmað,
"roderas reótað.   Nu is ræd gelang
"eft ät þe ânum!   Eard git ne const,
"frêcne stôwe,   þær þu findan miht
"sinnigne secg: sêc gif þu dyrre!
"Ic þe þâ fæhðe   feó leánige,
"eald-gestreónum,   swâ ic ær dyde,
"wundnum golde,   gyf þu on weg cymest."

XXII - BEÓWULF SEEKS THE MONSTER IN THE HAUNTS OF THE NIXIES

Beówulf maðelode,   bearn Ecgþeówes:
"Ne sorga, snotor guma!   sêlre bið æghwæm,
"þät he his freónd wrece,   þonne he fela murne;
"ûre æghwylc sceal   ende gebîdan
"worolde lîfes;   wyrce se þe môte
"dômes ær deáðe!   þät bið driht-guman
"unlifgendum   äfter sêlest.
"Ârîs, rîces weard;   uton hraðe fêran,
"Grendles mâgan   gang sceáwigan!
"Ic hit þe gehâte: nô he on helm losað,
"ne on foldan fäðm,   ne on fyrgen-holt,
"ne on gyfenes grund,   gâ þær he wille.
"Þys dôgor þu   geþyld hafa
"weána gehwylces,   swâ ic þe wêne tô!"
Âhleóp þâ se gomela,   gode þancode,
mihtigan drihtne,   þäs se man gespräc.

Þâ wäs Hrôðgâre   hors gebæted,
wicg wunden-feax.   Wîsa fengel
geatolîc gengde;   gum-fêða stôp
lind-häbbendra.   Lâstas wæron
äfter wald-swaðum   wîde gesýne,
gang ofer grundas;   gegnum fôr þâ
ofer myrcan môr,   mago-þegna bär
þone sêlestan   sâwol-leásne,
þâra þe mid Hrôðgâre   hâm eahtode.
Ofer-eode þâ   äðelinga bearn
steáp stân-hlíðo,   stîge nearwe,
enge ân-paðas,   un-cûð gelâd,
neowle nässas,   nicor-hûsa fela;
he feára sum   beforan gengde
wîsra monna,   wong sceáwian,
ôð þät he færinga   fyrgen-beámas
ofer hârne stân   hleonian funde,
wyn-leásne wudu;   wäter under stôd
dreórig and gedrêfed.   Denum eallum wäs,
winum Scyldinga,   weorce on môde,
tô geþolianne   þegne monegum,
oncýð eorla gehwæm,   syððan Äsc-heres
on þam holm-clife   hafelan mêtton.
Flôd blôde weól   (folc tô sægon)
hâtan heolfre.   Horn stundum song
fûslîc fyrd-leóð.   Fêða eal gesät;
gesâwon þâ äfter wätere   wyrm-cynnes fela,
sellîce sæ-dracan   sund cunnian,
swylce on näs-hleoðum   nicras licgean,
þâ on undern-mæl   oft bewitigað
sorh-fulne sîð   on segl-râde,
wyrmas and wil-deór;   hie on weg hruron
bitere and gebolgne,   bearhtm ongeâton,
gûð-horn galan.   Sumne Geáta leód
of flân-bogan   feores getwæfde,
ýð-gewinnes,   þät him on aldre stôd
here-stræl hearda;   he on holme wäs
sundes þe sænra,   þe hyne swylt fornam.
Hräðe wearð on ýðum   mid eofer-spreótum
heoro-hôcyhtum   hearde genearwod,
nîða genæged   and on näs togen
wundorlîc wæg-bora;   weras sceáwedon
gryrelîcne gist.   Gyrede hine Beówulf
eórl-gewædum,   nalles for ealdre mearn:
scolde here-byrne   hondum gebroden,
sîd and searo-fâh,   sund cunnian,
seó þe bân-côfan   beorgan cûðe,
þät him hilde-grâp   hreðre ne mihte,
eorres inwit-feng,   aldre gesceððan;

ac se hwîta helm   hafelan werede,
se þe mere-grundas   mengan scolde,
sêcan sund-gebland   since geweorðad,
befongen freá-wrâsnum,   swâ hine fyrn-dagum
worhte wæpna smið,   wundrum teóde,
besette swîn-lîcum,   þät hine syððan nô
brond ne beado-mêcas   bîtan ne meahton.
Näs þät þonne mætost   mägen-fultuma,
þät him on þearfe lâh   þyle Hrôðgâres;
wäs þäm häft-mêce   Hrunting nama,
þät wäs ân foran   eald-gestreóna;
ecg wäs îren   âter-teárum fâh,
âhyrded heaðo-swâte;   næfre hit ät hilde ne swâc
manna ængum   þâra þe hit mid mundum bewand,
se þe gryre-sîðas   gegân dorste,
folc-stede fâra;   näs þät forma sîð,
þät hit ellen-weorc   äfnan scolde.
Hûru ne gemunde   mago Ecglâfes
eafoðes cräftig,   þät he ær gespräc
wîne druncen,   þâ he þäs wæpnes onlâh
sêlran sweord-frecan: selfa ne dorste
under ýða gewin   aldre geneðan,
driht-scype dreógan;   þær he dôme forleás,
ellen-mærðum.   Ne wäs þäm ôðrum swâ,
syððan he hine tô gûðe   gegyred häfde.

XXIII - THE BATTLE WITH THE WATER-DRAKE

Beówulf maðelode,   bearn Ecgþeówes:
"geþenc nu, se mæra   maga Healfdenes,
"snottra fengel,   nu ic eom sîðes fûs,
"gold-wine gumena,   hwät wit geó spræcon,
"gif ic ät þearfe   þînre scolde
"aldre linnan,   þät þu me â wære
"forð-gewitenum   on fäder stäle;
"wes þu mund-bora mînum   mago-þegnum,
"hond-gesellum,   gif mec hild nime:
"swylce þu þâ mâdmas,   þe þu me sealdest,
"Hrôðgâr leófa,   Higelâce onsend.
"Mäg þonne on þäm golde ongitan   Geáta dryhten,
"geseón sunu Hrêðles,   þonne he on þät sinc staráð,
"þät ic gum-cystum   gôdne funde
"beága bryttan,   breác þonne môste.
"And þu Ûnferð læt   ealde lâfe,
"wrätlîc wæg-sweord   wîd-cûðne man
"heard-ecg habban;   ic me mid Hruntinge
"dôm gewyrce,   oððe mec deáð nimeð."
Äfter þæm wordum   Weder-Geáta leód
êfste mid elne,   nalas andsware
bîdan wolde;   brim-wylm onfêng

hilde-rince.   Þâ wäs hwîl däges,
ær he þone grund-wong   ongytan mehte.
Sôna þät onfunde,   se þe flôda begong
heoro-gîfre beheóld   hund missera,
grim and grædig,   þät þær gumena sum
äl-wihta eard   ufan cunnode.
Grâp þâ tôgeánes,   gûð-rinc gefêng
atolan clommum;   nô þý ær in gescôd
hâlan lîce: hring ûtan ymb-bearh,
þät heó þone fyrd-hom   þurh-fôn ne mihte,
locene leoðo-syrcan   lâðan fingrum.
Bär þâ seó brim-wylf,   þâ heó tô botme com,
hringa þengel   tô hofe sînum,
swâ he ne mihte nô   (he þäs môdig wäs)
wæpna gewealdan,   ac hine wundra þäs fela
swencte on sunde,   sæ-deór monig
hilde-tuxum   here-syrcan bräc,
êhton aglæcan.   Þâ se eorl ongeat,
þät he in nið-sele   nât-hwylcum wäs,
þær him nænig wäter   wihte ne sceðede,
ne him for hrôf-sele   hrînan ne mehte
fær-gripe flôdes: fýr-leóht geseah,
blâcne leóman   beorhte scînan.
Ongeat þâ se gôda   grund-wyrgenne,
mere-wîf mihtig;   mägen-ræs forgeaf
hilde-bille,   hond swenge ne ofteáh,
þät hire on hafelan   hring-mæl âgôl
grædig gûð-leóð.   Þâ se gist onfand,
þät se beado-leóma   bîtan nolde,
aldre sccðan,   ac seó ecg geswâc
þeódne ät þearfe: þolode ær fela
hond-gemôta,   helm oft gescär,
fæges fyrd-hrägl: þät wäs forma sîð
deórum mâðme,   þät his dôm âläg.
Eft wäs ân-ræd,   nalas elnes lät,
mærða gemyndig   mæg Hygelâces;
wearp þâ wunden-mæl   wrättum gebunden
yrre oretta,   þät hit on eorðan läg,
stîð and stýl-ecg;   strenge getrûwode,
mund-gripe mägenes.   Swâ sceal man dôn,
þonne he ät gûðe   gegân þenceð
longsumne lof,   nâ ymb his lîf cearað.
Gefêng þâ be eaxle   (nalas for fæhðe mearn)
Gûð-Geáta leód   Grendles môdor;
brägd þâ beadwe heard,   þâ he gebolgen wäs,
feorh-genîðlan,   þät heó on flet gebeáh.
Heó him eft hraðe   and-leán forgeald
grimman grâpum   and him tôgeánes fêng;
oferwearp þâ wêrig-môd   wîgena strengest,

fêðe-cempa,	þät he on fylle wearð.
Ofsät þâ þone sele-gyst	and hyre seaxe geteáh,
brâd and brûn-ecg	wolde hire bearn wrecan,
ângan eaferan.	Him on eaxle läg
breóst-net broden;	þät gebearh feore,
wið ord and wið ecge	ingang forstôd.
Häfde þâ forsîðod	sunu Ecgþeówes
under gynne grund,	Geáta cempa,
nemne him heaðo-byrne	helpe gefremede,
here-net hearde,	and hâlig god
geweóld wîg-sigor,	witig drihten;
rodera rædend	hit on ryht gescêd,
ýðelîce	syððan he eft âstôd.

XXIV - BEÓWULF SLAYS THE SPRITE

Geseah þâ on searwum	sige-eádig bil,
eald sweord eotenisc	ecgum þyhtig,
wîgena weorð-mynd:	þät wäs wæpna cyst,
bûton hit wäs mâre	þonne ænig mon ôðer
tô beadu-lâce	ätberan meahte
gôd and geatolîc	giganta geweorc.
He gefêng þâ fetel-hilt,	freca Scildinga,
hreóh and heoro-grim	hring-mæl gebrägd,
aldres orwêna,	yrringa slôh,
þät hire wið halse	heard grâpode,
bân-hringas bräc,	bil eal þurh-wôd
fægne flæsc-homan,	heó on flet gecrong;
sweord wäs swâtig,	secg weorce gefeh.
Lixte se leóma,	leóht inne stôd,
efne swâ of hefene	hâdre scîneð
rodores candel.	He äfter recede wlât,
hwearf þâ be wealle,	wæpen hafenade
heard be hiltum	Higelâces þegn,
yrre and ân-ræd.	Näs seó ecg fracod
hilde-rince,	ac he hraðe wolde
Grendle forgyldan	gûð-ræsa fela
þâra þe he geworhte	tô West-Denum
oftor micle	þonne on ænne sîð,
þonne he Hrôðgâres	heorð-geneátas
slôh on sweofote,	slæpende frät
folces Denigea	fýf-tyne men
and ôðer swylc	ût of-ferede,
lâðlîcu lâc.	He him þäs leán forgeald,
rêðe cempa,	tô þäs þe he on räste geseah
gûð-wêrigne	Grendel licgan,
aldor-leásne,	swâ him ær gescôd
hild ät Heorote;	hrâ wîde sprong,
syððan he äfter deáðe	drepe þrowade,
heoro-sweng heardne,	and hine þâ heáfde becearf,

Sôna þät gesâwon   snottre ceorlas,
þâ þe mid Hrôðgâre   on holm wliton,
þät wäs ýð-geblond   eal gemenged,
brim blôde fâh: blonden-feaxe
gomele ymb gôdne   ongeador spræcon,
þät hig þäs äðelinges   eft ne wêndon,
þät he sige-hrêðig   sêcean côme
mærne þeóden;   þâ þäs monige gewearð,
þät hine seó brim-wylf   âbroten häfde.
Þâ com nôn däges.   Näs ofgeâfon
hwate Scyldingas; gewât him hâm þonon
gold-wine gumena.   Gistas sêtan,
môdes seóce,   and on mere staredon,
wiston and ne wêndon,   þät hie heora wine-drihten
selfne gesâwon.   Þâ þät sweord ongan
äfter heaðo-swâte   hilde-gicelum
wîg-bil wanian;   þät wäs wundra sum,
þät hit eal gemealt   îse gelîcost,
þonne forstes bend   fäder onlæteð,
onwindeð wäl-râpas,   se þe geweald hafað
sæla and mæla;   þät is sôð metod.
Ne nom he in þæm wîcum,   Weder-Geáta leód,
mâðm-æhta mâ,   þêh he þær monige geseah,
bûton þone hafelan   and þâ hilt somod,
since fâge;   sweord ær gemealt,
forbarn broden mæl: wäs þät blôd tô þäs hât,
ættren ellor-gæst,   se þær inne swealt.
Sôna wäs on sunde,   se þe ær ät säcce gebâd
wîg-hryre wrâðra,   wäter up þurh-deáf;
wæron ýð-gebland   eal gefælsod,
eácne eardas,   þâ se ellor-gâst
oflêt lîf-dagas   and þâs lænan gesceaft.
Com þâ tô lande   lid-manna helm
swîð-môd swymman,   sæ-lâce gefeah,
mägen-byrðenne   þâra þe he him mid häfde.
Eodon him þâ tôgeánes,   gode þancodon,
þryðlîc þegna heáp,   þeódnes gefêgon,
þäs þe hi hyne gesundne   geseón môston.
Þâ wäs of þäm hrôran   helm and byrne
lungre âlýsed: lagu drusade,
wäter under wolcnum,   wäl-dreóre fâg.
Fêrdon forð þonon   fêðe-lâstum
ferhðum fägne,   fold-weg mæton,
cûðe stræte;   cyning-balde men
from þäm holm-clife   hafelan bæron
earfoðlîce   heora æghwäðrum
fela-môdigra: feówer scoldon
on ðäm wäl-stenge   weorcum geferian
tô þäm gold-sele   Grendles heáfod,

óð þät semninga   tô sele cômon
frome fyrd-hwate   feówer-tyne
Geáta gongan;   gum-dryhten mid
môdig on gemonge   meodo-wongas träd.
Þâ com in gân   ealdor þegna,
dæd-cêne mon   dôme gewurðad,
häle hilde-deór.   Hróðgâr grêtan:
Þâ wäs be feaxe   on flet boren
Grendles heáfod,   þær guman druncon,
egeslîc for eorlum   and þære idese mid:
wlite-seón wrätlîc   weras onsâwon.

XXV - HROTHGAR'S GRATITUDE: HE DISCOURSES

Beówulf maðelode,   bearn Ecgþeówes:
"Hwät! we þe þâs sæ-lâc,   sunu Healfdenes,
"leód Scyldinga,   lustum brôhton,
"tîres tô tâcne,   þe þu her tô lôcast.
"Ic þät unsôfte   ealdre gedîgde:
"wîge under wätere   weorc geneðde
"earfoðlîce,   ät-rihte wäs
"gûð getwæfed,   nymðe mec god scylde.
"Ne meahte ic ät hilde   mid Hruntinge
"wiht gewyrcan,   þeáh þät wæpen duge,
"ac me geûðe   ylda waldend,
"þät ic on wage geseah   wlitig hangian
"eald sweord eácen   (oftost wîsode
"winigea leásum)   þät ic þý wæpne gebräd.
"Ofslôh þâ ät þære säcce   (þâ me sæl âgeald)
"hûses hyrdas.   Þâ þät hilde-bil
"forbarn, brogden mæl,   swâ þät blôd gesprang,
"hâtost heaðo-swâta: ic þät hilt þanan
"feóndum ätferede;   fyren-dæda wräc,
"deáð-cwealm Denigea,   swâ hit gedêfe wäs.
"Ic hit þe þonne gehâte,   þät þu on Heorote môst
"sorh-leás swefan   mid þînra secga gedryht,
"and þegna gehwylc   þînra leóda,
"duguðe and iogoðe,   þät þu him ondrædan ne þearft,
"þeóden Scyldinga,   on þâ healfe,
"aldor-bealu eorlum,   swâ þu ær dydest."
Þâ wäs gylden hilt   gamelum rince.
hârum hild-fruman,   on hand gyfen,
enta ær-geweorc,   hit on æht gehwearf
äfter deófla hryre   Denigea freán,
wundor-smiða geweorc,   and þâ þâs worold ofgeaf
grom-heort guma,   godes andsaca,
morðres scyldig,   and his môdor eác;
on geweald gehwearf   worold-cyninga
þäm sêlestan   be sæm tweónum
þâra þe on Sceden-igge   sceattas dælde.

Hrôðgâr maðelode,   hylt sceáwode,
ealde lâfe,   on þäm wäs ôr writen
fyrn-gewinnes: syððan flôd ofslôh,
gifen geótende,   giganta cyn,
frêcne gefêrdon: þät wäs fremde þeód
êcean dryhtne,   him þäs ende-leán
þurh wäteres wylm   waldend sealde.
Swâ wäs on þæm scennum   scîran goldes
þurh rûn-stafas   rihte gemearcod,
geseted and gesæd,   hwâm þät sweord geworht,
îrena cyst   ærest wære,
wreoðen-hilt and wyrm-fâh.   Þâ se wîsa spräc
sunu Healfdenes   (swîgedon ealle):
"Þät lâ mäg secgan,   se þe sôð and riht
"fremeð on folce,   (feor eal gemon
"eald êðel-weard),   þät þes eorl wære
"geboren betera!   Blæd is âræred
"geond wîd-wegas,   wine mîn Beówulf,
"þîn ofer þeóda gehwylce.   Eal þu hit geþyldum healdest,
"mägen mid môdes snyttrum.   Ic þe sceal mîne gelæstan
"freóde, swâ wit furðum spræcon;   þu scealt tô frôfre weorðan
"eal lang-twidig   leódum þînum,
"häleðum tô helpe.   Ne wearð Heremôd swâ
"eaforum Ecgwelan,   Âr-Scyldingum;
"ne geweôx he him tô willan,   ac tô wäl-fealle
"and tô deáð-cwalum   Deniga leódum;
"breát bolgen-môd   beód-geneátas,
"eaxl-gesteallan,   ôð þät he âna hwearf,
"mære þeóden.   mon-dreámum from:
"þeáh þe hine mihtig god   mägenes wynnum,
"eafeðum stêpte,   ofer ealle men
"forð gefremede,   hwäðere him on ferhðe greów
"breóst-hord blôd-reów: nallas beágas geaf
"Denum äfter dôme;   dreám-leás gebâd,
"þät he þäs gewinnes   weorc þrowade,
"leód-bealo longsum.   Þu þe lær be þon,
"gum-cyste ongit!   ic þis gid be þe
"âwräc wintrum frôd.   Wundor is tô secganne,
"hû mihtig god   manna cynne
"þurh sîdne sefan   snyttru bryttað,
"eard and eorl-scipe,   he âh ealra geweald.
"Hwîlum he on lufan   læteð hworfan
"monnes môd-geþonc   mæran cynnes,
"seleð him on êðle   eorðan wynne,
"tô healdanne   hleó-burh wera,
"gedêð him swâ gewealdene   worolde dælas,
"sîde rîce,   þät he his selfa ne mäg
"for his un-snyttrum   ende geþencean;
"wunað he on wiste,   nô hine wiht dweleð,

"âdl ne yldo,   ne him inwit-sorh
"on sefan sweorceð,   ne gesacu ôhwær,
"ecg-hete eóweð,   ac him eal worold
"wendeð on willan;   he þät wyrse ne con,
"ôð þät him on innan   ofer-hygda dæl
"weaxeð and wridað,   þonne se weard swefeð,
"sâwele hyrde: bið se slæp tô fäst,
"bisgum gebunden,   bona swîðe neáh,
"se þe of flân-bogan   fyrenum sceóteð.

XXVI - THE DISCOURSE IS ENDED--BEÓWULF PREPARES TO LEAVE

"Þonne bið on hreðre   under helm drepen
"biteran stræle: him bebeorgan ne con
"wom wundor-bebodum   wergan gâstes;
"þinceð him tô lytel,   þät he tô lange heóld,
"gýtsað grom-hydig,   nallas on gylp seleð
"fätte beágas   and he þâ forð-gesceaft
"forgyteð and forgýmeð,   þäs þe him ær god sealde
"wuldres waldend,   weorð-mynda dæl.
"Hit on ende-stäf   eft gelimpeð,
"þät se lîc-homa   læne gedreóseð,
"fæge gefealleð;   fêhð ôðer tô,
"se þe unmurnlîce   mâdmas dæleð,
"eorles ær-gestreón,   egesan ne gýmeð.
"Bebeorh þe þone bealo-nîð,   Beówulf leófa,
"secg se betsta,   and þe þät sêlre geceós,
"êce rædas;   oferhyda ne gým,
"mære cempa!   Nu is þînes mägnes blæd
"âne hwîle;   eft sôna bið,
"þät þec âdl oððe ecg   eafoðes getwæfeð,
"oððe fýres feng   oððe flôdes wylm,
"oððe gripe mêces   oððe gâres fliht,
"oððe atol yldo,   oððe eágena bearhtm
"forsiteð and forsworceð;   semninga bið,
"þät þec, dryht-guma,   deáð oferswýðeð.
"Swâ ic Hring-Dena   hund missera
"weóld under wolcnum,   and hig wîge beleác
"manigum mægða   geond þysne middan-geard,
"äscum and ecgum,   þät ic me ænigne
"under swegles begong   gesacan ne tealde.
"Hwät! me þäs on êðle   edwenden cwom,
"gyrn äfter gomene,   seoððan Grendel wearð,
"eald-gewinna,   in-genga mîn:
"ic þære sôcne   singales wäg
"môd-ceare micle.   Þäs sig metode þanc,
"êcean drihtne,   þäs þe ic on aldre gebâd,
"þät ic on þone hafelan   heoro-dreórigne
"ofer eald gewin   eágum starige!

"Gâ nu tô setle,   symbel-wynne dreóh
"wîgge weorðad: unc sceal worn fela
"mâðma gemænra,   siððan morgen bið."
Geát wäs gläd-môd,   geóng sôna tô,
setles neósan,   swâ se snottra hêht.
Þâ wäs eft swâ ær   ellen-rôfum,
flet-sittendum   fägere gereorded
niówan stefne.   Niht-helm geswearc
deorc ofer dryht-gumum.   Duguð eal ârâs;
wolde blonden-feax   beddes neósan,
gamela Scylding.   Geát ungemetes wel,
rôfne rand-wîgan   restan lyste:
sôna him sele-þegn   sîðes wêrgum,
feorran-cundum   forð wîsade,
se for andrysnum   ealle beweotede
þegnes þearfe,   swylce þý dôgore
heáðo-lîðende   habban scoldon.
Reste hine þâ rûm-heort;   reced hlifade
geáp and gold-fâh,   gäst inne swäf,
ôð þät hrefn blaca   heofones wynne
blîð-heort bodode.   Þâ com beorht sunne
scacan ofer grundas;   scaðan onetton,
wæron äðelingas   eft tô leódum
fûse tô farenne,   wolde feor þanon
cuma collen-ferhð   ceóles neósan.
Hêht þâ se hearda   Hrunting beran,
sunu Ecglâfes,   hêht his sweord niman,
leóflîc îren;   sägde him þäs leánes þanc,
cwäð he þone gûð-wine   gôdne tealde,
wîg-cräftigne,   nales wordum lôg
mêces ecge: þät wäs môdig secg.
And þâ sîð-frome   searwum gearwe
wîgend wæron,   eode weorð Denum
äðeling tô yppan,   þær se ôðer wäs
häle hilde-deór,   Hrôðgâr grêtte.

XXVII - THE PARTING WORDS

Beówulf maðelode,   bearn Ecgþeówes:
"Nu we sæ-lîðend   secgan wyllað
"feorran cumene,   þät we fundiað
"Higelâc sêcan.   Wæron her tela
"willum bewenede;   þu ûs wel dohtest.
"Gif ic þonne on eorðan   ôwihte mäg
"þînre môd-lufan   mâran tilian,
"gumena dryhten,   þonne ic gyt dyde,
"gûð-geweorca   ic beó gearo sôna.
"Gif ic þät gefricge   ofer flôda begang,
"þät þec ymbe-sittend   egesan þýwað,
"swâ þec hetende   hwîlum dydon,

"ic þe þûsenda   þegna bringe,
"häleða tô helpe.   Ic on Higelâce wât,
"Geáta dryhten,   þeáh þe he geong sý,
"folces hyrde,   þät he mec fremman wile
"wordum and worcum,   þät ic þe wel herige,
"and þe tô geóce   gâr-holt bere
"mägenes fultum,   þær þe bið manna þearf;
"gif him þonne Hrêðrîc   tô hofum Geáta
"geþingeð, þeódnes bearn,   he mäg þær fela
"freónda findan: feor-cýððe beóð
"sêlran gesôhte   þäm þe him selfa deáh."
Hrôðgâr maðelode   him on andsware:
"Þe þâ word-cwydas   wittig drihten
"on sefan sende!   ne hýrde ic snotorlîcor
"on swâ geongum feore   guman þingian:
"þu eart mägenes strang   and on môde frôd,
"wîs word-cwida.   Wên ic talige,
"gif þät gegangeð,   þät þe gâr nymeð,
"hild heoru-grimme   Hrêðles eaferan,
"âdl oððe îren   ealdor þînne,
"folces hyrde,   and þu þîn feorh hafast,
"þät þe Sæ-Geátas   sêlran näbben
"tô geceósenne   cyning ænigne,
"hord-weard häleða,   gif þu healdan wylt
"mâga rîce.   Me þîn môd-sefa
"lîcað leng swâ wel,   leófa Beówulf:
"hafast þu gefêred,   þät þâm folcum sceal,
"Geáta leódum   and Gâr-Denum
"sib gemænum   and sacu restan,
"inwit-nîðas,   þe hie ær drugon;
"wesan, þenden ic wealde   wîdan rîces,
"mâðmas gemæne,   manig ôðerne
"gôdum gegrêtan   ofer ganotes bäð;
"sceal hring-naca   ofer heáðu bringan
"lâc and luf-tâcen.   Ic þâ leóde wât
"ge wið feónd ge wið freónd   fäste geworhte
"æghwäs untæle   ealde wîsan."
Þâ git him eorla hleó   inne gesealde,
mago Healfdenes   mâðmas twelfe,
hêt hine mid þæm lâcum   leóde swæse
sêcean on gesyntum,   snûde eft cuman.
Gecyste þâ   cyning äðelum gôd,
þeóden Scildinga,   þegen betstan
and be healse genam;   hruron him teáras,
blonden-feaxum: him wäs bega wên,
ealdum infrôdum,   ôðres swîðor,
þät hî seoððan   geseón môston
môdige on meðle.   Wäs him se man tô þon leóf,
þät he þone breóst-wylm   forberan ne mehte,
ac him on hreðre   hyge-bendum fäst

äfter deórum men   dyrne langað
beorn wið blôde.   Him Beówulf þanan,
gûð-rinc gold-wlanc   gräs-moldan träd,
since hrêmig: sæ-genga bâd
âgend-freán,   se þe on ancre râd.
Þâ wäs on gange   gifu Hrôðgâres
oft geæhted: þät wäs ân cyning
æghwäs orleahtre,   ôð þät hine yldo benam
mägenes wynnum,   se þe oft manegum scôd.

XXVIII - BEÓWULF RETURNS TO GEATLAND--THE QUEENS HYGD AND THRYTHO

Cwom þâ tô flôde   fela-môdigra
häg-stealdra heáp;   hring-net bæron,
locene leoðo-syrcan.   Land-weard onfand
eft-sîð eorla,   swâ he ær dyde;
nô he mid hearme   of hliðes nosan
gästas grêtte,   ac him tôgeánes râd;
cwäð þät wilcuman   Wedera leódum
scawan scîr-hame   tô scipe fôron.
Þâ wäs on sande   sæ-geáp naca
hladen here-wædum,   hringed-stefna
mearum and mâðmum: mäst hlifade
ofer Hrôðgâres   hord-gestreónum.
He þäm bât-wearde   bunden golde
swurd gesealde,   þät he syððan wäs
on meodu-bence   mâðme þý weorðra,
yrfe-lâfe.   Gewât him on ýð-nacan,
drêfan deóp wäter,   Dena land ofgeaf.
Þâ wäs be mäste   mere-hrägla sum,
segl sâle fäst.   Sund-wudu þunede,
nô þær wêg-flotan   wind ofer ýðum
sîðes getwæfde;   sæ-genga fôr,
fleát fâmig-heals   forð ofer ýðe,
bunden-stefna   ofer brim-streámas,
þät hie Geáta clifu   ongitan meahton,
cûðe nässas.   Ceól up geþrang,
lyft-geswenced   on lande stôd.
Hraðe wäs ät holme   hýð-weard gearo,
se þe ær lange tîd,   leófra manna
fûs, ät faroðe   feor wlâtode;
sælde tô sande   sîd-fäðme scip
oncer-bendum fäst,   þý läs hym ýða þrym
wudu wynsuman   forwrecan meahte.
Hêt þâ up beran   äðelinga gestreón,
frätwe and fät-gold;   näs him feor þanon
tô gesêcanne   sinces bryttan:
Higelâc Hrêðling   þær ät hâm wunað,

selfa mid gesîðum   sæ-wealle neáh;
bold wäs betlîc,   brego-rôf cyning,
heá on healle,   Hygd swîðe geong,
wîs, wel-þungen,   þeáh þe wintra lyt
under burh-locan   gebiden häbbe
Häreðes dôhtor: näs hió hnâh swâ þeáh,
ne tô gneáð gifa   Geáta leódum,
mâðm-gestreóna.   Mod Þryðo wäg,
fremu folces cwên,   firen ondrysne:
nænig þät dorste   deór genêðan
swæsra gesîða,   nefne sin-freá,
þät hire an däges   eágum starede;
ac him wäl-bende   weotode tealde,
hand-gewriðene: hraðe seoððan wäs
äfter mund-gripe   mêce geþinged,
þät hit sceaðen-mæl   scyran môste,
cwealm-bealu cýðan.   Ne bið swylc cwênlîc þeáw
idese tô efnanne,   þeáh þe hió ænlîcu sý,
þätte freoðu-webbe   feores onsäce
äfter lîge-torne   leófne mannan.
Hûru þät onhôhsnode   Heminges mæg;
ealo drincende   ôðer sædan,
þät hió leód-bealewa   läs gefremede,
inwit-nîða,   syððan ærest wearð
gyfen gold-hroden   geongum cempan,
äðelum dióre,   syððan hió Offan flet
ofer fealone flôd   be fäder lâre
sîðe gesôhte,   þær hió syððan wel
in gum-stôle,   gôde mære,
lîf-gesceafta   lifigende breác,
hióld heáh-lufan   wið häleða brego,
ealles mon-cynnes   mîne gefræge
þone sêlestan   bî sæm tweónum
eormen-cynnes;   forþam Offa wäs
geofum and gûðum   gâr-cêne man,
wîde geweorðod;   wîsdôme heóld
êðel sînne,   þonon Eómær wôc
häleðum tô helpe,   Heminges mæg,
nefa Gârmundes,   nîða cräftig.

XXIX - HIS ARRIVAL. HYGELAC'S RECEPTION

Gewât him þâ se hearda   mid his hond-scole
sylf äfter sande   sæ-wong tredan,
wîde waroðas.   Woruld-candel scân,
sigel sûðan fûs;   hî sîð drugon,
elne geeodon,   tô þäs þe eorla hleó,
bonan Ongenþeówes   burgum on innan,
geongne gûð-cyning   gôdne gefrunon
hringas dælan.   Higelâce wäs

sîð Beówulfes   snûde gecýðed,
þät þær on worðig   wîgendra hleó,
lind-gestealla   lifigende cwom,
heaðo-lâces hâl   tô hofe gongan.
Hraðe wäs gerýmed,   swâ se rîca bebeád,
fêðe-gestum   flet innan-weard.
Gesät þâ wið sylfne,   se þâ säcce genäs,
mæg wið mæge,   syððan man-dryhten
þurh hleóðor-cwyde   holdne gegrêtte
meaglum wordum.   Meodu-scencum
hwearf geond þät reced   Häreðes dôhtor:
lufode þâ leóde,   lîð-wæge bär
hælum tô handa.   Higelâc ongan
sînne geseldan   in sele þam heán
fägre fricgean,   hyne fyrwet bräc,
hwylce Sæ-Geáta   sîðas wæron:
"Hû lomp eów on lâde,   leófa Biówulf,
"þâ þu færinga   feorr gehogodest,
"säcce sêcean   ofer sealt wäter,
"hilde tô Hiorote?   Ac þu Hrôðgâre
"wîd-cûðne weán   wihte gebêttest,
"mærum þeódne?   Ic þäs môd-ceare
"sorh-wylmum seáð,   sîðe ne trûwode
"leófes mannes;   ic þe lange bäd,
"þät þu þone wäl-gæst   wihte ne grêtte,
"lête Sûð-Dene   sylfe geweorðan
"gûðe wið Grendel.   Gode ic þanc secge,
"þäs þe ic þe gesundne   geseón môste."
Biówulf maðelode,   bearn Ecgþiówes:
"Þät is undyrne,   dryhten Higelâc,
"mære gemêting   monegum fira,
"hwylc orleg-hwîl   uncer Grendles
"wearð on þam wange,   þær he worna fela
"Sige-Scildingum   sorge gefremede,
"yrmðe tô aldre;   ic þät eal gewräc,
"swâ ne gylpan þearf   Grendeles mâga
"ænig ofer eorðan   uht-hlem þone,
"se þe lengest leofað   lâðan cynnes,
"fenne bifongen.   Ic þær furðum cwom,
"tô þam hring-sele   Hrôðgâr grêtan:
"sôna me se mæra   mago Healfdenes,
"syððan he môd-sefan   mînne cûðe,
"wið his sylfes sunu   setl getæhte.
"Weorod wäs on wynne;   ne seah ic wîdan feorh
"under heofenes hwealf   heal-sittendra
"medu-dreám mâran.   Hwîlum mæru cwên,
"friðu-sibb folca   flet eall geond-hwearf,
"bædde byre geonge;   oft hió beáh-wriðan
"secge sealde,   ær hió tô setle geóng.

Beowulf: Scholar's Edition

"Hwîlum for duguðe   dôhtor Hrôðgâres
"eorlum on ende   ealu-wæge bär,
"þâ ic Freáware   flet-sittende
"nemnan hýrde,   þær hió nägled sinc
"häleðum sealde: sió gehâten wäs,
"geong gold-hroden,   gladum suna Frôdan;
"hafað þäs geworden   wine Scyldinga
"rîces hyrde   and þät ræd talað,
"þät he mid þý wîfe   wäl-fæhða dæl,
"säcca gesette.   Oft nô seldan hwær
"äfter leód-hryre   lytle hwîle
"bon-gâr bûgeð,   þeáh seó brýd duge!

XXX - BEÓWULF'S STORY OF THE SLAYINGS

"Mäg þäs þonne ofþyncan   þeóden Heaðobeardna
"and þegna gehwâm   þâra leóda,
"þonne he mid fæmnan   on flett gæð,
"dryht-bearn Dena   duguða biwenede:
"on him gladiað   gomelra lâfe
"heard and hring-mæl,   Heaðobeardna gestreón,
"þenden hie þâm wæpnum   wealdan môston,
"ôð þät hie forlæddan   tô þam lind-plegan
"swæse gesîðas   ond hyra sylfra feorh.
"Þonne cwið ät beóre,   se þe beáh gesyhð,
"eald äsc-wîga,   se þe eall geman
"gâr-cwealm gumena   (him bið grim sefa),
"onginneð geômor-môd   geongne cempan
"þurh hreðra gehygd   higes cunnian,
"wîg-bealu weccean   and þät word âcwyð:
"'Meaht þu, mîn wine,   mêce gecnâwan,
"'þone þin fäder   tô gefeohte bär
"'under here-grîman   hindeman sîðe,
"'dýre îren,   þær hyne Dene slôgon,
"'weóldon wäl-stôwe,   syðdan wiðer-gyld läg,
"'äfter häleða hryre,   hwate Scyldungas?
"'Nu her þâra banena   byre nât-hwylces,
"'frätwum hrêmig   on flet gæð,
"'morðres gylpeð   and þone mâððum byreð,
"'þone þe þu mid rihte   rædan sceoldest!'"
"Manað swâ and myndgað   mæla gehwylce
"sârum wordum,   ôð þät sæl cymeð,
"þät se fæmnan þegn   fore fäder dædum
"äfter billes bite   blôd-fâg swefeð,
"ealdres scyldig;   him se ôðer þonan
"losað lifigende,   con him land geare.
"Þonne bióð brocene   on bâ healfe
"âð-sweord eorla;   syðdan Ingelde
"weallað wäl-nîðas   and him wîf-lufan
"äfter cear-wälmum   côlran weorðað.

> *Beowulf: Scholar's Edition*

"Þý ic Heaðobeardna   hyldo ne telge,
"dryht-sibbe dæl   Denum unfæcne,
"freónd-scipe fästne.   Ic sceal forð sprecan
"gen ymbe Grendel,   þät þu geare cunne,
"sinces brytta,   tô hwan syððan wearð
"hond-ræs häleða.   Syððan heofones gim
"glâd ofer grundas,   gäst yrre cwom,
"eatol æfen-grom,   ûser neósan,
"þær we gesunde   säl weardodon;
"þær wäs Hondscio   hild onsæge,
"feorh-bealu fægum,   he fyrmest läg,
"gyrded cempa;   him Grendel wearð,
"mærum magu-þegne   tô mûð-bonan,
"leófes mannes   lîc eall forswealg.
"Nô þý ær ût þâ gen   îdel-hende
"bona blôdig-tôð   bealewa gemyndig,
"of þam gold-sele   gongan wolde,
"ac he mägnes rôf   mîn costode,
"grâpode gearo-folm.   Glôf hangode
"sîd and syllîc   searo-bendum fäst,
"sió wäs orþoncum   eall gegyrwed
"deófles cräftum   and dracan fellum:
"he mec þær on innan   unsynnigne,
"diór dæd-fruma,   gedôn wolde,
"manigra sumne: hyt ne mihte swâ,
"syððan ic on yrre   upp-riht âstôd.
"Tô lang ys tô reccenne,   hû ic þam leód-sceaðan
"yfla gehwylces   ond-leán forgeald;
"þær ic, þeóden mîn,   þîne leóde
"weorðode wcorcum.   He on weg losade,
"lytle hwîle   lîf-wynna breác;
"hwäðre him sió swîðre   swaðe weardade
"hand on Hiorte   and he heán þonan,
"môdes geômor   mere-grund gefeóll.
"Me þone wäl-ræs   wine Scildunga
"fättan golde   fela leánode,
"manegum mâðmum,   syððan mergen com
"and we tô symble   geseten häfdon.
"Þær wäs gidd and gleó;   gomela Scilding
"fela fricgende   feorran rehte;
"hwîlum hilde-deór   hearpan wynne,
"gomen-wudu grêtte;   hwîlum gyd âwräc
"sôð and sârlîc;   hwîlum syllîc spell
"rehte äfter rihte   rûm-heort cyning.
"Hwîlum eft ongan   eldo gebunden,
"gomel gûð-wîga   gioguðe cwîðan
"hilde-strengo;   hreðer inne weóll,
"þonne he wintrum frôd   worn gemunde.
"Swâ we þær inne   andlangne däg

"nióde nâman,   ôð þät niht becwom
"ôðer tô yldum.   Þâ wäs eft hraðe
"gearo gyrn-wräce   Grendeles môdor,
"sîðode sorh-full;   sunu deáð fornam,
"wîg-hete Wedra.   Wîf unhýre
"hyre bearn gewräc,   beorn âcwealde
"ellenlîce;   þær wäs Äsc-here,
"frôdan fyrn-witan,   feorh ûðgenge;
"nôðer hy hine ne môston,   syððan mergen cwom,
"deáð-wêrigne   Denia leóde
"bronde forbärnan,   ne on bæl hladan
"leófne mannan: hió þät lîc ätbär
"feóndes fäðmum   under firgen-streám.
"Þät wäs Hrôðgâre   hreówa tornost
"þâra þe leód-fruman   lange begeâte;
"þâ se þeóden mec   þîne lîfe
"healsode hreóh-môd,   þät ic on holma geþring
"eorl-scipe efnde,   ealdre geneðde,
"mærðo fremede: he me mêde gehêt.
"Ic þâ þäs wälmes,   þe is wîde cûð,
"grimne gryrelîcne   grund-hyrde fond.
"Þær unc hwîle wäs   hand gemæne;
"holm heolfre weóll   and ic heáfde becearf
"in þam grund-sele   Grendeles môdor
"eácnum ecgum,   unsôfte þonan
"feorh ôðferede;   näs ic fæge þâ gyt,
"ac me eorla hleó   eft gesealde
"mâðma menigeo,   maga Healfdenes.

XXXI - HE GIVES PRESENTS TO HYGELAC. HYGELAC REWARDS HIM. HYGELAC'S DEATH. BEÓWULF REIGNS

"Swâ se þeód-kyning   þeáwum lyfde;
"nealles ic þâm leánum   forloren häfde,
"mägnes mêde,   ac he me mâðmas geaf,
"sunu Healfdenes,   on sînne sylfes dôm;
"þâ ic þe, beorn-cyning,   bringan wylle,
"êstum geýwan.   Gen is eall ät þe
"lissa gelong: ic lyt hafo
"heáfod-mâga,   nefne Hygelâc þec!"
Hêt þâ in beran   eafor, heáfod-segn,
heaðo-steápne helm,   hâre byrnan,
gûð-sweord geatolîc,   gyd äfter wräc:
"Me þis hilde-sceorp   Hrôðgâr sealde,
"snotra fengel,   sume worde hêt,
"þät ic his ærest   þe eft gesägde,
"cwäð þät hyt häfde   Hiorogâr cyning,
"leód Scyldunga   lange hwîle:
"nô þý ær suna sînum   syllan wolde,
"hwatum Heorowearde,   þeáh he him hold wære,

"breóst-gewædu.   Brûc ealles well!"
Hýrde ic þät þâm frätwum   feówer mearas
lungre gelîce   lâst weardode,
äppel-fealuwe;   he him êst geteáh
meara and mâðma.   Swâ sceal mæg dôn,
nealles inwit-net   ôðrum bregdan,
dyrnum cräfte   deáð rênian
hond-gesteallan.   Hygelâce wäs,
nîða heardum,   nefa swýðe hold
and gehwäðer ôðrum   hrôðra gemyndig.
Hýrde ic þät he þone heals-beáh   Hygde gesealde,
wrätlîcne wundur-mâððum,   þone þe him Wealhþeó geaf,
þeódnes dôhtor,   þrió wicg somod
swancor and sadol-beorht;   hyre syððan wäs
äfter beáh-þege   breóst geweorðod.
Swâ bealdode   bearn Ecgþeówes,
guma gûðum cûð,   gôdum dædum,
dreáh äfter dôme,   nealles druncne slôg
heorð-geneátas;   näs him hreóh sefa,
ac he man-cynnes   mæste cräfte
gin-fästan gife,   þe him god sealde,
heóld hilde-deór.   Heán wäs lange,
swâ hyne Geáta bearn   gôdne ne tealdon,
ne hyne on medo-bence   micles wyrðne
drihten wereda   gedôn wolde;
swýðe oft sägdon,   þät he sleac wære,
 äðeling unfrom: edwenden cwom
tîr-eádigum menn   torna gehwylces.
Hêt þâ eorla hleó   in gefetian,
heaðo-rôf cyning,   Hrêðles lâfe,
golde gegyrede;   näs mid Geátum þâ
sinc-mâððum sêlra   on sweordes hâd;
þät he on Biówulfes   bearm âlegde,
and him gesealde   seofan þûsendo,
bold and brego-stôl.   Him wäs bâm samod
on þam leód-scipe   lond gecynde,
eard êðel-riht,   ôðrum swîðor
sîde rîce,   þam þær sêlra wäs.
Eft þät geiode   ufaran dôgrum
hilde-hlämmum,   syððan Hygelâc läg
and Heardrêde   hilde-mêceas
under bord-hreóðan   tô bonan wurdon,
þâ hyne gesôhtan   on sige-þeóde
hearde hilde-frecan,   Heaðo-Scilfingas,
nîða genægdan   nefan Hererîces.
Syððan Beówulfe   brâde rîce
on hand gehwearf: he geheóld tela
fîftig wintru   (wäs þâ frôd cyning,
eald êðel-weard),   ôð þät ân ongan

deorcum nihtum   draca rîcsian,
se þe on heáre hæðe   hord beweotode,
stân-beorh steápne: stîg under läg,
eldum uncûð.   Þær on innan gióng
niða nât-hwylces   neóde gefêng
hæðnum horde   hond . d . . geþ . . hwylc
since fâhne,   he þät syððan . . . . .
. . . þ . . . lð . þ . . l . g
slæpende be fýre,   fyrena hyrde
þeófes cräfte,   þät sie . . . . ðioð . . . . .
. idh . folc-beorn,   þät he gebolgen wäs.

XXXII - THE FIRE-DRAKE. THE HOARD

Nealles mid geweoldum   wyrm-horda . . . cräft
sôhte sylfes willum,   se þe him sâre gesceôd,
ac for þreá-nêdlan   þeów nât-hwylces
häleða bearna   hete-swengeas fleáh,
for ofer-þearfe   and þær inne fealh
secg syn-bysig.   Sôna in þâ tîde
þät . . . . . þam gyste   . . . . br . g . stôd,
hwäðre earm-sceapen . . . .
. . ð . . . sceapen o . . . . i r . . e se fäs begeat,
sinc-fät geseah: þær wäs swylcra fela
in þam eorð-scräfe   ær-gestreóna,
swâ hy on geâr-dagum   gumena nât-hwylc
eormen-lâfe   äðelan cynnes
þanc-hycgende   þær gehýdde,
deóre mâðmas.   Ealle hie deáð fornam
ærran mælum,   and se ân þâ gen
leóda duguðe,   se þær lengest hwearf,
weard wine-geômor   wîscte þäs yldan,
þät he lytel fäc   long-gestreóna
brûcan môste.   Beorh eal gearo
wunode on wonge   wäter-ýðum neáh,
niwe be nässe   nearo-cräftum fäst:
þær on innan bär   eorl-gestreóna
hringa hyrde   hard-fyrdne dæl
fättan goldes,   feá worda cwäð:
"Heald þu nu, hruse,   nu häleð ne môston,
"eorla æhte.   Hwät! hit ær on þe
"gôde begeâton;   gûð-deáð fornam,
"feorh-bealo frêcne   fyra gehwylcne,
"leóda mînra,   þâra þe þis lîf ofgeaf,
"gesâwon sele-dreám.   Nâh hwâ sweord wege
"oððe fetige   fäted wæge,
"drync-fät deóre: duguð ellor scôc.
"Sceal se hearda helm   hyrsted golde
"fätum befeallen: feormiend swefað,
"þâ þe beado-grîman   býwan sceoldon,

"ge swylce seó here-pâd,   sió ät hilde gebâd
"ofer borda gebräc   bite îrena,
"brosnað äfter beorne.   Ne mäg byrnan hring
"äfter wîg-fruman   wîde fêran
"häleðum be healfe;   näs hearpan wyn,
"gomen gleó-beámes,   ne gôd hafoc
"geond säl swingeð,   ne se swifta mearh
"burh-stede beáteð.   Bealo-cwealm hafað
"fela feorh-cynna   feorr onsended!"
Swâ giômor-môd   giohðo mænde,
ân äfter eallum   unblîðe hweóp,
däges and nihtes,   ôð þät deáðes wylm
hrân ät heortan.   Hord-wynne fond
eald uht-sceaða   opene standan,
se þe byrnende   biorgas sêceð
nacod nîð-draca,   nihtes fleógeð
fýre befangen;   hyne fold-bûend
wîde gesâwon.   He gewunian sceall
hlâw under hrusan,   þær he hæðen gold
waráð wintrum frôd;   ne byð him wihte þê sêl.
Swâ se þeód-sceaða   þreó hund wintra
heóld on hrusan   hord-ärna sum
eácen-cräftig,   ôð þät hyne ân âbealh
mon on môde: man-dryhtne bär
fäted wæge,   frioðo-wære bäd
hlâford sînne.   Þâ wäs hord râsod,
onboren beága hord,   bêne getîðad
feá-sceaftum men.   Freá sceáwode
fira fyrn-geweorc   forman sîðe.
Þâ se wyrm onwôc,   wrôht wäs geniwad;
stonc þâ äfter stâne,   stearc-heort onfand
feóndes fôt-lâst;   he tô forð gestôp,
dyrnan cräfte,   dracan heáfde neáh.
Swâ mäg unfæge   eáðe gedîgan
weán and wräc-sîð,   se þe waldendes
hyldo gehealdeð.   Hord-weard sôhte
georne äfter grunde,   wolde guman findan,
þone þe him on sweofote   sâre geteóde:
hât and hreóh-môd   hlæw oft ymbe hwearf,
ealne ûtan-weardne;   ne þær ænig mon
wäs on þære wêstenne.   Hwäðre hilde gefeh,
beado-weorces: hwîlum on beorh äthwearf,
sinc-fät sôhte;   he þät sôna onfand,
þät häfde gumena sum   goldes gefandod
heáh-gestreóna.   Hord-weard onbâd
earfoðlîce,   ôð þät æfen cwom;
wäs þâ gebolgen   beorges hyrde,
wolde se lâða   lîge forgyldan
drinc-fät dýre.   Þâ wäs däg sceacen

wyrme on willan,   nô on wealle leng
bîdan wolde,   ac mid bæle fôr,
fýre gefýsed.   Wäs se fruma egeslîc
leódum on lande,   swâ hyt lungre wearð
on hyra sinc-gifan   sâre geendod.

XXXIII - BEOWULF RESOLVES TO KILL THE FIRE-DRAKE

Þâ se gäst ongan   glêdum spîwan,
beorht hofu bärnan;   bryne-leóma stôd
eldum on andan;   nô þær âht cwices
lâð lyft-floga   læfan wolde.
Wäs þäs wyrmes wîg   wîde gesýne,
nearo-fâges nîð   neán and feorran,
hû se gûð-sceaða   Geáta leóde
hatode and hýnde: hord eft gesceát,
dryht-sele dyrnne   ær däges hwîle.
Häfde land-wara   lîge befangen,
bæle and bronde;   beorges getrûwode,
wîges and wealles: him seó wên geleáh.
Þâ wäs Biówulfe   brôga gecýðed
snûde tô sôðe,   þät his sylfes him
bolda sêlest   bryne-wylmum mealt,
gif-stôl Geáta.   Þät þam gôdan wäs
hreów on hreðre,   hyge-sorga mæst:
wênde se wîsa,   þät he wealdende,
ofer ealde riht,   êcean dryhtne
bitre gebulge: breóst innan weóll
þeóstrum geþoncum,   swâ him geþýwe ne wäs.
Häfde lîg-draca   leóda fästen,
eá-lond ûtan,   eorð-weard þone
glêdum forgrunden.   Him þäs gûð-cyning,
Wedera þióden,   wräce leornode.
Hêht him þâ gewyrcean   wîgendra hleó
eall-îrenne,   eorla dryhten
wîg-bord wrätlîc;   wisse he gearwe,
þät him holt-wudu   helpan ne meahte,
lind wið lîge.   Sceolde læn-daga
äðeling ær-gôd   ende gebîdan
worulde lîfes   and se wyrm somod;
þeáh þe hord-welan   heólde lange.
Oferhogode þâ   hringa fengel,
þät he þone wîd-flogan   weorode gesôhte,
sîdan herge;   nô he him þâ säcce ondrêd,
ne him þäs wyrmes wîg   for wiht dyde,
eafoð and ellen;   forþon he ær fela
nearo nêðende   nîða gedîgde,
hilde-hlemma,   syððan he Hrôðgâres,
sigor-eádig secg,   sele fälsode
and ät gûðe forgrâp   Grendeles mægum,

lâðan cynnes.　　Nô þät läsest wäs
hond-gemota,　　þær mon Hygelâc slôh,
syððan Geáta cyning　　gûðe ræsum,
freá-wine folces　　Freslondum on,
Hrêðles eafora　　hioro-dryncum swealt,
bille gebeáten;　　þonan Biówulf com
sylfes cräfte,　　sund-nytte dreáh;
+ häfde him on earme　　... XXX
hilde-geatwa,　　þâ he tô holme stâg.
Nealles Hetware　　hrêmge þorfton
fêðe-wîges,　　þe him foran ongeán
linde bæron:　　lyt eft becwom
fram þam hild-frecan　　hâmes niósan.
Oferswam þâ sióleða bigong　　sunu Ecgþeówes,
earm ân-haga　　eft tô leódum,
þær him Hygd gebeád　　hord and rîce,
beágas and brego-stôl:　　bearne ne trûwode,
þät he wið äl-fylcum　　êðel-stôlas
healdan cûðe,　　þâ wäs Hygelâc deád.
Nô þý ær feá-sceafte　　findan meahton
ät þam äðelinge　　ænige þinga,
þät he Heardrêde　　hlâford wære,
oððe þone cyne-dôm　　ciósan wolde;
hwäðre he him on folce　　freónd-lârum heóld,
êstum mid âre,　　ôð þät he yldra wearð,
Weder-Geátum weóld.　　Hyne wräc-mäcgas
ofer sæ sôhtan,　　suna Ôhteres:
häfdon hy forhealden　　helm Scylfinga,
þone sêlestan　　sæ-cyninga,
þâra þe in Swió-rîce　　sinc brytnade,
mærne þeóden.　　Him þät tô mearce wearð;
he þær orfeorme　　feorh-wunde hleát
sweordes swengum,　　sunu Hygelâces;
and him eft gewât　　Ongenþiówes bearn
hâmes niósan,　　syððan Heardrêd läg;
lêt þone brego-stôl　　Biówulf healdan,
Geátum wealdan:　　þät wäs gôd cyning.

XXXIV - RETROSPECT OF BEÓWULF--STRIFE BETWEEN SWEONAS AND GEATAS

Se þäs leód-hryres　　leán gemunde
uferan dôgrum,　　Eádgilse wearð
feá-sceaftum feónd.　　Folce gestepte
ofer sæ sîde　　sunu Ôhteres
wîgum and wæpnum:　　he gewräc syððan
cealdum cear-sîðum,　　cyning ealdre bineát.
Swâ he nîða gehwane　　genesen häfde,
slîðra geslyhta,　　sunu Ecgþiówes,

ellen-weorca,   ôð þone ânne däg,
þe he wið þam wyrme   gewegan sceolde.
Gewât þâ twelfa sum   torne gebolgen
dryhten Geáta   dracan sceáwian;
häfde þâ gefrunen,   hwanan sió fæhð ârâs,
bealo-nîð biorna;   him tô bearme cwom
mâððum-fät mære   þurh þäs meldan hond,
Se wäs on þam þreáte   þreotteoða secg,
se þäs orleges   ôr onstealde,
häft hyge-giômor,   sceolde heán þonon
wong wîsian: he ofer willan gióng
tô þäs þe he eorð-sele   ânne wisse,
hlæw under hrusan   holm-wylme nêh,
ýð-gewinne,   se wäs innan full
wrätta and wîra: weard unhióre,
gearo gûð-freca,   gold-mâðmas heóld,
eald under eorðan;   näs þät ýðe ceáp,
tô gegangenne   gumena ænigum.
Gesät þâ on nässe   nîð-heard cyning,
þenden hælo âbeád   heorð-geneátum
gold-wine Geáta: him wäs geômor sefa,
wäfre and wäl-fûs,   Wyrd ungemete neáh,
se þone gomelan   grêtan sceolde,
sêcean sâwle hord,   sundur gedælan
lîf wið lîce: nô þon lange wäs
feorh äðelinges   flæsce bewunden.
Biówulf maðelade,   bearn Ecgþeówes:
"Fela ic on giogoðe   guð-ræsa genäs,
"orleg-hwîla: ic þät eall gemon.
"Ic wäs syfan-wintre,   þâ mec sinca baldor,
"freá-wine folca   ät mînum fäder genam,
"heóld mec and häfde   Hrêðel cyning,
"geaf me sinc and symbel,   sibbe gemunde;
"näs ic him tô lîfe   lâðra ôwihte
"beorn in burgum,   þonne his bearna hwylc,
"Herebeald and Hæðcyn,   oððe Hygelâc mîn.
"Wäs þam yldestan   ungedêfelîce
"mæges dædum   morðor-bed strêd,
"syððan hyne Hæðcyn   of horn-bogan,
"his freá-wine   flâne geswencte,
"miste mercelses   and his mæg ofscêt,
"brôðor ôðerne,   blôdigan gâre:
"þät wäs feoh-leás gefeoht,   fyrenum gesyngad
"hreðre hyge-mêðe;   sceolde hwäðre swâ þeáh
"äðeling unwrecen   ealdres linnan.
"Swâ bið geômorlîc   gomelum ceorle
"tô gebîdanne,   þät his byre rîde
"giong on galgan,   þonne he gyd wrece,
"sârigne sang,   þonne his sunu hangað
"hrefne tô hrôðre   and he him helpe ne mäg,

"eald and in-frôd,   ænige gefremman.
"Symble bið gemyndgad   morna gehwylce
"eaforan ellor-sîð;   ôðres ne gýmeð
"tô gebîdanne   burgum on innan
"yrfe-weardes,   þonne se ân hafað
"þurh deáðes nýd   dæda gefondad.
"Gesyhð sorh-cearig   on his suna bûre
"wîn-sele wêstne,   wind-gereste,
"reóte berofene;   rîdend swefað
"häleð in hoðman;   nis þær hearpan swêg,
"gomen in geardum,   swylce þær iú wæron.

XXXV - MEMORIES OF PAST TIME--THE FEUD WITH THE FIRE-DRAKE

"Gewîteð þonne on sealman,   sorh-leóð gäleð
"ân äfter ânum: þûhte him eall tô rûm,
"wongas and wîc-stede.   Swâ Wedra helm
"äfter Herebealde   heortan sorge
"weallende wäg,   wihte ne meahte
"on þam feorh-bonan   fæhðe gebêtan:
"nô þý ær he þone heaðo-rinc   hatian ne meahte
"lâðum dædum,   þeáh him leóf ne wäs.
"He þâ mid þære sorge,   þe him sió sâr belamp,
"gum-dreám ofgeaf,   godes leóht geceás;
"eaferum læfde,   swâ dêð eádig mon,
"lond and leód-byrig,   þâ he of lîfe gewât.
"Þâ wäs synn and sacu   Sweona and Geáta,
"ofer wîd wäter   wrôht gemæne,
"here-nîð hearda,   syððan Hrêðel sweallt,
"oððe him Ongenþeówes   eaferan wæran
"frome fyrd-hwate,   freóde ne woldon
"ofer heafo healdan,   ac ymb Hreosna-beorh
"eatolne inwit-scear   oft gefremedon.
"Þät mæg-wine   mîne gewræcan,
"fæhðe and fyrene,   swâ hyt gefræge wäs,
"þeáh þe ôðer hit   ealdre gebohte,
"heardan ceápe: Hæðcynne wearð,
"Geáta dryhtne,   gûð onsæge.
"Þâ ic on morgne gefrägn   mæg ôðerne
"billes ecgum   on bonan stælan,
"þær Ongenþeów   Eofores niósade:
"gûð-helm tôglâd,   gomela Scylfing
"hreás heoro-blâc;   hond gemunde
"fæhðo genôge,   feorh-sweng ne ofteáh.
"Ic him þâ mâðmas,   þe he me sealde,
"geald ät gûðe,   swâ me gifeðe wäs,
"leóhtan sweorde: he me lond forgeaf,
"eard êðel-wyn.   Näs him ænig þearf,

"þät he tô Gifðum   oððe tô Gâr-Denum
"oððe in Swió-ríce   sêcean þurfe
"wyrsan wîg-frecan,   weorðe gecýpan;
"symle ic him on fêðan   beforan wolde,
"âna on orde,   and swâ tô aldre sceall
"säcce fremman,   þenden þis sweord þolað,
"þät mec ær and sîð   oft gelæste,
"syððan ic for dugeðum   Däghrefne wearð
"tô hand-bonan,   Hûga cempan:
"nalles he þâ frätwe   Fres-cyninge,
"breóst-weorðunge   bringan môste,
"ac in campe gecrong   cumbles hyrde,
"äðeling on elne.   Ne wäs ecg bona,
"ac him hilde-grâp   heortan wylmas,
"bân-hûs gebräc.   Nu sceall billes ecg,
"hond and heard sweord   ymb hord wîgan."
Beówulf maðelode,   beót-wordum spräc
niéhstan sîðe: "Ic geneðde fela
"gûða on geogoðe;   gyt ic wylle,
"frôd folces weard,   fæhðe sêcan,
"mærðum fremman,   gif mec se mân-sceaða
"of eorð-sele   ût gesêceð!"
Gegrêtte þâ   gumena gehwylcne,
hwate helm-berend   hindeman sîðe,
swæse gesîðas: "Nolde ic sweord beran,
"wæpen tô wyrme,   gif ic wiste hû
"wið þam aglæcean   elles meahte
"gylpe wiðgrîpan,   swâ ic gió wið Grendle dyde;
"ac ic þær heaðu-fýres   hâtes wêne,
"rêðes and-hâttres: forþon ic me on hafu
"bord and byrnan.   Nelle ic beorges weard
"oferfleón fôtes trem,   feónd unhýre,
"ac unc sceal weorðan ät wealle,   swâ unc Wyrd geteóð,
"metod manna gehwäs.   Ic eom on môde from,
"þät ic wið þone gûð-flogan   gylp ofersitte.
"Gebîde ge on beorge   byrnum werede,
"secgas on searwum,   hwäðer sêl mæge
"äfter wäl-ræse   wunde gedýgan
"uncer twega.   Nis þät eówer sîð,
"ne gemet mannes,   nefne mîn ânes,
"þät he wið aglæcean   eofoðo dæle,
"eorl-scype efne.   Ic mid elne sceall
"gold gegangan   oððe gûð nimeð,
"feorh-bealu frêcne,   freán eówerne!"
Ârâs þâ bî ronde   rôf oretta,
heard under helm,   hioro-sercean bär
under stân-cleofu,   strengo getrûwode
ânes mannes: ne bið swylc earges sîð.
Geseah þâ be wealle,   se þe worna fela,
gum-cystum gôd,   gûða gedîgde,

hilde-hlemma,   þonne hnitan fêðan,
(stôd on stân-bogan)   streám ût þonan
brecan of beorge;   wäs þære burnan wälm
heaðo-fýrum hât: ne meahte horde neáh
unbyrnende   ænige hwîle
deóp gedýgan   for dracan lêge.
Lêt þâ of breóstum,   þâ he gebolgen wäs,
Weder-Geáta leód   word ût faran,
stearc-heort styrmde;   stefn in becom
heaðo-torht hlynnan   under hârne stân.
Hete wäs onhrêred,   hord-weard oncniów
mannes reorde;   näs þær mâra fyrst,
freóde tô friclan.   From ærest cwom
oruð aglæcean   ût of stâne,
hât hilde-swât;   hruse dynede.
Biorn under beorge   bord-rand onswâf
wið þam gryre-gieste,   Geáta dryhten:
þâ wäs hring-bogan   heorte gefýsed
sæcce tô sêceanne.   Sweord ær gebräd
gôd gûð-cyning   gomele lâfe,
ecgum ungleáw,   æghwäðrum wäs
bealo-hycgendra   brôga fram ôðrum.
Stîð-môd gestôd   wið steápne rond
winia bealdor,   þâ se wyrm gebeáh
snûde tôsomne: he on searwum bâd.
Gewât þâ byrnende   gebogen scrîðan tô,
gescîfe scyndan.   Scyld wel gebearg
lîfe and lîce   lässan hwîle
mærum þeódne,   þonne his myne sôhte,
þær he þý fyrste   forman dôgore
wealdan môste,   swâ him Wyrd ne gescrâf
hrêð ät hilde.   Hond up âbräd
Geáta dryhten,   gryre-fâhne slôh
incge lâfe,   þät sió ecg gewâc
brûn on bâne,   bât unswîðor,
þonne his þiód-cyning   þearfe häfde,
bysigum gebæded.   Þâ wäs beorges weard
äfter heaðu-swenge   on hreóum môde,
wearp wäl-fýre,   wîde sprungon
hilde-leóman: hrêð-sigora ne gealp
gold-wine Geáta,   gûð-bill geswâc
nacod ät nîðe,   swâ hyt nô sceolde,
îren ær-gôd.   Ne wäs þät êðe sîð,
þät se mæra   maga Ecgþeówes
grund-wong þone   ofgyfan wolde;
sceolde wyrmes willan   wîc eardian
elles hwergen,   swâ sceal æghwylc mon
âlætan læn-dagas.   Näs þâ long tô þon,
þät þâ aglæcean   hy eft gemêtton.

Hyrte hyne hord-weard,   hreðer æðme weóll,
niwan stefne: nearo þrowode
fýre befongen   se þe ær folce weóld.
Nealles him on heápe   hand-gesteallan,
äðelinga bearn   ymbe gestôdon
hilde-cystum,   ac hy on holt bugon,
ealdre burgan.   Hiora in ânum weóll
sefa wið sorgum: sibb æfre ne mäg
wiht onwendan,   þam þe wel þenceð.

XXXVI - WIGLAF HELPS BEÓWULF IN THE FEUD

Wîglâf wäs hâten   Weoxstânes sunu,
leóflîc lind-wiga,   leód Scylfinga,
mæg Älfheres: geseah his mon-dryhten
under here-grîman   hât þrowian.
Gemunde þâ þâ âre,   þe he him ær forgeaf
wîc-stede weligne   Wægmundinga,
folc-rihta gehwylc,   swâ his fäder âhte;
ne mihte þâ forhabban,   hond rond gefêng,
geolwe linde,   gomel swyrd geteáh,
þät wäs mid eldum   Eánmundes lâf,
suna Ôhteres,   þam ät säcce wearð
wracu wine-leásum   Weohstânes bana
mêces ecgum,   and his mâgum ätbär
brûn-fâgne helm,   hringde byrnan,
eald sweord eotonisc,   þät him Onela forgeaf,
his gädelinges   gûð-gewædu,
fyrd-searo fûslîc: nô ymbe þâ fæhðe spräc,
þeáh þe he his brôðor   bearn âbredwade.
He frätwe geheóld   fela missera,
bill and byrnan,   ôð þät his byre mihte
eorl-scipe efnan,   swâ his ær-fäder;
geaf him þâ mid Geátum   gûð-gewæda
æghwäs unrîm;   þâ he of ealdre gewât,
frôd on forð-weg.   Þâ wäs forma sîð
geongan cempan,   þät he gûðe ræs
mid his freó-dryhtne   fremman sceolde;
ne gemealt him se môd-sefa,   ne his mæges lâf
gewâc ät wîge: þät se wyrm onfand,
syððan hie tôgädre   gegân häfdon.
Wîglâf maðelode   word-rihta fela,
sägde gesîðum,   him wäs sefa geômor:
"Ic þät mæl geman,   þær we medu þêgun,
"þonne we gehêton   ûssum hlâforde
"in biór-sele,   þe ûs þâs beágas geaf,
"þät we him þâ gûð-geatwa   gyldan woldon,
"gif him þyslîcu   þearf gelumpe,
"helmas and heard sweord: þê he ûsic on herge geceás
"tô þyssum sîð-fate   sylfes willum,

"onmunde ûsic mærða   and me þâs mâðmas geaf,
"þê he ûsic gâr-wîgend   gôde tealde,
"hwate helm-berend,   þeáh þe hlâford ûs
"þis ellen-weorc   âna âþôhte
"tô gefremmanne,   folces hyrde,
"forþam he manna mæst   mærða gefremede,
"dæda dollîcra.   Nu is se däg cumen,
"þät ûre man-dryhten   mägenes behôfað
"gôdra gûð-rinca: wutun gangan tô,
"helpan hild-fruman,   þenden hyt sý,
"glêd-egesa grim!   God wât on mec,
"þät me is micle leófre,   þät mînne lîc-haman
"mid mînne gold-gyfan   glêd fäðmie.
"Ne þynceð me gerysne,   þät we rondas beren
"eft tô earde,   nemne we æror mægen
"fâne gefyllan,   feorh ealgian
"Wedra þiódnes.   Ic wât geare,
"þät næron eald-gewyrht,   þät he âna scyle
"Geáta duguðe   gnorn þrowian,
"gesîgan ät säcce: sceal ûrum þät sweord and helm,
"byrne and byrdu-scrûd   bâm gemæne."
Wôd þâ þurh þone wäl-rêc,   wîg-heafolan bär
freán on fultum,   feá worda cwäð:
"Leófa Biówulf,   læst eall tela,
"swâ þu on geoguð-feore   geâra gecwæde,
"þät þu ne âlæte   be þe lifigendum
"dôm gedreósan: scealt nu dædum rôf,
"äðeling ân-hydig,   ealle mägene
"feorh ealgian;   ic þe fullæstu!"
Äfter þâm wordum   wyrm yrre cwom,
atol inwit-gäst   ôðre sîðe,
fýr-wylmum fâh   fiónda niósan,
lâðra manna;   lîg-ýðum forborn
bord wið ronde: byrne ne meahte
geongum gâr-wigan   geóce gefremman:
ac se maga geonga   under his mæges scyld
elne geeode,   þâ his âgen wäs
glêdum forgrunden.   Þâ gen gûð-cyning
mærða gemunde,   mägen-strengo,
slôh hilde-bille,   þät hyt on heafolan stôd
nîðe genýded: Nägling forbärst,
geswâc ät säcce   sweord Biówulfes
gomol and græg-mæl.   Him þät gifeðe ne wäs,
þät him îrenna   ecge mihton
helpan ät hilde;   wäs sió hond tô strong,
se þe mêca gehwane   mîne gefræge
swenge ofersôhte,   þonne he tô säcce bär
wæpen wundrum heard,   näs him wihte þê sêl.
Þâ wäs þeód-sceaða   þriddan sîðe,

frêcne fýr-draca   fæhða gemyndig,
ræsde on þone rôfan,   þâ him rûm âgeald,
hât and heaðo-grim,   heals ealne ymbefêng
biteran bânum;   he geblôdegod wearð
sâwul-driôre;   swât ýðum weóll.

XXXVII - BEÓWULF WOUNDED TO DEATH

Þâ ic ät þearfe gefrägn   þeód-cyninges
and-longne eorl   ellen cýðan,
cräft and cênðu,   swâ him gecynde wäs;
ne hêdde he þäs heafolan,   ac sió hand gebarn
môdiges mannes,   þær he his mæges healp,
þät he þone nîð-gäst   nioðor hwêne slôh,
secg on searwum,   þät þät sweord gedeáf
fâh and fäted,   þät þät fýr ongon
sweðrian syððan.   Þâ gen sylf cyning
geweóld his gewitte,   wäll-seaxe gebräd,
biter and beadu-scearp,   þät he on byrnan wäg:
forwrât Wedra helm   wyrm on middan.
Feónd gefyldan   (ferh ellen wräc),
and hi hyne þâ begen   âbroten häfdon,
sib-äðelingas: swylc sceolde secg wesan,
þegn ät þearfe.   Þät þam þeódne wäs
sîðast sîge-hwîle   sylfes dædum,
worlde geweorces.   Þâ sió wund ongon,
þe him se eorð-draca   ær geworhte,
swêlan and swellan.   He þät sôna onfand,
þät him on breóstum   bealo-nîð weóll,
âttor on innan.   Þâ se äðeling gióng,
þät he bî wealle,   wîs-hycgende,
gesät on sesse;   seah on enta geweorc,
hû þâ stân-bogan   stapulum fäste
êce eorð-reced   innan heóldon.
Hyne þâ mid handa   heoro-dreórigne
þeóden mærne   þegn ungemete till,
wine-dryhten his   wätere gelafede,
hilde-sädne   and his helm onspeón.
Biówulf maðelode,   he ofer benne spräc,
wunde wäl-bleáte   (wisse he gearwe,
þät he däg-hwîla   gedrogen häfde
eorðan wynne;   þâ wäs eall sceacen
dôgor-gerîmes,   deáð ungemete neáh):
"Nu ic suna mînum   syllan wolde
"gûð-gewædu,   þær me gifeðe swâ
"ænig yrfe-weard   äfter wurde,
"lîce gelenge.   Ic þâs leóde heóld
"fîftig wintra: näs se folc-cyning
"ymbe-sìttendra   ænig þâra,
"þe mec gûð-winum   grêtan dorste,

"egesan þeón.   Ic on earde bâd
"mæl-gesceafta,   heóld mîn tela,
"ne sôhte searo-nîðas,   ne me swôr fela
"âða on unriht.   Ic þäs ealles mäg,
"feorh-bennum seóc,   gefeán habban:
"forþam me wîtan ne þearf   waldend fira
"morðor-bealo mâga,   þonne mîn sceaceð
"lîf of lîce.   Nu þu lungre
"geong, hord sceáwian   under hârne stân,
"Wîglâf leófa,   nu se wyrm ligeð,
"swefeð sâre wund,   since bereáfod.
"Bió nu on ôfoste,   þät ic ær-welan,
"gold-æht ongite,   gearo sceáwige
"swegle searo-gimmas,   þät ic þý sêft mæge
"äfter mâððum-welan   mîn âlætan
"lîf and leód-scipe,   þone ic longe heóld."

XXXVIII - THE JEWEL-HOARD. THE PASSING OF BEOWULF

Þâ ic snûde gefrägn   sunu Wihstânes
äfter word-cwydum   wundum dryhtne
hýran heaðo-siócum,   hring-net beran,
brogdne beadu-sercean   under beorges hrôf.
Geseah þâ sige-hrêðig,   þâ he bî sesse geóng,
mago-þegn môdig   mâððum-sigla fela,
gold glitinian   grunde getenge,
wundur on wealle   and þäs wyrmes denn,
ealdes uht-flogan,   orcas stondan,
fyrn-manna fatu   feormend-leáse,
hyrstum behrorene: þær wäs helm monig,
eald and ômig,   earm-beága fela,
searwum gesæled.   Sinc eáðe mäg,
gold on grunde,   gumena cynnes
gehwone ofer-higian,   hýde se þe wylle!
Swylce he siomian geseah   segn eall-gylden
heáh ofer horde,   hond-wundra mæst,
gelocen leoðo-cräftum: of þam leóma stôd,
þät he þone grund-wong   ongitan meahte,
wräte giond-wlîtan.   Näs þäs wyrmes þær
onsýn ænig,   ac hyne ecg fornam.
Þâ ic on hlæwe   gefrägn hord reáfian,
eald enta geweorc   ânne mannan,
him on bearm hladan   bunan and discas
sylfes dôme,   segn eác genom,
beácna beorhtost;   bill ær-gescôd
(ecg wäs îren)   eald-hlâfordes
þam þâra mâðma   mund-bora wäs
longe hwîle,   lîg-egesan wäg

hâtne for horde,   hioro-weallende,
middel-nihtum,   ôð þät he morðre swealt.
Âr wäs on ôfoste   eft-sîðes georn,
frätwum gefyrðred: hyne fyrwet bräc,
hwäðer collen-ferð   cwicne gemêtte
in þam wong-stede   Wedra þeóden,
ellen-siócne,   þær he hine ær forlêt.
He þâ mid þâm mâðmum   mærne þióden,
dryhten sînne   dríorigne fand
ealdres ät ende: he hine eft ongon
wäteres weorpan,   ôð þät wordes ord
breóst-hord þurhbräc.   Beówulf maðelode,
gomel on giohðe   (gold sceáwode):
"Ic þâra frätwa   freán ealles þanc
"wuldur-cyninge   wordum secge,
"êcum dryhtne,   þe ic her on starie,
"þäs þe ic môste   mînum leódum
"ær swylt-däge   swylc gestrýnan.
"Nu ic on mâðma hord   mîne bebohte
"frôde feorh-lege,   fremmað ge nu
"leóda þearfe;   ne mäg ic her leng wesan.
"Hâtað heaðo-mære   hlæw gewyrcean,
"beorhtne äfter bæle   ät brimes nosan;
"se scel tô gemyndum   mînum leódum
"heáh hlifian   on Hrones nässe,
"þät hit sæ-lîðend   syððan hâtan
"Biówulfes biorh,   þâ þe brentingas
"ofer flôda genipu   feorran drîfað."
Dyde him of healse   hring gyldenne
þióden þrîst-hydig,   þegne gesealde,
geongum gâr-wigan,   gold-fâhne helm,
beáh and byrnan,   hêt hyne brûcan well:
"Þu eart ende-lâf   ûsses cynnes,
"Wægmundinga;   ealle Wyrd forsweóf,
"mîne mâgas   tô metod-sceafte,
"eorlas on elne: ic him äfter sceal."
Þät wäs þam gomelan   gingeste word
breóst-gehygdum,   ær he bæl cure,
hâte heaðo-wylmas: him of hreðre gewât
sâwol sêcean   sôð-fästra dôm.

XXXIX - THE COWARD-THANES

Þâ wäs gegongen   guman unfrôdum
earfoðlîce,   þät he on eorðan geseah
þone leófestan   lîfes ät ende
bleáte gebæran.   Bona swylce läg,
egeslîc eorð-draca,   ealdre bereáfod,
bealwe gebæded: beáh-hordum leng
wyrm woh-bogen   wealdan ne môste,

ac him îrenna   ecga fornâmon,
hearde heaðo-scearpe   homera lâfe,
þät se wîd-floga   wundum stille
hreás on hrusan   hord-ärne neáh,
nalles äfter lyfte   lâcende hwearf
middel-nihtum,   mâðm-æhta wlonc
ansýn ýwde: ac he eorðan gefeóll
for þäs hild-fruman   hond-geweorce.
Hûru þät on lande   lyt manna þâh
mägen-âgendra   mîne gefræge,
þeáh þe he dæda gehwäs   dyrstig wære,
þät he wið âttor-sceaðan   oreðe geræsde,
oððe hring-sele   hondum styrede,
gif he wäccende   weard onfunde
bûan on beorge.   Biówulfe wearð
dryht-mâðma dæl   deáðe forgolden;
häfde æghwäðer   ende gefêred
lænan lîfes.   Näs þâ lang tô þon,
þät þâ hild-latan   holt ofgêfan,
tydre treów-logan   tyne ätsomne,
þâ ne dorston ær   dareðum lâcan
on hyra man-dryhtnes   miclan þearfe;
ac hy scamiende   scyldas bæran,
gûð-gewædu,   þær se gomela läg:
wlitan on Wîglâf.   He gewêrgad sät,
fêðe-cempa   freán eaxlum neáh,
wehte hyne wätre;   him wiht ne speów;
ne meahte he on eorðan,   þeáh he ûðe wel,
on þam frum-gâre   feorh gehealdan,
ne þäs wealdendes willan   wiht oncirran;
wolde dôm godes   dædum rædan
gumena gehwylcum,   swâ he nu gen dêð.
Þâ wäs ät þam geongan   grim andswaru
êð-begête þâm þe ær   his elne forleás.
Wîglâf maðelode,   Weohstânes sunu,
secg sârig-ferð   seah on unleófe:
"Þät lâ mäg secgan,   se þe wyle sôð sprecan,
"þät se mon-dryhten,   se eów þâ mâðmas geaf,
"eóred-geatwe,   þe ge þær on standað,
"þonne he on ealu-bence   oft gesealde
"heal-sittendum   helm and byrnan,
"þeóden his þegnum,   swylce he þryðlîcost
"ôhwær feor oððe neáh   findan meahte,
"þät he genunga   gûð-gewædu
"wrâðe forwurpe.   Þâ hyne wîg beget,
"nealles folc-cyning   fyrd-gesteallum
"gylpan þorfte;   hwäðre him god ûðe,
"sigora waldend,   þät he hyne sylfne gewräc
"âna mid ecge,   þâ him wäs elnes þearf,

Beowulf: Scholar's Edition
"Ic him lîf-wraðe   lytle meahte
"ätgifan ät gûðe   and ongan swâ þeáh
"ofer mîn gemet   mæges helpan:
"symle wäs þý sæmra,   þonne ic sweorde drep
"ferhð-genîðlan,   fýr unswîðor
"weóll of gewitte.   Wergendra tô lyt
"þrong ymbe þeóden,   þâ hyne sió þrag becwom.
"Nu sceal sinc-þego   and swyrd-gifu
"eall êðel-wyn   eówrum cynne,
"lufen âlicgean: lond-rihtes môt
"þære mæg-burge   monna æghwylc
"îdel hweorfan,   syððan äðelingas
"feorran gefricgean   fleám eówerne,
"dôm-leásan dæd.   Deáð bið sêlla
"eorla gehwylcum   þonne edwît-lîf!"

XL - THE SOLDIER'S DIRGE AND PROPHECY

Hêht þâ þät heaðo-weorc   tô hagan biódan
up ofer êg-clif,   þær þät eorl-weorod
morgen-longne däg   môd-giômor sät,
bord-häbbende,   bega on wênum
ende-dôgores   and eft-cymes
leófes monnes.   Lyt swîgode
niwra spella,   se þe näs gerâd,
ac he sôðlîce   sägde ofer ealle;
"Nu is wil-geofa   Wedra leóda,
"dryhten Geáta   deáð-bedde fäst,
"wunað wäl-reste   wyrmes dædum;
"him on efn ligeð   ealdor-gewinna,
"siex-bennum seóc: sweorde ne meahte
"on þam aglæcean   ænige þinga
"wunde gewyrcean.   Wîglâf siteð
"ofer Biówulfe,   byre Wihstânes,
"eorl ofer ôðrum   unlifigendum,
"healdeð hige-mêðum   heáfod-wearde
"leófes and lâðes.   Nu ys leódum wên
"orleg-hwîle,   syððan underne
"Froncum and Frysum   fyll cyninges
"wîde weorðeð.   Wäs sió wrôht scepen
"heard wið Hûgas,   syððan Higelâc cwom
"faran flot-herge   on Fresna land,
"þær hyne Hetware   hilde gehnægdon,
"elne geeodon   mid ofer-mägene,
"þät se byrn-wîga   bûgan sceolde,
"feóll on fêðan: nalles frätwe geaf
"ealdor dugoðe;   ûs wäs â syððan
"Merewioinga   milts ungyfeðe.
"Ne ic tô Sweó-þeóde   sibbe oððe treówe
"wihte ne wêne;   ac wäs wîde cûð,

"þätte Ongenþió   ealdre besnyðede
"Hæðcyn Hrêðling   wið Hrefna-wudu,
"þâ for on-mêdlan   ærest gesôhton
"Geáta leóde   Gûð-scilfingas.
"Sôna him se frôda   fäder Ôhtheres,
"eald and eges-full   ond-slyht âgeaf,
"âbreót brim-wîsan,   brýd âheórde,
"gomela ió-meowlan   golde berofene,
"Onelan môdor   and Ôhtheres,
"and þâ folgode   feorh-genîðlan
"ôð þät hî ôðeodon   earfoðlîce
"in Hrefnes-holt   hlâford-leáse.
"Besät þâ sin-herge   sweorda lâfe
"wundum wêrge,   weán oft gehêt
"earmre teohhe   andlonge niht:
"cwäð he on mergenne   mêces ecgum
"getan wolde,   sume on galg-treówum
"fuglum tô gamene.   Frôfor eft gelamp
"sârig-môdum   somod ær-däge,
"syððan hie Hygelâces   horn and býman
"gealdor ongeâton.   Þâ se gôda com
"leóda dugoðe   on lâst faran.

XLI - HE TELLS OF THE SWEDES AND THE GEATAS

"Wäs sió swât-swaðu   Sweona and Geáta,
"wäl-ræs wera   wîde gesýne,
"hû þâ folc mid him   fæhðe tôwehton.
"Gewât him þâ se gôda   mid his gädelingum,
"frôd fela geômor   fästen sêcean,
"eorl Ongenþió   ufor oncirde;
"häfde Higelâces   hilde gefrunen,
"wlonces wîg-cräft,   wiðres ne trûwode,
"þät he sæ-mannum   onsacan mihte,
"heáðo-lîðendum   hord forstandan,
"bearn and brýde;   beáh eft þonan
"eald under eorð-weall.   Þâ wäs æht boden
"Sweona leódum,   segn Higelâce.
"Freoðo-wong þone   forð ofereodon,
"syððan Hrêðlingas   tô hagan þrungon.
"Þær wearð Ongenþió   ecgum sweorda,
"blonden-fexa   on bîd wrecen,
"þät se þeód-cyning   þafian sceolde
"Eofores ânne dôm: hyne yrringa
"Wulf Wonrêding   wæpne geræhte,
"þät him for swenge   swât ædrum sprong
"forð under fexe.   Näs he forht swâ þêh,
"gomela Scilfing,   ac forgeald hraðe
"wyrsan wrixle   wäl-hlem þone,
"syððan þeód-cyning   þyder oncirde:

"ne meahte se snella   sunu Wonrêdes
"ealdum ceorle   ond-slyht giofan,
"ac he him on heáfde   helm ær gescer,
"þät he blôde fâh   bûgan sceolde,
"feóll on foldan;   näs he fæge þâ git,
"ac he hyne gewyrpte,   þeáh þe him wund hrîne,
"Lêt se hearda   Higelâces þegn
"brâdne mêce,   þâ his brôðor läg,
"eald sweord eotonisc,   entiscne helm,
"brecan ofer bord-weal: þâ gebeáh cyning,
"folces hyrde,   wäs in feorh dropen.
"Þâ wæron monige,   þe his mæg wriðon,
"ricone ârærdon,   þâ him gerýmed wearð,
"þät hie wäl-stôwe   wealdan môston.
"Þenden reáfode   rinc ôðerne,
"nam on Ongenþió   îren-byrnan,
"heard swyrd hilted   and his helm somod;
"hâres hyrste   Higelâce bär.
"He þâm frätwum fêng   and him fägre gehêt
"leána fore leódum   and gelæste swâ:
"geald þone gûð-ræs   Geáta dryhten,
"Hrêðles eafora,   þâ he tô hâm becom,
"Jofore and Wulfe   mid ofer-mâðmum,
"sealde hiora gehwäðrum   hund þûsenda
"landes and locenra beága;   ne þorfte him þâ leán ôðwîtan
"mon on middan-gearde,   syððan hie þâ mærða geslôgon;
"and þâ Jofore forgeaf   ângan dôhtor,
"hâm-weorðunge,   hyldo tô wedde.
"Þät ys sió fæhðo   and se feónd-scipe,
"wäl-nîð wera,   þäs þe ic wên hafo,
"þe ûs sêceað tô   Sweona leóde,
"syððan hie gefricgeað   freán ûserne
"ealdor-leásne,   þone þe ær geheóld
"wið hettendum   hord and rîce,
"äfter häleða hryre   hwate Scylfingas,
"folc-ræd fremede   oððe furður gen
"eorl-scipe efnde.   Nu is ôfost betost,
"þät we þeód-cyning   þær sceáwian
"and þone gebringan,   þe ûs beágas geaf,
"on âd-färe.   Ne scel ânes hwät
"meltan mid þam môdigan,   ac þær is mâðma hord.
"gold unrîme   grimme geceápod
"and nu ät sîðestan   sylfes feore
"beágas gebohte;   þâ sceal brond fretan,
"äled þeccean,   nalles eorl wegan
"mâðdum tô gemyndum,   ne mägð scýne
"habban on healse   hring-weorðunge,
"ac sceall geômor-môd   golde bereáfod
"oft nalles æne   el-land tredan,
"nu se here-wîsa   hleahtor âlegde,

"gamen and gleó-dreám.   Forþon sceall gâr wesan
"monig morgen-ceald   mundum bewunden,
"häfen on handa,   nalles hearpan swêg
"wîgend weccean,   ac se wonna hrefn
"fûs ofer fægum,   fela reordian,
"earne secgan,   hû him ät æte speów,
"þenden he wið wulf   wäl reáfode."
Swâ se secg hwata   secgende wäs
lâðra spella;   he ne leág fela
wyrda ne worda.   Weorod eall árâs,
eodon unblîðe   under Earna näs
wollen-teáre   wundur sceáwian.
Fundon þâ on sande   sâwul-leásne
hlim-bed healdan,   þone þe him hringas geaf
ærran mælum: þâ wäs ende-däg
gôdum gegongen,   þät se gûð-cyning,
Wedra þeóden,   wundor-deáðe swealt.
Ær hî gesêgan   syllîcran wiht,
wyrm on wonge   wiðer-rähtes þær
lâðne licgean: wäs se lêg-draca,
grimlîc gryre-gäst,   glêdum beswæled,
se wäs fîftiges   fôt-gemearces.
lang on legere,   lyft-wynne heóld
nihtes hwîlum,   nyðer eft gewât
dennes niósian;   wäs þâ deáðe fäst,
häfde eorð-scrafa   ende genyttod.
Him big stôdan   bunan and orcas,
discas lâgon   and dýre swyrd,
ômige þurh-etone,   swâ hie wið eorðan fäðm
þûsend wintra   þær eardodon:
þonne wäs þät yrfe   eácen-cräftig,
iú-monna gold   galdre bewunden,
þät þam hring-sele   hrînan ne môste
gumena ænig,   nefne god sylfa,
sigora sôð-cyning,   sealde þam þe he wolde
(he is manna gehyld)   hord openian,
efne swâ hwylcum manna,   swâ him gemet þûhte.

XLII - WÎGLAF SPEAKS. THE BUILDING OF THE BALE-FIRE

Þâ wäs gesýne,   þät se sîð ne þâh
þam þe unrihte   inne gehýdde
wräte under wealle.   Weard ær ofslôh
feára sumne;   þâ sió fæhð gewearð
gewrecen wrâðlîce.   Wundur hwâr, þonne
eorl ellen-rôf   ende gefêre
lîf-gesceafta,   þonne leng ne mäg
mon mid his mâgum   medu-seld bûan.

Beowulf: Scholar's Edition

Swâ wäs Biówulfe,   þâ he biorges weard
sôhte, searo-nîðas: seolfa ne cûðe,
þurh hwät his worulde gedâl   weorðan sceolde;
swâ hit ôð dômes däg   diópe benemdon
þeódnas mære,   þâ þät þær dydon,
þät se secg wære   synnum scildig,
hergum geheaðerod,   hell-bendum fäst,
wommum gewitnad,   se þone wong strâde.
Näs he gold-hwät: gearwor häfde
âgendes êst   ær gesceáwod.
Wîglâf maðelode,   Wihstânes sunu:
"Oft sceall eorl monig   ânes willan
"wræc âdreógan,   swâ ûs geworden is.
"Ne meahton we gelæran   leófne þeóden,
"rîces hyrde   ræd ænigne,
"þät he ne grêtte   gold-weard þone,
"lête hyne licgean,   þær he longe wäs,
"wîcum wunian   ôð woruld-ende.
"Heóldon heáh gesceap: hord ys gesceáwod,
"grimme gegongen;   wäs þät gifeðe tô swîð,
"þe þone þeóden   þyder ontyhte.
"Ic wäs þær inne   and þät eall geond-seh,
"recedes geatwa,   þâ me gerýmed wäs,
"nealles swæslîce   sîð âlýfed
"inn under eorð-weall.   Ic on ôfoste gefêng
"micle mid mundum   mägen-byrðenne
"hord-gestreóna,   hider ût ätbär
"cyninge mînum: cwico wäs þâ gena,
"wîs and gewittig;   worn eall gespräc
"gomol on gehðo   and eówic grêtan hêt,
"bäd þät ge geworhton   äfter wines dædum
"in bæl-stede   beorh þone heán
"micelne and mærne,   swâ he manna wäs
"wîgend weorð-fullost   wîde geond eorðan,
"þenden he burh-welan   brûcan môste.
"Uton nu êfstan   ôðre sîðe
"seón and sêcean   searo-geþräc,
"wundur under wealle!   ic eów wîsige,
"þät ge genôge   neán sceáwiað
"beágas and brâd gold.   Sîe sió bær gearo
"ädre geäfned,   þonne we ût cymen,
"and þonne geferian   freán ûserne,
"leófne mannan,   þær he longe sceal
"on þäs waldendes   wære geþolian."
Hêt þâ gebeódan   byre Wihstânes,
häle hilde-diór,   häleða monegum
bold-âgendra,   þät hie bæl-wudu
feorran feredon,   folc-âgende
gôdum tôgênes: "Nu sceal glêd fretan
"(weaxan wonna lêg)   wîgena strengel,

"þone þe oft gebâd   îsern-scûre,
"þonne stræla storm,   strengum gebæded,
"scôc ofer scild-weall,   sceft nytte heóld,
"feðer-gearwum fûs   flâne full-eode."
Hûru se snotra   sunu Wihstânes
âcîgde of corðre   cyninges þegnas
syfone tôsomne   þâ sêlestan,
eode eahta sum   under inwit-hrôf;
hilde-rinc sum   on handa bär
äled-leóman,   se þe on orde geóng.
Näs þâ on hlytme,   hwâ þät hord strude,
syððan or-wearde   ænigne dæl
secgas gesêgon   on sele wunian,
læne licgan: lyt ænig mearn,
þät hi ôfostlice   ût geferedon
dýre mâðmas;   dracan êc scufun,
wyrm ofer weall-clif,   lêton wæg niman,
flôd fäðmian   frätwa hyrde.
Þær wäs wunden gold   on wæn hladen,
æghwäs unrîm,   äðeling boren,
hâr hilde-rinc   tô Hrones nässe.

XLIII - BEÓWULF'S FUNERAL PYRE

Him þâ gegiredan   Geáta leóde
âd on eorðan   un-wâclîcne,
helmum behongen,   hilde-bordum,
beorhtum byrnum,   swâ he bêna wäs;
âlegdon þâ tô-middes   mærne þeóden
häleð hiófende,   hlâford leófne.
Ongunnon þâ on beorge   bæl-fýra mæst
wîgend weccan: wudu-rêc âstâh
sweart ofer swioðole,   swôgende lêg,
wôpe bewunden   (wind-blond geläg)
ôð þät he þâ bân-hûs   gebrocen häfde,
hât on hreðre.   Higum unrôte
môd-ceare mændon   mon-dryhtnes cwealm;
swylce giômor-gyd   + lat . con meowle
. . . . .   wunden heorde . . .
serg (?) cearig sælde   geneahhe
þät hio hyre . . . . gas hearde
. . . . . ede   wälfylla wonn . .
hildes egesan   hyðo
haf mid   heofon rêce swealh (?)
Geworhton þâ   Wedra leóde
hlæw on hliðe,   se wäs heáh and brâd,
wæg-lîðendum   wîde gesýne,
and betimbredon   on tyn dagum
beadu-rôfes bêcn: bronda betost
wealle beworhton,   swâ hyt weorðlîcost

fore-snotre men   findan mihton.
Hî on beorg dydon   bêg and siglu,
eall swylce hyrsta,   swylce on horde ær
nîð-hydige men   genumen häfdon;
forlêton eorla gestreón   eorðan healdan,
gold on greóte,   þær hit nu gen lifað
eldum swâ unnyt,   swâ hit æror wäs.
Þâ ymbe hlæw riodan   hilde-deóre,
äðelinga bearn   ealra twelfa,
woldon ceare cwîðan,   kyning mænan,
word-gyd wrecan   and ymb wer sprecan,
eahtodan eorl-scipe   and his ellen-weorc
duguðum dêmdon,   swâ hit ge-dêfe bið,
þät mon his wine-dryhten   wordum hêrge,
ferhðum freóge,   þonne he forð scile
of lîc-haman   læne weorðan.
Swâ begnornodon   Geáta leóde
hlâfordes hryre,   heorð-geneátas,
cwædon þät he wære   woruld-cyning
mannum mildust   and mon-þwærust,
leódum lîðost   and lof-geornost.

APPENDIX

THE ATTACK IN FINNSBURG
[Footnote: See v. 1069 seqq.]
". . . . . näs byrnað næfre."
Hleoðrode þâ heaðo-geong cyning:
"Ne þis ne dagað eástan, ne her draca ne fleógeð,
"ne her þisse healle hornas ne byrnað,
"ac fêr forð berað fugelas singað,
"gylleð græg-hama, gûð-wudu hlynneð,
"scyld scefte oncwyð. Nu scýneð þes môna
"waðol under wolcnum; nu ârîsað weá-dæda,
"þe þisne folces nîð fremman willað.
"Ac onwacnigeað nu, wîgend mîne,
"hebbað eówre handa, hicgeað on ellen,
"winnað on orde, wesað on môde!"
Þâ ârâs monig gold-hladen þegn, gyrde hine his swurde;
þâ tô dura eodon drihtlîce cempan,
Sigeferð and Eaha, hyra sweord getugon,
and ät ôðrum durum Ordlâf and Gûðlâf,
and Hengest sylf; hwearf him on lâste.
Þâ git Gârulf Gûðere styrode,
þät hie swâ freólîc feorh forman sîðe
tô þære healle durum hyrsta ne bæran,
nu hyt nîða heard ânyman wolde:
ac he frägn ofer eal undearninga,
deór-môd häleð, hwâ þâ duru heólde.
"Sigeferð is mîn nama (cwäð he), ic eom Secgena leód,
"wrecca wîde cûð. Fela ic weána gebâd,
"heardra hilda; þe is gyt her witod,
"swäðer þu sylf tô me sêcean wylle."
Þâ wäs on wealle wäl-slihta gehlyn,
sceolde cêlod bord cênum on handa
bân-helm berstan. Buruh-þelu dynede,
ôð þät ät þære gûðe Gârulf gecrang,
ealra ærest eorð-bûendra,
Gûðlâfes sunu; ymbe hine gôdra fela.
Hwearf flacra hræw hräfn, wandrode
sweart and sealo-brûn; swurd-leóma stôd
swylce eal Finns-buruh fýrenu wære.
Ne gefrägn ic næfre wurðlîcor ät wera hilde
sixtig sige-beorna sêl gebæran,
ne næfre swânas swêtne medo sêl forgyldan,
þonne Hnäfe guldon his häg-stealdas.

Beowulf: Scholar's Edition
Hig fuhton fîf dagas,　　swâ hyra nân ne feól
driht-gesîða,　　ac hig þâ duru heóldon.
Þâ gewât him wund häleð　　on wäg gangan,
sæde þät his byrne　　âbrocen wære,
here-sceorpum hrôr,　　and eác wäs his helm þyrl.
Þâ hine sôna frägn　　folces hyrde,
hû þâ wîgend　　hyra wunda genæson
oððe hwäðer þæra hyssa . . . .

LIST OF NAMES; NOTES; AND GLOSSARY

ABBREVIATIONS
m.: masculine.
f.: feminine.
n.: neuter.
nom., gen.: nominative, genitive, etc.
w.: weak.
w. v.: weak verb.
st.: strong.
st. v.: strong verb.
I., II., III.: first, second, third person.
comp.: compound.
imper.: imperative.
w.: with.
instr.: instrumental.
G. and Goth.: Gothic.
O.N.: Old Norse.
O.S.: Old Saxon.
O.H.G.: Old High German.
M.H.G.: Middle High German.

The vowel ä = a in glad}
The diphthong æ = a in hair} approximately.
The names Leo, Bugge, Rieger, etc., refer to authors of emendations.
Words beginning with ge- will be found under their root-word.
Obvious abbreviations, like subj., etc., are not included in this list.

LIST OF NAMES

Abel, Cain's brother.
Älf-here (gen. Älf-heres), a kinsman of Wîglâf's.
Äsc-here, confidential adviser of King Hrôðgâr, older brother of Yrmenlâf, killed by Grendel's mother.
Bân-stân, father of Breca.
Beó-wulf, son of Scyld, king of the Danes. After the death of his father, he succeeds to the throne of the Scyldings. His son is Healfdene.
Beó-wulf (Biówulf; gen. Beówulfes, etc., Biówulfes; dat. Beówulfe, Biówulfe), of the race of the Geátas. His father is the Wægmunding Ecgþeów; his mother a daughter of Hrêðel, king of the Geátas, at whose court he is brought up after his seventh year with Hrêðel's sons, Herebeald, Hæðcyn, and Hygelâc. In his youth lazy and unapt; as man he attains in the gripe of his hand the strength of thirty men. Hence his victories in his combats with bare hands, while fate denies him the victory in the battle with swords. His swimming-match with Breca in his youth, goes with fourteen Geátas to the assistance of the Danish king, Hrôðgâr, against

Grendel, his combat with Grendel, and his victory. He is, in consequence, presented with rich gifts by Hrôðgâr. His combat with Grendel's mother having again received gifts, he leaves Hrôðgâr, and returns to Hygelâc.--After Hygelâc's last battle and death, he flees alone across the sea. In this battle he crushes Däghrefn, one of the Hûgas, to death. He rejects at the same time Hygelâc's kingdom and the hand of his widow, but carries on the government as guardian of the young Heardrêd, son of Hygelâc. After Heardrêd's death, the kingdom falls to Beówulf.-- Afterwards, on an expedition to avenge the murdered Heardrêd, he kills the Scylfing, Eádgils, and probably conquers his country.

Breca (acc. Brecan), son of Beánstân. Chief of the Brondings. His swimming-match with Beówulf.

Brondingas (gen. Brondinga), Breca, their chief.

Brosinga mene, corrupted from, or according to Müllenhoff, written by mistake for, Breosinga mene (O.N., Brisinga men, cf. Haupts Zeitschr. XII.), collar, which the Brisingas once possessed.

Cain (gen. Caines): descended from him are Grendel and his kin.

Däg-hrefn (dat. Däghrefne), a warrior of the Hûgas, who seems to have been the slayer of King Hygelâc, in his battle against the allied Franks, Frisians, and Hûgas. Is crushed to death by Beówulf in a hand-to-hand combat.

Dene (gen. Dena, Denia, Deniga, Denum), as subjects of Scyld and his descendants, they are also called Scyldings; and after the first king of the East Danes, Ing (Runenlied), Ing-wine. They are also once called Hrêðmen. On account of their renowned warlike character, they bore the names Gâr-Dene, Hring-Dene (Armor-Danes), Beorht-Dene. The great extent of this people is indicated by their names from the four quarters of the heavens: Eást-Dene, West-Dene, Sûð-Dene, Norð-Dene.--Their dwelling-place "in Scedelandum," "on Scedenigge," "be sæm tweónum."

Ecg-lâf (gen. Ecglâfes), Hûnferð's father.

Ecg-þeów (nom. Ecgþeów, Ecgþeó; gen. Ecgþeówes, Ecgþiówes), a far-famed hero of the Geátas, of the house of the Wægmundings. Beówulf is the son of Ecgþeów, by the only daughter of Hrêðel, king of the Geátas. Among the Wylfings, he has slain Heaðolâf, and in consequence he goes over the sea to the Danes, whose king, Hrôðgâr, by means of gold, finishes the strife for him.

Ecg-wela (gen. Ecg-welan). The Scyldings are called his descendants. Grein considers him the founder of the older dynasty of Danish kings, which closes with Heremôd. See Heremôd.

Elan, daughter of Healfdene, king of the Danes. According to the restored text, she is the wife of Ongenþeów, the Scylfing.

Earna-näs, the Eagle Cape in the land of the Geátas, where occurred Beówulf's fight with the drake.

Eádgils (dat. Eádgilse), son of Ôhthere, and grandson of Ongenþeów, the Scylfing. His older brother is

Eánmund (gen. Eánmundes). What is said about both in our poem is obscure, but the following may be conjectured:--

The sons of Ôhthere, Eánmund and Eádgils, have rebelled against their father, and must, in consequence, depart with their followers from Swiórîce. They come into the country of the Geátas to Heardrêd, but whether with friendly or hostile intent is not stated; but, we are to presume that they came against Heardrêd with designs of conquest. At a banquet (on feorme; or feorme, MS.) Heardrêd falls, probably through treachery, by the hand of one of the brothers. The murderer must have been Eánmund, to whom, "in battle the revenge of Weohstân brings death." Weohstân takes revenge for his murdered king, and exercises upon Eánmund's body the booty-right, and robs it of helm, breastplate, and sword, which the slain man had received as gifts from his uncle, Onela. But Weohstân does not speak willingly of this fight, although he has slain Onela's brother's son.--After Heardrêd's and Eánmund's death, the descendant of Ongenþeów, Eádgils, returns to his home. He must give way before Beówulf, who has, since Heardrêd's death, ascended the throne of the Geátas. But Beówulf remembers it against him in after days, and the old feud breaks out anew. Eádgils makes an invasion into the land of the Geátas, during which he falls at the hands of Beówulf. The latter must have then obtained the sovereignty over the Sweonas.

Eofor (gen. Eofores; dat. Jofore), one of the Geátas, son of Wonrêd and brother of Wulf, kills the Swedish king, Ongenþeów, for which he receives from King Hygelâc, along with other gifts, his only daughter in marriage.

Eormen-rîc (gen. Eormenrîces), king of the Goths (cf. about him, W. Grimm, Deutsche Heldensage. Hâma has wrested the Brosinga mene from him.

Eomær, son of Offa and Þryðo (cf. Þryðo).

Finn (gen. Finnes; dat. Finne), son of Folcwalda, king of the North Frisians, i.e. of the Eotenas, husband of Hildeburg, a daughter of Hôc. He is the hero of the inserted poem on the Attack in Finnsburg, the obscure incidents of which are, perhaps, as follows: In Finn's castle, Finnsburg, situated in Jutland, the Hôcing, Hnäf, a relative--perhaps a brother--of Hildeburg is spending some time as guest. Hnäf, who is a liegeman of the Danish king, Healfdene, has sixty men with him. These are treacherously attacked one night by Finn's men. For five days they hold the doors of their lodging-place without losing one of their number. Then, however, Hnäf is slain, and the Dane, Hengest, who was among Hnäf's followers, assumes the command of the beleaguered band. But on the attacking side the fight has brought terrible losses to Finn's men. Their numbers are diminished, and Hildeburg bemoans a son and a brother among the fallen. Therefore the Frisians offer the Danes peace under the conditions mentioned, and it is confirmed with oaths, and money is given by Finn in propitiation. Now all who have survived the battle go together to Friesland, the homo proper of Finn, and here Hengest remains during the winter, prevented by ice and storms from returning home (Grein). But in spring the feud breaks out anew. Gûðlâf and Oslâf avenge Hnäf's fall, probably after they have brought help from home. In the battle, the hall is filled with the corpses of the enemy. Finn himself is killed, and the queen is captured and carried away, along with the booty, to the land of the Danes.

Finna land. Beówulf reaches it in his swimming-race with Breca.

Fitela, the son and nephew of the Wälsing, Sigemund, and his companion in arms. (Sigemund had begotten Fitela by his sister, Signý. Cf. more at length Leo on Beówulf, where an extract from the legend of the Walsungs is given.)

Folc-walda (gen. Folc-waldan), Finn's father.

Francan (gen. Francna; dat. Froncum). King Hygelâc fell on an expedition against the allied Franks, Frisians, and Hûgas.

Fresan, Frisan, Frysan (gen. Fresena, Frysna, Fresna: dat. Frysum). To be distinguished, are: 1) North Frisians, whose king is Finn; 2) West Frisians, in alliance with the Franks and Hûgas, in the war against whom Hygelâc falls. The country of the former is called Frysland; that of the latter, Fresna land.

Fr..es wäl (in Fr..es wäle), mutilated proper name.

Freáwaru, daughter of the Danish king, Hrôðgâr; given in marriage to Ingeld, the son of the Heaðobeard king, Frôda, in order to end a war between the Danes and the Heaðobeardnas.

Frôda (gen. Frôdan), father of Ingeld, the husband of Freáware.

Gârmund (gen. Gârmundes) father of Offa. His grandson is Eómær.

Geátas (gen. Geáta; dat. Geátum), a tribe in Southern Scandinavia, to which the hero of this poem belongs; also called Wedergeátas; or, Wederas, etc.; Gûðgeátas; Sægeátas. Their kings named in this poem are: Hrêðel; Hæðcyn, second son of Hrêðel; Hygelâc, the brother of Hæðcyn; Heardrêd, son of Hygelâc; then Beówulf.

Gifðas (dat. Gifðum), Gepidæ, mentioned in connection with Danes and Swedes.

Grendel, a fen-spirit of Cain's race. He breaks every night into Hrôðgâr's hall and carries off thirty warriors. He continues this for twelve years, till Beówulf fights with him, and gives him a mortal wound, in that he tears out one of his arms, which is hung up as a trophy in the roof of Heorot. Grendel's mother wishes to avenge her son, and the following night breaks into the hall and carries off Äschere. Beówulf seeks for and finds her home in the fen-lake, fights with her, and kills her; and cuts off the head of Grendel, who lay there dead, and brings it to Hrôðgâr.

Gûð-lâf and Oslâf, Danish warriors under Hnäf, whose death they avenge on Finn.

Hâlga, with the surname, til, the younger brother of the Danish king, Hrôðgâr. His son is Hrôðulf.

Hâma wrests the Brosinga mene from Eormenrîc.

Häreð (gen. Häreðes), father of Hygd, the wife of Hygelâc.

Hæðcyn (dat. Hæðcynne), second son of Hrêðel, king of the Geátas. Kills his oldest brother, Herebeald, accidentally, with an arrow. After Hrêðel's death, he obtains the kingdom. He falls at Ravenswood, in the battle against the Swedish king, Ongenþeów. His successor is his younger brother, Hygelâc.

Helmingas (gen. Helminga). From them comes Wealhþeów, Hrôðgâr's wife.

Heming (gen. Heminges). Offa is called Heminges mæg; Eómær. According to Bachlechner (Pfeiffer's Germania, I), Heming is the son of the sister of Gârmund, Offa's father.

Hengest (gen. Hengestes; dat. Hengeste): about him and his relations to Hnäf and Finn, see Finn.

Here-beald (dat. Herebealde), the oldest son of Hrêðel, king of the Geátas, accidentally killed with an arrow by his younger brother, Hæðcyn.

Here-môd (gen. Heremôdes), king of the Danes, not belonging to the Scylding dynasty, but, according to Grein, immediately preceding it; is, on account of his unprecedented cruelty, driven out.

Here-rîc (gen. Hererîces) Heardrêd is called Hererîces nefa. Nothing further is known of him.

Het-ware or Franks, in alliance with the Frisians and the Hûgas, conquer Hygelâc, king of the Geátas.

Healf-dene (gen. Healfdenes), son of Beówulf, the Scylding; rules the Danes long and gloriously; has three sons, Heorogâr, Hrôðgâr, and Hâlga (61), and a daughter, Elan, who, according to the renewed text of the passage, wäs married to the Scylfing, Ongenþeów.

Heard-rêd (dat. Heardrêde), son of Hygelâc, king of the Geátas, and Hygd. After his father's death, while still under age, he obtains the throne; wherefore

Beówulf, as nephew of Heardrêd's father, acts as guardian to the youth till he becomes older. He is slain by Ôhthere's sons. This murder Beówulf avenges on Eádgils.

Heaðo-beardnas (gen. -beardna), the tribe of the Lombards. Their king, Frôda, has fallen in a war with the Danes. In order to end the feud, King Hrôðgâr has given his daughter, Freáwaru, as wife to the young Ingeld, the son of Frôda, a marriage that does not result happily; for Ingeld, though he long defers it on account of his love for his wife, nevertheless takes revenge for his father (Wîdsîð).

Heaðo-lâf (dat. Heaðo-lâfe), a Wylfingish warrior. Ecgþeów, Beówulf's father, kills him.

Heaðo-ræmas reached by B. in the swimming-race with Beówulf.

Heoro-gâr (nom; Heregâr; Hiorogâr), son of Healfdene, and older brother of Hrôðgâr. His death is mentioned. He has a son, Heoroweard. His coat of mail Beówulf has received from Hrôðgâr, and presents it to Hygelâc.

Heoro-weard (dat. Heorowearde), Heorogâr's son.

Heort. Heorot (gen. Heorotes; dat. Heorote, Heorute, Hiorte). Hrôðgâr's throne-room and banqueting hall and assembly-room for his liegemen, built by him with unusual splendor. In it occurs Beówulf's fight with Grendel. The hall receives its name from the stag's antlers, of which the one-half crowns the eastern gable, the other half the western.

Hildeburh, daughter of Hôc, relative of the Danish leader, Hnäf, consort of the Frisian king, Finn. After the fall of the latter, she becomes a captive of the Danes. See also under Finn.

Hnäf (gen. Hnäfes), a Hôcing (Wîdsîð), the Danish King Healfdene's general. For his fight with Finn, his death and burial, see under Finn.

Hond-scio, warrior of the Geátas: dat.

Hôc (gen. Hôces), father of Hildeburh; probably also of Hnäf (Wîdsîð).

Hrêðel (gen. Hrêðles), son of Swerting. King of the Geátas. He has, besides, a daughter, who is married to Ecgþeów, and has borne him Beówulf, three sons, Herebeald, Hæðcyn, and Hygelâc. The eldest of these is accidentally killed by the second. On account of this inexpiable deed, Hrêðel becomes melancholy and dies.

Hrêðla (gen. Hrêðlan, MS. Hrædlan), the same as Hrêðel (cf. Müllenhoff in Haupts Zeitschrift), the former owner of Beówulf's coat of mail.

Hrêð-men (gen. Hrêð-manna), the Danes are so called.

Hrêð-rîc, son of Hrôðgâr.

Hrefna-wudu, or Hrefnes-holt, the thicket near which the Swedish king, Ongenþeów, slew Hæðcyn, king of the Geátas, in battle.

Hreosna-beorh, promontory in the land of the Geátas, near which Ongenþeów's sons, Ôhthere and Onela, had made repeated robbing incursions into the country after Hrêðel's death. These were the immediate cause of the war in which Hrêðel's son, King Hæðcyn, fell.

Hrôð-gâr (gen. Hrôðgâres; dat. Hrôðgâre), of the dynasty of the Scyldings; the second of the three sons of King Healfdene. After the death of his elder brother, Heorogâr, he assumes the government of the Danes (yet it is not certain whether Heorogâr was king of the Danes before Hrôðgâr, or whether his death occurred while his father, Healfdene, was still alive). His consort is Wealhþeów, of the stock of the Helmings, who has borne him two sons, Hrêðrîc and Hrôðmund, and a daughter, Freáware, who has been given in marriage to the king of the Heaðobeardnas, Ingeld. His throne-room, which has been built at great cost, is visited every night by Grendel, who, along with his mother, is slain by Beówulf. Hrôðgâr's rich gifts to Beówulf, in consequence; he is praised as being generous; as being brave; and wise.--Other information about Hrôðgâr's reign for the most part only suggested: his expiation of the murder which Ecgþeów, Beówulf's father, committed upon Heaðolâf; his war with the Heaðobeardnas; his adjustment of it by giving his daughter, Freáware, in marriage to their king, Ingeld; evil results of this marriage.--Treachery of his brother's son, Hrôðulf, intimated.

Hrôð-mund, Hrôðgâr's son.

Hrôð-ulf, probably a son of Hâlga, the younger brother of King Hrôðgâr. Wealhþeów expresses the hope that, in case of the early death of Hrôðgâr, Hrôð-ulf would prove a good guardian to Hrôðgâr's young son, who would succeed to the government; a hope which seems not to have been accomplished, since it appears from that Hrôð-ulf has abused his trust towards Hrôðgâr.

Hrones-näs (dat. -nässe), a promontory on the coast of the country of the Geátas, visible from afar. Here is Beówulf's grave-mound.

Hrunting (dat. Hruntinge), Hûnferð's sword, is so called.

Hûgas (gen. Hûga), Hygelâc wars against them allied with the Franks and Frisians, and falls. One of their heroes is called Däghrefn, whom Beówulf slays.

[H]ûn-ferð, the son of Ecglâf, þyle of King Hrôðgâr. As such, he has his place near the throne of the king. He lends his sword, Hrunting, to Beówulf for his battle with Grendel's mother. According to, he slew his brothers. Since his name is always alliterated with vowels, it is probable that the original form was, as Rieger (Zachers Ztschr) conjectures, Unferð.

Hûn-lâfing, name of a costly sword, which Finn presents to Hengest See Note.

Hygd (dat. Hygde), daughter of Häreð; consort of Hygelâc, king of the Geátas; her son, Heardrêd.--Her noble, womanly character is emphasized.

Hyge-lâc (gen. Hige-lâces, Hygelâces; dat. Higelâce, Hygelâce), king of the Geátas. His grandfather is Swerting; his father, Hrêðel; his older brothers, Herebeald and Hæðcyn; his sister's son, Beówulf. After his brother, Hæðcyn, is killed by Ongenþeów, he undertakes the government. To Eofor he gives, as reward for slaying Ongenþeów, his only daughter in marriage. But much later, at the time of the return of Beówulf from his expedition to Hrôðgâr, we see him married to the very young Hygd, the daughter of Häreð. The latter seems, then, to have been his second wife. Their son is Heardrêd.--Hygelâc falls during an expedition against the Franks, Frisians, and Hûgas.

Ingeld (dat. Ingelde), son of Frôda, the Heaðobeard chief, who fell in a battle with the Danes, in order to end the war, Ingeld is married to Freáwaru, daughter of the Danish king, Hrôðgâr. Yet his love for his young wife can make him forget only for a short while his desire to avenge his father. He finally carries it out, excited thereto by the repeated admonitions of an old warrior (Wîdsîð).

Ing-wine (gen. Ingwina), friends of Ing, the first king of the East Danes. The Danes are so called.

Mere-wioingas (gen. Mere-wioinga), as name of the Franks.

Nägling, the name of Beówulf's sword.

Offa (gen. Offan), king of the Angles (Wîdsîð), the son of Gârmund; married to Þryðo, a beautiful but cruel woman, of unfeminine spirit, by whom he has a son, Eómær.

Ôht-here (gen. Ôhtheres; Ôhteres), son of Ongenþeów, king of the Swedes. His sons are Eánmund and Eádgils.

Onela (gen. Onelan), Ôhthere's brother.

Ongen-þeów (nom. -þeów, -þió; gen. -þeówes, -þiówes; dat. -þió), of the dynasty of the Scylfings; king of the Swedes. His wife is, perhaps, Elan, daughter of the Danish king, Healfdene, and mother of two sons, Onela and Ôhthere. She is taken prisoner by Hæðcyn, king of the Geátas, on an expedition into Sweden, which he undertakes on account of her sons' plundering raids into his country. She is set free by Ongenþeów, who kills Hæðcyn, and encloses the Geátas, now deprived of their leader, in the Ravenswood, till they are freed by Hygelâc. A battle then follows, which is unfavorable to Ongenþeów's army. Ongenþeów himself, attacked by the brothers, Wulf and Eofor, is slain by the latter.

Ôs-lâf, a warrior of Hnäf's, who avenges on Finn his leader's death.

Scede-land. Sceden-îg (dat. Sceden-îgge), O.N., Scân-ey, the most southern portion of the Scandinavian peninsula, belonging to the Danish kingdom, and, in the above-mentioned passages of our poem, a designation of the whole Danish kingdom.

Scêf or Sceáf. See Note.

Scyld (gen. Scyldes), a Scêfing. His son is Beówulf: his grandson, Healfdene; his great-grandson, Hrôðgâr, who had two brothers and a sister.--Scyld dies, 26; his body, upon a decorated ship, is given over to the sea, just as he, when a child, drifted alone, upon a ship, to the land of the Danes. After him his descendants bear his name.

Scyldingas (Scyldungas; gen. Scyldinga, Scyldunga; dat. Scyldingum), a name which is extended also to the Danes, who are ruled by the Scyldings. They are also called Âr-Scyldingas; Sige-Scyldingas,; Þeód-Scyldingas; Here-Scyldingas.

Scylfingas, a Swedish royal family, whose relationship seems to extend to the Geátas, since Wîglâf, the son of Wihstân, who in another place, as a kinsman of Beówulf, is called a Wægmunding, is also called leód Scylfinga. The Scylfings are also called Heaðo-Scilfingas, Gûð-Scylfingas.

Sige-mund (dat. -munde), the son of Wäls. His (son and) nephew is Fitela. His fight with the drake.

Swerting (gen. Swertinges), Hygelâc's grandfather, and Hreðel's father.

Sweon (gen. Sweona), also Sweó-þeód. The dynasty of the Scylfings rules over them. Their realm is called Swiórice.

Þryðo, consort of the Angle king, Offa. Mother of Eómær, notorious on account of her cruel, unfeminine character. She is mentioned as the opposite to the mild, dignified Hygd, the queen of the Geátas.

Wäls (gen. Wälses), father of Sigemund.

Wæg-mundingas (gen. Wægmundinga). The Wægmundings are on one side, Wihstân and his son Wîglâf; on the other side, Ecgþeów and his son Beówulf. See under Scylfingas.

Wederas (gen. Wedera), or Weder-geátas. See Geátas.

Wêland (gen. Wêlandes), the maker of Beówulf's coat of mail.

Wendlas (gen. Wendla): their chief is Wulfgâr. See Wulfgâr. The Wendlas are, according to Grundtvig and Bugge, the inhabitants of Vendill, the most northern part of Jutland, between Limfjord and the sea.

Wealh-þeów (Wealh-þeó), the consort of King Hrôðgâr, of the stock of the Helmings. Her sons are Hreðrîc and Hrôðmund; her daughter, Freáwaru.

Weoh-stân (gen. Weox-stânes, Weoh-stânes, Wih-stânes), a Wægmunding, father of Wîglâf. In what relationship to him Älfhere, mentioned, stands, is not clear.--Weohstân is the slayer of Eánmund, in that, as it seems, he takes revenge for his murdered king, Heardrêd. See Eánmund.

Wîg-lâf, Weohstân's son, a Wægmunding, and so also a Scylfing; a kinsman of Älfhere. For his relationship to Beówulf, see the genealogical table under Scylfingas.--He supports Beówulf in his fight with the drake. The hero gives him, before his death, his ring, his helm, and his coat of mail.

Won-rêd (gen. Wonrêdes), father of Wulf and Eofor.

Wulf (dat. Wulfe), one of the Geátas, Wonrêd's son. He fights in the battle between the armies of Hygelâc and Ongenþeów with Ongenþeów himself, and gives him a wound, whereupon Ongenþeów, by a stroke of his sword, disables him. Eofor avenges his brother's fall by dealing Ongenþeów a mortal blow.

Wulf-gâr, chief of the Wendlas, lives at Hrôðgâr's court, and is his "âr and ombiht."

Wylfingas (dat. Wylfingum). Ecgþeów has slain Heoðolâf, a warrior of this tribe.

Yrmen-lâf, younger brother of Äschere.

ADDITIONAL

Eotenas (gen. pl. Eotena; dat. Eotenum), the subjects of Finn, the North Frisians: distinguished from eoton, giant. Vid eoton.

Hrêðling, son of Hrêðel, Hygelâc: nom. sg; nom. pl., the subjects of Hygelâc, the Geats.

Scêfing, the son (?) of Scêf, or Sceáf, reputed father of Scyld. See Note.

ABBREVIATIONS

B.: Bugge.
Br.: S.A. Brooke, Hist. of Early Eng. Lit.
C.: Cosijn.
E.: Earle, Deeds of Beowulf in Prose.
G.: Garnett, Translation of Beowulf
Gr.: Grein.
H.: Heyne.
Ha.: Hall, Translation of Beowulf.
H.-So.: Heyne-Socin, 5th ed.
Ho.: Holder.
K.: Kemble.
Kl.: Kluge.
Müllenh.: Müllenhoff.
R.: Rieger.
S.: Sievers.
Sw.: Sweet, Anglo-Saxon Reader, 6th ed.
Ten Br.: Ten Brink.
Th.: Thorpe.
Z.: Zupitza.

PERIODICALS

Ang.: Anglia.
Beit.: Paul und Branne's Beiträge.
Eng. Stud.: Englische Studien.

Germ.: Germania.
Haupts Zeitschr.: Haupts Zeitschrift, etc.
Mod. Lang. Notes: Modern Language Notes.
Tidskr.: Tidskrift for Philologi.
Zachers Zeitschr.: Zachers Zeitschrift, etc.

Footnotes:

l. 1. hwät: for this interjectional formula opening a poem, cf. Andreas, Daniel, Juliana, Exodus, Fata Apost., Dream of the Rood, and the "Listenith lordinges!" of mediaeval lays.--E. Cf. Chaucer, Prologue, ed. Morris, l. 853:

"Sin I shal beginne the game,
What, welcome be the cut, a Goddes name!"

we ... gefrunon is a variant on the usual epic formulæ ic gefrägn (l. 74) and mîne gefræge (l. 777). Exodus, Daniel, Phoenix, etc., open with the same formula.

l. 1. "Gâr was the javelin, armed with two of which the warrior went into battle, and which he threw over the 'shield-wall.' It was barbed."--Br. 124. Cf. Maldon, l. 296; Judith, l. 224; Gnom. Verses, l. 22; etc.

l. 4. "Scild of the Sheaf, not 'Scyld the son of Scaf'; for it is too inconsistent, even in myth, to give a patronymic to a foundling. According to the original form of the story, Sceáf was the foundling; he had come ashore with a sheaf of corn, and from that was named. This form of the story is preserved in Ethelwerd and in William of Malmesbury. But here the foundling is Scyld, and we must suppose he was picked up with the sheaf, and hence his cognomen."--E., p. 105. Cf. the accounts of Romulus and Remus, of Moses, of Cyrus, etc.

l. 6. egsian is also used in an active sense (not in the Gloss.), = to terrify.

l. 15. S. suggests þâ (which) for þät. as object of dreógan; and for aldor-leáse, Gr. suggested aldor-ceare.--Beit. ix. 136.

S. translates: "For God had seen the dire need which the rulerless ones before endured."

l. 18. "Beowulf (that is, Beaw of the Anglo-Saxon genealogists, not our Beowulf, who was a Geat, not a Dane), 'the son of Scyld in Scedeland.' This is our ancestral myth,--the story of the first culture-hero of the North; 'the patriarch,' as Rydberg calls him, 'of the royal families of Sweden, Denmark, Angeln, Saxland, and England.'"--Br., p. 78. Cf. A.-S. Chron. an. 855.

H.-So. omits parenthetic marks, and reads (after S., Beit. ix. 135) eaferan; cf. Fata Apost.: lof wîde sprang þeódnes þegna.

"The name Beowulf means literally 'Beewolf,' wolf or ravager of the bees, = bear. Cf. beorn, 'hero,' originally 'bear,' and beohata, 'warrior,' in Cædmon, literally 'bee-hater' or 'persecutor,' and hence identical in meaning with beowulf."--Sw.

Cf. "Arcite and Palamon, That foughten breme, as it were bores two." --Chaucer, Knightes Tale, l. 841, ed. Morris.

Cf. M. Müller, Science of Lang., Sec. Series, pp. 217, 218; and Hunt's Daniel, 104.

l. 19. Cf. l. 1866, where Scedenig is used, = Scania, in Sweden(?).

l. 21. wine is pl.; cf. its apposition wilgesîðas below. H.-So. compares Héliand, 1017, for language almost identical with ll. 20, 21.

l. 22. on ylde: cf. "In elde is bothe wisdom and usage." --Chaucer, Knightes Tale, l. 1590, ed. Morris.

l. 26. Reflexive objects often pleonastically accompany verbs of motion; cf. ll. 234, 301, 1964, etc.

l. 28. faroð = shore, strand, edge. Add these to the meanings in the Gloss.

l. 31. The object of âhte is probably geweald, to be supplied from wordum weóld of l. 30.--H.-So.

R., Kl., and B. all hold conflicting views of this passage: Beit. xii. 80, ix. 188; Zachers Zeitschr. iii. 382, etc. Kl. suggests lændagas for lange.

l. 32. "hringed-stefna is sometimes translated 'with curved prow,' but it means, I think, that in the prow were fastened rings through which the cables were passed that tied it to the shore."--Br., p. 26. Cf. ll. 1132, 1898. Hring-horni was the mythic ship of the Edda. See Toller-Bosworth for three different views; and cf. wunden-stefna (l. 220), hring-naca (l. 1863).

ll. 34-52. Cf. the burial of Haki on a funeral-pyre ship, Inglinga Saga; the burial of Balder, Sinfiötli, Arthur, etc.

l. 35. "And this [their joy in the sea] is all the plainer from the number of names given to the ship-names which speak their pride and affection. It is the Ætheling's vessel, the Floater, the Wave-swimmer, the Ring-sterned, the Keel, the Well-bound wood, the Seawood, the Sea-ganger, the Sea-broad ship, the Wide-bosomed, the Prow-curved, the Wood of the curved neck, the Foam-throated floater that flew like a bird."--Br., p. 168.

l. 49. "We know from Scandinavian graves ... that the illustrious dead were buried ... in ships, with their bows to sea-ward; that they were however not sent to sea, but were either burnt in that position, or mounded over with earth."--E. See Du Chaillu, The Viking Age, xix.

l. 51. (1) sele-rædende (K., S., C.); (2) sêle-rædenne (H.); (3) sele-rædende (H.-So.). Cf. l. 1347; and see Ha.

l. 51. E. compares with this canto Tennyson's "Passing of Arthur" and the legendary burial-journey of St. James of Campostella, an. 800.

l. 53. The poem proper begins with this, "There was once upon a time," the first 52 lines being a prelude. Eleven of the "fitts," or cantos, begin with the monosyllable þâ, four with the verb gewîtan, nine with the formula Hrôðgâr (Beówulf, Unferð) maðelode, twenty-four with monosyllables in general (him, swâ, sê, hwät, þâ, hêht, wäs, mäg, cwôm, stræt).

l. 58. gamel. "The ... characteristics of the poetry are the use of archaic forms and words, such as mec for mé, the possessive sín, gamol, dógor, swat for eald, dæg, blód, etc., after they had become obsolete in the prose language, and the use of special compounds and phrases, such as hildenædre (war-adder) for 'arrow,' gold-gifa (gold-giver) for 'king,' ... goldwine gumena (goldfriend of men, distributor of gold to men) for 'king,'" etc.--Sw. Other poetic words are ides, ielde (men), etc.

l. 60. H.-So. reads ræswa (referring to Heorogâr alone), and places a point (with the Ms.) after Heorogâr instead of after ræswa. Cf. l. 469; see B., Zachers Zeitschr. iv. 193.

l. 62. Elan here (OHG. Elana, Ellena, Elena, Elina, Alyan) is thought by B. (Tidskr. viii. 43) to be a remnant of the masc. name Onela, and he reads: [On-]elan ewên, Heaðoscilfingas(=es) healsgebedda.

l. 68. For hê, omitted here, cf. l. 300. Pronouns are occasionally thus omitted insubord. clauses.--Sw.

l. 70. þone, here = þonne, than, and micel = mâre? The passage, by a slight change, might be made to read, medo-ärn micle mâ gewyrcean,--þone = by much larger than,--in which þone (þonne) would come in naturally.

l. 73. folc-scare. Add folk-share to the meanings in the Gloss.; and cf. gûð-scearu.

l. 74. ic wide gefrägn: an epic formula very frequent in poetry, = men said. Cf. Judith, ll. 7, 246; Phoenix, l. 1; and the parallel (noun) formula, mîne gefræge, ll. 777, 838, 1956, etc.

ll. 78-83. "The hall was a rectangular, high-roofed, wooden building, its long sides facing north and south. The two gables, at either end, had stag-horns on their points, curving forwards, and these, as well as the ridge of the roof, were probably covered with shining metal, and glittered bravely in the sun."--Br., p. 32.

Beowulf: Scholar's Edition

l. 84. Son-in-law and father-in-law; B., a so-called dvanda compound. Cf. l. 1164, where a similar compound means uncle and nephew; and Wîdsîð's suhtorfædran, used of the same persons.

l. 88. "The word dreám conveys the buzz and hum of social happiness, and more particularly the sound of music and singing."--E. Cf. l. 3021; and Judith, l. 350; Wanderer, l. 79, etc.

ll. 90-99. There is a suspicious similarity between this passage and the lines attributed by Bede to Cædmon:

Nû wê sculan herian heofonrices Weard, etc.   --Sw., p. 47.

ll. 90-98 are probably the interpolation of a Christian scribe.

ll. 92-97. "The first of these Christian elements [in Beówulf] is the sense of a fairer, softer world than that in which the Northern warriors lived.... Another Christian passage (ll. 107, 1262) derives all the demons, eotens, elves, and dreadful sea-beasts from the race of Cain. The folly of sacrificing to the heathen gods is spoken of (l. 175).... The other point is the belief in immortality (ll. 1202, 1761)."--Br. 71.

l. 100. Cf. l. 2211, where the third dragon of the poem is introduced in the same words. Beowulf is the forerunner of that other national dragon-slayer, St. George.

l. 100. onginnan in Beówulf is treated like verbs of motion and modal auxiliaries, and takes the object inf. without tô; cf. ll. 872, 1606, 1984, 244. Cf. gan (= did) in Mid. Eng.: gan espye (Chaucer, Knightes Tale, l. 254, ed. Morris).

l. 101. B. and H.-So. read, feónd on healle; cf. l. 142.--Beit. xii.

ll. 101-151. "Grimm connects [Grendel] with the Anglo-Saxon grindel (a bolt or bar).... It carries with it the notion of the bolts and bars of hell, and hence a fiend. ... Ettmüller was the first ... to connect the name with grindan, to grind, to crush to pieces, to utterly destroy. Grendel is then the tearer, the destroyer."--Br., p. 83.

l. 102. gäst = stranger (Ha.); cf. ll. 1139, 1442, 2313, etc.

l. 103. See Ha., p. 4.

l. 106. "The perfect and pluperfect are often expressed, as in Modern English, by hæfð and hæfde with the past participle."--Sw. Cf. ll. 433, 408, 940, 205 (p. p. inflected in the last two cases), etc.

l. 106. S. destroys period here, reads in Caines, etc., and puts þone ... drihten in parenthesis.

l. 108. þäs þe = because, especially after verbs of thanking (cf. ll. 228, 627, 1780, 2798); according to (l. 1351).

Beowulf: Scholar's Edition

l. 108. The def. article is omitted with Drihten (Lord) and Deofol (devil; cf. l. 2089), as it is, generally, sparingly employed in poetry; cf. tô sæ (l. 318), ofer sæ (l. 2381), on lande (l. 2311), tô räste (l. 1238), on wicge (l. 286), etc., etc.

l. 119. weras (S., H.-So.); wera (K., Th.).--Beit. ix. 137.

l. 120. unfælo = uncanny (R.).

l. 131. E. translates, majestic rage; adopting Gr.'s view that swyð is = Icel. sviði, a burn or burning. Cf. l. 737.

l. 142. B. supposes heal-þegnes to be corrupted from helþegnes; cf. l. 101.--Beit. xii. 80. See Gûðlâc, l. 1042.

l. 144. See Ha., p. 6, for S.'s rearrangement.

l. 146. S. destroys period after sêlest, puts wäs ... micel in parenthesis, and inserts a colon after tîd.

l. 149. B. reads sârcwidum for syððan.

l. 154. B. takes sibbe for accus. obj. of wolde, and places a comma after Deniga.--Beit. xii. 82.

l. 159. R. suggests ac se for atol.

l. 168. H.-So. plausibly conjectures this parenthesis to be a late insertion, as, at ll. 180-181, the Danes also are said to be heathen. Another commentator considers the throne under a "spell of enchantment," and therefore it could not be touched.

l. 169. ne ... wisse: nor had he desire to do so (W.). See Ha., p. 7, for other suggestions.

l. 169. myne wisse occurs in Wanderer, l. 27.

l. 174. The gerundial inf. with tô expresses purpose, defines a noun or adjective, or, with the verb be, expresses duty or necessity passively; cf. ll. 257, 473, 1004, 1420, 1806, etc. Cf. tô + inf. at ll. 316, 2557.

ll. 175-188. E. regards this passage as dating the time and place of the poem relatively to the times of heathenism. Cf. the opening lines, In days of yore, etc., as if the story, even then, were very old.

l. 177. gâst-bona is regarded by Ettmüller and G. Stephens (Thunor, p. 54) as an epithet of Thor (= giant-killer), a kenning for Thunor or Thor, meaning both man and monster.--E.

l. 189. Cf. l. 1993, where similar language is used. H.-So. takes both môd-ceare and mæl-ceare as accus., others as instr.

ll. 190, 1994. seáð: for this use of seóðan cf. Bede, Eccles. Hist., ed. Miller, p. 128, where p. p. soden is thus used.

l. 194. fram hâm = in his home (S., H.-So.); but fram hâm may be for fram him (from them, i.e. his people, or from Hrothgar's). Cf. Ha., p. 8.

l. 197. Cf. ll. 791, 807, for this fixed phrase.

l. 200. See Andreas, Elene, and Juliana for swan-râd (= sea). "The swan is said to breed wild now no further away than the North of Sweden." --E. Cf. ganotes bäð, l. 1862.

l. 203. Concessive clauses with þeáh, þeáh þe, þeáh ... eal, vary with subj. and ind., according as fact or contingency is dominant in the mind; cf. ll. 526, 1168, 2032, etc. (subj.), 1103, 1614 (ind.). Cf. gif, nefne.

l. 204. hæl, an OE. word found in Wülker's Glossaries in various forms, = augury, omen, divination, etc. Cf. hælsere, augur; hæl, omen; hælsung, augurium, hælsian, etc. Cf. Tac., Germania, 10.

l. 207. C. adds "= impetrare" to the other meanings of findan given in the Gloss.

l. 217. Cf. l. 1910; and Andreas, l. 993.--E. E. compares Byron's "And fast and falcon-like the vessel flew," --Corsair, i.17. and Scott's "Merrily, merrily bounds the bark." --Lord of the Isles, iv. 7.

l. 218. Cf. "The fomy stedes on the golden brydel Gnawinge." --Chaucer, Knightes Tale, l. 1648, ed. Morris.

l. 219. Does ân-tîd mean hour (Th.), or corresponding hour = ând-tîd (H.-So.), or in due time (E.), or after a time, when ôþres, etc., would be adv. gen.? See C., Beit. viii. 568.

l. 224. eoletes may = (1) voyage; (2) toil, labor; (3) hurried journey; but sea or fjord appears preferable.

ll. 229-257. "The scenery ... is laid on the coast of the North Sea and the Kattegat, the first act of the poem among the Danes in Seeland, the second among the Geats in South Sweden."--Br., p. 15.

l. 239. "A shoal of simple terms express in Beówulf the earliest sea-thoughts of the English.... The simplest term is Sæ.... To this they added Wæter, Flod, Stream, Lagu, Mere, Holm, Grund, Heathu, Sund, Brim, Garsecg, Eagor, Geofon, Fifel, Hron-rad, Swan-rad, Segl-rad, Ganotes-bæð."--Br., p. 163-166.

l. 239. "The infinitive is often used in poetry after a verb of motion where we should use the present participle."--Sw. Cf. ll. 711, 721, 1163 1803, 268, etc. Cf. German spazieren fahren reiten, etc., and similar constructions in French, etc.

l. 240, W. reads hringed-stefnan for helmas bæron. B. inserts (?) after holmas and begins a new line at the middle of the verse. S. omits B.'s "on the wall."

l. 245. Double and triple negatives strengthen each other and do not produce an affirmative in A.-S. or M. E. The neg. is often prefixed to several emphatic words in the sentence, and readily contracts with vowels, and h or w; cf. ll. 863, 182, 2125, 1509, 575, 583, 3016, etc.

l. 249. seld-guma = man-at-arms in another's house (Wood); = low-ranking fellow (Ha.); stubenhocker, stay-at-home (Gr.); Scott's "carpet knight," Marmion, i. 5.

l. 250. näfne (nefne, nemne) usually takes the subj., = unless; cf. ll. 1057, 3055, 1553. For ind., = except, see l. 1354. Cf. bûtan, gif, þeáh.

l. 250. For a remarkable account of armor and weapons in Beówulf, see S. A. Brooke, Hist. of Early Eng. Lit. For general "Old Teutonic Life in Beówulf," see J. A. Harrison, Overland Monthly.

l. 252. ær as a conj. generally has subj., as here; cf. ll. 264, 677, 2819, 732. For ind., cf. l. 2020.

l. 253. leás = loose, roving. Ettmüller corrected to leáse.

l. 256. This proverb (ôfest, etc.) occurs in Exod. (Hunt), l. 293.

l. 258. An "elder" may be a very young man; hence yldesta, = eminent, may be used of Beowulf. Cf. Laws of Ælfred, C. 17: Nâ þät ælc eald sý, ac þät he eald sý on wîsdôme.

l. 273. Verbs of hearing and seeing are often followed by acc. with inf.; cf. ll. 229, 1024, 729, 1517, etc. Cf. German construction with sehen, horen, etc., French construction with voir, entendre, etc., and the classical constructions.

l. 275. dæd-hata = instigator. Kl. reads dæd-hwata.

l. 280. ed-wendan, n. (B.; cf. 1775), = edwenden, limited by bisigu. So ten Br. = Tidskr. viii. 291.

l. 287. "Each is denoted ... also by the strengthened forms 'æghwæðer ('ægðer), éghwæðer, etc. This prefixed 'æ, óe corresponds to the Goth, aiw, OHG. eo, io, and is umlauted from á, ó by the i of the gi which originally followed."--Cook's Sievers' Gram., p. 190.

l. 292. "All through the middle ages suits of armour are called 'weeds.'"--E.

l. 303. "An English warrior went into battle with a boar-crested helmet, and a round linden shield, with a byrnie of ringmail ... with two javelins or a single ashen spear some eight or ten feet long, with a long two-edged sword naked or held in an ornamental scabbard.... In his belt was a short, heavy, one-edged sword, or rather a long knife, called the seax ... used for close quarters."--Br., p. 121.

l. 303. For other references to the boar-crest, cf. ll. 1112, 1287, 1454; Grimm, Myth. 195; Tacitus, Germania, 45. "It was the symbol of their [the Baltic Æstii's] goddess, and they had great faith in it as a preservative from hard knocks."--E. See the print in the illus. ed. of Green's Short History, Harper & Bros.

l. 303. "See Kemble, Saxons in England, chapter on heathendom, and Grimm's Teutonic Mythology, chapter on Freyr, for the connection these and other writers establish between the Boar-sign and the golden boar which Freyr rode, and his worship."--Br., p. 128. Cf. Elene, l. 50.

l. 304. Gering proposes hleór-bergan = cheek-protectors; cf. Beit. xii. 26. "A bronze disk found at Öland in Sweden represents two warriors in helmets with boars as their crests, and cheek-guards under; these are the hleór-bergan."--E. Cf. hauberk, with its diminutive habergeon, < A.-S. heals, neck + beorgan, to cover or protect; and harbor, < A.-S. here, army + beorgan, id.--Zachers Zeitschr. xii. 123. Cf. cinberge, Hunt's Exod. l. 175.

l. 305. For ferh wearde and gûðmôde grummon, B. and ten Br. read ferh-wearde (l. 305) and gûðmôdgum men (l. 306), = the boar-images ...guarded the lives of the warlike men.

l. 311. leóma: cf. Chaucer, Nonne Preestes Tale, l. 110, ed. Morris:

"To dremen in here dremes
Of armes, and of fyr with rede lemes."

l. 318. On the double gender of sæ, cf. Cook's Sievers' Gram., p. 147; and note the omitted article at ll. 2381, 318, 544, with the peculiar tmesis of between at ll. 859, 1298, 1686, 1957. So Cædmon, l. 163 (Thorpe), Exod. l. 562 (Hunt), etc.

l. 320. Cf. l. 924; and Andreas, l. 987, where almost the same words occur. "Here we have manifestly before our eye one of those ancient causeways, which are among the oldest visible institutions of civilization." --E.

l. 322. S. inserts comma after scîr, and makes hring-îren (= ring-mail) parallel with gûð-byrne.

l. 325. Cf. l. 397. "The deposit of weapons outside before entering a house was the rule at all periods.... In provincial Swedish almost everywhere a church porch is called våkenhus,... i.e. weapon-house, because the worshippers deposited their arms there before they entered the house."--E., after G. Stephens.

l. 333. Cf. Dryden's "mingled metal damask'd o'er with gold."--E.

l. 336. "æl-, el-, kindred with Goth. aljis, other, e.g. in ælþéodig, elþéodig, foreign."-- Cook's Sievers' Gram., p. 47.

l. 336. Cf. l. 673 for the functions of an ombiht-þegn.

l. 343. Cf. l. 1714 for the same beód-geneátas,--"the predecessor title to that of the Knights of the Table Round."--E. Cf. Andreas (K.), l. 2177.

l. 344. The future is sometimes expressed by willan + inf., generally with some idea of volition involved; cf. ll. 351, 427, etc. Cf. the use of willan as principal vb. (with omitted inf.) at ll. 318, 1372, 543, 1056; and sculan, ll. 1784, 2817.

l. 353. sîð here, and at l. 501, probably means arrival. E. translates the former by visit, the latter by adventure.

l. 357. unhâr = hairless, bald (Gr., etc.).

l. 358. eode is only one of four or five preterits of gân (gongan, gangan, gengan), viz. geóng (gióng: ll. 926, 2410, etc.), gang (l. 1296, etc.), gengde (ll. 1402, 1413). Sievers, p. 217, apparently remarks that eode is "probably used only in prose." (?!). Cf. geng, Gen. ll. 626, 834; Exod. (Hunt) l. 102.

l. 367. The MS. and H.-So. read with Gr. and B. glädman Hrôðgâr, abandoning Thorkelin's glädnian. There is a glass. hilaris glädman.--Beit. xii. 84; same as gläd.

l. 369. dugan is a "preterit-present" verb, with new wk. preterit, like sculan, durran, magan, etc. For various inflections, see ll. 573, 590, 1822, 526. Cf. do in "that will do"; doughty, etc.

l. 372. Cf. l. 535 for a similar use; and l. 1220. Bede, Eccles. Hist., ed. Miller, uses the same expression several times. "Here, and in all other places where cniht occurs in this poem, it seems to carry that technical sense which it bore in the military hierarchy [of a noble youth placed out and learning the elements of the art of war in the service of a qualified warrior, to whom he is, in a military sense, a servant], before it bloomed out in the full sense of knight."--E.

l. 373. E. remarks of the hyphened eald-fäder, "hyphens are risky toys to play with in fixing texts of pre-hyphenial antiquity"; eald-fäder could only = grandfather. eald here can only mean honored, and the hyphen is unnecessary. Cf. "old fellow," "my old man," etc.; and Ger. alt-vater.

l. 378. Th. and B. propose Geátum, as presents from the Danish to the Geatish king.--Beit. xii.

l. 380. häbbe. The subj. is used in indirect narration and question, wish and command, purpose, result, and hypothetical comparison with swelce = as if.

ll. 386, 387. Ten Br. emends to read: "Hurry, bid the kinsman-throng go into the hall together."

l. 387. sibbe-gedriht, for Beowulf's friends, occurs also at l. 730. It is subject-acc. to seón. Cf. ll. 347, 365, and Hunt's Exod. l. 214.

l. 404. "Here, as in the later Icelandic halls, Beowulf saw Hrothgar enthroned on a high seat at the east end of the hall. The seat is sacred. It has a supernatural quality. Grendel, the fiend, cannot approach it."--Br., p. 34. Cf. l. 168.

l. 405. "At Benty Grange, in Derbyshire, an Anglo-Saxon barrow, opened in 1848, contained a coat of mail. 'The iron chain work consists of a large number of links of two kinds attached to each other by small rings half an inch in diameter; one kind flat and lozenge-shaped ... the others all of one kind, but of different lengths.'"--Br., p. 126.

l. 407. Wes ... hâl: this ancient Teutonic greeting afterwards grew into wassail. Cf. Skeat's Luke, i. 28; Andreas (K.), 1827; Layamon, l. 14309, etc.

l. 414. "The distinction between wesan and weorðan [in passive relations] is not very clearly defined, but wesan appears to indicate a state, weorðan generally an action."--Sw. Cf. Mod. German werden and sein in similar relations.

l. 414. Gr. translates hâdor by receptaculum; cf. Gering, Zachers Zeitschr. xii. 124. Toller-Bosw. ignores Gr.'s suggestion.

ll. 420, 421. B. reads: þær ic (on) fifelgeban (= ocean) ýðde eotena cyn. Ten Br. reads: þær ic fifelgeban ýðde, eotena hâm. Ha. suggests fifelgeband = monster-band, without further changes.

l. 420. R. reads þæra = of them, for þær.--Zachers Zeitschr. iii. 399; Beit. xii. 367.

l. 420. "niht has a gen., nihtes, used for the most part only adverbially, and almost certainly to be regarded as masculine."--Cook's Sievers' Gram., p. 158.

l. 425. Cf. also ll. 435, 635, 2345, for other examples of Beowulf's determination to fight single-handed.

l. 441. þe hine = whom, as at l. 1292, etc. The indeclinable þe is often thus combined with personal pronouns, = relative, and is sometimes separated from them by a considerable interval.--Sw.

l. 443. The MS. has Geotena. B. and Fahlbeck, says H.-So., do not consider the Geátas, but the Jutes, as the inhabitants of Swedish West-Gothland. Alfred translates Juti by Geátas, but Jutland by Gotland. In the laws they are called Guti.--Beit. xii. 1, etc.

l. 444. B., Gr., and Ha. make unforhte an adv. = fearlessly, modifying etan. Kl. reads anforhte = timid.

l. 446. Cf. l. 2910. Th. translates: thou wilt not need my head to hide (i.e. bury). Simrock supposes a dead-watch or lyke-wake to be meant. Wood, thou wilt not have to bury so much as my head! H.-So. supposes heáfod-weard, a guard of honor, such as sovereigns or presumptive rulers had, to be meant by hafalan hýdan; hence, you need not give me any guard, etc. Cf. Schmid, Gesetze der A., 370-372.

l. 447. S. places a colon after nimeð.

l. 451. H.-So., Ha., and B. (Beit. xii. 87) agree essentially in translating feorme, food. R. translates consumption of my corpse. Maintenance, support, seems preferable to either.

l. 452. Rönning (after Grimm) personifies Hild.--Beovulfs Kvadet, l. 59. Hildr is the name of one of the Scandinavian Walkyries, or battle-maidens, who transport the spirits of the slain to Walhalla. Cf. Kent's Elene, l. 18, etc.

l. 455. "The war-smiths, especially as forgers of the sword, were garmented with legend, and made into divine personages. Of these Weland is the type, husband of a swan maiden, and afterwards almost a god."-- Br., p. 120. Cf. A. J. C. Hare's account of "Wayland Smith's sword with which Henry II. was knighted," and which hung in Westminster Abbey to a late date.--Walks in London, ii. 228.

l. 455. This is the ælces mannes wyrd of Boethius (Sw., p. 44) and the wyrd bið swîðost of Gnomic Verses, 5. There are about a dozen references to it in Beówulf.

l. 455. E. compares the fatalism of this concluding hemistich with the Christian tone of l. 685 seq.

ll. 457, 458. B. reads wære-ryhtum (= from the obligations of clientage).

l. 480. Cf. l. 1231, where the same sense, "flown with wine," occurs.

l. 488. "The duguð, the mature and ripe warriors, the aristocracy of the nation, are the support of the throne."--E. The M. E. form of the word, douth, occurs often. Associated with geogoð, ll. 160 and 622.

l. 489. Kl. omits comma after meoto and reads (with B.) sige-hrêð-secgum, = disclose thy thought to the victor-heroes. Others, as Körner, convert meoto into an imperative and divide on sæl = think upon happiness. But cf. onband beadu-rûne, l. 501. B. supposes onsæl meoto =speak courteous words. Tidskr. viii. 292; Haupts Zeitschr. xi. 411; Eng. Stud. ii. 251.

l. 489. Cf. the invitation at l. 1783.

l. 494. Cf. Grimm's Andreas, l. 1097, for deal, =proud, elated, exulting; Phoenix (Bright), l. 266.

l. 499. MS. has Hunferð, but the alliteration requires Ûnferð, as at ll. 499, 1166, 1489; and cf. ll. 1542, 2095, 2930. See List of Names.

l. 501. sîð = arrival (?); cf. l. 353.

l. 504. þon mâ = the more (?), may be added to the references under þon.

l. 506. E. compares the taunt of Eliab to David, I Sam. xvii. 28.

l. 509. dol-gilp = idle boasting. The second definition in the Gloss. is wrong.

l. 513. "Eagor-stream might possibly be translated the stream of Eagor, the awful terror-striking stormy sea in which the terrible [Scandinavian] giant dwelt, and through which he acted."--Br., p. 164. He remarks, "The English term eagre still survives in provincial dialect for the tide-wave or bore on rivers. Dryden uses it in his Threnod. Angust. 'But like an eagre rode in triumph o'er the tide.' Yet we must be cautious," etc. Cf. Fox's Boethius, ll. 20, 236; Thorpe's Cædmon, 69, etc.

l. 524. Krüger and B. read Bânstânes.--Beit. ix. 573.

l. 525. R. reads wyrsan (= wyrses: cf. Mod. Gr. guten Muthes) geþinges; but H.-So. shows that the MS. wyrsan ... þingea = wyrsena þinga, can stand; cf. gen. pl. banan, Christ, l. 66, etc.

l. 534. Insert, under eard-lufa (in Gloss.), earfoð, st. n., trouble, difficulty, struggle; acc. pl. earfeðo, 534.

l. 545 seq. "Five nights Beowulf and Breca kept together, not swimming, but sailing in open boats (to swim the seas is to sail the seas), then storm drove them asunder ... Breca is afterwards chief of the Brondings, a tribe mentioned in Wîdsíth. The story seems legendary, not mythical."--Br., pp. 60, 61.

ll. 574-578. B. suggests swâ þær for hwäðere, = so there it befell me. But the word at l. 574 seems = however, and at l. 578 = yet; cf. l. 891; see S.; Beit. ix. 138; Tidskr. viii. 48; Zacher, iii. 387, etc.

l. 586. Gr. and Grundt. read fâgum sweordum (no ic þæs fela gylpe!), supplying fela and blending the broken half-lines into one. Ho. and Kl. supply geflites.

l. 599. E. translates nýd-bâde by blackmail; adding "nêd bâd, toll; nêd bâdere, tolltaker."--Land Charters, Gloss, v.

l. 601. MS. has ond = and in three places only (601, 1149, 2041); elsewhere it uses the symbol 7 = and.

l. 612. seq. Cf. the drinking ceremony at l. 1025. "The royal lady offers the cup to Beowulf, not in his turn where he sate among the rest, but after it has gone the round; her approach to Beowulf is an act apart."--E.

l. 620. "The [loving] cup which went the round of the company and was tasted by all," like the Oriel and other college anniversary cups.--E.

l. 622. Cf. ll. 160, 1191, for the respective places of young and old.

l. 623. Cf. the circlet of gold worn by Wealhþeów at l. 1164.

Beowulf: Scholar's Edition

l. 631. gyddode. Cf. Chaucer, Prol. l. 237 (ed. Morris): "Of yeddynges he bar utterly the prys." Cf. giddy.

l. 648. Kl. suggests a period after geþinged, especially as B. (Tidskr. viii. 57) has shown that oþþe is sometimes = ond. Th. supplies ne.

l. 650. oþþe here and at ll. 2476, 3007, probably = and.

l. 651. Cf. 704, where sceadu-genga (the night-ganger of Leechdoms, ii. 344) is applied to the demon.--E.

l. 659. Cf. l. 2431 for same formula, "to have and to hold" of the Marriage Service.--E.

l. 681. B. considers þeáh ... eal a precursor of Mod. Eng. although.

l. 682. gôdra = advantages in battle (Gr.), battle-skill (Ha.), skill in war (H.-So.). Might not nât be changed to nah = ne + âh (cf. l. 2253), thus justifying the translation ability (?) --he has not the ability to, etc.

l. 695. Kl. reads hiera.--Beit. ix. 189. B. omits hîe as occurring in the previous hemistich.--Beit. xii. 89.

l. 698. "Here Destiny is a web of cloth."- -E., who compares the Greek Clotho, "spinster of fate." Women are also called "weavers of peace," as l. 1943. Cf. Kent's Elene, l. 88; Wîdsîð, l. 6, etc.

l. 711. B. translates þâ by when and connects with the preceding sentences, thus rejecting the ordinary canto-division at l. 711. He objects to the use of com as principal vb. at ll. 703, 711, and 721. (Beit, xii.)

l. 711. "Perhaps the Gnomic verse which tells of Thyrs, the giant, is written with Grendel in the writer's mind,--þyrs sceal on fenne gewunian âna inuan lande, the giant shall dwell in the fen, alone in the land (Sweet's Read., p. 187)."--Br. p. 36.

l. 717. Dietrich, in Haupt. xi. 419, quotes from Ælfric, Hom. ii. 498: hê beworhte þâ bigelsas mid gyldenum læfrum, he covered the arches with gold-leaf,--a Roman custom derived from Carthage. Cf. Mod. Eng. oriel = aureolum, a gilded room.--E. (quoting Skeat). Cf. ll. 2257, 1097, 2247, 2103, 2702, 2283, 333, 1751, for various uses of gold-sheets.

l. 720. B. and ten Br. suggest hell-thane (Grendel) for heal-þegnas, and make häle refer to Beowulf. Cf. l. 142.

l. 723. Z. reads [ge]hrân.

l. 727. For this use of standan, cf. ll. 2314, 2770; and Vergil, Ecl. ii. 26:
"Cum placidum ventis staret mare."

l. 757. gedräg. Tumult is one of the meanings of this word. Here, appar. = occupation, lair.

l. 759. R. reads môdega for gôda, "because the attribute cannot be separated from the word modified unless the two alliterate."

l. 762. Cf. Andreas, l. 1537, for a similar use of ût = off.--E.

l. 769. The foreign words in Beówulf (as ceaster-here) are not numerous; others are (aside from proper names like Cain, Abel, etc.) deófol (diabolus), candel (l. 1573), ancor (l. 303), scrîfan (for- ge-), segn (l. 47), gigant (l. 113), mîl- (l. 1363), stræt (l. 320), ombeht (l. 287), gim (l. 2073), etc.

l. 770. MS. reads cerwen, a word conceived by B. and others to be part of a fem. compd.: -scerwen like -wenden in ed- wenden, -ræden, etc. (cf. meodu-scerpen in Andreas, l. 1528); emended to -scerwen, a great scare under the figure of a mishap at a drinking-bout; one might compare bescerwan, to deprive, from bescyrian (Grein, i. 93), hence ealu-seerwen would = a sudden taking away, deprivation, of the beer.--H.-So., p. 93. See B., Tidskr. viii. 292.

l. 771. Ten Br. reads rêðe, rênhearde, = raging, exceeding bold.

l. 792. Instrumental adverbial phrases like ænige þinga, nænige þinga (not at all), hûru þinga (especially) are not infrequent. See Cook's Sievers' Gram., p. 178; March, A.-S. Gram., p. 182.

l. 811. myrðe. E. translates in wanton mood. Toller-Bosw. does not recognize sorrow as one of the meanings of this word.

ll. 850, 851. S. reads deóp for deóg and erases semicolon after weól, = the death-stained deep welled with sword-gore; cf. l. 1424. B. reads deáð-fæges deóp, etc., = the deep welled with the doomed one's gore.-- Beit. xii. 89.

l. 857. The meaning of blaneum is partly explained by fealwe mearas below, l. 866. Cf. Layamon's "and leop on his blancke" = steed, l. 23900; Kent's Elene, l. 1185.

l. 859. Körner, Eng. Stud. i. 482, regards the oft-recurring be sæm tweónum as a mere formula = on earth; cf. ll. 1298, 1686. tweóne is part of the separable prep. between; see be-. Cf. Baskerville's Andreas, l. 558.

l. 865. Cf. Voyage of Ôhthere and Wulfstân for an account of funeral horse-racing, Sweet's Read., p. 22.

l. 868. See Ha., p. 31, for a variant translation.

l. 871 seq. R. considers this a technical description of improvised alliterative verse, suggested by and wrought out on the spur of the moment.

l. 872. R. and B. propose secg[an], = rehearse, for secg, which suits the verbs in the next two lines.

ll. 878-98. "It pleases me to think that it is in English literature we possess the first sketch of that mighty saga [the Volsunga Saga = Wälsinges gewin] which has for so many centuries engaged all the arts, and at last in the hands of Wagner the art of music."--Br., p. 63. Cf. Nibelung. Lied, l. 739.

l. 894. Intransitive verbs, as gân, weorðan, sometimes take habban, "to indicate independent action."--Sw. Cf. hafað ... geworden, l. 2027.

l. 895. "brûcan (enjoy) always has the genitive."--Sw.; cf. l. 895; acc., gen., instr., dat., according to March, A.-S. Gram., p. 151.

l. 898. Scherer proposes hâte, = from heat, instr. of hât, heat; cf. l. 2606.

l. 901. hê þäs âron þâh = he throve in honor (B.). Ten Br. inserts comma after þâh, making siððan introduce a depend. clause.--Beit. viii. 568. Cf. weorð-myndum þâh, l. 8; ll. 1155, 1243.--H.-So.

l. 902. Heremôdes is considered by Heinzel to be a mere epithet = the valiant; which would refer the whole passage to Sigmund (Sigfrid), the eotenas, l. 903, being the Nibelungen. This, says H.-So., gets rid of the contradiction between the good "Heremôd" here and the bad one, l. 1710 seq.--B. however holds fast to Heremôd.--Beit. xii. 41. on feónda geweald, l. 904,--into the hands of devils, says B.; cf. ll. 809, 1721, 2267; Christ, l. 1416; Andreas, l. 1621; for hine fyren onwôd, cf. Gen. l. 2579; Hunt's Dan. 17: hîe wlenco anwôd.

l. 902 seq. "Heremôd's shame is contrasted with the glory of Sigemund, and with the prudence, patience, generosity, and gentleness of Beowulf as a chieftain."--Br., p. 66.

l. 906. MS. has lemede. Toller-Bosw. corrects to lemedon.

l. 917. Cf. Hunt's Exod., l. 170, for similar language.

l. 925. hôs, G. hansa, company, "the word from which the mercantile association of the 'Hanseatic' towns took their designation."--E.

l. 927. on staþole = on the floor (B., Rask, ten Br.).--Beit. xii. 90.

l. 927. May not steápne here = bright, from its being immediately followed by golde fâhne? Cf. Chaucer's "his eyen stepe," Prol. l. 201 (ed. Morris); Cockayne's Ste. Marherete, pp. 9, 108; St. Kath., l. 1647.

l. 931. grynna may be for gyrnna (= sorrows), gen. plu. of gyrn, as suggested by one commentator.

l. 937. B. (Beit. xii. 90) makes gehwylcne object of wîd-scofen (häfde). Gr. makes weá nom. absolute.

l. 940. scuccum: cf. G. scheuche, scheusal; Prov. Eng. old-shock; perhaps the pop. interjection O shucks! (!)

l. 959. H. explains we as a "plur. of majesty," which Beówulf throws off at l. 964.

l. 963. feónd þone frätgan (B. Beit. xii. 90).

l. 976. synnum. "Most abstract words in the poetry have a very wide range of meanings, diverging widely from the prose usage, synn, for instance, means simply injury, mischief, hatred, and the prose meaning sin is only a secondary one; hata in poetry is not only hater, but persecutor, enemy, just as nîð is both hatred and violence, strength; heard is sharp as well as hard."--Sw.

l. 986. S. places wäs at end of l. 985 and reads stîðra nägla, omitting gehwylc and the commas after that and after sceáwedon. Beit. ix. 138; stêdra (H.-So.); hand-sporu (H.-So.) at l. 987.

l. 986. Miller (Anglia, xii. 3) corrects to æghwylene, in apposition to fingras.

l. 987. hand-sporu. See Anglia, vii. 176, for a discussion of the intrusion of u into the nom. of n-stems.

l. 988. Cf. ll. 2121, 2414, for similar use of unheóru = ungeheuer.

l. 992. B. suggests heátimbred for hâten, and gefrätwon for -od; Kl., hroden (Beit. ix. 189).

l. 995, 996. Gold-embroidered tapestries seem to be meant by web = aurifrisium.

l. 997. After þâra þe = of those that, the depend. vb. often takes sg. for pl.; cf. ll. 844, 1462, 2384, 2736.--Sw.; Dietrich.

l. 998. "Metathesis of l takes place in seld for setl, bold for botl," etc.--Cook's Sievers' Gram., p. 96. Cf. Eng. proper names, Bootle, Battle field, etc.--Skeat, Principles, i. 250.

l. 1000. heorras: cf. Chaucer, Prol. (ed. Morris) l. 550:

"Ther was no dore that he nolde heve of harre."

ll. 1005-1007. See Zachers Zeitschr. iii. 391, and Beit. xii. 368, for R.'s and B.'s views of this difficult passage.

l. 1009. Cf. l. 1612 for sæl and mæl, surviving still in E. Anglia in "mind your seals and meals," = times and occasions, i.e. have your wits about you.--E.

ll. 1012, 1013. Cf. ll. 753, 754 for two similar comparatives used in conjunction.

l. 1014. Cf. l. 327 for similar language.

ll. 1015, 1016. H.-So. puts these two lines in parentheses (fylle ...þâra). Cf. B., Beit. xii. 91.

l. 1024. One of the many famous swords spoken of in the poem. See Hrunting, ll. 1458, 1660; Hûnlâfing, l. 1144, etc. Cf. Excalibur, Roland's sword, the Nibelung Balmung, etc.

l. 1034. scûr-heard. For an ingenious explanation of this disputed word see Professor Pearce's article in Mod. Lang. Notes, Nov. 1, 1892, and ensuing discussion.

l. 1039. eoderas is of doubtful meaning. H. and Toller-Bosw. regard the word here = enclosure, palings of the court. Cf. Cædmon, ll. 2439, 2481. The passage throws interesting light on horses and their trappings

l. 1043. Grundt. emends wîg to wicg, = charger; and E. quotes Tacitus, Germania, 7.

l. 1044. "Power over each and both"; cf. "all and some," "one and all."

For Ingwin, see List of Names.

l. 1065. Gr. contends that fore here = de, concerning, about (Ebert's Jahrb., 1862, p. 269).

l. 1069. H.-So. supplies fram after eaferum, to govern it, = concerning (?). Cf. Fight at Finnsburg, Appendix.

l. 1070. For the numerous names of the Danes, "bright-" "spear-" "east-" "west-" "ring-" Danes, see these words.

l. 1073. Eotenas = Finn's people, the Frisians; cf. ll. 1089, 1142, 1146, etc., and Beit. xii. 37. Why they are so called is not known.

l. 1084. R. proposes wiht Hengeste wið gefeohtan (Zachers Zeitschr. iii. 394). Kl., wið H. wiht gefeohtan.

ll. 1085 and 1099. weá-lâf occurs in Wulfstan, Hom. 133, ed. Napier.--E. Cf. daroða lâf, Brunanb., l. 54; âdes lâfe, Phoenix, 272 (Bright), etc.

l. 1098. elne unflitme = so dass der eid (der inhalt des eides) nicht streitig war.--B., Beit. iii. 30. But cf. 1130, where Hengist and Finn are again brought into juxtaposition and the expression ealles (?) unhlitme occurs.

l. 1106. The pres. part. + be, as myndgiend wære here, is comparatively rare in original A.-S. literature, but occurs abundantly in translations from the Latin. The periphrasis is generally meaningless. Cf. l. 3029.

l. 1108. Körner suggests ecge, = sword, in reference to a supposed old German custom of placing ornaments, etc., on the point of a sword or spear (Eng. Stud. i. 495). Singer, ince-gold = bright gold; B., andiége = Goth, andaugjo, evidently. Cf. incge lâfe, l. 2578. Possibly: and inge (= young men) gold âhôfon of horde. For inge, cf. Hunt's Exod. l. 190.

ll. 1115-1120. R. proposes (hêt þâ ...) bânfatu bärnan ond on bæl dôn, earme on eaxe = to place the arms in the ashes, reading gûðrêc = battle-reek, for -rinc (Zachers Zeitschr. iii. 395). B., Sarrazin (Beit. xi. 530), Lichtenfeld (Haupts Zeitschr. xvi. 330), C., etc., propose various emendations. See H.-So., p. 97, and Beit. viii. 568. For gùðrinc âstâh, cf. Old Norse, stiga á bál, "ascend the balefire."

l. 1116. sweoloðe. "On Dartmoor the burning of the furze up the hillsides to let new grass grow, is called zwayling."--E. Cf. sultry, G. schwül, etc.

l. 1119. Cf. wudu-rêc âstâh, l. 3145; and Exod. (Hunt), l. 450: wælmist âstâh.

l. 1122. ätspranc = burst forth, arose (omitted from the Gloss.), < ät + springan.

l. 1130. R. and Gr. read elne unflitme, = loyally and without contest, as at l. 1098. Cf. Ha., p. 39; H.-So., p. 97.

l. 1137. scacen = gone; cf. ll. 1125, 2307, 2728.

l. 1142. "The sons of the Eotenas" (B., Beit. xii. 31, who conjectures a gap after 1142).

l. 1144. B. separates thus: Hûn Lâfing, = Hûn placed the sword Lâfing, etc.--Beit. xii. 32; cf. R., Zachers Zeitschr. iii. 396. Heinzel and Homburg make other conjectures (Herrig's Archiv, 72, 374, etc.).

l. 1143. B., H.-So., and Möller read: worod rædenne, þonne him Hûn Lâfing, = military brotherhood, when Hûn laid upon his breast (the sword) Lâfing. There is a sword Laufi, Lövi in the Norse sagas; but swords, armor, etc., are often called the leaving (lâf) of files, hammers, etc., especially a precious heirloom; cf. ll. 454, 1033, 2830, 2037, 2629, 796, etc., etc.

l. 1152. roden = reddened (B., Tidskr. viii. 295).

l. 1160. For ll. 1069-1160, containing the Finn episode, cf. Möller, Alteng. Volksepos, 69, 86, 94; Heinzel, Anz. f. dtsch. Altert., 10, 226; B., Beit. xii. 29-37. Cf. Wîdsîð, l. 33, etc.

ll. 1160, 1161. leóð (lied = song, lay) and gyd here appear synonyms.

ll. 1162-1165. "Behind the wars and tribal wanderings, behind the contentions of the great, we watch in this poem the steady, continuous life of home, the passions and thoughts of men, the way they talked and moved and sang and drank and lived and loved among one another and for one another."--Br., p. 18.

l. 1163. Cf. wonderwork. So wonder-death, wonder-bidding, wonder-treasure, -smith, -sight, etc. at ll. 1748, 3038, 2174, 1682, 996, etc. Cf. the German use of the same intensive, = wondrous, in wunder-schön, etc.

l. 1165. þâ gyt points to some future event when "each" was not "true to other," undeveloped in this poem, suhtor-gefäderan = Hrôðgâr and Hrôðulf, l. 1018. Cf. âðumswerian, l. 84.

l. 1167 almost repeats l. 500, ät fôtum, etc., where Ûnferð is first introduced.

l. 1191. E. sees in this passage separate seats for youth and middle-aged men, as in English college halls, chapels, convocations, and churches still.

l. 1192. ymbutan, round about, is sometimes thus separated: ymb hie ûtan; cf. Voyage of Ôhthere, etc. (Sw.), p. 18, l. 34, etc.; Beówulf, ll. 859, 1686, etc.

l. 1194. bewägned, a [Greek: hapax legomenon], tr. offered by Th. Probably a p. p. wägen, made into a vb. by -ian, like own, drown, etc. Cf. hafenian (< hafen, < hebban), etc.

l. 1196. E. takes the expression to mean "mantle and its rings or broaches." "Rail" long survived in Mid. Eng. (Piers Plow., etc.).

l. 1196. This necklace was afterwards given by Beowulf to Hygd, ll. 2173, 2174.

ll. 1199-1215. From the obscure hints in the passage, a part of the poem may be approximately dated,--if Hygelâc is the Chochi-laicus of Gregory of Tours, Hist. Francorum, iii. 3,--about A.D. 512-20.

l. 1200. The Breosinga men (Icel. Brísinga men) is the necklace of the goddess Freya; cf. Elder Edda, Hamarshemt. Hâma stole the necklace from the Gothic King Eormenrîc; cf. Traveller's Song, ll. 8, 18, 88, 111. The comparison of the two necklaces leads the poet to anticipate Hygelâc's history,--a suggestion of the poem's mosaic construction.

l. 1200. For Brôsinga mene, cf. B., Beit. xii. 72. C. suggests fleáh, = fled, for fealh, placing semicolon after byrig, and making hê subject of fleáh and geceás.

l. 1202. B. conjectures geceás êcne ræd to mean he became a pious man and at death went to heaven. Heime (Hâma) in the Thidrekssaga goes into a cloister = to choose the better part (?). Cf. H.-So., p. 98. But cf. Hrôðgâr's language to Beowulf, ll. 1760, 1761.

l. 1211. S. proposes feoh, = property, for feorh, which would be a parallel for breóst-gewædu ... beáh below.

l. 1213. E. remarks that in the Laws of Cnut, i. 26, the devil is called se wôdfreca werewulf, the ravening werewolf.

l. 1215. C. proposes heals-bêge onfèng. Beit. viii. 570. For hreâ- Kl. suggests hræ-.

l. 1227. The son referred to is, according to Ettmüller, the one that reigns after Hrôðgâr.

l. 1229. Kl. suggests sî, = be, for is.

l. 1232. S. gives wine-elated as the meaning of druncne.--Beit. ix. 139; Kl. ibid. 189, 194. But cf. Judith, ll. 67, 107.

l. 1235. Cf. l. 119 for similarity of language.

l. 1235. Kl. proposes gea-sceaft; but cf. l. 1267.

l. 1246. Ring armor was common in the Middle Ages. E. points out the numerous forms of byrne in cognate languages,--Gothic, Icelandic, OHG., Slavonic, O. Irish, Romance, etc. Du Chaillu, The Viking Age, i. 126. Cf. Murray's Dict. s. v.

l. 1248. ânwîg-gearwe = ready for single combat (C.); but cf. Ha. p. 43; Beit. ix. 210, 282.

l. 1252. Some consider this fitt the beginning of Part (or Lay) II. of the original epic, if not a separate work in itself.

l. 1254. K., W., and Ho. read farode = wasted; Kolbing reads furode; but cf. wêsten warode, l. 1266. MS. has warode.

ll. 1255-1258. This passage is a good illustration of the constant parallelism of word and phrase characteristic of A.-S. poetry, and is quoted by Sw. The changes are rung on ende and swylt, on gesýne and wîdcûð, etc.

l. 1259. "That this story of Grendel's mother was originally a separate lay from the first seems to be suggested by the fact that the monsters are described over again, and many new details added, such as would be inserted by a new singer who wished to enhance and adorn the original tale."--Br., p. 41.

l. 1259. Cf. l. 107, which also points to the ancestry of murderers and monsters and their descent from "Cain."

l. 1261. The MS. has se þe, m.; changed by some to seo þe. At ll. 1393, 1395, 1498, Grendel's mother is referred to as m.; at ll. 1293, 1505, 1541-1546, etc., as f., the uncertain pronoun designating a creature female in certain aspects, but masculine in demonic strength and savageness.--H.-So.; Sw. p. 202. Cf. the masc. epithets at ll. 1380, 2137, etc.

l. 1270. âglæca = Grendel, though possibly referring to Beowulf, as at l. 1513.--Sw.

l. 1273. "It is not certain whether anwalda stands for onwealda, or whether it should be read ânwealda, = only ruler.--Sw.

l. 1279. The MS. has sunu þeod wrecan, which R. changes to sunu þeód-wrecan, þeód- = monstrous; but why not regard þeód as opposition to sunu, = her son, the prince? See Sweet's Reader, and Körner's discussion, Eng. Stud. i. 500.

l. 1281. Ten Br. suggests (for sôna) sâra = return of sorrows.

l. 1286. "geþuren (twice so written in MSS.) stands for geþrúen, forged, and is an isolated p. p."--Cook's Sievers' Gram., 209. But see Toller-Bosw. for examples; Sw., Gloss.; March, p. 100, etc.

ll. 1292. þe hine = whom; cf. ll. 441, 1437, 1292; Hêliand, l. 1308.

l. 1298. be sæm tweonum; cf. l. 1192; Hunt's Exod. l. 442; and Mod. Eng. "to us-ward, etc.--Earle's Philol., p. 449. Cf. note, l. 1192.

l. 1301. C. proposes ôðer him ärn = another apartment was assigned him.

l. 1303. B. conjectures under hrôf genam; but Ha., p. 45, shows this to be unnecessary, under also meaning in, as in (or under) these circumstances.

l. 1319. E. and Sw. suggest nægde or nêgde, accosted, < nêgan = Mid. Ger. nêhwian, pr. p. nêhwiandans, approach. For hnægan, press down, vanquish, see ll. 1275, 1440, etc.

l. 1321. C. suggests neád-lâðum for neódlaðu, after crushing hostility; but cf. freóndlaðu, l. 1193.

l. 1334. K. and ten Br. conjecture gefägnod = rejoicing in her fill, a parallel to æse wlanc, l. 1333.

l. 1340. B. translates: "and she has executed a deed of blood-vengeance of far-reaching consequence."--Beit. xii. 93.

l. 1345. B. reads geó for eów (Zachers Zeitschr. iv. 205).

ll. 1346-1377. "This is a fine piece of folk-lore in the oldest extant form.... The authorities for the story are the rustics (ll. 1346, 1356)." --E.

l. 1347. Cf. sele-rædende at l. 51.

l. 1351. "The ge [of gewitan] may be merely a scribal error,--a repetition (dittography) of the preceding ge of gewislîcost."--Sw.

l. 1352. ides, like firas, men, etc., is a poetic word supposed by Grimm to have been applied, like Gr. [Greek: númphæ], to superhuman or semi-divine women.

ll. 1360-1495 seq. E. compares this Dantesque tarn and scenery with the poetical accounts of Æneid, vii. 563; Lucretius, vi. 739, etc.

l. 1360. firgenstreám occurs also in the Phoenix (Bright, p. 168) l. 100; Andreas, ll. 779, 3144 (K.); Gnomic Verses, l. 47, etc.

l. 1363. The genitive is often thus used to denote measure = by or in miles; cf. l. 3043; and contrast with partitive gen. at l. 207.

l. 1364. The MS. reads hrinde = hrînende (?), which Gr. adopts; K. and Th. read hrinde-bearwas; hringde, encircling (Sarrazin, Beit. xi. 163); hrîmge = frosty (Sw.); with frost-whiting covered (Ha.). See Morris, Blickling Hom., Preface, vi., vii.

l. 1364. Cf. Ruin, hrîmige edoras behrofene, rimy, roofless halls.

l. 1366. nîðwundor may = nið- (as in nið-sele, q. v.) wundor, wonder of the deep.

l. 1368. The personal pronoun is sometimes omitted in subordinate and even independent clauses; cf. wite here; and Hunt's Exod., l. 319.

l. 1370. hornum. Such "datives of manner or respect" are not infrequent with adj.

l. 1371. "seleð is not dependent on ær, for in that case it would be in the subjunctive, but ær is simply an adverb, correlative with the conjunction ær in the next line: 'he will (sooner) give up his life, before he will,' etc."--Sw.

l. 1372. Cf. ll. 318 and 543 for willan with similar omitted inf.

l. 1373. heafola is found only in poetry.--Sw. It occurs thirteen or fourteen times in this poem. Cf. the poetic gamol, swât (l. 2694), etc., for eald, blôd.

l. 1391. uton: hortatory subj. of wîtan, go, = let us go; cf. French allons, Lat. eamus, Ital. andiamo, etc. + inf. Cf. ll. 2649, 3102.

l. 1400. H. is dat. of person indirectly affected, = advantage.

l. 1402. geatolîc probably = in his equipments, as B. suggests (Beit. xii. 83), comparing searolîc.

ll. 1402, 1413 reproduce the wk. form of the pret. of gân (Goth. gaggida). Cf. Andreas, l. 1096, etc.

l. 1405. S. (Beit. ix. 140) supplies [þær heó] gegnum fôr; B. (ibid. xii. 14) suggests hwær heó.

l. 1411. B., Gr., and E. take ân-paðas = paths wide enough for only one, like Norwegian einstig; cf. stîge nearwe, just above. Trail is the meaning. Cf. enge ânpaðas, uncûð gelâd, Exod. (Hunt), l. 58.

l. 1421. Cf. oncýð, l. 831. The whole passage (ll. 1411-1442) is replete with suggestions of walrus-hunting, seal-fishing, harpooning of sea-animals (l. 1438), etc.

l. 1425. E. quotes from the 8th cent. Corpus Gloss., "Falanx foeða."

l. 1428. For other mention of nicors, cf. ll. 422, 575, 846. E. remarks, "it survives in the phrase 'Old Nick' ... a word of high authority ... Icel. nykr, water-goblin, Dan. nök, nisse, Swed. näcken, G. nix, nixe, etc." See Skeat, Nick.

l. 1440. Sw. reads gehnæged, prostrated, and regards nîða as gen. pl. "used instrumentally," = by force.

l. 1441. -bora = bearer, stirrer; occurs in other compds., as mund-, ræd-, wæg-bora.

l. 1447. him = for him, a remoter dative of reference.--Sw.

l. 1455. Gr. reads brondne, = flaming.

l. 1457. león is the inf. of lâh; cf. onlâh (< onleón) at l. 1468. lîhan was formerly given as the inf.; cf. læne = læhne.

l. 1458. Cf. the similar dat. of possession as used in Latin.

l. 1458. H.-So. compares the Icelandic saga account of Grettir's battle with the giant in the cave. häft-mêce may be = Icel. heptisax (Anglia, iii. 83), "hip-knife."

l. 1459. "The sense seems to be 'pre-eminent among the old treasures.' ... But possibly foran is here a prep. with the gen.: 'one before the old treasures.'".--Sw. For other examples of foran, cf. ll. 985, 2365.

l. 1460. âter-teárum = poison-drops (C., Beit. viii. 571; S., ibid. xi. 359).

l. 1467. þät, comp. relative, = that which; "we testify that we do know."

l. 1480. forð-gewitenum is in appos. to me, = mihi defuncto.--M. Callaway, Am. Journ. of Philol., October, 1889.

l. 1482. nime. Conditional clauses of doubt or future contingency take gif or bûton with subj.; cf. ll. 452, 594; of fact or certainty, the ind.; cf. ll. 442, 447, 527, 662, etc. For bûton, cf. ll. 967, 1561.

l. 1487. "findan sometimes has a preterit funde in W. S. after the manner of the weak preterits."--Cook's Sievers' Cram., p, 210.

l. 1490. Kl. reads wäl-sweord, = battle-sword.

l. 1507. "This cave under the sea seems to be another of those natural phenomena of which the writer had personal knowledge (ll. 2135, 2277), and which was introduced by him into the mythical tale to give it a local color. There are many places of this kind. Their entrance is under the lowest level of the tide."--Br., p. 45.

l. 1514. B. (Beit. xii. 362) explains niðsele, hrôfsele as roof-covered hall in the deep; cf. Grettir Saga (Anglia , iii. 83).

l. 1538. Sw., R., and ten Br. suggest feaxe for eaxle, = seized by the hair.

l. 1543. and-leán (R.); cf. l. 2095. The MS. has hand-leán.

l. 1546. Sw. and S. read seax.--Beit. ix. 140.

l. 1557. H.-So. omits comma and places semicolon after ýðelîce; Sw. and S. place comma after gescêd.

l. 1584. ôðer swylc = another fifteen (Sw.); = fully as many (Ha.).

ll. 1592-1613 seq. Cf. Anglia, iii; 84 (Grettir Saga).

l. 1595. blondenfeax = grizzly-haired (Bright, Reader, p. 258); cf. Brunanb, l. 45 (Bright).

l. 1599. gewearð, impers. vb., = agree, decide = many agreed upon this, that, etc. (Ha., p. 55; cf. ll. 2025-2027, 1997; B., Beit. xii. 97).

l. 1605. C. supposes wiston = wîscton = wished.--Beit. viii. 571.

l. 1607. broden mæl is now regarded as a comp. noun, = inlaid or damascened sword.-- W., Ho.

l. 1611. wäl-râpas = water-ropes = bands of frost (l. 1610) (?). Possibly the Prov. Eng. weele, whirlpool. Cf. wæl, gurges, Wright, Voc., Gnom. Verses, l. 39.--E.

l. 1611. wægrâpas (Sw.) = wave-bands (Ha.).

l. 1622. B. suggests eatna = eotena, eardas, haunts of the giants (Northumbr. ea for eo).

l. 1635. cyning-holde (B., Beit. xii. 369); cf. l. 290.

l. 1650. H., Gr., and Ettmüller understand idese to refer to the queen.

l. 1651. Cf. Anglia, iii. 74, Beit. xi. 167, for coincidences with the Grettir Saga (13th cent.).

l. 1657. Restore MS. reading wigge in place of wîge.

l. 1664. B. proposes eotenise ... èste for eácen ... oftost, omitting brackets (Zackers Zeitschr. iv. 206). G. translates mighty ... often.

l. 1675. ondrædan. "In late texts the final n of the preposition on is frequently lost when it occurs in a compound word or stereotyped phrase, and the prefix then appears as a: abútan, amang, aweg, aright, adr'ædan."-- Cook's Sievers' Gram., p. 98.

ll. 1680-1682. Giants and their work are also referred to at ll. 113, 455, 1563, 1691, etc.

l. 1680. Cf. ceastra ... orðanc enta geweorc, Gnomic Verses, l. 2; Sweet's Reader, p. 186.

ll. 1687-1697. "In this description of the writing on the sword, we see the process of transition from heathen magic to the notions of Christian times .... The history of the flood and of the giants ... were substitutes for names of heathen gods, and magic spells for victory."--E. Cf. Mohammedan usage.

ll. 1703, 1704. þät þê eorl nære geboren betera (B., Tidskr. 8, 52).

l. 1715. âna hwearf = he died solitary and alone (B., Beit. xii. 38); = lonely (Ha.); = alone (G.).

l. 1723. leód-bealo longsum = eternal hell-torment (B., Beit. xii. 38, who compares Ps. Cott. 57, lîf longsum).

l. 1729. E. translates on lufan, towards possession; Ha., to possessions.

l. 1730. môdgeþonc, like lig, sæ, segn, niht, etc., is of double gender (m., n. in the case of môdgeþ.).

l. 1741. The doctrine of nemesis following close on [Greek: hubris], or overweening pride, is here very clearly enunciated. The only protector against the things that "assault and hurt" the soul is the "Bishop and Shepherd of our souls" (l. 1743).

l. 1745 appears dimly to fore-shadow the office of the evil archer Loki, who in the Scandinavian mythology shoots Balder with a mistletoe twig. The language closely resembles that of Psalm 64.

Beowulf: Scholar's Edition

l. 1748. Kl. regards wom = wô(u)m; cf. wôh-bogen, l. 2828. See Gloss., p. 295, under wam. Contrast the construction of bebeorgan a few lines below (l. 1759), where the dat. and acc. are associated.

l. 1748. See Cook's Sievers' Gram., p. 167, for declension of wôh, wrong = gen. wôs or wôges, dat. wô(u)m, etc.; pl. gen. wôra, dat. wô(u)m, etc.; and cf. declension of heáh, hreóh, rûh, etc.

l. 1748. wergan gâstes; cf. Blickl. Hom. vii.; Andreas, l. 1171. "Auld Wearie is used in Scotland, or was used a few years ago, ... to mean the devil."--E. Bede's Eccles. Hist. contains (naturally) many examples of the expression = devil.

l. 1750. on gyld = in reward (B. Beit. xii. 95); Ha. translates boastfully; G., for boasting; Gr., to incite to boastfulness. Cf. Christ, l. 818.

l. 1767. E. thinks this an allusion to the widespread superstition of the evil eye (mal occhio, mauvais æil). Cf. Vergil, Ecl. iii. 103. He remarks that Pius IX., Gambetta, and President Carnot were charged by their enemies with possessing this weapon.

l. 1784. wigge geweorðad (MS. wigge weorðad) is C.'s conjecture; cf. Elene, l. 150. So G., honored in war.

l. 1785. The future generally implied in the present of beón is plainly seen in this line; cf. ll. 1826, 661, 1830, 1763, etc.

l. 1794. Some impers. vbs. take acc. (as here, Geat) of the person affected; others (as þyncan) take the dat. of the person, as at ll. 688, 1749, etc. Cf. verbs of dreaming, being ashamed, desiring, etc.--March, A.-S. Gram., p. 145.

l. 1802. E. remarks that the blaca hrefn here is a bird of good omen, as opposed to se wonna hrefn of l. 3025. The raven, wolf, and eagle are the regular epic accompaniments of battle and carnage. Cf. ll. 3025-3028; Maldon, 106; Judith, 205-210, etc.

l. 1803. S. emends to read: "then came the light, going bright after darkness: the warriors," etc. Cf. Ho., p. 41, l. 23. G. puts period before "the warriors." For onettan, cf. Sw.'s Gloss, and Bright's Read., Gloss.

ll. 1808-1810. Müllenh. and Grundt. refer se hearda to Beowulf, correct sunu (MS.) to suna Ecgláfes (i.e. Unferth); [he] (Beo.) thanked him (Un.) for the loan. Cf. ll. 344, 581, 1915.

ll. 1823-1840. "Beowulf departing pledges his services to Hroðgar, to be what afterwards in the mature language of chivalry was called his 'true knight'"--E.

l. 1832. Kl. corrects to dryhtne, in appos. with Higeláce.

l. 1835 gâr-holt more properly means spear-shaft; cf. äsc-holt.

l. 1855. sêl = better (Grundt.; B., Beit. xii. 96), instead of MS. wel.

ll. 1855-1866. "An ideal picture of international amity according to the experience and doctrine of the eighth century."--E.

l. 1858. S. and Kl. correct to gemæne, agreeing with sib.--Beit. ix. 140, 190.

l. 1862. "The gannet is a great diver, plunging down into the sea from a considerable height, such as forty feet."--E.

l. 1863. Kl. suggests heafu, = seas.

l. 1865. B. proposes geþôhte, = with firm thought, for geworhte; cf. l. 611.

l. 1876. geseón = see again (Kl., Beit. ix. 190). S. and B. insert nâ to modify geseón and explain Hrôðgâr's tears. Ha. and G. follow Heyne's text. Cf. l. 567.

l. 1881. Is beorn here = bearn (be-arn?) of l. 67? or more likely = born, barn, = burned?--S., Th.

l. 1887. orleahtre is a [Greek: hapax legomenon]. E. compares Tennyson's "blameless" king. Cf. also ll. 2015, 2145; and the gôd cyning of l. 11.

l. 1896. scaðan = warriors (cf. l. 1804) has been proposed by C.; but cf. l. 253.

l. 1897. The boat had been left, at ll. 294-302, in the keeping of Hrôðgâr's men; at l. 1901 the bât-weard is specially honored by Beowulf with a sword and becomes a "sworded squire."--E. This circumstance appears to weld the poem together. Cf. also the speed of the journey home with ymb ân-tîd ôþres dôgores of l. 219, and the similarity of language in both passages (fâmig-heals, clifu, nässas, sælde, brim, etc.).--The nautical terms in Beowulf would form an interesting study.

l. 1904. R. proposes gewât him on naca, = the vessel set out, on alliterating as at l. 2524 (Zachers Zeitschr. iii. 402). B. reads on nacan, but inserts irrelevant matter (Beit. xii. 97).

l. 1913. Cf. the same use of ceól, = ship, in the A.-S. Chron., ed. Earle-Plummer; Gnomic Verses, etc.

l. 1914. S. inserts þät hê before on lande.

l. 1916. B. makes leófra manna depend on wlâtode, = looked for the dear men ready at the coast (Beit. xii. 97).

l. 1924. Gr., W., and Ho. propose wunade, = remained; but cf. l. 1929. S. conceives ll. 1924, 1925 as "direct speech" (Beit. ix. 141).

l. 1927 seq. "The women of Beowulf are of the fine northern type; trusted and loved by their husbands and by the nobles and people; generous, gentle, and holding their place with dignity."--Br., p. 67. Thrytho is the exception, l. 1932 seq.

l. 1933. C. suggests frêcnu, = dangerous, bold, for Thrytho could not be called "excellent." G. writes "Modthrytho" as her name. The womanly Hygd seems purposely here contrasted with the terrible Thrytho, just as, at l. 902 seq., Sigemund and Heremôd are contrasted. For Thrytho, etc., cf. Gr., Jahrb. für rom. u. eng. Lit. iv. 279; Müllenhoff, Haupts Zeitschr. xiv. 216; Matthew Paris; Suchier, Beit. iv. 500-521; R. Zachers Zeitschr. iii. 402; B., ibid. iv. 206; Körner, Eng. Stud. i. 489-492; H.-So., p. 106.

l. 1932-1963. K. first pointed out the connection between the historical Offa, King of Mercia, and his wife Cwendrida, and the Offa and Þryðo (Gr.'s Drida of the Vita Offæ Secundi) of the present passage. The tale is told of her, not of Hygd.

l. 1936. Suchier proposes andæges, = eye to eye; Leo proposes ândæges, = the whole day; G., by day. No change is necessary if an be taken to govqern hire, = on her, and däges be explained (like nihtes, etc.) as a genitive of time, = by day.

l. 1943. R. and Suchier propose onsêce, = seek, require; but cf. 2955.

l. 1966. Cf. the heofoncandel of Exod. l. 115 (Hunt). Shak.'s 'night's candles.'

l. 1969. Cf. l. 2487 seq. for the actual slayer of Ongenþeów, i.e. Eofor, to whom Hygelâc gave his only daughter as a reward, l. 2998.

l. 1981. meodu-scencum = with mead-pourers or mead-cups (G., Ha.); draught or cup of mead (Toller-Bosw.).

l. 1982. K., Th., W., H. supply [heal-]reced; Holler [heá-].

l. 1984. B. defends the MS., reading hæ nû (for hæðnû), which he regards as = Heinir, the inhabitants of the Jutish "heaths" (hæð). Cf. H.-So., p. 107; Beit. xii. 9.

l. 1985. sînne. "In poetry there is a reflexive possessive of the third person, sîn (declined like mîn). It is used not only as a true reflexive, but also as a non-reflexive (= Lat. ejus)"--Sw.; Cook's Sievers' Gram., p. 185. Cf. ll. 1508, 1961, 2284, 2790.

l. 1994. Cf. l. 190 for a similar use of seáð; cf. to "glow" with emotion, "boil" with indignation, "burn" with anger, etc. weallan is often so used; cf. ll. 2332, 2066, etc.

l. 2010. B. proposes fâcne, = in treachery, for fenne. Cf. Juliana, l. 350; Beit. xii. 97.

l. 2022. Food of specific sorts is rarely, if at all, mentioned in the poem. Drink, on the other hand, occurs in its primitive varieties,--ale (as here: ealu-wæg), mead, beer, wine, lîð (cider? Goth. leiþus, Prov. Ger. leit- in leithaus, ale-house), etc.

l. 2025. Kl. proposes is for wäs.

l. 2027. Cf. l. 1599 for a similar use of weorðan, = agree, be pleased with (Ha.); appear (Sw., Reader, 6th ed.).

ll. 2030, 2031. Ten Br. proposes: oft seldan (= gave) wære äfter leód-hryre: lytle hwîle bongâr bûgeð, þeáh seó brýd duge = oft has a treaty been given after the fall of a prince: but little while the murder-spear resteth, however excellent the bride be. Cf. Kl., Beit. ix. 190; B., Beit. xii. 369; R., Zachers Zeitschr. in. 404; Ha., p. 69; G., p. 62.

l. 2036. Cf. Kl, Beit. ix. 191; R., Zachers Zeitschr. iii. 404.

l. 2042. For beáh B. reads bâ, = both, i.e. Freaware and the Dane.

l. 2063. Thorkelin and Conybeare propose wîgende, = fighting, for lifigende.

l. 2068. W.'s edition begins section xxx. (not marked in the MS.) with this line. Section xxxix. (xxxviii. in copies A and B, xxxix. in Thorkelin) is not so designated in the MS., though þâ (at l. 2822) is written with capitals and xl. begins at l. 2893.

l. 2095. Cf. l. 1542, and note.

l. 2115 seq. B. restores thus:
Þær on innan gióng
niðða nâthwylc,   neóde tô gefêng
hæðnum horde;   hond ätgenam
seleful since fâh;   nê hê þät syððan âgeaf,
þeáh þe hê slæpende   besyrede hyrde
þeófes cräfte: þät se þióden onfand,
bý-folc beorna,   þät hê gebolgen wäs.
--Beit. xii. 99; Zachers Zeitschr. iv. 210.

l. 2128. ätbär here = bear away, not given in the Gloss.

l. 2129. B. proposes færunga, = suddenly, for Gr.'s reading in the text.--Beit. xii. 98.

l. 2132. MS. has þine life, which Leo translates by thy leave (= ON. leyfi); B., by thy life.--Beit. xii. 369.

l. 2150. B. renders gen, etc., by "now I serve thee alone again as my gracious king" (Beit. xii. 99).

l. 2151. The forms hafu [hafo], hafast, hafað, are poetic archaisms.--Sw.

l. 2153. Kl. proposes ealdor, = prince, for eafor. W. proposes the compd. eafor-heáfodsegn, = helm; cf. l. 1245.

l. 2157. The wk. form of the adj. is frequent in the vocative, especially when postponed: "Beowulf leófa," l. 1759. So, often, in poetry in nom.: wudu selesta, etc.

l. 2158. ærest is possibly the verbal subs. from arîsan, to arise, = arising, origin. R. suggested ærist, arising, origin. Cf. Bede, Eccles. Hist., ed. Miller, where the word is spelt as above, but = (as usual) resurrection. See Sweet, Reader, p. 211; E.-Plummer's Chronicle, p. 302, etc. The MS. has est. See Ha., p. 73; S., Beit. x. 222; and cf. l. 2166.

l. 2188. Gr., W., H. supply [wên]don, = weened, instead of Th.'s [oft säg]don.

l. 2188. The "slack" Beowulf, like the sluggish Brutus, ultimately reveals his true character, and is presented with a historic sword of honor. It is "laid on his breast" (l. 2195) as Hun laid Lâfing on Hengest's breast, l. 1145.

l. 2188. "The boy was at first slothful, and the Geats thought him an unwarlike prince, and long despised him. Then, like many a lazy third son in the folk tales, a change came, he suddenly showed wonderful daring and was passionate for adventure."-- Br., p. 22.

l. 2196. "Seven of thousands, manor and lordship" (Ha.). Kl., Beit. ix. 191, thinks with Ettm. that þúsendo means a hide of land (see Schmid, Ges. der Angl, 610), Bede's familia = 1/2 sq. meter; seofan being used (like hund, l. 2995) only for the alliteration.

l. 2196. "A vast Honour of 7000 hides, a mansion, and a judgment-seat" [throne].--E.

l. 2210. MS. has the more correct wintra.

l. 2211. Cf. similar language about the dragon at l. 100. Beowulf's "jubilee" is fitly solemnized by his third and last dragon-fight.

l. 2213. B. proposes sê þe on hearge hæðen hord beweotode; cf. Ha., p. 75.

l. 2215. "The dragon lies round the treasures in a cave, as Fafnir, like a Python, lay coiled over his hoard. So constant was this habit among the dragons that gold is called Worms' bed, Fafnir's couch, Worms' bed-fire. Even in India, the cobras ... are guardians of treasure."--Br., p. 50.

l. 2216. neóde. E. translates deftly; Ha., with ardor. H.-So. reads neóde, = with desire, greedily, instr. of neód.

l. 2223. E. begins his "Part Third" at this point as he begins "Part Second" at l. 1252, each dragon-fight forming part of a trilogy.

ll. 2224, 2225. B. proposes: nealles mid gewealdum wyrmes weard gäst sylfes willum.--Zachers Zeitschr. iv. 211; Beit. xii. 100.

l. 2225. For þeów read þegn.--K. and Z.

l. 2225. þeów, st. m., slave, serf (not in H.-So.).

l. 2227. For ofer-þearfe read ærnes þearfa.--Z.

ll. 2229-2231. B. proposes:
secg synbysig   sôna onwlâtode,
þeáh þâm gyste   gryrebrôga stôd,
hwäðre earmsceapen   innganges þearfa
. . . .
feásceapen,   þâ hyne se fær begeat.
-- Beit. xii. 101. Cf. Ha., p. 69.

l. 2232. W. suggests seah or seîr for geseah, and Gr. suggests searolîc.

l. 2233. Z. surmises eorð-hûse (for -scräfe).

l. 2241. B. proposes læn-gestreóna, = transitory, etc.; Th., R. propose leng (= longer) gestreóna; S. accepts the text but translates "the long accumulating treasure."

l. 2246. B. proposed (1) hard-fyndne, = hard to find; (2) hord-wynne dæl,--a deal of treasure-joy (cf. l. 2271).--Zachers Zeitschr. iv. 211; Beit. xii. 102.

l. 2247. fecword = banning words (?) MS. has fec.

l. 2254. Others read feor-[mie], = furbish, for fetige: I own not one who may, etc.

l. 2261. The Danes themselves were sometimes called the "Ring-Danes," = clad in ringed (or a ring of) armor, or possessing rings. Cf. ll. 116, 1280.

l. 2264. Note the early reference to hawking. Minstrelsy (hearpan wyn), saga-telling, racing, swimming, harpooning of sea-animals, feasting, and the bestowal of jewels, swords, and rings, are the other amusements most frequent in Beówulf.

l. 2264. Cf. Maldon, ll. 8, 9, for a reference to hawking.

l. 2276. Z. suggests swýðe ondrædað; Ho. puts gesêcean for Gr.'s gewunian.

l. 2277. Z. and K. read: hord on hrûsan. "Three hundred winters," at l. 2279, is probably conventional for "a long time," like hund missera, l. 1499; hund þúsenda, l. 2995; þritig (of Beowulf's strength), l. 379; þritig (of the men slain by Grendel), l. 123; seofan þúsendo, l. 2196, etc.

l. 2285. B. objects to hord as repeated in ll. 2284, 2285; but cf. Ha., p. 77. C. prefers sum to hord. onboren = inminutus; cf. B., Beit. xii. 102.

l. 2285. onberan is found also at line 991, = carry off, with on- = E. un--(un-bind, -loose, -tie, etc.), G. ent-. The negro still pronounces on-do, etc.

l. 2299. Cf. H.-So., p. 112, for a defense of the text as it stands. B. proposes "nor was there any man in that desert who rejoiced in conflict," etc. So ten Br.

l. 2326. B. and ten Br,. propose hâm, = home, for him.--Beit. xii. 103.

l. 2335. E. translates eálond utan by the sea-board front, the water-washed land on the (its) outside. See B., Beit. xii. 1, 5.

l. 2346. Cf. l. 425, where Beowulf resolves to fight the dragon single-handed. E. compares Guy of Warwick, ll. 49, 376.

l. 2355. Ten Br. proposes laðan cynne as apposition to mægum.

l. 2360. Cf. Beowulf's other swimming-feat with Breca, ll. 506 seq.

l. 2362. Gr. inserts âna, = lone-going. before xxx.: approved by B.; and Krüger, Beit. ix. 575. Cf. l. 379.

l. 2362. "Beowulf has the strength of thirty men in the original tale. Here, then, the new inventor makes him carry off thirty coats of mail."--Br., p. 48.

l. 2364. Hetware = Chattuarii, a nation allied against Hygelâc in his Frisian expedition; cf. ll. 1208 seq., 2917, etc.

l. 2368. B. proposes quiet sea as trans, of sióleða bigong, and compares Goth. anasilan, to be still; Swed. dial, sil, still water between waterfalls.--Zachers Zeitschr. iv. 214.

l. 2380. hyne--Heardrêd; so him, l. 2358.

l. 2384. E. calls attention to Swió-rîce as identical with the modern Sverige = Sweden; cf. l. 2496.

l. 2386. Gr. reads on feorme, = at the banquet; cf. Möller, Alteng. Volksepos, 111, who reads (f)or feorme. The MS. has or.

l. 2391. Cf. l. 11.

l. 2394. B., Gr., and Mûllenh. understand ll. 2393-2397 to mean that Eádgils, Ôhthere's son, driven from Sweden, returns later, supported by Beowulf, takes the life of his uncle Onela, and probably becomes himself O.'s successor and king of Sweden. For another view see H.-So., p. 115. MS. has freond (l. 2394), which Leo, etc., change to feónd. G. translates friend.--Beit. xii. 13; Anzeiger f. d. Altert. iii. 177.

l. 2395. Eádgils is Ôhthere's son; cf. l. 2381; Onela is Ôhthere's brother; cf. ll. 2933, 2617.

l. 2402. "Twelfsome"; cf. "fifteensome" at l. 207, etc. As Beówulf is essentially the Epic of Philanthropy, of the true love of man, as distinguished from the ordinary love-epic, the number twelve in this passage may be reminiscent of another Friend of Man and another Twelve. In each case all but one desert the hero.

l. 2437. R. proposes stýred, = ordered, decreed, for strêd.—Zachers Zeitschr. iii. 409.

l. 2439. B. corrects to freó-wine = noble friend, asking, "How can Herebeald be called Hæðcyn's freá-wine [MS.], lord?"

l. 2442. feohleás gefeoht, "a homicide which cannot be atoned for by money--in this case an unintentional fratricide."--Sw.

l. 2445. See Ha., pp. 82, 83, for a discussion of ll. 2445-2463. Cf. G., p. 75.

l. 2447. MS. reads wrece, justified by B. (Tidskr. viii. 56). W. conceives wrece as optative or hortative, and places a colon before þonne.

l. 2449. For helpan read helpe.--K., Th., S. (Zeitschr. f. D. Phil. xxi. 3, 357).

ll. 2454-2455. (1) Müllenh. (Haupts Zeitschr. xiv. 232) proposes:
  þonne se ân hafað
  þurh dæda nýd   deáðes gefandod.
(2) B. proposes:
  þurh dæda nîð   deáðes gefondad.
--Zachers Zeitschr. iv. 215.

l. 2458. Cf. sceótend, pl., ll. 704, 1155; like rîdend. Cf. Judith, l. 305, etc.

l. 2474. Th. considers the "wide water" here as the Mälar lake, the boundary between Swedes and Goths.

l. 2477. On oþþe = and, cf. B., Tidskr. viii. 57. See Ha., p. 83.

l. 2489. B. proposes hreá-blâc for Gr.'s heoro-.--Tikskr. viii. 297.

l. 2494. S. suggests êðel-wynne.

l. 2502. E. translates for dugeðum, of my prowess; so Ettmüller.

ll. 2520-2522. Gr. and S. translate, "if I knew how else I might combat the monster's boastfulness."--Ha., p. 85.

l. 2524. and-hâttres is H.'s invention. Gr. reads oreðes and âttres, blast and venom. Cf. oruð, l. 2558, and l. 2840 (where âttor- also occurs).

l. 2526. E. quotes fleón fôtes trym from Maldon, l. 247.

l. 2546. Gr., H.-So., and Ho. read standan stân-bogan (for stôd on stân-bogan) depending on geseah.

l. 2550. Grundt. and B. propose deór, brave one, i.e. Beowulf, for deóp.

L. 2565. MS. has ungleaw (K., Th.), unglaw (Grundt.). B. proposes unslâw, = sharp.--Beit. xii. 104. So H.-So., Ha., p. 86.

ll. 2570, 2571. (1) May not gescîfe (MS. to gscipe) = German schief, "crooked," "bent," "aslant," and hence be a parallel to gebogen, bent, coiled? cf. l. 2568, þâ se wyrm gebeáh snûde tôsomne, and l. 2828. Coiled serpents spring more powerfully for the coiling. (2) Or perhaps destroy comma after tô and read gescäpe, = his fate; cf. l. 26: him þâ Scyld gewât tô gescäp-hwîle. G. appar. adopts this reading, p. 78.

l. 2589. grund-wong = the field, not the earth (so B.); H.-So., cave, as at l. 2771. So Ha., p. 87.

l. 2595. S. proposes colon after stefne.--Beit. ix. 141.

l. 2604. Müllenh. explains leód Scylfinga in Anzeiger f. d. Altert. iii. 176-178.

l. 2607. âre = possessions, holding (Kl., Beit. ix. 192; Ha., p. 88).

l. 2609. folcrihta. Add "folk-right" to the meanings in the Gloss.; and cf. êðel-, land-riht, word-riht.

l. 2614. H.-So. reads with Gr. wræccan wineleásum Weohstân bana, = whom, a friendless exile, W. had slain.

ll. 2635-61. E. quotes Tacitus, Germania, xiv.: "turpe comitatui virtutem principis non adaequare." Beowulf had been deserted by his comitatus.

l. 2643. B. proposes ûser.--Zachers Zeitschr. iv. 216.

l. 2649. wutun; l. 3102, uton = pres. subj. pl. 1st person of wîtan, to go, used like Mod. Eng. let us + inf., Lat. eamus, Ital. andiamo, Fr. allons; M. E. (Layamon) uten. Cf. Psa. ii. 3, etc. March, A.-S. Gram., pp. 104, 196.

l. 2650. B. suggests hât for hyt,.--Beit. xii. 105.

l. 2656. fâne = fâh-ne; cf. fâra = fâh-ra, l. 578; so heánne (MS.) = heáh-ne, etc., l. 984. See Cook's Sievers' Gram.

ll. 2660, 2661. Why not read beadu-scrûd, as at l. 453, = battle-shirt? B. and R. suppose two half-verses omitted between byrdu-scrûd and bâm gemæne. B. reads býwdu, = handsome, etc. Gr. suggests unc nû, = to us two now, for ûrum; and K. and Grundt. read beón gemæne for bâm, etc. This makes sense. Cf. Ha., p. 89.

l. 2666. Cf. the dat. absolute without preposition.

l. 2681. Nägling; cf. Hrunting, Lâfing, and other famous wundor-smiða geweorc of the poem.

l. 2687. B. changes þonne into þone (rel. pro.) = which.--Beit. xii. 105.

l. 2688. B. supports the MS. reading, wundum.

l. 2688. Cf. l. 2278 for similar language.

l. 2698. B. (Beit. xii. 105) renders: "he did not heed the head of the dragon (which Beowulf with his sword had struck without effect), but he struck the dragon somewhat further down." Cf. Saxo, vi. p. 272.

l. 2698. Cf. the language used at ll. 446 and 1373, where hafelan also occurs; and hýdan.

l. 2700. hwêne; cf. Lowl. Sc. wheen, a number; Chaucer's woon, number.

l. 2702. S. proposes þâ (for þät) þät fýr, etc., = when the fire began, etc.

l. 2704. "The (hup)-seax has often been found in Saxon graves on the hip of the skeleton."--E.

l. 2707. Kl. proposes: feorh ealne wräc, = drove out all the life; cf. Gen. l. 1385.--Beit. ix. 192. S. suggests gefylde,--he felled the foe, etc.--Ibid. Parentheses seem unnecessary.

l. 2727. däg-hwîl = time allotted, lifetime.

l. 2745, 2745. Ho. removes geong from the beginning of l. 2745 and places it at the end of l. 2744.

l. 2750. R. proposes sigle searogimmas, as at l. 1158.

l. 2767. (1) B. proposes doubtfully oferhîgean or oferhîgan, = Goth, ufarhauhjan, p. p. ufarhauhids (Gr. [Greek: tuphwtheis]) = exceed in value.-- Tidskr . viii. 60. (2) Kl. proposes oferhýdian, = to make arrogant, infatuate; cf. oferhýd.--Beit. ix. 192.

l. 2770. gelocen leoðocräftum = (1) spell-bound (Th., Arnold, E.); (2) wrought with hand-craft (G.); (3) meshed, linked together (H., Ho.); cf. Elene, ll. 1251, 522.

l. 2778. B. considers bill ... ealdhlâfordes as Beowulf's short sword, with which he killed the dragon, l. 2704 (Tidskr. viii. 299). R. proposes ealdhlâforde. Müllenh. understands ealdhlâford to mean the former possessor of the hoard. W. agrees to this, but conceives ærgescôd as a compd. = ære calceatus, sheathed in brass. Ha. translates ærgescôd as vb. and adv.

l. 2791. Cf. l. 224, eoletes ät ende; landes ät ende, Exod. (Hunt).

l. 2792. MS. reads wäteres weorpan, which R. would change to wätere sweorfan.

l. 2806. "Men saw from its height the whales tumbling in the waves, and called it Whale's Ness (Hrones-næs)."--Br. p. 28. Cf. l. 3137.

l. 2815. Wîglâf was the next of kin, the last of the race, and hence the recipient of Beowulf's kingly insignia. There is a possible play on the word lâf (Wîg-lâf, ende-lâf).

l. 2818. gingeste word; cf. novissima verba, and Ger. jüngst, lately.

l. 2837. E. translates on lande, in the world, comparing on lîfe, on worulde.

l. 2840. geræsde = pret. of geræsan (omitted from the Gloss.), same as ræsan; cf. l. 2691.

l. 2859. B. proposes deáð ârædan, = determine death.--Beit. xii. 106.

l. 2861. Change geongum to geongan as a scribal error (?), but cf. Lichtenheld, Haupts Zeitschr. xvi. 353-355.

l. 2871. S. and W. propose ôwêr.--Beit. ix. 142.

l. 2873. S. punctuates: wrâðe forwurpe, þâ, etc.

l. 2874. H.-So. begins a new sentence with nealles, ending the preceding one with beget.

l. 2879. ätgifan = to render, to afford; omitted in Gloss.

ll. 2885-2892. "This passage ... equals the passage in Tacitus which describes the tie of chief to companion and companion to chief among the Germans, and which recounts the shame that fell on those who survived their lord."--Br., p. 56.

l. 2886. cyn thus has the meaning of gens or clan, just as in many Oriental towns all are of one blood. E. compares Tacitus, Germania, 7; and cf. "kith and kin."

l. 2892. Death is preferable to dishonor. Cf. Kemble, Saxons, i. 235.

l. 2901. The [Greek: angelos] begins his [Greek: angelia] here.

l. 2910. S. proposes higemêðe, sad of soul; cf. ll. 2853 and 2864 (Beit. ix. 142). B. considers higemêðum a dat. or instr. pl. of an abstract in -u (Beit. xii. 106). H. makes it a dat. pl. = for the dead. For heafod-wearde, etc., cf. note on l. 446.

l. 2920-2921. B. explains "he could not this time, as usual, give jewels to his followers."--Beit. xii. 106.

l. 2922. The Merovingian or Frankish race.

l. 2940 seq. B. conjectures:
cwäð hîe on mergenne   mêces ecgum
gêtan wolde,   sumon galgtreowu
âheáwan on holte   ond hîe âhôan on þâ
fuglum tô gamene.
--Beit. xii. 107, 372. Cf. S., Beit. ix. 143. gêtan = cause blood to be shed.

l. 2950. B. proposes gomela for gôda; "a surprising epithet for a Geat to apply to the 'terrible' Ongentheow."--Ha. p. 99. But "good" does not necessarily mean "morally excellent," as a "good" hater, a "good" fighter.

l. 2959. See H.-So. for an explanatory quotation from Paulus Diaconus, etc. B., K., and Th. read segn Higelâces, = H.'s banner uplifted began to pursue the Swede-men.--Beit. xii. 108. S. suggests sæce, = pursuit.

l. 2977. gewyrpton: this vb. is also used reflexively in Exod. (Hunt), l. 130: wyrpton hie wêrige.

l. 2989. bär is Grundt.'s reading, after the MS. "The surviving victor is the heir of the slaughtered foe."--H.-So. Cf. Hildebrands Lied, ll. 61, 62.

l. 2995. "A hundred of thousands in land and rings" (Ha., p. 100). Cf. ll. 2196, 3051. Cf. B., Beit. xii. 20, who quotes Saxo's bis senas gentes and remarks: "Hrolf Kraki, who rewards his follower, for the slaying of the foreign king, with jewels, rich lands, and his only daughter's hand, answers to the Jutish king Hygelâc, who rewards his liegeman, for the slaying of Ongentheów, with jewels, enormous estates, and his only daughter's hand."

l. 3006. H.-So. suggests Scilfingas for Scyldingas, because, at l. 2397, Beowulf kills the Scylfing Eádgils and probably acquires his lands. Thus ll. 3002, 3005, 3006, would indicate that, after Beowulf's death, the Swedes desired to shake off his hated yoke. Müllenh., however, regards l. 3006 as a thoughtless repetition of l. 2053.--Haupts Zeitschr. xiv. 239.

l. 3008. Cf. the same proverb at l. 256; and Exod. (Hunt.) l. 293.

l. 3022. E. quotes:
"Thai token an harp gle and game
And maked a lai and yaf it name."
--Weber, l. 358.
and from Percy, "The word glee, which peculiarly denoted their art (the minstrels'), continues still in our own language ... it is to this day used in a musical sense, and applied to a peculiar piece of composition."

l. 3025. "This is a finer use than usual of the common poetic attendants of a battle, the wolf, the eagle, and the raven. The three are here like three Valkyrie, talking of all that they have done."--Br., p. 57.

l. 3033. Cf. Hunt's Dan. l. 731, for similar language.

l. 3039. B. supplies a supposed gap here:
[banan eác fundon   bennum seócne
(nê) ær hî þæm   gesêgan syllîcran wiht]
wyrm on wonge...
-- Beit. xii. 372.
Cf. Ha., p. 102. W. and Ho. insert [þær] before gesêgan.

l. 3042. Cf. l. 2561, where gryre-giest occurs as an epithet of the dragon. B. proposes gry[re-fâh].

l. 3044. lyft-wynne, in the pride of the air, E.; to rejoice in the air, Ha.

l. 3057. (1) He (God) is men's hope; (2) he is the heroes' hope; (3) gehyld = the secret place of enchanters; cf. hêlsmanna gehyld, Gr.'s reading, after A.-S. hælsere, haruspex, augur.

l. 3060. B. suggests gehýðde, = plundered (i.e. by the thief), for gehýdde.

ll. 3063-3066. (1) B. suggests wundur [deáðe] hwâr þonne eorl ellenrof ende gefère = let a brave man then somewhere meet his end by wondrous venture, etc.--Zachers Zeitschr. iv. 241; cf. l. 3038. (2) S. supposes an indirect question introduced by hwâr and dependent upon wundur, = a mystery is it when it happens that the hero is to die, if he is no longer to linger among his people.--Beit. ix. 143. (3) Müllenh. suggests: is it to be wondered at that a man should die when he can no longer live?--Zachers Zeitschr. xiv. 241. (4) Possibly thus:
Wundrað hwät þonne,
eorl ellen-rôf,   ende gefère
lîf-gesceafta,   þonne leng ne mäg (etc.),
in which hwät would = þurh hwät at l. 3069, and eorl would be subject of the conjectural vb. wundrað: "the valiant earl wondereth then through what he shall attain his life's end, when he no longer may live.... So Beówulf knew not (wondered how) through what his end should come," etc. W. and Ho. join þonne to the next line. Or, for hwâr read wære: Wundur wære þonne (= gif), etc., = "would it be any wonder if a brave man," etc., which is virtually Müllenhoff's.

l. 3053. galdre bewunden, spell-bound, throws light on l. 2770, gelocen leoðo-cräftum. The "accursed" gold of legend is often dragon-guarded and placed under a spell. Even human ashes (as Shakespeare's)

Beowulf: Scholar's Edition

are thus banned. ll. 3047-3058 recall the so-called "Treasury of Atreus."

l. 3073. herh, hearh, temple, is conjectured by E. to survive in Harrow. Temple, barrow, etc., have thus been raised to proper names. Cf. Biówulfes biorh of l. 2808.

l. 3074. H.-So. has strude, = ravage, and compares l. 3127. MS. has strade. S. suggests stride, = tread.

l. 3074. H.-So. omits strâdan, = tread, stride over, from the Gloss., referring ll. 3174 and 3074 to strûdan, q. v.

l. 3075. S. proposes: næs hê goldhwätes gearwor häfde, etc., = Beowulf had not before seen the greedy possessor's favor.--Beit. ix. 143. B. reads, goldhwäte gearwor häfde, etc., making goldhwäte modify êst, = golden favor; but see Beit. xii. 373, for B.'s later view.

l. 3086-3087. B. translates, "that which (i.e. the treasure) drew the king thither was granted indeed, but it overwhelmed us."--Beit. xii. 109.

l. 3097. B. and S. propose äfter wine deádum, = in memory of the dead friend.--Beit. ix. 144.

l. 3106. The brâd gold here possibly includes the iú-monna gold of l. 3053 and the wunden gold of l. 3135. E. translates brâd by bullion.

l. 3114. B. supposes folc-âgende to be dat. sg. to gôdum, referring to Beowulf.

l. 3116. C. considers weaxan, = Lat. vescor, to devour, as a parallel to fretan, and discards parentheses.--Beit. viii. 573.

l. 3120. fûs = furnished with; a meaning which must be added to those in the Gloss.

ll. 3124-3125. S. proposes:
eóde eahta sum   under inwit-hrôf
hilderinca: sum on handa bär, etc.
--Beit. ix. 144.

l. 3136. H.-So. corrects (after B.) to äðeling c, the MS. having e.

l. 3145. "It was their [the Icelanders'] belief that the higher the smoke rose in the air the more glorious would the burnt man be in heaven."-- Ynglinga Saga, 10 (quoted by E.). Cf. the funeral pyre of Herakles.

l. 3146-3147. B. conjectures:
... swôgende lêc
wôpe bewunden   windblonda lêg
(lêc from lâcan, see Gloss.).--Beit. xii. 110. Why not windblonda lâc?

l. 3147. Müllenhoff rejected wind-blond geläg because a great fire raises rather than "lays" the wind; hence B., as above, = "swoughing sported the flame wound with the howling of wind-currents."

l. 3151 seq. B. restores conjecturally:
swylce giômor-gyd   sio geó-meowle
[äfter Beówulfe]   bunden-heorde
[song] sorg-cearig,   sæde geneahhe,
þät hió hyre [hearm-]dagas   hearde on [dr]êde,
wälfylla worn,   [w]îgendes egesan,
hý[n]ðo ond häftnýd,   heóf on rîce wealg.
--Beit. xii. 100.

Here geó-meowle = old woman or widow; bunden-heorde = with bound locks; heóf = lamentation; cf. l. 3143. on rîce wealg is less preferable than the MS. reading, heofon rêce swealg = heaven swallowed the smoke.-- H.-So. B. thinks Beowulf's widow (geómeowle) was probably Hygd; cf. ll. 2370, 3017-3021.

l. 3162. H.-So. reads (with MS.) bronda be lâfe, for betost, and omits colon after bêcn. So B., Zachers Zeitschr. iv. 224.

l. 3171. E. quotes Gibbon's accounts of the burial of Attila when the "chosen squadrons of the Hun, wheeling round in measured evolutions, chanted a funeral song to the memory of a hero."

ll. 3173-3174. B. proposes:
woldon gên cwîðan   [ond] kyning
wordgyd wrecan   ond ymb wel sprecan.
-- Beit. xii. 112.

l. 3183. Z., K., Th. read manna for mannum.

l. 3184. "It is the English ideal of a hero as it was conceived by an Englishman some twelve hundred years ago."--Br., p. 18.

NOTES TO THE FIGHT AT FINNSBURG.

The original MS. of this fragment has vanished, but a copy had been made and printed by Hickes in his Thesaurus Linguarum Septentrionalium, i. 192. The original was written on a single sheet attached to a codex of homilies in the Lambeth Library. Möller, Alteng. Epos, p. 65, places the fragment in the Finn episode, between ll. 1146 and 1147. Bugge (Beit. xii. 20) makes it illustrate the conflict in which Hnäf fell, i.e. as described in Beówulf as antecedent to the events there given. Heinzel (Anzeiger f. d. Altert.), however, calls attention to the fact that Hengest in the fragment is called cyning, whereas in Beówulf, l. 1086, he is called þegn. See H.-So., p. 125.

"The Fight at Finnsburg and the lays from which our Beówulf was composed were, as it seems to me, sung among the English who dwelt in the north of Denmark and the south of Sweden, and whose tribal name was the Jutes or Goths."--Br., p. 101.

l. 1. R. supposes [hor]nas, and conjectures such an introductory conversation as follows: "Is it dawning in the east, or is a fiery dragon flying about, or are the turrets of some castle burning?" questions which the king negatives in the same order. Then comes the positive declaration, "rather they are warriors marching whose armor gleams in the moonlight." --Alt- und Angels. Lesebuch, 1861. Heinzel and B. conjecture, [beorhtor hor]nas byrnað næfre. So. G.--Beit. xii. 22; Anzeiger f. d. Altert. x. 229.

l. 5. B. conjectures fugelas to mean arrows, and supplies:

    ac hêr forð berað   [fyrdsearu rincas,
    flacre flânbogan],   fugelas singað.

He compares Saxo, p. 95, cristatis galeis hastisque sonantibus instant, as explanatory of l. 6.--Beit. xii. 22. But see Brooke, Early Eng. Literature, who supposes fugelas = raven and eagle, while græg-hama is = wulf (the "grey-coated one"), the ordinary accompaniers of battle.

l. 11. hicgeað, etc.: cf. Maldon, l. 5; Exod. l. 218.

l. 15. Cf. B. (Beit. xii. 25), etc., and Saxo, p. 101, for l. 13.

ll. 18-21. H.-So. remarks: "If, according to Möller and Bugge, Gârulf is one of the attackers, one of Finn's men, this does not harmonize with his character as Gûðlâf's son (l. 33), who (l. 16, and Beówulf, l. 1149) is a Dane, therefore one of Finn's antagonists." B. (Beit. xii. 25) conjectures:

    þâ gyt Gûðdene   Gârulf styrode,
    þät hê swâ freólîc feorh   forman sîðe
    tô þære healle durum   hyrsta ne bære,
    nû hîe nîða heard   ânyman wolde;

in which Gûðdene is the same as Sigeferð, l. 24; hê (l. 22) refers to Gârulf; and hîe (l. 21) to hyrsta.

l. 27. swäðer = either (bad or good, life or death).--H.-So.

l. 29. cêlod: meaning doubtful; cf. Maldon , l. 283. G. renders "curved board"; Sw. suggests "round"? "hollow"?

l. 30. B. suggests bâr-helm, = boar-helm. Cf. Saxo, p. 96.-- Beit. xii. 26.

l. 34. B. conjectures: (1) hwearf flacra hræw hräfen, wandrode; (2) hwearf flacra hræw hräfen fram ôðrum = flew from one corpse to another .-- Beit. xii. 27.

l. 43. B. supposes wund häleð to be a Dane, folces hyrde to be Hnäf, in opposition to Holtzmann (Germania , viii. 494), who supposes the wounded man to be a Frisian, and folces hyrde to be their king, Finn.-- Beit. xii. 28.

l. 45. B. adopts Th.'s reading heresceorp unhrôr = equipments useless .-- Beit. xii. 28.

l. 47. "Though wounded, they had retained their strength and activity in battle."-- B., Beit. xii. 28.

ADDENDA.

ll. 105 and 218. MS. and Ho. read wonsæli and fâmi-heals.

ll. 143, 183, 186, etc. Read þæm for þäm.

l. 299. MS. reads gôd-fremmendra. So H.-So.

l. 338. Ho. marks wräc- and its group long.

l. 530. Hwät should here probably be printed as an interj., hwät! Cf. ll. 1, 943, 2249.

l. 2263. Koeppel suggests nis for näs.

The editors are much indebted to E. Koeppel (in Eng. Stud. xiii. 3) for numerous corrections in text and glossary.

l. 3070. H.-So. begins a new line with swâ.

GLOSSARY

A

ac, conj. denoting contrariety: hence 1) but (like N.H.G. sondern), 109, 135, 339, etc.--2) but (N.H.G. aber), nevertheless , 602, 697, etc.--3) in direct questions: nonne, numquid, 1991.

aglæca, ahlæca, äglæca, -cea, w. m. (cf. Goth, aglo, trouble , O.N. agi, terror , + lâc, gift, sport: = misery, vexation, = bringer of trouble ; hence): 1) evil spirit, demon, a demon-like being ; of Grendel, 159, 433, 593, etc.; of the drake, 2535, 2906, etc.--2) great hero, mighty warrior ; of Sigemund, 894; of Beówulf: gen. sg. aglæcan(?), 1513; of Beówulf and the drake: nom. pl. þâ aglæcean, 2593.

aglæc-wîf, st. n., demon, devil, in the form of a woman ; of Grendel's mother, 1260.

aldor. See ealdor.

al-wealda. See eal-w.

am-biht (from and-b., Goth, and-baht-s), st. m., servant, man-servant : nom. sg. ombeht, of the coast-guard, 287; ombiht, of Wulfgâr, 336.

ambiht-þegn (from ambiht n. officium and þegn, which see), servant, man-servant : dat. sg. ombiht-þegne, of Beówulf's servant, 674.

an, prep, with the dat., on, in, with respect to , 678; with, among, at, upon (position after the governed word), 1936; with the acc., 1248. Elsewhere on, which see.

ancor, st. m., anchor : dat. sg. ancre, 303, 1884.

ancor-bend, m. (?) f. (?), anchor-cable : dat. pl. oncer-bendum, 1919.

and, conj. (ond is usual form; for example, 601, 1149, 2041), and 33, 39, 40, etc. (See Appendix.)

anda, w. m., excitement, vexation, horror : dat. wrâðum on andan, 709, 2315.

and-git, st. n., insight, understanding : nom. sg., 1060. See gitan.

and-hâtor, st. m. n., heat coming against one : gen. sg. rêðes and-hâttres, 2524.

and-lang, -long, adj., very long. hence 1) at whole length, raised up high : acc. andlongne eorl, 2696 (cf. Bugge upon this point, Zachers Ztschr., 4, 217).--2) continual, entire ; andlangne däg, 2116, the whole day ; andlonge niht, 2939.

and-leán, st. n., reward, payment in full : acc. sg., 1542, 2095 (hand-, hond-lean, MS.).

and-risno, st. f. (see rîsan, surgere, decere), that which is to be observed, that which is proper, etiquette : dat. pl. for andrysnum, according to etiquette , 1797.

and-saca, w. m., adversary : godes andsaca (Grendel), 787, 1683.

and-slyht, st. m., blow in return : acc. sg., 2930, 2973 (MS. both times hond-slyht).

and-swaru, st. f., act of accosting : 1) to persons coming up, an address , 2861.--2) in reply to something said, an answer , 354, 1494, 1841.

and-weard, adj., present, existing : acc. sg. n. swîn ofer helme and-weard (the image of the boar, which stands on his helm), 1288.

and-wlita, w. m., countenance : acc. sg. -an, 690.

an-sund, adj., entirely unharmed : nom. sg. m., 1001.

an-sýn, f., the state of being seen : hence 1) the exterior, the form , 251: ansýn ýwde, showed his form , i.e. appeared, 2835.--2) aspect, appearance , 929; on-sýn, 2773.

an-walda, w. m., He who rules over all, God , 1273. See Note.

atol, adj. (also eatol, 2075, etc.), hostile, frightful, cruel : of Grendel, 159, 165, 593, 2075, etc.; of Grendel's mother's hands (dat. pl. atolan), 1503; of the undulation of the waves, 849; of battle, 597, 2479.--cf. O.N. atall, fortis, strenuus.

atelîc, adj., terrible, dreadful : atelîc egesa, 785.

Â

â, adv. (Goth, áiv, acc. from aiv-s aevum), ever, always , 455, 882, 931, 1479: â syððan, ever afterwards, ever, ever after , 283, 2921.-- ever , 780.--Comp. nâ.

âd st. m. funeral pile : acc. sg. âd, 3139; dat. sg. âde, 1111, 1115.

âd-faru, st. f., way to the funeral pile , dat. sg. on âd-färe, 3011.

âdl, st. f. sickness , 1737, 1764, 1849.

âð, st. m., oath in general , 2740; oath of allegiance , 472 (?); oath of reconciliation of two warring peoples , 1098, 1108.

âð-sweord, st. n., the solemn taking of an oath, the swearing of an oath : nom. pl., 2065. See sweord.

âðum-swerian, m. pl., son-in-law and father-in-law : dat. pl., 84.

âgan, verb, pret. and pres., to have, to possess , w. acc.: III. prs. sg. âh, 1728; inf. âgan, 1089; prt. âhte, 487, 522, 533; with object, geweald, to be supplied, 31. Form contracted with the negative: prs. sg. I. nâh hwâ sweord wege (I have no one to wield the sword), 2253.

âgen, adj., own, peculiar , 2677.

âgend (prs. part. of âgan), possessor, owner, lord : gen. sg. âgendes, of God , 3076.--Compounds: blæd-, bold-, folc-, mägen-âgend.

âgend-freá, w. m., owner, lord : gen. sg. âgend-freán, 1884.

âhsian, ge-âhsian, w. v.: 1) to examine, to find out by inquiring : pret. part. ge-âhsod, 433.--2) to experience, to endure : pret. âhsode, 1207; pl. âhsodon, 423.

âht, st. n. (contracted from â-wiht, which see), something, anything : âht cwices, 2315.

ân, num. The meaning of this word betrays its apparent demonstrative character: 1) this, that , 2411, of the hall in the earth mentioned before; similarly, 100 (of Grendel; already mentioned), cf. also 2775.--2) one , a particular one among many, a single one, in numerical sense: ymb âne niht (the next night), 135; þurh ânes cräft, 700; þâra ânum, 1038; ân äfter ânum, one for the other (Hrêðel for Herebeald), 2462: similarly, ân äfter eallum, 2269; ânes hwät, some single thing, a part , 3011; se ân leóda duguðe, the one of the heroes of the people , 2238; ânes willan, for the sake of a single one , 3078, etc.--Hence, again, 3) alone, distinguished , 1459, 1886.--4) a , in the sense of an indefinite article: ân ... feónd, 100; gen. sg. ânre bêne (or to No.2[?]), 428; ân ... draca, 2211--5) gen. pl. ânra, in connection with a pronoun, single ; ânra gehwylces, every single one , 733; ânra gehwylcum, 785. Similarly, the dat. pl. in this sense: nemne feáum ânum, except a few single ones , 1082.--6) solus, alone : in the strong form, 1378, 2965; in the weak form, 145, 425, 431, 889, etc.; with the gen., âna Geáta duguðe, alone of the warriors of the Geátas , 2658.--7) solitarius, alone, lonely , see æn.--Comp. nân.

ân-feald, adj., simple, plain, without reserve : acc. sg. ânfealdne geþôht, simple opinion , 256.

ân-genga, -gengea, w. m., he who goes alone , of Grendel, 165, 449.

ân-haga, w. m., he who stands alone , solitarius, 2369.

ân-hydig, adj. (like the O.N. ein-râd-r, of one resolve , i.e. of firm resolve), of one opinion , i.e. firm, brave, decided, 2668.

ânga, adj. (only in the weak form), single, only : acc. sg. ângan dôhtor, 375, 2998; ângan eaferan, 1548; dat. sg. ângan brêðer, 1263.

ân-päð, st. m., lonely way, path : acc. pl. ânpaðas, 1411.

ân-ræd, adj. (cf. under ân-hydig), of firm resolution, resolved , 1530, 1576.

ân-tîd, st. f., one time , i.e. the same time, ymb ân-tîd ôðres dôgores, about the same time the second day (they sailed twenty-four hours), 219.--ân stands as in ân-mod, O.H.G. ein-muoti, harmonious, of the same disposition .

ânunga, adv., throughout, entirely, wholly , 635.

âr, st. m., ambassador, messenger , 336, 2784.

âr, st. f., 1) honor, dignity : ârum healdan, to hold in honor , 296; similarly, 1100, 1183.--2) favor, grace, support : acc. sg. âre, 1273, 2607; dat. sg. âre, 2379; gen. pl. hwät ... ârna, 1188.--Comp. worold-âr; also written ær.

âr-fäst, adj., honorable, upright , 1169; of Hûnferð (with reference to 588). See fäst.

ârian, w. v., (to be gracious), to spare : III. sg. prs. w. dat. nænegum ârað; of Grendel, 599.

âr-stäf, st. m.,(elementum honoris), grace, favor : dat. pl. mid ârstafum, 317.-- Help, support : dat. pl. for âr-stafum, to the assistance , 382, 458. See stäf.

âter-teár, m., poisonous drop : dat. pl. îren âter-teárum fâh (steel which is dipped in poison or in poisonous sap of plants), 1460.

âttor, st. n., poison , here of the poison of the dragon's bite: nom., 2716.

âttor-sceaða, w. m., poisonous enemy, of the poisonous dragon : gen. sg. -sceaðan, 2840.

âwâ, adv. (certainly not the dative, but a reduplicated form of â, which see), ever : âwâ tô aldre, fôr ever and ever , 956.

Ä

ädre, adv., hastily, directly, immediately , 77, 354, 3107. [ædre.]

äðele, adj., noble : nom. sg., of Beówulf, 198, 1313; of Beówulf's father, 263, where it can be understood as well in a moral as in a genealogical sense; the latter prevails decidedly in the gen. sg. äðelan cynnes, 2235.

äðeling, st. m., nobleman, man of noble descent , especially the appellation of a man of royal birth; so of the kings of the Danes, 3; of Scyld, 33; of Hrôðgâr, 130; of Sigemund, 889; of Beówulf, 1226, 1245, 1597, 1816, 2189, 2343, 2375, 2425, 2716, 3136; perhaps also of Däghrefn, 2507;--then, in a broader sense, also denoting other noble-born men: Äschere, 1295; Hrôðgâr's courtiers, 118, 983; Heremôd's courtiers, 907; Hengest's warriors, 1113; Beówulf's retinue, 1805, 1921, 3172; noble-born in general, 2889. --Comp. sib-äðeling.

äðelu, st. n., only in the pl., noble descent, nobility , in the sense of noble lineage: acc. pl. äðelu, 392; dat. pl. cyning äðelum gôd, the king, of noble birth , 1871; äðelum dióre, worthy on account of noble lineage , 1950; äðelum (hæleþum, MS.), 332.--Comp. fäder-äðelu.

äfnan, w. v. w. acc., to perform, to carry out, to accomplish : inf. ellen-weorc äfnan, to do a heroic deed , 1465; pret. unriht äfnde, perpetrated wrong , 1255.

ge-äfnan, 1) to carry out, to do, to accomplish : pret. pl. þät geäfndon swâ, so carried that out, 538; pret. part. âð wäs geäfned, the oath was sworn, 1108.--2) get ready, prepare : pret. part. geäfned, 3107. See efnan.

äfter (comparative of af, Ags. of, which see; hence it expresses the idea of forth, away, from, back), a) adv., thereupon, afterwards, 12, 341, 1390, 2155.--ic him äfter sceal, I shall go after them, 2817; in word äfter cwäd, 315, the sense seems to be, spoke back, having turned ; b) prep. w. dat., 1) (temporal) after, 119, 128, 187, 825, 1939, etc.; äfter beorne, after the (death of) the hero, 2261, so 2262; äfter mâððum-welan, after (obtaining) the treasure, 2751.--2) (causal) as proceeding from something, denoting result and purpose, hence, in consequence of, conformably to : äfter rihte, in accordance with right, 1050, 2111; äfter faroðe, with the current, 580; so 1321, 1721, 1944, 2180, etc., äfter heaðo-swâte, in consequence of the blood of battle, 1607; äfter wälnîðe, in consequence of mortal enmity, 85; in accordance with, on account of, after, about : äfter äðelum (hæleþum, MS.) frägn, asked about the descent, 332; ne frin þu äfter sælum, ask not after my welfare, 1323; äfter sincgyfan greóteð, weeps for the giver of treasure, 1343; him äfter deórum men dyrne langað, longs in secret for the dear man, 1880; ân äfter ânum, one for the other, 2462, etc.--3) (local), along : äfter gumcynnum, throughout the races of men, among men, 945; sôhte bed äfter bûrum, sought a bed among the rooms of the castle (the castle was fortified, the hall was not), 140; äfter recede wlât, looked along the hall, 1573; stone äfter stâne, smelt along the rocks, 2289; äfter lyfte, along the air through the air, 2833; similarly, 996, 1068, 1317, etc.

äf-þunca, w. m., anger, chagrin, vexatious affair : nom., 502.

äglæcea. See aglæcea.

äled (Old Sax. eld, O.N. edl-r), st. m., fire, 3016. [æled.]

äled-leóma, w. m., (fire-light), torch : acc. sg. leóman, 3126. See leóma.

äl-fylce (from äl-, Goth. ali-s, [Greek: allos], and fylce, O.N. fylki, collective form from folc), st. n., other folk, hostile army : dat. pl. wið älfylcum, 2372.

äl-mihtig (for eal-m.), adj., almighty : nom. sg. m., of the weak form, se älmihtiga, 92.

äl-wiht, st. m., being of another species, monster : gen. pl. äl-wihta eard, of the dwelling-place of Grendel's kindred, 1501.

äppel-fealu, adj., dappled sorrel, or apple-yellow : nom. pl. äppel-fealuwe mearas, apple-yellow steeds, 2166.

ärn, st. n., house, in the compounds heal-, hord-, medo-, þryð-, win-ärn.

äsc, st. m., ash (does not occur in Beówulf in this sense), lance, spear, because the shaft consists of ash wood: dat. pl. (quâ instr.) äscum and ecgum, with spears and swords, 1773.

äsc-holt, st. n., ash wood, ashen shaft : nom. pl. äsc-holt ufan græg, the ashen shafts gray above (spears with iron points), 330.

äsc-wîga, w. m., spear-fighter, warrior armed with the spear : nom. sg., 2043.

ät, prep. w. dat., with the fundamental meaning of nearness to something, hence 1) local, a) with, near, at, on, in (rest): ät hýðe, in harbor, 32; ät symle, at the meal, 81, ät âde, on the funeral-pile, 1111, 1115; ät þe ânum, with thee alone, 1378; ät wîge, in the fight, 1338; ät hilde, 1660, 2682; ät æte, in eating, 3027, etc. b) to, towards, at, on (motion to): deáðes wylm hrân ät heortan, seized upon the heart, 2271; gehêton ät härgtrafum, vowed at (or to) the temples of the gods, 175. c) with verbs of taking away, away from (as starting from near an object): geþeah þät ful ät Wealhþeón, took the cup from W., 630; fela ic gebâd grynna ät Grendle, from Grendel, 931; ät mînum fäder genam, took me from my father to himself, 2430.--2) temporal, at, in, at the time of : ät frumsceafte, in the beginning, 45; ät ende, at an end, 224; fand sînne dryhten ealdres ät ende, at the end of life, dying, 2791; similarly, 2823; ät feohgyftum, in giving gifts, 1090; ät sîðestan, finally, 3014.

ät-græpe, adj., laying hold of, prehendens, 1270.

ät-rihte, adv., almost, 1658.

Æ

ædre, êdre, st. f., aqueduct, canal (not in Beów.), vein (not in Beów.), stream, violent pouring forth : dat. pl. swât ædrum sprong, the blood sprang in streams, 2967; blôd êdrum dranc, drank the blood in streams (?), 743.

æðm, st. m., breath, gasp, snort : instr. sg. hreðer æðme weóll, the breast (of the drake) heaved with snorting, 2594.

æfen, st. m., evening, 1236.

æfen-gram, adj., hostile at evening, night-enemy : nom. sg. m. æfen-grom, of Grendel, 2075.

æfen-leóht, st. n., evening-light : nom. sg., 413.

æfen-räst, st. f., evening-rest : acc. sg. -räste, 647, 1253.

æfen-spræc, st. f., evening-talk : acc. sg. gemunde ...æfen-spræce, thought about what he had spoken in the evening, 760.

æfre, adv., ever, at any time, 70, 280, 504, 693, etc.: in negative sentences, æfre ne, never, 2601.--Comp. næfre.

æg-hwâ (O.H.G. êo-ga-hwër), pron., every, each : dat. sg. æghwæm, 1385. The gen. sg. in adverbial sense, in all, throughout, thoroughly : æghwäs untæle, thoroughly blameless, 1866; æghwäs unrîm, entirely innumerable quantity, i.e. an enormous multitude, 2625, 3136.

æg-hwäðer (O.H.G. êo-ga-hwëdar): 1) each (of two): nom. sg. häfde æghwäðer ende gefêred, each of the two (Beówulf and the drake) had reached the end, 2845; dat. sg. æghwäðrum wäs brôga fram ôðrum, to each of the two (Beówulf and the drake) was fear of the other, 2565; gen. sg. æghwäðres ... worda and worca, 287.--2) each (of several): dat. sg. heora æghwäðrum, 1637.

æg-hwær, adv., everywhere, 1060.

æg-hwilc (O.H.G. êo-gi-hwëlih), pron., unusquisque, every (one): 1) used as an adj.: acc. sg. m. dæl æghwylcne, 622.--2) as substantive, a) with the partitive genitive: nom. sg. æg-hwylc, 9, 2888; dat. sg. æghwylcum, 1051. b) without gen.: nom. sg. æghwylc, 985, 988; (wäs) æghwylc ôðrum trýwe, each one (of two) true to the other, 1166.

æg-weard, st. f., watch on the sea shore : acc. sg. æg-wearde, 241.

æht (abstract form from âgan, denoting the state of possessing), st. f.: 1) possession, power : acc. sg. on flôdes æht, 42; on wäteres æht, into the power of the water, 516; on æht gehwearf Denigea freán, passed over into the possession of a Danish master, 1680.--2) property, possessions, goods : acc. pl. æhte, 2249.--Comp. mâðm-, gold-æht.

æht (O.H.G. âhta), st. f., pursuit : nom. þâ wäs æht boden Sweona leódum, segn Higelâce, then was pursuit offered to the people of the Sweonas, (their) banner to Hygelâc (i.e. the banner of the Swedes, taken during their flight, fell into the hands of Hygelâc), 2958.

ge-æhtan, w. v., to prize, to speak in praise of : pret. part. geæhted, 1866. [geähtan.]

ge-æhtla, w. m., or ge-æhtle, w. f., a speaking of with praise, high esteem : gen. sg. hy ... wyrðe þinceað eorla geæhtlan, seem worthy of the high esteem of the noble-born , 369. [geähtla.]

æn (oblique form of ân), num., one : acc. sg. m. þone ænne þone..., the one whom ..., 1054; oftor micle þonne on ænne sîð, much oftener than one time , 1580; forð onsendon ænne, sent him forth alone , 46.

æne, adv., once : oft nalles æne, 3020.

ænig, pron., one, any one , 474, 503, 510, 534, etc.: instr. sg. nolde ... 0nige þinga, would in no way, not at all , 792; lyt ænig mearn, little did any one sorrow (i.e. no one), 3130.--With the article: näs se folccyning ... ænig, no people's king , 2735.--Comp. nænig.

æn-lîc, adj., alone, excellent, distinguished : ænlîc ansýn, distinguished appearance , 251; þeáh þe hió ænlîcu sý, though she be beautiful , 1942.

ær (comparative form, from â): 1) adv., sooner, before, beforehand , 15, 656, 695, 758, etc., for a long time , 2596; eft swâ ær, again as formerly , 643; ær ne siððan, neither sooner nor later , 719; ær and sîð, sooner and later (all times), 2501; nô þý ær (not so much the sooner), yet not , 755, 1503, 2082, 2161, 2467.-- 2) conjunct., before, ere : a) with the ind.: ær hió tô setle geóng, 2020. b) w. subjunc.: ær ge fyr fêran, before you travel farther , 252; ær he on hwurfe 164, so 677, 2819; ær þon däg cwôme, ere the day break , 732; ær correlative to ær adv.: ær he feorh seleð, aldor an ôfre, ær he wille ..., he will sooner (rather) leave his life upon the shore, before (than) he will ..., 1372.--3) prepos. with dat., before ær deáðe, before death , 1389; ær däges hwîle, before daybreak , 2321; ær swylt-däge, before the day of death , 2799.

æror, comp. adv., sooner, before-hand , 810; formerly , 2655.

ærra, comp. adj., earlier ; instr. pl., ærran mælum, in former times , 908, 2238, 3036.

ærest, supcrl.: 1) adv., first of all, foremost , 6, 617, 1698, etc.--2) as subst. n., relation to, the beginning : acc. þät ic his ærest þe eft gesägde (to tell thee in what relation it stood at first to the coat of mail that has been presented), 2158. See Note.

ær-däg, st. m. (before-day), morning-twilight, gray of morning : dat. sg. mid ærdäge, 126; samod ærdäge, 1312, 2943.

ærende, st. n., errand, trust : acc. sg., 270, 345.

ær-fäder, st. m., late father, deceased father : nom sg. swâ his ærfäder, 2623.

ær-gestreón, st. n., old treasure, possessions dating from old times : acc sg., 1758; gen. sg. swylcra fela ærgestreóna, much of such old treasure , 2233. See gestreón.

ær-geweorc, st. n., work dating from old times : nom. sg. enta ær-geweorc, the old work of the giants (of the golden sword-hilt from Grendel's water-hall), 1680. See geweorc.

ær-gôd, adj., good since old times, long invested with dignity or advantages : äðeling ærgôd, 130; (eorl) ærgôd, 1330; îren ærgôd (excellent sword), 990, 2587.

ær-wela, w. m., old possessions, riches dating from old times : acc. sg. ærwelan, 2748. See wela.

æs, st. n., carcass, carrion : dat. (instr.) sg. æse, of Äschere's corpse, 1333.

æt, st. m., food, meat : dat, sg., hû him ät æte speów, how he fared well at meat , 3027.

ættren (see âttor), adj., poisonous : wäs þät blôd tô þäs hât, ættren ellorgâst, se ær inne swealt, so hot was the blood, (and) poisonous the demon (Grendel's mother) who died therein , 1618

B

bana, bona, w. m., murderer , 158, 588, 1103, etc.: acc. sg. bonan Ongenþeówes, of Hygelâc, although in reality his men slew Ongenþeów (2965 ff.), 1969. Figuratively of inanimate objects: ne wäs ecg bona, 2507; wearð wracu Weohstânes bana, 2614.--Comp.: ecg-, feorh-, gâst-, hand-, mûð-bana.

bon-gâr, st. m. murdering spear , 2032.

ge-bannan, st. v. w. acc. of the thing and dat. of the person, to command, to bid : inf., 74.

bâd, st. f., pledge , only in comp.: nýd-bâd.

bân, st. n., bone : dat. sg. on bâne (on the bony skin of the drake), 2579; dat. pl. heals ealne ymbefêng biteran bânum (here of the teeth of the drake), 2693.

bân-côfa, w. m., "cubile ossium" (Grimm) of the body: dat. sg. -côfan, 1446.

bân-fâg, adj., variegated with bones , either with ornaments made of bone-work, or adorned with bone, perhaps deer-antlers; of Hrôðgâr's hall, 781. The last meaning seems the more probable.

bân-fät, st. n., bone-vessel , i.e. the body: acc. pl. bân-fatu, 1117.

bân-hring, st. m., the bone-structure, joint, bone-joint : acc. pl. hire wið halse ... bânhringas bräc (broke her neck-joint), 1568.

bân-hûs, st. n., bone-house , i.e. the body: acc. sg. bânhûs gebräc, 2509; similarly, 3148.

bân-loca, w. m., the enclosure of the bones , i.e. the body: acc. sg. bât bânlocan, bit the body , 743; nom. pl. burston bânlocan, the body burst (of Grendel, because his arm was torn out), 819.

bât, st. m., boat, craft, ship , 211.--Comp. sæ-bât.

bât-weard, st. m., boat-watcher, he who keeps watch over the craft. dat. sg. -wearde, 1901.

bäð, st. n., bath : acc. sg. ofer ganotes bäð, over the diver's bath (i.e. the sea), 1862.

bärnan, w. v., to cause to burn, to burn : inf. hêt ... bânfatu bärnan, bade that the bodies be burned , 1117; ongan ... beorht hofu bärnan, began to consume the splendid country-seats (the dragon), 2314.

for-bärnan, w. v., consume with fire : inf. hy hine ne môston ... brondefor-bärnan, they (the Danes) could not burn him (the dead Äschere) upon the funeral-pile , 2127.

bædan (Goth, baidjan, O.N. beðia), to incite, to encourage : pret. bædde byre geonge, encouraged the youths (at the banquet), 2019.

ge-bædan, w. v., to press hard : pret. part. bysigum gebæded, distressed by trouble, difficulty, danger (of battle), 2581; to drive, to send forth : stræla storm strengum gebæded, the storm of arrows sent with strength , 3118; overcome : draca ... bealwe gebæded, the dragon ... overcome by the ills of battle , 2827.

bæl (O.N. bâl), st. n., fire, flames : (wyrm) mid bæle fôr, passed (through the air) with fire , 2309; häfde landwara lîge befangan, bæle and bronde, with fire and burning , 2323.--Especially, the fire of the funeral-pile, the funeral-pile , 1110, 1117, 2127; ær he bæl cure, ere he sought the burning (i.e. died), 2819; hâtað ...

hlæw gewyrcean ... äfter bæle, after I am burned, let a burial mound be thrown up (Beówulf's words), 2804.

    bæl-fýr, st. n., bale-fire, fire of the funeral-pile : gen. pl. bælfýra mæst, 3144.

    bæl-stede, st. m., place for the funeral-pile : dat. sg. in bæl=stede, 3098.

    bæl-wudu, st. m., wood for the funeral-pile , 3113.

    bær, st. f., bier , 3106.

    ge-bæran, w. v., to conduct one's self, behave : inf. w. adv., ne gefrägen ic þâ mægðe ... sêl gebæran, I did not hear that a troop bore itself better, maintained a nobler deportment , 1013; he on eorðan geseah þone leófestan lîfes ät ende bleáte gebæran, saw the best-beloved upon the earth, at the end of his life, struggling miserably (i.e. in a helpless situation), 2825.

    ge-bætan (denominative from bæte, the bit), w. v., to place the bit in the mouth of an animal, to bridle : pret. part. þâ wäs Hrôðgâre hors gebæted, 1400.

    be, prep. w. dat. (with the fundamental meaning near , "but not of one direction, as ät, but more general"): 1) local, near by, near, at, on (rest): be ýdlâfe uppe lægon, lay above, upon the deposit of the waves (upon the strand, of the slain nixies), 566; häfde be honda, held by the hand (Beówulf held Grendel), 815; be sæm tweonum, in the circuit of both the seas , 859, 1686; be mäste, on the mast , 1906; by fýre, by the fire , 2220; be nässe, at the promontory , 2244; sät be þæm gebrôðrum twæm, sat by the two brothers , 1192; wäs se gryre lässa efne swâ micle swâ bið mägða cräft be wæpnedmen, the terror was just so much less, as is the strength of woman to the warrior (i.e. is valued by), 1285, etc.--2) also local, but of motion from the subject in the direction of the object, on, upon, by : gefêng be eaxle, seized by the shoulder , 1538; âlêdon leófne þeóden be mäste, laid the dear lord near the mast , 36; be healse genam, took him by the neck, fell upon his neck , 1873; wæpen hafenade be hiltum, grasped the weapon by the hilt , 1757, etc.--3) with this is connected the causal force, on account of, for, according to : ic þis gid be þe âwräc, I spake this solemn speech for thee, for thy sake , 1724; þû þe lær be þon, learn according to this, from this , 1723; be fäder lâre, according to her father's direction , 1951.--4) temporal, while, during : be þe lifigendum, while thou livest, during thy life , 2666. See bî.

    bed, st. n., bed, couch : acc. sg. bed, 140, 677; gen. sg. beddes, 1792; dat. pl. beddum, 1241.--Comp: deað-, hlin-, läger-, morðor-, wäl-bed.

    ge-bedde, w. f., bed-fellow : dat. sg. wolde sêcan ewên tô gebeddan, wished to seek the queen as bed-fellow, to go to bed with her , 666.--Comp. heals-gebedde.

    begen, fem. bâ, both : nom. m., 536, 770, 2708; acc. fem. on bâ healfa, on two sides (i.e. Grendel and his mother), 1306; dat. m. bâm, 2197; and in connection with the possessive instead of the personal pronouen, ûrum bâm, 2661; gen. n. bega, 1874, 2896; bega gehwäðres, each one of the two , 1044; bega folces, of both peoples , 1125.

    ge-belgan, st. v. (properly, to cause to swell, to swell), to irritate : w. dat. (pret. subj.) þät he êcean dryhtne bitre gebulge, that he had bitterly angered the eternal Lord , 2332; pret. part. gebolgen, 1540; (gebolge, MS.), 2222; pl. gebolgne, 1432; more according to the original meaning in torne gebolgen, 2402.

    â-belgan, to anger : pret. sg. w. acc. ôð þät hyne ân âbealh mon on môde, till a man angered him in his heart , 2281; pret. part. âbolgen, 724.

    ben, st. f., wound : acc. sg. benne, 2725.--Comp.: feorh-, seax-ben.

    benc, st. f., bench : nom. sg. benc, 492; dat. sg. bence, 327, 1014, 1189, 1244.--Comp.: ealu-, medu-benc.

benc-swêg, st. m., (bench-rejoicing), rejoicing which resounds from the benches, 1162.

benc-þel, st. n., bench-board, the wainscotted space where the benches stand : nom. pl. benc-þelu, 486; acc. pl. bencþelu beredon, cleared the bench-boards (i.e. by taking away the benches, so as to prepare couches), 1240.

bend, st. m. f., bond, fetter : acc. sg. forstes bend, frost's bond, 1610; dat. pl. bendum, 978.--Comp.: fýr-, hell-, hyge-, îren-, oncer-, searo-, wäl-bend.

ben-geat, st. n., (wound-gate), wound-opening : nom. pl. ben-geato, 1122.

bera (O.N. beri), w. m., bearer : in comp. hleor-bera.

beran, st. v. w. acc., to carry ; III. sg. pres. byreð, 296, 448; þone mâððum byreð, carries the treasure (upon his person), 2056; pres. subj. bere, 437; pl. beren, 2654; inf. beran, 48, 231, 291, etc.; hêht þâ se hearda Hrunting beran, to bring Hrunting, 1808; up beran, 1921; in beran, 2153; pret. bär, 495, 712, 847, etc.; mandryhtne bär fäted wæge, brought the lord the costly vessel, 2282; pl. bæron, 213, 1636, etc.; bæran, 2851; pret. part. boren, 1193, 1648, 3136.--The following expressions are poetic paraphrases of the forms go, come : þät we rondas beren eft tô earde, 2654; gewîtað forð beran wæpen and gewædu, 291; ic gefrägn sunu Wihstânes hringnet beran, 2755; wîgheafolan bär, 2662; helmas bæron, 240 (conjecture); scyldas bæran, 2851: they lay stress upon the connection of the man with his weapons.

ät-beran, to carry to : inf. tô beadulâce (battle) ätberan, 1562; pret. þâ hine on morgentîd on Heaðoræmas holm up ätbär, the sea bore him up to the Heaðoræmas, 519; hió Beówulfe medoful ätbär brought Beówulf the mead-cup, 625; mägenbyrðenne ... hider ût ätbär cyninge mînum, bore the great burden hither to my king, 3093; pl. hî hyne ätbæron tô brimes faroðe, 28.

for-beran, to hold, to suppress : inf. þät he þone breóstwylm forberan ne mehte, that he could not suppress the emotions of his breast, 1878.

ge-beran, to bring forth, to bear : pret. part. þät lâ mäg secgan se þe sôð and riht fremeð on folce ... þät þes eorl wære geboren betera (that may every just man of the people say, that this nobleman is better born), 1704.

ôð-beran, to bring hither : pret. þâ mec sæ ôðbär on Finna land, 579.

on-beran (O.H.G. in bëran, intpëran, but in the sense of carere), auferre, to carry off, to take away : inf. îren ærgôd þät þäs ahlæcan blôdge beadufolme onberan wolde, excellent sword which would sweep off the bloody hand of the demon, 991; pret. part. (wäs) onboren beága hord, the treasure of the rings had been carried off, 2285.--Compounds with the pres. part.: helm-, sâwl-berend.

berian (denominative from bär, naked), w. v., to make bare, to clear : pret. pl. bencþelu beredon, cleared the bench-place (by removing the benches), 1240.

berstan, st. v., to break, to burst : pret. pl. burston bânlocan, 819; bengeato burston, 1122.-- to crack, to make the noise of breaking : fingras burston, the fingers cracked (from Beówulf's gripe), 761.

for-berstan, break, to fly asunder : pret. Nägling forbärst, Nägling (Beówulf's sword) broke in two, 2681.

betera, adj. (comp.), better : nom. sg. m. betera, 469, 1704.

bet-lîc, adj., excellent, splendid : nom. sg. n., of Hrôðgâr's hall, 781; of Hygelâc's residence, 1926.

betst, betost (superl.), best, the best : nom. sg. m. betst beadurinca, 1110; neut. nu is ôfost betost, þät we ..., now is haste the best, that we... , 3008; voc. m. secg betsta, 948; neut. acc. beaduscrûda betst, 453; acc. sg. m. þegn betstan, 1872.

bêcn, st. n., (beacon), token, mark, sign : acc. sg. betimbredon beadu-rôfes bêcn (of Beówulf's grave-mound), 3162. See beacen.

bêg. See beág.

bên, st. f., entreaty : gen. sg. bêne, 428, 2285.

bêna, w. m., suppliant, supplex: nom. sg. swâ þu bêna eart (as thou entreatest), 352; swâ he bêna wäs (as he had asked), 3141; nom. pl. hy bênan synt, 364.

ge-betan: 1) to make good, to remove : pret. ac þu Hrôðgâre wîdcûðne wean wihte gebêttest, hast thou in any way relieved Hrôðgâr of the evil known afar, 1992; pret. part. acc. sg. swylce oncýððe ealle gebêtte, removed all trouble, 831. -- 2) to avenge : inf. wihte ne meahte on þam feorhbonan fæhðe gebêtan, could in no way avenge the death upon the slayer, 2466.

beadu, st. f., battle, strife, combat : dat. sg. (as instr.) beadwe, in combat, 1540; gen. pl. bâd beadwa ge-þinges, waited for the combats (with Grendel) that were in store for him, 710.

beadu-folm, st. f., battle-hand : acc. sg. -folme, of Grendel's hand, 991.

beado-grîma, w. m., (battle-mask), helmet : acc. pl. -grîman, 2258.

beadu-hrägl, st. n., (battle-garment), corselet, shirt of mail, 552.

beadu-lâc, st. n., (exercise in arms, tilting), combat, battle : dat. sg. tô beadu-lâce, 1562.

beado-leóma, w. m., (battle-light), sword : nom. sg., 1524.

beado-mêce, st. m., battle-sword : nom. pl. beado-mêcas, 1455.

beado-rinc, st. m., battle-hero, warrior : gen. pl. betst beadorinca, 1110.

beadu-rôf, adj., strong in battle : gen. sg. -rôfes, of Beówulf, 3162.

beadu-rûn, st. f., mystery of battle : acc. sg. onband beadu-rûne, solved the mystery of the combat, i.e. gave battle, commenced the fight, 501.

beadu-scearp, adj., battle-sharp, sharp for the battle, 2705.

beadu-scrûd, st. n., (battle-dress), corselet, shirt of mail : gen. pl. beaduscrûda betst, 453.

beadu-serce, w. f., (battle-garment), corselet, shirt of mail : acc. sg. brogdne beadu-sercean (because it consists of interlaced metal rings), 2756.

beado-weorc, st. n., (battle-work), battle : gen. sg. gefeh beado-weorces, rejoiced at the battle, 2300.

beald, adj., bold, brave : in comp. cyning-beald.

bealdian, w. v., to show one's self brave : pret. bealdode gôdum dædum (through brave deeds), 2178.

bealdor, st. m., lord, prince : nom. sg. sinca baldor, 2429; winia bealdor, 2568.

bealu, st. n., evil, ruin, destruction : instr. sg. bealwe, 2827; gen. pl. bealuwa, 281; bealewa, 2083; bealwa, 910.--Comp.: cwealm-, ealdor-, hreðer-, leód-, morðor-, niht-, sweord-, wîg-bealu.

bealu, adj., deadly, dangerous, bad : instr. sg. hyne sâr hafað befongen balwon bendum, pain has entwined him in deadly bands, 978.

bealo-cwealm, st. m., violent death, death by the sword (?), 2266.

bealo-hycgende, pres. part., thinking of death, meditating destruction : gen. pl. æghwäðrum bealo-hycgendra, 2566.

bealo-hydig, adj., thinking of death, meditating destruction : of Grendel, 724.

bealo-nîð, st. m., (zeal for destruction), deadly enmity : nom. sg., 2405; destructive struggle : acc. sg. bebeorh þe þone bealonîð, beware of destructive striving , 1759; death-bringing rage : nom. sg. him on breóstum bealonîð weóll, in his breast raged deadly fury (of the dragon's poison), 2715.

bearhtm (see beorht): 1) st. m., splendor, brightness, clearness : nom. sg. eágena bearhtm, 1767.--2) sound, tone : acc. sg. bearhtm ongeâton, gûðhorn galan, they heard the sound, (heard) the battle-horn sound , 1432.

bearm, m., gremium, sinus, lap, bosom : nom. sg. foldan bearm, 1138; acc. sg. on bearm scipes, 35, 897; on bearm nacan, 214; him on bearm hladan bunan and discas, 2776.--2) figuratively, possession, property , because things bestowed were placed in the lap of the receiver (1145 and 2195, on bearm licgan, âlecgan); dat. sg. him tô bearme cwom mâððumfät mære, came into his possession , 2405.

bearn, st. n., 1) child, son : nom. sg. bearn Healfdenes, 469, etc.; Ecglâfes bearn, 499, etc.; dat. sg. bearne, 2371; nom. pl. bearn, 59; dat. pl. bearnum, 1075.--2) in a broader sense, scion, offspring, descendant : nom. sg. Ongenþeów's bearn, of his grandson, 2388; nom. pl. yldo. bearn, 70; gumena bearn, children of men , 879; häleða bearn, 1190; äðelinga bearn, 3172; acc. pl. ofer ylda bearn, 606; dat. pl. ylda bearnum, 150; gen. pl. niðða bearna, 1006.--Comp.: brôðor-, dryht-bearn.

bearn-gebyrdu, f., birth, birth of a son : gen. sg. þät hyre ealdmetod êste wære bearn-gebyrdo, has been gracious through the birth of such a son (i.e. as Beówulf), 947.

bearu, st. m., (the bearer , hence properly only the fruit-tree, especially the oak and the beech), tree , collectively forest : nom. pl. hrîmge bearwas, rime-covered or ice-clad , 1364.

beácen, st. n., sign, banner , vexillum: nom. sg. beorht beácen godes, of the sun , 570; gen. pl. beácna beorhtost, 2778. See bêcn.

ge-beácnian, w. v., to mark, to indicate : pret. part. ge-beácnod, 140.

beág, st. m., ring, ornament : nom. sg. beáh (neck-ring), 1212; acc. sg. beáh (the collar of the murdered king of the Heaðobeardnas), 2042; bêg (collective for the acc. pl.), 3165; dat. sg. cwom Wealhþeó forð gân under gyldnum beáge, she walked along under a golden head-ring, wore a golden diadem , 1164; gen. sg. beáges (of a collar), 1217; acc. pl. beágas (rings in general), 80, 523, etc.; gen. pl. beága, 35, 352, 1488, 2285, etc.-- Comp.: earm-, heals-beág.

beág-gyfa, w. m., ring-giver , designation of the prince: gen. sg. -gyfan, 1103.

beág-hroden, adj., adorned with rings, ornamented with clasps : nom. sg. beághroden, cwên, of Hrôðgâr's consort, perhaps with reference to her diadem (cf. 1164), 624.

beáh-hord, st. m. n., ring-hoard, treasure consisting of rings : gen. sg. beáh-hordes, 895; dat. pl. beáh-hordum, 2827; gen. pl. beáh-horda weard, of King Hrôðgâr, 922.

beáh-sele, st. m., ring-hall, hall in which the rings were distributed : nom. sg., of Heorot, 1178.

beáh-þegu, st. f., the receiving of the ring : dat. sg. äfter beáh-þege, 2177.

beáh-wriða, w. m. ring-band , ring with prominence given to its having the form of a band: acc. sg. beáh-wriðan, 2019.

beám, st. m., tree , only in the compounds fyrgen-, gleó-beám.

beátan, st. v., thrust, strike : pres. sg. mearh burhstede beáteð, the steed beats the castle-ground (place where the castle is built), i.e. with his hoofs, 2266; pret. part. swealt bille ge-beáten, died, struck by the battle-axe , 2360.

beorh, st. m.: 1) mountain, rock : dat. sg. beorge, 211; gen. sg. beorges, 2525, 2756; acc. pl. beorgas, 222.--2) grave-mound, tomb-hill : acc. sg. biorh, 2808;

beorh, 3098, 3165. A grave-mound serves the drake as a retreat (cf. 2277, 2412): nom. sg. beorh, 2242; gen. sg. beorges, 2323.--Comp. stân-beorh.

beorh, st. f., veil, covering, cap ; only in the comp. heáfod-beorh.

beorgan, st. v. (w. dat. of the interested person or thing), to save, to shield : inf. wolde feore beorgan, place her life in safety , 1294; here-byrne ... seó þe bâncôfan beorgan cûðe, which could protect his body , 1446; pret. pl. ealdre burgan, 2600.

be-beorgan (w. dat. refl. of pers. and acc. of the thing), to take care, to defend one's self from : inf. him be-beorgan ne con wom, cannot keep himself from stain (fault), 1747; imp. bebeorh þe þone bealontð, 1759.

ge-beorgan (w, dat. of person or thing to be saved), to save, to protect : pret. sg. þät gebearh feore, protected the life , 1549; scyld wel gebearg lîfe and lîce, 2571.

ymb-beorgan, to surround protectingly : pret. sg. bring ûtan ymb-bearh, 1504.

beorht, byrht, adj.: 1) gleaming, shining, radiant, shimmering : nom. sg. beorht, of the sun, 570, 1803; beorhta, of Heorot, 1178; þät beorhte bold, 998; acc. sg. beorhtne, of Beówulf's grave-mound, 2804; dat. sg. tô þære byrhtan (here-byrhtan, MS.) byrig, 1200; acc. pl. beorhte frätwe, 214, 897; beorhte randas, 231; bordwudu beorhtan, 1244; n. beorht hofu, 2314. Superl.: beácna beorhtost, 2778. -- 2) excellent, remarkable : gen. sg. beorhtre bôte, 158. --Comp.: sadol-, wlite-beorht.

beorhte, adv., brilliantly, brightly, radiantly , 1518.

beorhtian, w. v., to sound clearly : pret. sg. beorhtode benc-swêg, 1162.

beorn, st. m., hero, warrior, noble man : nom. sg. (Hrôðgâr), 1881, (Beówulf), 2434, etc.; acc. sg. (Beów.), 1025, (Äschere), 1300; dat. sg. beorne, 2261; nom. pl. beornas (Beówulf and his companions), 211, (Hrôðgâr's guests), 857; gen. pl. biorna (Beówulf's liege-men), 2405.--Comp.: folc-, gûð-beorn.

beornan, st. v., to burn : pres. part. byrnende (of the drake), 2273.--Comp. un-byrnende.

for-beornan, to be consumed, to burn : pret. sg. for-barn, 1617, 1668; for-born, 2673.

ge-beornan, to be burned : pret. gebarn, 2698.

beorn-cyning, st. m., king of warriors, king of heroes : nom. sg. (as voc.), 2149.

beódan, st. v.: 1) to announce, to inform, to make known : inf. biódan, 2893.-- 2) to offer, to proffer (as the notifying of a transaction in direct reference to the person concerned in it): pret. pl. him geþingo budon, offered them an agreement , 1086; pret. part. þâ wäs äht boden Sweona leódum, then was pursuit offered the Swedish people , 2958; inf. ic þäm gôdan sceal mâðmas beódan, I shall offer the excellent man treasures , 385.

â-beódan, to present, to announce : pret. word inne âbeád, made known the words within , 390; to offer, to tender, to wish : pret. him häl âbeád, wished him health (greeted him), 654. Similarly, hälo âbeád, 2419; eoton weard âbeád, offered the giant a watcher , 669.

be-beódan, to command, to order : pret. swâ him se hearda bebeád, as the strong man commanded them , 401. Similarly, swâ se rîca bebeád, 1976.

ge-beódan: 1) to command, to order : inf. hêt þâ gebeódan byre Wihstânes häleða monegum, þät hie..., the son of Wihstan caused orders to be given to many of the men... , 3111.--2) to offer : him Hygd gebeád hord and ríce, offered him the treasure and the chief power , 2370; inf. gûðe gebeódan, to offer battle , 604.

beód-geneát, st. m., table-companion : nom. and acc. pl. geneátas, 343, 1714.

beón, verb, to be , generally in the future sense, will be : pres. sg. I. gûðgeweorca ic beó gearo sôna, I shall immediately be ready for warlike deeds , 1826; sg. III. wâ bið þäm þe sceal..., woe to him who ...! 183; so, 186; gifeðe bið is given, 299; ne bið þe wilna gâd (no wish will be denied thee), 661; þær þe bið manna þearf, if thou shalt need the warriors , 1836; ne bið swylc cwênlîc þeáw, is not becoming, honorable to a woman , 1941; eft sôna bið will happen directly , 1763; similarly, 1768, etc.; pl. þonne bióð brocene, then are broken , 2064; feor cýðe beóð sêlran gesôhte þam þe..., "terrae longinquae meliores sunt visitatu ei qui..." (Grein), 1839; imp. beó (bió) þu on ôfeste, hasten! 386, 2748; beó wið Geátas gläd, be gracious to the Geátas , 1174.

beór, st. n., beer : dat. sg. ät beóre, at beer-drinking , 2042; instr. sg. beóre druncen, 531; beóre druncne, 480.

beór-scealc, st. m., keeper of the beer, cup-bearer : gen. pl. beór-scealca sum (one of Hrôðgâr's followers, because they served the Geátas at meals), 1241.

beór-sele, st. m., beer-hall, hall in which beer is drunk : dat. sg. in (on) beórsele, 482, 492, 1095; biórsele, 2636.

beór-þegu, st. f., beer-drinking, beer-banquet : dat. sg. äfter beórþege, 117; ät þære beórþege, 618.

beót, st. n., promise, binding agreement to something that is to be undertaken : acc. sg. he beót ne âlêh, did not break his pledge , 80; beót eal ... gelæste, performed all that he had pledged himself to , 523.

ge-beótian, w. v., to pledge one's self to an undertaking, to bind one's self : pret. gebeótedon, 480, 536.

beót-word, st. n., same as beót: dat. pl. beót-wordum spräc, 2511.

biddan, st. v., to beg, to ask, to pray : pres. sg. I. dôð swâ ic bidde! 1232; inf. (w. acc. of the pers. and gen. of the thing asked for) ic þe biddan wille ânre bêne, beg thee for one , 427; pret. swâ he selfa bäd, as he himself had requested , 29; bäd hine blîðne (supply wesan) ät þære beórþege, begged him to be cheerful at the beer-banquet , 618; ic þe lange bäd þät þu..., begged you a long time that you , 1995; frioðowære bäd hlâford sînne, begged his lord for protection (acc. of pers. and gen. of thing), 2283; bäd þät ge geworhton, asked that you ..., 3097; pl. wordum bædon þät..., 176.

on-bidian, w. v., to await : inf. lætað hilde-bord her onbidian ... worda geþinges, let the shields await here the result of the conference (lay the shields aside here), 397.

bil, st. n. sword : nom. sg. bil, 1568; bill, 2778; acc. sg. bil, 1558; instr. sg. bille, 2360; gen. sg. billes, 2061, etc.; instr. pl. billum, 40; gen. pl. billa, 583, 1145.--Comp.: gûð-, hilde-, wîg-bil.

bindan, st. v., to bind, to tie : pret. part. acc. sg. wudu bundenne, the bound wood , i.e. the built ship, 216; bunden golde swurd, a sword bound with gold , i.e. either having its hilt inlaid with gold, or having gold chains upon the hilt (swords of both kinds have been found), 1901; nom. sg. heoru bunden, 1286, has probably a similar meaning.

ge-bindan, to bind : pret. sg. þær ic fîfe geband, where I had bound five (?), 420; pret. part. cyninges þegn word ôðer fand sôðe gebunden, the king's man found (after many had already praised Beówulf's deed) other words (also referring to Beówulf, but in connection with Sigemund) rightly bound together , i.e. in good alliterative verses, as are becoming to a gid, 872; wundenmæl wrättum gebunden, sword bound with ornaments, i.e. inlaid, 1532; bisgum gebunden, bound together by sorrow, 1744; gomel gûðwîga eldo gebunden, hoary hero bound by old age (fettered, oppressed), 2112.

 on-bindan, to unbind, to untie, to loose : pret. onband, 501.

 ge-bind, st. n. coll., that which binds, fetters : in comp. îs-gebind.

 bite, st. m., bite, figuratively of the cut of the sword: acc. sg. bite îrena, the swords' bite, 2260; dat. sg. äfter billes bite, 2061.--Comp. lâð-bite.

 biter (primary meaning that of biting), adj.: 1) sharp, cutting, cutting in : acc. sg. biter (of a short sword), 2705; instr. sg. biteran stræle, 1747; instr. pl. biteran bânum, with sharp teeth, 2693.--2) irritated, furious : nom. pl. bitere, 1432.

 bitre, adv., bitterly (in a moral sense), 2332.

 bî, big (fuller form of the prep. be, which see), prep. w. dat.: 1) near, at, on, about, by (as under be, No. 1): bî sæm tweónum, in the circuit of both seas, 1957; ârâs bî ronde, raised himself up by the shield, 2539; bî wealle gesät, sat by the wall, 2718. With a freer position: him big stôdan bunan and orcas, round about him, 3048.--2) to, towards (motion): hwearf þâ bî bence, turned then towards the bench, 1189; geóng bî sesse, went to the seat, 2757.

 bîd (see bîdan), st. n., tarrying hesitation : þær wearð Ongenþió on bîd wrecen, forced to tarry, 2963.

 bîdan, st. v.: 1) to delay, to stay, to remain, to wait : inf. nô on wealle leng bîdan wolde, would not stay longer within the wall (the drake), 2309; pret. in þýstrum bâd, remained in darkness, 87; flota stille bâd, the craft lay still, 301; receda ... on þäm se rîca bâd, where the mighty one dwelt, 310; þær se snottra bâd, where the wise man (Hrôðgâr) waited, 1314; he on searwum bâd, he (Beówulf) stood there armed, 2569; ic on earde bâd mælgesceafta, lived upon the paternal ground the time appointed me by fate, 2737; pret. pl. sume þær bidon, some remained, waited there, 400.--2) to await, to wait for, with the gen. of that which is awaited: inf. bîdan woldon Grendles gûðe, wished to await the combat with Grendel, to undertake it, 482; similarly, 528; wîges bîdan, await the combat, 1269; nalas andsware bîdan wolde, would await no answer, 1495; pret. bâd beadwa geþinges, awaited the event of the battle, 710; sægenga bâd âgend-freán, the sea-goer (boat) awaited its owner, 1883; sele ... heaðowylma bâd, lâðan lîges (the poet probably means to indicate by these words that the hall Heorot was destroyed later in a fight by fire; an occurrence, indeed, about which we know nothing, but which 1165 and 1166, and again 2068 ff. seem to indicate), 82.

 â-bîdan, to await, with the gen.: inf., 978.

 ge-bîdan: 1) to tarry, to wait : imp. gebîde ge on beorge, wait ye on the mountain, 2530; pret. part. þeáh þe wintra lyt under burhlocan gebiden häbbe Häreðes dôhtor although H's daughter had dwelt only a few years in the castle, 1929.--2) to live through, to experience, to expect (w. acc.): inf. sceal endedäg mînne gebîdan, shall live my last day, 639; ne wênde ... bôte gebîdan, did not hope ... to live to see reparation, 935; fela sceal gebîdan leófes and lâðes, experience much good and much affliction, 1061; ende gebîdan, 1387, 2343; pret. he þäs frôfre gebâd, received consolation (compensation) therefore, 7; gebâd wintra worn, lived a great number of years, 264; in a similar construction, 816, 930, 1619, 2259, 3117. With gen.: inf. tô gebîdanne ôðres yrfeweardes, to await another heir, 2453. With depend. clause: inf. tô gebîdanne þät his byre rîde on galgan, to live to see it, that his son hang upon the gallows, 2446; pret. dreám-leás gebâd þät he..., joyless he experienced it, that he ..., 1721; þäs þe ic on aldre gebâd þät ic..., for this, that I, in my old age, lived to see that ..., 1780.

on-bîdan, to wait, to await : pret. hordweard onbâd earfoðlîce ôð þät æfen cwom, scarcely waited, could scarcely delay till it was evening , 2303.

bîtan, st. v., to bite , of the cutting of swords: inf. bîtan, 1455, 1524; pret. bât bânlocan, bit into his body (Grendel), 743; bât unswîðor, cut with less force (Beówulf's sword), 2579.

blanca, w. m., properly that which shines here of the horse, not so much of the white horse as the dappled: dat. pl. on blancum, 857.

ge-bland, ge-blond, st. n., mixture, heaving mass, a turning .--Comp.: sund-, ŷð-geblond, windblond.

blanden-feax, blonden-feax, adj., mixed , i.e. having gray hair, gray-headed , as epithet of an old man: nom. sg. blondenfeax, 1792; blondenfexa, 2963; dat. sg. blondenfeaxum, 1874; nom. pl. blondenfeaxe, 1595.

bläc, adj., dark, black : nom. sg, hrefn blaca, 1802.

blâc, adj.: 1) gleaming, shining : acc. sg. blâcne leóman, a brilliant gleam , 1518.--2) of the white death-color, pale ; in comp. heoroblâc.

blæd, st. m.: 1) strength, force, vigor : nom. sg. wäs hira blæd scacen (of both tribes), strength was gone , i.e. the bravest of both tribes lay slain, 1125; nu is þînes mägnes blæd âne hwîle, now the fulness of thy strength lasts for a time , 1762.--2) reputation, renown, knowledge (with stress upon the idea of filling up, spreading out): nom. sg. blæd, 18; (þîn) blæd is âræred, thy renown is spread abroad , 1704.

blæd-âgend, pt., having renown, renowned : nom. pl. blæd-âgende, 1014.

blæd-fäst, adj., firm in renown, renowned, known afar : acc. sg. blædfästne beorn (of Äschere, with reference to 1329), 1300.

bleát, adj., miserable, helpless ; only in comp. wäl-bleát.

bleáte, adv., miserably, helplessly , 2825.

blîcan, st. v., shine, gleam : inf., 222

blîðe, adj.: 1) blithe, joyous, happy acc. sg. blîðne, 618.--2) gracious, pleasing : nom. sg. blîðe, 436.--Comp. un-blîðe.

blîð-heort, adj., joyous in heart, happy : nom. sg., 1803.

blôd, st. n., blood : nom. sg., 1122; acc. sg., 743; dat. sg. blôde, 848; äfter deórum men him langað beorn wið blôde, the hero (Hrôðgâr) longs for the beloved man contrary to blood , i.e. he loves him although he is not related to him by blood, 1881; dat. as instr. blôde, 486, 935, 1595, etc.

blôd-fâg, adj., spotted with blood, bloody , 2061.

blôdig, adj., bloody : acc. sg. f. blôdge, 991; acc. sg. n. blôdig, 448; instr. sg. blôdigan gâre, 2441.

ge-blôdian, w. v., to make bloody, to sprinkle with blood : pret. part. ge-blôdegod, 2693.

blôdig-tôð, adj., with bloody teeth : nom. sg. bona blôdig-tôð (of Grendel, because he bites his victims to death), 2083.

blôd-reów, adj., bloodthirsty, bloody-minded : nom. sg. him on ferhðe greów breóst-hord blôd-reów, in his bosom there grew a bloodthirsty feeling , 1720.

be-bod, st. n., command, order ; in comp. wundor-bebod.

bodian, w. v., (to be a messenger), to announce, to make known : pret. hrefn blaca heofones wynne blîð-heort bodode, the black raven announced joyfully heaven's delight (the rising sun), 1803.

boga, w. m., bow, of the bended form; here of the dragon, in comp. hring-boga; as an instrument for shooting, in the comp. flân-, horn-boga; bow of the arch, in comp. stân-boga.

bolca, w. m., "forus navis" (Grein), gangway ; here probably the planks which at landing are laid from the ship to the shore: acc. sg. ofer bolcan, 231.

bold, st. n., building, house, edifice : nom. sg. (Heorot), 998; (Hygelâc's residence), 1926; (Beówulfs residence), 2197, 2327.--Comp. fold-bold.

bold-âgend, pt., house-owner, property-holder : gen. pl. monegum boldâgendra, 3113.

bolgen-môd, adj., angry at heart, angry , 710, 1714.

bolster, st. m., bolster, cushion, pillow : dat. pl. (reced) geond-bræded wearð beddum and bolstrum, was covered with beds and bolsters , 1241.--Comp. hleór-bolster.

bon-. See ban-.

bora, w. m., carrier, bringer, leader : in the comp. mund-, ræd-, wæg-bora.

bord, st. n., shield : nom. sg., 2674; acc. sg., 2525; gen. pl. ofer borda gebræc, over the crashing of the shields , 2260.--Comp.: hilde-, wîg-bord.

bord-häbbend, pt., one having a shield, shield-bearer : nom. pl. häbbende, 2896.

bord-hreóða, w. m., shield-cover, shield with particular reference to its cover (of hides or linden bark): dat. sg. -hreóðan, 2204.

bord-rand, st. m., shield : acc. sg., 2560.

bord-weall, st. m., shield-wall, wall of shields : acc. sg., 2981.

bord-wudu, st. m., shield-wood, shield : acc. pl. beorhtan beord-wudu, 1244.

botm, st. m., bottom : dat. sg. tô botme (here of the bottom of the fen-lake), 1507.

bôt (emendation, cf. bêtan), st. f.: 1) relief, remedy : nom. sg., 281; acc. sg. bôte, 935; acc. sg. bôte, 910.--2) a performance in expiation, a giving satisfaction, tribute : gen. sg. bôte, 158.

brand, brond, st. m.: 1) burning, fire : nom. sg. þâ sceal brond fretan (the burning of the body), 3015; instr. sg. by hine ne môston ... bronde forbärnan (could not bestow upon him the solemn burning), 2127; häfde landwara lîge befangen, bæle and bronde, with glow, fire, and flame , 2323.--2) in the passage, þät hine nô brond ne beadomêcas bîtan ne meahton, 1455, brond has been translated sword, brand (after the O.N. brand-r). The meaning fire may be justified as well, if we consider that the old helmets were generally made of leather, and only the principal parts were mounted with bronze. The poet wishes here to emphasize the fact that the helmet was made entirely of metal, a thing which was very unusual.--3) in the passage, forgeaf þâ Beówulfe brand Healfdenes segen gyldenne, 1021, our text, with other editions, has emendated, bearn, since brand, if it be intended as a designation of Hrôðgâr (perhaps son), has not up to this time been found in this sense in A.-S.

brant, bront, adj., raging, foaming, going-high , of ships and of waves: acc. sg. brontne, 238, 568.

brâd, adj.: 1) extended, wide : nom. pl. brâde rîce, 2208.--2) broad : nom. sg. heáh and brâd (of Beówulf's grave-mound), 3159; acc. sg. brâdne mêce, 2979; (seax) brâd [and] brûnecg, the broad, short sword with bright edge , 1547.--3) massive, in abundance . acc, sg. brâd gold, 3106.

ge-bräc, st. n., noise, crash : acc. sg. borda gebräc, 2260.

geond-brædan, w. v., to spread over, to cover entirely : pret. part. geond-bræded, 1240.

brecan, st. v.: 1) to break, to break to pieces : pret. bânhringas bräc, (the sword) broke the joints , 1568. In a moral sense: pret. subj. þät þær ænig mon wære ne bræce, that no one should break the agreement , 1101; pret. part. þonne bióð brocene ... âð-sweord eorla, then are the oaths of the men broken , 2064.--2) probably also simply to break in upon something, to press upon , w. acc.: pret. sg. sædeór monig hildetuxum heresyrcan bräc, many a sea-animal pressed with his battle-teeth upon the shirt of mail (did not break it, for, according to 1549 f., 1553 f., it was still unharmed). 1512.--3) to break out, to spring out : inf. geseah ... streám ût brecan of beorge, saw a stream break out from the rocks , 2547; lêt se hearda Higelâces þegn brâdne mêce ... brecan ofer bordweal, caused the broadsword to spring out over the wall of shields , 2981.--4) figuratively, to vex, not to let rest : pret. hine fyrwyt bräc, curiosity tormented (N.H.G. brachte die Neugier um), 232, 1986, 2785.

ge-brecan, to break to pieces : pret. bânhûs gebräc, broke in pieces his body (Beówulf in combat with Däghrefn), 2509.

tô-brecan, to break in pieces : inf., 781; pret. part. tô-brocen, 998.

þurh-brecan, to break through , pret. wordes ord breósthord þurh-bräc, the word's point broke through his closed breast , i.e. a word burst out from his breast, 2793.

brecð, st. f., condition of being broken, breach : nom. pl. môdes brecða (sorrow of heart), 171.

â-bredwian, w. v. w. acc., to fell to the ground, to kill (?): pret. âbredwade, 2620.

bregdan, st. v., properly to swing round , hence: 1) to swing : inf. under sceadu bregdan, swing among the shadows, to send into the realm of shadows , 708; pret. brägd ealde lâfe, swung the old weapon , 796; brägd feorh-genîðlan, swung his mortal enemy (Grendel's mother), threw her down, 1540; pl. git eágorstreám ... mundum brugdon, stirred the sea with your hands (of the movement of the hands in swimming), 514; pret. part. broden (brogden) mæl, the drawn sword , 1617, 1668.--2) to knit, to knot, to plait : inf., figuratively, inwitnet ôðrum bregdan, to weave a waylaying net for another (as we say in the same way, to lay a trap for another, to dig a pit for another), 2168; pret. part. beadohrägl broden, a woven shirt of mail (because it consisted of metal rings joined together), 552; similarly, 1549; brogdne beadusercean, 2756.

â-bregdan, to swing : pret. hond up â-bräd, swung, raised his hand , 2576.

ge-bregdan: 1) swing : pret. hring-mæl gebrägd, swung the ringed sword , 1565; eald sweord eácen ... þät ic þý wæpne gebrägd, an old heavy sword that I swung as my weapon , 1665; with interchanging instr. and acc. wällseaxe gebräd, biter and beadu-scearp, 2704; also, to draw out of the sheath : sweord ær gebräd, had drawn the sword before , 2563.--2) to knit, to knot, to plait : pret. part. bere-byrne hondum gebroden, 1444.

on-bregdan, to tear open, to throw open : pret. onbräd þâ recedes mûðan, had then thrown open the entrance of the hall (onbregdan is used because the opening door swings upon its hinges), 724.

brego, st. m., prince, ruler : nom. sg. 427, 610.

brego-rôf, adj., powerful, like a ruler, of heroic strength : nom. sg. m., 1926.

brego-stôl, st. m., throne , figuratively for rule : acc. sg. him gesealde seofon þûsendo, bold and brego-stôl, seven thousand see under sceat), a country-seat, and the dignity of a prince, 2197; þær him Hygd gebeád ... brego-stôl, where H. offered him the chief power, 2371; lêt þone bregostôl Beówulf healdan, gave over to Beówulf the chief power (did not prevent Beówulf from entering upon the government), 2390.

breme, adj., known afar, renowned. nom. sg., 18.

brenting (see brant), st. m., ship craft : nom. pl. brentingas, 2808.

â-breátan, st. v., to break, to break in pieces, to kill : pret. âbreót brimwîsan, killed the sea-king (King Hæðcyn), 2931. See breótan.

breóst, st. n.: 1) breast : nom. sg., 2177; often used in the pl., so acc. þät mîne breóst wereð, which protects my breast, 453; dat. pl. beadohrägl broden on breóstum läg. 552.--2) the inmost thoughts, the mind, the heart, the bosom : nom. sg. breóst innan weóll þeóstrum geþoncum, his breast heaved with troubled thoughts, 2332; dat. pl. lêt þâ of breóstum word ût faran, caused the words to come out from his bosom, 2551.

breóst-gehygd, st. n. f., breast-thought, secret thought : instr. pl. -gehygdum, 2819.

breóst-gewædu, st. n. pl., breast-clothing, garment covering the breast, of the coat of mail: nom., 1212; acc., 2163.

breóst-hord, st. m., breast-hoard, that which is locked in the breast, heart, mind, thought, soul : nom. sg., 1720; acc. sg., 2793.

breóst-net, st. n., breast-net, shirt of chain-mail, coat of mail : nom. sg. breóst-net broden, 1549.

breóst-weorðung, st. f., ornament that is worn upon the breast : acc. sg. breóst-weorðunge, 2505: here the collar is meant which Beówulf receives from Wealhþeów (1196, 2174) as a present, and which B., according to 2173, presents to Hygd, while, according to 1203, it is in the possession of her husband Hygelâc. In front the collar is trimmed with ornaments (frätwe), which hang down upon the breast, hence the name breóst-weorðung.

breóst-wylm, st. m., heaving of the breast, emotion of the bosom : acc. sg, 1878.

breótan, st. v., to break, to break in pieces, to kill : pret. breát beódgeneátas, killed his table-companions (courtiers), 1714.

â-breótan, same as above: pret. þone þe heó on räste âbreát, whom she killed upon his couch, 1299; pret. part. þâ þät monige gewearð, þät hine seó brimwylf âbroten häfde, many believed that the sea-wolf (Grendel's mother) had killed him, 1600; hî hyne ... âbroten häfdon, had killed him (the dragon), 2708.

brim, st. n., flood, the sea : nom. sg., 848, 1595; gen. sg. tô brimes faroðe, to the sea, 28; ät brimes nosan, at the sea's promontory, 2804; nom. pl. brimu swaðredon, the waves subsided, 570.

brim-clif, st. n., sea-cliff, cliff washed by the sea : acc. pl. -clifu, 222.

brim-lâd, st. f., flood-way, sea-way : acc. sg. þâra þe mid Beówulfe brimlâde teáh, who had travelled the sea-way with B., 1052.

brim-lîðend, pt, sea-farer, sailor acc. p. -lîðende, 568.

brim-streám, st. m., sea-stream, the flood of the sea : acc. pl. ofer brim-streámas, 1911.

brim-wîsa, w. m., sea-king : acc. sg. brimwîsan, of Hæðcyn, king of the Geátas, 2931.

brim-wylf, st. f., sea-wolf (designation of Grendel's mother): nom. sg. seó brimwylf, 1507, 1600.

brim-wylm, st. m., sea-wave : nom. sg., 1495.

bringan, anom. v., to bring, to bear : prs. sg. I. ic þe þûsenda þegna bringe tô helpe, bring to your assistance thousands of warriors, 1830; inf. sceal hringnaca ofer heáðu bringan lâc and luftâcen, shall bring gifts and love-tokens over the high sea, 1863; similarly, 2149, 2505; pret. pl. we þâs sælâc ... brôhton, brought this sea-offering (Grendel's head), 1654.

ge-bringan, to bring : pres. subj. pl. þat we þone gebringan ... on âdfäre, that we bring him upon the funeral-pile, 3010.

brosnian, w. v., to crumble, to become rotten, to fall to pieces : prs. sg. III. herepâd ... brosnað äfter beorne, the coat of mail falls to pieces after (the death of) the hero, 2261.

brôðor, st. m., brother : nom. sg., 1325, 2441; dat sg. brêðer, 1263; gen. sg. his brôðor bearn, 2620; dat. pl. brôðrum, 588, 1075.

ge-brôðru, pl., brethren, brothers : dat. pl. sät be þæm gebrôðrum twæm, sat by the two brothers, 1192.

brôga, w. m., terror, horror : nom. sg., 1292, 2325, 2566; acc. sg. billa brôgan, 583.--Comp.: gryre-, here-brôga.

brûcan, st. v. w. gen., to use, to make use of : prs. sg. III. se þe longe her worolde brûceð, who here long makes use of the world, i.e. lives long, 1063; imp. brûc manigra mêda, make use of many rewards, give good rewards, 1179; to enjoy : inf. þät he beáhhordes brûcan môste, could enjoy the ring-hoard, 895; similarly, 2242, 3101; pret. breác lîfgesceafta, enjoyed the appointed life, lived the appointed time, 1954. With the genitive to be supplied: breác þonne môste, 1488; imp. brûc þisses beáges, enjoy this ring, take this ring, 1217. Upon this meaning depends the form of the wish, wel brûcan (compare the German geniesze froh!): inf. hêt hine wel brûcan, 1046; hêt hine brûcan well, 2813; imp. brûc ealles well, 2163.

brûn, adj., having a brown lustre, shining : nom. sg. sió ecg brûn, 2579.

brûn-ecg, adj., having a gleaming blade : acc. sg. n. (hyre seaxe) brâd [and] brûnecg, her broad sword with gleaming blade, 1547.

brûn-fâg, adj., gleaming like metal : acc. sg. brûnfâgne helm, 2616.

bryne-leóma, w. m., light of a conflagration, gleam of fire : nom. sg., 2314.

bryne-wylm, st. m., wave of fire : dat. pl. -wylmum, 2327.

brytnian (properly to break in small pieces, cf. breótan), w. v., to bestow, to distribute : pret. sinc brytnade, distributed presents, i.e. ruled (since the giving of gifts belongs especially to rulers), 2384.

brytta, w. m., giver, distributer, always designating the king: nom. sg. sinces brytta, 608, 1171, 2072; acc. sg. beága bryttan, 35, 352, 1488; sinces bryttan, 1923.

bryttian (to be a dispenser), w. v., to distribute, to confer : prs. sg. III. god manna cynne snyttru bryttað, bestows wisdom upon the human race, 1727.

brýd, st. f.: 1) wife, consort : acc. sg. brýd, 2931; brýde, 2957, both times of the consort of Ongenþeów (?).--2) betrothed, bride : nom. sg., of Hrôðgâr's daughter, Freáware, 2032.

brýd-bûr, st. n., woman's apartment : dat. sg. eode ... cyning of brýdbûre, the king came out of the apartment of his wife (into which, according to 666, he had gone), 922.

bunden-stefna, w. m., (that which has a bound prow), the framed ship : nom. sg., 1911.

bune, w. f., can or cup, drinking-vessel : nom. pl. bunan, 3048; acc. pl. bunan, 2776.

burh, burg, st. f., castle, city, fortified house : acc. sg. burh, 523; dat. sg. byrig, 1200; dat. pl. burgum, 53, 1969, 2434.--Comp.: freó, freoðo-, heá-, hleó-, hord-, leód-, mæg-burg.

burh-loca, w. m., castle-bars : dat. sg. under burh-locan, under the castle-bars, i.e. in the castle (Hygelâc's), 1929.

burh-stede, st. m., castle-place, place where the castle or city stands : acc. sg. burhstede, 2266.

burh-wela, w. m., riches, treasure of a castle or city : gen. sg. þenden he burh-welan brûcan môste, 3101.

burne, w. f., spring, fountain : gen. þære burnan wälm, the bubbling of the spring, 2547.

bûan, st. v.: 1) to stay, to remain, to dwell : inf. gif he weard onfunde bûan on beorge, if he had found the watchman dwelling on the mountain, 2843.--2) to inhabit, w. acc.: meduseld bûan, to inhabit the mead-house, 3066.

ge-bûan, w. acc., to occupy a house, to take possession : pret. part. heán hûses, hû hit Hring Dene äfter beórþege gebûn häfdon, how the Danes, after their beer-carouse, had occupied it (had made their beds in it), 117.--With the pres. part. bûend are the compounds ceaster-, fold-, grund-, lond-bûend.

bûgan, st. v., to bend, to bow, to sink; to turn, to flee : prs. sg. III. bon-gâr bûgeð, the fatal spear sinks, i.e. its deadly point is turned down, it rests, 2032; inf. þät se byrnwîga bûgan sceolde, that the armed hero had to sink down (having received a deadly blow), 2919; similarly, 2975; pret. sg. beáh eft under eorðweall, turned, fled again behind the earth-wall, 2957; pret. pl. bugon tô bence, turned to the bench, 327, 1014; hy on holt bugon, fled to the wood, 2599.

â-bûgan, to bend off, to curve away from : pret. fram sylle âbeág medubenc monig, from the threshold curved away many a mead-bench, 776.

be-bûgan, w. acc., to surround, to encircle : prs. swâ (which) water bebûgeð, 93; efne swâ sîde swâ sæ bebûgeð windige weallas, as far as the sea encircles windy shores, 1224.

ge-bûgan, to bend, to bow, to sink : a) intrans.: heó on flct gcbeáh, sank on the floor, 1541; þâ gebeáh cyning, then sank the king, 2981; þâ se wyrm gebeáh snûde tôsomne (when the drake at once coiled itself up), 2568; gewât þâ gebogen scrîðan tô, advanced with curved body (the drake), 2570.--b) w. acc. of the thing to which one bends or sinks: pret. selereste gebeáh, sank upon the couch in the hall, 691; similarly gebeág, 1242.

bûr, st. n., apartment, room : dat. sg. bûre, 1311, 2456; dat. pl. bûrum, 140.--Comp. brýd-bûr.

bûtan, bûton (from be and ûtan, hence in its meaning referring to what is without, excluded): 1) conj. with subjunctive following, lest : bûtan his lîc swice, lest his body escape, 967. With ind. following, but : bûton hit wäs mâre þonne ænig mon ôðer tô beadulâce ätberan meahte, but it (the sword) was greater than any other man could have carried to battle, 1561. After a preceding negative verb, except : þâra þe gumena bearn gearwe ne wiston bûton Fitela mid hine, which the children of men did not know at all, except Fitela, who was with him, 880; ne nom he mâðm-æhta mâ bûton þone hafelan, etc., he took no more of the rich treasure than the head alone, 1615.--2) prep. with dat., except : bûton folcscare, 73; bûton þe, 658; ealle bûton ânum, 706.

bycgan, w. v., to buy, to pay : inf. ne wäs þät gewrixle til þät hie on bâ healfa bicgan scoldon freónda feorum, that was no good transaction, that they, on both sides (as well to Grendel as to his mother), had to pay with the lives of their friends, 1306.

be-bycgan, to sell : pret. nu ic on mâðma hord mîne bebohte frôde feorhlege (now I, for the treasure-hoard, gave up my old life), 2800.

ge-bycgan, to buy, to acquire; to pay : pret. w. acc. nô þær ænige ... frôfre gebohte, obtained no sort of help, consolation, 974; hit (his, MS.) ealdre gebohte, paid it with his life, 2482; pret. part. sylfes feore beágas [geboh]te, bought rings with his own life, 3015.

byldan, w. v. (to make beald, which see), to excite, to encourage, to brave deeds : inf. w. acc. swâ he Fresena cyn on beórsele byldan wolde (by distributing gifts), 1095.

ge-byrd, st. n., "fatum destinatum" (Grein) (?): acc. sg. hie on gebyrd hruron gâre wunde, 1075.

ge-byrdu, st. f., birth ; in compound, bearn-gebyrdu.

byrdu-scrûd, st. n., shield-ornament, design upon a shield (?): nom. sg., 2661.

byre, st. m., (born) son : nom. sg., 2054, 2446, 2622, etc.; nom. pl. byre, 1189. In a broader sense, young man, youth : acc. pl. bædde byre geonge, encouraged the youths (at the banquet), 2019.

byrðen, st. f., burden ; in comp. mägen-byrðen.

byrele, st. m., steward, waiter, cupbearer : nom. pl. byrelas, 1162.

byrgan, w. v., to feast, to eat : inf., 448.

ge-byrgea, w. m., protector ; in comp. leód-gebyrgea.

byrht. See beorht.

byrne, w. f., shirt of mail, mail : nom. sg. byrne, 405, 1630, etc.; hringed byrne, ring-shirt, consisting of interlaced rings, 1246; acc. sg. byrnan, 1023, etc.; sîde byrnan, large coat of mail, 1292; hringde byrnan, 2616; hâre byrnan, gray coat of mail (of iron), 2154; dat. sg. on byrnan, 2705; gen. sg. byrnan hring, the ring of the shirt of mail (i.e. the shirt of mail), 2261; dat. pl. byrnum, 40, 238, etc.; beorhtum byrnum, with gleaming mail, 3141.--Comp.: gûð-, here-, heaðo-, îren-, îsern-byrne.

byrnend. See beornan.

byrn-wîga, w. m., warrior dressed in a coat of mail : nom. sg., 2919.

bysgu, bisigu, st. f., trouble, difficulty, opposition : nom. sg. bisigu, 281; dat. pl. bisgum, 1744, bysigum, 2581.

bysig, adj., opposed, in need, in the compounds lîf-bysig, syn-bysig.

býme, w. f., a wind-instrument, a trumpet, a trombone : gen. sg. býman gealdor, the sound of the trumpet, 2944.

býwan, w. v., to ornament, to prepare : inf. þâ þe beado-grîman býwan sceoldon, who should prepare the helmets, 2258.

C

camp, st. m., combat, fight between two : dat. sg. in campe (Beówulf's with Däghrefn; cempan, MS.), 2506.

candel, st. f., light, candle : nom. sg. rodores candel, of the sun, 1573.--Comp. woruld-candel.

cempa, w. m., fighter, warrior, hero : nom. sg. äðele cempa, 1313; Geáta cempa, 1552; rêðe cempa, 1586; mære cempa (as voc.), 1762; gyrded cempa, 2079; dat. sg. geongum (geongan) cempan, 1949, 2045, 2627; Hûga cempan, 2503; acc. pl. cempan, 206.--Comp. fêðe-cempa.

cennan, w. v.: 1) to bear, w. acc.: efne swâ hwylc mägða swâ þone magan cende, who bore the son, 944; pret. part. þäm eafera wäs äfter cenned, to him was a son born, 12.--2) reflexive, to show one's self, to reveal one's self: imp. cen þec mid cräfte, prove yourself by your strength, 1220.

â-cennan, to bear: pret. part. nô hie fäder cunnon, hwäðer him ænig wäs ær âcenned dyrnra gâsta, they (the people of the country) do not know his (Grendel's) father, nor whether any evil spirit has been before born to him (whether he has begotten a son), 1357.

cênðu, st. f., boldness: acc. sg. cênðu, 2697.

cêne, adj., keen, warlike, bold: gen. p.. cênra gehwylcum, 769. Superl., acc. pl. cênoste, 206.--Comp.: dæd-, gâr-cêne.

ceald, adj., cold: acc. pl. cealde streámas, 1262; dat. pl. cealdum cearsîðum, with cold, sad journeys, 2397. Superl. nom. sg. wedera cealdost, 546;--Comp. morgen-ceald.

cearian, w. v., to have care, to take care, to trouble one's self: prs. sg. III. nâ ymb his lîf cearað, takes no care for his life, 1537.

cearig, adj., troubled, sad: in comp. sorh-cearig.

cear-sîð, st. m., sorrowful way, an undertaking that brings sorrow, i.e. a warlike expedition: dat. pl. cearsîðum (of Beówulf's expeditions against Eádgils), 2397.

cearu, st. f., care, sorrow, lamentation: nom. sg., 1304; acc. sg. [ceare], 3173.--Comp.: ealdor-, gûð-, mæl-, môd-cearu.

cear-wälm, st. m., care-agitation, waves of sorrow in the breast: dat. pl. äfter cear-wälmum, 2067.

cear-wylm, st. m., same as above; nom. pl. þâ cear-wylmas, 282.

ceaster-bûend, pt, inhabitant of a fortified place, inhabitant of a castle: dat. pl. ceaster-bûendum, of those established in Hrôðgâr's castle, 769.

ceáp, st. m., purchase, transaction: figuratively, nom. sg. näs þät ýðe ceáp, no easy transaction, 2416; instr. sg. þeáh þe ôðer hit ealdre gebohte, heardan ceápe, although the one paid it with his lifc, a dcar purchasc, 2483.

ge-ceápian, w. v., to purchase: pret. part. gold unrîme grimme geceápod, gold without measure, bitterly purchased (with Beówulf's life), 3013.

be-ceorfan, st. v., to separate, to cut off (with acc. of the pers. and instr. of the thing): pret. hine þâ heáfde becearf, cut off his head, 1591; similarly, 2139.

ceorl, st. m., man: nom. sg. snotor ceorl monig, many a wise man, 909; dat. sg. gomelum ceorle, the old man (of King Hrêðel), 2445; so, ealdum ceorle, of King Ongenþeów, 2973; nom. pl. snotere ceorlas, wise men, 202, 416, 1592.

ceól, st. m., keel, figuratively for the ship: nom. sg., 1913; acc. sg. ceól, 38, 238; gen. sg. ceóles, 1807.

ceósan, st. v., to choose, hence, to assume: inf. þone cynedôm ciósan wolde, would assume the royal dignity, 2377; to seek: pret. subj. ær he bæl cure, before he sought his funeral-pile (before he died), 2819.

ge-ceósan, to choose, to elect: gerund, tô geceósenne cyning ænigne (sêlran), to choose a better king, 1852; imp. þe þät sêlre ge-ceós, choose thee the better (of two: bealonîð and êce rædas), 1759; pret. he ûsic on herge geceás tô þyssum siðfate, selected us among the soldiers for this undertaking, 2639; geceás êcne ræd, chose the everlasting gain, i.e. died, 1202; similarly, godes leóht geceás, 2470; pret. part. acc. pl. häfde ... cempan gecorone, 206.

on-cirran, w. v., to turn, to change : inf. ne meahte ... þäs wealdendes [willan] wiht on-cirran, could not change the will of the Almighty , 2858; pret. ufor oncirde, turned higher , 2952; þyder oncirde, turned thither , 2971.

â-cîgan, w. v., to call hither : pret. âcîgde of corðre cyninges þegnas syfone, called from the retinue of the king seven men , 3122.

clam, clom, st. m., f. n.? fetter , figuratively of a strong gripe: dat. pl. heardan clammum, 964; heardum clammum, 1336; atolan clommum (horrible claws of the mother of Grendel), 1503.

clif, cleof, st. n., cliff, promontory : acc. pl. Geáta clifu, 1912.--Comp.: brim-, êg-, holm-, stân-clif.

ge-cnâwan, st. v., to know, to recognize : inf. meaht þu, mîn wine, mêce gecnâwan, mayst thou, my friend, recognize the sword , 2048.

on-cnâwan, to recognize, to distinguish : hordweard oncniów mannes reorde, distinguished the speech of a man , 2555.

cniht, st. m., boy, youth : dat. pl. þyssum cnyhtum, to these boys (Hrôðgâr's sons), 1220.

cniht-wesende, prs. part., being a boy or a youth : acc. sg. ic hine cûðe cniht-wesende, knew him while still a boy , 372; nom. pl. wit þät gecwædon cniht-wesende, we both as young men said that , 535.

cnyssan, w. v., to strike, to dash against each other : pret. pl. þonne ... eoferas cnysedan, when the bold warriors dashed against each other, stormed (in battle), 1329.

collen-ferhð, -ferð, adj., (properly, of swollen mind), of uncommon thoughts, in his way of thinking, standing higher than others, high-minded : nom. sg. cuma collen-ferhð, of Beówulf, 1807; collen-ferð, of Wîglâf, 2786.

corðer, st. n., troop, division of an army, retinue : dat. sg. þâ wäs ... Fin slägen, cyning on corðre, then was Fin slain, the king in the troop (of warriors), 1154; of corðre cyninges, out of the retinue of the king , 3122.

costian, w. v., to try ; pret. (w. gen.) he mîn costode, tried me , 2085.

côfa, w. m., apartment, sleeping-room, couch : in comp. bân-côfa.

côl, adj., cool : compar. cearwylmas côlran wurðað, the waves of sorrow become cooler , i.e. the mind becomes quiet, 282; him wîflufan ... côlran weorðað, his love for his wife cools , 2067.

cräft, st. m., the condition of being able , hence: 1) physical strength : nom. sg. mägða cräft, 1284; acc. sg. mägenes cräft, 418; þurh ânes cräft, 700; cräft and cênðu, 2697; dat. (instr.) sg. cräfte, 983, 1220, 2182, 2361.--2) art, craft, skill : dat. sg. as instr. dyrnum cräfte, with secret (magic) art , 2169; dyrnan cräfte, 2291; þeófes cräfte, with thief's craft , 2221; dat. pl. deófles cräftum, by devil's art (sorcery), 2089.--3) great quantity (?): acc. sg. wyrm-horda cräft, 2223.--Comp.: leoðo-, mägen-, nearo-, wîg-cräft.

cräftig, adj.: 1) strong, stout : nom. sg. eafoðes cräftig, 1467; nîða cräftig, 1963. Comp. wîg-cräftig.--2) adroit, skilful : in comp. lagu-cräftig.--3) rich (of treasures); in comp. eácen-cräftig.

cringan, st. v., to fall in combat, to fall with the writhing movement of those mortally wounded : pret. subj. on wäl crunge, would sink into death, would fall , 636; pret. pl. for the pluperfect, sume on wäle crungon, 1114.

ge-cringan, same as above: pret. he under rande gecranc, fell under his shield , 1210; ät wîge gecrang, fell in battle , 1338; heó on flet gecrong, fell to the ground , 1569; in campe gecrong, fell in single combat , 2506.

cuma (he who comes), w. m., newcomer, guest : nom. sg. 1807.--Comp.: cwealm-, wil-cuma.

cuman, st. v., to come : pres. sg. II. gyf þu on weg cymest, if thou comest from there , 1383; III. cymeð, 2059; pres. subj. sg. III. cume, 23; pl. þonne we ût cymen, when we come out , 3107; inf. cuman, 244, 281, 1870; pret. sg. com, 430, 569, 826, 1134, 1507, 1601, etc.; cwom, 419, 2915; pret. subj. sg. cwôme, 732; pret. part. cumen, 376; pl. cumene, 361. Often with the inf. of a verb of motion, as, com gongan, 711; com sîðian, 721; com in gân, 1645; cwom gân, 1163; com scacan, 1803; cwômon lædan, 239; cwômon sêcean, 268; cwôman scrîðan, 651, etc. [pret. côm, etc.]

be-cuman, to come, to approach, to arrive : pret. syððan niht becom, after the night had come , 115; þe on þâ leóde becom, that had come over the people , 192; þâ he tô hâm becom, 2993. And with inf. following: stefn in becom ... hlynnan under hârne stân, 2553; lyt eft becwom ... hâmes niósan, 2366; ôð þät ende becwom, 1255; similarly, 2117. With acc. of pers.: þâ hyne sió þrag becwom, when this time of battle came over him , 2884.

ofer-cuman, to overcome, to compel : pret. þý he þone feónd ofercwom, thereby he overcame the foe , 1274: pl. hie feónd heora ... ofercômon, 700; pret. part. (w. gen.) nîða ofercumen, compelled by combats , 846.

cumbol, cumbor, st. m., banner : gen. sg. cumbles hyrde, 2506.--Comp. hilte-cumbor.

cund, adj., originating in, descended from : in comp. feorran-cund.

cunnan, verb pret. pres.: 1) to know, to be acquainted with (w. acc. or depend. clause): sg. pres. I. ic mînne can glädne Hrôðulf þät he ... wile, I know my gracious H., that he will ..., 1181; II. eard git ne const, thou knowest not yet the land , 1378; III. he þät wyrse ne con, knows no worse , 1740. And reflexive: con him land geare, knows the land well , 2063; pl. men ne cunnon hwyder helrûnan scrîðað, men do not know whither ..., 162; pret. sg. ic hine cûðe, knew him , 372; cûðe he duguð þeáw, knew the customs of the distinguished courtiers , 359; so with the acc., 2013; seolfa nc cûðc þurh hwät..., he himself did not know through what ..., 3068; pl. sorge ne cûðon, 119; so with the acc., 180, 418, 1234. With both (acc. and depend. clause): nô hie fäder cunnon (scil. nô hie cunnon) hwäðer him ænig wäs ær âcenned dyrnra gâsta, 1356.--2) with inf. following, can, to be able : prs. sg. him bebeorgan ne con, cannot defend himself , 1747; prs. pl. men ne cunnon secgan, cannot say , 50; pret. sg. cûðe reccan, 90; beorgan cûðe, 1446; pret. pl. hêrian ne cûðon, could not praise , 182; pret. subj. healdan cûðe, 2373.

cunnian, w. v., to inquire into, to try , w. gen. or acc.: inf. sund cunnian (figurative for roam over the sea), 1427, 1445; geongne cempan higes cunnian, to try the young warrior's mind , 2046; pret. eard cunnode, tried the home , i.e. came to it, 1501; pl. wada cunnedon, tried the flood , i.e. swam through the sea, 508.

cûð, adj.: 1) known, well known; manifest, certain : nom. sg. undyrne cûð, 150, 410; wîde cûð, 2924; acc. sg. fern. cûðe folme, 1304; cûðe stræte, 1635; nom. pl. ecge cûðe, 1146; acc. pl. cûðe nässas, 1913.--2) renowned : nom. sg. gûðum cûð, 2179; nom. pl. cystum cûðe, 868.--3) also, friendly, dear, good (see un-cûð).--Comp.: un-, wîd-cûð.

cûð-lîce, adv., openly, publicly : comp. nô her cûðlîcor cuman ongunnon lind-häbbende, no shield-bearing men undertook more boldly to come hither (the coast-watchman means by this the secret landing of the Vikings), 244.

cwalu, st. f., murder, fall : in comp. deáð-cwalu.

cweccan (to make alive , see cwic), w. v., to move, to swing : pret. cwehte mägen-wudu, swung the wood of strength (= spear), 235.

cweðan, st. v., to say, to speak : a) absolutely: prs. sg. III. cwið ät beóre, speaks at beer-drinking , 2042.--b) w. acc.: pret. word äfter cwäð, 315; feá worda cwäð, 2247, 2663.--c) with þät following: pret. sg. cwäð, 92, 2159; pl. cwædon, 3182.--d) with þät omitted: pret. cwäð he gûð-cyning sêcean wolde, said he would seek out the war-king , 199; similarly, 1811, 2940.

â-cweðan, to say, to speak , w. acc.: prs. þät word âcwyð, speaks the word , 2047; pret. þät word âcwäð, 655.

ge-cweðan, to say, to speak : a) absolutely: pret. sg. II. swâ þu gecwæde, 2665.--b)w. acc.: pret. wel-hwylc gecwäð, spoke everything , 875; pl. wit þät gecwædon, 535.--c) w. þät following: pret. gecwäð, 858, 988.

cwellan, w. v., (to make die), to kill, to murder : pret. sg. II. þu Grendel cwealdest, 1335.

â-cwellan, to kill : pret. sg. (he) wyrm âcwealde, 887; þone þe Grendel ær mâne âcwealde, whom Grendel had before wickedly murdered , 1056; beorn âcwealde, 2122.

cwên, st. f.: 1) wife, consort (of noble birth): nom. sg. cwên, 62; (Hrôðgâr's), 614, 924; (Finn's), 1154.--2) particularly denoting the queen: nom. sg. beághroden cwên (Wealhþeów), 624; mæru cwên, 2017; fremu folces cwên (Þryðo), 1933; acc. sg. cwên (Wealhþeów), 666.-Comp. folc-cwên.

cwên-lîc, adj., feminine, womanly : nom. sg. ne bið swylc cwênlîc þeáw (such is not the custom of women, does not become a woman), 1941.

cwealm, st. m., violent death, murder, destruction : acc. sg. þone cwealm gewräc, avenged the death (of Abel by Cain), 107; mændon mondryhtnes cwealm, lamented the ruler's fall , 3150.--Comp.: bealo-, deáð-, gâr-cwealm.

cwealm-bealu, st. n., the evil of murder : acc. sg., 1941.

cwealm-cuma, w. m., one coming for murder, a new-comer who contemplates murder : acc. sg. þone cwealm-cuman (of Grendel), 793.

cwic and cwico, adj., quick, having life, alive : acc. sg. cwicne, 793, 2786; gen. sg. âht cwices, something living , 2315; nom. pl. cwice, 98; cwico wäs þâ gena, was still alive , 3094.

cwide, st. m., word, speech, saying : in comp. gegn-, gilp-, hleó-, ðor- [non-existant form--KTH], word-cwide.

cwîðan, st. v., to complain, to lament : inf. w. acc. ongan ... gioguðe cwîðan hilde-strengo, began to lament the (departed) battle-strength of his youth , 2113 [ceare] cwîðan, lament their cares , 3173.

cyme, st. m., coming, arrival : nom. pl. hwanan eówre cyme syndon, whence your coming is , i. e. whence ye are, 257.--Comp. eft-cyme.

cymlîce, adv., (convenienter), splendidly, grandly : comp. cymlîcor, 38.

cyn, st. n., race , both in the general sense, and denoting noble lineage: nom. sg. Fresena cyn, 1094; Wedera (gara, MS.) cyn, 461; acc. sg. eotena cyn, 421; giganta cyn, 1691; dat. sg. Caines cynne, 107; manna cynne, 811, 915, 1726; eówrum (of those who desert Beówulf in battle) cynne, 2886; gen. sg. manna (gumena) cynnes, 702, etc.; mæran cynnes, 1730; lâðan cynnes, 2009, 2355; ûsses cynnes Wægmundinga, 2814; gen. pl. cynna gehwylcum, 98.--Comp.: eormen-, feorh-, frum-, gum-, man-, wyrm-cyn.

cyn, st. n., that which is suitable or proper : gen. pl. cynna (of etiquette) gemyndig, 614.

ge-cynde, adj., innate, peculiar, natural : nom. sg., 2198, 2697.

cyne-dôm, st. m., kingdom, royal dignity : acc. sg., 2377.

cyning, st. m., king : nom. acc. sg. cyning, II, 864, 921, etc.; kyning, 620, 3173; dat. sg. cyninge, 3094; gen. sg. cyninges, 868, 1211; gen. pl. kyning[a] wuldor, of God, 666.--Comp. beorn-, eorð-, folc-, guð-, heáh-, leód-, sæ-, sôð-, þeód-, worold-, wuldor-cyning.

cyning-beald, adj., " nobly bold " (Thorpe), excellently brave (?): nom. pl. cyning-balde men, 1635.

ge-cyssan, w. v., to kiss : pret. gecyste þâ cyning ... þegen betstan, kissed the best thane (Beówulf), 1871.

cyst (choosing , see ceósan), st. f., the select, the best of a thing, good quality, excellence : nom. sg. îrenna cyst, of the swords , 803, 1698; wæpna cyst, 1560; symbla cyst, choice banquet , 1233; acc. sg. îrena cyst, 674; dat. pl. foldwegas ... cystum cûðe, known through excellent qualities , 868; (cyning) cystum gecýðed, 924.--Comp. gum-, hilde-cyst.

cýð. See on-cýð.

cýðan (see cûð), w. v., to make known, to manifest, to show : imp. sg. mägen-ellen cýð, show thy heroic strength , 660; inf. cwealmbealu cýðan, 1941; ellen cýðan, 2696.

ge-cýðan (to make known , hence): 1) to give information, to announce : inf. andsware gecýðan, to give answer , 354; gerund, tô gecýðanne hwanan eówre cyme syndon (to show whence ye come), 257; pret. part. sôð is gecýðed þät ... (the truth has become known , it has shown itself to be true), 701; Higelâce wäs sîð Beówulfes snûde gecýðed, the arrival of B. was quickly announced , 1972; similarly, 2325.--2) to make celebrated , in pret. part.: wäs mîn fäder folcum gecýðed (my father was known to warriors), 262; wäs his môdsefa manegum gecýðed, 349; cystum gecýðed, 924.

cýððu (properly, condition of being known , hence relationship), st. f., home, country, land : in comp. feor-cýððu. [should be cýð, feor-cýð--KTH]

ge-cýpan, w. v., to purchase : inf. näs him ænig þearf þät he ... þurfe wyrsan wîgfrecan weorðe gecýpan, had need to buy with treasures no inferior warrior , 2497.

D

daroð, st. m., spear : dat. pl. dareðum lâcan (to fight), 2849.

ge-dâl, st. n., parting, separation : nom. sg. his worulde gedâl, his separation from the world (his death), 3069.--Comp. ealdor-, lîf-gedâl.

däg, st. m., day : nom. sg. däg, 485, 732, 2647; acc. sg. däg, 2400; andlangne däg, the whole day , 2116; morgenlongne däg (the whole morning), 2895; ôð dômes däg, till judgment-day , 3070; dat. sg. on þäm däge þysses lîfes (eo tempore, tunc), 197, 791, 807; gen. sg. däges, 1601, 2321; hwîl däges, a day's time, a whole day , 1496; däges and nihtes, day and night , 2270; däges, by day , 1936; dat. pl. on tyn dagum, in ten days , 3161.--Comp. ær-, deáð-, ende-, ealdor-, fyrn-, geâr-, læn-, lîf-, swylt-, win-däg, an-däges.

däg-hwîl, st. f., day-time : acc. pl. þät he däghwîla gedrogen häfde eorðan wynne, that he had enjoyed earth's pleasures during the days (appointed to him), i.e. that his life was finished, 2727.--(After Grein.)

däg-rîm, st. n., series of days, fixed number of days : nom. sg. dôgera dägrîm (number of the days of his life), 824.

dæd, st. f., deed, action : acc. sg. deórlîce dæd, 585; dômleásan dæd, 2891; frêcne dæde, 890; dæd, 941; acc. pl. Grendles dæda, 195; gen. pl. dæda, 181, 479, 2455, etc.; dat. pl. dædum, 1228, 2437, etc.--Comp. ellen-, fyren-, lof-dæd.

dæd-cêne, adj., bold in deed : nom. sg. dæd-cêne mon, 1646.

dæd-fruma, w. m., doer of deeds, doer : nom. sg., of Grendel, 2091.

dæd-bata, w. m., he who pursues with his deeds : nom. sg., of Grendel, 275.

dædla, w. m., doer : in comp. mân-for-dædla.

dæl, st. m., part, portion : acc. sg. dæl, 622, 2246, 3128; acc. pl. dælas, 1733.-- Often dæl designates the portion of a thing or of a quality which belongs in general to an individual, as, ôð þät him on innan oferhygda dæl weaxeð, till in his bosom his portion of arrogance increases : i.e. whatever arrogance he has, his arrogance, 1741. Biówulfe wearð dryhtmâðma dæl deáðe, forgolden, to Beówulf his part of the splendid treasures was paid with death , i.e. whatever splendid treasures were allotted to him, whatever part of them he could win in the fight with the dragon, 2844; similarly, 1151, 1753, 2029, 2069, 3128.

dælan, w. v., to divide, to bestow, to share with , w. acc.: pres. sg. III. mâdmas dæleð, 1757; pres. subj. þät he wið aglæcean eofoðo dæle, that he bestow his strength upon (strive with) the bringer of misery the drake), 2535; inf. hringas dælan, 1971; pret. beágas dælde, 80; sceattas dælde, 1687.

be-dælan, w. instr., (to divide), to tear away from, to strip of : pret. part. dreámum (dreáme) bedæled, deprived of the heavenly joys (of Grendel), 722, 1276.

ge-dælan: 1) to distribute : inf. (w. acc. of the thing distributed); bær on innan eall gedælan geongum and ealdum swylc him god sealde, distribute therein to young and old all that God had given him , 71.--2) to divide, to separate , with acc.: inf. sundur gedælan lîf wið lîce, separate life from the body , 2423; so pret. subj. þät he gedælde ... ânra gehwylces lîf wið lîce, 732.

denn (cf. denu, dene, vallis), st. n., den, cave : acc. sg. þäs wyrmes denn, 2761; gen. sg. (draca) gewât dennes niósian, 3046.

ge-defe, adj.: 1) (impersonal) proper, appropriate : nom. sg. swâ hit gedêfe wäs (bið), as was appropriate, proper , 561, 1671, 3176.--2) good, kind, friendly ; nom sg. beó þu suna mînum dædum gedêfe, be friendly to my son by deeds (support my son in deed, namely, when he shall have attained to the government), 1228.-- Comp. un-ge-dêfelîce.

dêman (see dôm), w. v.: 1) to judge, to award justly : pres. subj. mærðo dême, 688.--2) to judge favorably, to praise, to glorify : pret. pl. his ellenweorc duguðum dêmdon, praised his heroic deed with all their might , 3176.

dêmend, judge : dæda dêmend (of God), 181.

deal, adj., "superbus, clarus, fretus" (Grimm): nom. pl. þryðum dealle, 494.

deád, adj., dead : nom. sg. 467, 1324, 2373; acc. sg. deádne, 1310.

deáð, st. m., death, dying : nom. sg, deáð, 441, 447, etc.; acc. sg. deáð, 2169; dat. sg. deáðe, 1389, 1590, (as instr.) 2844, 3046; gen. sg. deáðes wylm, 2270; deáðes nýd, 2455.--Comp. gûð-, wäl-, wundor-deáð.

deáð-bed, st. n., death-bed : dat. sg. deáð-bedde fäst, 2902.

deáð-cwalu, st. f., violent death , ruin and death : dat. pl. tô deáð-cwalum, 1713.

deáð-cwealm, st. m., violent death, murder : nom. sg. 1671.

deáð-däg, st. m., death-day, dying day : dat. sg. äfter deáð-däge (after his death), 187, 886.

deáð-fǽge, adj., given over to death : nom. sg. (Grendel) deáð-fǽge deóg, had hidden himself, being given over to death (mortally wounded), 851.

deáð-scûa, w. m., death-shadow, ghostly being, demon of death : nom. sg. deorc deáð-scûa (of Grendel), 160.

deáð-wêrig, adj., weakened by death, i.e. dead: acc. sg. deáð-wêrigne, 2126. See wêrig.

deáð-wîc, st. n. death's house, home of death : acc. sg. gewât deáðwîc seón (had died), 1276.

deágan (O.H.G. pret. part. tougan, hidden), to conceal one's self, to hide : pret. (for pluperf.) deóg, 851.--Leo.

deorc, adj., dark : of the night, nom. sg. (nihthelm) deorc, 1791; dat. pl. deorcum nihtum, 275, 2212; of the terrible Grendel, nom. sg. deorc deáð-scûa, 160.

deófol, st. m. n., devil : gen. sg. deófles, 2089; gen. pl. deófla, of Grendel and his troop, 757, 1681.

deógol, dýgol, adj., concealed, hidden, inaccessible, beyond information, unknown : nom. sg. deógol dǽdhata (of Grendel), 275; acc. sg. dýgel lond, inaccessible land, 1358.

deóp, st. n., deep, abyss : acc. sg., 2550.

deóp, adv. deeply : acc. sg. deóp wäter, 509, 1905.

diópe, adj., deep : hit ôð dômes däg diópe benemdon þeódnas mǽre, the illustrious rulers had charmed it deeply till the judgment-day, had laid a solemn spell upon it, 3070.

deór, st. n., animal, wild animal : in comp. mere-, sǽ-deór.

deór, adj.: 1) wild, terrible : nom. sg. diór dǽd-fruma (of Grendel), 2091.-- 2) bold, brave : nom. nænig ... deór, 1934.--Comp.: heaðu-, hilde-deór.

deóre, dýre, adj.: 1) dear, costly (high in price): acc. sg. dýre îren, 2051; drincfät dýre (deóre), 2307, 2255; instr. sg. deóran sweorde, 561; dat. sg. deórum mâðme, 1529; nom. pl. dýre swyrd, 3049; acc. pl. deóre (dýre) mâðmas, 2237, 3132.--2) dear, beloved, worthy : nom. sg. f., äðelum dióre, worthy by reason of origin, 1950; dat. sg. äfter deórum men, 1880; gen. sg. deórre duguðe, 488; superl. acc. sg. aldorþegn þone deórestan, 1310.

deór-lîc, adj., bold, brave : acc. sg. deórlîce dǽd, 585. See deór.

disc, st. m., disc, plate, flat dish : nom. acc. pl. discas, 2776, 3049.

ge-dîgan. See ge-dýgan.

dol-gilp, st. m., mad boast, foolish pride, vain-glory, thoughtless audacity : dat. sg. for dolgilpe, 509.

dol-lîc, adj., audacious : gen. pl. mǽst ... dǽda dollîcra, 2647.

dol-sceaða, w. m., bold enemy : acc. sg. þone dol-scaðan (Grendel), 479.

dôgor, st. m. n., day ; 1) day as a period of 24 hours: gen. sg. ymb ântîd ôðres dôgores, at the same time of the next day, 219; morgen-leóht ôðres dôgores, the morning-light of the second day, 606.--2) day in the usual sense: acc. sg. n. þys dôgor, during this day, 1396; instr. þý dôgore, 1798; forman dôgore, 2574; gen. pl. dôgora gehwâm, 88; dôgra gehwylce, 1091; dôgera dägrim, the number of his days (the days of his life), 824.--3) day in the wider sense of time: dat. pl. ufaran dôgrum, in later days, times, 2201, 2393.--Comp. ende-dôgor.

dôgor-gerîm, st. n., series of days : gen. sg. wäs eall sceacen dôgor-gerîmes, the whole number of his days (his life) was past, 2729.

dôhtor, st. f., daughter : nom. acc. sg. dôhtor, 375, 1077, 1930, 1982, etc.

dôm, st. m.: I., condition, state in general ; in comp. cyne-, wis-dôm.--II., having reference to justice, hence: 1) judgment, judicial opinion : instr. sg. weotena dôme, according to the judgment of the Witan , 1099. 2) custom : äfter dôme, according to custom , 1721. 3) court, tribunal : gen. sg. miclan dômes, 979; ôð dômes däg, 3070, both times of the last judgment.--III., condition of freedom or superiority , hence: 4) choice, free will : acc. sg. on sînne sylfes dôm, according to his own choice , 2148; instr. sg. selfes dôme, 896, 2777. 5) might, power : nom. sg. dôm godes, 2859; acc. sg. Eofores ânne dôm, 2965; dat. sg. drihtnes dôme, 441. 6) glory, honor, renown : nom. sg. [dôm], 955; dôm unlytel, not a little glory , 886; þät wäs forma sîð deórum mâðme þät his dôm âläg, it was the first time to the dear treasure (the sword Hrunting) that its fame was not made good , 1529; acc. sg. ic me dôm gewyrce, make renown for myself , 1492; þät þu ne âläete dôm gedreósan, that thou let not honor fall , 2667; dat. instr. sg. þær he dôme forleás, here he lost his reputation , 1471; dôme gewurðad, adorned with glory , 1646; gen. sg. wyrce se þe môte dômes, let him make himself reputation, whoever is able , 1389. 7) splendor (in heaven): acc. sôð-fästra dôm, the glory of the saints , 2821.

dôm-leás, adj., without reputation, inglorious : acc. sg. f. dômleásan däd, 2891.

dôn, red. v., to do, to make, to treat : 1) absolutely: imp. dôð swâ ic bidde, do as I beg , 1232.--2) w. acc.: inf. hêt hire selfre sunu on bäl dôn, 1117; pret. þâ he him of dyde îsernbyrnan, took off the iron corselet , 672; (þonne) him Hûnlâfing, ... billa sêlest, on bearm dyde, when he made a present to him of Hûnlâfing, the best of swords , 1145; dyde him of healse hring gyldenne, took off the gold ring from his neck , 2810; ne him þäs wyrmes wîg for wiht dyde, eafoð and ellen, nor did he reckon as anything the drake's fighting, power, and strength , 2349; pl. hi on beorg dydon bêg and siglu, placed in the (grave-) mound rings and ornaments , 3165.--3) representing preceding verbs: inf. tô Geátum sprec mildum wordum! swâ sceal man dôn, as one should do , 1173; similarly, 1535, 2167; pres. metod eallum weóld, swâ he nu git dêð, the creator ruled over all, as he still does , 1059; similarly, 2471, 2860, and (sg. for pl.) 1135; pret. II. swâ þu ær dydest, 1677; III. swâ he nu gyt dyde, 957; similarly, 1382, 1892, 2522; pl. swâ hie oft ær dydon, 1239; similarly, 3071. With the case also which the preceding verb governs: wên' ic þät he wille ... Geátena leóde etan unforhte, swâ he oft dyde mägen Hreðmanna, I believe he will wish to devour the Geát people, the fearless, as he often did (devoured) the bloom of the Hreðmen , 444; gif ic þät gefricge ... þät þec ymbesittend egesan þýwað, swâ þec hetende hwîlum dydon, that the neighbors distress thee as once the enemy did thee (i.e. distressed), 1829; gif ic ôwihte mäg þînre môd-lufan mâran tilian þonne ic gyt dyde, if I can with anything obtain thy greater love than I have yet done , 1825; similarly, pl. þonne þâ dydon, 44.

ge-dôn, to do, to make , with the acc. and predicate adj.: prs. (god) gedêð him swâ gewealdene worolde dælas, makes the parts of the world (i.e. the whole world) so subject that ... , 1733; inf. ne hyne on medo-bence micles wyrðne drihten wereda gedôn wolde, nor would the leader of the people much honor him at the mead-banquet , 2187. With adv.: he mec þær on innan ... gedôn wolde, wished to place me in there , 2091.

draca, w. m., drake, dragon : nom. sg., 893, 2212; acc. sg. dracan, 2403, 3132; gen. sg., 2089, 2291, 2550.--Comp.: eorð-, fŷr-, lêg-, lîg-, nîð-draca.

on-drædan, st. v., w. acc. of the thing and dat. of the pers., to fear, to be afraid of : inf. þät þu him on-drædan ne þearft ... aldorbealu, needest not fear death for them , 1675; pret. nô he him þâ säcce ondrêd, was not afraid of the combat , 2348.

ge-dräg (from dragan, in the sense se gerere), st. n., demeanor, actions : acc. sg. sêcan deófla gedräg, 757.

drepan, st. v., to hit, to strike : pret. sg. sweorde drep ferhð-genîðlan, 2881; pret. part. bið on hreðre ... drepen biteran stræle, struck in the breast with piercing arrow , 1746; wäs in feorh dropen (fatally hit), 2982.

drepe, st. m., blow, stroke : acc. sg. drepe, 1590.

drêfan, ge-drêfan, w. v., to move, to agitate, to stir up : inf. gewât ... drêfan deóp wäter (to navigate), 1905; pret. part. wäter under stôd dreórig and gedrêfed, 1418.

dreám, st. m., rejoicing, joyous actions, joy : nom. sg. häleða dreám, 497; acc. sg. dreám hlûdne, 88; þu ... dreám healdende, thou who livest in rejoicing (at the drinking-carouse), who art joyous , 1228: dat. instr. sg. dreáme bedæled, 1276; gen. pl. dreáma leás, 851; dat. pl. dreámum (here adverbial) lifdon, lived in rejoicing, joyously , 99; dreámum bedæled, 722; the last may refer also to heavenly joys.--Comp. gleó-, gum-, man-, sele-dreám.

dreám-leás, adj., without rejoicing, joyless : nom. sg. of King Heremôd, 1721.

dreógan, st. v.: 1) to lead a life, to be in a certain condition : pret. dreáh äfter dôme, lived in honor, honorably , 2180; pret. pl. fyren-þearfe ongeat, þät hie ær drugon aldorleáse lange hwile, (God) had seen the great distress, (had seen) that they had lived long without a ruler (?), 15.--2) to experience, to live through, to do, to make, to enjoy : imp. dreóh symbelwynne, pass through the pleasure of the meal, to enjoy the meal , 1783; inf. driht-scype dreógan (do a heroic deed), 1471; pret. sundnytte dreáh (had the occupation of swimming , i.e. swam through the sea), 2361; pret. pl. hie gewin drugon (fought), 799; hî sîð drugon, made the way, went , 1967.--3) to experience, to bear, to suffer : scealt werhðo dreógan, shall suffer damnation , 590; pret. þegn-sorge dreáh, bore sorrow for his heroes , 131; nearoþcarfc drcáh, 422; pret. pl. inwidsorge þe hie ær drugon, 832, similarly, 1859.

â-dreógan, to suffer, to endure : inf. wræc âdreógan, 3079.

ge-dreógan, to live through, to enjoy , pret. part. þät he ... gedrogen häfde eorðan wynne, that he had now enjoyed the pleasures of earth (i.e. that he was at his death), 2727.

dreór, st. m., blood dropping or flowing from wounds : instr. sg. dreóre, 447.--Comp. heoru-, sâwul-, wäl-dreór.

dreór-fâh, adj., colored with blood, spotted with blood : nom. sg. 485.

dreórig, adj., bloody, bleeding : nom. sg. wäter stôd dreórig, 1418; acc. sg. dryhten sînne driórigne fand, 2790.--Comp. heoru-dreórig.

ge-dreósan, st. v., to fall down, to sink : pres. sg. III. lîc-homa læne gedreóseð, the body, belonging to death, sinks down , 1755; inf. þät þu ne âlæte dôm gedreósan, honor fall, sink , 2667.

drincan, st. v., to drink (with and without the acc.): pres. part. nom. pl. ealo drincende, 1946; pret. blôd êdrum dranc, drank the blood in streams (?), 743; pret. pl. druncon wîn weras, the men drank wine , 1234; þær guman druncon, where the men drank , 1649. The pret. part., when it stands absolutely, has an active sense: nom. pl. druncne dryhtguman, ye warriors who have drunk, are drinking , 1232; acc. pl. nealles druncne slog heorð-geneátas, slew not his hearth-companions who had drunk with him , i.e. at the banquet, 2180. With the instr. it means drunken : nom. sg. beóre (wîne) druncen, 531, 1468; nom. pl. beóre druncne, 480.

drîfan, st. v., to drive : pres. pl. þâ þe brentingas ofer flôda genipu feorran drîfað, who drive their ships thither from afar over the darkness of the sea , 2809; inf. (w. acc.) þeáh þe he [ne] meahte on mere drîfan hringedstefnan, although he could not drive the ship on the sea , 1131.

to-drîfan, to drive apart, to disperse : pret. ôð þät unc flôd tôdrâf, 545.

drohtoð, st. m., mode of living or acting, calling, employment : nom. sg. ne wäs his drohtoð þær swylce he ær gemêtte, there was no employment for him (Grendel) there such as he had found formerly , 757.

drusian, w. v. (cf. dreósan, properly, to be ready to fall ; here of water), to stagnate, to be putrid . pret. lagu drusade (through the blood of Grendel and his mother), 1631.

dryht, driht, st. f., company, troop, band of warriors; noble band : in comp. mago-driht.

ge-dryht, ge-driht, st. f., troop, band of noble warriors : nom. sg. mînra eorla gedryht, 431; acc. sg. äðelinga gedriht, 118; mid his eorla (häleða) gedriht (gedryht), 357, 663; similarly, 634, 1673.--Comp. sibbe-gedriht.

dryht-bearn, st. n., youth from a noble warrior band, noble young man : nom. sg. dryhtbearn Dena, 2036.

dryhten, drihten, st. m., commander, lord : a) temporal lord : nom. sg. dryhten, 1485, 2001, etc.; drihten, 1051; dat. dryhtne, 2483, etc.; dryhten, 1832.--b) God : nom. drihten, 108, etc.; dryhten, 687, etc.; dat. sg. dryhtne, 1693, etc.; drihtne, 1399, etc.; gen. sg. dryhtnes, 441; drihtnes, 941.--Comp.: freá-, freó-, gum-, man-, sige-, wine-dryhten.

dryht-guma, w. m., one of a troop of warriors, noble warrior : dat. sg. drihtguman, 1389; nom. pl. drihtguman, 99; dryhtguman, 1232; dat. pl. ofer dryhtgumum, 1791 (of Hrôðgâr's warriors).

dryht-lîc, adj., (that which befits a noble troop of warriors), noble, excellent : dryhtlîc îren, excellent sword , 893; acc. sg. f. (with an acc. sg. n.) drihtlîce wîf (of Hildeburh), 1159.

dryht-mâðum, st. m., excellent jewel, splendid treasure : gen. pl. dryhtmâðma, 2844.

dryht-scipe, st. m., (lord-ship) warlike virtue, bravery; heroic deed : acc. sg. drihtscype dreógan, to do a heroic deed , 1471.

dryht-sele, st. m., excellent, splendid hall : nom. sg. driht-sele, 485; dryhtsele, 768; acc. sg. dryhtsele, 2321.

dryht-sib, st. f., peace or friendship between troops of noble warriors : gen. sg. dryhtsibbe, 2069.

drync, st. m., drink : in comp. heoru-drync.

drync-fät, st. n., vessel for drink, to receive the drink : acc. sg., 2255; drinc-fät, 2307.

drysmian, w. v., to become obscure, gloomy (through the falling rain): pres. sg. III. lyft drysmað, 1376.

drysne, adj. See on-drysne.

dugan, v., to avail, to be capable, to be good : pres. sg. III. hûru se aldor deáh, especially is the prince capable , 369; ðonne his ellen deáh, if his strength avails, is good , 573; þe him selfa deáh, who is capable of himself, who can rely on himself , 1840; pres. subj. þeáh þîn wit duge, though, indeed, your understanding be good, avail , 590; similarly, 1661, 2032; pret. sg. þu ûs wel dohtest, you did us good, conducted yourself well towards us , 1822; similarly, nu seó hand ligeð se þe eów welhwylcra wilna dohte, which was helpful to each one of your desires , 1345; pret. subj. þeáh þu heaðoræsa gehwær dohte, though thou wast everywhere strong in battle , 526.

duguð (state of being fit, capable), st. f.: 1) capability, strength : dat. pl. for dugeðum, in ability (?), 2502; duguðum dêmdon, praised with all their might (?), 3176.--2) men capable of bearing arms, band of warriors , esp., noble warriors : nom. sg. duguð unlytel, 498; duguð, 1791, 2255; dat. sg. for duguðe, before the heroes , 2021; nalles frätwe geaf ealdor duguðe, gave the band of heroes no treasure (more), 2921; leóda duguðe on lâst, upon the track of the heroes of the people , i.e. after them, 2946; gen. sg. cûðe he duguðe þeáw, the custom of the noble warriors , 359; deórre duguðe, 488; similarly, 2239, 2659; acc. pl. duguða, 2036.--3) contrasted with geogoð, duguð designates the noted warriors of noble birth (as in the Middle Ages, knights in contrast with squires): so gen. sg. duguðe and geogoðe, 160; gehwylc ... duguðe and iogoðe, 1675; duguðe and geogoðe dæl æghwylcne, 622.

durran, v. pret. and pres. to dare ; prs. sg. II. þu dearst bîdan, darest to await , 527; III. he gesêcean dear, 685; pres. subj. sêc gyf þu dyrre, seek (Grendel's mother), if thou dare , 1380; pret. dorste, 1463, 1469, etc.; pl. dorston, 2849.

duru, st. f., door, gate, wicket : nom. sg., 722; acc. sg. [duru], 389.

ge-dûfan, st. v., to dip in, to sink into : pret. þät sweord gedeáf (the sword sank into the drake , of a blow), 2701.

þurh-dûfan, to dive through; to swim through, diving : pret. wäter up þurh-deáf, swam through the water upwards (because he was before at the bottom), 1620.

dwellan, w. v., to mislead, to hinder : prs. III. nô hine wiht dweleð, âdl ne yldo, him nothing misleads, neither sickness nor age , 1736.

dyhtig, adj., useful, good for : nom. sg. n. sweord ... ecgum dyhtig, 1288.

dynnan, w. v., to sound, to groan, to roar : pret. dryhtsele (healwudu, hruse) dynede, 768, 1318, 2559.

dyrne, adj.: 1) concealed, secret, retired : nom. sg. dyrne, 271; acc. sg. dryhtsele dyrnne (of the drake's cave-hall), 2321.--2) secret, malicious, hidden by sorcery : dat. instr. sg. dyrnan cräfte, with secret magic art , 2291; dyrnum cräfte, 2169; gen. pl. dyrnra gâsta, of malicious spirits (of Grendel's kin), 1358.--Comp. un-dyrne.

dyrne, adv., in secret, secretly : him ...äfter deórum men dyrne langað, longs in secret for the dear man , 1880.

dyrstig, adj., bold, daring : þeáh þe he dæda gehwäs dyrstig wære, although he had been courageous for every deed , 2839.

ge-dýgan, ge-dîgan, w. v., to endure, to overcome , with the acc. of the thing endured: pres. sg. II. gif þu þät ellenweorc aldre gedîgest, if thou survivest the heroic work with thy life , 662; III. þät þone hilderæs hâl gedîgeð, that he survives the battle in safety , 300; similarly, inf. unfæge gedîgan weán and wräcsîð, 2293; hwäðer sêl mæge wunde gedýgan, which of the two can stand the wounds better (come off with life), 2532; ne meahte unbyrnende deóp gedýgan, could not endure the deep without burning (could not hold out in the deep), 2550; pret. sg. I. III. ge-dîgde, 578, 1656, 2351, 2544.

dýgol. See deógol.

dýre. See deóre.

E

ecg, st. f., edge of the sword, point : nom. sg. sweordes ecg, 1107; ecg, 1525, etc.; acc. sg. wið ord and wið ecge ingang forstôd, defended the entrance against point and edge (i.e. against spear and sword), 1550; mêces ecge, 1813; nom. pl. ecge, 1146.-- Sword, battle-axe, any cutting weapon : nom. sg. ne wäs ecg bona (not the sword killed him), 2507; sió ecg brûn (Beówulf's sword Nägling), 2578; hyne ecg fornam, the sword snatched him away , 2773, etc.; nom. pl. ecga, 2829; dat. pl. äscum and ecgum, 1773; dat. pl. (but denoting only one sword) eácnum ecgum, 2141; gen. pl. ecga, 483, 806, 1169;-- blade : ecg wäs îren, 1460.--Comp.: brûn-, heard-, stýl-ecg, adj.

ecg-bana, w. m., murderer by the sword : dat. sg. Cain wearð tô ecg-banan ângan brêðer, 1263.

ecg-hete, st. m., sword-hate, enmity which the sword carries out : nom. sg., 84, 1739.

ecg-þracu, st. f., sword-storm (of violent combat): acc. atole ecg-þräce, 597.

ed-hwyrft, st. m., return (of a former condition): þâ þær sôna wearð edhwyrft eorlum, siððan inne fealh Grendles môdor (i.e. after Grendel's mother had penetrated into the hall, the former perilous condition, of the time of the visits of Grendel, returned to the men), 1282.

ed-wendan, w. v., to turn back, to yield, to leave off : inf. gyf him edwendan æfre scolde bealuwa bisigu, if for him the affliction of evil should ever cease , 280.

ed-wenden, st. f., turning, change : nom. sg. edwenden, 1775; ed-wenden torna gehwylces (reparation for former neglect), 2189.

edwît-lîf, st. n., life in disgrace : nom. sg., 2892.

efn, adj., even, like , with preceding on, and with depend. dat., upon the same level, near : him on efn ligeð ealdorgewinna, lies near him , 2904.

efnan (see äfnan) w. v., to carry out, to perform, to accomplish : pres. subj. eorlscype efne (accomplish knightly deeds), 2536; inf. eorlscipe efnan, 2623; sweorda gelâc efnan (to battle), 1042; gerund. tô efnanne, 1942; pret. eorlscipe efnde, 2134, 3008.

efne, adv., even, exactly, precisely, just , united with swâ or swylc: efne swâ swîðe swâ, just so much as , 1093; efne swâ sîde swâ, 1224; wäs se gryre lässa efne swâ micle swâ, by so much the less as ... , 1284; leóht inne stôd efne swâ ... scîneð, a gleam stood therein (in the sword) just as when ... shines , 1572; efne swâ hwylc mägða swâ þone magan cende (a woman who has borne such a son), 944; efne swâ hwylcum manna swâ him gemet þûhte, to just such a man as seemed good to him , 3058; efne swylce mæla swylce ... þearf gesælde, just at the times at which necessity commanded it , 1250.

eft, adv.: l) thereupon, afterwards : 56, 1147, 2112, 3047, etc.; eft sôna bið, then it happens immediately , 1763; bôt eft cuman, help come again , 281.-- 2) again, on the other side : þät hine on ylde eft gewunigen wilgesîðas, that in old age again (also on their side) willing companions should be attached to him , 22;-- anew, again : 135, 604, 693, 1557, etc.; eft swâ ær, again as formerly , 643.--3) retro, rursus, back : 123, 296, 854, etc.; þät hig äðelinges eft ne wêndon (did not believe that he would come back), 1597.

eft-cyme, st. m., return : gen. sg. eftcymes, 2897.

eft-sîð, st. m., journey back, return : acc. sg. 1892; gen. sg. eft-sîðes georn, 2784; acc. pl. eftsîðas teáh, went the road back , i.e. returned, 1333.

egesa, egsa (state of terror , active or passive): l) frightfulness : acc. sg. þurh egsan, 276; gen. egesan ne gýmeð, cares for nothing terrible, is not troubled about future terrors (?), 1758.--2) terror, horror, fear : nom. sg. egesa, 785; instr. sg. egesan, 1828, 2737.--Comp.: glêd-, lîg-, wäter-egesa.

eges-full, adj., horrible (full of fear, fearful) , 2930.

eges-lîc, adj., terrible, bringing terror : of Grendel's head, 1650; of the beginning of the fight with the drake, 2310; of the drake, 2826.

egle, adj., causing aversion, hideous : nom. pl. neut., or, more probably, perhaps, adverbial, egle (MS. egl), 988.

egsian (denominative from egesa), w. v., to have terror, distress : pret. (as pluperf.) egsode eorl(?), 6.

ehtian, w. v., to esteem, to make prominent with praise : III. pl. pres. þät þe ... weras ehtigað, that thee men shall esteem, praise , 1223.

elde (those who generate , cf. O.N. al-a, generare), st. m. only in the pl., men : dat. pl. eldum, 2215; mid eldum, among men , 2612.--See ylde.

eldo, st. f., age : instr. sg. eldo gebunden, 2112.

el-land, st. n., foreign land, exile : acc. sg. sceall ... elland tredan, (shall be banished), 3020.

ellen, st. n., strength, heroic strength, bravery : nom. sg. ellen, 573; eafoð and ellen, 903; Geáta ... eafoð and ellen, 603; acc. sg. eafoð and ellen, 2350; ellen cýðan, show bravery , 2696; ellen fremedon, exercised heroic strength, did heroic deeds , 3; similarly, ic gefremman sceal eorlîc ellen, 638; ferh ellen wräc, life drove out the strength , i.e. with the departing life (of the dragon) his strength left him, 2707; dat. sg. on elne, 2507, 2817; as instr. þâ wäs ät þam geongum grim andswaru êðbegête þâm þe ær his elne forleás, then it was easy for (every one of) those who before had lost his hero-courage, to obtain rough words from the young man (Wîglâf), 2862; mid elne, 1494, 2536; elne, alone, in adverbial sense, strongly, zealously , and with the nearly related meaning, hurriedly, transiently , 894, 1098, 1968, 2677, 2918; gen. sg. elnes lät, 1530; þâ him wäs elnes þearf, 2877.--Comp. mägen-ellen.

ellen-dæd, st. f., heroic deed : dat. pl. -dædum, 877, 901.

ellen-gæst, st. m., strength-spirit, demon with heroic strength : nom. sg. of Grendel, 86.

ellen-lîce, adv., strongly, with heroic strength , 2123.

ellen-mærðu, st. f., renown of heroic strength , dat. pl. -mærðum, 829, 1472.

ellen-rôf, adj., renowned for strength : nom. sg. 340, 358, 3064; dat. pl. -rôfum, 1788.

ellen-seóc, adj., infirm in strength : acc. sg. þeóden ellensiócne (the mortally wounded king, Beówulf), 2788.

ellen-weorc, st. n., (strength-work), heroic deed, achievement in battle : acc. sg. 662, 959, 1465, etc.; gen. pl. ellen-weorca, 2400.

elles, adv., else, otherwise : a (modal), in another manner , 2521.--b (local), elles hwær, somewhere else , 138; elles hwergen, 2591.

ellor, adv., to some other place , 55, 2255.

ellor-gâst, -gæst, st. m., spirit living elsewhere (standing outside of the community of mankind): nom. sg. se ellorgâst (Grendel), 808; (Grendel's mother), 1622; ellorgæst (Grendel's mother), 1618; acc. pl. ellorgæstas, 1350.

ellor-sîð, st. m., departure, death : nom. sg. 2452.

elra, adj. (comparative of a not existing form, ele, Goth. aljis, alius), another : dat. sg. on elran men, 753.

el-þeódig, adj., of another people: foreign : acc. pl. el-þeódige men, 336.

ende, st. m., the extreme : hence, 1) end : nom. sg. aldres (lîfes) ende, 823, 2845; ôð þät ende becwom (scil. unrihtes), 1255; acc. sg. ende lîfgesceafta (lîfes, læn-daga), 3064, 1387, 2343; häfde eorðscrafa ende genyttod, had used the end of the earth-caves (had made use of the caves for the last time), 3047; dat. sg. ealdres (lîfes) ät ende, 2791, 2824; eoletes ät ende, 224.--2) boundary : acc. sg. sîde rîce þät he his selfa ne mäg ... ende geþencean, the wide realm, so that he himself cannot comprehend its boundaries , 1735.--3) summit, head : dat. sg. eorlum on ende, to the nobles at the end (the highest courtiers), 2022.--Comp. woruld-ende.

ende-däg, st. m., last day, day of death : nom. sg. 3036; acc. sg. 638.

ende-dôgor, st. m., last day, day of death : gen. sg. bega on wênum endedôgores and eftcymes leótes monnes (hesitating between the belief in the death and in the return of the dear man), 2897.

ende-lâf, st. f., last remnant : nom. sg. þu eart ende-lâf ûsses cynnes, art the last of our race , 2814.

ende-leán, st. n., final reparation : acc. sg. 1693.

ende-sæta, w. m., he who sits on the border, boundary-guard : nom. sg. (here of the strand-watchman), 241.

ende-stäf, st. m. (elementum finis), end : acc. sg. hit on endestäf eft gelimpeð, then it draws near to the end , 1754.

ge-endian, w. v., to end : pret. part. ge-endod, 2312.

enge, adj., narrow : acc. pl. enge ânpaðas, narrow paths , 1411.

ent, st. m., giant : gen. pl. enta ær-geweorc (the sword-hilt out of the dwelling-place of Grendel), 1680; enta geweorc (the dragon's cave), 2718; eald-enta ær-geweorc (the costly things in the dragon's cave), 2775.

entisc, adj., coming from giants : acc. sg. entiscne helm, 2980.

etan, st. v., to eat, to consume : pres. sg. III. blôdig wäl ... eteð ân-genga, he that goes alone (Grendel) will devour the bloody corpse , 448; inf. Geátena leóde ... etan, 444.

þurh-etan, to eat through : pret. part. pl. nom. swyrd ... þurhetone, swords eaten through (by rust), 3050.

Ê

êc. See eác.

êce, adj., everlasting ; nom. êce drihten (God), 108; acc. sg. êce eorðreced, the everlasting earth-hall (the dragon's cave), 2720; geceás êcne ræd, chose the everlasting gain (died), 1202; dat. sg. êcean dryhtne, 1693, 1780, 2331; acc. pl. geceós êce rædas, 1761.

êdre. See ædre.

êð-begête, adj., easy to obtain, ready : nom. sg. þâ wäs ät þam geongum grim andswaru êð-begête, then from the young man (Wîglâf) it was an easy thing to get a gruff answer , 2862.

êðe. See eáðe.

êðel, st. m., hereditary possessions, hereditary estate : acc. sg. swæsne êðel, 520; dat. sg. on êðle, 1731.--In royal families the hereditary possession is the whole realm: hence, acc. sg. êðel Scyldinga, of the kingdom of the Scyldings , 914; (Offa) wîsdôme heóld êðel sînne, ruled with wisdom his inherited kingdom , 1961.

êðel-riht, st. n., hereditary privileges (rights that belong to a hereditary estate): nom. sg. eard êðel-riht, estate and inherited privileges , 2199.

êðel-stôl, st. m., hereditary seat, inherited throne : acc. pl. êðel-stôlas, 2372.

êðel-turf, st. f., inherited ground, hereditary estate : dat. sg. on mînre êðeltyrf, 410.

êðel-weard, st. m., lord of the hereditary estate (realm): nom. sg. êðelweard (king), 1703, 2211; dat. sg. Eást-Dena êðel wearde (King Hrôðgâr), 617.

êðel-wyn, st. f., joy in , or enjoyment of, hereditary possessions : nom. sg. nu sceal ... eall êðelwyn eówrum cynne, lufen âlicgean, now shall your race want all home-joy, and subsistence (?) (your race shall be banished from its hereditary abode), 2886; acc. sg. he me lond forgeaf, eard êðelwyn, presented me with land, abode, and the enjoyment of home , 2494.

eð-gesýne, ýð-gesêne, adj., easy to see, visible to all : nom. sg. 1111, 1245.

êfstan, w. v., to be in haste, to hasten : inf. uton nu êfstan, let us hurry now , 3102; pret. êfste mid elne, hastened with heroic strength , 1494.

êg-clif, st. n., sea-cliff : acc. sg. ofer êg-clif (ecg-clif, MS.), 2894.

êg-streám, st. m., sea-stream, sea-flood : dat. pl. on êg-streámum, in the sea-floods , 577. See eágor-streám.

êhtan (M.H.G. æchten; cf. æht and ge-æhtla), w. v. w. gen., to be a pursuer, to pursue : pres. part. äglæca êhtende wäs duguðe and geogoðe, 159; pret. pl. êhton aglæcan, they pursued the bringer of sorrow (Beówulf)(?), 1513.

êst, st. m. f., favor, grace, kindness : acc. sg. he him êst geteáh Meara and mâðma (honored him with horses and jewels), 2166; gearwor häfde âgendes êst ær gesceáwod, would rather have seen the grace of the Lord (of God) sooner , 3076.--dat. pl., adverbial, libenter: him on folce heóld, êstum mid âre, 2379; êstum geýwan (to present), 2150; him wäs ... wunden gold êstum geeáwed (presented), 1195; we þät ellenweorc êstum miclum fremedon, 959.

êste, adj., gracious : w. gen. êste bearn-gebyrdo, gracious through the birth (of such a son as Beówulf), 946.

EA

eafoð, st. n., power, strength : nom, sg. eafoð and ellen, 603, 903; acc. sg. eafoð and ellen, 2350; we frêcne geneðdon eafoð uncûðes, we have boldly ventured against the strength of the enemy (Grendel) have withstood him , 961; gen. sg. eafoðes cräftig, 1467; þät þec âdl oððe ecg eafoðes getwæfed, shall rob of strength , 1764; acc. pl. eafeðo (MS. earfeðo) [This reading cancelled. See note to l. 534--KTH], 534; dat. pl. hine mihtig god ... eafeðum stêpte, made him great through strength , 1718. See Note for l. 534.

eafor, st. m., boar ; here the image of the boar as banner: acc. sg. eafor, 2153.

eafora (offspring), w. m.: 1) son : nom. sg. eafera, 12, 898; eafora, 375; acc. sg. eaferan, 1548, 1848; gen. sg. eafera, 19; nom. pl. eaferan, 2476; dat. pl. eaferum, 1069, 2471; uncran eaferan, 1186.--2) in broader sense, successor : dat. pl. eaforum, 1711.

eahta, num., eight : acc. pl. eahta mearas, 1036; eode eahta sum, went as one of eight, with seven others , 3124.

eahtian, w. v.: 1) to consider; to deliberate : pret. pl. w. acc. ræd eahtedon, consulted about help , 172; pret. sg. (for the plural) þone sêlestan þâra þe mid Hrôðgâre hâm eahtode, the best one of those who with Hrôðgâr deliberated about their home (ruled), 1408.--2) to speak with reflection of (along with the idea of praise): pret. pl. eahtodan eorlscipe, spoke of his noble character , 3175.

eal, eall, adj., all, whole : nom. sg. werod eall, 652; pl. eal bencþelu, 486; sg. eall êðelwyn, 2886; eal worold, 1739, etc.; þät hit wearð eal gearo, healärna mæst,

77; þät hit (wîgbil) eal gemealt, 1609. And with a following genitive: þær wäs eal geador Grendles grâpe, there was all together Grendel's hand, the whole hand of Grendel, 836; eall ... lissa, all favor, 2150; wäs eall sceacen dôgorgerîmes, 2728. With apposition: þûhte him eall tô rûm, wongas and wîcstede, 2462; acc. sg. beót eal, 523; similarly, 2018, 2081; oncýððe ealle, all distress, 831; heals ealne, 2692; hlæw ... ealne ûtan-weardne, 2298; gif he þät eal gemon, 1186, 2428; þät eall geondseh, recedes geatwa, 3089; ealne wîde-ferhð, through the whole wide life, through all time, 1223; instr. sg. ealle mägene, with all strength, 2668; dat. sg. eallum ... manna cynne, 914; gen. sg. ealles moncynnes, 1956. Subst. ic þäs ealles mäg ... gefeán habban, 2740; brûc ealles well, 2163; freán ealles þanc secge, give thanks to the Lord of all, 2795; nom. pl. untydras ealle, 111; sceótend ... ealle, 706; we ealle, 942; acc. pl. feónd ealle, 700; similarly, 1081, 1797, 2815; subst. ofer ealle, 650; ealle hie deáð fornam, 2237; lîg ealle forswealg þâra þe þær gûð fornam, all of those whom the war had snatched away, 1123; dat. pl. eallum ceaster-bûendum, 768; similarly, 824, 907, 1418; subst. âna wið eallum, one against all, 145; with gen. eallum gumena cynnes, 1058; gen. pl. äðelinga bearn ealra twelfa, the kinsmen of all twelve nobles (twelve nobles hold the highest positions of the court), 3172; subst. he âh ealra geweald, has power over all, 1728.

Uninflected: bil eal þurhwôd flæschoman, the battle-axe cleft the body through and through, 1568; häfde ... eal gefeormod fêt and folma, had devoured entirely feet and hands, 745; se þe eall geman gâr-cwealm gumena, who remembers thoroughly the death of the men by the spear, 2043, etc.

Adverbial: þeáh ic eal mæge, although I am entirely able, 681; hî on beorg dydon bêg and siglu eall swylce hyrsta, they placed in the grave-mound rings, and ornaments, all such adornments, 3165.--The gen. sg. ealles, adverbial in the sense of entirely, 1001, 1130.

eald, adj., old : a) of the age of living beings: nom. sg. eald, 357, 1703, 2211, etc.; dat. sg. ealdum, 2973; gen. sg. ealdes uhtflogan (dragon), 2761; dat. sg. ealdum, 1875; geongum and ealdum, 72.--b) of things and of institutions: nom. sg. helm monig eald and ômig, 2764; acc. sg. ealde lâfe (sword), 796, 1489; ealde wîsan, 1866; eald sweord, 1559, 1664, etc.; eald gewin, old (lasting years), distress, 1782; eald enta geweorc (the precious things in the drake's cave), 2775; acc. pl. ealde mâðmas, 472; ofer ealde riht, against the old laws (namely, the Ten Commandments; Beówulf believes that God has sent him the drake as a punishment, because he has unconsciously, at some time, violated one of the commandments), 2331.

yldra, compar. older : mîn yldra mæg, 468; yldra brôðor, 1325; ôð þät he (Heardrêd) yldra wearð, 2379.

yldesta, superl. oldest, in the usual sense; dat. sg. þam yldestan, 2436; in a moral sense, the most respected : nom. sg. se yldesta, 258; acc. sg. þone yldestan, 363, both times of Beówulf.

eald-fäder, st. m., old-father, grandfather, ancestor : nom. sg. 373.

eald-gesegen, st. f., traditions from old times : gen. pl. eal-fela eald-gesegena, very many of the old traditions, 870.

eald-gesîð, st. m., companion ever since old times, courtier for many years : nom. pl. eald-gesîðas, 854.

eald-gestreón, st. n., treasure out of the old times : dat. pl. eald-gestreónum, 1382; gen. pl. -gestreóna, 1459.

eald-gewinna, w. m., old-enemy, enemy for many years : nom. sg. of Grendel, 1777.

eald-gewyrht, st. n., merit on account of services rendered during many years : nom. pl. þät næron eald-gewyrht, þät he âna scyle gnorn þrowian, that has not been his desert ever since long ago, that he should bear the distress alone , 2658.

eald-hlâford, st. m., lord through many years : gen. sg. bill eald-hlâfordes (of the old Beówulf(?)), 2779.

eald-metod, st. m., God ruling ever since ancient times : nom. sg. 946.

ealdor, aldor, st. m., lord, chief (king or powerful noble): nom. sg. ealdor, 1645, 1849, 2921; aldor, 56, 369, 392; acc. sg. aldor, 669; dat. sg. ealdre, 593; aldre, 346.

ealdor, aldor, st. n., life : acc. sg. aldor, 1372; dat. sg. aldre, 1448, 1525; ealdre, 2600; him on aldre stôd herestræl hearda (in vitalibus), 1435; nalles for ealdre mearn, was not troubled about his life , 1443; of ealdre gewât, went out of life, died , 2625; as instr. aldre, 662, 681, etc.; ealdre, 1656, 2134, etc.; gen. sg. aldres, 823; ealdres, 2791, 2444; aldres orwêna, despairing of life , 1003, 1566; ealdres scyldig, having forfeited life , 1339, 2062; dat. pl. aldrum nêðdon, 510, 538.-- Phrases: on aldre (in life), ever , 1780; tô aldre (for life), always , 2006, 2499; âwa tô aldre, for ever and ever , 956.

ealdor-bealu, st. n., life's evil : acc. sg. þu ... ondrædan ne þearft ... aldorbealu eorlum, thou needest not fear death for the courtiers , 1677.

ealdor-cearu, st. f., trouble that endangers life, great trouble : dat. sg. he his leódum wearð ... tô aldor-ceare, 907.

ealdor-dagas, st. m. pl., days of one's life : dat. pl. næfre on aldor-dagum (never in his life), 719; on ealder-dagum ær (in former days), 758.

ealdor-gedâl, st. n., severing of life, death, end : nom. sg. aldor-gedâl, 806.

ealdor-gewinna, w. m., life-enemy, one who strives to take his enemy's life (in N.H.G. the contrary conception, Tod-feind): nom. sg. ealdorgewinna (the dragon), 2904.

ealdor-leás, adj., without a ruler (?): nom. pl. aldor-leáse, 15.

ealdor-leás, adj., lifeless, dead : acc. sg. aldor-leásne, 1588; ealdor-leásne, 3004.

ealdor-þegn, st. m., nobleman at the court, distinguished courtier : acc. sg. aldor-þegn (Hrôðgâr's confidential adviser, Äschere), 1309.

eal-fela, adj., very much : with following gen., eal-fela eald-gesegena, very many old traditions , 870; eal-fela eotena cynnes, 884.

ealgian, w. v., to shield, to defend, to protect : inf. w. acc. feorh ealgian, 797, 2656, 2669; pret. siððan he (Hygelâc) under segne sinc eal-gode, wälreáf werede, while under his banner he protected the treasures, defended the spoil of battle (i.e. while he was upon the Viking expeditions), 1205.

eal-gylden, adj., all golden, entirely of gold : nom. sg. swýn ealgylden, 1112; acc. sg. segn eallgylden, 2768.

eal-îrenne, adj., entirely of iron : acc. sg. eall-îrenne wîgbord, a wholly iron battle-shield , 2339.

ealu, st. n., ale, beer : acc. sg. ealo drincende, 1946.

ealu-benc, st. f., ale-bench, bench for those drinking ale : dat. sg. in ealo-bence, 1030; on ealu-bence, 2868.

ealu-scerwen, st. f., terror , under the figure of a mishap at an ale-drinking, probably the sudden taking away of the ale: nom. sg. Denum eallum wearð ... ealuscerwen, 770.

ealu-wæge, st. n., ale-can, portable vessel out of which ale is poured into the cups : acc. sg. 2022; hroden ealowæge, 495; dat. sg. ofer ealowæge (at the ale-carouse), 481.

eal-wealda, w. adj., all ruling (God): nom. sg. fäder alwalda, 316; alwalda, 956, 1315; dat. sg. al-wealdan, 929.

eard, st. m., cultivated ground, estate, hereditary estate ; in a broader sense, ground in general, abode, place of sojourn : nom. sg. him wäs bâm ... lond gecynde, eard êðel-riht, the land was bequeathed to them both, the land and the privileges attached to it. 2199; acc. sg. fîfel-cynnes eard, the ground of the giant race, place of sojourn , 104; similarly, älwihta eard, 1501; eard gemunde, thought of his native ground, his home , 1130; eard git ne const, thou knowest not yet the place of sojourn. 1378; eard and eorlscipe, prædium et nobilitatem , 1728; eard êðelwyn, land and the enjoyment of home , 2494; dat. sg. ellor hwearf of earde, went elsewhere from his place of abode , i.e. died, 56; þät we rondas beren eft tô earde, that we go again to our homes , 2655; on earde, 2737; nom. pl. eácne eardas, the broad expanses (in the fen-sea where Grendel's home was), 1622.

eardian, w. v.: 1) to have a dwelling-place, to live; to rest : pret. pl. dýre swyrd swâ hie wið eorðan fäðm þær eardodon, costly swords, as they had rested in the earth's bosom , 3051.--2) also transitively, to inhabit : pret. sg. Heorot eardode, 166; inf. wîc eardian elles hwergen, inhabit a place elsewhere (i.e. die), 2590.

eard-lufa, w. m., the living upon one's land, home-life : acc. sg. eard-lufan, 693.

earfoð-lîce, adv., with trouble, with difficulty , 1637, 1658; with vexation, angrily , 86; sorrowfully , 2823; with difficulty, scarcely , 2304, 2935.

earfoð-þrag, st. f., time full of troubles, sorrowful time : acc. sg. -þrage, 283.

earh, adj., cowardly : gen. sg. ne bið swylc earges sîð (no coward undertaken that), 2542.

earm, st. m., arm : acc. sg. earm, 836, 973; wið earm gesät, supported himself with his arm , 750; dat. pl. earmum, 513.

earm, adj., poor, miserable, unhappy : nom. sg. earm, 2369; earme ides, the unhappy woman , 1118; dat. sg. earmre teohhe, the unhappy band , 2939.--Comp. acc. sg. earmran mannan, a more wretched, more forsaken man , 577.

earm-beág, st. m., arm-ring, bracelet : gen. pl. earm-beága fela searwum gesæled, many arm-rings interlaced , 2764.

earm-hreád, st. f., arm-ornament . nom. pl. earm-hreáde twâ, 1195 (Grein's conjecture, MS. earm reade).

earm-lîc, adj., wretched, miserable : nom. sg. sceolde his ealdor-gedâl earmlîc wurðan, his end should be wretched , 808.

earm-sceapen, pret. part. as adj. (properly, wretched by the decree of fate), wretched : nom. sg. 1352.

earn, st. m., eagle : dat. sg. earne, 3027.

eatol. See atol.

eaxl, st. f., shoulder : acc. sg. eaxle, 836, 973; dat. sg. on eaxle, 817, 1548; be eaxle, 1538; on eaxle ides gnornode, the woman sobbed on the shoulder (of her son, who has fallen and is being burnt), 1118; dat. pl. sät freán eaxlum neáh, sat near the shoulders of his lord (Beówulf lies lifeless upon the earth, and Wîglâf sits by his side, near his shoulder, so as to sprinkle the face of his dead lord), 2854; he for eaxlum gestôd Deniga freán, he stood before the shoulders of the lord of the Danes (i.e. not directly before him, but somewhat to the side, as etiquette demanded), 358.

eaxl-gestealla, w. m., he who has his position at the shoulder (sc. of his lord), trusty courtier, counsellor of a prince : nom. sg. 1327; acc. pl. -gesteallan, 1715.

EÁ

eác, conj., also : 97, 388, 433, etc.; êc, 3132.

eácen (pret. part. of a not existing eacan, augere), adj., wide-spread , large : nom. pl. eácne eardas, broad plains , 1622.-- great, heavy : eald sweord eácen, 1664; dat. pl. eácnum ecgum, 2141, both times of the great sword in Grendel's habitation.-- great, mighty, powerful : äðele and eácen, of Beówulf, 198.

eácen-cräftig, adj., immense (of riches), enormously great : acc. sg. hord-ärna sum eácen-cräftig, that enormous treasure-house , 2281; nom. sg. þät yrfe eácen-cräftig, iúmonna gold, 3052.

eádig, adj., blessed with possessions, rich, happy by reason of property : nom. sg. wes, þenden þu lifige, äðeling eádig, be, as long as thou livest, a prince blessed with riches , 1226; eádig mon, 2471.--Comp. sige-, sigor-, tîr-eádig.

eádig-lîce, adv., in abundance, in joyous plenty : dreámum lifdon eádiglîce, lived in rejoicing and plenty , 100.

eáðe, êðe, ýðe, adj., easy, pleasant : nom. pl. gode þancedon þäs þe him ýð-lâde eáðe wurdon, thanked God that the sea-ways (the navigation) had become easy to them , 228; ne wäs þät êðe sîð, no pleasant way , 2587; näs þät ýðe ceáp, no easy purchase , 2416; nô þät ýðe byð tô befleónne, not easy (as milder expression for in no way, not at all), 1003.

eáðe, ýðe, adv., easily . eáðe, 478, 2292, 2765.

eáð-fynde, adj., easy to find : nom. sg. 138.

eáge, w. n., eye : dat. pl. him of eágum stôd leóht unfäger, out of his eyes came a terrible gleam , 727; þät ic ... eágum starige, see with eyes, behold , 1782; similarly, 1936; gen. pl. eágena bearhtm, 1767.

eágor-streám, st. m., sea-stream sea : acc. sg. 513.

eá-land, st. n., land surrounded by water (of the land of the Geátas): acc. sg. eá-lond, 2335; island .

eám, st. m., uncle, mothers brother : nom. sg. 882.

eástan, adv., from the east , 569.

eáwan, w. v., to disclose, to show, to prove : pres. sg. III. eáweð ... uncûðne nîð, shows evil enmity , 276. See eówan, ýwan.

ge-eáwan, to show, to offer : pret. part. him wäs ... wunden gold êstum ge-eáwed, was graciously presented , 1195.

EO

eode. See gangan.

eodor, st. m., fence, hedge, railing . Among the old Germans, an estate was separated by a fence from the property of others. Inside of this fence the laws of peace and protection held good, as well as in the house itself. Hence eodor is sometimes used instead of house : acc. pl. hêht eahta mearas on flet teón, in under eoderas, gave orders to lead eight steeds into the hall, into the house , 1038.--2) figuratively, lord, prince , as protector: nom. sg. eodor, 428, 1045; eodur, 664.

eofoð, st. n., strength : acc. pl. eofoðo, 2535. See eafoð.

eofer, st. m.: 1) boar , here of the metal boar-image upon the helmet: nom. sg. eofer îrenheard, 1113.--2) figuratively, bold hero, brave fighter (O.N. iöfur): nom.

411

pl. þonne ... eoferas cnysedan, when the heroes rushed upon each other, 1329, where eoferas and fêðan stand in the same relation to each other as cnysedan and hniton.

eofor-lîc, st. n. boar-image (on the helmet): nom. pl. eofor-lîc scionon, 303.

eofor-spreót, st. m., boar-spear : dat. pl. mid eofer-spreótum heóro-hôcyhtum, with hunting-spears which were provided with sharp hooks, 1438.

eoguð, ioguð. See geogoð.

eolet, st. m. n., sea (?): gen. sg. eoletes, 224.

eorclan-stân, st. m., precious stone : acc. pl. -stânas, 1209.

eorð-cyning, st. m., king of the land : gen. sg. eorð-cyninges (Finn), 1156.

eorð-draca, w. m., earth-drake, dragon that lives in the earth : nom. sg. 2713, 2826.

eorðe, w. f.: 1) earth (in contrast with heaven), world : acc. sg. älmihtiga eorðan worhte, 92; wîde geond eorðan, far over the earth, through the wide world, 266; dat. sg. ofer eorðan, 248, 803; on eorðan, 1823, 2856, 3139; gen. sg. eorðan, 753.--2) earth, ground : acc. sg. he eorðan gefeóll, fell to the ground, 2835; forlêton eorla gestreón eorðan healdan, let the earth hold the nobles' treasure, 3168; dat. sg. þät hit on eorðan läg, 1533; under eorðan, 2416; gen. sg. wið eorðan fäðm (in the bosom of the earth), 3050.

eorð-reced, st. n., hall in the earth, rock-hall : acc. sg. 2720.

eorð-scräf, st. n., earth-cavern, cave : dat. sg. eorð-[scräfe], 2233; gen. pl. eorð-scräfe, 3047.

eorð-sele, st. m., hall in the earth, cave : acc. sg. eorð-sele, 2411; dat sg. of eorðsele, 2516.

eorð-weall, st. m., earth-wall : acc. sg. (Ongenþeów) beáh eft under eorðweall, fled again under the earth-wall (into his fortified camp), 2958; þâ me wäs ... sîð âlýfed inn under eorðweall, then the way in, under the earth-wall was opened to me (into the dragon's cave), 3091.

eorð-weard, st. m., land-property, estate : acc. sg. 2335.

eorl, st. m., noble born man, a man of the high nobility : nom. sg. 762, 796, 1229, etc.; acc. sg. eorl, 573, 628, 2696; gen. sg. eorles, 690, 983, 1758, etc.; acc. pl. eorlas, 2817; dat. pl. eorlum, 770, 1282, 1650, etc.; gen. pl. eorla, 248, 357, 369, etc.--Since the king himself is from the stock of the eorlas, he is also called eorl, 6, 2952.

eorl-gestreón, st. n., wealth of the nobles : gen. pl. eorl-gestreóna ... hardfyrdne dæl, 2245.

eorl-gewæde, st. n., knightly dress, armor : dat. pl. -gewædum, 1443.

eorlîc (i.e. eorl-lîc), adj., what it becomes a noble born man to do, chivalrous : acc. sg. eorlîc ellen, 638.

eorl-scipe, st. m., condition of being noble born, chivalrous nature, nobility : acc. sg. eorl-scipe, 1728, 3175; eorl-scipe efnan, to do chivalrous deeds, 2134, 2536, 2623, 3008.

eorl-weorod, st. n., followers of nobles : nom. sg. 2894.

eormen-cyn, st. n., very extensive race, mankind : gen. sg. eormen-cynnes, 1958.

eormen-grund, st. m., immensely wide plains, the whole broad earth : acc. sg. ofer eormen-grund, 860.

eormen-lâf, st. f., enormous legacy : acc. sg. eormen-lâfe äðelan cynnes (the treasures of the dragon's cave) 2235.

eorre, adj., angry, enraged : gen. sg. eorres, 1448.

eoton, st. m.: 1) giant : nom. sg. eoten (Grendel), 762; dat. sg. uninflected, eoton (Grendel), 669; nom. pl. eotenas, 112.--2) Eotens, subjects of Finn, the N. Frisians: 1073, 1089, 1142; dat. pl. 1146. See
List of Names, p. 114.

eotonisc, adj., gigantic, coming from giants : acc. sg. eald sweord eotenisc (eotonisc), 1559, 2980, (etonisc, MS.) 2617.

EÓ

eóred-geatwe, st. f. pl., warlike adornments : acc. pl., 2867.

eówan, w. v., to show, to be seen : pres. sg. III. ne gesacu ôhwær, ecghete eóweð, nowhere shows itself strife, sword-hate , 1739. See eáwan, ýwan.

eówer: 1) gen. pl. pers. pron., vestrum: eówer sum, that one of you (namely, Beówulf), 248; fæhðe eówer leóde, the enmity of the people of you (of your people), 597; nis þät eówer sîð ... nefne mîn ânes, 2533.--2) poss. pron., your , 251, 257, 294, etc.

F

ge-fandian, -fondian, w. v., to try, to search for, to find out, to experience : w. gen. pret. part. þät häfde gumena sum goldes gefandod, that a man had discovered the gold , 2302; þonne se ân hafað þurh deâðes nýd dæda gefondad, now the one (Herebeald) has with death's pang experienced the deeds (the unhappy bow-shot of Hæðcyn), 2455.

fara, w. m., farer, traveller : in comp. mere-fara.

faran, st. v., to move from one place to another, to go, to wander : inf. tô hâm faran, to go home , 124; lêton on geflît faran fealwe mearas, let the fallow horses go in emulation , 865; cwom faran flotherge on Fresna land, had come to Friesland with a fleet , 2916; com leóda dugoðe on last faran, came to go upon the track of the heroes of his people , i.e. to follow them, 2946; gerund wæron äðelingas eft tô leódum fûse tô farenne, the nobles were ready to go again to their people , 1806; pret. sg. gegnum fôr [þâ] ofer myrcan mör, there had (Grendel's mother) gone away over the dark fen , 1405; sægenga fôr, the seafarer (the ship) drove along , 1909; (wyrm) mid bæle fôr, (the dragon) fled away with fire , 2309; pret. pl. þät ... scawan scîrhame tô scipe fôron, that the visitors in glittering attire betook themselves to the ship , 1896.

gefaran, to proceed, to act : inf. hû se mânsceaða under færgripum gefaran wolde, how he would act in his sudden attacks , 739.

ût faran, to go out : w. acc. lêt of breóstum ... word ût faran, let words go out of his breast, uttered words , 2552.

faroð, st. m., stream, flood of the sea : dat. sg. tô brimes faroðe, 28; äfter faroðe, with the stream , 580; ät faroðe, 1917.

faru, st. f., way, passage, expedition : in comp. âd-faru.

fâcen-stäf (elementum nequitiae), st. m., wickedness, treachery, deceit . acc. pl. fâcen-stafas, 1019.

fâh, fâg, adj., many-colored, variegated, of varying color (especially said of the color of gold, of bronze, and of blood, in which the beams of light are refracted): nom. sg. fâh (covered with blood), 420; blôde fâh, 935; âtertânum fâh (sc. îren) [This is the MS reading; emmended to âterteárum in text--KTH], 1460; sadol searwum fâh (saddle artistically ornamented with gold), 1039; sweord swâte fâh, 1287; brim blôde fâh, 1595; wäldreóre fâg, 1632; (draca) fýrwylmum fâh

(because he spewed flame), 2672; sweord fâh and fäted, 2702; blôde fâh, 2975; acc. sg. dreóre fâhne, 447; goldsele fättum fâhne, 717; on fâgne flôr treddode, trod the shining floor (of Heorot), 726; hrôf golde fâhne, the roof shining with gold , 928; nom. pl. eoforlîc ... fâh and fýr-beard, 305; acc. pl. þâ hilt since fâge, 1616; dat. pl. fâgum sweordum, 586.--Comp. bân-, blôd-, brûn-, dreór-, gold-, gryre-, searo-, sinc-, stân-, swât-, wäl-, wyrm-fâh.

fâh, fâg, fâ, adj.: 1) hostile : nom. sg. fâh feónd-scaða, 554; he wäs fâg wið god (Grendel), 812; acc. sg. fâne (the dragon), 2656; gen. pl. fâra, 578, 1464.-- 2) liable to pursuit, without peace, outlawed : nom. sg. fâg, 1264; mâne fâh, outlawed through crime , 979; fyren-dædum fâg, 1002.--Comp. nearo-fâh.

fâmig-heals, adj., with foaming neck : nom. sg. flota fâmig-heals, 218; (sægenga) fâmig-heals, 1910.

fäc, st. n., period of time : acc. sg. lytel fäc, during a short time , 2241.

fäder, st. m., father : nom. sg. fäder, 55, 262, 459, 2609; of God, 1610; fäder alwalda, 316; acc. sg. fäder, 1356; dat. sg. fäder, 2430; gen. sg. fäder, 21, 1480; of God, 188--Comp.: ær, eald-fäder.

fädera, w. m., father's brother in comp. suhter-gefäderan.

fäder-äðelo, st. n. pl., paternus principatus (?): dat. pl. fäder-äðelum, 912.

fäderen-mæg, st. m., kinsman descended from the same father, co-descendant : dat. sg. fäderen-mæge, 1264.

fäðm, st. m.: 1) the outspread, encircling arms : instr. pl. feóndes fäð[mum], 2129.--2) embrace, encircling : nom. sg. lîges fäðm, 782; acc. sg. in fýres fäðm, 185.--3) bosom, lap : acc. sg. on foldan fäðm, 1394; wið eorðan fäðm, 3050; dat. pl. tô fäder (God's) fäðmum, 188.--4) power, property : acc. in Francna fäðm, 1211.--Cf. sîd-fäðmed, sîð-fäðme.

fäðmian, w. v., to embrace, to take up into itself : pres. subj. þät mine lîchaman ... glêd fäðmie, 2653; inf. lêton flôd fäðmian frätwa hyrde, 3134.

ge-fäg, adj., agreeable, desirable (Old Eng., fawe, willingly): comp. ge-fägra, 916.

fägen, adj., glad, joyous : nom. pl. ferhðum fägne, the glad at heart , 1634.

fäger, adj., beautiful, lovely : nom. sg. fäger fold-bold, 774; fäger foldan bearm, 1138; acc. sg. freoðoburh fägere, 522; nom. pl. þær him fold-wegas fägere þûhton, 867.--Comp. un-fäger.

fägere, fägre, adv., beautifully, well, becomingly, according to etiquette : fägere geþægon medoful manig, 1015; þâ wäs flet-sittendum fägere gereorded, becomingly the repast was served , 1789; Higelâc ongan ... fägre fricgean, 1986; similarly, 2990.

fär, st. n., craft, ship : nom. sg., 33.

fäst, adj., bound, fast : nom. sg. bið se slæp tô fäst, 1743; acc. sg. freóndscipe fästne, 2070; fäste frioðuwære, 1097.--The prep. on stands to denote the where or wherein: wäs tô fäst on þâm (sc. on fæhðe and fyrene), 137; on ancre fäst, 303. Or, oftener, the dative: feónd-grâpum fäst, (held) fast in his antagonist's clutch , 637; fýrbendum fäst, fast in the forged hinges , 723; handa fäst, 1291, etc.; hygebendum fäst (beorn him langað), fast (shut) in the bonds of his bosom, the man longs for (i.e. in secret), 1879.--Comp: âr-, blæd-, gin-, sôð-, tîr-, wîs-fäst.

fäste, adv., fäst 554, 761, 774, 789, 1296.--Comp. fästor, 143.

be-fästan, w. v., to give over : inf. hêt Hildeburh hire selfre sunu sweoloðe befästan, to give over to the flames her own son , 1116.

fästen, st. n., fortified place, or place difficult of access : acc. sg. leóda fästen, the fastness of the Geátas (with ref. to 2327), 2334; fästen (Ongenþeów's castle or fort), 2951; fästen (Grendel's house in the fen-sea), 104.

fäst-ræd, adj., firmly resolved : acc. sg. fäst-rædne geþôht, firm determination , 611.

fät, st. m., way, journey : in comp. sîð-fät.

fät, st. n., vessel; vase, cup : acc. pl. fyrn-manna fatu, the (drinking-) vessels of men of old times , 2762.--Comp.: bân-, drync-, mâððum-, sinc-, wundor-fät.

fät, st. n. (?), plate, sheet of metal , especially gold plate (Dietrich Hpt. Ztschr. XI. 420): dat. pl. gold sele ... fättum fâhne, shining with gold plates (the walls and the inner part of the roof were partly covered with gold), 717; sceal se hearda helm hyrsted golde fätum befeallen (sc. wesan), the gold ornaments shall fall away from it , 2257.

fäted, fätt, part., ornamented with gold beaten into plate-form : gen. sg. fättan goldes, 1094, 2247; instr. sg. fättan golde, 2103. Elsewhere, covered, ornamented with gold plate : nom. sg. sweord ... fäted, 2702; acc. sg. fäted wæge, 2254, 2283; acc. pl. fätte scyldas, 333; fätte beágas, 1751. [fæted, etc.]

fäted-hleór, adj., phaleratus gena (Dietr.): acc. pl. eahta mearas fäted-hleóre (eight horses with bridles covered with plates of gold), 1037.

fät-gold, st. n., gold in sheets or plates : acc. sg., 1922.

fæge, adj.: 1) forfeited to death, allotted to death by fate : nom. sg. fæge, 1756, 2142, 2976; fæge and ge-flýmed, 847; fûs and fæge, 1242; acc. sg. fægne flæschoman, 1569; dat. sg. fægum, 2078; gen. sg. fæges, 1528.--2) dead : dat. pl. ofer fægum (over the warriors fallen in the battle), 3026.--Comp.: deáð-, un-fæge.

fæhð (state of hostility , see fâh), st. f., hostile act, feud, battle : nom. sg. fæhð, 2404, 3062; acc. sg. fæhðe, 153, 459, 470, 596, 1334, etc.; also of the unhappy bowshot of the Hrêðling, Hæðcyn, by which he killed his brother, 2466; dat. sg. fore fæhðe and fyrene, 137; nalas for fæhðe mearn (did not recoil from the combat), 1538; gen. sg, ne gefeah he þære fæhðe, 109; gen. pl. fæhða gemyndig, 2690.--Comp. wäl-fæhð.

fæhðo, st. f., same as above: nom. sg. sió fæhðo, 3000; acc. fæhðo, 2490.

fælsian, w. v., to bring into a good condition, to cleanse : inf. þät ic môte ... Heorot fælsian (from the plague of Grendel), 432; pret. Hrôðgâres ... sele fælsode, 2353.

ge-fælsian, w. v., same as above: pret. part. häfde gefælsod ... sele Hrôðgâres, 826; Heorot is gefælsod, 1177; wæron ýð-gebland eal gefælsod, 1621.

fæmne, w. f., virgin, recens nupta : dat. sg. fæmnan, 2035; gen. sg. fæmnan, 2060, both times of Hrôðgâr's daughter Freáware.

fær, st. m., sudden, unexpected attack : nom. sg. (attack upon Hnäf's band by Finn's), 1069, 2231.

fær-gripe, st. m., sudden, treacherous gripe, attack : nom. sg. fær-gripe flôdes, 1517; dat. pl. under færgripum, 739.

fær-gryre, st. m., fright caused by a sudden attack : dat. pl. wið fær-gryrum (against the inroads of Grendel into Heorot), 174.

færinga, adv., suddenly, unexpectedly , 1415, 1989.

fær-nîð, st. m., hostility with sudden attacks : gen. pl. hwät me Grendel hafað ... færnîða gefremed, 476.

feðer-gearwe, st. f. pl. (feather-equipment), the feathers of the shaft of the arrow : dat. (instr.) pl. sceft feðer-gearwum fûs, 3120.

fel, st. n., skin, hide : dat. pl. glôf ... gegyrwed dracan fellum, made of the skins of dragons , 2089.

fela, I., adj. indecl., much, many : as subst.: acc. sg. fela fricgende, 2107. With worn placed before: hwät þu worn fela ... ymb Brecan spræce, how very much you spoke about Breca , 530.--With gen. sg.: acc. sg. fela fyrene, 810; wyrm-cynnes fela, 1426; worna fela sorge, 2004; tô fela micles ... Denigea leóde, too much of the race of the Danes , 695; uncûðes fela, 877; fela lâðes, 930; fela leófes and lâðes, 1061.--With gen. pl.: nom. sg. fela mâdma, 36; fela þæra wera and wîfa, 993, etc.; acc. sg. fela missera, 153; fela fyrena, 164; ofer landa fela, 311; mâððum-sigla fela (falo, MS.), 2758; ne me swôr fela âða on unriht, swore no false oaths , 2739, etc.; worn fela mâðma, 1784; worna fela gûða, 2543.--Comp. eal-fela.

II., adverbial, very , 1386, 2103, 2951.

fela-hrôr, adj., valde agitatus, very active against the enemy, very warlike , 27.

fela-môdig, adj., very courageous : gen. pl. -môdigra, 1638, 1889.

fela-synnig, adj., very criminal, very guilty : acc. sg. fela-sinnigne secg (in MS., on account of the alliteration, changed to simple sinnigne), 1380.

feólan, st. v., to betake one's self into a place, to conceal one's self : pret. siððan inne fealh Grendles môdor (in Heorot), 1282; þær inne fealh secg syn-bysig (in the dragon's cave), 2227.-- to fall into, undergo, endure : searonîðas fealh, 1201.

ät-feólan, w. dat., insistere, adhærere: pret. nô ic him þäs georne ätfealh (held him not fast enough , 969.

fen, st. n., fen, moor : acc. sg. fen, 104; dat. sg. tô fenne, 1296; fenne, 2010.

fen-freoðo, st. f., refuge in the fen : dat. sg. in fen-freoðo, 852.

feng, st. m., gripe, embrace : nom. sg. fýres feng, 1765; acc. sg. fâra feng (of the hostile sea-monsters), 578.--Comp. inwit-feng.

fengel (probably he who takes possession , cf. tô fôn, 1756, and fôn tô rîce, to enter upon the government), st. m., lord, prince, king : nom. sg. wîsa fengel, 1401; snottra fengel, 1476, 2157; hringa fengel, 2346.

fen-ge-lâd, st. n., fen-paths, fen with paths : acc. pl. frêcne fengelâd (fens difficult of access), 1360.

fen-hlið, st. n., marshy precipice : acc. pl. under fen-hleoðu, 821.

fen-hop, st. n., refuge in the fen : acc. pl. on fen-hopu, 765.

ferh, st. m. n., life ; see feorh.

ferh, st. m., hog, boar , here of the boar-image on the helmet: nom. sg., 305.

ferhð, st. m., heart, soul : dat. sg. on ferhðe, 755, 949, 1719; gehwylc hiora his ferhðe treówde, þät ..., each of them trusted to his (Hûnferð's) heart, that ..., 1167; gen. sg. ferhðes fore-þanc, 1061; dat. pl. (adverbial) ferhðum fägne, happy at heart , 1634; þät mon ... ferhðum freóge, that one ... heartily love , 3178.--Comp.: collen-, sarig-, swift-, wide-ferhð.

ferhð-frec, adj., having good courage, bold, brave : acc. sg. ferhð-frecan Fin, 1147.

ferhð-genîðla, w. m., mortal enemy : acc. sg. ferhð-genîðlan, of the drake, 2882.

ferian, w. v. w. acc., to bear, to bring, to conduct : pres. II. pl. hwanon ferigeað fätte scyldas, 333; pret. pl. tô scypum feredon eal ingesteald eorðcyninges, 1155; similarly, feredon, 1159, 3114.

ät-ferian, to carry away, to bear off : pret. ic þät hilt þanan feóndum ätferede, 1669.

ge-ferian, bear, to bring, to lead : pres. subj. I. pl. þonne (we) geferian freán ûserne, 3108; inf. geferian ... Grendles heáfod, 1639; pret. þät hi ût geferedon dýre mâðmas, 3131; pret. part. her syndon geferede feorran cumene ... Geáta leóde, men of the Geátas, come from afar, have been brought hither (by ship), 361.

ôð-ferian, to tear away, to take away : pret. sg. I. unsôfte þonan feorh ôð-ferede, 2142.

of-ferian, to carry off, to take away, to tear away : pret. ôðer swylc ût offerede, took away another such (sc. fifteen), 1584.

fetel-hilt, st. n., sword-hilt, with the gold chains fastened to it: acc. (sg. or pl.?), 1564. (See "Leitfaden f. nord. Altertumskunde," pp.45, 46.)

fetian, w. v., to bring near, bring : pres. subj. nâh hwâ ... fe[tige] fäted wæge, bring the gold-chased tankard , 2254; pret. part. hraðe wäs tô bûre Beówulf fetod, 1311.

ge-fetian, to bring : inf. hêt þâ eorla hleó in gefetian Hrêðles lâfe, caused Hrêðel's sword to be brought , 2191.

â-fêdan, w. v., to nourish, to bring up : pret. part. þær he âfêded wäs, 694.

fêða (O.H.G. fendo), w. m.: 1) foot-soldiers : nom. pl. fêðan, 1328, 2545.--2) collective in sing., band of foot-soldiers, troop of warriors : nom. fêða eal gesät, 1425; dat. on fêðan, 2498, 2920.--Comp. gum-fêða.

fêðe, st. n., gait, going, pace : dat. sg. wäs tô foremihtig feónd on fêðe, the enemy was too strong in going (i.e. could flee too fast), 971.

fêðe-cempa, w. m., foot-soldier : nom. sg., 1545, 2854.

fêðe-gäst, st. m., guest coming on foot : dat. pl. fêðe-gestum, 1977.

fêðe-lâst, st. m., signs of going, footprint : dat. pl. fêrdon forð þonon fêðe-lâstum, went forth from there upon their trail , i.e. by the same way that they had gone, 1633.

fêðe-wîg, st. m., battle on foot : gen. sg. nealles Hetware hrêmge þorfton (sc. wesan) fêðe-wîges, 2365.

fêl (= feól), st. f. file : gen. pl. fêla lâfe, what the files have left behind (that is, the swords), 1033.

fêran, w. v., iter (A.S. fôr) facere, to come, to go, to travel : pres. subj. II. pl. ær ge ... on land Dena furður fêran, ere you go farther into the land of the Danes , 254; inf. fêran on freán wære (to die), 27; gewiton him þâ fêran (set out upon their way), 301; mæl is me tô fêran, 316; fêran ... gang sceáwigan, go, so as to see the footprints , 1391; wîde fêran, 2262; pret. fêrdon folctogan ... wundor sceáwian, the princes came to see the wonder , 840; fêrdon forð, 1633.

ge-fêran: 1) adire, to arrive at : pres. subj. þonne eorl ende gefêre lîfgesceafta, reach the end of life , 3064; pret. part. häfde æghwäðer ende gefêred lænan lîfes, frail life's end had both reached , 2845.--2) to reach, to accomplish, to bring about : pret. hafast þu gefêred þät ..., 1222, 1856.--3) to behave one's self, to conduct one's self : pret. frêcne gefêrdon, had shown themselves daring , 1692.

feal, st. m., fall : in comp. wäl-feal.

feallan, st. v., to fall, to fall headlong : inf. feallan, 1071; pret. sg. þät he on hrusan ne feól, that it (the hall) did not fall to the ground , 773; similarly, feóll on foldan, 2976; feóll on fêðan (dat. sg.), fell in the band (of his warriors), 2920; pret. pl. þonne walu feóllon, 1043.

be-feallen, pret. part. w. dat. or instr., deprived of, robbed : freóndum befeallen, robbed of friends , 1127; sceal se hearda helm ... fätum befeallen (sc.

wesan), be robbed of its gold mountings (the gold mounting will fall away from it moldering), 2257.

ge-feallan, to fall, to sink down : pres. sg. III. þät se lîc-homa ... fæge gefealleð, that the body doomed to die sinks down, 1756.--Also, with the acc. of the place whither: pret. meregrund gefeóll, 2101; he eorðan gefeóll, 2835.

fealu, adj., fallow, dun-colored, tawny : acc. sg. ofer fealone flôd (over the sea), 1951; fealwe stræte (with reference to 320), 917; acc. pl. lêton on geflît faran fealwe mearas, 866.--Comp. äppel-fealo.

feax, st. n., hair, hair of the head : dat. sg. wäs be feaxe on flet boren Grendles heáfod, was carried by the hair into the hall, 1648; him ... swât ... sprong forð under fexe, the blood sprang out under the hair of his head, 2968.--Comp.: blonden-, gamol-, wunden-feax.

ge-feá, w. m., joy : acc. sg. þære fylle gefeán, joy at the abundant repast, 562; ic þäs ealles mäg ... gefeán habban (can rejoice at all this), 2741.

feá, adj., few dat. pl. nemne feáum ânum, except some few, 1082; gen. pl. feára sum, as one of a few, with a few, 1413; feára sumne, one of a few (some few), 3062. With gen. following: acc. pl. feá worda cwäð, spoke few words, 2663, 2247.

feá-sceaft, adj., miserable, unhappy, helpless : nom. sg. syððan ærest wearð feásceaft funden, 7; feásceaft guma (Grendel), 974; dat. sg. feásceaftum men, 2286; Eádgilse ... feásceaftum, 2394; nom. pl. feásceafte (the Geátas robbed of their king, Hygelâc), 2374.

feoh, feó, st. n., (properly cattle, herd) here, possessions, property, treasure : instr. sg. ne wolde ... feorh-bealo feó þingian, would not allay life's evil for treasure (tribute), 156; similarly, þâ fæhðe feó þingode, 470; ic þe þâ fæhðe feó leánige, 1381.

ge-feohan, ge-feón, st. v. w. gen. and instr., to enjoy one's self, to rejoice at something : a) w. gen.: pret. sg. ne gefeah he þære fæhðe, 109; hilde gefeh, beado-weorces, 2299; pl. fylle gefægon, enjoyed themselves at the bounteous repast, 1015; þeódnes gefêgon, rejoiced at (the return of) the ruler, 1628.--b) w. instr.: niht-weorce gefeh, ellen-mærðum, 828; secg weorce gefeh, 1570; sælâce gefeah, mägen-byrðenne þâra þe he him mid häfde, rejoiced at the gift of the sea, and at the great burden of that (Grendel's head and the sword-hilt) which he had with him, 1625.

feoh-gift, -gyft, st. f., bestowing of gifts or treasures : gen. sg. þære feoh-gyfte, 1026; dat. pl. ät feohgyftum, 1090; fromum feohgiftum, with rich gifts, 21.

feoh-leás, adj., that cannot be atoned for through gifts : nom. sg. þät wäs feoh-leás gefeoht, a deed of arms that cannot be expiated (the killing of his brother by Hæðcyn), 2442.

ge-feoht, st. n., combat; warlike deed : nom. sg. (the killing of his brother by Hæðcyn), 2442; dat. sg. mêce þone þîn fader tô gefeohte bär, the sword which thy father bore to the combat, 2049.

ge-feohtan, st. v., to fight : inf. w. acc. ne mehte ... wîg Hengeste with gefeohtan (could by no means offer Hengest battle), 1084.

feohte, w. f., combat : acc. sg. feohtan, 576, 960. See were-fyhte.

feor, adj., far, remote : nom. sg. nis þät feor heonon, 1362; näs him feor þanon tô gesêcanne sinces bryttan, 1922; acc. sg. feor eal (all that is far, past), 1702.

feor, adv., far, far away : a) of space, 42, 109, 809, 1806, 1917; feor and (oððe) neáh, far and (or) near, 1222, 2871; feorr, 2267.--b) of time: ge feor hafað fæhðe gestæled (has placed us under her enmity henceforth), 1341.

Comparative, fyr, feorr, and feor: fyr and fæstor, 143; fyr, 252; feorr, 1989; feor, 542.

feor-bûend, pt., dwelling far away : nom. pl. ge feor-bûend, 254.

feor-cýð, st. f., home of those living far away, distant land : nom, pl. feor-cýððe beóð sêlran gesôhte þäm þe him selfa deáh, foreign lands are better sought by him who trusts to his own ability , 1839.

feorh, ferh (Goth. fairhvu-s, world), st. m. and n., life, principle of life, soul : nom. sg. feorh, 2124; nô þon lange wäs feorh äðelinges flæsce bewunden, not for much longer was the soul of the prince enveloped in the body (he was near death), 2425; ferh ellen wräc, life expelled the strength (i.e. with the departing life the strength disappeared also), 2707; acc. sg. feorh ealgian, 797, 2656, 2669; feorh gehealdan, preserve his life , 2857; feorh âlegde, gave up his life , 852; similarly, ær he feorh seleð, 1371; feorh oðferede, tore away her life , 2142; ôð þät hie forlæddan tô þam lindplegan swæse gesîðas ond hyra sylfra feorh, till in an evil hour they carried into battle their dear companions and their lives (i.e. led them to their death), 2041; gif þu þîn feorh hafast, 1850; ymb feorh sacan (to fight for life), 439; wäs in feorh dropen, was wounded into his life , i.e. mortally, 2982; wîdan feorh, as temporal acc., through a wide life , i.e. always, 2015; dat. sg. feore, 1294, 1549; tô wîdan feore, for a wide life , i.e. at all times, 934; on swâ geongum feore (at a so youthful age), 1844; as instr., 578, 3014; gen. sg. feores, 1434, 1943; dat. pl. bûton ... feorum gumena, 73; freónda feorum, 1307.-- Also, body, corpse : þâ wäs heal hroden feónda feorum (the hall was covered with the slain of the enemy), 1153; gehwearf þâ in Francna fäðm feorh cyninges, then the body of the king (Hygelâc) fell into the power of the Franks , 1211. --Comp. geogoð-feorh.

feorh-bana, w. m., (life-slayer), man-slayer, murderer : dat. sg. feorh-bonan, 2466.

feorh-ben, st. f., wound that takes away life, mortal wound : dat. (instr.) pl. feorh-bennum seóc, 2741.

feorh-bealu, st. n., evil destroying life, violent death : nom. sg., 2078, 2251, 2538; acc. sg., 156.

feorh-cyn, st. n., race of the living, mankind : gen. pl. fela feorh-cynna, 2267.

feorh-genîðla, w. m., he who seeks life, life's enemy (N.H.G. Todfeind), mortal enemy : acc. sg. -genîðlan, 1541; dat. sg. -genîðlan, 970; acc. sg. brægd feorh-genîðlan, 1541; acc. pl. folgode feorh-genîðlan, (Ongenþeów) pursued his mortal enemies , 2934.

feorh-lagu, st. f., the life allotted to anyone, life determined by fate : acc. sg. on mâðma hord mine (mînne, MS.) bebohte frôde feorh-lege, for the treasure-hoard I sold my old life , 2801.

feorh-lâst, st. m., trace of (vanishing) life, sign of death : acc. pl. feorh-lâstas bär, 847.

feorh-seóc, adj., mortally wounded : nom. sg., 821.

feorh-sweng, st. m., (stroke robbing of life), fatal blow : acc. sg., 2490.

feorh-wund, st. f., mortal wound, fatal injury : acc. sg. feorh-wunde hleát, 2386.

feorm, st. f., subsistence, entertainment : acc. sg. nô þu ymb mînes ne þearft lîces feorme leng sorgian, thou needest no longer have care for the sustenance of my body , 451.--2) banquet : dat. on feorme (or feorme, MS.), 2386.

feormend-leás, adj., wanting the. cleanser : acc. pl. geseah ... fyrn-manna fatu feormend-leáse, 2762.

feormian, w. v., to clean, to cleanse, to polish : pres. part. nom pl. feormiend swefað (feormynd, MS.), 2257.

ge-feormian, w. v., to feast, to eat ; pret. part. sôna häfde unlyfigendes eal gefeormod fêt and folma, 745.

feorran, w. v., w. acc., to remove : inf. sibbe ne wolde wið manna hwone mägenes Deniga feorh-bealo feorran, feó þingian, (Grendel) would not from friendship free any one of the men of the Danes of life's evil, nor allay it for tribute , 156.

feorran, adv., from afar : a) of space, 361, 430, 826, 1371, 1820, etc.; siððan äðelingas feorran gefricgean fleám eówerne, when noble men afar learn of your flight (when the news of your flight reaches distant lands), 2890; fêrdon folctogan feorran and neán, from far and from near , 840; similarly, neán and feorran þu nu [friðu] hafast, 1175; wäs þäs wyrmes wîg wîde gesýne ... neán and feorran, visible from afar, far and near , 2318.--b) temporal: se þe cûðe frumsceaft fira feorran reccan (since remote antiquity), 91; similarly, feorran rehte, 2107.

feorran-cund, adj., foreign-born : dat. sg. feorran-cundum, 1796.

feor-weg, st. m., far way : dat. pl. mâdma fela of feorwegum, many precious things from distant paths (from foreign lands), 37.

ge-feón. See feohan.

feónd, st. m., enemy : nom. sg., 164, 726, 749; feónd on helle (Grendel), 101; acc. sg., 279, 1865, 2707; dat. sg. feónde, 143, 439; gen. sg. feóndes, 985, 2129, 2290; acc, pl. feónd, 699; dat. pl. feóndum, 420, 1670; gen. pl. feonda 294, 809, 904.

feónd-grâp, st. f., foe's clutch : dat. (instr.) pl. feónd-grâpum fäst, 637.

feónd-sceaða, w. m., one who is an enemy and a robber : nom. sg. fâh feónd-scaða (a hostile sea-monster), 554.

feónd-scipe, st. m., hostility : nom. sg., 3000.

feówer, num., four : nom. feówer bearn, 59; feówer mearas, 2164; feówer, as substantive, 1638; acc. feówer mâðmas, 1028.

feówer-tyne, num., fourteen : nom. with following gen. pl. feówertyne Geáta, 1642.

findan, st. v., to find, to invent, to attain : a) with simple object in acc.: inf. þâra þe he cênoste findan mihte, 207; swylce hie at Finnes-hâm findan meahton sigla searo-gimma, 1157; similarly, 2871; mäg þär fela freónda findan, 1839; wolde guman findan, 2295; swâ hyt weorðlîcost fore-snotre men findan mihton, so splendidly as only very wise men could devise it , 3164; pret. sg. healþegnas fand, 720; word ôðer fand, found other words , i.e. went on to another narrative, 871; grimne gryrelîcne grund-hyrde fond, 2137; þät ic gôdne funde beága bryttan, 1487; pret. part. syððan ärest wearð feásceaft funden (discovered), 7.--b) with acc. and pred. adj.: pret. sg. dryhten sînne driórigne fand, 2790.--c) with acc. and inf.: pret. fand þâ þär inne äðelinga gedriht swefan, 118; fand wäccendne wer wîges bîdan, 1268; hord-wynne fond opene standan, 2271; ôð þät he fyrgen-beámas ... hleonian funde, 1416; pret. pl. fundon þâ sâwulleásne hlim-bed healdan, 3034.--d) with dependent clause: inf. nô þý är feásceafte findan meahton ät þam äðelinge þät he Heardrêde hlâford wäre (could by no means obtain it from the prince), 2374.

on-findan, to be sensible of, to perceive, to notice : a) w. acc.: pret. sg. landweard onfand eftsîð eorla, the coast-guard observed the return of the earls ,

1892; pret. part. þâ heó onfunden wäs (was discovered), 1294.--b) w. depend, clause: pret. sg. þâ se gist onfand þät se beado-leóma bîtan nolde, the stranger (Beówulf) perceived that the sword would not cut , 1523; sôna þät onfunde, þät ..., immediately perceived that ..., 751; similarly, 810, 1498.

 finger, st. m., finger : nom. pl. fingras, 761; acc. pl. fingras, 985; dat. (instr.) pl. fingrum, 1506; gen. pl. fingra, 765.

 firas, fyras (O.H.G. firahî, i.e. the living ; cf. feorh), st. m., only in pl., men : gen. pl. fira, 91, 2742; monegum fira, 2002; fyra gehwylcne leóda mînra, 2251; fira fyrngeweorc, 2287.

 firen, fyren, st. f., cunning waylaying, insidious hostility, malice, outrage : nom. sg. fyren, 916; acc. sg. fyrene and fæhðe, 153; fæhðe and fyrene, 880, 2481; firen' ondrysne, 1933; dat. sg. fore fæhðe and fyrene, 137; gen. pl. fyrena, 164, 629; and fyrene, 812; fyrena hyrde (of Grendel), 751. The dat. pl., fyrenum, is used adverbially in the sense of maliciously , 1745, or fallaciously , with reference to Hæðcyn's killing Herebeald, which was done unintentionally, 2442.

 firen-dæd, st. f., wicked deed : acc. pl. fyren-dæda, 1670; instr. pl. fyren-dædum, 1002; both times of Grendel and his mother, with reference to their nocturnal inroads.

 firen-þearf, st. f., misery through the malignity of enemies : acc. sg. fyren-þearfe, 14.

 firgen-beám, st. m., tree of a mountain-forest : acc. pl. fyrgen-beámas, 1415.

 firgen-holt, st. m., mountain-wood, mountain-forest : acc. sg. on fyrgen-holt, 1394.

 firgen-streám, st. m., mountain-stream : nom. sg. fyrgen-streám, 1360; acc. sg. under fyrgen-streám (marks the place where the mountain-stream, according to 1360, empties into Grendel's sea), 2129.

 fisc, st. m., fish : in comp. hron-, mere-fisc.

 fîf, num., five : uninflect. gen. fîf nihta fyrst, 545; acc. fîfe (?), 420.

 fîfel-cyn (O.N. fîfl, stultus and gigas), st. n., giant-race : gen. sg. fîfelcynnes eard, 104.

 fîf-tene, fîf-tyne, num., fifteen : acc. fýftyne, 1583; gen. fîftena sum, 207.

 fîf-tig, num., fifty : 1) as substantive with gen. following; acc. fîftig wintra, 2734; gen. se wäs fîftiges fôt-gemearces lang, 3043.--2) as adjective: acc. fîftig wintru, 2210.

 flân, st. m., arrow : dat. sg. flâne, 3120; as instr., 2439.

 flân-boga, w. m., bow which shoots the flân, bow : dat. sg. of flân-bogan, 1434, 1745.

 flæsc, st. n., flesh, body in contrast with soul : instr. sg. nô þon lange wäs feorh äðelinges flæsce bewunden, not much longer was the son of the prince contained in his body , 2425.

 flæsc-hama, w. m., clothing of flesh , i.e. the body: acc. sg. flæsc-homan, 1569.

 flet, st. n.: 1) ground, floor of a hall : acc. sg. heó on flet gebeáh, fell to the ground , 1541; similarly, 1569.--2) hall, mansion : nom. sg. 1977; acc. sg. flet, 1037, 1648, 1950, 2018, etc.; flett, 2035; þät hie him ôðer flet eal gerýmdon, that they should give up entirely to them another hall , 1087; dat. sg. on flette, 1026.

 flet-räst, st. f., resting-place in the hall : acc. sg. flet-räste gebeág, reclined upon the couch in the hall , 1242.

 flet-sittend, pres. part., sitting in the hall : acc. pl -sittende, 2023; dat. pl. -sittendum, 1789.

flet-werod, st. n., troop from the hall : nom. sg., 476.

fleám, st. m., flight : acc. sg. on fleám gewand, had turned to flight , 1002; fleám eówerne, 2890.

fleógan, st. v., to fly : prs. sg. III. fleógeð, 2274.

fleón, st. v., to flee : inf. on heolster fleón, 756; fleón on fenhopu, 765; fleón under fen-hleoðu, 821; pret. hete-swengeas fleáh, 2226.

be-fleón, w. acc., to avoid, to escape : gerund nô þät ýðe byð tô befleónne, that is not easy (i.e. not at all) to be avoided , 1004.

ofer-fleón, w. acc., to flee from one, to yield : inf. nelle ic beorges weard oferfleón fôtes trem, will not yield to the warder of the mountain (the drake) a foot's breadth , 2526.

fleótan, st. v., to float upon the water, to swim : inf. nô he wiht fram me flôd-ýðum feor fleótan meahte. hraðor on helme, no whit, could he swim from me farther on the waves (regarded as instrumental, so that the waves marked the distance), more swiftly in the sea , 542; pret. sægenga fleát fâmigheals forð ofer ýðe, floated away over the waves , 1910.

flîht. See flyht.

flitme. See un-flitme.

flîtan, st. v., to exert one's self, to strive, to emulate : pres. part. flîtende fealwe stræte mearum mæton (rode a race), 917; pret. sg. II. eart þu se Beówulf, se þe wið Brecan ... ymb sund flite, art thou the Beówulf who once contended with Breca for the prize in swimming? 507.

ofer-flîtan, to surpass one in a contest, to conquer, to overcome : pret. w. acc. he þe ät sunde oferflât (overcome thee in a swimming-wager), 517.

ge-flît, st. n., emulation : acc. sg. lêton on geflît faran fealwe mearas, let the fallow horses go in emulation , 866.

floga, w. m., flyer ; in the compounds: gûð-, lyft-, uht-, wîð-floga.

flota (see fleótan), w. m., float, ship, boat : nom. sg., 210, 218, 301; acc. sg. flotan eówerne, 294.--Comp. wæg-flota.

flot-here, st. m., fleet : instr. sg. cwom faran flotherge on Fresna land, 2916.

flôd, st. m., flood, stream, sea-current : nom. sg., 545, 580, 1362, etc.; acc. sg. flôd, 3134; ofer fealone flôd, 1951; dat. sg. tô flôde, 1889; gen. pl. flôda begong, the region of floods , i.e. the sea, 1498, 1827; flôda genipu, 2809.

flôd-ýð, st. f., flood-wave : instr. pl. flôd-ýðum, 542.

flôr, st. m., floor, stone-floor : acc. sg. on fâgne flôr (the floor was probably a kind of mosaic, made of colored flags), 726; dat. sg. gang þâ äfter flôre, along the floor (i.e. along the hall), 1317.

flyht, flîht, st. m., flight : nom. sg. gâres fliht, flight of the spear , 1766.

ge-flýman, w. v., to put to flight : pret. part. geflýmed, 847, 1371.

folc, st. n., troop, band of warriors; folk , in the sense of the whole body of the fighting men of a nation: acc. sg. folc, 522, 694, 912; Sûðdene folc, 464; folc and rîce, 1180; dat. sg. folce, 14, 2596; folce Deninga, 465; as instr. folce gestepte ofer sæ sîde, went with a band of warriors over the wide sea , 2394; gen. sg. folces, 1125; folces Denigea, 1583.--The king is called folces hyrde, 611, 1833, 2645, 2982; freáwine folces, 2358; or folces weard, 2514. The queen, folces cwên, 1933.--The pl., in the sense of warriors, fighting men : nom. pl. folc, 1423, 2949; dat. pl. folcum, 55, 262, 1856; gen. pl. freó- (freá-) wine folca, of the king , 430, 2430; friðu-sibb folca, of the queen , 2018.--Comp. sige-folc.

folc-âgend, pres. part., leader of a band of warriors : nom. pl. folc-âgende, 3114.

folc-beorn, st. m., man of the multitude, a common man : nom. sg. folc-beorn, 2222.

folc-cwên, st. f., queen of a warlike host : nom. sg., of Wealhþeów, 642.

folc-cyning, st. m., king of a warlike host : nom. sg., 2734, 2874.

folc-ræd, st. m, what best serves a warlike host : acc. sg., 3007.

folc-riht, st. n., the rights of the fighting men of a nation : gen. pl. him ær forgeaf ... folcrihta gehwylc, swâ his fäder âhte, 2609.

folc-scearu, st. f., part of a host of warriors, nation : dat. sg. folc-scare, 73.

folc-stede, st. m., position of a band of warriors, place where a band of warriors is quartered : acc. sg. folcstede, of the hall, Heorot, 76; folcstede fâra (the battle-field), 1464.

folc-toga, w. m., leader of a body of warriors, duke : nom. pl., powerful liegemen of Hrôðgâr are called folc-togan, 840.

fold-bold, st. n., earth-house (i.e. a house on earth in contrast with a dwelling in heaven): nom. sg. fäger fold-bold, of the hall, Heorot, 774.

fold-bûend, pres. part. dweller on earth, man : nom. pl. fold-bûend, 2275; fold-bûende, 1356; dat. pl. fold-bûendum, 309.

folde, w. f., earth, ground : acc. sg. under foldan, 1362; feóll on foldan, 2976; gen. sg. foldan bearm, the bosom of the earth , 1138; foldan sceátas, 96; foldan fäðm, 1394.--Also, earth, world : dat. sg. on foldan, 1197.

fold-weg, st. m., field-way, road through the country : acc. sg. fold-weg, 1634; acc. pl. fold-wegas, 867.

folgian, w. v.: 1) to perform vassal-duty, to serve, to follow : pret. pl. þeáh hie hira beággyfan banan folgedon, although they followed the murderer of their prince , 1103.--2) to pursue, to follow after : folgode feorh-geníðlan (acc. pl.) 2934.

folm, st. f, hand : acc. sg. folme, 971, 1304; dat. sg. mid folme, 743; acc. pl. fêt and folma, feet and hands , 746; dat. pl. tô banan folmum, 158; folmum (instr.), 723, 993.--Comp.: heado-, gearo-folm.

for, prep. w. dat., instr., and acc.: 1) w. dat. local, before , ante: þät he for eaxlum gestôd Deniga freán, 358; for hlâwe, 1121.--b) before , coram, in conspectu: no he þære feohgyfte for sceótendum scamigan þorfte, had no need to be ashamed of the gift before the warriors , 1027; for þäm werede, 1216; for eorlum, 1650; for duguðe, before the noble band of warriors , 2021.--Causal, a) to denote a subjective motive, on account of, through, from : for wlenco, from bravery, through warlike courage , 338, 1207; for wlence, 508; for his wonhýdum, 434; for onmêdlan, 2927, etc.--b) objective, partly denoting a cause, through, from, by reason of : for metode, for the creator, on account of the creator , 169; for þreánýdum, 833; for þreánêdlan, 2225; for dolgilpe, on account of, in accordance with the promise of bold deeds (because you claimed bold deeds for yourself), 509; him for hrôfsele hrînan ne mehte fær-gripe flôdes, on account of the roofed hall the malicious grasp of the flood could not reach him , 1516; lîg-egesan wäg for horde, on account of (the robbing of) the treasure , 2782; for mundgripe mînum, on account of, through the gripe of my hand , 966; for þäs hildfruman hondgeweorce, 2836; for swenge, through the stroke , 2967; ne meahte ... deóp gedýgan for dracan lêge, could not hold out in the deep on account of the heat of the drake , 2550. Here may be added such passages as ic þäm gôdan sceal for his môdþräce mâðmas beódan, will offer him treasures on account of his boldness of character, for his high courage , 385; ful-oft for lässan leán teohhode, gave often reward for what was inferior , 952; nalles for ealdre mearn, was not uneasy about his life , 1443; similarly, 1538. Also denoting purpose: for ârstafum, to the assistance , 382, 458.--2) w. instr. causal, because of, for : he hine feor forwräc for þý mane, 110.--3) w. acc., for, as, instead of : for sunu freógan, love as a son , 948; for sunu habban, 1176; ne him þäs wyrmes wîg for wiht dyde, held the drake's fighting as nothing , 2349.

foran, adv., before, among the first, forward : siððan ... sceáwedon feóndes fingras, foran æghwylc (each before himself), 985; þät wäs ân foran ealdgestreóna, that was one among the first of the old treasures , i.e. a splendid old treasure, 1459; þe him foran ongeán linde bæron, bore their shields forward against him (went out to fight against him), 2365.

be-foran: 1) adv., local, before : he ... beforan gengde, went before , 1413; temporal, before, earlier , 2498.--2) prep. w. acc. before , in conspectu: mære mâððum-sweord manige gesâwon beforan beorn beran, 1025.

ford, st. m., ford, water-way : acc. sg. ymb brontne ford, 568.

forð: 1) local, forth, hither, near : forð near ätstôp, approached nearer , 746; þâ cwom Wealhþeó forð gân, 1163; similarly, 613; him seleþegn forð wîsade, led him (Beówulf) forth (to the couch that had been prepared for him in Heorot), 1796; þät him swât sprong forð under fexe, forth under the hair of his head , 2968. Forward, further : gewîtað forð beran wæpen and gewædu, 291; he tô forð gestôp, 2290; freoðo-wong þone forð ofereodon, 2960. Away, forth , 45, 904; fyrst forð gewât, the time (of the way to the ship) was out , i.e. they had arrived at the ship, 210; me ... forð-gewitenum, to me the departed , 1480; fêrdon forð, went forth (from Grendel's sea), 1633; þonne he forð scile, when he must (go) forth , i.e. die, 3178; hine mihtig god ... ofer ealle men forð gefremede, carried him forth, over all men , 1719.--2) temporal, forth, from now on : heald forð tela niwe sibbe, 949; ic sceal forð sprecan gen ymbe Grendel, shall from now on speak again of Grendel , 2070. See furðum and furðor.

forð-gerîmed, pres. part., in unbroken succession , 59.

forð-gesceaft, st. f., that which is determined for farther on, future destiny : acc. sg. he þâ forð-gesceaft forgyteð and forgýmeð, 1751.

forð-weg, st. m., road that leads away, journey : he of ealdre gewât frôd on forð-weg (upon the way to the next world), 2626.

fore, prep. w. dat., local, before , coram, in conspectu: heó fore þäm werede spräc, 1216. Causal, through, for, because of : nô mearn fore fæhðe and fyrene, 136; fore fäder dædum, because of the father's deeds , 2060,--Allied to this is the meaning, about , de, super: þær wäs sang and swêg samod ätgädere fore Healfdenes hildewîsan, song and music about Healfdene's general (the song of Hnäf), 1065.

fore-mære, adj., renowned beyond (others) , præclarus: superl. þät wäs foremærost foldbûendum receda under roderum, 309.

fore-mihtig, adj., able beyond (others) , præpotens: nom. sg. wäs tô foremihtig feónd on fêðe, the enemy was too strong in going (could flee too rapidly), 970.

fore-snotor, adj., wise beyond (others) , sapientissimus: nom. pl. foresnotre men, 3164.

fore-þanc, st. m., forethought, consideration, deliberation : nom. sg., 1061.

forht, adj., fearful, cowardly : nom. sg. forht, 2968; he on môde wearð forht on ferhðe, 755.--Comp. unforht.

forma, adj., foremost, first : nom. sg. forma sîð (the first time), 717, 1464, 1528, 2626; instr. sg. forman sîðe, 741, 2287; forman dôgore, 2574.

fyrmest, adv. superl., first of all, in the first place : he fyrmest läg, 2078.

forst, st. m., frost, cold : gen. sg. forstes bend, 1610.

for-þam, for-þan, for-þon, adv. and conj., therefore, on that account, then : forþam, 149; forþan, 418, 680, 1060; forþon þe, because , 503.

fôn, st. v., to catch, to grasp, to take hold, to take : prs. sg. III. fêhð ôðer tô, another lays hold (takes possession), 1756; inf. ic mid grâpe sceal fôn wið feónde, 439; pret. sg. him tôgeánes fêng, caught at him, grasped at him , 1543; w. dat. he þäm frätwum fêng, received the rich adornments (Ongenþeów's equipment), 2990.

be-fôn, to surround, to ensnare, to encompass, to embrace : pret. part. hyne sâr hafað ... nearwe befongen balwon bendum, 977; heó äðelinga ânne häfde fäste befangen (had seized him firmly), 1296; helm ... befongen freáwrâsnum (encircled by an ornament like a diadem), 1452; fenne bifongen, surrounded by the fen , 2010; (draca) fŷre befongen, encircled by fire , 2275, 2596; häfde landwara lîge befangen, encompassed by fire , 2322.

ge-fôn, w. acc., to seize, to grasp : pret. he gefêng slæpendne rinc, 741; gûðrinc gefêng atolan clommum, 1502; gefêng þâ be eaxle ... Gûðgeáta leód Grendles môdor, 1538; gefêng þâ fetelhilt, 1564; hond rond gefêng, geolwe linde, 2610; ic on ôfoste gefêng micle mid mundum mägen-byrðenne, hastily I seized with my hands the enormous burden , 3091.

on-fôn, w. dat., to receive, to accept, to take : pres. imp. sg. onfôh þissum fulle, accept this cup , 1170; inf. þät þät þeódnes bearn ... scolde fäder-äðelum onfôn, receive the paternal rank , 912; pret. sg. hwâ þäm hläste onfêng, who received the ship's lading , 52; hleór-bolster onfêng eorles andwlitan, the pillow received the nobleman's face , 689; similarly, 853, 1495; heal swêge onfêng, the hall received the loud noise , 1215; he onfêng hraðe inwit-þancum, he (Beówulf) at once clutched him (Grendel) devising malice , 749.

þurh-fôn, w. acc., to break through with grasping, to destroy by grasping : inf. þät heó þone fyrd-hom þurh-fôn ne mihte, 1505.

wið-fôn, w. dat., (to grasp at), to seize, to lay hold of : pret. sg. hǐm fäste wið-fêng, 761.

ymbe-fôn, w. acc., to encircle : pret. heals ealne ymbefêng biteran bânum, encircled his (Beówulf's) whole neck with sharp bones (teeth), 2692.

fôt, st. m., foot : gen. sg. fôtes trem (the measure of a foot, a foot broad), 2526; acc. pl. fêt, 746; dat. pl. ät fôtum, at the feet , 500, 1167.

fôt-gemearc, st. n., measure, determining by feet, number of feet : gen. sg. se wäs fîftiges fôtgemearces lang (fifty feet long), 3043.

fôt-lâst, st. m., foot-print : acc. sg. (draca) onfand feóndes fôt-lâst, 2290.

fracod, adj., objectionable, useless . nom. sg. näs seó ecg fracod hilde-rince, 1576.

fram, from, I. prep. w. dat. loc. away from something : þær fram sylle âbeág medubenc monig, 776, 1716; þanon eft gewiton ealdgesîðas ... fram mere, 856; cyning-balde men from þäm holmclife hafelan bæron, 1636; similarly, 541, 543, 2367. Standing after the dat.: he hine feor forwräc ... mancynne fram, 110; similarly, 1716. Also, hither from something : þâ ic cwom ... from feóndum, 420; æghwäðrum wäs ... brôga fram ôðrum, 2566.--Causal with verbs of saying and hearing, of, about, concerning : sägdest from his sîðe, 532; nô ic wiht fram þe swylcra searo-nîða secgan hŷrde, 581; þät he fram Sigemunde secgan hyrde, 876. II adv., away, thence : nô þŷ ær fram meahte, 755; forth, out : from ærest cwom oruð aglæcean ût of stâne, the breath of the dragon came forth first from the rock 2557.

fram, from, adj.: 1) directed forwards, striving forwards ; in comp. sîð-fram.-- 2) excellent, splendid , of a man with reference to his warlike qualities: nom. sg. ic eom on môde from, 2528; nom. pl. frome fyrd-hwate, 1642, 2477. Of things: instr. pl. fromum feoh-giftum, 21.--Comp. un-from; see freme, forma.

ge-frägen. See frignan.

frätwe, st. f. pl., ornament, anything costly , originally carved objects (cf. Dietrich in Hpts. Ztschr. X. 216 ff.), afterwards of any costly and artistic work: acc. pl. frätwe, 2920; beorhte frätwe, 214; beorhte frätwa, 897; frätwe.. eorclan-stânas, 1208; frätwe,... breóst-weorðunge, 2504, both times of Hygelâc's collar; frätwe and fät-gold, 1922; frätwe (Eanmund's sword and armor), 2621; dat. instr. pl. þâm frätwum, 2164; on frätewum, 963; frätwum (Heaðobeard sword) hrêmig, 2055; frätwum, of the drake's treasures, 2785; frätwum (Ongenþeów's armor), 2990; gen. pl. fela ... frätwa, 37; þâra frätwa (drake's treasure), 2795; frätwa hyrde (drake), 3134.

frätwan, w. v., to supply with ornaments, to adorn : inf. folc-stede frätwan, 76.

ge-frätwian, w. v., to adorn : pret. sg. gefrätwade foldan sceátas leomum and leáfum, 96; pret. part. þâ wäs hâten Heort innanweard folmum gefrätwod, 993.

ge-fræge, adj., known by reputation, renowned : nom. sg. leód-cyning ... folcum gefræge, 55; swâ hyt gefræge wäs, 2481.

ge-fræge, st. n., information through hearsay : instr. sg. mine gefræge (as I learned through the narrative of others), 777, 838, 1956, etc.

ge-frægnian, w. v., to become known through hearsay : pret. part. fylle gefrægnod (of Grendel's mother, who had become known through the carrying off of Äschere), 1334?

freca, w. m., properly a wolf , as one that breaks in, robs; here a designation of heroes: nom. sg. freca Scildinga, of Beówulf, 1564.--Comp.: gûð-, hilde-, scyld-, sweord-, wîg-freca; ferð-frec (adj.).

fremde, adj., properly distant, foreign ; then estranged, hostile : nom sg. þät wäs fremde þeód êcean dryhtne, of the giants, 1692.

freme, adj., excellent, splendid : nom. sg. fem. fremu folces cwên, of Þryðo, 1933(?).

fremman, w. v., to press forward, to further , hence: 1) in general, to perform, to accomplish, to do, to make : pres. subj. without an object, fremme se þe wille, let him do (it) whoever will , 1004. With acc.: imp. pl. fremmað ge nu leóda þearfe, 2801; inf. fyrene fremman, 101; säcce fremman, 2500; fæhðe ... mærðum fremman, 2515, etc.; pret. sg. folcræd fremede (did what was best for his men , i.e. ruled wisely), 3007; pl. hû þâ äðelingas ellen fremedon, 3; feohtan fremedon, 960; nalles fâcenstafas ... þenden fremedon, 1020; pret. subj. þät ic ... mærðo fremede, 2135. --2) to help on, to support : inf. þät he mec fremman wile wordum and worcum (to an expedition), 1833.

ge-fremman, w. acc., to do, to make, to render : inf. gefremman eorlîc ellen, 637; helpan gefremman, to give help , 2450; äfter weáspelle wyrpe gefremman, to work a change after sorrow (to give joy after sorrow), 1316; gerund, tô gefremmanne, 174, 2645; pret. sg. gefremede, 135, 165, 551, 585, etc.; þeáh þe hine mihtig god ... ofer ealle men forð gefremede, placed him away, above all men , i.e. raised him, 1719; pret. pl. gefremedon, 1188, 2479; pret. subj. gefremede, 177; pret. part. gefremed, 476; fem, nu scealc hafað ... dæd gefremede,

941; absolutely, þu þe self hafast dædum gefremed, þät ..., hast brought it about by thy deeds that , 955.

fretan, st. v., to devour, to consume : inf. þâ (the precious things) sceal brond fretan, 3015; nu sceal glêd fretan wîgena strengel, 3115; pret. sg. (Grendel) slæpende frät folces Denigea fýftyne men, 1582.

frêcne, adj., dangerous, bold : nom. sg. frêcne fýr-draca, 2690; feorh-bealo frêcne, 2251, 2538; acc. sg. frêcne dæde, 890; frêcne fengelâd, 1360; frêcne stôwe, 1379; instr. sg. frêcnan spræce (through provoking words), 1105.

frêcne, adv., boldly, audaciously , 960, 1033, 1692.

freá, w. m., ruler, lord , of a temporal ruler: nom. sg. freá, 2286; acc. sg. freán, 351, 1320, 2538, 3003, 3108; gen. sg. freán, 359, 500, 1167, 1681; dat. sg. freán, 271, 291, 2663. Of a husband: dat. sg. eode ... tô hire freán sittan, 642. Of God: dat. sg. freán ealles, the Lord of all , 2795; gen. sg. freán, 27.-- Comp.: âgend-, lîf-, sin-freá.

freá-dryhten, st. m., lord, ruling lord : gen. sg. freá-drihtnes, 797.

freá-wine, st. m., lord and friend, friendly ruler : nom. sg. freá-wine folces (folca), 2358, 2430; acc. sg. his freá-wine, 2439.

freá-wrâsn, st. f., encircling ornament like a diadem : instr. pl. helm ... befongen freáwrâsnum, 1452; see wrâsn.

freoðu, friðu, f., protection, asylum, peace : acc. sg. wel bið þäm þe môt ... tô fäder fäðmum freoðo wilnian, who may obtain an asylum in God's arms , 188; neán and feorran þu nu [friðu] hafast, 1175.--Comp. fen-freoðo.

freoðo-burh, st. f., castle, city affording protection : acc. sg. freoðoburh fägere, 522.

freoðo-wong, st. m., field of peace, field of protection : acc. sg., 2960; seems to have been the proper name of a field.

freoðo-wær, st. f., peace-alliance, security of peace : acc. sg. þâ hie getrûwedon on twâ healfa fäste frioðu-wære, 1097; gen. sg. frioðowære bäd hlâford sînne, entreated his lord for the protection of peace (i.e. full pardon for his delinquency), 2283.

freoðo-webbe, w. f., peace-weaver , designation of the royal consort (often one given in marriage as a confirmation of a peace between two nations): nom. sg., 1943.

freó-burh, st. f., = freá-burg (?), ruler's castle (?) (according to Grein, arx ingenua): acc. sg. freóburh, 694.

freód, st. f., friendship : acc. sg. freóde ne woldon ofer heafo healdan, 2477; gen. sg. näs þær mâra fyrst freóde tô friclan, was no longer time to seek for friendship , 2557; -- favor, acknowledgement : acc. sg. ic þe sceal mîne gelæstan freóde (will show myself grateful , with reference to 1381 ff.), 1708.

freó-dryhten (= freá-dryhten), st. m., lord, ruler ; according to Grein, dominus ingenuus vel nobilis: nom. sg. as voc. freó-drihten min! 1170; dat. sg. mid his freó-dryhtne, 2628.

freógan, w. v., to love; to think of lovingly : pres. subj. þät mon his wine-dryhten ... ferhðum freóge, 3178; inf. nu ic þec ... me for sunu wylle freógan on ferhðe, 949.

freó-lîc, adj., free, free-born (here of the lawful wife in contrast with the bond concubine): nom. sg. freólîc wîf, 616; freólîcu folc-cwên, 642.

freónd, st. m., friend : acc. sg. freónd, 1386, 1865; dat. pl. freóndum, 916, 1019, 1127; gen. pl. freónda, 1307, 1839.

freónd-laðu, st. f., friendly invitation : nom. sg. him wäs ful boren and freónd-laðu (friendly invitation to drink) wordum bewägned, 1193.

freónd-lâr, st. f., friendly counsel : dat. (instr.) pl. freónd-lârum, 2378.

freónd-lîce, adv., in a friendly manner, kindly : compar. freónd-lîcor, 1028.

freónd-scipe, st. m., friendship : acc. sg. freónd-scipe fästne, 2070.

freó-wine, st. m. (see freáwine), lord and friend, friendly ruler ; according to Grein, amicus nobilis, princeps amicus: nom. sg. as voc. freó-wine folca! 430.

fricgean, w. v., to ask, to inquire into : inf. ongan sînne geseldan fägre fricgean hwylce Sæ-Geáta sîðas wæron, 1986; pres. part, gomela Scilding fela fricgende feorran rehte, the old Scilding, asking many questions (having many things related to him), told of old times (the conversation was alternate), 2107.

ge-fricgean, to learn, to learn by inquiry : pres. pl. syððan hie ge-fricgeað freán ûserne ealdorleásne, when they learn that our lord is dead , 3003; pres. subj. gif ic þät gefricge, þät..., 1827; pl. syððan äðelingas feorran gefricgean fleám eówerne, 2890.

friclan (see freca), w. v. w. gen., to seek, to desire, to strive for : inf. näs þær mâra fyrst freóde tô friclan, 2557.

friðo-sib, st. f., kin for the confirming of peace , designation of the queen (see freoðo--webbe), peace-bringer : nom. sg. friðu-sibb folca, 2018.

frignan, fringan, frinan, st. v., to ask, to inquire : imp. ne frin þu äfter sælum, ask not after the well-being! 1323; inf. ic þäs wine Deniga frinan wille ... ymb þînne sîð, 351; pret. sg. frägn, 236, 332; frägn gif ..., asked whether ..., 1320.

ge-frignan, ge-fringan, ge-frinan, to find out by inquiry, to learn by narration. pret. sg. (w. acc.) þät fram hâm gefrägn Higelâces þegn Grendles dæda, 194; nô ic gefrägn heardran feohtan, 575; (w. acc. and inf.) þâ ic wîde gefrägn weorc gebannan, 74; similarly, 2485, 2753, 2774; ne gefrägen ic þâ mægðe mâran weorode ymb hyra sincgyfan sêl gebæran, I never heard that any people, richer in warriors, conducted itself better about its chief , 1012; similarly, 1028; pret. pl. (w. acc.) we þeódcyninga þrym gefrunon, 2; (w. acc. and inf.) geongne gûðcyning gôdne gefrunon hringas dælan, 1970; (parenthetical) swâ guman gefrungon, 667, (after þonne) medo-ärn micel (greater) ... þone yldo bearn æfre gefrunon, 70; pret. part. häfde Higelâces hilde gefrunen, 2953; häfdon gefrunen þät..., had learned that ..., 695; häfde gefrunen hwanan sió fæhð ârâs, 2404; healsbeága mæst þâra þe ic on foldan gefrägen häbbe, 1197.

from, See fram.

frôd, adj.: 1) ætate provectus, old, gray : nom. sg. frôd, 2626, 2951; frôd cyning, 1307, 2210; frôd folces weard, 2514; wintrum frôd, 1725, 2115, 2278; se frôda, 2929; ac. sg. frôde feorhlege (the laying down of my old life), 2801; dat. sg. frôdan fyrnwitan (may also, from its meaning, belong under No. 2), 2124.--2) mente excellentior, intelligent, experienced, wise : nom. sg. frôd, 1367; frôd and gôd, 279; on môde frôd, 1845.--Comp.: in-, un-frôd.

frôfor, st. f., consolation, compensation, help : nom. sg. frôfor, 2942; acc. sg. frôfre, 7, 974; fyrena frôfre, 629; frôfre and fultum, 1274; frôfor and fultum, 699; dat. sg. tô frôfre, 14, 1708; gen. sg. frôfre, 185.

fruma (see forma), w. m., the foremost , hence: l) beginning : nom. sg. wäs se fruma egeslîc leódum on lande, swâ hyt lungre wearð on hyra sincgifan sâre geendod (the beginning of the dragon-combat was terrible, its end distressing through the death of Beówulf), 2310.--2) he who stands first, prince ; in comp. dæd-, hild-, land-, leód-, ord-, wîg-fruma.

frum-cyn, st. n., (genus primitivum), descent, origin : acc. sg. nu ic eówer sceal frumcyn witan, 252.

frum-gâr, st. m., primipilus, duke, prince : dat. sg. frumgâre (of Beówulf), 2857.

frum-sceaft, st. f., prima creatio, beginning : acc. sg. se þe cûðe frumsceaft fira feorran reccan, who could tell of the beginning of mankind in old times , 91; dat. sg. frum-sceafte, in the beginning , i.e at his birth, 45.

fugol, st. m., bird : dat. sg. fugle gelîcost, 218; dat. pl. [fuglum] tô gamene, 2942.

ful, adj., full, filled : nom. sg. w. gen. pl. se wäs innan full wrätta and wîra, 2413.--Comp.: eges-, sorh-, weorð-ful.

ful, adv., plene, very : ful oft, 480; ful-oft, 952.

ful, st. n., cup, beaker : nom. sg., 1193; acc. sg. ful, 616, 629, 1026; ofer ýða ful, over the cup of the waves (the basin of the sea filled with waves), 1209; dat. sg. onfôh þissum fulle, 1170.--Comp.: medo-, sele-full.

fullæstian, w. v. w. dat, to give help : pres. sg. ic þe fullæstu, 2669.

fultum, st. m., help, support, protection : acc. sg. frôfor (frôfre) and fultum, 699, 1274; mägenes fultum, 1836; on fultum, 2663.--Comp. mägen-fultum.

fundian, w. v., to strive, to have in view : pres. pl. we fundiað Higelâc sêcan, 1820; pret. sg. fundode of geardum, 1138.

furðum, adv., primo, just, exactly; then first : þâ ic furðum weóld folce Deninga, then first governed the people of the Danes (had just assumed the government), 465; þâ hie tô sele furðum ... gangan cwômon, 323; ic þær furðum cwom tô þam hringsele, 2010;-- before, previously : ic þe sceal mine gelæstan freóde, swâ wit furðum spræcon, 1708.

furður, adv., further, forward, more distant , 254, 762, 3007.

fûs, adj., inclined to, favorable, ready : nom. sg. nu ic eom sîðes fûs, 1476; leófra manna fûs, prepared for the dear men , i.e. expecting them, 1917; sigel sûðan fûs, the sun inclined from the south (midday sun), 1967; se wonna hrefn fûs ofer fægum, eager over the slain , 3026; sceft ... feðer-gearwum fûs, 3120; nom. pl. wæron ... eft to leódum fûse tô farenne, 1806.--Sometimes fûs means ready for death , moribundus: fûs and fæge, 1242.--Comp.: hin-, ût-fûs.

fûs-lîc, adj., prepared, ready : acc. sg. fûs-lîc f[yrd]-leóð, 1425; fyrd-searo fûs-lîc, 2619; acc. pl. fyrd-searu fûs-lîcu, 232.

fyl, st. m., fall : nom. sg. fyll cyninges, the fall of the king (in the dragon-fight), 2913; dat. sg. þät he on fylle wearð, that he came to a fall, fell , 1545.--Comp. hrâ-fyl.

fylce (collective form from folc), st. n., troop, band of warriors : in comp. äl-fylce.

ge-fyllan (see feal), w. v., to fell, to slay in battle : inf. fâne gefyllan, to slay the enemy , 2656; pret. pl. feónd gefyldan, they had slain the enemy , 2707.

â-fyllan (see ful), w. v., to fill : pret. part. Heorot innan wäs freóndum âfylled (was filled with trusted men), 1019.

fyllo, st. f. (plenty, abundant meal : dat. (instr.) sg. fylle gefrægnod, 1334; gen. sg. näs hie þære fylle gefeán häfdon, 562; fylle gefægon, 1015.--Comp.: wäl-, wist-fyllo.

fyl-wêrig, adj., weary enough to fall, faint to death , moribundus: acc. sg. fyl-wêrigne, 963.

fyr. See feor.

fyrian, w. v. w. acc. (= ferian) to bear, to bring, carry : pret. pl. þâ þe gif-sceattas Geáta fyredon þyder tô þance, 378.

fyras. See firas.

fyren. See firen.

fyrde, adj., movable, that can be moved .--Comp. hard-fyrde.--Leo.

fyrd-gestealla, w. m., comrade on an expedition, companion in battle : dat. pl. fyrd-gesteallum, 2874

fyrd-ham, st. m., war-dress, coat of mail : acc. sg. þone fyrd-hom, 1505.

fyrd-hrägl, st. n., coat of mail, war-dress : acc. sg. fyrd-hrägl, 1528.

fyrd-hwät, adj., sharp, good in war, warlike : nom. pl. frome fyrd-hwate, 1642, 2477.

fyrd-leóð, st. n., war-song, warlike music : acc. sg. horn stundum song fûslîc f[yrd]leoð, 1425.

fyrd-searu, st. n., equipment for an expedition : acc. sg. fyrd-searu fûslîc, 2619; acc. pl. fyrd-searu fûslîcu, 232.

fyrd-wyrðe, adj., of worth in war, excellent in battle : nom. sg. fyrd-wyrðe man (Beówulf), 1317.

ge-fyrðran (see forð), w. v., to bring forward, to further : pret. part. âr wäs on ôfoste, eftsîðes georn, frätwum gefyrðred, he was hurried forward by the treasure (i.e. after he had gathered up the treasure, he hasted to return, so as to be able to show it to the mortally-wounded Beówulf), 2785.

fyrmest. See forma.

fyrn-dagas, st. m. pl., by-gone days : dat. pl. fyrndagum (in old times), 1452.

fyrn-geweorc, st. n., work, something done in old times : acc. sg. fira fyrn-geweorc (the drinking-cup mentioned in 2283), 2287.

fyrn-gewin, st. n., combat in ancient times : gen. sg. ôr fyrn-gewinnes (the origin of the battles of the giants), 1690.

fyrn-man, st. m., man of ancient times : gen. pl. fyrn-manna fatu, 2762.

fyrn-wita, w. m., counsellor ever since ancient times, adviser for many years : dat. sg. frôdan fyrnwitan, of Äschere, 2124.

fyrst, st. m., portion of time, definite time, time : nom. sg. näs hit lengra fyrst, ac ymb âne niht ..., 134; fyrst forð gewât, the time (of going to the harbor) was past , 210; näs þær mâra fyrst freóde tô friclan, 2556; acc. sg. niht-longne fyrst, 528; fîf nihta fyrst, 545; instr. sg. þý fyrste, 2574; dat. sg. him on fyrste gelomp ..., within the fixed time , 76.

fyr-wit, -wet, -wyt, st. n., prying spirit, curiosity : nom. sg. fyrwyt, 232; fyrwet, 1986, 2785.

ge-fýsan (fûs), w. v., to make ready, to prepare : part. winde gefýsed flota, the ship provided with wind (for the voyage), 217; (wyrm) fýre gefýsed, provided with fire , 2310; þâ wäs hringbogan (of the drake) heorte gefýsed säcce tô sêceanne, 2562; with gen., in answer to the question, for what? gûðe gefýsed, ready for battle, determined to fight , 631.

fýr, st. n., fire : nom. sg., 1367, 2702, 2882; dat. sg. fýre, 2220; as instr. fýre, 2275, 2596; gen. sg. fýres fäðm, 185; fýres feng, 1765.-- Comp.: âd-, bäl-, heaðu-, wäl-fýr.

fýr-bend, st. m., band forged in fire : dat. pl. duru ... fýr-bendum fäst, 723.

fýr-draca, w. m., fire-drake, fire-spewing dragon : nom. sg., 2690.

fýr-heard, adj., hard through fire, hardened in fire : nom. pl. (eoforlîc) fâh and fýr-heard, 305.

fýr-leóht, st. n., fire-light : acc. sg., 1517.

fýr-wylm, st. m., wave of fire, flame-wave : dat. pl. wyrm ... fýrwylmum fâh, 2672.

G

galan, st. v., to sing, to sound : pres. sg. sorh-leóð gäleð, 2461; inf. gryre-leóð galan, 787; bearhtm ongeâton, gûðhorn galan, heard the clang, the battle-trumpet sound , 1433.

â-galan, to sing, to sound : pret. sg. þät hire on hafelan hringmæl âgôl grædig gûðleóð, that the sword caused a greedy battle-song to sound upon her head , 1522.

gamban, or, according to Bout., gambe, w. f., tribute, interest : acc. sg. gomban gyldan, 11.

gamen, st. n., social pleasure, rejoicing, joyous doings : nom. sg. gamen, 1161; gomen, 2460; gomen gleóbeámes, the pleasure of the harp , 2264; acc. sg. gamen and gleódreám, 3022; dat. sg. gamene, 2942; gomene, 1776.--Comp. heal-gamen.

gamen-wâð, st. f., way offering social enjoyment, journey in joyous society : dat. sg. of gomen-wâðe, 855.

gamen-wudu, st. m., wood of social enjoyment , i.e. harp: nom. sg. þær wäs ... gomenwudu grêted, 1066; acc. sg. gomenwudu grêtte, 2109.

gamol, gomol, gomel, adj., old ; of persons, having lived many years, gray : gamol, 58, 265; gomol, 3096; gomel, 2113, 2794; se gomela, 1398; gamela (gomela) Scylding, 1793, 2106; gomela, 2932; acc. sg. þone gomelan, 2422; dat. sg. gamelum rince, 1678; gomelum ceorle, 2445; þam gomelan, 2818; nom. pl. blondenfeaxe gomele, 1596.--Also, late, belonging to former time : gen. pl. gomelra lâfe (legacy), 2037.--Of things, old, from old times : nom. sg. sweord ... gomol, 2683; acc. sg. gomele lâfe, 2564; gomel swyrd, 2611; gamol is a more respectful word than eald.

gamol-feax, adj., with gray hair : nom. sg., 609.

gang, st. m.: 1) gait, way : dat. sg. on gange, 1885; gen. sg. ic hine ne mihte ... ganges ge-twæman, could not keep him from going , 969.--2) step, foot-step : nom. sg. gang (the foot-print of the mother of Grendel), 1405; acc. sg. uton hraðe fêran Grendles mâgan gang sceáwigan, 1392.--Comp. in-gang.

be-gang, bi-gang, st. m., (so far as something goes), extent : acc. sg. ofer geofenes begang, over the extent of the sea , 362; ofer flôda begang, 1827; under swegles begong, 861, 1774; flôda begong, 1498; sioleða bigong, 2368.

gangan. See under gân.

ganot, st. m., diver , fulica marina: gen. sg. ofer ganotes bäð (i.e. the sea), 1862.

gâd, st. n., lack : nom. sg. ne bið þe wilna gâd (thou shalt have no lack of desirable [valuable] things), 661; similarly, 950.

gân, expanded = gangan, st. v., to go : pres. sg. III. gæð â Wyrd swâ hió scel, 455; gæð eft ... tô medo, 605; þonne he ... on flett gæð, 2035; similarly, 2055; pres. subj. III. sg. gâ þær he wille, let him go whither he will , 1395; imp. sg. II. gâ nu tô setle, 1783; nu þu lungre geong, hord sceáwian, under hârne stân, 2744; inf. in gân, to go in , 386, 1645 'forð gân, to go forth, to go thither , 1164; þat hie him tô mihton gegnum gangan, to go towards, to go to , 314; tô sele ... gangan cwômon, 324; in a similar construction, gongan, 1643; nu ge môton gangan ... Hrôðgâr geseón, 395; þâ com of môre ... Grendel gongan, there came Grendel (going) from the fen , 712; ongeán gramum gangan, to go to meet the enemy, to go to the war , 1035; cwom ... tô hofe gongan, 1975; wutun gangan tô, let us go thither , 2649.-- As preterite, serve, 1) geóng or gióng: he tô healle geóng, 926; similarly, 2019; se þe on orde geóng, who went at the head, went in front, 3126; on innan gióng, went in , 2215; he ... gióng tô þäs þe he eorðsele ânne wisse, went thither, where he knew of that earth-hall, 2410; þâ se äðeling, gióng, þät he bî wealle gesät, then went the prince (Beówulf) that he might sit down by the wall , 2716.-- 2) gang: tô healle gang Healfdenes sunu, 1010; similarly, 1296; gang þâ äfter flôre, went along the floor, along the hall , 1317.--3) gengde (Goth. gaggida): he ... beforan gengde ..., wong sceáwian, went in front to inspect the fields , 1413; gengde, also of riding, 1402.--4) from another stem, eode (Goth. iddja): eode ellenrôf, þät he for eaxlum gestôd Deniga freán, 358; similarly, 403; [wið duru healle Wulfgâr eode], went towards the door of the hall , 390; eode Wealhþeów forð, went forth , 613; eode tô hire freán sittan, 641; eode yrremôd, went with angry feeling , 727; eode ... tô sele, 919; similarly, 1233; eode ... þær se snottra bâd, 1313; eode weorð Denum äðeling tô yppan, the prince (Beówulf), honored by the Danes, went to the high seat , 1815; eode ... under inwit-hrôf, 3124; pl. þær swîðferhðe sittan eodon, 493; eodon him þâ tôgeánes, went to meet him , 1627; eodon under Earna näs, 3032.

â-gangan, to go out, to go forth, to befall : pret. part. swâ bit âgangen wearð eorla manegum (as it befell many a one of the earls), 1235.

full-gangan, to emulate, to follow after : pret. sg. þonne ... sceft nytte heóld, feðer-gearwum fûs flâne full-eode, when the shaft had employment, furnished with feathers it followed the arrow, did as the arrow , 3120.

ge-gân, ge-gangan: 1) to go, to approach : inf. (w. acc.) his môdor ... gegân wolde sorhfulne sîð, 1278; se þe gryre-sîðas gegân dorste, who dared to go the ways of terror (to go into the combat), 1463; pret. sg. se maga geonga under his mæges scyld elne geeode, went quickly under his kinsman's shield , 2677; pl. elne geeodon tô þäs þe ..., went quickly thither where ..., 1968; pret. part. syððan hie tô-gädre gegân häfdon, when they (Wîglâf and the drake) had come together , 2631; þät his aldres wäs ende gegongen, that the end of his life had come , 823; þâ wäs endedäg gôdum gegongen, þät se gûðcyning ... swealt, 3037.--2) to obtain, to reach : inf. (w. acc.) þonne he ät gûðe gegân þenceð longsumne lof, 1536; ic mid elne sceall gold gegangan, 2537; gerund, näs þät ýðe ceáp tô gegangenne gumena ænigum, 2417; pret. pl. elne geeodon ... þät se byrnwîga bûgan sceolde, 2918; pret. part. häfde ... gegongen þät, had attained it, that ..., 894; hord ys gesceáwod, grimme gegongen, 3086.--3) to occur, to happen : pres. sg. III. gif þät gegangeð þät ..., if that happen, that ..., 1847; pret. sg. þät geiode ufaran dôgrum hilde-hlämmum, it happened in later times to the warriors (the Geátas), 2201; pret. part. þâ wäs gegongen guman unfrôdum earfoðlîce þät, then it had happened to the young man in sorrowful wise that ..., 2822.

ôð-gangan, to-go thither : pret. pl. oð þät hi ôðeodon ... in Hrefnesholt, 2935.

ofer-gangan, w. acc., to go over : pret. sg. ofereode þâ äðelinga bearn steáp stân-hlîðo, went over steep, rocky precipices , 1409; pl. freoðo-wong þone forð ofereodon, 2960.

ymb-gangan, w. acc., to go around : pret. ymb-eode þâ ides Helminga duguðe and geogoðe dæl æghwylcne, went around in every part, among the superior and the inferior warriors , 621.

gâr, st. m., spear, javelin, missile : nom. sg., 1847, 3022; instr. sg. gâre, 1076; blôdigan gâre, 2441; gen. sg. gâres fliht, 1766; nom. pl. gâras, 328; gen. pl., 161(?).--Comp.: bon-, frum-gâr.

gâr-cêne, adj., spear-bold : nom. sg., 1959.

gâr-cwealm, st. m., murder, death by the spear : acc. sg. gâr-cwealm gumena, 2044.

gâr-holt, st. n., forest of spears, i.e. crowd of spears: acc. sg., 1835.

gâr-secg, st. m. (cf. Grimm, in Haupt l. 578), sea, ocean : acc. sg. on gâr-secg, 49, 537; ofer gâr-secg, 515.

gâr-wîga, w. m., one who fights with the spear : dat. sg. geongum gâr-wîgan, of Wîglâf, 2675, 2812.

gâr-wîgend, pres. part., fighting with spear, spear-fighter : acc. pl. gâr-wîgend, 2642.

gâst, gæst, st. m., ghost, demon : acc. sg. helle gâst (Grendel), 1275; gen. sg. wergan gâstes (of Grendel), 133; (of the tempter), 1748; gen. pl. dyrnra gâsta (Grendel's race), 1358; gæsta gîfrost (flames consuming corpses), 1124.--Comp.: ellor-, geó-sceaft-gâst; ellen-, wäl-gæst.

gâst-bana, w. m., slayer of the spirit, i.e. the devil: nom. sg. gâst-bona, 177.

gädeling, st. m., he who is connected with another, relation, companion : gen. sg. gädelinges, 2618; dat. pl. mid his gädelingum, 2950.

ät-gädere, adv., together, united : 321, 1165, 1191; samod ätgädere, 329, 387, 730, 1064.

tô-gadere, adv., together, 2631.

gäst, gist, gyst, st. m., stranger, guest : nom. sg. gäst, 1801; se gäst (the drake), 2313; se grimma gäst (Grendel), 102; gist, 1139, 1523; acc. sg. gryre-lîcne gist (the nixy slain by Beówulf), 1442; dat. sg. gyste, 2229; nom. pl. gistas, 1603; acc. pl. gäs[tas], 1894.--Comp.: fêðe-, gryre-, inwit-, nîð-, sele-gäst (-gyst).

gäst-sele, st. m., hall in which the guests spend their time, guest-hall : acc. sg., 995.

ge, conj., and, 1341; ge ... ge ..., as well ... as ... , 1865; ge ... ge ..., ge ..., 1249; ge swylce, and likewise, and moreover, 2259.

ge, pron., ye, you, plur. of þu, 237, 245, etc.

gegn-cwide, st. m., reply : gen. pl. þînra gegn-cwida, 367. gegnum, adv., thither, towards, away, with the prep. tô, ofer, giving the direction: þät hie him tô mihton gegnum gangan (that they might go thither), 314; gegnum fôr [þâ] ofer myrcan môr, away over the dark moor, 1405.

gehðu, geohðu, st. f., sorrow, care : instr. sg. giohðo mænde, 2268; dat. sg. on gehðo, 3096; on giohðe, 2794.

gen (from gegn), adv., yet, again. ne wäs hit lenge þâ gen, þät ..., it was not then long before ..., 83; ic sceal forð sprecan gen ymb Grendel, shall from now on speak again of Grendel, 2071; nô þý ær ût þâ gen ... gongan wolde (still he would not yet go out), 2082; gen is eall ät þe lissa gelong (yet all my favor belongs to thee), 2150; þâ gen, then again, 2678, 2703; swâ he nu gen dêð, as he still does, 2860; furður gen, further still, besides, 3007; nu gen, now again, 3169; ne gen, no more, no farther : ne wäs þät wyrd þâ gen, that was no more fate (fate no longer willed that), 735.

gena, still : cwico wäs þâ gena, was still living, 3094.

genga, w. m., goer ; in comp. in-, sæ-, sceadu-genga.

gengde. See gân(3).

genge. See ûð-genge.

genunga (from gegnunga), adv., precisely, completely, 2872.

gerwan, gyrwan, w. v.: 1) to prepare, to make ready, to put in condition : pret. pl. gestsele gyredon, 995.--2) to equip, to arm for battle : pret. sg. gyrede hine Beówulf eorl-gewædum (dressed himself in the armor), 1442.

ge-gyrwan: 1) to make, to prepare : pret. pl. him þâ gegiredan Geáta leóde âd ... unwâclîcne, 3138; pret. part. glôf ... eall gegyrwed deófles cräftum and dracan fellum, 2088.--2) to fit out, to make ready : inf. ceól gegyrwan hilde-wæpnum and heaðowædum, 38; hêt him ýðlidan gôdne gegyrwan, had (his) good ship fitted up for him, 199. Also, to provide warlike equipment : pret. part. syððan he hine tô gûðe gegyred häfde, 1473.--3) to endow, to provide, to adorn : pret. part. nom. sg. beado-hrägl ... golde gegyrwed, 553; acc. sg. lâfe ... golde gegyrede, 2193; acc. pl. mâdmas ... golde gegyrede, 1029.

getan, w. v., to injure, to slay : inf., 2941.

be-gête, adj., attainable ; in comp. êð-begête.

geador, adv., unitedly, together, jointly, 836; geador ätsomne, 491.

on-geador, adv., unitedly, together, 1596.

gealdor, st. n.: 1) sound : acc. sg. býman gealdor, 2944.--2) magic song, incantation, spell : instr. sg. þonne wäs þät yrfe ... galdre bewunden (placed under a spell), 3053.

gealga, w. m., gallows : dat. sg. þät his byre rîde giong on galgan, 2447.

gealg-môd, adj., gloomy : nom. sg. gîfre and galgmôd, 1278.

gealg-treów, st. n., gallows : dat. pl. on galg-treówu[m], 2941.

geard, st. m., residence ; in Beówulf corresponding to the house-complex of a prince's residence, used only in the plur.: acc. in geardas (in Finn's castle), 1135; dat. in geardum, 13, 2460; of geardum, 1139; ær he on weg hwurfe ... of geardum, before he went away from his dwelling-place, i.e. died, 265.--Comp. middan-geard.

gearo, adj., properly, made, prepared ; hence, ready, finished, equipped : nom. sg. þät hit wearð eal gearo, heal-ärna mæst, 77; with unhælo ... gearo sôna wäs, the demon of destruction was quickly ready, did not delay long, 121; Here-Scyldinga betst beadorinca wäs on bæl gearu, was ready for the funeral-pile (for the solemn burning), 1110; þeód (is) eal gearo, the warriors are altogether ready, always prepared, 1231; hraðe wäs ät holme hýð-weard gearo (geara, MS.), 1915; gearo gûð-freca, 2415; sîe sió bær gearo ädre geäfned, let the bier be made ready at once, 3106. With gen.: gearo gyrnwräce, ready for revenge for harm done, 2119, acc. sg. gearwe stôwe, 1007; nom. pl. beornas gearwe, 211; similarly, 1814.

gearwe, gearo, geare, adv., completely, entirely : ne ge ... gearwe ne wisson, you do not know at all ..., 246; similarly, 879; hine gearwe geman witena welhwyle (remembers him very well), 265; wisse he gearwe þät ..., he knew very well that ..., 2340, 2726; þät ic ... gearo sceáwige swegle searogimmas (that I may see the treasures altogether, as many as they are), 2749; ic wât geare þät ..., 2657.--Comp. gearwor, more readily, rather, 3077.--Superl. gearwost, 716.

gearo-folm, adj., with ready hand, 2086.

gearwe, st. f., equipment, dress ; in comp. feðer-gearwe.

geat, st. n., opening, door ; in comp. ben-, hilde-geat.

geato-lîc, adj., well prepared, handsome, splendid : of sword and armor, 215, 1563, 2155; of Heorot, 308. Adv.: wîsa fengel geatolîc gengde, passed on in a stately manner, 1402.

geatwe, st. f. pl., equipment, adornment : acc. recedes geatwa, the ornaments of the dragon's cave (its treasures), 3089.--Comp.: eóred-, gryre-, gûð-, hilde-, wîg-geatwe.

geán (from gegn), adv. in

on-geán, adv. and prep., against, towards : þät he me ongeán sleá, 682; ræhte ongeán feónd mid folme, 748; foran ongeán, forward towards , 2365. With dat.: ongeán gramum, against the enemy , 1035.

tô-geánes, tô-genes, prep. against, towards : Grendle tôgeánes, towards Grendel, against Grendel , 667; grâp þâ tôgeánes, she grasped at (Beówulf), 1502; similarly, him tôgeánes fêng, 1543; eodon him þâ tôgeánes, went towards him , 1627; hêt þâ gebeódan ... þät hie bæl-wudu feorran feredon gôdum tôgênes, had it ordered that they should bring the wood from far for the funeral-pyre towards the good man (i.e. to the place where the dead Beówulf lay), 3115.

geáp, adj., roomy, extensive, wide : nom. sg. reced ... geáp, the roomy hall , 1801; acc. sg. under geápne hrôf, 837.--Comp.: horn-, sæ-geáp.

geâr, st. n., year : nom. sg., 1135; gen. pl. geâra, in adverbial sense, olim, in former times , 2665. See un-geâra.

geâr-dagas, st. m. pl., former days : dat. pl. in (on) geâr-dagum, 1, 1355.

geofe. See gifu.

geofon, gifen, gyfen (see Kuhn Zeitschr. I. 137), st. n., sea, flood : nom. sg. geofon, 515; gifen geótende, the streaming flood , 1691; gen. sg. geofenes begang, 362; gyfenes, 1395.

geogoð, st. f.: 1) youth, time of youth : dat. sg. on geogoðe, 409, 466, 2513; on giogoðe, 2427; gen. gioguðe, 2113.--2) contrasted with duguð, the younger warriors of lower rank (about as in the Middle Ages, the squires with the knights): nom. sg. geogoð, 66; giogoð, 1191; acc. sg. geogoðe, 1182; gen. duguðe and geogoðe, 160; duguðe and iogoðe (geogoðe), 1675, 622.

geoguð-feorh, st. n., age of youth , i.e. age in which one still belongs in the ranks of the geogoð: on geogoð- (geoguð-) feore, 537, 2665.

geohðo. See gehðo.

geolo, adj., yellow : acc. sg. geolwe linde (the shield of yellow linden bark), 2611.

geolo-rand, st. m., yellow shield (shield with a covering of interlaced yellow linden bark): acc. sg., 438.

geond, prep. w. acc., through, throughout, along, over : geond þisne middangeard, through the earth, over the earth , 75; wide geond eorðan, 266, 3100; fêrdon folctogan ... geond wîd-wegas, went along the ways coming from afar , 841; similarly, 1705; geond þät säld, through the hall, through the extent of the hall , 1281; similarly, 1982, 2265.

geong, adj., young, youthful : nom. sg., 13, 20, 855, etc.; giong, 2447; w. m. se maga geonga, 2676; acc. sg. geongne gûðcyning, 1970; dat. sg. geongum, 1949, 2045, 2675, etc.; on swâ geongum feore, at a so youthful age , 1844; geongan cempan, 2627; acc. pl. geonge, 2019; dat. pl. geongum and ealdum, 72.--Superl. **gingest**, the last : nom. sg. w. f. gingeste word, 2818.

georn, adj., striving, eager , w. gen. of the thing striven for: eft sîðes georn, 2784.--Comp. lof-georn.

georne, adv., readily, willingly : þät him wine-mâgas georne hýrdon, 66; georne trûwode, 670.-- zealously, eagerly : sôhte georne äfter grunde, eagerly searched over the ground , 2295.-- carefully, industriously : nô ic him þäs georne ätfealh (held him not fast enough), 969.-- completely, exactly : comp. wiste þê geornor, 822.

geó, iú, adv., once, formerly, earlier , 1477; gió, 2522; iú, 2460.

geóc, st. f., help, support : acc. sg. geóce gefremman, 2675; þät him gâst-bona geóce gefremede wið þeód-þreáum, 177; geóce gelýfde, believed in the help (of Beówulf), 609; dat. sg. tô geóce, 1835.

geócor, adj., ill, bad : nom. sg., 766.--See Haupt's Zeitschrift 8, p. 7.

geó-man, iú-man, st. m., man of former times : gen. pl. iú-manna, 3053.

geó-meowle, w. f., (formerly a virgin), wife : acc. sg. ió-meowlan, 2932.

geômor, adj., with depressed feelings, sad, troubled : nom. sg. him wäs geômor sefa, 49, 2420, 2633, 2951; môdes geômor, 2101; fem. þät wäs geômuru ides, 1076.

geômore, adv., sadly , 151.

geômor-gid, st. n., dirge : acc. sg. giômor-gyd, 3151.

geômor-lîc, adj., sad, painful : swâ bið geômorlîc gomelum ceorle tô gebîdanne þät..., it is painful to an old man to experience it, that ... , 2445.

geômor-môd, adj., sad, sorrowful : nom. sg., 2045, 3019; giômor-môd, 2268.

geômrian, w. v., to complain, to lament : pret. sg. geômrode giddum, 1119.

geó-sceaft, st. f., (fixed in past times), fate : acc. sg. geósceaft grimme, 1235.

geósceaft-gâst, st. m., demon sent by fate : gen. pl. fela geósceaft-gâsta, of Grendel and his race, 1267.

geótan, st. v. intrans., to pour, to flow, to stream : pres. part. gifen geótende, 1691.

gicel, st. m., icicle : in comp. hilde-gicel.

gid, gyd, st. n., speech, solemn alliterative song : nom. sg. þær wäs ... gid oft wrecen, 1066; leóð wäs âsungen, gleómannes gyd, the song was sung, the gleeman's lay , 1161; þær wäs gidd and gleó, 2106; acc. sg. ic þis gid âwräc, 1724; gyd âwräc, 2109; gyd äfter wräc, 2155; þonne he gyd wrece, 2447; dat. pl. giddum, 151, 1119; gen. pl. gidda gemyndig, 869.--Comp.: geômor-, word-gid.

giddian, w. v., to speak, to speak in alliteration : pret. gyddode, 631.

gif, conj.: 1) if , w. ind., 442, 447, 527, 662, etc.; gyf, 945, etc. With subj., 452, 594, 1482, etc.; gyf, 280, 1105, etc.--2) whether , w. ind., 272; w. subj., 1141, 1320.

gifa, geofa, w. m., giver ; in comp. gold-, sinc-, wil-gifa (-geofa).

gifan, st. v., to give : inf. giofan, 2973; pret. sg. nallas beágas geaf Denum, 1720; he me [mâðmas] geaf, 2147; and similarly, 2174, 2432, 2624, etc.; pret. pl. geâfon (hyne) on gârsecg, 49; pret. part. þâ wäs Hrôðgâre here-spêd gyfen, 64; þâ wäs gylden hilt gamelum rince ... on hand gyfen, 1679; syððan ærest wearð gyfen ... geongum cempan (given in marriage), 1949.

â-gifan, to give, to impart : inf. andsware ... âgifan, to give an answer , 355; pret. sg. sôna him se frôda fäder Ôhtheres ... ondslyht âgeaf (gave him a counter-blow), (hand-blow ?), 2930.

for-gyfan, to give, to grant : pret. sg. him þäs lîf-freá ... worold-âre forgeaf, 17; þäm tô hâm forgeaf Hrêðel Geáta ângan dôhtor (gave in marriage), 374; similarly, 2998; he me lond forgeaf, granted me land , 2493; similarly, 697, 1021, 2607, 2617; mägen-ræs forgeaf hilde-bille, he gave with his battle-sword a mighty blow , i.e. he struck with full force, 1520.

of-gifan, (to give up), to leave : inf. þät se mæra maga Ecgþeówes grund-wong þone ofgyfan wolde (was fated to leave the earth-plain), 2589; pret. sg. þâs worold ofgeaf gromheort guma, 1682; similarly, gumdreám ofgeaf, 2470; Dena land ofgeaf, 1905; pret. pl. näs ofgeâfon hwate Scyldingas, left the promontory , 1601; þät þâ hildlatan holt ofgêfan, that the cowards left the wood (into which they had fled), 2847; sg. pret. for pl. þâra þe þis [lîf] ofgeaf, 2252.

gifeðe, adj., given, granted : Gûðfremmendra swylcum gifeðe bið þät..., to such a warrior is it granted that ..., 299; similarly, 2682; swâ me gifeðe wäs, 2492; þær me gifeðe swâ ænig yrfeweard äfter wurde, if an heir , (living) after me, had been given me , 2731.--Neut. as subst.: wäs þät gifeðe tô swîð, þe þone [þeóden] þyder ontyhte, the fate was too harsh that has drawn hither the king , 3086; gyfeðe, 555, 820.--Comp. un-gifeðe.

gif-heal, st. f., hall in which fiefs were bestowed, throne-hall : acc. sg. ymb þâ gifhealle, 839.

gif-sceat, st. m., gift of value : acc. pl. gif-sceattas, 378.

gif-stôl, st. m., seat from which fiefs are granted, throne : nom. sg., 2328; acc. sg., 168.

gift, st. f., gift, present : in comp. feoh-gift.

gifu, geofu, st. f., gift, present, grant; fief : nom. sg. gifu, 1885 acc. sg. gimfäste gife þe him god sealde, the great gift that God had granted him (i.e. the enormous strength), 1272; ginfästan gife þe him god sealde, 2183; dat. pl. (as instr.) geofum, 1959; gen. pl. gifa, 1931; geofena, 1174.--Comp.: mâððum-, sinc-gifu.

gigant, st. m., giant : nom. pl. gigantas, 113; gen. pl. giganta, 1563, 1691.

gild, gyld, st. n., reparation : in comp. wiðer-gyld(?).

gildan, gyldan, st. v., to do something in return, to repay, to reward, to pay : inf. gomban gyldan, pay tribute , 11; he mid gôde gyldan wille uncran eaferan, 1185; we him þâ gûðgeatwa gyldan woldon, 2637; pret. sg. heaðoræsas geald mearum and mâðmum, repaid the battles with horses and treasures , 1048; similarly, 2492; geald þone gûðræs ... Jofore and Wulfe mid ofermâðmum, repaid Eofor and Wulf the battle with exceedingly great treasures , 2992.

an-gildan, to pay for : pret. sg. sum sâre angeald æfenräste, one (Äschere) paid for the evening-rest with death's pain , 1252.

â-gildan, to offer one's self : pret. sg. þâ me sæl âgeald, when the favorable opportunity offered itself , 1666; similarly, þâ him rûm âgeald, 2691.

for-gildan, to repay, to do something in return, to reward : pres. subj. sg. III. alwalda þec gôde forgylde, may the ruler of all reward thee with good , 957; inf. þone änne hêht golde forgyldan, he ordered that the one (killed by Grendel) be paid for (atoned for) with gold , 1055; he ... wolde Grendle for-gyldan gûðræsa fela, wished to pay Grendel for many attacks , 1578; wolde se lâða lîge forgyldan drinc-fät dýre, the enemy wished to repay with fire the costly drinking vessel (the theft of it), 2306; pret. sg. he him þäs leán forgeald, he gave them the reward therefore , 114; similarly, 1542, 1585, 2095; forgeald hraðe wyrsan wrixle wälhlem þone, repaid the murderous blow with a worse exchange , 2969.

gilp, gylp, st. m., speech in which one promises great things for himself in a coming combat, defiant speech, boasting speech : acc. sg. häfde ... Geát-mecga leôd gilp gelæsted (had fulfilled what he had claimed for himself before the battle), 830; nallas on gylp seleð fätte beágas, gives no chased gold rings for a boastful speech , 1750; þät ic wið þone gûðflogan gylp ofersitte, restrain myself from the speech of defiance , 2529; dat. sg. gylpe wiðgrîpan (fulfil my promise of battle), 2522.--Comp. dol-gilp.

gilpan, gylpan, st. v. w. gen., acc., and dat., to make a defiant speech, to boast, to exult insolently : pres. sg. I. nô ic þäs gilpe (after a break in the text), 587; sg. III. morðres gylpeð, boasts of the murder, 2056; inf. swâ ne gylpan þearf Grendles maga ænig ... uhthlem þone, 2007; nealles folc-cyning fyrdgesteallum gylpan þorfte, had no need to boast of his fellow-warrior, 2875; pret. sg. hrêðsigora ne gealp goldwine Geáta, did not exult at the glorious victory (could not gain the victory over the drake), 2584.

gilp-cwide, st. m., speech in which a man promises much for himself for a coming combat, speech of defiance : nom. sg., 641.

gilp-hläden, pret. part., laden with boasts of defiance (i.e. he who has made many such boasts, and consequently has been victorious in many combats), covered with glory : nom. sg. guma gilp-hläden, 869.

gilp-spræc, same as gilp-cwide, speech of defiance, boastful speech : dat. sg. on gylp-spræce, 982.

gilp-word, st. n., defiant word before the coming combat, vaunting word : gen. pl. gespräc ... gylp-worda sum, 676.

gim, st. m., gem, precious stone, jewel : nom. sg. heofones gim, heaven's jewel, i.e. the sun, 2073. Comp. searo-gim.

gimme-rîce, adj., rich in jewels : acc. sg. gimme-rîce hord-burh häleða, 466.

gin (according to Bout., ginne), adj., properly gaping, hence, wide, extended : acc. sg. gynne grund (the bottom of the sea), 1552.

gin-fäst, adj., extensive, rich : acc. sg. gim-fäste gife (gim-, on account of the following f), 1272; in weak form, gin-fästan gife, 2183.

ginnan, st. v., original meaning, to be open, ready ; in

on-ginnan, to begin, to undertake : pret. ôð þät ân ongan fyrene fremman feónd on helle, 100; secg eft ongan sîð Beówulfes snyttrum styrian, 872; þâ þät sweord ongan ... wanian, the sword began to diminish, 1606; Higelâc ongan sînne geseldan ... fägre fricgean, began with propriety to question his companion, 1984, etc.; ongon, 2791; pret. pl. nô her cûðlîcor cuman ongunnon lindhäbbende, no shield-bearing men e'er undertook more openly to come hither, 244; pret. part. häbbe ic mærða fela ongunnen on geogoðe, have in my youth undertaken many deeds of renown, 409.

gist. See gäst.

gistran, adv., yesterday : gystran niht, yesterday night, 1335.

git, pron., ye two, dual of þu, 508, 512, 513, etc.

git, gyt, adv., yet; then still, 536, 1128, 1165, 2142; hitherto, 957; næfre git, never yet, 583; still, 945, 1059, 1135; once more, 2513; moreover, 47, 1051, 1867.

gitan (original meaning, to take hold of, to seize, to attain), in

be-gitan, w. acc., to grasp, to seize, to reach : pret. sg. begeat, 1147, 2231; þâ hine wîg beget, when war seized him, came upon him, 2873; similarly, begeat, 1069; pret. pl. hit ær on þe gôde be-geâton, good men received it formerly from thee, 2250; subj. sg. for pl. þät wäs Hrôðgâre hreówa tornost þâra þe leódfruman lange begeâte, the bitterest of the troubles that for a long time had befallen the people's chief, 2131.

for-gitan, w. acc., to forget : pres. sg. III. he þâ forðgesceaft forgyteð and forgýmeð, 1752.

an-gitan, on-gitan, w. acc.: 1) to take hold of, to grasp : imp. sg. gumcyste ongit, lay hold of manly virtue, of what becomes the man, 1724; pret. sg. þe hine se brôga angeat, whom terror seized, 1292.--2) to grasp intellectually, to comprehend, to perceive, to distinguish, to behold : pres. subj. I. þät ic ærwelan ... ongite, that I may behold the ancient wealth (the treasures of the drake's cave), 2749; inf. säl timbred ... ongytan, 308, 1497; Geáta clifu ongitan, 1912; pret. sg. fyren-þearfe ongeat, had perceived their distress from hostile snares, 14; ongeat ... grund-wyrgenne, beheld the she-wolf of the bottom, 1519; pret. pl. bearhtm ongeâton, gûðhorn galan, perceived the noise, (heard) the battle-trumpet sound, 1432; syððan hie Hygelâces horn and býman gealdor ongeâton, 2945.

gîfre, adj., greedy, eager : nom. sg. gîfre and galgmôd, of Grendel's mother, 1278.--Superl.: lîg..., gæsta gîfrost, 1124.--Comp. heoro-gîfre.

gîtsian, w. v., to be greedy : pres. sg. III. gýtsað, 1750.

gio-, gió-. See geo-, geó-.

gladian, w. v., to gleam, to shimmer : pres. pl. III. on him gladiað gomelra lâfe, upon him gleams the legacy of the men of ancient times (armor), 2037.

gläd, adj., gracious, friendly (as a form of address for princes): nom. sg. beó wið Geátas gläd, 1174; acc. sg. glädne Hrôðgâr, 864; glädne Hrôðulf, 1182; dat. sg. gladum suna Frôdan, 2026.

gläde, adv., in a gracious, friendly way, 58.

glädnian, w. v., to rejoice : inf. w. gen., 367.

gläd-môd, adj., joyous, glad, 1786.

glêd, st. f., fire, flame : nom. sg., 2653, 3115; dat. (instr.) pl. glêdum, 2313, 2336, 2678, 3042.

glêd-egesa, w. m., terror on account of fire, fire-terror : nom. sg. glêd-egesa grim (the fire-spewing of the drake), 2651.

gleáw (Goth, glaggwu-s), adj., considerate, well-bred, of social conduct; in comp. un-gleáw.

gleó, st. n., social entertainment, (especially by music, play, and jest): nom. sg. þær wäs gidd and gleó, 2106.

gleó-beám, st. m., (tree of social entertainment, of music), harp. gen. sg. gleó-beámes, 2264.

gleó-dreám, st. m., joyous carrying-on in social entertainment, mirth, social gaiety : acc. sg. gamen and gleó-dreám, 3022.

gleó-man, m., (gleeman, who enlivens the social entertainment, especially with music), harper : gen. sg. gleómannes gyd, 1161.

glitinian (O.H.G. glizinôn), w. v., to gleam, to light, to glitter : inf. geseah þâ ... gold glitinian, 2759.

glîdan, st. v., to glide : pret. sg. syððan heofones gim glâd ofer grundas, after heaven's gem had glided over the fields (after the sun had set), 2074; pret. pl. glidon ofer gârsecg, you glided over the ocean (swimming), 515.

tô-glîdan (to glide asunder), to separate, to fall asunder : pret. gûð-helm tô-glâd (Ongenþeów's helmet was split asunder by the blow of Eofor), 2488.

glôf, st. f., glove : nom. sg. glôf hangode, (on Grendel) a glove hung, 2086.

gneáð, adj., niggardly : nom. sg. f. näs hió ... tô gneáð gifa Geáta leódum, was not too niggardly with gifts to the people of the Geátas, 1931.

gnorn, st. m., sorrow, sadness : acc. sg. gnorn þrowian, 2659.

gnornian, w. v., to be sad, to complain : pret. sg. earme ... ides gnornode, 1118.

be-gnornian, w. acc., to bemoan, to mourn for : pret. pl. begnornodon ... hlâfordes [hry]re, bemoaned their lord's fall, 3180.

god, st. m., god : nom. sg., 13, 72, 478, etc.; hâlig god, 381, 1554; witig god, 686; mihtig god, 702; acc. sg. god, 812; ne wiston hie drihten god, did not know the Lord God , 181; dat. sg. gode, 113, 227, 626, etc.; gen. sg. godes, 570, 712, 787, etc.

gold, st. n., gold : nom. sg., 3013, 3053; icge gold, 1108; wunden gold, wound gold, gold in ring-form , 1194, 3136; acc. sg. gold, 2537, 2759, 2794, 3169; hæðen gold, heathen gold (that from the drake's cave), 2277; brâd gold, massive gold , 3106; dat. instr. sg. golde, 1055, 2932, 3019; fättan golde, with chased gold, with gold in plate-form , 2103; gehroden golde, covered with gold, gilded , 304; golde gegyrwed (gegyrede), provided with, ornamented with gold , 553, 1029, 2193; golde geregnad, adorned with gold , 778; golde fâhne (hrôf), the roof shining with gold , 928; bunden golde, bound with gold (see under bindan), 1901; hyrsted golde (helm), the helmet ornamented with, mounted with gold , 2256; gen. sg. goldes, 2302; fättan goldes, 1094, 2247; scîran goldes, of pure gold , 1695. -- Comp. fät-gold.

gold-æht, st. f., possessions in gold, treasure : acc. sg., 2749.

gold-fâh, adj., variegated with gold, shining with gold : nom. sg. reced ... gold-fâh, 1801; acc. sg. gold-fâhne helm, 2812; nom. pl. gold-fâg scinon web äfter wagum, variegated with gold, the tapestry gleamed along the walls , 995.

gold-gifa, w. m., gold-giver , designation of the prince: acc. sg. mid mînne goldgyfan, 2653.

gold-hroden, pret. part., (covered with gold), ornamented with gold : nom. sg., 615, 641, 1949, 2026; epithet of women of princely rank.

gold-hwät, adj., striving after gold, greedy for gold : näs he goldhwät, he (Beówulf) was not greedy for gold (he did not fight against the drake for his treasure, cf. 3067 ff.) 3075.

gold-mâðm, st. m., jewel of gold : acc. pl. gold-mâðmas (the treasures of the drake's cave), 2415.

gold-sele, st. m., gold-hall , i.e. the hall in which the gold was distributed, ruler's hall: acc. sg., 716, 1254; dat. sg. gold-sele, 1640, 2084.

gold-weard, st. m., gold-ward, defender of the gold : acc. sg. (of the drake), 3082.

gold-wine, st. m., friend who distributes gold , i.e. ruler, prince: nom. sg. (partly as voc.) goldwine gumena, 1172, 1477, 1603; goldwine Geáta, 2420, 2585.

gold-wlanc, adj., proud of gold : nom. sg. gûðrinc goldwlanc (Beówulf rewarded with gold by Hrôðgâr on account of his victory), 1882.

gomban, gomel, gomen. See gamban, gamal, gamen.

gong, gongan. See gang, gangan.

gôd, adj., good, fit , of persons and things: nom. sg., 11, 195, 864, 2264, 2391, etc.; frôd and gôd, 279; w. dat. cyning äðelum gôd, the king noble in birth , 1871; gumcystum gôd, 2544; w. gen. wes þu ûs lârena gôd, be good to us with teaching (help us thereto through thy instruction), 269; in weak form, se gôda, 205, 355, 676, 1191, etc.; acc. sg. gôdne, 199, 347, 1596, 1970, etc.; gumcystum gôdne, 1487; neut. gôd, 1563; dat. sg. gôdum, 3037, 3115; þäm gôdan, 384, 2328; nom. pl. gôde, 2250; þâ gôdan, 1164; acc. pl. gôde, 2642; dat. pl. gôdum dædum, 2179; gen. pl. gôdra gûðrinca, 2649.--Comp. ær-gôd.

gôd, st. n.: 1) good that is done, benefit, gift : instr. sg. gôde, 20, 957, 1185; gôde mære, renowned on account of her gifts (Þryðo), 1953; instr. pl. gôdum, 1862.--2) ability , especially in fight: gen. pl. nât he þara gôda, 682.

gram, adj., hostile : gen. sg. on grames grâpum, in the gripe of the enemy (Beówulf), 766; nom. pl. þâ graman, 778; dat. pl. gramum, 424, 1035.

gram-heort, adj., of a hostile heart, hostile : nom. sg. grom-heort guma, 1683.

gram-hydig, adj., with hostile feeling, maliciously inclined : nom. sg. gromhydig, 1750.

grâp, st. f., the hand ready to grasp, hand, claw : dat. sg. mid grâpe, 438; on grâpe, 555; gen. sg. eal ... Grendles grâpe, all of Grendel's claw, the whole claw, 837; dat. pl. on grames grâpum, 766; (as instr.) grimman grâpum, with grim claws, 1543.--Comp.: feónd-, hilde-grâp.

grâpian, w. v., to grasp, to lay hold of, to seize : pret. sg. þät hire wið halse heard grâpode, that (the sword) griped hard at her neck, 1567; he ... grâpode gearofolm, he took hold with ready hand, 2086.

gräs-molde, w. f., grass-plot : acc. sg. gräsmoldan träd, went over the grass-plot, 1882.

grædig, adj., greedy, hungry, voracious : nom. sg. grim and grædig, 121, 1500; acc. sg. grædig gûðleóð, 1523.

græg, adj., gray : nom. pl. äsc-holt ufan græg, the ashen wood, gray above (the spears with iron points) 330; acc. pl. græge syrcan, gray (i.e. iron) shirts of mail, 334.

græg-mæl, adj., having a gray color, here = iron : nom. sg. sweord Beówulfes gomol and grægmæl, 2683.

græpe. See ät-græpe.

grêtan, w. v. w. acc.: 1) to greet, to salute : inf. hine swâ gôdne grêtan, 347; Hrôðgâr grêtan, 1647, 2011; eówic grêtan hêt (bade me bring you his last greeting), 3096; pret. sg. grêtte Geáta leód, 626; grêtte þâ guma ôðerne, 653; Hrôðgâr grêtte, 1817.-- 2) to come on, to come near, to seek out; to touch; to take hold of : inf. gifstôl grêtan, take possession of the throne, mount it as ruler, 168; näs se folccyning ænig ... þe mec gûðwinum grêtan dorste (attack with swords), 2736; Wyrd ... se þone gomelan grêtan sceolde, 2422; þät þone sin-scaðan gûðbilla nân grêtan nolde, that no sword would take hold upon the irreconcilable enemy, 804; pret. sg. grêtte goldhroden guman on healle, the gold-adorned (queen) greeted the men in the hall, 615; nô he mid hearme ... gästas grêtte, did not approach the strangers with insults, 1894; gomenwudu grêtte, touched the wood of joy, played the harp, 2109; pret. subj. II. sg. þät þu þone wælgæst wihte ne grêtte, that thou shouldst by no means seek out the murderous spirit (Grendel), 1996; similarly, sg. III. þät he ne grêtte goldweard þone, 3082; pret. part. þær wäs ... gomenwudu grêted, 1066.

ge-grêtan, w. acc.: 1) to greet, to salute, to address : pret. sg. holdne gegrêtte meaglum wordum, greeted the dear man with formal words, 1981; gegrêtte þâ gumena gehwylcne ... hindeman siðe, spoke then the last time to each of the men, 2517.--2) to approach, to come near, to seek out : inf. sceal ... manig ôðerne gôdum gegrêtan ofer ganotes bäð, many a one will seek another across the sea with gifts, 1862.

greót, st. m., grit, sand, earth : dat. sg. on greóte, 3169.

greótan, st. v., to weep, to mourn, to lament : pres. sg. III. se þe äfter sincgyfan on sefan greóteð, who laments in his heart for the treasure-giver, 1343.

grim, adj., grim, angry, wild, hostile : nom. sg., 121, 555, 1500, etc.; weak form, se grimma gäst, 102; acc. sg. m. grimne, 1149, 2137; fem. grimme, 1235; gen. sg. grimre gûðe, 527; instr. pl. grimman grâpum, 1543.--Comp.: beado-, heaðo-, heoro-, searo-grim.

grimme, adv., grimly, in a hostile manner, bitterly, 3013, 3086.

grim-lîc, adj., grim, terrible : nom. sg. grimlîc gry[re-gäst], 3042.

grimman, st. v., (properly to snort), to go forward hastily, to hasten : pret. pl. grummon, 306.

grindan, st. v., to grind , in

for-grindan, to destroy, to ruin : pret. sg. w. dat. forgrand gramum, destroyed the enemy, killed them (?), 424; pret. part. w. acc. häfde lîgdraca leóda fästen ... glêdum forgrunden, had with flames destroyed the people's feasts , 2336; þâ his âgen (scyld) wäs glêdum forgrunden, since his own (shield) had been destroyed by the fire , 2678.

gripe, st. m., gripe, attack : nom. sg. gripe mêces, 1766; acc. sg. grimne gripe, 1149.--Comp.: fær-, mund-, nîð-gripe.

grîma, w. m., mask, visor : in comp. beado-, here-grîma.

grîm-helm, st. m., mask-helmet, helmet with visor : acc. pl. grîm-helmas, 334.

grîpan, st. v., to gripe, to seize, to grasp : pret. sg. grâp þâ tôgeánes, then she caught at , 1502.

for-grîpan (to gripe vehemently), to gripe so as to kill, to kill by the grasp , w. dat.: pret. sg. ät gûðe forgrâp Grendeles mægum, 2354. wið-grîpan, w. dat., (to seize at), to maintain, to hold erect : inf. hû wið þam aglæcean elles meahte gylpe wið-grîpan, how else I might maintain my boast of battle against the monster , 2522.

grôwan, st. v., to grow, to sprout : pret. sg. him on ferhðe greów breósthord blôdreów, 1719.

grund, st. m.: 1) ground, plain, fields in contrast with highlands; earth in contrast with heaven: dat. sg. sôhte ... äfter grunde, sought along the ground , 2295; acc. pl. ofer grundas, 1405, 2074.--2) bottom, the lowest part : acc. sg. grund (of the sea of Grendel), 1368; on gyfenes grund, 1395; under gynne grund (bottom of the sea) 1552; dat. sg. tô grunde (of the sea), 553; grunde (of the drake's cave) getenge, 2759; so, on grunde, 2766.--Comp.: eormen-, mere-, sæ-grund.

grund-bûend, pres. part., inhabitant of the earth : gen. pl. grund-bûendra, 1007.

grund-hyrde, st. m., warder of the bottom (of the sea): acc. sg. (of Grendel's mother), 2137.

grund-sele, st. m., hall at the bottom (of the sea): dat sg. in þam [grund]sele, 2140.

grund-wang, st. m., ground surface, lowest surface : acc. sg. þone grund-wong (bottom of the sea), 1497; (bottom of the drake's cave), 2772, 2589.

grund-wyrgen, st. f., she-wolf of the bottom (of the sea): acc. sg. grund-wyrgenne (Grendel's mother), 1519.

gryn (cf. Gloss. Aldh. "retinaculum, rete grin," Hpts. Ztschr. IX. 429), st. n., net, noose, snare : gen. pl. fela ... grynna, 931. See gyrn.

gryre, st. m., horror, terror, anything causing terror : nom. sg., 1283; acc. sg. wið Grendles gryre, 384; hie Wyrd forsweóp on Grendles gryre, snatched them away into the horror of Grendel, to the horrible Grendel , 478; dat. pl. mid gryrum ecga, 483; gen. pl. swâ fela gryra, 592.--Comp.: fær-, wîg-gryre.

gryre-brôga, w. m., terror and horror, amazement : nom. sg. [gryre-]br[ô]g[a], 2229.

gryre-fâh, adj., gleaming terribly : acc. sg. gryre-fâhne (the fire-spewing drake , cf. also [draca] fýrwylmum fâh, 2672), 2577.

gryre-gäst, st. m., terror-guest, stranger causing terror : nom. sg. grimlîc gry[regäst], 3042; dat. sg. wið þam gryregieste (the dragon), 2561.

gryre-geatwe, st. f. pl., terror-armor, warlike equipment : dat. pl. in hyra gryre-geatwum, 324.

gryre-leóð, st. n., terror-song, fearful song : acc. sg. gehýrdon gryreleóð galan godes and-sacan (heard Grendel's cry of agony), 787.

gryre-lîc, adj., terrible, horrible : acc. sg. gryre-lîcne, 1442, 2137.

gryre-sîð, st. m., way of terror, way causing terror , i.e. warlike expedition: acc. pl. se þe gryre-sîðas gegân dorste, 1463.

guma, w. m., man, human being : nom. sg., 653, 869, etc.; acc. sg. guman, 1844, 2295; dat. sg. guman (gumum, MS.), 2822; nom pl. guman, 215, 306, 667, etc.; acc. pl. guman, 615; dat. pl. gumum, 127, 321; gen. pl. gumena, 73, 328, 474, 716, etc.--Comp.: driht-, seld-guma.

gum-cyn, st. n., race of men, people, nation : gen. sg. we synt gumcynnes Geáta leóde, people from the nation of the Geátas , 260; dat. pl. äfter gum-cynnum, along the nations, among the nations , 945.

gum-cyst, st. f., man's excellence, man's virtue : acc. sg. (or pl.) gumcyste, 1724; dat. pl. as adv., excellently, preeminently : gumcystum gôdne beága bryttan, 1487; gumcystum gôd ... hilde-hlemma (Beówulf), 2544.

gum-dreám, st. m., joyous doings of men : acc. sg. gum-dreám ofgeaf (died), 2470.

gum-dryhten, st. m., lord of men : nom. sg. 1643.

gum-fêða, w. m., troop of men going on foot : nom. sg., 1402.

gum-man, st. m., man : gen. pl. gum-manna fela, 1029.

gum-stôl, st. m., man's seat [Greek: kat'ezochæn] ruler's seat, throne : dat. sg. in gumstôle, 1953.

gûð, st. f., combat, battle : nom. sg., 1124, 1659, 2484, 2537; acc. sg. gûðe, 604; instr. sg. gûðe, 1998; dat. sg. tô (ät) gûðe, 438, 1473. 1536, 2354, etc.; gen. sg. gûðe, 483, 527, 631, etc.; dat. pl. gûðum, 1959, 2179; gen. pl. gûða, 2513, 2544.

gûð-beorn, st. m., warrior : gen. pl. gûð-beorna sum (the strand-guard on the Danish coast), 314.

gûð-bil, st. n., battle-bill : nom. sg. gûðbill, 2585; gen. pl. gûð-billa nân, 804.

gûð-byrne, w. f., battle-corselet : nom. sg., 321.

gûð-cearu, st. f., sorrow which the combat brings : dat. sg. äfter gûð-ceare, 1259.

gûð-cräft, st. m., warlike strength, power in battle : nom. sg. Grendles gûð-cräft, 127.

gûð-cyning, st. m., king in battle, king directing a battle : nom. sg., 199, 1970, 2336, etc.

gûð-deáð, st. m., death in battle : nom. sg., 2250.

gûð-floga, w. m., flying warrior : acc. sg. wið þone gûðflogan (the drake), 2529.

gûð-freca, w. m., hero in battle, warrior (see freca): nom. sg. gearo gûð-freca, of the drake, 2415.

gûð-fremmend, pres. part., fighting a battle, warrior : gen. pl. gûð-fremmendra, 246; gûð- (gôd-, MS.) fremmendra swylcum, such a warrior (meaning Beówulf), 299.

gûð-gewæde, st. n., battle-dress, armor : nom. pl. gûð-gewædo, 227; acc. pl. -gewædu, 2618, 2631(?), 2852, 2872; gen. pl. -gewæda, 2624.

gûð-geweorc, st. n., battle-work warlike deed : gen. pl., -geweorca, 679, 982, 1826.

gûð-geatwe, st. f. pl., equipment for combat : acc. þâ gûð-geatwa (-getawa, MS.), 2637; dat. in eówrum gûð-geatawum, 395.

gûð-helm, st. m., battle-helmet : nom. sg., 2488.

gûð-horn, st. n., battle-horn : acc. sg., 1433.

gûð-hrêð, st. f., battle-fame : nom. sg., 820.

gûð-leóð, st. n., battle-song : acc., sg., 1523.

gûð-môd, adj., disposed to battle, having an inclination to battle . nom. pl. gûð-môde, 306.

gûð-ræs, st. m., storm of battle, attack : acc. sg., 2992; gen. pl. gûð-ræsa, 1578, 2427.

gûð-reów, adj., fierce in battle : nom. sg., 58.

gûð-rinc, st. m., man of battle, fighter, warrior : nom. sg., 839, 1119, 1882; acc. sg., 1502; gen. pl. gûð-rinca, 2649.

gûð-rôf, adj., renowned in battle : nom. sg., 609.

gûð-sceaða, w. m., battle-foe, enemy in combat : nom. sg., of the drake, 2319.

gûð-scearu, st. f., decision of the battle : dat. sg. äfter gûð-sceare, 1214.

gûð-sele, st. m., battle-hall, hall in which a battle takes place : dat sg. in þäm gûðsele (in Heorot), 443.

gûð-searo, st. n. pl., battle-equipment, armor ; acc., 215, 328.

gûð-sweord, st. n., battle-sword : acc. sg., 2155.

gûð-wêrig, adj., wearied by battle dead : acc. sg. gûð-wêrigne Grendel, 1587.

gûð-wine, st. m., battle-friend, comrade in battle designation of the sword: acc. sg., 1811; instr. pl. þe mec gûð-winum grêtan dorste, who dared to attack me with his war-friends , 2736.

gûð-wîga, w. m., fighter of battles, warrior : nom. sg., 2112.

gyd. See gid.

gyfan. See gifan.

gyldan. See gildan.

gylden, adj., golden : nom. sg. gylden hilt, 1678; acc. sg. segen gyldenne, 47, 1022; bring gyldenne, 2810; dat. sg. under gyldnum beáge, 1164.--Comp. eal-gylden.

gylp. See gilp.

gyrdan, w. v., to gird, to lace : pret. part. gyrded cempa, the (sword-) girt warrior , 2079.

gyrn, st. n., sorrow, harm : nom. sg., 1776.

gyrn-wracu, st. f., revenge for harm : dat. sg. tô gyrn-wräce, 1139; gen. sg. þâ wäs eft hraðe gearo gyrn-wräce Grendeles môdor, then was Grendel's mother in turn immediately ready for revenge for the injury , 2119.

gyrwan. See gerwan.

gystran. See gistran.

gýman, w. v. w. gen., to take care of, to be careful about : pres. III. gýmeð, 1758, 2452; imp. sg. oferhyda ne gým! do not study arrogance (despise it), 1761.

for-gýman, w. acc., to neglect, to slight : pres. sg. III. he þâ forð-gesceaft forgyteð and forgýmeð, 1752.

gýtsian. See gîtsian.

gyt. See git.

H

habban, w. v., to have : 1) w. acc.: pres. sg. I. þäs ic wên häbbe (as I hope), 383; þe ic geweald häbbe, 951; ic me on hafu bord and byrnan, have on me shield and coat of mail , 2525; hafo, 3001; sg. II. þu nu [friðu] hafast, 1175; pl. I. habbað we ... micel ærende, 270; pres. subj. sg. III. þät he þrittiges manna mägencräft on his mundgripe häbbe, 381. Blended with the negative: pl. III. þät be Sæ-Geátas sêlran näbben tô geceósenne cyning ænigne, that the Sea-Geátas will have no better king than you to choose, 1851; imp. hafa nu and geheald hûsa sêlest, 659; inf. habban, 446, 462, 3018; pret. sg. häfde, 79, 518, 554; pl. häfdon, 539.--2) used as an auxiliary with the pret. part.: pres. sg. I. häbbe ic ... ongunnen, 408; häbbe ic ... geâhsod, 433; II. hafast, 954, 1856; III. hafað, 474, 596; pret. sg. häfde, 106, 220, 666, 2322, 2334, 2953, etc.; pl. häfdon, 117, 695, 884, 2382, etc. Pret. part. inflected: nu scealc hafað dæd gefremede, 940; häfde se gôda ... cempan gecorone, 205. With the pres. part. are formed the compounds: bord-, rond-häbbend.

 for-habban, to hold back, to keep one's self : inf. ne meahte wäfre môd forhabban in hreðre, the expiring life could not hold itself back in the breast, 1152; ne mihte þâ for-habban, could not restrain himself, 2610.

 wið-habban, to resist, to offer resistance : pret. þät se wînsele wið-häfde heaðo-deórum, that the hall resisted them furious in fight, 773.

 hafela, heafola, w. m., head : acc. sg. hafelan, 1373, 1422, 1615, 1636, 1781; nâ þu mînne þearft hafalan hýdan, 446; þonne we on orlege hafelan weredon, protected our heads, defended ourselves, 1328; se hwîta helm hafelan werede, 1449; dat. sg. hafelan, 673, 1522; heafolan, 2680; gen. sg. heafolan, 2698; nom. pl. hafelan, 1121.--Comp. wîg-heafola.

 hafenian, w. v., to raise, to uplift : pret. sg. wæpen hafenade heard be hiltum, raised the weapon, the strong man, by the hilt, 1574.

 hafoc, st. m., hawk : nom. sg., 2264.

 haga, w. m., enclosed piece of ground, hedge, farm-enclosure : dat. sg. tô hagan, 2893, 2961.

 haga, w. m. See ân-haga.

 hama, homa, w. m., dress : in the comp. flæsc-, fyrd-, lîc-hama, scîr-ham (adj.).

 hamer, st. m., hammer : instr. sg. hamere, 1286; gen. pl. homera lâfe (swords), 2830.

 hand, hond, st. f., hand : nom. sg. 2138; sió swîðre ... hand, the right hand, 2100; hond, 1521, 2489, 2510; acc. sg. hand, 558, 984; hond, 657, 687, 835, 928, etc.; dat. sg. on handa, 495, 540; mid handa, 747, 2721; be honda, 815; dat. pl. (as instr.) hondum, 1444, 2841.

 hand-bana, w. m., murderer with the hand, or in hand-to-hand combat : dat. sg. tô hand-bonan (-banan), 460, 1331.

 hand-gemôt, st. n., hand-to-hand conflict, battle : gen. pl. (ecg) þolode ær fela hand-gemôta, 1527; nô þät läsest wäs hond-gemôta, 2356.

 hand-gesella, w. m., hand-companion, man of the retinue : dat. pl. hond-gesellum, 1482.

 hand-gestealla, w. m., (one whose position is near at hand), comrade, companion, attendant : dat. sg. hond-gesteallan, 2170; nom. pl. hand-gesteallan, 2597.

 hand-geweorc, st. n., work done with the hands, i.e. achievement in battle: dat. sg. for þäs hild-fruman hondgeweorce, 2836.

 hand-gewriðen, pret. part. hand-wreathed, bound with the hand. acc. pl. wälbende ... hand-gewriðene, 1938.

 hand-locen, pret. part., joined, united by hand : nom. sg. (gûð-byrne, lîc-syrce) hondlocen (because the shirts of mail consisted of interlaced rings), 322, 551.

 hand-ræs, st. m., hand-battle, i.e. combat with the hands: nom. sg. hond-ræs, 2073.

hand-scalu, st. f., hand-attendance, retinue : dat. sg. mid his hand-scale (hond-scole), 1318, 1964.

hand-sporu, st. f., finger (on Grendel's hand), under the figure of a spear: nom. pl. hand-sporu, 987.

hand-wundor, st. n., wonder done by the hand, wonderful handwork : gen. pl. hond-wundra mæst, 2769.

hangan. See hôn.

hangian, w. v., to hang : pres. sg. III. þonne his sunu hangað hrefne to hrôðre, when his son hangs, a joy to the ravens , 2448; pl. III. ofer þäm (mere) hongiað hrîmge bearwas, over which frosty forests hang , 1364; inf. hangian, 1663; pret. hangode, hung down , 2086.

hatian, w. v. w. acc., to hate, to be an enemy to, to hurt : inf. he þone heaðo-rinc hatian ne meahte lâðum dædum (could not do him any harm), 2467; pret. sg. hû se gûð-sceaða Geáta leóde hatode and hýnde, 2320.

hâd, st. m., form, condition, position, manner : acc. sg. þurh hæstne hâd, in a powerful manner , 1336; on gesîðes hâd, in the position of follower, as follower , 1298; on sweordes hâd, in the form of a sword , 2194. See under on.

hâdor, st. m., clearness, brightness : acc. sg. under heofenes hâdor, 414.

hâdor, adj., clear, fresh, loud : nom. sg. scop hwîlum sang hâdor on Heorote, 497.

hâdre, adv., clearly, brightly , 1572.

hâl, adj., hale, whole, sound, unhurt : nom. sg. hâl, 300. With gen. heaðo-lâces hâl, safe from battle , 1975. As form of salutation, wes ... hâl, 407; dat. sg. hâlan lîce, 1504.

hâlig, adj., holy : nom. sg. hâlig god, 381, 1554; hâlig dryhten, 687.

hâm, st. m., home, residence, estate, land : acc. sg. hâm, 1408; Hrôðgâres hâm, 718. Usually in adverbial sense: gewât him hâm, betook himself home , 1602; tô hâm, 124, 374, 2993; fram hâm, at home , 194; ät hâm, at home , 1249, 1924, 1157; gen. sg. hâmes, 2367; acc. pl. hâmas, 1128.--Comp. Finnes-hâm, 1157.

hâm-weorðung, st. f., honor or ornament of home : acc. sg. hâm-weorðunge (designation of the daughter of Hygelâc, given in marriage to Eofor), 2999.

hâr, adj., gray : nom. sg. hâr hilde-rinc, 1308, 3137; acc. sg. under (ofer) hârne stân, 888, 1416, 2554; hâre byrnan (i.e. iron shirt of mail), 2154; dat. sg. hârum hildfruman, 1679; f. on heáre hæðe (on heaw ... h ... ðe, MS.), 2213; gen. sg. hâres, of the old man , 2989.--Comp. un-hâr.

hât, adj., hot, glowing, flaming nom sg., 1617, 2297, 2548, 2559, etc.; wyrm hât gemealt, the drake hot (of his own heat) melted , 898; acc. sg., 2282(?); inst. sg. hâtan heolfre, 850, 1424; g. sg. heaðu-fýres hâtes, 2523; acc. pl. hâte heaðo-wylmas, 2820.--Sup.: hâtost heaðo-swâta, 1669.

hât, st. n., heat, fire : acc. sg. geseah his mondryhten ... hât þrowian, saw his lord endure the (drake's) heat , 2606.

hata, w. m., persecutor ; in comp. dæd-hata.

hâtan, st. v.: 1) to bid, to order, to direct , with acc. and inf., and acc. of the person: pres. sg. I. ic maguþegnas mîne hâte ... flotan eówerne ârum healdan, I bid my thanes take good care of your craft , 293; imp. sg. II. hât in gân ... sibbegedriht, 386; pl. II. hâtað heaðo-mære hlæw gewyrcean, 2803; inf. þät healreced hâtan wolde ... men gewyrcean, that he wished to command men to build a hall-edifice , 68. Pret. sg. hêht: hêht ... eahta mearas ... on flet teón, gave command to bring eight horses into the hall , 1036; þonne ænne hêht golde forgyldan, commanded to make good that one with gold , 1054; hêht þâ þät heaðo-weorc tô hagan biódan, ordered the combat to be announced at the hedge (?), 2893; swâ se snottra hêht, as the wise (Hrôðgâr) directed, 1787; so, 1808, 1809. hêt: hêt him ýðlidan gôdne gegyrwan, ordered a good vessel to be prepared for him, 198; so, hêt, 391, 1115, 3111. As the form of a wish: hêt hine wel brûcan, 1064; so, 2813; pret. part. þâ wäs hâten hraðe Heort innan-weard folmum gefrätwod, forthwith was ordered Heorot, adorned by hand on the inside (i.e. that the edifice should be adorned by hand on the inside), 992.--2) to name, to call : pres. subj. III. pl. þät hit sælîðend ... hâtan Biówulfes biorh, that mariners may call it Beówulf's grave-mound, 2807; pret. part. wäs se grimma gäst Grendel hâten, 102; so, 263, 373, 2603.

ge-hâtan, to promise, to give one's word, to vow, to threaten : pres. sg. I. ic hit þe gehâte, 1393; so, 1672; pret. sg. he me mêde gehêt, promised me reward, 2135; him fägre gehêt leána (gen. pl.), promised them proper reward, 2990; weán oft gehêt earmre teohhe, with woe often threatened the unhappy band, 2938; pret. pl. gehêton ät härgtrafum wig-weorðunga, vowed offerings at the shrines of the gods, 175; þonne we gehêton ûssum hlâforde þät ..., when we promised our lord that ..., 2635; pret. part. sió gehâten [wäs] ... gladum suna Frôdan, betrothed to the glad son of Froda, 2025.

hâtor, st. m. n., heat : in comp. and-hâtor.

häft, adj., held, bound, fettered : nom. sg., 2409; acc. sg. helle häftan, him fettered by hell (Grendel), 789.

häft-mêce, st. m., sword with fetters or chains (cf. fetel-hilt): dat. sg. þäm häft-mêce, 1458. See Note.

häg-steald, st. m., man, liegeman, youth : gen. pl. häg-stealdra, 1890.

häle, st. m., man : nom. sg., 1647, 1817, 3112; acc. sg. häle, 720; dat. pl. hælum (hænum, MS.), 1984.

häleð, st. m., hero, fighter, warrior, man : nom. sg., 190, 331, 1070; nom. pl. häleð, 52, 2248, 2459, 3143; dat. pl. häleðum 1710, 1962, etc.; gen. pl. häleða, 467, 497, 612, 663, etc.

härg. See hearg.

hæð, st. f., heath : dat. sg. hæðe, 2213.

hæðen, adj., heathenish ; acc. sg. hæðene sâwle, 853; dat. sg. hæðnum horde, 2217; gen. sg. hæðenes, of the heathen (Grendel), 987; gen. pl. hæðenra, 179.

hæð-stapa, w. m., that which goes about on the heath (stag): nom. sg., 1369

hæl, st. f.: 1) health, welfare, luck : acc. sg. him hæl âbeád, 654; mid hæle, 1218.--2) favorable sign, favorable omen : hæl sceáwedon, observed favorable signs (for Beówulf's undertaking), 204.

hælo, st. f., health, welfare, luck : acc. sg. hælo âbeád heorð-geneátum, 2419.-- Comp. un-hælo.

hæst (O.H.G. haisterâ hantî, manu violenta; heist, ira; heistigo, iracunde), adj., violent, vehement : acc. sg. þurh hæstne hâd, 1336.

he, fem. heó, neut. hit, pers. pron., he, she, it ; in the oblique cases also reflexive, himself, herself, itself : acc. sg. hine, hî, hit; dat. sg. him, hire, him; gen. sg. his, hire, his; plur. acc. nom. hî, hig, hie; dat. him; gen. hira, heora, hiera, hiora.--he omitted before the verb, 68, 300, 2309, 2345.

hebban, st. v., to raise, to lift, w. acc.: inf. siððan ic hond and rond hebban mihte, 657; pret. part. hafen, 1291; häfen, 3024.

â-hebban, raise, to lift from, to take away : wäs ... icge gold âhafen of horde, taken up from the hoard, 1109; þâ wäs ... wôp up âhafen, a cry of distress raised, 128

ge-hegan [ge-hêgan], w. v., to enclose, to fence : þing gehegan, to mark off the court, hold court. Here figurative: inf. sceal ... âna gehegan þing wið þyrse (shall alone decide the matter with Grendel), 425.

hel, st. f., hell : nom. sg., 853; acc. sg. helle, 179; dat. sg. helle, 101, 589; (as instr.), 789; gen. sg. helle, 1275.

hel-bend, st. m. f. bond of hell : instr. pl. hell-bendum fäst, 3073.

hel-rûna, w. m., sorcerer : nom. pl. helrûnan, 163.

be-helan, st. v., to conceal, to hide : pret. part. be-holen, 414.

helm, st. m.: 1) protection in general, defence, covering that protects : acc. sg. on helm, 1393; under helm, 1746.--2) helmet : nom. sg., 1630; acc. sg. helm, 673, 1023, 1527, 2988; (helo, MS.), 2724; brûn-fâgne, gold-fâhne helm, 2616, 2812; dat. sg. under helme, 342, 404; gen. sg. helmes, 1031; acc. pl. helmas, 240, 2639.--3) defence, protector, designation of the king: nom. sg. helm Scyldinga (Hrôðgâr), 371, 456, 1322; acc. sg. heofena helm (the defender of the heavens = God), 182; helm Scylfinga, 2382.--Comp.: grîm-, gûð-, heaðo-, niht-helm.

ofer-helmian, w. v. w. acc., to cover over, to overhang : pres. sg. III. ofer-helmað, 1365.

helm-berend, pres. part., helm-wearing (warrior): acc. pl. helmberend, 2518, 2643.

helpan, st. v., to help : inf. þät him holt-wudu helpan ne meahte, lind wið lîge, that a wooden shield could not help him, a linden shield against flame, 2341; þät him îrenna ecge mihton helpan ät hilde, 2685; wutun gangan to, helpan hildfruman, let us go thitherto help the battle-chief, 2650; w. gen. ongan ... mæges helpan, began to help my kinsman, 2880; so, pret. sg. þær he his mæges (MS. mägenes) healp, 2699.

help, m. and f., help, support, maintenance : acc. sg. helpe, 551, 1553; dat. sg. tô helpe, 1831; acc. sg. helpe, 2449.

hende, -handed : in comp. îdel-hende.

her, adv., here, 397, 1062, 1229, 1655, 1821, 2054, 2797, etc.; hither, 244, 361, 376.

here (Goth, harji-s), st. m., army, troops : dat. sg. on herge, in the army, on a warlike expedition, 1249; in the army, among the fighting men, 2639; as instr. herge, 2348.--Comp.: flot-, scip-, sin-here.

here-brôga, w. m., terror of the army, fear of war : dat. sg. for here-brôgan, 462.

here-byrne, w. f., battle-mail, coat of mail : nom. sg., 1444.

here-grîma, w. m., battle-mask, i.e. helmet (with visor): dat. sg. -grîman, 396, 2050, 2606.

here-net, st. n., battle-net, i.e. coat of mail (of interlaced rings): nom. sg., 1554.

here-nîð, st. m., battle-enmity, battle of armies : nom. sg., 2475.

here-pâd, st. f., army-dress, i.e. coat of mail, armor: nom. sg., 2259.

here-rinc, st. m., army-hero, hero in battle, warrior : acc. sg. here-rinc (MS. hère ric), 1177.

here-sceaft, st. m., battle-shaft, i.e. spear: gen. pl. here-sceafta heáp, 335.

here-spêd, st. f., (war-speed), luck in war : nom. sg., 64.

here-stræl, st. m., war-arrow, missile : nom. sg., 1436.

here-syrce, w. f., battle-shirt, shirt of mail : acc. sg. here-syrcan, 1512.

here-wæd, st. f., army-dress, coat of mail, armor : dat. pl. (as instr.) here-wædum, 1898.

here-wæsma, w. m., war-might, fierce strength in battle : dat. pl. an here-wæsmum, 678.--Leo.

here-wîsa, w. m., leader of the army, i.e. ruler, king: nom. sg., 3021.

herg, hearg, st. m., image of a god, grove where a god was worshipped, hence to the Christian a wicked place(?): dat. pl. hergum geheaðerod, confined in wicked places (parallel with hell-bendum fäst), 3073.

herigean, w. v. w. dat. of pers., to provide with an army, to support with an army : pres. sg. I. ic þe wel herige, 1834.--Leo.

hete, st. m., hate, enmity : nom. sg. 142, 2555.--Comp.: ecg-, morðor-, wîg-hete.

hete-lîc, adj., hated : nom. sg., 1268.

hetend, hettend, (pres. part. of hetan, see hatian), enemy, hostis: nom. pl. hetende, 1829; dat. pl. wið hettendum, 3005.

hete-nîð, st. m., enmity full of hate : acc. pl. hete-nîðas, 152.

hete-sweng, st. m., a blow from hate : acc. pl. hete-swengeas, 2226.

hete-þanc, st. m., hate-thought, a hostile design : dat. pl. mid his hete-þancum, 475.

hêdan, ge-hêdan, w. v. w. gen.: 1) to protect : pret. sg. ne hêdde he þäs heafolan, did not protect his head, 2698.--2) to obtain : subj. pret. sg. III. gehêdde, 505.

hêrian, w. v. w. acc., to praise, to commend : with reference to God, to adore : inf. heofena helm hêrian ne cûðon, could not worship the defence of the heavens (God), 182; ne hûru Hildeburh hêrian þorfte Eotena treówe, had no need to praise the fidelity of the Eotens, 1072; pres. subj. þät mon his wine-dryhten wordum hêrge, 3177.

ge-heaðerian, w. v., to force, to press in : pret. part. ge-heaðerod, 3073.

heaðo-byrne, w. f., battle-mail, shirt of mail : nom. sg., 1553.

heaðo-deór, adj., bold in battle, brave : nom. sg., 689; dat. pl. heaðo-deórum, 773.

heaðo-fyr, st. n., battle-fire, hostile fire : gen. sg. heaðu-fýres, 2523; instr. pl. heaðo-fýrum, 2548, of the drake's fire-spewing.

heaðo-grim, adj., grim in battle, 548.

heaðo-helm, st. m., battle-helmet, war-helmet : nom. sg., 3157(?).

heaðo-lâc, st. n., battle-play, battle : dat. sg. ät heaðo-lâce, 584; gen. sg. heaðo-lâces hâl, 1975.

heaðo-mære, adj., renowned in battle : acc. pl. -mære, 2803.

heaðo-ræs, st. m., storm of battle, attack in battle, entrance by force : nom. sg., 557; acc. pl. -ræsas, 1048; gen. pl. -ræsa, 526.

heaðo-reáf, st. n., battle-dress, equipment for battle : acc. sg. heaðo-reáf heóldon (kept the equipments), 401.

heaðo-rinc, st. m., battle-hero, warrior : acc. sg. þone heaðo-rinc (Hrêðel's son, Hæðcyn), 2467; dat. pl. þæm heaðo-rincum, 370.

heaðo-rôf, adj., renowned in battle : nom. sg., 381; nom. pl. heaðo-rôfe, 865.

heaðo-scearp, adj., sharp in battle, bold : n. m. pl. (-scearde, MS.), 2830.

heaðo-seóc, adj., battle-sick : dat. sg. -siócum, 2755.

heaðo-steáp, adj., high in battle, excelling in battle : nom. sg. in weak form, heaðo-steápa, 1246; acc. sg. heaðo-steápne, 2154, both times of the helmet.

heaðo-swât, st. m., blood of battle : dat. sg. heaðo-swâte, 1607; as instr., 1461; gen. pl. hâtost heaðo-swâta, 1669.

heaðo-sweng, st. m., battle-stroke (blow of the sword): dat. sg. äfter heaðu-swenge, 2582.

heaðo-torht, adj., loud, clear in battle : nom. sg. stefn ... heaðo-torht, the voice clear in battle , 2554.

heaðo-wæd, st. f., battle-dress, coat of mail, armor : instr. pl. heaðo-wædum, 39.

heaðo-weorc, st. n., battle-work, battle : acc. sg., 2893.

heaðo-wylm, st. m., hostile (flame-) wave : acc. pl. hâte heaðo-wylmas, 2820; gen. pl. heaðo-wylma, 82.

heaf, st. n., sea : acc. pl. ofer heafo, 2478. See Note.

heafola. See hafela.

heal, st. f., hall, main apartment, large building (consisting of an assembly-hall and a banqueting-hall): nom. sg. heal, 1152, 1215; heall, 487; acc. sg. healle, 1088; dat. sg. healle, 89, 615, 643, 664, 926, 1010, 1927, etc.; gen. sg. [healle], 389.-- Comp.: gif-, meodo-heal.

heal-ärn, st. n., hall-building, hall-house : gen. sg. heal-ärna, 78.

heal-gamen, st. n., social enjoyment in the hall, hall-joy : nom. sg., 1067.

heal-reced, st. n., hall-building : acc. sg., 68.

heal-sittend, pres. part., sitting in the hall (at the banquet): dat. pl. heal-sittendum, 2869; gen. pl. heal-sittendra, 2016.

heal-þegn, st. m., hall-thane , i.e. a warrior who holds the hall: gen. sg. heal-þegnes, of Grendel, 142; acc. pl. heal-þegnas, of Beówulfs band, 720.

heal-wudu, hall-wood , i.e. hall built of wood: nom. sg., 1318.

healdan, st. v. w. acc.: 1) to hold, to hold fast; to support : pret. pl. hû þâ stânbogan ... êce eorðreced innan heóldon (MS. healde), how the arches of rock within held the everlasting earth-house , 2720. Pret. sg., with a person as object: heóld hine to fäste, held him too fast , 789; w. the dat. he him freóndlârum heóld, supported him with friendly advice , 2378.--2) to hold, to watch, to preserve, to keep ; reflexive, to maintain one's self, to keep one's self : pres. sg. II. eal þu hit geþyldum healdest, mägen mid môdes snyttrum, all that preservest thou continuously, strength and wisdom of mind , 1706; III. healdeð hige-mêðum heáfod-wearde, holds for the dead the head-watch , 2910; imp. sg. II. heald forð tela niwe sibbe, keep well, from now on, the new relationship , 949; heald (heold, MS.) þu nu hruse ... eorla æhte, preserve thou now, Earth, the noble men's possessions , 2248; inf. se þe holmclifu healdan scolde, watch the sea-cliffs , 230; so, 705; nacan ... ârum healdan, to keep well your vessel , 296; wearde healdan, 319; forlêton eorla gestreón eorðan healdan, 3168; pres. part. dream healdende, holding rejoicing (i.e. thou who art rejoicing), 1228; pret. sg. heóld hine syððan fyr and fästor, kept himself afterwards afar and more secure , 142; ægwearde heóld, I have (hitherto) kept watch on the sea , 241; so, 305; hióld heáh-lufan wið häleða brego, preserved high love , 1955; ginfästan gife ... heóld, 2184; gold-mâðmas heóld, took care of the treasures of gold , 2415; heóld mîn tela, protected well mine own , 2738; þonne ... sceft ... nytte heóld, had employment, was employed , 3119; heóld mec, protected , i.e. brought me up, 2431; pret. pl. heaðo-reáf heóldon, watched over the armor , 401; sg. for pl. heáfodbeorge ... walan ûtan heóld, outwards, bosses kept guard over the head , 1032.--Related to the preceding meaning are the two following: 3) to rule and protect the fatherland : inf. gif þu healdan wylt maga rice, 1853; pret. heóld, 57, 2738.--4) to hold, to have, to possess, to inhabit : inf. lêt þone brego-stôl Beówulf healdan, 2390; gerund. tô healdanne hleóburh wera, 1732; pret. sg. heóld, 103, 161,

466, 1749, 2752; lyftwynne heóld nihtes hwîlum, at night-time had the enjoyment of the air , 3044; pret. pl. Geáta leóde hreâwic heóldon, the Geátas held the place of corpses (lay dead upon it), 1215; pret. sg. þær heó ær mæste heóld worolde wynne, in which she formerly possessed the highest earthly joy , 1080.--5) to win, to receive : pret. pl. I. heoldon heáh gesceap, we received a heavy fate, heavy fate befell us , 3085.

be-healdan, w. acc.: 1) to take care of, to attend to : pret. sg. þegn nytte beheóld, a thane discharged the office , 494; so, 668.--2) to hold : pret. sg. se þe flôda begong ... beheóld, 1499.--3) to look at, to behold : þryðswyð beheóld mæg Higelâces hû ..., great woe saw H.'s kinsman, how ... , 737.

for-healdan, w. acc., (to hold badly), to fall away from, to rebel : pret. part. häfdon hy forhealden helm Scylfinga, had rebelled against the defender of the Scylfings , 2382.

ge-healdan: 1) to hold, to receive, to hold fast : pres. sg. III. se þe waldendes hyldo gehealdeð, who receives the Lord's grace , 2294; pres. subj. fäder alwalda ... eówic gehealde sîða gesunde, keep you sound on your journey , 317; inf. ne meahte he ... on þam frum-gâre feorh gehealdan, could not hold back the life in his lord , 2857.--2) to take care, to preserve, to watch over; to stop : imp. sg. hafa nu and geheald hûsa sêlest, 659; inf. gehealdan hêt hilde-geatwe, 675; pret. sg. he frätwe geheóld fela missera, 2621; þone þe ær geheóld wið hettendum hord and rîce, him who before preserved treasure and realm , 3004.--3) to rule : inf. folc gehealdan, 912; pret. sg. geheóld tela (brâde rîce), 2209.

healf, st. f., half, side, part : acc. sg. on þâ healfe, towards this side , 1676; dat. sg. häleðum be healfe, at the heroes' side , 2263; acc. pl. on twâ healfa, upon two sides, mutually , 1096; on bâ healfa (healfe), on both sides (to Grendel and his mother), 1306; on two sides, on both sides , 2064; gen. pl. on healfa gehwone, in half, through the middle , 801.

healf, adj., half : gen. sg. healfre, 1088.

heals, st. m., neck : acc. sg. heals, 2692; dat. sg. wið halse, 1567; be healse, 1873.--Comp.: the adjectives fämig-, wunden-heals.

heals-beáh, st. m., neck-ring, collar : acc. sg. þone heals-beáh, 2173; gen. pl. heals-beága, 1196.

heals-gebedde, w. f., beloved bedfellow, wife : nom. sg. healsgebedde (MS. healsgebedda), 63.

healsian, w. v. w. acc., to entreat earnestly, to implore : pret. sg. þâ se þeóden mec ... healsode hreóh-môd þät..., entreated me sorrowful, that ..., 2133.

heard, adj.: 1) of persons, able, efficient in war, strong, brave : nom. sg. heard, 342, 376, 404, 1575, 2540, etc.; in weak form, se hearda, 401, 1964; se hearda þegn, 2978; þes hearda heáp, 432; nom. pl. hearde hilde-frecan, 2206; gen. pl. heardra, 989. Comparative: acc. sg. heardran häle, 720. With accompanying gen.: wîges heard, strong in battle , 887; dat. sg. nîða heardum, 2171.--2) of the implements of war, good, firm, sharp, hard : nom. sg. (gûð-byrne, lîc-syrce) heard, 322, 551. In weak form: masc. here-stræl hearda, 1436; se hearda helm, 2256; neutr. here-net hearde, 1554; acc. sg. (swurd, wæpen), heard, 540, 2688, 2988; nom. pl. hearde ... homera lâfe, 2830; heard and hring-mæl Heaðobeardna gestreón, 2038; acc. pl. heard sweord, 2639. Of other things, hard, rough, harsh, hard to bear : acc. sg. hreðer-bealo hearde, 1344; nom. sg. wrôht ... heard, 2915; here-nîð hearda, 2475; acc. sg. heoro-sweng heardne, 1591; instr. sg. heardan ceápe, 2483; instr. pl. heardan, heardum clammum, 964, 1336; gen. pl. heardra hýnða, 166. Compar.: acc. sg. heardran feohtan, 576.--Comp.: fýr-, îren-, nîð-, regn-, scûr-heard.

hearde, adv., hard, very , 1439.

heard-ecg, adj., sharp-edged, hard, good in battle : nom. sg., 1289.

heard-fyrde, adj., hard to take away, heavy : acc. sg. hard-fyrdne, 2246.--Leo.

heard-hycgend, pres. part. of a warlike disposition, brave : nom. pl. -hicgende, 394, 800.

hearg-träf, st. n., tent of the gods, temple : dat. pl. ät härg-trafum (MS. hrærg trafum), 175.

hearm, st. m., harm, injury, insult : dat. sg. mid hearme, 1893.

hearm-sceaða, w. m., enemy causing injury or grief : nom. sg. hearm-scaða, 767.

hearpe, w. f., harp : gen. sg. hearpan swêg, 89, 3024; hearpan wynne (wyn), 2108, 2263.

heáðu, st. f., sea, waves : acc. sg. heáðu, 1863?

heáðu-lîðend, pres. part., sea-farer, sailor : nom. pl. -lîðende, 1799; dat. pl. -lîðendum (designation of the Geátas), 2956.

heáfod, st. n., head : acc. sg., 48, 1640; dat. sg. heáfde, 1591, 2291, 2974; dat. pl. heáfdum, 1243.

heáfod-beorh, st. f., head-defence, protection for the head : acc. sg. heáfod-beorge, 1031.

heáfod-mæg, st. m., head-kinsman, near blood-relative : dat. pl. heáfod-mægum (brothers), 589; gen. pl. heáfod-mâga, 2152.

heáfod-segn, st. n., head-sign, banner : acc. sg., 2153.

heáfod-weard, st. f., head-watch acc. sg. healdeð ... heáfod-wearde leófes and lâðes, for the friend and the foe (Beówulf and the drake, who lie dead near each other), 2910.

heáh, heá, adj., high, noble (in composition, also primus): nom. sg. heáh Healfdene, 57; heá (Higelâc), 1927; heáh (sele), 82; heáh hlæw, 2806, 3159; acc. sg. heáh (segn), 48, 2769; heáhne (MS. heánne) hrôf, 984; dat. sg. in (tô) sele þam heán, 714, 920; gen. sg. heán hûses, 116.-- high, heavy : acc. heáh gesceap (an unusual, heavy fate), 3085.

heá-burh, st. f., high city, first city of a country : acc. sg., 1128.

heáh-cyning, st. m., high king, mightiest of the kings : gen. sg. -cyninges (of Hrôðgâr), 1040.

heáh-gestreón, st. n., splendid treasure : gen. pl. -gestreóna, 2303.

heáh-lufe, w. f., high love : acc. sg. heáh-lufan, 1955.

heáh-sele, st. m., high hall, first hall in the land, hall of the ruler : dat. sg. heáh-sele, 648.

heáh-setl, st. n., high seat, throne : acc. sg., 1088.

heáh-stede, st. m., high place, ruler's place : dat. sg. on heáh-stede, 285.

heán, adj., depressed, low, despised, miserable : nom. sg., 1275, 2100, 2184, 2409.

heáp, st. m., heap, crowd, troop : nom. sg. þegna heáp, 400; þes hearda heáp, this brave band , 432; acc. sg. here-sceafta heáp, the crowd of spears , 335; mago-rinca heáp, 731; dat. sg. on heápe, in a compact body , as many as there were of them, 2597.--Comp. wîg-heáp.

heáwan, st. v., to hew, to cleave : inf., 801.

ge-heáwan, cleave : pres. subj. ge-heáwe, 683.

heoðu, st. f., the interior of a building : dat. sg. þät he on heoðe gestôd, in the interior (of the hall, Heorot), 404.

heofon, st. m., heaven : nom. sg., 3157; dat. sg. hefene, 1572; gen. sg. heofenes, 414, 576, 1802, etc.; gen. pl. heofena, 182; dat. pl. under heofenum, 52, 505.

heolfor, st. n., gore, fresh or crude blood : dat. instr. sg. hâtan heolfre, 850, 1424; heolfre, 2139; under heolfre, 1303.

heolster, st. n., haunt, hiding-place : acc. sg. on heolster, 756.

heonan, adv., hence, from here : heonan, 252; heonon, 1362.

heor, st. m., door-hinge : nom. pl. heorras, 1000.

heorde, adj. See wunden-heorde.

heorð-geneát, st. m., hearth-companion , i.e. a vassal of the king, in whose castle he receives his livelihood: nom. pl. heorð-geneátas, 261, 3181; acc. pl. heorð-geneátas, 1581, 2181; dat. pl. heorð-geneátum, 2419.

heorot, st. m., stag : nom. sg., 1370.

heorte, w. f., heart : nom. sg., 2562; dat. sg. ät heortan, 2271; gen. sg. heortan, 2464, 2508.--Comp.: the adjectives blîð-, grom-, rûm-, stearc-heort.

heoru, st. m., sword : nom. sg. heoru bunden (cf. under bîndan), 1286. In some of the following compounds heoru- seems to be confounded with here-(see here).

heoru-blâc, adj., pale through the sword, fatally wounded : nom. sg. [heoru-]blâc, 2489.

heoru-dreór, st. m., sword-blood : instr. sg. heoru-dreóre, 487; heoro-dreóre, 850.

heoro-dreórig, adj., bloody through the sword : nom. sg., 936; acc. sg. heoro-dreórigne, 1781, 2721.

heoro-drync, st. m., sword-drink , i.e. blood shed by the sword: instr. pl. hiorodryncum sant, died through sword-drink , i.e. struck by the sword, 2359.

heoro-gîfre, adj., eager for hostile inroads : nom. sg., 1499.

heoro-grim, adj., sword-grim, fierce in battle : nom. sg. m., 1565; fem. -grimme, 1848.

heoro-hôcihte, adj., provided with barbs, sharp like swords : instr. pl. mid eofer-spreótum heoro-hôcyhtum, 1439.

heoro-serce, w. f., shirt of mail : acc. sg. hioro-sercean, 2540.

heoro-sweng, st. m., sword-stroke : acc. sg. 1591.

heoro-weallende, pres. part., rolling around fighting , of the drake, 2782. See weallian.

heoro-wearh, st. m. he who is sword-cursed, who is destined to die by the sword : nom. sg., 1268.

heófan, w. v., to lament, to moan : part. nom. pl. hiófende, 3143.

â-heóran, to free (?): w. acc. pret. sg. brýd âheórde, 2931.

heóre, adj., pleasant, not haunted, secure : nom. sg. fem, nis þät heóru stôw, that is no secure place , 1373.--Comp. un-heóre (-hýre).

hider, adv., hither , 240, 370, 394, 3093, etc.

ofer-higian, w. v. (according to the connection, probably), to exceed , 2767. (O.H.G. ubar-hugjan, to be arrogant .)

hild, st. f., battle, combat : nom. sg., 452, 902, 1482, 2077; hild heoru-grimme, 1848; acc. sg. hilde, 648; instr. sg. hilde, through combat , 2917; dat. sg. ät hilde, 1461.

hilde-bil, st. n., battle-sword : nom. sg., 1667; instr. dat. sg. hilde-bille, 557, 1521.

hilde-bord, st. n., battle-shield : acc. pl. hilde-bord, 397; instr. pl. -bordum, 3140.

hilde-cyst, st. f., excellence in battle, bravery in battle : instr. pl. -cystum, 2599.

hilde-deór, adj., bold in battle, brave in battle : nom. sg., 312, 835, 1647, 1817; hilde-diór, 3112; nom. pl. hilde-deóre, 3171.

hilde-freca, w. m., hero in battle : nom. pl. hilde-frecan, 2206; dat. sg. hild-frecan, 2367.

hilde-geatwe, st. f. pl., equipment for battle, adornment for combat : acc. hilde-geatwe, 675; gen. -geatwa, 2363.

hilde-gicel, st. m., battle-icicle , i.e. the blood which hangs upon the sword-blades like icicles: instr. pl. hilde-gicelum, 1607.

hilde-grâp, st. f., battle-gripe : nom. sg., 1447, 2508.

hilde-hlemma, w. m., one raging in battle, warrior, fighter : nom. sg., 2352, 2545; dat. pl. eft þät ge-eode ... hilde-hlämmum, it happened to the warriors (the Geátas), 2202.

hilde-leóma, w. m., battle-light, gleam of battle , hence: 1) the fire-spewing of the drake in the fight: nom. pl. -leóman, 2584.--2) the gleaming sword : acc. sg. -leóman, 1144.

hilde-mecg, st. m., man of battle, warrior : nom. pl. hilde-mecgas, 800.

hilde-mêce, st. m., battle-sword : nom. pl. -mêceas, 2203.

hilde-rand, st. m., battle-shield : acc. pl. -randas, 1243.

hllde-ræs, st. m., storm of battle : acc. sg., 300.

hilde-rinc, st. m., man of battle, warrior, hero : nom. sg., 1308, 3125, 3137; dat. sg. hilde-rince, 1496; gen. sg. hilde-rinces, 987.

hilde-säd, adj., satiated with battle, not wishing to fight any more : acc. sg. hilde-sädne, 2724.

hilde-sceorp, st. n., battle-dress, armor, coat of mail : acc. sg., 2156.

hilde-setl, st. n., battle-seat (saddle): nom. sg., 1040.

hilde-strengo, st. f., battle-strength, bravery in battle : acc., 2114.

hilde-swât, st. m., battle-sweat : nom. sg. hât hilde-swât (the hot, damp breath of the drake as he rushes on), 2559.

hilde-tux, st. m., battle-tooth : instr. pl. hilde-tuxum, 1512.

hilde-wæpen, st. m., battle-weapon : instr. pl. -wæpnum, 39.

hilde-wîsa, w. m., leader in battle, general : dat. sg. fore Healfdenes hildewîsan, Healfdene's general (Hnäf), 1065.

hild-freca. See hilde-freca

hild-fruma, st. m., battle-chief : dat. sg. -fruma, 1679, 2650; gen. sg. þäs hild-fruman, 2836.

hlld-lata, w. m., he who is late in battle, coward : nom. pl. þâ hild-latan, 2847.

hilt, st. n., sword-hilt : nom. gylden hilt, 1678; acc. sg. þät hilt, 1669; hylt, 1668. Also used in the plural; acc. þâ hilt, 1615; dat. pl, be hiltum, 1575.--Comp.: fetel-, wreoðen-hilt.

hilte-cumbor, st. n., banner with a staff : acc. sg., 1023.

hilted, pret. part., provided with a hilt or handle : acc. sg. heard swyrd hiked, sword with a (rich) hilt , 2988.

hin-fûs, adj., ready to die : nom. sg. hyge wäs him hinfûs (i.e. he felt that he should not survive), 756.

hindema, adj. superl., hindmost, last : instr. sg. hindeman sîðe, the last time, for the last time , 2050, 2518.

hirde, hyrde, st. m., (herd) keeper, guardian, possessor : nom. sg. folces hyrde, 611, 1833, 2982; rîces hyrde, 2028; fyrena hyrde, the guardian of mischief, wicked one , 751, 2220; wuldres hyrde, the king of glory, God , 932; hringa hyrde, the keeper of the rings , 2246; cumbles hyrde, the possessor of the banner, the bearer of the banner , 2506; folces hyrde, 1850; frätwa hyrde, 3134; rîces hyrde, 3081; acc. pl. hûses hyrdas, 1667.--Comp.: grund-hyrde.

hit (O.N. hita), st. f. (?), heat : nom. sg. þenden hyt sý, 2650.

hladan, st. v.: 1) to load, to lay : inf. on bæl hladan leófne mannan, lay the dear man on the funeral-pile , 2127; him on bearm hladan bunan and discas, laid cups and plates upon his bosom, loaded himself with them , 2776; pret. part. þær wäs wunden gold on wæn hladen, laid upon the wain , 3135.--2) to load, to burden : pret. part. þâ wäs ... sægeáp naca hladen herewædum, loaded with armor , 1898.--Comp. gilp-hläden.

ge-hladan, w. acc., to load, to burden : pret. sg. sæbât gehlôd (MS gehleod), 896.

hlâford, st. m., lord, ruler : nom. sg., 2376; acc. sg., 267; dat. sg. hlâforde, 2635; gen. sg. hlâfordes, 3181.--Comp. eald-hlâford.

hlâford-leás; adj., without a lord : nom. pl. hlâford-leáse, 2936.

hlâw, hlæw, st. m., grave-hill : acc. sg. hlæw, 2803, 3159, 3171; dat. sg. for hlâwe, 1121. Also, grave-chamber (the interior of the grave-hill), cave : acc. sg. hlâw [under] hrusan, 2277; hlæw under hrusan, 2412; dat. sg. on hlæwe, 2774. The drake dwells in the rocky cavern which the former owner of his treasure had chosen as his burial-place, 2242-2271.

hläst, st. n., burden, load : dat. sg. hläste, 52.

hlem, st. m., noise, din of battle, noisy attack : in the compounds, uht-, wäl-hlem.

hlemma, w. m., one raging, one who calls ; see hilde-hlemma.

â-hlehhan, st. v., to laugh aloud, to shout, to exult : pret. sg. his môd âhlôg, his mood exulted , 731.

hleahtor, st. m., laughter : nom. sg., 612; acc. sg., 3021.

hleápan, st. v., to run, to trot, to spring : inf. hleápan lêton ... fealwe mearas, 865.

â-hleapan, to spring up : pret. âhleóp, 1398.

hleoðu. See hlið.

hleonian, w. v., to incline, to hang over : inf. oð þät he ... fyrgen-beámas ofer hârne stân hleonian funde, till he found mountain-trees hanging over the gray rocks , 1416.

hleó, st. m., shady, protected place; defence, shelter ; figurative designation of the king, or of powerful nobles: wîgendra hleó, of Hrôðgâr, 429; of Sigemund, 900; of Beówulf, 1973, 2338; eorla hleó, of Hrôðgâr, 1036, 1867; of Beówulf, 792; of Hygelâc, 2191.

hleó-burh, st. f., ruler's castle or city : acc. sg., 913, 1732.

hleóðor-cwyde, st. m., speech of solemn sound, ceremonious words , 1980.

hleór, st. n., cheek, jaw : in comp. fäted-hleór (adj.).

hleór-bera, w. m., cheek-bearer , the part of the helmet that reaches down over the cheek and protects it: acc. pl. ofer hleór-beran (visor ?), 304.

hleór-bolster, st. m., cheek-bolster, pillow : nom. sg., 689.

hleótan, st. v. w. acc., to obtain by lot, to attain, to get : pret. sg. feorh-wunde hleát, 2386.

hlifian, w. v., to rise, to be prominent : inf. hlifian, 2806; pret. hlifade, 81, 1800, 1899.

hlið, st. n., cliff, precipice of a mountain : dat. sg. on hliðe, 3159; gen. sg. hliðes, 1893; pl. hliðo in composition, stân-hliðo; hleoðu in the compounds fen-, mist-, näs-, wulf-hleoðu.

hlin-bed (Frisian hlen-bed, Richthofen 206^28, for which another text has cronk-bed), st. n., [Greek: klinidion], bed for reclining, sick-bed : acc. sg. hlim-bed, 3035.

tô-hlîdan, st. v., to spring apart, to burst : pret. part. nom. pl. tô-hlidene, 1000.

hlûd, adj., loud : acc. sg. dreám ... hlûdne, 89.

hlyn, st. m., din, noise, clatter : nom. sg., 612.

hlynnan, hlynian, w. v., to sound, to resound : inf. hlynnan (of the voice), 2554; of fire, to crackle : pret. sg. hlynode, 1121.

hlynsian, w. v., to resound, to crash : pret. sg. reced hlynsode, 771.

hlytm, st. m., lot : dat. sg. näs þâ on hlytme, hwâ þät hord strude, it did not depend upon lot who should plunder the hoard, i.e. its possession was decided, 3127.

hnâh, adj.: 1) low, inferior : comp. acc. sg. hnâgran, 678; dat. sg. hnâhran rince, an inferior hero, one less brave, 953.--2) familiarly intimate : nom. sg. näs hió hnâh swâ þeáh, was nevertheless not familiarly intimate (with the Geátas, i.e. preserved her royal dignity towards them), (niggardly ?), 1930.

hnægan, w. v. w. acc., (for nægan), to speak to, to greet : pret. sg. þät he þone wîsan wordum hnægde freán Ingwina, 1319.

ge-hnægan, w. acc., to bend, to humiliate, to strike down, to fell : pret. sg. ge-hnægde helle gâst, 1275; þær hyne Hetware hilde gehnægdon, 2917.

hnitan, st. v., to dash against, to encounter, here of the collision of hostile bands: pret. pl. þonne hniton (hnitan) fêðan, 1328, 2545.

hoðma, w. m., place of concealment, cave, hence, the grave : dat. sg. in hoðman, 2459.

hof, st. n., enclosed space, court-yard, estate, manor-house : acc. sg. hof (Hrôðgâr's residence), 312; dat. sg. tô hofe sînum (Grendel's home in the sea), 1508; tô hofe (Hygelâc's residence), 1975; acc. pl. beorht hofu, 2314; dat. pl. tô hofum Geáta, 1837.

hogode. See hycgan.

hold, adj., inclined to, attached to, gracious, dear, true : nom. sg. w. dat. of the person, hold weorod freán Scyldinga, a band well disposed to the lord of the Scyldings, 290; mandrihtne hold, 1230; Hygelâce wäs ... nefa swýðe hold, to H. was his nephew (Beówulf) very much attached, 2171; acc. sg. þurh holdne hige, from a kindly feeling, with honorable mind, 267; holdne wine, 376; holdne, 1980; gen. pl. holdra, 487.

hold. See healdan.

holm, st. m., deep sea : nom. sg., 519, 1132, 2139; acc. sg., 48, 633; dat. sg. holme, 543, 1436, 1915; acc. pl. holmas, 240.--Comp. wæg-holm.

holm-clif, st. n., sea-cliff : dat. sg. on þam holm-clife, 1422; from þäm holmclife, 1636; acc. pl. holm-clifu, 230.

holm-wylm, st. m., the waves of the sea : dat. sg. holm-wylme, 2412.

holt, st. n., wood, thicket, forest. acc. sg. on holt, 2599; holt, 2847.--Comp.: äsc-, fyrgen-, gâr-, Hrefnes-holt.

holt-wudu, st. m., forest-wood : 1) of the material: nom. sg., 2341.--2) = forest : acc. sg., 1370.

hord, st. m. and n., hoard, treasure : nom. sg., 2284, 3085; beága hord, 2285; mâðma hord, 3012; acc. sg. hord, 913, 2213, 2320, 2510, 2745, 2774, 2956, 3057; sâwle hord, 2423; þät hord, 3127; dat. sg. of horde, 1109; for horde, on account of (the robbing of) the hoard, 2782; hæðnum horde, 2217; gen. sg. hordes, 888.--Comp.: beáh-, breóst-, word-, wyrm-hord.

hord-ärn, st. n., place in which a treasure is kept, treasure-room : dat. hord-ärne, 2832; gen. pl. hord-ärna, 2280.

hord-burh, st. f., city in which is the treasure (of the king's), ruler's castle : acc. sg., 467.

hord-gestreón, st. n., hoard-treasure, precious treasure : dat. pl. hord-gestreónum, 1900; gen. pl. mägen-byrðenne hord-gestreóna, the great burden of rich treasures, 3093.

hord-mâððum, st. m., treasure-jewel, precious jewel : acc. sg. (-madmum, MS.), 1199.

hord-wela, w. m., treasure-riches, abundance of treasures : acc. sg. hord-welan, 2345.

hord-weard, st. m., warder of the treasure, hoard-warden : 1) of the king: nom. sg., 1048; acc. sg., 1853.--2) of the drake: nom. sg., 2294, 2303, 2555, 2594.

hord-weorðung, st. f., ornament out of the treasure, rich ornament : acc. sg.--weorðunge, 953.

hord-wyn, st. f., treasure-joy, joy-giving treasure : acc. sg. hord-wynne, 2271.

horn, st. m., horn : 1) upon an animal: instr. pl. heorot hornum trum, 1370.--2) wind-instrument: nom. sg., 1424; acc. sg., 2944.--Comp. gûð-horn.

horn-boga, w. m., bow made of horn : dat. sg. of horn-bogan, 2438.

horn-geáp, adj., of great extent between the (stag-)horns adorning the gables(?): nom. sg. sele ... heáh and horn-geáp, 82.

horn-reced, st. n., building whose two gables are crowned by the halves of a stag's antler(?): acc. sg., 705. Cf. Heyne's Treatise on the Hall, Heorot, p. 44.

hors, st. n., horse : nom. sg., 1400.

hôciht, adj., provided with hooks, hooked : in comp. heoro-hôciht.

be-hôfian, w. v. w. gen., to need, to want : pres. sg. III. nu is se däg cumen þat ûre man-dryhten mägenes behôfað gôdra gûðrinca, now is the day come when our lord needs the might of strong warriors, 2648.

on-hôhsnian, w. v., to hinder : pret. sg. þät onhôhsnode Heminges mæg (on hohsnod, MS.), 1945.

hôlinga, adv., in vain, without reason, 1077.

be-hôn, st. v., to hang with : pret. part. helmum behongen, 3140.

hop, st. n., protected place, place of refuge, place of concealment, in the compounds fen-, môr-hop.

hôs (Goth. hansa), st. f., accompanying troop, escort : instr. sg. mägða hôse, with an accompanying train of servingwomen, 925.

hräðe, adv., hastily, quickly, immediately, 224, 741, 749, 1391, etc.; hraðe, 1438; hreðe, 992; compar. hraðor, 543.

hran-fix, st. m., whale : acc. pl. hron-fixas, 540.

hran-râd, st. f., whale-road, i.e. sea: dat. sg. ofer hron-râde, 10.

hrâ, st. n., corpse : nom. sg., 1589.

hrâ-fyl, st. m., fall of corpses, killing, slaughter : acc. sg., 277.

hrädlîce, adv., hastily, immediately, 356, 964.

hräfn, hrefn, st. m., raven : nom. sg. hrefn blaca, black raven, 1802; se wonna hrefn, the dark raven, 3025; dat. sg. hrefne, 2449.

hrägl, st. n., dress, garment, armor : nom. sg., 1196; gen. sg., hrägles, 1218; gen. pl. hrägla, 454--Comp.: beado-, fyrd-, mere-hrägl.

hreðe. See hraðe.

hreðer, st. m., breast, bosom nom. sg. hreðer inne weóll (it surged in his breast), 2114; hreðer æðme weóll, 2594; dat. sg. in hreðre, 1152; of hreðre, 2820.-- Breast as the seat of feeling, heart : dat. sg. þät wäs ... hreðre hygemêðe, that was depressing to the heart (of the slayer, Hæðcyn), 2443; on hreðre, 1879, 2329; gen. pl. þurh hreðra gehygd, 2046.-- Breast as seat of life: instr. sg. hreðre, parallel with aldre, 1447.

hreðer-bealo, st. n., evil that takes hold on the heart, evil severely felt : acc. sg., 1344.

hrefn. See hräfn.

hrêð, st. f., glory ; in composition, gûð-hrêð; renown, assurance of victory, in sige-hrêð.

hrêðe, adj., renowned in battle : nom. sg. hrêð (on account of the following ät, final e is elided, as wênic for wêne ic, 442; frôfor and fultum for frôfre and fultum, 699; firen ondrysne for firene ondr., 1933), 2576.

hrêð-sigor, st. m., glorious victory : dat. sg. hrêð-sigora, 2584.

hrêmig, adj., boasting, exulting : with instr. and gen. hûðe hrêmig, 124; since hrêmig, 1883; frätwum hrêmig, 2055; nom. pl. nealles Hetware hrêmge þorfton (sc. wesan) fêðe-wîges, 2365.

on-hrêran, w. v., to excite, to stir up : pret. part. on-hrêred, 549, 2555.

hreâ-wîc, st. n., place of corpses : acc. sg. Geáta leóde hreâ-wîc heóldon, held the place of corpses, 1215.

hreád, st. f., ornament (?), in comp. earm-hreád. See hreóðan.

hreám, st. m., noise, alarm :: nom. sg., 1303.

hreóða, w. m., cover, in the compound bord-hreóða.

hreóðan, ge-hreóðan, st. v., to cover, to clothe ; only in the pret. part. hroden, gehroden, dressed, adorned : hroden, 495, 1023; þâ wäs heal hroden feónda feorum, then was the hall covered with the corpses of the enemy, 1152; ge-hroden golde, adorned with gold, 304.--Comp.: beág-, gold-hroden.

hreóh, hreów, hreó, adj., excited, stormy, wild, angry, raging; sad, troubled : nom. sg. (Beówulf) hreóh and heoro-grim, 1565; þät þam gôdan wäs hreów on hreðre, (that came with violence upon him, pained his heart), 2329; hreó wæron ýða, the waves were angry, the sea stormy, 548; näs him hreóh sefa, his mind was not cruel, 2181; dat. sg. on hreón môde, of sad heart, 1308; on hreóum môde, angry at heart, 2582.

hreóh-môd, adj., of sad heart, 2133; angry at heart, 2297.

hreósan, st. v., to fall, to sink, to rush : pret. hreás, 2489, 2832; pret. pl. hruron, 1075; hie on weg hruron, they rushed away, 1431; hruron him teáras, tears burst from him, 1873.

be-hreósan, to fall from, to be divested of : pret. part. acc. pl. fyrn-manna fatu ... hyrstum behrorene, divested of ornaments (from which the ornaments had fallen away), 2760.

hreów, st. f., distress, sorrow : gen. pl. þät wäs Hrôðgâre hreówa tornost, that was to Hrôðgâr the bitterest of his sorrows, 2130.

hring, st. m.: 1) ring : acc. sg. þone hring, 1203; hring gyldenne, 2810; acc. pl. hringas, 1196, 1971, 3035; gen. pl. hringa, 1508, 2246.--2) shirt of mail (of interlaced rings): nom. sg. hring, 1504; byrnan hring, 2261.--Comp. bân-hring.

hringan, w. v., to give forth a sound, to ring, to rattle : pret. pl. byrnan hringdon, 327.

hring-boga, w. m., one who bends himself into a ring : gen. sg. hring-bogan (of the drake, bending himself into a circle), 2562.

hringed, pret. part., made of rings : nom. sg. hringed byrne, 1246; acc. sg. hringde byrnan, 2616.

hringed-stefna, w. m., ship whose stem is provided with iron rings (cramp-irons), especially of sea-going ships (cf. Frið-þiofs saga, I: þorsteinn âtti skip þat er Ellidi hêt, ... borðit war spengt iarni): nom. sg., 32, 1898; acc. sg. hringed-stefnan, 1132.

hring-îren, st. n., ring-iron, ring-mail : nom. sg., 322.

hring-mæl, adj., marked with rings , i.e. ornamented with rings, or marked with characters of ring-form: nom. acc. sg., of the sword, 1522, 1562(?); nom. pl. heard and hring-mæl Heaðobeardna gestreón (rich armor), 2038.

hring-naca, w. m., ship with iron rings, sea-going ship : nom. sg., 1863.

hring-net, st. n., ring-net , i.e. a shirt of interlaced rings: acc. sg., 2755; acc. pl. hring-net, 1890.

hring-sele, st. m., ring-hall , i.e. hall in which are rings, or in which rings are bestowed: acc. sg., 2841; dat. sg., 2011, 3054.

hring-weorðung, st. f., ring-ornament : acc. sg. -weorðunge, 3018.

hrînan, st. v. w. dat.: 1) to touch, lay hold of : inf. þät him heardra nân hrînan wolde îren ærgôd (that no good sword of valiant men would make an impression on him), 989; him for hrôf-sele hrînan ne mehte færgripe flôdes (the sudden grip of the flood might not touch him owing to the hall-roof), 1516; þät þam hring-sele hrînan ne môste gumena ænig (so that none might touch the ringed-hall), 3054; pret. sg. siððan he hire folmum [hr]ân (as soon as he touched it with his hands), 723; ôð þät deáðes wylm hrân ät heortan (seized his heart), 2271. Pret. subj. þeáh þe him wund hrîne (although he was wounded), 2977.--2) (O.N. hrîna, sonare, clamare), to resound, rustle : pres. part. nom. pl. hrînde bearwas (for hrînende) 1364; but see Note.

hroden. See hreóðan.

hron-fix. See hran-fix.

hrôðor, st. m., joy, beneficium : dat sg. hrefne tô hrôðre, 2449; gen. pl. hrôðra, 2172.

hrôf, st. m., roof, ceiling of a house : nom. sg., 1000; acc. sg. under Heorotes hrôf, 403; under geápne hrôf, 838; geseah steápne hrôf (here inner roof, ceiling), 927; so, ofer heáhne hrôf, 984; ymb þäs helmes hrôf, 1031; under beorges hrôf, 2756.--Comp. inwit-hrôf.

hrôf-sele, st. m., covered hall : dat. sg. hrôf-sele, 1516.

hrôr, adj., stirring, wide-awake, valorous : dat. sg. of þäm hrôran, 1630.--Comp. fela-hrôr.

hruron. See hreósan.

hruse, w. f., earth, soil : nom. sg., 2248, 2559; acc. sg. on hrusan, 773, 2832; dat. sg. under hrusan, 2412.

hrycg, st. m., back : acc. sg. ofer wäteres hrycg (over the water's back, surface), 471.

hryre, st. m., fall, destruction, ruin : acc. sg., 3181; dat. sg., 1681, 3006.--Comp.: leód-, wîg-hryre.

hrysian, w. v., to shake, be shaken, clatter : pret. pl. syrcan hrysedon (corselets rattled , of men in motion), 226.

hund, st. m., dog : instr. pl. hundum, 1369.

hund, num., hundred : þreó hund, 2279; w. gen. pl. hund missera, 1499; hund þûsenda landes and locenra beága, 2995.

hû, adv., how, quomodo , 3, 116, 279, 738, 845, 2319, 2520, 2719, etc.

huð, st. f., booty, plunder : dat. (instr.) sg. hûðe, 124.

hûru, adv., above all, certainly , 369; indeed, truly , 182, 670, 1072, 1466, 1945, 2837; yet, nevertheless , 863; now , 3121.

hûs, st. n., house : gen. sg. hûses, 116; gen. pl. hûsa sêlest (Heorot), 146, 285, 659, 936.

hwan, adv., whither : tô hwan syððan wearð hondræs häleða (what issue the hand-to-hand fight of the heroes had), 2072.

hwanan, hwanon, adv., whence : hwanan, 257, 2404; hwanon, 333.

hwâ, interrog. and indef. pron., who : nom. sg. m. hwâ, 52, 2253, 3127; neut. hwät, 173; ânes hwät (a part only), 3011; hwät þâ men wæron (who the men were), 233, etc.; hwät syndon ge searo-häbbendra (what armed men are ye?), 237; acc. sg. m. wið manna hwone (from (?) any man), 155; neut. þurh hwät, 3069; hwät wit geó spræcon, 1477; hwät ... hýnðo (gen.), fær-nîða (what shame and sudden woes), 474; so, hwät þu worn fela (how very much thou), 530; swylces hwät, 881; hwät ... ârna, 1187; dat. m. hwâm, 1697.--Comp. æg-hwâ.

hwät, interj., what! lo! indeed! 1, 943, 2249.

ge-hwâ, w. part, gen., each, each one : acc. sg. m. wið feónda gehwone, 294; nîða gehwane, 2398; mêca gehwane, 2686; gum-cynnes gehwone, 2766; fem, on healfa gehwone, 801; dat. sg. m. dôgora gehwâm, 88; ät nîða gehwâm, 883; þegna gehwâm, 2034; eorla gehwæm, 1421; fem. in mægða ge-hwære, 25; nihta gehwæm, 1366; gen. sing. m. manna gehwäs, 2528; fem. dæda gehwäs, 2839.

hwâr. See hwær.

hwäder. See hwider.

hwäðer, pron., which of two : nom. sg. hwäðer ... uncer twega, 2531; swâ hwäðer, utercunque : acc. sg. on swâ hwäðere hond swâ him gemet þince, 687.--Comp. æg-hwäðer.

ge-hwäðer, each of two, either-other : nom. sg. m. wäs gehwäðer ôðrum lifigende lâð, 815; wäs ... gehwäðer ôðrum hrôðra gemyndig, 2172; ne gehwäðer incer (nor either of you two), 584; nom. sg. neut. gehwäðer þâra (either of them , i.e. ready for war or peace), 1249; dat. sg. hiora gehwäðrum, 2995; gen. sg. bega gehwäðres, 1044.

hwäðer, hwäðere, hwäðre, 1) adv., yet, nevertheless : hwäðre, 555, 891, 1271, 2099, 2299, 2378, etc.; hwäðre swâ þeáh, however, notwithstanding , 2443; hwäðere, 574, 578, 971, 1719--2) conj., = utrum, whether : hwäðre, 1315; hwäðer, 1357, 2786.

hwät, adj., sharp, bold, valiant : nom. sg. se secg hwata, 3029; dat. sg. hwatum, 2162; nom. pl. hwate, 1602, 2053; acc. pl. hwate, 2643, 3006.--Comp.: fyrd-, gold-hwät.

hwät. See hwâ.

hwær, adv., where : elles hwær, elsewhere , 138; hwær, somewhere , 2030. In elliptical question: wundur hwâr þonne..., is it a wonder when...? 3063.--Comp. ô-hwær.

ge-hwær, everywhere : þeáh þu heaðo-ræsa gehwær dohte (everywhere good in battle), 526.

hwele. See hwyle.

hwergen, adv., anywhere : elles hwergen, elsewhere , 2591.

hwettan, w. v., to encourage, urge : pres. subj. swâ þin sefa hwette (as thy mind urges, as thou likest), 490; pret. pl. hwetton higerôfne (they whetted the brave one), 204.

hwêne, adv., a little, paululum , 2700.

hwealf, st. f., vault : acc. sg. under heofones hwealf, 576, 2016.

hweorfan, st. v., to stride deliberately, turn, depart, move, die : pres. pl. þâra þe cwice hwyrfað, 98; inf. hwîlum he on lufan læteð hworfan monnes môd-geþonc (sometimes on love (?) possessions (?) permits the thoughts of man to turn), 1729; londrihtes môt ... monna æghwylc îdel hweorfan (of rights of land each one of men must be deprived), 2889; pret. sg. fader ellor hwearf ... of earde (died), 55; hwearf þâ hrädlîce þær Hrôðgâr sät, 356; hwearf þâ bî bence (turned then to the bench), 1189; so, hwearf þâ be wealle, 1574; hwearf geond þät reced, 1982; hlæw oft ymbe hwearf (went oft round the cave), 2297; nalles äfter lyfte lâcende hwearf (not at all through the air did he go springing), 2833; subj. pret. sg, ær he on weg hwurfe ... of geardum (died), 264.

and-hweorfan, to move against : pret. sg. ôð þät ... norðan wind heaðo-grim and-hwearf (till the fierce north wind blew in our faces), 548.

ät-hweorfan, to go to : pret. sg. hwîlum he on beorh ät-hwearf (at times returned to the mountain), 2300.

ge-hweorfan, to go, come : pret. sg. gehwearf þâ in Francna fäðm feorh cyninges, 1211; hit on äht gehwearf ... Denigea freán, 1680; so, 1685, 2209.

geond-hweorfan, to go through from end to end : pres. sg. flet eall geond-hwearf, 2018.

hwider, adv., whither : hwyder, 163; hwäder (hwäðer, MS.), 1332.

hwîl, st. f., time, space of time : nom. sg. wäs seó hwîl micel (it was a long time), 146; þâ wäs hwîl däges (the space of a day), 1496; acc. sg. hwîle, for a time , 2138; a while , 105, 152; lange (longe) hwîle , a long while , 16, 2781; âne hwîle, a while , 1763; lytle hwîle, brief space , 2031, 2098; ænige hwîle , any while , 2549; lässan hwîle, a lesser while , 2572; dat. sg. ær däges hwîle, before daybreak , 2321; dat. pl. nihtes hwîlum, sometimes at night , 3045. Adv., sometimes, often : hwîlum, 175, 496, 917, 1729, 1829, 2017, 2112, etc.; hwîlum ... hwîlum, 2108-9-10.--Comp.: däg-, gescäp-, orleg-, sige-hwîl.

hwît, adj., brilliant, flashing : nom. sg. se hwîta helm, 1449.

hworfan. See hweorfan.

hwôpan, st. v., to cry, cry out mourn : pret. sg. hweóp, 2269.

hwyder. See hwider.

hwylc, pron., which, what, any : 1) adj.: nom. sg. m. sceaða ic nât hwylc, 274; fem, hwylc orleghwîl, 2003; nom. pl. hwylce Sægeáta sîðas wæron, 1987.--2) subst., w. gen. pl. nom. m.: Frisna hwylc, 1105; fem, efne swâ hwylc mägða swâ þone magan cende (whatever woman brought forth this son), 944; neut. þonne his bearna hwylc (than any one of his sons), 2434; dat. sg. efne swâ hwylcum manna swâ him gemet þûhte, 3058.--Comp.: æg-, nât-, wel-hwylc.

ge-hwylc, ge-hwilc, ge-hwelc, w. gen. pl., each : nom. sg. m. gehwylc, 986, 1167, 1674; acc. sg. m. gehwylcne, 937, 2251, 2517; gehwelcne, 148; fem, gehwylce, 1706; neut. gehwylc, 2609; instr. sg. dôgra gehwylce, 1091; so, 2058,

2451; dat. sg. m. gehwylcum, 412, 769, 785, etc.; fem, ecga gehwylcre, 806; neut. cynna gehwylcum, 98; gen. sg. m. and neut. gehwylces, 733, 1397, 2095.

hwyrft, st. m., circling movement, turn : dat. pl. adv. hwyrftum scrîðað (wander to and fro), 163.--Comp. ed-hwyrft.

hycgan, w. v., to think, resolve upon : pret. sg. ic þät hogode þät ... (my intention was that ...), 633.--Comp. w. pres. part.: bealo-, heard-, swîð-, þanc-, wîs-hycgend.

for-hycgan, to despise, scorn, reject with contempt : pres. sg. I. ic þät þonne for-hicge þät ..., reject with scorn the proposition that ... , 435.

ge-hycgan, to think, determine upon : pret. sg. þâ þu ... feorr gehogodest säcce sêcean, 1989.

ofer-hycgan, to scorn : pret. sg. ofer-hogode þâ hringa fengel þät he þone wîdflogan weorode gesôhte (scorned to seek the wide-flier with a host), 2346.

hydig (for hygdig), adj., thinking, of a certain mind : comp. ân-, bealo-, grom-, nîð-, þrîst-hydig.

ge-hygd, st. n., thought, sentiment : acc. sg. þurh hreðra gehygd, 2046.-- Comp.: breóst-, môd-gehygd, won-hyd.

hyge, hige, st. m., mind, heart, thought : nom. sg. hyge, 756; hige, 594; acc. sg. þurh holdne hige, 267; gen. sg. higes, 2046; dat. pl. higum, 3149.

hyge-bend, st. m. f., mind-fetter, heart-band : instr. pl. hyge-bendum fäst, fast in his mind's fetters, secretly , 1879.

hyge-geômor, adj., sad in mind : nom. sg. hyge-giômor, 2409.

hyge-mêðe, adj.: 1) sorrowful, soul-crushing : nom. sg., 2443.--2) life-weary, dead : dat. pl. hyge-mêðum (-mæðum, MS.), 2910.

hyge-rôf, adj., brave, valiant, vigorous-minded : nom. sg. [hygerôf], 403; acc. sg. hige-rôfne, 204.

hyge-sorh, st. f., heart-sorrow : gen. pl. -sorga, 2329.

hyge-þyhtig, adj., doughty, courageous : acc. sg. hige-þihtigne (of Beówulf), 747. See þyhtig.

hyge-þrym, st. m., animi majestas, high-mindedness : dat. pl. for hige-þrymmum, 339.

hyht, st. m., thought, pleasant thought, hope (Dietrich): nom. sg., 179.

ge-hyld (see healdan), st. n., support, protection : nom. sg., 3057.--Leo.

hyldan, w. v., to incline one's self, lie down to sleep : pret. sg. hylde hine, inclined himself, lay down , 689.

hyldo, st. f., inclination, friendliness, grace : acc. sg. hyldo, 2068, 2294; gen. sg. hyldo, 671, 2999.

â-hyrdan, w. v., harden : pret. part. â-hyrded, 1461.

hyrde. See hirde.

hyrst, st. f., accoutrements, ornament, armor : acc. sg. hyrste (Ongenþeów's equipments and arms), 2989; acc. pl. hyrsta, 3166; instr. pl. hyrstum, 2763.

hyrstan, w. v., to deck, adorn : pret. part. hyrsted sweord, 673; helm [hyr]sted gólde, 2256.

hyrtan, w. v., to take heart, be emboldened : pret. sg. hyrte hyne hord-weard (the drake took heart ; see 2566, 2568, 2570), 2594.

hyse, st. m., youth, young man : nom. sg. as voc., 1218.

hyt. See hit.

hýdan, w. v., to hide, conceal, protect, preserve : pres. subj. hýde [hine, himself] se þe wylle, 2767; inf. w. acc. nô þu mînne þearft hafalan hýdan,

446; ær he in wille hafelan [hýdan] (ere in it he [the stag] will hide his head), 1373.

ge-hýdan, w. acc., to conceal, preserve : pret. sg. gehýdde, 2236, 3060.

hýð, st. f., haven : dat. sg. ät hýðe, 32.

hýð-weard, st. m., haven-warden : nom. sg., 1915.

hýnan (see heán), w. v. w. acc., to crush, afflict, injure : pret. sg. hýnde, 2320.

hýnðu, st. f., oppression, affliction, injury : acc. sg. hýnðu, 277; gen. sg. hwät ... hýnðo, 475; fela ... hýnðo, 594; gen. pl. heardra hýnða, 166.

hýran, w. v.: 1) to hear, perceive, learn : a) w. inf. or acc. with inf.: I. pret. sg. hýrde ic, 38, 582, 1347, 1843, 2024; III. sg. þät he fram Sigemunde secgan hýrde, 876; I. pl. swâ we sôðlîce secgan hýrdon, 273. b) w. acc.: nænigne ic ... sêlran hýrde hordmâððum (I heard of no better hoard-jewel), 1198. c) w. dependent clause: I. sg. pret. hýrde ic þät ..., 62, 2164, 2173.--2) w. dat. of person, to obey : inf. ôð þät him æghwylc þâra ymbsittendra hýran scolde, 10; hýran heaðo-siócum, 2755; Pret. pl. þät him winemâgas georne hýrdon, 66.

ge-hýran, to hear, learn : a) w. acc.: II. pers. sg. pres. mînne gehýrað ânfealdne geþôht, 255; III. sg. pret. gehýrde on Beówulfe fästrædne geþôht, 610. b) w. acc. and inf.: III. pl. pret. gehýrdon, 786. c) w. depend. clause: I. pres. sg. ic þät gehýre þät ..., 290.

I

ic, pers. pron. I : acc. mec, dat. me, gen. mîn; dual nom. wit, acc. uncit, unc, dat. unc, gen. uncer; pl. nom. we, acc. ûsic, ûs, dat. ûs, gen. ûser. ic omitted before the verb, 470.

icge, gold (perhaps related to Sanskrit îç, = dominare, imperare, O.H.G. êht, wealth , opes), treasure?, sword (edge)?, 1108.--Körner.

ides, st. f., woman, lady, queen : nom. sg., 621, 1076, 1118, 1169; dat. sg. idese, 1650, 1942. Also of Grendel's mother: nom. sg., 1260; gen. sg. idese, 1352.

in. See inn.

in: I. prep. w. dat. and acc.: 1) w. dat. (local, indicating rest), in : in geardum, 13, 2460; in þäm gûðsele, 443; in beórsele, 2636; so, 89, 482, 589, 696, 729, 2140, 2233, etc.; in mægða gehwære, 25; in þýstrum, 87; in Caines cynne, 107; in hyra gryregeatwum (in their accoutrements of terror, war-weeds), 324; so, 395; in campe (in battle), 2506; hiora in ânum (in one of them), 2600. Prep. postpositive: Scedelandum in, 19. Also, on, upon , like on: in ealo-bence, 1030; in gumstôle, 1953; in þam wongstede (on the grassy plain, the battle-field), 2787; in bælstede, 3098. Temporal: in geâr-dagum, 1.--2) w. acc. (local, indicating motion), in, into : in woruld, 60; in fýres fäðm, 185; so, 1211; in Hrefnesholt, 2936. Temporal, in, at, about, toward : in þâ tîde (in watide, MS.), 2228.

II. adv., in (here or there), 386, 1038, 1372, 1503, 1645, 2153, 2191, 2228; inn, 3091.

incge, adj. (perhaps related to icge), instr. sg. incge lâfe (with the costly sword ? or with mighty sword ?), 2578.--[Edge : incge lâfe, edge of the sword .--K. Körner?]

in-frôd, adj., very aged : nom. sg., 2450; dat. sg. in-frôdum, 1875.

in-gang, st. m., entrance, access to : acc. sg., 1550.

in-genga, w. m., in-goer, visitor : nom. sg., of Grendel, 1777.

in-gesteald, st. m., house-property, possessions in the house : acc. sg., 1156.

inn, st. n., apartment, house : nom. sg. in, 1301.

innan, adv., within, inside , 775, 1018, 2413, 2720; on innan (in the interior), within , 1741, 2716; þær on innan (in there), 71; burgum on innan (within his city), 1969. Also, therein : þær on innan, 2090, 2215, 2245.

innan-weard, adv., inwards, inside, within , 992, 1977; inne-weard, 999.

inne, adv.: 1) inside, within , 643, 1282, 1571, 2114, 3060; word inne âbeád (called, sent word, in , i.e. standing in the hall door), 390; in it (i.e. the battle), 1142; þær inne (therein), 118, 1618, 2116, 2227, 3088.--2) = insuper, still further, besides , 1867.

inwit, st. n., evil, mischief, spite, cunning hostility , as in

inwit-feng, st. m., malicious grasp, grasp of a cunning foe : nom. sg., 1448.

inwit-gäst, st. m., evil guest, hostile stranger : nom. sg., 2671.

inwit-hrôf, st. m., hostile roof, hiding-place of a cunning foe : acc. sg. under inwit-hrôf, 3124.

inwit-net, st. n., mischief-net, cunning snare : acc. sg., 2168.

inwit-nîð, st. n., cunning hostility, hostile contest : nom. pl. inwit-nîðas (hostility through secret attack), 1859; gen. pl. inwit-nîða, 1948.

inwit-scear, st. m., massacre through cunning, murderous attack : acc. sg. eatolne inwit-scear, 2479.

inwit-searo, st. n., cunning, artful intrigue : acc. sg. þurh inwit-searo, 1102. See searo.

inwit-sorh, st. f., grief, remorse, mourning springing from hostile cunning : nom. sg., 1737; acc. sg. inwid-sorge, 832.

inwit-þanc, adj., ill-disposed, malicious : dat. sg. he onfêng hraðe inwit-þancum (he quickly grasped the cunning-in-mind [Grendel]), 749.

irnan (for rinnan), st. v., to run : so be-irnan, to run up to , occur : pret. sg him on môd be-arn (came into his mind), 67.

on-irnan, to open : pret. sg. duru sôna onarn, 722.

irre-môd, adj. See yrre-môd.

Î

îdel, adj., empty, bare; deprived of : nom. sg., 145, 413; w. gen. lond-rihtes þære mægburge îdel (deprived of his land-possessions among the people [of the Geátas]), 2889.

îdel-hende, adj., empty-handed , 2082.

îren, st. n., iron, sword : nom. sg. dryhtlîc îren (the doughty, lordly sword), 893; îren ær-gôd, 990; acc. sg. leóflîc îren, 1810; gen. pl. îrena cyst (choicest of swords), 674; îrenna cyst, 803; îrenna ecge (edges of swords), 2684.

îren, adj., of iron : nom. sg. ecg wäs îren, 1460.

îren-bend, st. f., iron band, bond, rivet : instr. pl. îren-bendum fast (bold), 775, 999.

îren-byrne, w. f., iron corselet : acc. sg. îren-byrnan, 2987. See îsern-byrne.

îren-heard, adj., hard as iron : nom. sg., 1113.

îrenne, adj., of iron : in comp. eall-îrenne.

îren-þreát, st. m., iron troop, armored band : nom. sg., 330.

îs, st. n., ice : dat. sg. îse, 1609.

îsern-byrne, w. f., iron corselet : acc. sg. îsern-byrnan, 672. See îren-byrne.

îsern-scûr, st. f., iron shower, shower of arrows : gen. sg. þone þe oft gebâd îsern-scûre, 3117.

îs-gebind, st. n., fetters of ice : instr. sg. îs-gebinde, 1134.

îsig, adj., shining, brilliant (like brass): nom. sg. îsig (said of a vessel covered with plates(?) of metal), 33.--Leo.

IO IU

iú. See geó.
iú-man. See geó-man.
ió-meówle. See geó-meówle.

L

laðu, st. f., invitation .--Comp.: freónd-, neód-laðu.

ge-lafian, w. v. w. acc. pers. and instr. of the thing, to refresh, lave : pret. sg. wine-dryhten his wätere gelafede, 2723.

lagu, st. m., lake, sea : nom. sg., 1631.

lagu-cräftig, adj., acquainted with the sea : nom. sg. lagu-cräftig mon (pilot), 209.

lagu-stræt, st. f., path over the sea : acc. sg. ofer lagu-stræte, 239.

lagu-streám, st. m., sea-current, flood : acc. pl. ofer lagu-streámas, 297.

land, st. n., land : nom. sg. lond, 2198; acc. sg. land, 221, 2063; lond, 2472, 2493; land Dena, 242, 253; lond Brondinga, 521; Finna land, 580; dat. sg. on lande (in the land), 2311, 2837; at near, land, shore , 1914; tô lande (to the land, ashore), 1624; gen. sg. landes, 2996; gen. pl. ofer landa fela (over much country, space; afar), 311.--Comp.: el-, eá-land.

land-bûend, part, pres., terricola, inhabitant of the land : nom. pl. lond-bûend, 1346; dat. pl. land-bûendum, 95.

land-fruma, w. m., ruler, prince of the country : nom. sg., 31.

land-gemyrcu, st. n. pl., frontier, land-mark : acc. pl., 209.

land-geweorc, st. n., land-work, fortified place : acc. sg. leóda land-geweorc, 939. See weorc, geweorc.

land-riht, st. n., prerogatives based upon land-possessions, right to possess land , hence real estate itself: gen. sg. lond-rihtes îdel, 2887.

land-waru, st. f., inhabitants, population : acc. pl. land-wara, 2322.

land-weard, st. m., guard, guardian of the frontier : nom. sg., 1891.

lang, long, adj., long : 1) temporal: nom. sg. tô lang, 2094; näs þâ long (lang) tô þon (not long after), 2592, 2846; acc. sg. lange hwîle (for a long time), 16, 2160, 2781; longe (lange) þrage, 54, 114, 1258; lange tîd, 1916. Compar. nom. sg. lengra fyrst, 134.--2) local, nom. sg. se wäs fîftiges fôtgemearces lang, 3044.-- Comp.: and-, morgen-, niht-, up-lang.

lange, longe, adv., long : lange, 31, 1995, 2131, 2345, 2424; longe, 1062, 2752, 3109; tô lange (too long, excessively long), 906, 1337, 1749. Compar. leng, 451, 1855, 2802, 3065; nô þý leng (none the longer), 975. Superl. lengest (longest), 2009, 2239.

ge-lang, adj., extending, reaching to something or somebody, hence ready, prepared : nû is ræd gelang eft ät þe ânum (now is help [counsel] at hand in thee alone), 1377; gen is eall ät þe lissa gelong (all of favor is still on thee dependent, is thine), 2151. See ge-lenge.

lang-ge-streón, st. n., long-lasting treasure : gen. pl. long-gestreóna, 2241.-- Leo.

langian, w. v., reflex, w. dat, to long, yearn : pres. sg. III. him ...äfter deórum men dyrne langað beorn (the hero longeth secretly after the dear man), 1880.

lang-sum, adj., long-lasting, continuing : nom. sg. longsum, 134, 192, 1723; acc. sg. long-sumne, 1537.

lang-twidig, adj., long-granted, assured : nom. sg., 1709.

lata, w. m., a lazy, cowardly one ; in comp. hild-lata.

lâ, interj., yes! indeed! 1701, 2865.

lâc, st. n.: 1) measured movement, play : in comp. beadu-, heaðo-lâc.--2) gift, offering : acc. pl. lâc, 1864; lâðlîcu lâc (loathly offering, prey), 1585; dat. pl. lâcum, 43, 1869.--Comp. sæ-lâc.

ge-lâc, st. n., sport, play : acc. pl. sweorda gelâc (battle), 1041; dat. pl. ät ecga gelâcum, 1169.

lâcan, st. v., to move in measured time, dancing, playing, fighting, flying , etc.: inf. dareðum lâcan (fight), 2849; part. pres. äfter lyfte lâcende (flying through the air), 2833.

for-lâcan, to deceive, betray : part. pret. he wearð on feónda geweald forð forlâcen (deceitfully betrayed into the enemy's hands), 904.

lâd, st. f., street, way, journey : dat. sg. on lâde, 1988; gen. sg. lâde, 569.--Comp.: brim-, sæ-lâd.

ge-lâd, st. n., way, path, road : acc. sg. uncûð gelâd, 1411.

lâð, adj., loathly, evil, hateful, hostile : nom. sg. lâð, 816; lâð lyft-floga, 2316; lâð (enemy), 440; ne leóf ne lâð, 511; neut. lâð, 134, 192; in weak form, se lâða (of the dragon), 2306; acc. sg. lâðne (wyrm), 3041; dat. sg. lâðum, 440, 1258; gen. sg. lâðes (of the enemy), 842; fela lâðes (much evil), 930; so, 1062; lâðan lîges, 83; lâðan cynnes, 2009, 2355; þäs lâðan (of the enemy), 132; acc. pl. neut. lâð gewidru (hateful storms), 1376; dat. instr. pl. wið lâðum, 550; lâðum scuccum and scinnum, 939; lâðum dædum (with evil deeds), 2468; lâðan fingrum, 1506; gen. pl. lâðra manna, spella, 2673, 3030; lâðra (the enemy), 242. Compar. nom. sg. lâðra ... beorn, 2433.

lâð-bite, st. m., hostile bite : dat. sg. lâð-bite lîces (the body's hostile bite = the wound), 1123.

lâð-geteóna, w. m., evil-doer, injurer : nom. sg., 975; nom. pl. lâð-geteónan, 559.

lâð-lîc, adj., loathly, hostile : acc. pl. lâð-lîcu, 1585.

lâf, st. f.: 1) what is left, relic; inheritance, heritage, legacy : nom. sg. Hrêðlan lâf (Beówulf's corselet), 454; nom. pl. fêla lâfe (the leavings of files = swords, Grein), 1033; so, homera lâfe, 2830; on him gladiað gomelra lâfe, heard and hringmæl Heaðobeardna gestreón (on him gleams the forefather's bequest, hard and ring-decked, the Heaðobeardas' treasure , i.e. the equipments taken from the slain king of the Heaðobeardas), 2037; acc. sg. sweorda lâfe (leavings of the sword , i.e. those spared by the sword), 2937.--2) the sword as a specially precious heir-loom : nom. sg., 2629; acc. sg. lâfe, 796, 1489, 1689, 2192, 2564; instr. sg. incge lâfe, 2578.--Comp.: ende-, eormen-, weá-, yrfe-, ýð-lâf.

lâr, st. f., lore, instruction, prescription : dat. sg. be fäder lâre, 1951; gen. pl. lâra, 1221; lârena, 269.--Comp. freónd-lâr.

lâst, st. m., footstep, track : acc. sg. lâst, 132, 972, 2165; on last (on the traces of, behind), 2946; nom. pl. lâstas, 1403; acc. pl. lâstas, 842.--Comp.: fêðe-, feorh-, fôt-, wräc-lâst.

läger. See leger.

läger-bed, st. n., bed to lie on : instr. sg. leger-bedde, 1008.

läs, adj., less , 1947; þý läs (the less), 487; conjunct, that not, lest , 1919.

lässa, adj., less, fewer : nom. sg. lässa, 1283; acc. sg. m. lässan, 43; fem, lässan hwîle, 2572; dat. sg. for lässan (for less, smaller), 952. Superl. nom. sg. nô þät läsest wäs hond-gemôt[a], 2355.

lät, adj., negligent, neglectful ; w. gen.: nom. sg. elnes lät, 1530.

lædan, w. v. w. acc.: to lead, guide, bring : inf. lædan, 239; pret. pl. læddon, 1160.

for-lædan, to mislead : pret. pl. for-læddan, 2440 (?).

ge-lædan, lead, bring : part. pret. ge-læded, 37.

læfan, w. v.: 1), to bequeathe, leave : imper. sg. þînum magum læf folc and rîce, 1179; pret. sg. eaferum læfde ... lond and leódbyrig, 2471.--2) spare, leave behind : âht cwices læfan (to spare aught living), 2316.

læn-dagas, st. m. pl., loan-days, transitory days (of earthly existence as contrasted with the heavenly, unending): acc. pl. læn-dagas, 2592; gen. pl. læn-daga, 2342.

læne, adj., inconstant, perishable, evanescent, given over to death or destruction : nom. sg., 1755, 3179; acc. sg. of rust-eaten treasures, 3130; þâs lænan gesceaft (this fleeting life), 1623; gen. sg. lænan lîfes, 2846.

læran, w. v., to teach, instruct : imper. sg. þu þe lær be þon (learn this, take this to heart), 1723.

ge-læran, to teach, instruct, give instruction : inf. ic þäs Hrôðgâr mäg ... ræd gelæran (I can give H. good advice about this), 278; so, 3080; pret. pl. þâ me þät ge-lærdon leóde mîne (gave me the advice), 415.

læstan, w. v.: 1) to follow, to sustain, serve : inf. þät him se lîc-homa læstan nolde (that his body would not sustain him), 813.--2) perform : imper. læst eall tela (do all well), 2664.

ge-læstan: 1) to follow, serve : pret. sg. (sweord) þät mec ær and oft gelæste, 2501.--2) to fulfil, grant : subj. pres. pl. þät ... wilgesîðas, þonne wîg cume, leóde gelæstan (render war service), 24; inf. ic þe sceal mîne gelæstan freóde (shall grant thee my friendship, be grateful), 1707; pret. sg. beót ... gelæste (fulfilled his boast), 524; gelæste swâ (kept his word), 2991; pres. part. häfde Eást-Denum ... gilp gelæsted (had fulfilled for the East Danes his boast), 830.

lætan, st. v., to let, allow , w. acc. and inf.: pres. sg. III. læteð, 1729; imper. pl. II. lætað, 397; sg. II. læt, 1489; pret. sg. lêt, 2390, 2551, 2978, 3151(?); pret. pl. lêton, 48, 865, 3133; subj. pret. sg. II. lête, 1997; sg. III. lête, 3083.

â-lætan: 1) to let, allow : subj. pres. sg. II. þät þu ne âlæte ... dôm ge-dreósan, 2666.--2) to leave, lay aside : inf. âlætan læn-dagas (die) 2592; so, âlætan lîf and leódscipe, 2751.

for-lætan: 1) to let, permit , w. acc. and inf.: pret. sg. for-lêt, 971; pret. pl. for-lêton, 3168. Also with inf. omitted: inf. nolde eorla hleó ... þone cwealmcuman cwicne (i.e. wesan) forlætan (would not let the murderous spirit go alive), 793.--2) to leave behind, leave : pret. sg. in þam wong-stede ... þær he hine ær forlêt (where he had previously left him), 2788.

of-lætan, to leave, lay aside : pres. sg. II. gyf þu ær þonne he worold oflætest (leavest the world, diest), 1184; so pret. sg. oflêt lîf-dagas and þâs lænan gesceaft, 1623.

on-lætan, to release, liberate : pres. sg. III. þonne forstes bend fader on-læteð (as soon as the Father looseth the frost's fetters), 1610.

â-lecgan, w. v.: 1) to lay, lay down : pret. sg. syððan hilde-deór hond â-legde ... under geápne hrôf, 835; þät he on Beówulfes bearm â-legde (this [the sword] he laid in B.'s bosom, presented to him), 2195; pret. pl. â-ledon þâ leófne þeóden ... on bearm scipes, 34; â-legdon þâ tô middes mærne þeóden (laid the mighty prince in the midst [of the pyre]), 3142.--2) to lay aside, give up : siððan ... in fen-freoðo feorh â-legde (laid down his life, died), 852; nu se here-wîsa hleahtor â-legde, gamen and gleó-dreám (now the war-chief has left laughter , etc.), 3021.

leger, st. n., couch, bed, lair : dat. sg. on legere, 3044.

lemian, w. v., to lame, hinder, oppress : pret. sg. (for pl.) hine sorh-wylmas lemede tô lange, 906. MS.

leng. See lang.

lenge, adj., extending along or to, near (of time): nom. sg. neut. ne wäs hit lenge þâ gen (nor was it yet long), 83.

ge-lenge, adj., extending, reaching to, belonging : nom. sg. yrfe-weard ... lîce gelenge (an heir belonging to one's body), 2733.

let, st. m., place of rest, sojourn? in comp. eo-let (voyage?).

lettan, w. v., to hinder : pret. pl. (acc. pers. and gen. thing), þät syððan nâ ... brim-lîðende lâde ne letton (might no longer hinder seafarers from journeying), 569.

â-lêdon. See â-lecgan.

lêg, st. m., flame, fire : nom. sg. wonna lêg (the lurid flame), 3116; swôgende lêg, 3146; dat. sg. for dracan lêge, 2550. See lîg.

lêg-draca, w. m., fire-drake, flaming dragon : nom. sg., 3041.

*leahan, leán, st. v. w. acc. to scold, blame : pres. sg. III. lyhð, 1049; pret. sg. lôg, 1812; pret. pl. lôgon, 203, 863.

be-leán, to dissuade, prevent : inf. ne inc ænig mon ... beleán mihte sorhfullne sîð (no one might dissuade you twain from your difficult journey), 511.

leahtre. See or-leahtre.

leáf, st. n., leaf, foliage : instr. pl. leáfum, 97.

leáfnes-word, st. n., permission, leave : acc. pl., 245.

leán. See leahan.

leán, st. n., reward, compensation : acc. sg., 114, 952, 1221, 1585, 2392; dat. sg. leáne, 1022. Often in the pl.: acc. þâ leán, 2996; dat. þam leánum, 2146; gen. leána, 2991.--Comp.: and-, ende-leán.

leân (for læn, O.H.G. lêhan), st. n, loan , 1810.

leánian, w. v., to reward, compensate : pres. sg. I. ic þe þâ fæhðe feó leánige (repay thee for the contest with old-time treasures), 1381; pret. sg. me þone wälræs wine Scyldinga fättan golde fela leánode (the friend of the Scyldings rewarded me richly for the combat with plated gold), 2103.

leás, adj., false : nom. pl. leáse, 253.

leás, adj., deprived of, free from , w. gen.: nom. sg. dreáma leás, 851; dat. sg. winigea leásum, 1665.--Comp.: dôm-, dreám-, ealdor-, feoh-, feormend-, hlâford-, sâwol-, sige-, sorh-, tîr-, þeóden-, wine-, wyn-leás.

leásig, adj., concealing one's self ; in comp. sin-leásig(?).

leoðo-cräft, st. m., the art of weaving or working in meshes, wire , etc.: instr. pl. segn eall-gylden ... gelocen leoðo-cräftum (a banner all hand-wrought of interlaced gold), 2770.

leoðo-syrce, w. f., shirt of mail (limb-sark) : acc. sg. locene leoðo-syrcan (locked linked sark), 1506; acc. pl. locene leoðo-syrcan, 1891.

leomum. See lim.

leornian, w. v., to learn, devise, plan : pret. him þäs gûð-cyning ... wräce leornode (the war-king planned vengeance therefor), 2337.

leód, st. m., prince : nom. sg., 341, 348, 670, 830, 1433, 1493, 1613, 1654, etc.; acc. leód, 626.

leód, st. f., people : gen. sg. leóde, 597, 600, 697. In pl. indicates individuals, people, kinsmen : nom. pl. leóde, 362, 415, 1214, 2126, etc.; gum-cynnes Geáta leóde (people of the race of the Geátas), 260; acc. pl. leóde, 192, 443, 1337, 1346, etc.; dat. pl. leódum, 389, 521, 619, 698, 906, 1160, etc.; gen. pl. leóda, 205, 635, 794, 1674, 2034, etc.

leód-bealo, st. n., (mischief, misfortune affecting an entire people), great, unheard-of calamity : acc. sg., 1723; gen. pl. leód-bealewa, 1947.

leód-burh, st. f., princely castle, stronghold of a ruler, chief city : acc. pl. -byrig, 2472.

leód-cyning, st. m., king of the people : nom. sg., 54.

leód-fruma, w. m., prince of the people, ruler : acc. sg. leód-fruman, 2131.

leód-gebyrgea, w. m., protector of the people, prince : acc. sg. -gebyrgean, 269.

leód-hryre, st. m., fall, overthrow, of the prince, ruler : dat. sg. äfter leód-hryre (after the fall of the king of the Heaðobeardas , Frôda, cf. 2051), 2031; gen. sg. þäs leód-hryres (of the fall of Heardred, cf. 2389), 2392.

leód-sceaða, w. m., injurer of the people : dat. sg. þam leód-sceaðan, 2094.

leód-scipe, st. m., the whole nation, people : acc. sg., 2752; dat. sg. on þam leód-scipe, 2198.

leóð, st. n., song, lay : nom. sg., 1160.--Comp.: fyrd-, gryre-, gûð-, sorh-leóð.

leóf, adj., lief, dear : nom. sg., 31, 54, 203, 511, 521, 1877, 2468; weak form m., leófa, 1217, 1484, 1855, 2664; acc. sg. m. leófne, 34, 297, 619, 1944, 2128, 3109, 3143; gen. sg. leófes (m.), 1995, 2081, 2898; (neut.), 1062, 2911; dat. pl. leófum, 1074; gen. pl. leófra, 1916. Compar. nom. sg. neut. leófre, 2652. Superl. nom. sg. m. leófost, 1297; acc. sg. þone leófestan, 2824.

leóflîc, dear, precious, valued : nom. sg. m. leóflîc lind-wîga, 2604; acc. sg. neut. leóflîc îren, 1810.

leógan, st. v., to lie, belie, deceive . subj. pres. näfne him his wlite leóge (unless his looks belie him), 250; pret. sg. he ne leág fela wyrda ne worda, 3030.

â-leógan, to deceive, leave unfulfilled : pret. sg. he beót ne â-lêh (he left not his promise unfulfilled), 80.

ge-leógan, to deceive, betray : pret. sg. him seó wên geleáh (hope deceived him), 2324.

leóht, st. n., light, brilliance : nom. sg., 569, 728, 1751 (?); acc. sg. sunnan leóht, 649; godes leóht geceás (chose God's light, died), 2470; dat. sg. tô leóhte, 95.--Comp.: æfen-, fýr-, morgen-leóht.

leóht, adj., luminous, bright : instr. sg. leóhtan sweorde, 2493.

leóma, w. m.: 1) light, splendor : nom. sg., 311, 2770; acc. sg. leóman, 1518; sunnan and mônan leóman (light of sun and moon), 95.--2) (as beadu- and hilde-leóma), the glittering sword : nom. sg. lixte se leóma (the blade-gleam flashed), 1571.

leósan, st. v., = amitti, in

be-leósan, to deprive, be deprived of : pres. part. (heó) wearð beloren leófum bearnum and brôðrum (was deprived of her dear children and brethren), 1074.

for-leósan, with dat. instr., to lose something : pret. sg. þær he dome for-leás, ellen-mærðum (there lost he the glory, the repute, of his heroic deeds), 1471; pret. sg. for pl. þâm þe ær his elne for-leás (to him who, before, had lost his valor),

2862; part. pret. nealles ic þâm leánum for-loren häfde (not at all had I lost the rewards), 2146.

libban, w. v., to live, be, exist : pres. sing. III. lifað, 3169; lyfað, 945; leofað, 975, 1367, 2009; subj. pres. sg. II. lifige, 1225; pres. part. lifigende, 816, 1954, 1974, 2063; dat. sg. be þe lifigendum (in thy lifetime), 2666; pret. sg. lifde, 57, 1258; lyfde, 2145; pret. pl. lifdon, 99. See unlifigende.

licgan, st. v.: 1) to lie, lie down or low : pres. sg. nu seó hand ligeð (now the hand lies low), 1344; nu se wyrm ligeð, 2746, so 2904; inf. licgan, 3130; licgean, 967, 3083; pret. sg. läg, 40, 552, 2078; syððan Heardrêd läg (after Heardrêd had fallen), 2389; pret. pl. lâgon, 3049; lægon, 566.--2) to lie prostrate, rest, fail : pret. sg. næfre on ôre läg wîd-cûðes wîg (never failed the far-famed one's valor at the front), 1042; syððan wiðer-gyld läg (after vengeance failed, or, when Withergyld lay dead, if W. is a proper name), 2052.

â-licgan, to succumb, fail, yield : inf. 2887; pret. sg. þät his dôm â-läg (that its power failed it), 1529.

ge-licgan, to rest, lie still : pret. sg. wind-blond geläg, 3147.

lida, w. m., boat, ship (as in motion); in comp.: sund-, ýð-lida.

lid-man, st. m., seafarer, sailor : gen. pl. lid-manna, 1624.

lim, st. n., limb, branch : instr. pl. leomum, 97.

limpan, st. v., to happen, befall (well or ill); impers. w. dat. pret. sg. hû lomp eów on lâde (how went it with you on the journey?), 1988.

â-limpan, to come about, offer itself : pret. sg. ôð þät sæl â-lamp (till the opportunity presented itself), 623; pret. part, þâ him â-lumpen wäs wistfylle wên (since a hope of a full meal had befallen him), 734.

be-limpan, to happen to, befall : pret. sg. him sió sâr belamp, 2469.

ge-limpan, to happen, occur, turn out : pres. sg. III. hit eft gelimpeð þät..., 1754; subj. pres. þisse ansýne alwealdan þanc lungre gelimpe (thanks to the Almighty forthwith for this sight!), 930; pret. sg. him on fyrste gelamp þät..., 76; swâ him ful-oft gelamp (as often happened to them), 1253; þäs þe hire se willa gelamp þät ... (because her wish had been fulfilled), 627; frôfor eft gelamp sârig-môdum, 2942; subj. pret. gif him þyslîcu þearf gelumpe, 2638; pret. part. Denum eallum wearð ... willa gelumpen, 825.

lind, st. f. (properly linden ; here, a a wooden shield covered with linden-bark or pith): nom. sg., 2342; acc. sg. geolwe linde, 2611; acc. pl. linde, 2366.

lind-gestealla, w. m., shield-comrade, war-comrade : nom. sg., 1974.

lind-häbbend, pres. part., provided with a shield, i.e. warrior: nom. pl. -häbbende, 245; gen. pl. häbbendra, 1403.

lind-plega, w. m., shield-play, i.e. battle: dat. sg. lind-plegan, 1074, 2040.

lind-wîga, w. m., shield-fighter, warrior : nom. sg., 2604.

linnan, st. v., to depart, be deprived of : inf. aldre linnan (depart from life), 1479; ealdres linnan, 2444.

lis, st. f., favor, affection : gen. pl. eall ... lissa, 2151.

list, st. m., art, skill, cleverness, cunning : dat. pl. adverbial, listum (cunningly), 782.

lixan, w. v., to shine, flash : pret. sg. lixte, 311, 485, 1571.

lîc, st. n.: 1) body, corpse : nom. sg., 967; acc. sg. lîc, 2081; þät lîc (the body, corpse), 2128; dat. sg. lîce, 734, 1504, 2424, 2572, 2733, 2744; gen. sg. lîces, 451, 1123.--2) form, figure : in comp. eofor-, swîn-lîc.

ge-lîc, adj., like, similar : nom. pl. m. ge-lîce, 2165. Superl. ge-lîcost, 218, 728, 986, 1609.

lîc-hama, -homa, w. m. (body-home, garment), body : nom. sg. lîc-homa, 813, 1008, 1755; acc. sg. lîc-haman, 2652; dat. sg. lîc-haman, 3179.

lîcian, w. v., to please, like (impers.): pres. sg. III. me þîn môd-sefa lîcað leng swâ wel, 1855; pret. pl. þam wîfe þâ word wel lîcodon, 640.

lîcnes. See on-lîcnes.

lîc-sâr, st. n., bodily pain : acc. sg. lîc-sâr, 816.

lîc-syrce, w. f., body-sark, shirt of mail covering the body : nom. sg., 550.

lîðan, st. v., to move, go : pres. part. nom. pl. þâ lîðende (navigantes, sailors), 221; þâ wäs sund liden (the water was then traversed), 223.--Comp.: heáðu-, mere-, wæg-lîðend.

lîðe (O.H.G. lindi), adj., gentle, mild, friendly : nom. sg. w. instr. gen. lâra lîðe, 1221. Superl. nom. sg. lîðost, 3184.

lið-wæge, st. n., can in which lið (a wine-like, foaming drink) is contained : acc. sg., 1983.

lîf, st. n., life : acc. sg. lîf, 97, 734, 1537, 2424, 2744, 2752; dat. sg. lîfe, 2572; tô lîfe (in one's life, ever) 2433; gen. sg. lîfes, 197, 791, 807, 2824, 2846; worolde lîfes (of the earthly life), 1388, 2344.--Comp. edwît-lîf.

lîf-bysig, adj. (striving for life or death), weary of life, in torment of death : nom. sg., 967.

lîf-dagas, st. m. pl., lifetime : acc.-dagas, 794, 1623.

lîf-freá, w. m., lord of life, God : nom. sg., 16.

lîf-gedâl, st. n., separation from life : nom. sg., 842.

lîf-gesceaft, st. f., fate, destiny : gen. pl.-gesceafta, 1954, 3065.

lîf-wraðu, st. f., protection for one's life, safety : acc. sg. lîf-wraðe, 2878; dat. sg. tô lîf-wraðe, 972.

lîf-wyn, st. f., pleasure, enjoyment, joy (of life): gen. pl. lîf-wynna, 098.

lîg, st. m. n., flame, fire : nom. sg., 1123; dat. instr. sg. lîge, 728, 2306, 2322, 2342; gen. sg. lîges, 83, 782. See lêg.

lîg-draca, w. m., fire-drake, flaming dragon ; nom. pl., 2334. See lêg-draca.

lîg-egesa, w. m., horror arising through fire, flaming terror : acc. sg., 2781.

lîge-torn, st. m., false, pretended insult or injury, fierce anger (?): dat. sg. äfter lîge-torne (on account of a pretended insult? or fierce anger? cf. Bugge in Zacher's Zeits. 4, 208), 1944.

lîg-ýð, st. m., wave of fire : instr. pl. lîg-ýðum, 2673.

león, st. v., to lend : pret. sg. þät him on þearfe lâh þyle Hrôðgâres (which H.'s spokesman lent him in need), 1457.

on-leóon, to lend, grant as a loan , with gen. of thing and dat. pers.: pret. sg. þâ he þäs wæpnes on-lâh sêlran sweord-frecan, 1468.

loca, w. m., bolt, lock : in comp. bân-, burh-loca.

locen. See lûcan.

lond, long. See land, lang.

lof, st. m. n., praise, repute : acc. sg. lof, 1537.

lof-dæd, st. f., deed of praise : instr. pl. lof-dædum, 24.

lof-georn, adj., eager for praise, ambitious : superl. nom. sg. lof-geornost, 3184.

loga, w. m., liar ; in comp. treów-loga.

losian, w. v., to escape, flee : pres. sg. III. losað, 1393, 2063; pret. sg. he on weg losade (fled away), 2097.

lôcian, w. v., to see, look at : pres. sg. II. sæ-lâc ... þe þu her tô lôcast (booty of the sea that thou lookest on), 1655.

ge-lôme, adv., often, frequently , 559.

lufe, w. f., love : in comp. heáh-, môd-, wîf-lufe.

lufa (cf. and-leofa, big-leofa, nourishment), w. m., food, subsistence; property, real estate : acc. sg. on lufan (on possessions), 1729.--Comp. eard-lufa.

lufen, st. f. (cf. lufa), subsistence, food; real estate, (enjoyment?) : nom. sg. lufen (parallel with êðel-wyn), 2887.

luf-tâcen, st. n., love-token : acc. pl. luf-tâcen, 1864.

lufian, w. v., to love, serve affectionately : pret. sg. III. lufode þâ leóde (was on affectionate terms with the people), 1983.

lungre, adv.: 1) hastily, quickly, forthwith , 930, 1631, 2311, 2744.--2) quite, very, fully : feówer mearas lungre gelîce (four horses quite alike), 2165.

lust, st. m., pleasure, joy : dat. pl. adv. lustum (joyfully), 1654; so, on lust, 619, cf. 600.

lûcan, st. v., to twist, wind, lock, interweave : pret. part. acc. sg. and pl. locene leoðo-syrcan (shirt of mail wrought of meshes or rings interlocked), 1506, 1891; gen. pl. locenra beága (rings wrought of gold wire), 2996.

be-lûcan: 1) to shut, close in or around : pret. sg. winter ýðe be-leác îs-gebinde (winter locked the waves with icy bond), 1133.-- 2) to shut in, off, preserve, protect : pret. sg. I. hig wîge beleác manegum mægða (I shut them in, protected them, from war arising from many a tribe), 1771. Cf. me wîge belûc wrâðum feóndum (protect me against mine enemies), Ps. 34, 3.

ge-lûcan, to unite, link together, make : pret. part. gelocen, 2770.

on-lûcan, to unlock, open : pret. sg. word-hord on-leác (opened the word-hoard, treasure of speech), 259.

tô-lucan, (to twist, wrench, in two) to destroy : inf., 782.

lyft, st. f. (m. n.?), air : nom. sg., 1376; dat. sg. äfter lyfte (along, through, the air), 2833.

lyft-floga, w. m., air-flier : nom. sg. (of the dragon), 2316.

lyft-geswenced, pret. part., urged, hastened on, by the wind , 1914.

lyft-wyn, st. f., enjoyment of the air : acc. sg. lyft-wynne, 3044.

lyhð. See leahan.

lystan, w. v., to lust after, long for : pret. sg. Geát ungemetes wel ... restan lyste(the Geát [Beówulf] longed sorely to rest), 1794.

lyt, adj. neut. (= parum), little, very little, few : lyt eft becwom ... hâmes niósan (few escaped homeward), 2366; lyt ænig (none at all), 3130; usually with gen.: wintra lyt, 1928; lyt ... heáfod-mâga, 2151; wergendra tô lyt (too few defenders), 2883; lyt swîgode nîwra spella (he kept to himself little, none at all, of the new tidings), 2898; dat. sg. lyt manna (too few of men), 2837.

lytel, adj., small, little : nom. sg. neut. tô lytel, 1749; acc. sg. f. lytle hwîle (a little while), 2031, 2098; lif-wraðe lytle (little protection for his life), 2878.-- Comp. un-lytel.

lyt-hwôn, adv., little = not at all : lyt-hwôn lôgon, 204.

lýfe, st. n., leave, permission, (life?) : instr. sg. þîne lýfe (life, MS.), 2132.-- Leo. Cf. O.N. leyfi, n., leave, permission , in Möbius' Glossary, p. 266.

lýfan, w. v., (fundamental meaning to believe, trust) in

â-lýfan, to allow, grant, entrust : pret. sg. næfre ic ænegum men ær âlýfde ... þryð-ärn Dena (never before to any man have I entrusted the palace of the Danes),

656; pret. part. (þâ me wäs) sîð ... âlýfed inn under eorð-weall (the way in under the wall of earth was allowed me), 3090.

ge-lýfan, w. v., to believe, trust : 1) w. dat.: inf. þær gelýfan sceal dryhtnes dôme se þe hine deáð nimeð (whomever death carrieth away, shall believe it to be the judgment of God , i.e. in the contest between Beówulf and Grendel), 440.--2) w. acc.: pret. sg. geóce gelýfde brego Beorht-Dena (believed in, expected, help , etc.), 609; þät heó on ænigne eorl gelýfde fyrena frôfre (that she at last should expect from any earl comfort, help, out of these troubles), 628; se þe him bealwa tô bôte gelýfde (who trusted in him as a help out of evils), 910; him tô anwaldan âre gelýfde (relied for himself on the help of God), 1273.

â-lýsan, w. v., to loose, liberate : pret. part. þâ wäs of þäm hrôran helm and byrne lungre â-lýsed (helm and corselet were straightway loosed from him), 1631.

M

maðelian, w. v. (sermocinari), to speak, talk : pret. sg. maðelode, 286, 348, 360, 371, 405, 456, 499, etc.; maðelade, 2426.

maga, w. m., son, male descendant, young man : nom. sg. maga Healfdenes (Hrôðgâr), 189, 1475, 2144; maga Ecgþeówes (Beówulf), 2588: maga (Grendel), 979; se maga geonga (Wîglâf), 2676; Grendeles maga (a relative of Grendel), 2007; acc. sg. þone magan, 944.

magan, v. with pret.-pres. form, to be able : pres. sg. I. III. mäg, 277, 478, 931, 943, 1485, 1734, etc.; II. meaht þu, 2048; subj. pres. mæge, 2531, 2750; þeáh ic eal mæge (even though I could), 681; subj. pl. we mægen, 2655; pret. sg. meahte, 542, 755, 1131, 1660, 2465, etc.; mihte, 190, 207, 462, 511, 571, 657, 1509, 2092, 2610; mehte, 1083, 1497, 1516, 1878; pl. meahton, 649, 942, 1455, 1912, 2374, 3080; mihton, 308, 313, 2684, 3164; subj. pret. sg. meahte, 243, 763, 2521; pres. sg. mäg, sometimes = licet, may, can, will (fut.), 1366, 1701, 1838, 2865.

mago (Goth. magu-s), st. m., male, son : nom. sg. mago Ecglâfes (Hunferð), 1466; mago Healfdenes (Hrôðgâr), 1868, 2012.

mago-dryht, st. f., troop of young men, band of men : nom. sg. mago-driht, 67.

mago-rinc, st. m., hero, man (preeminently): gen. pl. mago-rinca, heáp, 731.

magu-þegn, mago-þegn, st. m., vassal, war-thane : nom. sg. 408, 2758; dat. sg. magu-þegne, 2080; acc. pl. magu-þegnas, 293; dat. pl. mago-þegnum, 1481; gen. pl. mago-þegna ... þone sêlestan (the best of vassals), 1406.

man, mon, st. m.: 1) man, human being : nom. sg. man, 25, 503, 534, 1049, 1354, 1399, 1535, 1877, etc.; mon, 209, 510, 1561, 1646, 2282, etc.; acc. sg. w. mannan, 297, 577, 1944, 2128, 2775; wîd-cûðne man, 1490; dat. sg. men, 656, 753, 1880; menn, 2190; gen. sg. mannes, 1195 (?), 2081, 2534, 2542; monnes, 1730; nom. pl. men, 50, 162, 233, 1635, 3167; acc. pl. men, 69, 337, 1583, 1718; dat. pl. mannum, 3183; gen. pl. manna, 155, 201, 380, 702, 713, 736, etc.; monna, 1414, 2888.--2) indef. pron. = one, they, people (Germ. man): man, 1173, 1176; mon, 2356, 3177.--Comp.: fyrn-, gleó-, gum-, iú-, lid-, sæ-, wæpned-man.

man. See munan.

man-cyn, st. n., mankind : dat. sg. man-cynne, 110; gen. sg. man-cynnes, 164, 2182; mon-cynnes, 196, 1956.

man-dreám, st. m., human joy, mundi voluptas : acc. sg. man-dreám, 1265; dat. pl. mon-dreámum, 1716.

man-dryhten, st. m. (lord of men), ruler of the people, prince, king : nom. sg. man-dryhten, 1979, 2648; mon-drihten, 436; mon-dryhten, 2866; acc. sg. mon-dryhten, 2605; dat. sg. man-drihtne, 1230; man-dryhtne, 1250, 2282; gen. sg. man-dryhtnes, 2850; mon-dryhtnes, 3150.

ge-mang, st. m., troop, company : dat. sg. on gemonge (in the troop [of the fourteen Geátas that returned from the sea]), 1644.

manian, w. v., to warn, admonish : pres. sg. III. manað swâ and myndgað ... sârum wordum (so warneth and remindeth he with bitter words), 2058.

manig, monig, adj., many, many a, much : 1) adjectively: nom. sg. rinc manig, 399; geong manig (many a young man), 855; monig snellîc sæ-rinc, 690; medu-benc monig, 777; so 839, 909, 919, 1511, 2763, 3023, etc.; acc. sg. medo-ful manig, 1016; dat. sg. m. þegne monegum, 1342, 1420; dat. sg. f. manigre mægðe, 75; acc. pl. manige men, 337; dat. pl. manegum mâðmum, 2104; monegum mægðum, 5; gen. pl. manigra mêda, 1179.--2) substantively: nom. sg. manig, 1861; monig, 858; dat. sg. manegum, 349, 1888; nom. pl. manige, 1024; monige, 2983; acc. pl. monige, 1599; gen. pl. manigra, 2092.--3) with depend. gen. pl.: dat. manegum mægða, 1772; monegum fira, 2002; häleða monegum bold-âgendra, 3112; acc. pl. rinca manige, 729; (mâðm)-æhta monige, 1614.

manig-oft, adv., very often, frequently , 171 [if manig and oft are to be connected].

man-lîce, adv., man-like, manly , 1047.

man-þwære, adj., kind, gentle toward men, philanthropic : nom. sg. superl. mon-þwærust, 3183.

mâ, contracted compar., more : with partitive gen., 504, 736, 1056.

mâðum, mâððum, st. m., gift, jewel, object of value : acc. sg. mâðum, 169, 1053, 2056, 3017; dat. instr. sg. mâðme, 1529, 1903; nom. pl. mâðmas, 1861; acc. pl. mâdmas, 385, 472, 1028, 1483, 1757, 1868, etc.; dat. instr. pl. mâðmum, mâdmum, 1049, 1899, 2104, 2789; gen. pl. mâðma, 1785, 2144, 2167, etc.; mâdma, 36, 41.--Comp.: dryht-, gold-, hord-, ofer-, sinc-, wundor-mâðum.

mâðm-æht, st. f., treasure in jewels, costly objects : gen. pl. mâðm-æhta, 1614, 2834.

mâððum-fät, st. n., treasure-casket or cup, costly vessel : nom. sg., 2406.

mâðm-gestreón, st. n., precious jewel : gen. pl. mâðm-gestreóna, 1932.

mâðum-gifu, st. f., gift of valuable objects, largess of treasure : dat. sg. äfter mâððum-gife, 1302.

mâðum-sigl, st. n., costly, sun-shaped ornament, valuable decoration : gen. pl. mâððum-sigla, 2758.

mâðum-sweord, st. n., costly sword (inlaid with gold and jewels): acc. sg., 1024.

mâðum-wela, w. m., wealth of jewels, valuables :: dat. sg. äfter-mâððum-welan (after the sight of the wealth of jewels), 2751.

mâgas. See mæg.

mâge, w. f., female relative : gen. sg. Grendles mâgan (mother), 1392.

mân, st. n., crime, misdeed : instr. sg. mâne, 110, 979; adv., criminally , 1056.

mân-for-dædla, w. m., evil-doer, criminal : nom. pl. mân-for-dædlan, 563.

mân-scaða, w. m., mischievous, hurtful foe, hostis nefastus : nom. sg. 713, 738, 1340; mân-sceaða, 2515.

mâra (comp. of micel), adj., greater, stronger, mightier : nom. sg. m. mâra, 1354, 2556; neut. mâre, 1561; acc. sg. m. mâran, 2017; mund-gripe mâran (a mightier hand-grip), 754; with following gen. pl. mâran ... eorla (a more powerful earl), 247; fem. mâran, 533, 1012; neut. mâre, 518; with gen. pl. morð-beala mâre (more, greater, deeds of murder), 136; gen. sg. f. mâran, 1824.

mæst (superl. of micel, mâra), greatest, strongest : nom. sg. neut. (with partitive gen.), mæst, 78, 193; fem. mæst, 2329; acc. sg. fem. fæhðe mæste, 459; mæste ... worolde wynne (the highest earthly pleasure), 1080; neut. n. (with partitive gen.) mæst mærða, 2646; hond-wundra mæst, 2769; bæl-fýra mæst, 3144; instr. sg. m. mæste cräfte, 2182.

mäcg. See mecg.

mägð, st. f., wife, maid, woman : nom. sg., 3017; gen. pl. mägða hôse (accompanied by her maids of honor), 925; mägða, 944, 1284.

mägen, st. n.: 1) might, bodily strength, heroic power : acc. sg. mägen, 518, 1707; instr. sg. mägene, 780(?), 2668; gen. sg. mägenes, 418, 1271, 1535, 1717, etc.; mägnes, 671, 1762; mägenes strang, strengest (great in strength), 1845, 196; mägenes rôf (id.), 2085.--2) prime, flower (of a nation), forces available in war : acc. sg. swâ he oft (i.e. etan) dyde mägen Hrêðmanna (the best of the Hreðmen), 445; gen. sg. wið manna hwone mägenes Deniga (from(?) any of the men of the Danes), 155.--Comp. ofer-mägen.

mägen-âgend, pres. part., having great strength, valiant : gen. pl. -âgendra, 2838.

mägen-byrðen, st. f., huge burthen : acc. sg. mägen-byrðenne, 3092; dat. (instr.) sg., 1626.

mägen-cräft, st. m., great, hero-like, strength : acc. sg., 380.

mägen-ellen, st. n. (the same), acc. sg., 660.

mägen-fultum, st. m., material aid : gen. pl. näs þät þonne mætost mägen-fultuma (that was not the least of strong helps , i.e. the sword Hrunting), 1456.

mägen-ræs, st. m., mighty attack, onslaught : acc. sg., 1520.

mägen-strengo, st. f., main strength, heroic power : acc. sg., 2679.

mägen-wudu, st. m., might-wood , i.e. the spear, lance: acc. sg., 236.

mäst, st. m., mast : nom. sg., 1899; dat. sg. be mäste (beside the mast), 36; to the mast , 1906.

mæðum. See mâðum, hyge-mæðum.

mæg, st. m., kinsman by blood : nom. sg. mæg, 408, 738, 759, 814, 915, 1531, 1945, etc; (brother), 468, 2605? acc. sg. mæg (son), 1340; (brother), 2440, 2485, 2983; dat. sg. mæge, 1979; gen. sg. mæges, 2629, 2676, 2699, 2880; nom. pl. mâgas, 1016; acc. pl. mâgas, 2816; dat. pl. mâgum, 1179, 2615, 3066; (to brothers), 1168; mægum, 2354; gen. pl. mâga, 247, 1080, 1854, 2007, 2743.--Comp.: fäderen-, heáfod-, wine-mæg.

mæg-burh, st. f., borough of blood-kinsmen, entire population united by ties of blood ; (in wider sense) race, people, nation : gen. sg. lond-rihtes ... þære mæg-burge (of land possessions among the people , i.e. of the Geátas), 2888.

mægð, st. f., race, people : acc. sg. mægðe, 1012; dat. sg. mægðe, 75; dat. pl. mægðum, 5; gen. pl. mægða, 25, 1772.

mæg-wine, st. m., blood kinsman, friend , 2480 (nom. pl.).

mæl, st. n.: l) time, point of time : nom. sg. 316; þâ wäs sæl and mæl (there was [appropriate] chance and time), 1009; acc. sg. mæl, 2634; instr. pl. ærran mælum, 908, 2238, 3036; gen. pl. mæla, 1250; sæla and mæla, 1612; mæla gehwylce (each time, without intermission), 2058.--2) sword, weapon : nom. sg. broden (brogden) mæl (the drawn sword), 1617, 1668 (cf. Grimm, Andreas and Elene, p. 156).--3) mole, spot, mark .--Comp.: græg-, hring-, sceaðen-, wunden-mæl.

mæl-cearu, st. f., long-continued sorrow, grief : acc. sg. mæl-ceare, 189.

mæl-gesceaft, st. f., fate, appointed time : acc. pl. ie on earde bâd mæl-gesceafta (awaited the time allotted for me by fate), 2738.

mænan, w. v., with acc. in the sense of (1) to remember, mention, proclaim : inf. mænan, 1068; pret. part. þær wäs Beówulfes mærðo mæned, 858.--2) to mention sorrowfully, mourn : inf. 3173; pret. sg. giohðo mænde (mourned sorrowfully), 2268; pret. pl. mændon, 1150, 3150.

ge-mænan (see mân), w. v. with acc., to injure maliciously, break : subj. pret. pl. ge-mænden, 1102.

ge-mæne, adj., common, in common : nom. sg. gemæne, 2474; þær unc hwîle wäs hand gemæne (i.e. in battle), 2138; sceal ûrum þät sweord and helm bâm gemæne (i.e. wesan), 2661; nom. pl. gemæne, 1861; dat. pl. þät þâm folcum sceal ... sib gemænum (attraction for gemæne, i.e. wesan), 1858; gen. pl. unc sceal (i.e. wesan) fela mâðma gemænra (we two shall share many treasures together), 1785.

mærðu, st. f.: 1) glory, a heroes fame : nom. sg. 858; acc. sg. mærðo, 660, 688; acc. pl. mærða, 2997; instr. pl. mærðum (gloriously), 2515: gen. pl. mærða, 504, 1531.--2) deed of glory, heroism : acc. sg. mærðo, 2135; gen. pl. mærða, 408, 2646.--Comp. ellen-mærðu.

mære, adj., memorable; celebrated, noble; well known, notorious : nom. sg. m. mære, 103, 129, 1716, 1762; se mæra, 763, 2012, 2588; also as vocative m. se mæra, 1475; nom. fem. mæru, 2017; mære, 1953; neut. mære, 2406; acc. sg. m. mærne, 36, 201, 353, 1599, 2385, 2722, 2789, 3099; neut. mære, 1024; dat. sg. mærum, 345, 1302, 1993, 2080, 2573; tô þäm mæran, 270; gen. sg. mæres, 798; mæran, 1730; nom. pl. mære, 3071; superl. mærost, 899,--Comp.: fore-, heaðo-mære.

mæst. See mâra.

mæte, adj., moderate, small : superl. nom. sg. mætost, 1456.

mecg, mäcg, st. m., son, youth, man . in comp. hilde-, oret-mecg, wräc-mäcg.

medla. See on-medla.

medu, st. m., mead : acc. sg. medu, 2634; dat. sg. tô medo, 605.

medo-ärn, st. n., mead-hall : acc. sg. medo-ärn (Heorot), 69.

medu-benc, st. f., mead-bench, bench in the mead-hall : nom. sg. medu-benc, 777; dat. sg. medu-bence, 1053; medo-bence, 1068, 2186; meodu-bence, 1903.

medu-dreám, st. m., mead-joy, joyous carousing during mead-drinking : acc. sg. 2017.

medo-ful, st. n., mead-cup : acc. sg. 625, 1016.

medo-heal, st. f., mead-hall : nom. sg., 484; dat. sg. meodu-healle, 639.

medu-scenc, st. m., mead-can, vessel : instr. pl. meodu-scencum, 1981.

medu-seld, st. n., mead-seat, mead-house : acc. sg., 3066.

medo-setl, st. n., mead-seat upon which one sits mead-drinking : gen. pl. meodo-setla, 5.

medo-stîg, st. f., mead-road, road to the mead-hall : acc. sg. medo-stîg, 925.

medo-wang, st. m., mead-field (where the mead-hall stood): acc. pl. medo-wongas, 1644.

meðel, st. n., assembly, council : dat. sg. on meðle, 1877.

meðel-stede, st. m., (properly place of speech, judgment-seat), here meeting-place, battle-field (so, also 425, the battle is conceived under the figure of a parliament or convention): dat. sg. on þäm meðel-stede, 1083.

meðel-word, st. n., words called forth at a discussion; address : instr. pl. meðel-wordum, 236.

melda, w. m., finder, informer, betrayer : gen. sg. þäs meldan, 2406.

meltan, st. v. intrans., to consume by fire, melt or waste away : inf., 3012; pret. sg. mealt, 2327; pl. multon, 1121.

ge-meltan, the same: pret. sg. gemealt, 898, 1609, 1616; ne gemealt him se môd-sefa (his courage did not desert him), 2629.

men. See man.

mene, st. m., neck ornament, necklace, collar : acc. sg., 1200.

mengan, w. v., to mingle, unite, with , w. acc. of thing: inf. se þe mere-grundas mengan scolde, 1450.

ge-mengan, to mix with, commingle : pret. part. 849, 1594.

menigu, st. f., multitude, many : nom. and acc. sg. mâðma menigeo (multitude of treasures, presents), 2144; so, mänigo, 41.

mercels, st. m., mark, aim : gen. sg. mercelses, 2440.

mere, st. m., sea, ocean : nom. sg. se mere, 1363; acc. sg. on mere, 1131, 1604; on nicera mere, 846; dat. sg. fram mere, 856.

mere-deór, st. n., sea-beast : acc. sg., 558.

mere-fara, w. m., seafarer : gen. sg. mere-faran, 502.

mere-fix, st. m., sea-fish : gen. pl. mere-fixa (the whale , cf. 540), 549.

mere-grund, st. m., sea-bottom : acc. sg., 2101; acc. pl. mere-grundas, 1450.

mere-hrägl, st. n., -sea-garment , i.e., sail: gen. pl. mere-hrägla sum, 1906.

mere-lîðend, pres. part., moving on the sea, sailor : nom. pl. mere-lîðende, 255.

mere-stræt, st. f., sea-street, way over the sea : acc. pl. mere-stræta 514.

mere-strengo, st. f., sea-power, strength in the sea : acc. sg., 533.

mere-wîf, st. n., sea-woman, mer-woman : acc. sg. (of Grendel's mother), 1520.

mergen. See morgen.

met, st. n., thought, intention (cf. metian = meditari): acc. pl. onsæl meoto, 489 (meaning doubtful; see Bugge, Journal 8, 292; Dietrich, Haupt's Zeits. 11, 411; Körner, Eng. Stud. 2, 251).

ge-met, st. n., an apportioned share; might, power, ability : nom. sg. nis þät ... gemet mannes nefne mîn ânes (nobody, myself excepted, can do that), 2534; acc. sg. ofer mîn gemet (beyond my power), 2880; dat. sg. mid gemete, 780.

ge-met, adj., well-measured, meet, good : nom. sg. swâ him gemet þince (þûhte), (as seemed meet to him), 688, 3058. See un-gemete, adv.

metan, st. v., to measure, pass over or along : pret. pl. fealwe stræte mearum mæton (measured the yellow road with their horses), 918; so, 514, 1634.

ge-metan, the same: pret. sg. medu-stîg gemät.(measured, walked over, the road to the mead-hall), 925.

metod, st. m. (the measuring, arranging) Creator, God : nom. sg., 110, 707, 968, 1058, 2528; scîr metod, 980; sôð metod, 1612; acc. sg. metod, 180; dat. sg. metode, 169, 1779; gen. sg. metodes, 671.--Comp. eald-metod.

metod-sceaft, st. f.: 1) the Creator's determination, divine purpose, fate : acc. sg. -sceaft, 1078.--2) the Creators glory : acc. sg. metod-sceaft seón (i.e. die), 1181; dat. sg. tô metod-sceafte, 2816.

mêce, st. m., sword : nom. sg., 1939; acc. sg. mêce, 2048; brâdne mêce, 2979; gen. sg. mêces, 1766, 1813, 2615, 2940; dat. pl. instr. mêcum, 565; gen. pl. mêca, 2686.--Comp.: beado-, häft-, hilde-mêce.

mêd, st. f., meed, reward : acc. sg. mêde, 2135; dat. sg. mêde, 2147; gen. pl. mêda, 1179.

ge-mêde, st. n., approval, permission (Grein): acc. pl. ge-mêdu, 247.

mêðe, adj., tired, exhausted, dejected : in comp. hyge-, sæ-mêðe.

mêtan, w. v., to meet, find, fall in with : with acc., pret. pl. syððan Äscheres ... hafelan mêtton, 1422; subj. pret. sg. þät he ne mêtte ... on elran man mundgripe mâran (that he never met, in any other man, with a mightier hand-grip), 752.

ge-mêtan, with acc., the same: pret. sg. gemêtte, 758, 2786; pl. näs þâ long tô þon, þät þâ aglæcean hy eft gemêtton (it was not long after that the warriors again met each other), 2593.

ge-mêting, st. f., meeting, hostile coming together : nom. sg., 2002.

meagol, adj., mighty, immense; formal, solemn : instr. pl. meaglum wordum, 1981.

mearc, st. f., frontier, limit, end : dat. sg. tô mearce (the end of life), 2385.-- Comp. Weder-mearc, 298.

ge-mearc, st. n., measure, distance : comp. fôt-, mîl-ge-mearc.

mearcian, w. v., to mark, stain : pres. ind. sg. mearcað môrhopu (will stain, mark, the moor with the blood of the corpse), 450.

ge-mearcian, the same: pret. part. (Cain) morðre gemearcod (murder-marked [cf. 1 Book Mos. IV. 15]), 1265; swâ wäs on þæm scennum ... gemearcod ... hwâm þät sweord geworht wære (engraved for whom the sword had been wrought), 1696.

mearc-stapa, w. m., march-strider, frontier-haunter (applied to Grendel and his mother): nom. sg., 103; acc. pl. mearc-stapan, 1349.

mearh, st. m., horse, steed : nom. pl. mearas, 2164; acc. pl. mearas, 866, 1036; dat. pl. inst. mearum, 856, 918; mearum and mâðmum, 1049, 1899; gen. pl. meara and mâðma, 2167.

mearn. See murnan.

meodu. See medu.

meoto. See met.

meotud. See metod.

meowle, w. f., maiden : comp. geó-meowle.

micel, adj., great, huge, long (of time): nom. sg. m., 129, 502; fem., 67, 146, 170; neut., 772; acc. sg. m. micelne, 3099; fem, micle, 1779, 3092; neut. micel, 270, 1168. The comp. mâre must be supplied before þone in: medo-ärn micel ... (mâre) þone yldo beam æfre ge-frunon, 69; instr. sg. ge-trume micle, 923; micle (by much, much); micle leófre (far dearer), 2652; efne swâ micle (lässa), ([less] even by so much), 1284; oftor micle (much oftener), 1580; dat. sg, weak form miclan, 2850; gen. sg. miclan, 979. The gen. sg. micles is an adv. = much, very : micles wyrðne gedôn (deem worthy of much , i.e. honor very highly), 2186; tô fela micles (far too much, many), 695; acc. pl. micle, 1349. Compar., see mâra.

mid, I. prep. w. dat., instr., and acc., signifying preëminently union, community, with , hence: 1) w. dat.: a) with, in company, community, with ; mid Finne, 1129; mid Hrôðgâre, 1593; mid scip-herge, 243; mid gesîðum (with his comrades), 1314; so, 1318, 1964, 2950, etc.; mid his freó-drihtne, 2628; mid þæm lâcum (with the gifts), 1869; so, 2789, 125; mid hæle (with good luck!), 1218; mid bæle fôr (sped off amid fire), 2309. The prep. postponed: him mid (with him, in his company), 41; with him , 1626; ne wäs him Fitela mid (was not with him), 890. b) with, among : mid Geátum (among the Geátas), 195, 2193, 2624; mid Scyldingum, 274; mid Eotenum, 903; mid yldum (eldum), 77, 2612; mid him (with, among, one another), 2949. In temporal sense: mid ær-däge (at dawn), 126.--2) with, with the help of, through , w. dat.: mid âr-stafum (through his grace), 317; so, 2379; mid grâpe (with the fist), 438; so, 1462, 2721; mid his

478

hete-þoncum (through his hatred), 475; mid sweorde, 574; so, 1660, 2877; mid gemete (through, by, his power), 780; so, 1220, 2536, 2918; mid gôde (with benefits), 1185; mid hearme (with harm, insult), 1893; mid þære sorge (with [through?] this sorrow), 2469; mid rihte (by rights), 2057. With instr.: mid þý wife (through [marriage with] the woman), 2029.--3) w. acc., with, in community, company, with : mid his eorla gedriht, 357; so, 634, 663, 1673; mid hine, 880; mid mînne gold-gyfan, 2653.

II. adv., mid, thereamong, in the company , 1643; at the same time, likewise , 1650.

middan-geard, st. m., globe, earth : acc. sg., 75, 1772; dat. sg. on middan-gearde, 2997; gen. sg. middan-geardes, 504, 752.

midde, w. f., middle = medius : dat. sg. on middan (through the middle, in two), 2706; gen. sg. (adv.) tô-middes (in the midst), 3142.

middel-niht, st. f., midnight : dat. pl. middel-nihtum, 2783, 2834.

miht, st. f., might, power, authority : acc. sg. þurh drihtnes miht (through the Lord's help, power), 941; instr. pl. selfes mihtum, 701.

mihtig, adj.: 1) physically strong, powerful : acc. sg. mihtig mere-deór, 558; mere-wîf mihtig, 1520.--2) possessing authority, mighty : nom. sg. mihtig god, 702, 1717, 1726; dat. sg. mihtigan drihtne, 1399.--Comp.: äl-, fore-mihtig.

milde, adj., kind, gracious, generous : nom. sg. môdes milde (kind-hearted), 1230; instr. pl. mildum wordum (graciously), 1173. Superl. nom. sg. worold-cyning mannum mildust (a king most liberal to men), 3183.

milts, st. f., kindness, benevolence : nom. sg., 2922.

missan, w. v. with gen., to miss, err in : pret. sg. miste mercelses (missed the mark), 2440.

missere, st. n., space of a semester, half a year : gen. pl. hund missera (fifty winters), 2734, 2210; generally, a long period of time, season, 1499, 1770; fela missera, 153, 2621.

mist-hlið, st. n., misty cliff, cloud-capped slope : dat. pl. under mist-hleoðum, 711.

mistig, adj., misty : acc. pl. mistige môras, 162.

mîl-gemearc, st. n., measure by miles : gen. sg. mîl-gemearces, 1363.

mîn: 1) poss. pron., my, mine , 255, 345, etc.; Hygelâc mîn (my lord , or king, H.), 2435.--2) gen. sg. of pers. pron. ic, of me , 2085, 2534, etc.

molde, w. f., dust; earth, field : in comp. gräs-molde.

mon. See man.

ge-mong. See ge-mang.

morð-bealu, st. n., murder, deadly hale or deed of murder : gen. pl. morð-beala, 136.

morðor, st. n., deed of violence, murder : dat. instr. sg. morðre, 893, 1265, 2783; gen. sg. morðres, 2056; morðres scyldig (guilty of murder), 1684.

morðor-bed, st. n., bed of death, murder-bed : acc. sg. wäs þam yldestan ... morðor-bed strêd (a bed of death was spread for the eldest , i.e. through murder his death-bed was prepared), 2437.

morðor-bealu, st. n., death-bale, destruction by murder : acc. sg. morðor-bealo, 1080, 2743.

morðor-hete, st. m., murderous hate : gen. sg. þäs morðor-hetes, 1106.

morgen, morn, mergen, st. m., morning, forenoon ; also morrow : nom. sg. morgen, 1785, 2125; (morrow), 2104; acc. sg. on morgen (in the morning), 838;

dat. sg. on morgne, 2485; on mergenne, 565, 2940; gen. pl. morna gehwylce (every morning), 2451.

morgen-ceald, adj., morning-cold, dawn-cold : nom. sg. gâr morgen-ceald (spear chilled by the early air of morn), 3023.

morgen-lang, adj., lasting through the morning : acc. sg. morgen-longne däg (the whole forenoon), 2895.

morgen-leóht, st. n., morning-light : nom. sg., 605, 918.

morgen-swêg, st. m., morning-cry, cry at morn : nom. sg., 129.

morgen-tîd, st. f., morning-tide : acc. sg. on morgen-tîde, 484, 818(?)

morn. See morgen.

môd, st. n.: 1) heart, soul, spirit, mood, mind, manner of thinking : nom. sg., 50, 731; wäfre môd (the flicker ing spirit, the fading breath), 1151; acc. sg. on môd (into his mind), 67; dat. instr. sg. môde geþungen (of mature, lofty spirit), 625; on môde (in heart, mind), 754, 1845, 2282? 2528; on hreóum môde (fierce of spirit), 2582; gen. sg. modes, 171, 811, 1707; modes blîðe (gracious-minded, kindly disposed), 436; so, môdes milde, 1230; môdes seóce (depressed in mind), 1604.--2) boldness, courage : nom. and acc. sg., 1058, 1168. 3) passion, fierceness : nom. sg., 549.--Comp. form adj.: galg-, geômor-, gläd-, gûð-, hreóh-, irre-, sârig-, stîð-, swîð-, wêrig-môd.

môd-cearu, st. f., grief of heart : acc. sg. môd-ceare, 1993, 3150.

môd-gehygd, st. f., thought of the heart; mind : instr. pl. môd-gehygdum, 233

môd-ge-þanc, st. n., mood-thought, meditation : acc. sg. môd-ge-þonc, 1730.

môd-giômor, adj., grieved at heart, dejected : nom. sg., 2895.

môdig, adj., courageous : nom. sg., 605, 1644, 1813, 2758; he þäs (þäm, MS.) môdig wäs (had the courage for it), 1509; se môdega, 814; dat. sg. mid þam môdigan, 3012; gen. sg. môdges, 502; môdiges, 2699; Geáta leód georne trûwode môdgan mägnes (trusted firmly in his bold strength), 671; nom. pl. môdge, 856; môdige, 1877; gen. pl. môdigra, 312, 1889.--Comp, fela-môdig.

môdig-lîc, adj., of bold appearance : compar. acc. pl. môdiglîcran, 337.

môd-lufe, w. f., hearts affection, love : gen. sg. þînre môd-lufan, 1824.

môd-sefa, w. m., thought of the heart; brave, bold temper; courage : nom. sg., 349, 1854, 2629; acc. sg. môd-sefan, 2013; dat. sg. môd-sefan, 180.

môd-þracu, st. f., boldness, courage, strength of mind : dat. sg. for his môd-þräce, 385.

môdor, f., mother : nom. sg., 1259, 1277, 1283, 1684, 2119; acc. sg. môdor, 1539, 2140, 2933.

môna, w. m., moon : gen. sg. mônan, 94.

môr, st. m., moor, morass, swamp : acc. sg. ofer myrcan môr, 1406; dat. sg. of môre, 711; acc. pl. môras, 103, 162, 1349.

môr-hop, st. n., place of refuge in the moor, hiding-place in the swamp : acc. pl. môr-hopu, 450.

ge-môt, st. n., meeting : in comp. hand-, torn-ge-môt.

môtan, pret.-pres. v.: 1) power or permission to have something, to be permitted; may, can : pres. sg. I., III. môt, 186, 442, 604; II. môst, 1672; pl. môton, 347, 365, 395; pres. subj. ic môte, 431; III. se þe môte, 1388; pret sg. môste, 168, 707, 736, 895, 1488, 1999, 2242, 2505, etc.; pl. môston, 1629, 1876, 2039, 2125, 2248; pres. subj. sg. II. þät þu hine selfne geseón môste (mightest see), 962.-- 2) shall, must, be obliged : pres. sg. môt, 2887; pret. sg. môste, 1940; þær he þý fyrste forman dôgore wealdan môste, swâ him Wyrd ne gescrâf, hrêð ät hilde (if he must for the first time that day be victorious, as Fate had denied him victory , cf. 2681, 2683 seqq.), 2575.

ge-munan, pret.-pres. v., to have in mind, be mindful; remember, think of , w. acc.: pres. sg. hine gearwe geman witena wel-hwylc (each of the knowing ones still remembers him well), 265; ic þe þäs leán geman (I shall not forget thy reward for this), 1221; ic þät eall gemon (I remember all that), 2428; so, 1702, 2043; gif he þät eall gemon hwät ... (if he is mindful of all that which ...), 1186; ic þät mæl gemon hwær... (I remember the time when ...), 2634; pret. sg. w. gemunde... æfen-spræce (recalled his evening speech), 759; so, 871, 1130, 1260, 1271, 1291, 2115, 2432, 2607, 2679; se þäs leód-hryres leán ge-munde (was mindful of reward for the fall of the ruler), 2392; þät he Eotena bearn inne gemunde (that he in this should remember, take vengeance on, the children of the Eotens), 1142; so, hond gemunde fæhðo genôge (his hand remembered strife enough), 2490; ne ge-munde mago Ecglâfes þät ... (remembered not that which ...), 1466; pret. pl. helle gemundon in môd-sefan (their thoughts [as heathens] fixed themselves on, remembered, hell), 179.

on-munan, w. acc. pers. and gen. of thing, to admonish, exhort : pret. sg. onmunde ûsic mærða (exhorted us to deeds of glory), 2641.

mund, st. f., hand : instr. pl. mundum, mid mundum, 236, 514, 1462, 3023, 3092.

mund-bora, w. m., protector, guardian, preserver : nom. sg., 1481, 2780.

mund-gripe, st. m., hand-grip, seizure : acc. sg. mund-gripe, 754; dat. sg. mund-gripe, 380, 1535; äfter mund-gripe (after having seized the criminal), 1939.

murnan, st. v., to shrink from, be afraid of, avoid : pret. sg. nô mearn fore fæhðe and fyrene, 136; so, 1538; nalles for ealdre mearn (was not apprehensive for his life), 1443.--2) to mourn, grieve : pres. part. him wäs ... murnende môd, 50; pres. subj., þonne he fela murne (than that he should mourn much), 1386.

be-murnan, be-meornan, with acc., to mourn over : pret. be-mearn, 908, 1078.

murn-lîce. See un-murn-lîce.

mûð-bana, w. m., mouth-destroyer : dat. sg. tô mûð-bonan (of Grendel because he bit his victim to death), 2080.

mûða, w. m., mouth, entrance : acc. sg. recedes mûðan (mouth of the house, door), 725.

ge-mynd, st. f., memory, memorial, remembrance : dat. pl. tô gemyndum, 2805, 3017. See weorð-mynd.

myhdgian, w. v., to call to mind, remember : pres. sg. myndgað, 2058; pres. part. w. gen. gif þonne Fresna hwylc ... þäs morðor-hetes myndgiend wære (were to call to mind the bloody feud), 1106.

ge-myndgian, w. v. w. acc., to remember : bið gemyndgad ... eaforan ellor-sîð (is reminded of his son's decease), 2451.

ge-myndig, adj., mindful : nom. sg. w. gen., 614, 869, 1174, 1531, 2083, etc.

myne, st. m.: 1) mind, wish : nom. sg., 2573.--2) love (?): ne his myne wisse (whose [God's] love he knew not), 169.

ge-mynian, w. v. w. acc., to be mindful of : imper. sg. gemyne mærðo! 660.

myntan, w. v., to intend, think of, resolve : pret. sg. mynte ... manna cynnes sumne besyrwan (meant to entrap all (?) [see sum], some one of (?), the men), 713; mynte þät he gedælde ... (thought to sever), 732; mynte se mæra, þær he meahte swâ, wîdre gewindan (intended to flee), 763.

myrce, adj., murky, dark : acc. sg. ofer myrcan môr, 1406.

myrð, st. f., joy, mirth : dat. (instr.) sg. môdes myrðe, 8n.

N

naca, w. m., vessel, ship : acc. sg. nacan, 295; gen. sg. nacan, 214.--Comp.: hring-, ýð-naca.

nacod, adj., naked : nom. and acc. sg. swurd, gûð-bill nacod, 539, 2586; nacod nîð-draca, 2274.

nalas, nales, nallas. See nealles.

nama, w. m., name : nom. sg. Beówulf is mîn nama, 343; wäs þäm häft-mêce Hrunting nama, 1458; acc. sg. scôp him Heort naman (gave it the name Hart), 78.

nâ (from ne-â), strength, negative, never, not all , 445, 567, 1537.

nâh, from ne-âh. See âgan.

nân (from ne-ân), indef. pron., none, no : with gen. pl. gûð-billa nân, 804; adjectively, nân ... îren ærgôd, 990.

nât, from ne-wât: I know not=nescio . See witan.

nât-hwylc (nescio quis, ne-wât-hwylc, know not who, which , etc.), indef. pron., any, a certain one, some or other : 1) w. partitive gen.: nom. sg. gumena nât-hwylc, 2234;. gen. sg. nât-hwylces (þâra banena), 2054; niða nât-hwylces(?), 2216; nât-hwylces häleða bearna, 2225.--2) adjectively: dat. sg. in nið-sele nât-hwylcum, 1514.

näbben, from ne-häbben (subj. pres.). See habban.

näfne. See nefne.

nägel, st. m., nail : gen. pl. nägla (of the finger-nails), 986.

nägled, part., nailed?, nail-like?, buckled? : acc. sg. neut. nägled (MS. gled) sinc, 2024.

näs, st. m., naze, rock projecting into the sea, cliff, promontory : acc. sg. näs, 1440, 1601, 2899; dat. sg. nässe, 2244, 2418; acc. pl. windige nässas, 1412; gen. pl. nässa, 1361.

näs, from ne-wäs (was not). See wesan.

näs, neg. adv., not, not at all , 562, 2263.

näs-hlið, st. n., declivity, slope of a promontory that sinks downward to the sea : dat. pl. on näs-hleoðum, 1428.

næfre, adv., never , 247, 583, 592, 656, 719, 1042, 1049, etc.; also strengthened by ne: næfre ne, 1461.

ge-nægan, w. v. w. acc. pers. and gen. of thing, to attack, press ; pret. pl. nîða genægdan nefan Hererîces (in combats pressed hard upon H.'s nephew), 2207; pret. part. wearð ... nîða genæged, 1440.

nænig (from ne-ænig), pron., not any, none, no : 1) substantively w. gen. pl.: nom. sg., 157, 242, 692; dat. sg. nænegum, 599; gen. pl. nænigra, 950.--2) adjectively: nom. sg. ôðer nænig, 860; nænig wäter, 1515; nænig ... deór, 1934; acc. sg. nænigne ... hord-mâððum, 1199.

nære, from ne-wære (were not, would not be). See wesan.

ne, simple neg., not , 38, 50, 80, 83, 109, etc.; before imper. ne sorga! 1385; ne gým! 1761, etc. Doubled = certainly not, not even that : ne ge ... gearwe ne wisson (ye certainly have not known , etc.), 245; so, 863; ne ic ... wihte ne wêne (nor do I at all in the least expect), 2923; so, 182. Strengthened by other neg.: nôðer ... ne, 2125; swâ he ne mihte nô ... (so that he absolutely could not), 1509.

ne ... ne, not ... and not, nor; neither ... nor , 154-157, 511, 1083-1085, etc. Another neg. may supply the place of the first ne: so, nô ... ne, 575-577, 1026-1028, 1393-1395, etc.; næfre ... ne, 583-584; nalles ... ne, 3016-3017. The neg. may be omitted the first time: ær ne siððan (neither before nor after, before nor since), 719; sûð ne norð (south nor north), 859; âdl ne yldo (neither illness nor old age), 1737; wordum ne worcum (neither by word nor deed), 1101; wiston and ne wêndon (knew not and weened not), 1605.

 nefa, w. m., nephew, grandson : nom. sg. nefa (grandson), 1204; so, 1963; (nephew), 2171; acc. sg. nefan (nephew), 2207; dat. sg. nefan (nephew), 882.

 nefne, näfne, nemne (orig. from ne-gif-ne): 1) subj.: a) with depend. clause = unless : nefne him witig god wyrd forstôde (if fate, the wise God, had not prevented him), 1057; nefne god sylfa ... sealde (unless God himself , etc.), 3055; näfne him his wlite leóge (MS. næfre) (unless his face belie him), 250; näfne he wäs mâra (except that he was huger), 1354; nemne him heaðo-byrne helpe ge-fremede, 1553; so, 2655.--b) w. follow. substantive = except, save, only : nefne sin-freá (except the husband), 1935; ic lyt hafo heáfod-mâga nefne Hygelâc þec (have no near kin but thee), 2152; nis þät eówer (gen. pl.) sîð ... nefne mîn ânes, 2534.--2) Prep. with dat., except : nemne feáum ânum, 1082.

 ge-nehost. See ge-neahhe.

 nelle, from ne-wille (I will not). See willan.

 nemnan, w. v. w. acc.: 1) to name, call : pres. pl. þone yldestan oret-mecgas Beówulf nemnað (the warriors call the most distinguished one Beówulf), 364; so inf. nemnan, 2024; pret. pl. nemdon, 1355.--2) to address , as in

 be-nemnan, to pronounce solemnly, put under a spell : pret. sg. Fin Hengeste ... âðum be-nemde þät (asserted, promised under oath that ...), 1098; pret. pl. swâ hit ôð dômes däg diópe benemdon þeódnas mære (put under a curse), 3070.

 nemne. See nefne.

 nerian, ge-nerian, w. v., to save, rescue, liberate : pres. sg. Wyrd oft nereð unfægne eorl, 573; pret. part. häfde ... sele Hrôðgâres ge-nered wið nîðe (saved from hostility), 828.

 ge-nesan, st. v.: 1) intrans., to remain over, be preserved : pret. sg. hrôf âna genäs ealles ansund (the roof alone was quite sound), 1000.--2) w. acc., to endure successfully, survive, escape from : pret. sg. se þâ säcce ge-näs, 1978; fela ic ... gûð-ræsa ge-näs, 2427; pret. part. swâ he nîða gehwane genesen häfde, 2398.

 net, st. n., net : in comp. breóst-, here-, hring-, inwit-, searo-net.

 nêdla, w. m., dire necessity, distress : in comp. þreá-nêdla.

 nêðan (G. nanþjan), w. v., to venture, undertake boldly : pres. part. nearo nêðende (encountering peril), 2351; pret. pl. þær git ... on deóp water aldrum nêðdon (where ye two risked your lives in the deep water), 510; so, 538.

 ge-nêðan, the same: inf. ne dorste under ýða gewin aldre ge-nêðan, 1470. With depend. clause: nænig þät dorste genêðan þät (none durst undertake to ...), 1934; pret. sg. he under hârne stân âna genêðde frêcne dæde (he risked alone the bold deed, venturing under the grey rock), 889; (ic) wîge under wätere weorc genêðde earfoð-lîce (I with difficulty stood the work under the water in battle , i.e. could hardly win the victory), 1657; ic genêðde fela gûða (ventured on, risked, many contests), 2512; pres. pl. (of majesty) we ... frêcne genêðdon eafoð uncûðes (we have boldly risked, dared, the monster's power), 961.

 nêh. See neáh.

 ge-neahhe, adv., enough, sufficiently , 784, 3153; superl. genehost brägd eorl Beówulfes ealde lâfe (many an earl of B.'s), 795.

nealles (from ne-ealles), adv., omnino non, not at all, by no means : nealles, 2146, 2168, 2180, 2223, 2597, etc.; nallas, 1720, 1750; nalles, 338, 1019, 1077, 1443, 2504, etc.; nalas, 43, 1494, 1530, 1538; nales, 1812.

nearo, st. n., strait, danger, distress : acc. sg. nearo, 2351, 2595.

nearo, adj., narrow : acc. pl. f. nearwe, 1410.

nearwe, adv., narrowly , 977.

nearo-cräft, st. m., art of rendering difficult of access?, inaccessibility (see 2214 seqq.): instr. pl. nearo-cräftum, 2244.

nearo-fâh, m., foe that causes distress, war-foe : gen. sg. nearo-fâges, 2318.

nearo-þearf, st. f., dire need, distress : acc. sg. nearo-þearfe, 422.

ge-nearwian, w. v., to drive into a corner, press upon : pret. part. genearwod, 1439.

neáh, nêh: 1) adj., near, nigh : nom. sg. neáh, 1744, 2729. In superl. also = last : instr. sg. nýhstan sîðe (for the last time), 1204; niéhstan sîðe, 2512.   2) adv., near : feor and (oððe) neáh, 1222, 2871; 3) prep, sæ-grunde neáh, 564; so, 1925, 2243; holm-wylme nêh, 2412. Compar. neár, 746.

neán, adv., near by, (from) close at hand , 528; (neon, MS.), 3105; feorran and neán, 840; neán and feorran, 1175, 2318.

ge-neát, st. m., comrade, companion : in comp. beód-, heorð-geneát. nioðor. See niðer.

neowol, adj., steep, precipitous : acc. pl. neowle, 1412.

neód, st. f., polite intercourse regulated by etiquette?, hall-joy? : acc. sg. nióde, 2117; inst. (= joy), 2216.

neód-laðu, st. f., polite invitation; wish : dat. sg. äfter neód-laðu (according to his wishes), 1321.

neósan, neósian, w. v. w. gen., to seek out, look for; to attack : inf. neósan, 125, 1787, 1792, 1807, 2075; niósan, 2389, 2672; neósian, 115, 1126; niósian, 3046; pret. sg. niósade, 2487.

neótan, st. v., to take, accept , w. gen.; to use, enjoy : imper. sg. neót, 1218.

be-neótan, w. dat., to rob, deprive of : inf. hine aldre be-neótan, 681; pret. sg. cyning ealdre bi-neát (deprived the king of life), 2397.

nicor, st. m., sea-horse, walrus, sea-monster (cf. Bugge in Zacher's Journal, 4, 197): acc. pl. niceras, 422, 575; nicras, 1428; gen. pl. nicera, 846.

nicor-hûs, st. n., house or den of sea-monsters : gen. pl. nicor-hûsa, 1412.

nið st. m., man, human being : gen. pl. niðða, 1006; niða? (passage corrupt), 2216.

niðer, nyðer, neoðor, adv., down, downward : niðer, 1361; nioðor, 2700; nyðer, 3045.

nið-sele, st. m., hall, room, in the deep (Grein): dat. sg. [in] nið-sele nât-hwylcum, 1514.

nigen, num., nine : acc. nigene, 575.

niht, st. f. night : nom. sg., 115, 547. 650, 1321, 2117; acc. sg. niht, 135, 737, 2939; gystran niht (yester-night), 1335; dat. sg. on niht, 575, 684; on wanre niht, 703; gen. sg. nihtes hwîlum (sometimes at night, in the hours of the night), 3045; as adv. = of a night, by night , G. nachts, 422, 2274; däges and nihtes, 2270; acc. pl. seofon niht (se'nnight, seven days , cf. Tac. Germ, 11), 517; dat. pl. sweartum nihtum, 167; deorcum nihtum, 275, 221; gen. pl. nihta, 545, 1366.--Comp.: middel-, sin-niht.

niht-bealu, st. n., night-bale, destruction by night : gen. pl. niht-bealwa, 193.

niht-helm, st. m., veil or canopy of night : nom. sg., 1790.

484

niht-long, adj., lasting through the night : acc. sg. m. niht-longne first (space of a night), 528.

niht-weorc, st. n., night-work, deed done at night : instr. sg. niht-weorce, 828.

niman, st. v. w. acc.: 1) to take, hold, seize, undertake : pret. sg. nam þâ mid handa hige-þihtigne rinc, 747; pret. pl. we . . . nióde nâman, 2117.--2) to take, take away, deprive of : pres. sg. se þe hine deáð nimeð (he whom death carrieth off), 441; so, 447; nymeð, 1847; nymeð nýd-bâde, 599; subj. pres. gif mec hild nime, 452, 1482; pret. sg. ind. nam on Ongenþió îren-byrnan, 2987; ne nom he ... mâðm-æhta mâ (he took no more of the rich treasures), 1613; pret. part. þâ wäs ... seó cwên numen (the queen carried off), 1154.

be-niman, to deprive of : pret. sg. ôð þät hine yldo benam mägenes wynnum (till age bereft him of joy in his strength), 1887.

for-niman, to carry off : pres. sg. þe þâ deáð for-nam (whom death carried off), 488; so, 557, 696, 1081, 1124, 1206, 1437, etc. Also, dat. for acc.: pret. pl. him îrenna ecge fornâmon, 2829.

ge-niman: 1) to take, seize : pret. sg. (hine) be healse ge-nam (clasped him around the neck, embraced him), 1873.--2) to take, take away : pret. on reste genam þritig þegna, 122; heó under heolfre genam cûðe folme, 1303; segn eác genom, 2777; þâ mec sinca baldor ... ät mînum fäder genam (took me at my father's hands, adopted me), 2430; pret. part. genumen, 3167.

ge-nip, st. n., darkness, mist, cloud : acc. pl. under nässa genipu, 1361; ofer flôda genipu, 2809.

nis, from ne-is (is not): see wesan.

niwe, niówe, adj., new, novel; unheard-of : nom. sg. swêg up â-stâg niwe geneahhe (a monstrous hubbub arose), 784; beorh ... niwe (a newly-raised(?) grave-mound), 2244; acc. sg. niwe sibbe (the new kinship), 950; instr. sg. niwan stefne (properly, novâ voce; here = de novo, iterum, again), 2595; niówan stefne (again), 1790; gen. pl. niwra spella (new tidings), 2899.

ge-niwian, w. v., to renew : pret. part. ge-niwod, 1304, 1323; geniwad, 2288.

niw-tyrwed, pret. part., newly-tarred : acc. sg. niw-tyrwedne (-tyrwydne, MS.) nacan, 295.

nîð, st. m., properly only zeal, endeavor ; then hostile endeavor, hostility, battle, war : nom. sg., 2318; acc. sg. nîð, 184, 276; Wedera nîð (enmity against the W., the sorrows of the Wedera), 423; dat. sg. wið (ät) nîðe, 828, 2586; instr. nîðe, 2681; gen. pl. nîða, 883, 2351, 2398, etc.; also instr. = by, in, battle , 846, 1440, 1963, 2171, 2207.--Comp.: bealo-, fær-, here-, hete-, inwit-, searo-, wäl-nîð.

nîð-draca, w. m., battle-dragon : nom. sg., 2274.

nîð-gast, st. m., hostile alien, fell demon : acc. sg. þone nîð-gäst (the dragon), 2700.

nîð-geweorc, st. n., work of enmity, deed of evil : gen. pl. -geweorca, 684.

nîð-grim, adj., furious in battle, savage : nom. sg., 193.

nîð-heard, adj., valiant in war : nom. sg., 2418.

nîð-hydig, adj., eager for battle, valorous : nom. pl. nîð-hydige men, 3167.

ge-nîðla, w. m., foe, persecutor, waylayer : in comp. ferhð-, feorh-genîðla.

nîð-wundor, st. n., hostile wonder, strange marvel of evil : acc. sg., 1366.

nîpan, st. v., to veil, cover over, obscure : pres. part. nîpende niht, 547, 650.

nolde, from ne-wolde (would not); see willan.

norð, adv., northward , 859.

norðan, adv., from the north , 547.

nose, w. f., projection, cliff, cape : dat. sg. of hliðes nosan, 1893; ät brimes nosan, 2804.

nô (strengthened neg.), not, not at all, by no means, 136, 244, 587, 755, 842, 969, 1736, etc.; strengthened by following ne, 459(?), 1509; nô ... nô (neither ... nor), 541-543; so, nô ... ne, 168. See ne.

nôðer (from nâ-hwäðer), neg., and not, nor, 2125.

ge-nôh, adj., sufficient, enough : acc. sg. fæhðo genôge, 2490; acc. pl. genôge ... beágas, 3105.

nôn, st. f., [Eng. noon], ninth hour of the day, three o'clock in the afternoon of our reckoning (the day was reckoned from six o'clock in the morning; cf. Bouterwek Screádunga, 24 2 : we hâtað ænne däg fram sunnan upgange ôð æfen): nom. sg. nôn, 1601.

nu, adv.: 1) now, at present, 251, 254, 375, 395, 424, 426, 489, etc.: nu gyt (up to now, hitherto), 957; nu gen (now still, yet), 2860; (now yet, still), 3169.--2) conj., since, inasmuch as : nu þu lungre geong ... nu se wyrm ligeð (go now quickly, since the dragon lieth dead), 2746; so, 2248; þät þu me ne forwyrne ... nu ic þus feorran com (that do not thou refuse me, since I am come so far), 430; so, 1476; nu ic on mâðma hord mîne bebohte frôde feorh-lege, fremmað ge nu (as I now..., so do ye), 2800; so, 3021.

nymðe, conj. w. subj., if not, unless, 782; nymðe mec god scylde (if God had not shielded me), 1659.

nyt, st. f., duty, service, office, employment : acc. sg. þegn nytte beheóld (did his duty), 494; so, 3119.--Comp.: sund-, sundor-nyt.

nyt, adj., useful : acc. pl. m. nytte, 795; comp. un-nyt.

ge-nyttian, w. v., to make use of, enjoy : pret. part. häfde eorð-scrafa ende ge-nyttod (had enjoyed, made use of), 3047.

nýd, st. f., force, necessity, need, pain : acc. sg. þurh deáðes nýd, 2455; instr. sg. nýde, 1006. In comp. (like nýd-maga, consanguineus, in Æthelred's Laws, VI. 12, Schmid, p. 228; nêd-maga, in Cnut's Laws, I. 7, ibid., p. 258); also, tie of blood. --Comp. þreá-nýd.

ge-nýdan, w. v.: 1) to force, compel : pret. part. nîðe ge-nýded (forced by hostile power), 2681.--2) to force upon : pret. part. acc. sg. f. nýde genýdde ... gearwe stôwe (the inevitable place prepared for each, i.e. the bed of death), 1006.

nýd-bâd, st. f., forced pledge, pledge demanded by force : acc. pl. nýd-bâde, 599.

nýd-gestealla, w. m., comrade in need or united by ties of blood : nom. pl. nýd-gesteallan, 883.

nýd-gripe, st. m., compelling grip : dat. sg. in nýd-gripe (mid-gripe, MS.), 977.

nýd-wracu, st. f., distressful persecution, great distress : nom. sg., 193.

nýhst. See neáh.

O

oððe, conj.: 1) or; otherwise, 283, 437, 636, 638, 694, 1492, 1765, etc.--2) and (?), till (?), 650, 2476, 3007.

of, prep. w. dat., from, off from : 1) from some point of view : ge-seah of wealle (from the wall), 229; so, 786; of hefene scîneð (shineth from heaven), 1572; of hliðes nosan gästas grêtte (from the cliff's projection), 1893; of þam leóma stôd (from which light streamed), 2770; þær wäs mâðma fela of feorwegum ... gelæded (from distant lands), 37; þâ com of môre (from the moor), 711, 922.--2) forth from, out of : hwearf of earde (wandered from his home, died), 56; so, 265, 855, 2472; þâ ic of searwum com (when I had escaped from the persecutions of the foe), 419; þâ him Hrôðgâr gewât ... ût of healle (out of the hall), 664; so, 2558, 2516; 1139, 2084, 2744; wudu-rêc â-stâh sweart of (ofer) swioðole (black wood-reek ascended from the smoking fire), 3145; (icge gold) â-häfen of horde (lifted from the hoard), 1109; lêt þâ of breóstum ... word ût faran (from his breast), 2551; dyde ... helm of hafelan (doffed his helmet), 673; so, 1130; sealdon wîn of wunder-fatum (presented wine from wondrous vessels), 1163; siððan hyne Hæðcyn of horn-bogan ... flâne geswencte (with an arrow shot from the horned bow), 2438; so, 1434. Prep. postponed: þâ he him of dyde îsern-byrnan (doffed his iron corselet), 672.

ofer, prep. w. dat. and acc., over, above : 1) w. dat, over (rest, locality): Wîglâf siteð ofer Biówulfe, 2908; ofer äðelinge, 1245; ofer eorðan, 248, 803, 2008; ofer wer-þeóde (over the earth, among mankind), 900; ofer ýðum, 1908; ofer hron-râde (over the sea), 10; so, 304, 1287, 1290, etc.; ofer ealowæge (over the beer-cup, drinking), 481.--2) w. acc. of motion: a) over (local): ofer ýðe (over the waves), 46, 1910; ofer swan-râde (over the swan-road, the sea), 200; ofer wægholm, 217; ofer geofenes be-gang, 362; so, 239, 240, 297, 393, 464, 471, etc.; ofer bolcan (over the gangway), 231; ofer landa fela (over many lands), 311; so, 1405, 1406; ofer heáhne hrôf (along upon (under?) the high roof), 984; ofer eormen-grund (over the whole earth), 860; ofer ealle (over all, on all sides), 2900, 650; so, 1718;--606, 900, 1706; ofer borda gebräc (over, above, the crashing of shields), 2260; ofer bord-(scild) weall, 2981, 3119. Temporal: ofer þâ niht (through the night, by night), 737. b) w. verbs of saying, speaking, about, of, concerning : he ofer benne spräc, 2725. c) beyond, over : ofer mîn ge-met (beyond my power), 2880;--hence, against, contrary to : he ofer willan gióng (went against his will), 2410; ofer ealde riht (against the ancient laws , i.e. the ten commandments), 2331;--also, without : wîg ofer wæpen (war sans, dispensing with, weapons), 686;--temporal = after : ofer eald-gewin (after long, ancient, suffering), 1782.

ofer-hygd, st. n., arrogance, pride, conceit : gen. pl. ofer-hygda, 1741; ofer-hyda, 1761.

ofer-mâðum, st. m., very rich treasure : dat. pl. ofer-mâðmum, 2994.

ofer-mägen, st. n., over-might, superior numbers : dat. sg. mid ofer-mägene, 2918.

ofer-þearf, st. f., dire distress, need : dat. sg. [for ofer] þea[rfe], 2227.

oft, adv., often , 4, 165, 444, 572, 858, 908, 1066, 1239, etc.; oft [nô] seldan, 2030; oft nalles æne, 3020; so, 1248, 1888. Compar. oftor, 1580. Superl. oftost, 1664.

om-, on-. See am-, an-.

ombiht. See ambiht.

oncer. See ancer.

ond. See and.

onsýn. See ansýn.

on, prep. w. dat. and acc., signifying primarily touching on, contact with : I. local, w. dat.: a) on, upon, in at (of exterior surface): on heáh-stede (in the high place), 285; on mînre êðel-tyrf (in my native place), 410; on þäm meðel-stede, 1083; so, 2004; on þam holmclife, 1422; so, 1428; on foldan (on earth), 1197; so, 1533, 2997; on þære medu-bence (on the mead-bench), 1053; beornas on blancum (the heroes on the dapple-greys), 857, etc.; on räste (in bed), 1299; on stapole

(at, near, the pillar), 927; on wealle, 892; on wage (on the wall), 1663; on þäm wäl-stenge (on the battle-lance), 1639; on eaxle (on his shoulder), 817, 1548; on bearme, 40; on breóstum, 552; on hafelan, 1522; on handa (in his hand), 495, 540; so, 555, 766; on him byrne scân (on him shone the corselet), 405; on ôre (at the front), 1042; on corðre (at the head of, among, his troop), 1154; scip on ancre (the ship at anchor), 303; þät he on heoðe ge-stôd (until he stood in the hall), 404; on fäder stäle (in a father's place), 1480; on ýðum (on the waves, in the water), 210, 421, 534, 1438; on holme, 543; on êg-streámum, 577; on segl-râde, 1438, etc.; on flôde, 1367. The prep. postponed: Freslondum on, 2358.--b) in, inside of (of inside surface): secg on searwum (a champion in armor), 249; so, 963; on wîg-geatwum, 368; (reced) on þäm se rîca bâd (in which the mighty one abode), 310; on Heorote (in Heorot), 475, 497, 594, 1303; on beór-sele, 492, 1095; on healle, 615, 643; so, 639, 1017, 1026, etc.; on burgum (in the cities, boroughs), 53; on helle, 101; on sefan mînum (in my mind), 473; on môde, 754; so, 755, 949, 1343, 1719, etc.; on aldre (in his vitals), 1435; on middan (in medio), 2706.--c) among, amid : on searwum (among the arms), 1558; on gemonge (among the troop), 1644; on þam leód-scipe (among the people), 2198; nymðe lîges fäðm swulge on swaðule (unless the embracing flame should swallow it in smoke), 783;-- in, with, touched by, possessing something : þâ wäs on sâlum sinces brytta (then was the dispenser of treasure in joy), 608; so, 644, 2015; wäs on hreón môde, 1308; on sweofote (in sleep), 1582, 2296; heó wäs on ôfste (she was in haste), 1293; so, 1736, 1870; þâ wäs on blôde brim weallende (there was the flood billowing in, with, blood), 848; (he) wäs on sunde (was a-swimming), 1619; wäs tô fore-mihtig feónd on fêðe (too powerful in speed), 971; þær wäs swîgra secg ... on gylpspræce (there was the champion more silent in his boasting speech), 982;-- in; full of, representing, something : on weres wästmum (in man's form), 1353.--d) attaching to , hence proceeding from; from something : ge-hýrde on Beówulfe fäst-rædne ge-þôht (heard in, from, B. the fixed resolve), 610; þät he ne mêtte ... on elran men mund-gripe mâran, 753;--hence, with verbs of taking: on räste genam (took from his bed), 122; so, 748, 2987; hit ær on þe gôde be-geâton (took it before from thee), 2249.--e) with : swâ hit lungre wearð on hyra sinc-gifan sâre ge-endod (as it, too, soon painfully came to an end with the dispenser of treasure), 2312.--f) by : mäg þonne on þäm golde ongitan Geáta dryhten (the lord of the Geatas may perceive by the gold), 1485.--g) to , after weorðan: þät he on fylle wearð (that he came to a fall), 1545.

With acc.: a) w. verbs of moving, doing, giving, seeing, etc., up to, on, upon, in : â-lêdon þâ leófne þeóden ... on bearm scipes, 35; on stefn (on wang) stigon, 212, 225; þâ him mid scoldon on flôdes æht feor ge-wîtan, 42; se þe wið Brecan wunne on sîdne sæ (who strovest in a swimming-match with B. on the broad sea), 507, cf. 516; þät ic on holma ge-þring eorlscipe efnde (that I should venture on the sea to do valiant deeds), 2133; on feónda geweald sîðian, 809; þâra þe on swylc starað, 997; so, 1781; on lufan læteð hworfan (lets him turn his thoughts to love?, to possessions?), 1729; him on môd bearn (came into his mind, occurred to him), 67; ræsde on þone rôfan (rushed on the powerful one), 2691; (cwom) on worðig (came into the palace), 1973; so, 27, 242, 253, 512, 539, 580, 677, 726, etc.; on weg (away), 764, 845, 1383, 1431, 2097.--b) towards, on : gôde gewyrcean ... on fäder wine (pl.), 21.--c) aim or object, to, for the object, for, as, in, on : on þearfe (in his need, in his strait), 1457; so, on hyra man-dryhtnes miclan þearfe, 2850; wrâðum on andan (as a terror to the foe), 709; Hrôðgâr maðelode him on andsware (said to him in reply), 1841; betst beado-rinca wäs on bæl gearu (on the pyre ready), 1110; wîg-heafolan bär freán on fultum (for help), 2663; wearð on bîd wrecen (forced to wait), 2963.--d) ground, reason, according to, in conformity with : rodera rædend hit on ryht gescêd (decided it in accordance with right), 1556; ne me swôr fela âða on unriht (swore no oaths unjustly, falsely), 2740; on spêd (skilfully), 874; nallas on gylp seleð fätte beágas (giveth no gold-wrought rings as he promised), 1750; on sînne selfes dôm (boastingly, at his own will), 2148; him eal worold wendeð on willan (according to his will), 1740.--e) w. verbs of buying, for, in exchange for : me ic on mâðma hord mîne be-bohte frôde feorh-lege (for the hoard of jewels), 2800.--f) of, as to : ic on Higelâce wât, Geáta dryhten (I know with respect to, as to, of, H.), 1831; so, 2651; þät heó on ænigne eorl ge-lýfde fyrena frôfre (that she should rely on any earl for help out of trouble), 628; þâ hie ge-trûwedon on twâ healfa (on both sides, mutually), 1096; so, 2064; þät þu him ondrædan ne þearft ... on þâ healfe (from, on this side), 1676.--g) after superlatives or virtual superlatives = among : näs ... sinc-mâððum sêlra (= þät wäs sinc-mâðma sêlest) on sweordes hâd (there was no better jewel in sword's shape , i.e. among all swords there was none better), 2194; se wäs Hrôðgâre häleða leófost on ge-sîðes hâd (dearest of men as, in the character of, follower , etc.), 1298.

II. Of time: a) w. dat., in, inside of, during, at : on fyrste (in time, within the time appointed), 76; on uhtan (at dawn), 126; on mergenne (at morn, on the morrow), 565, 2940; on niht, 575; on wanre niht, 703; on tyn dagum, 3161; so, 197, 719, 791, 1063, etc.; on geogoðe (in youth), 409, 466; on geogoð-feore, 537; so, 1844; on orlege (in, during, battle), 1327; hû lomp eów on lâde (on the way), 1988; on gange (in going, en route), 1885; on sweofote (in sleep), 1582.--b) w. acc., towards, about : on undern-mæl (in the morning, about midday), 1429; on morgen-tîd, 484, 518; on morgen, 838; on ende-stäf (toward the end, at last), 1754; oftor micle þonne on ænne sîð (far oftener than once), 1580.

III. With particles: him on efn (beside, alongside of, him), 2904; on innan (inside, within), 71, 1741, 1969, 2453, 2716; þær on innan (in there), 2090, 2215, 2245. With the relative þe often separated from its case: þe ic her on starie (that I here look on, at), 2797; þe ge þær on standað (that ye there stand in), 2867.

on-cýð (cf. Dietrich in Haupt's Zeits. XI., 412), st. f., pain, suffering : nom. sg., 1421; acc. sg. or pl. on-cýððe, 831.

on-drysne, adj., frightful, terrible : acc. sg. firen on-drysne, 1933.

onettan (for anettan, from root an-, Goth. inf. anan, to breathe, pant), w. v., to hasten : pret. pl. onetton, 306, 1804.

on-lîcnes, st. f., likeness, form, figure : nom. sg., 1352.

on-mêdla, w. m., pride, arrogance : dat. sg. for on-mêdlan, 2927. Cf. Bugge in Zacher's Zeits. 4, 218 seqq.

on-sæge, adj., tending to fall, fatal : nom. sg. þâ wäs Hondsció (dat.) hild on-sæge, 2077; Hæðcynne wearð ... gûð on-sæge, 2484.

on-weald, st. m., power, authority : acc. sg. (him) bega ge-hwäðres ... onweald ge-teáh (gave him power over, possession of, both), 1044.

open, adj., open : acc. sg. hord-wynne fond ... opene standan, 2272.

openian, w. v., to open , w. acc.: inf. openian, 3057.

orc (O.S. orc, Goth. aúrkei-s), st. m., crock, vessel, can : nom. pl. orcas, 3048; acc. pl. orcas, 2761.

orcnê, st. m., sea-monster : nom. pl. orcnêas, 112.

ord, st. n. point : nom. sg. ôð þät wordes ord breóst-hord þurh-bräc (till the word-point broke through his breast-hoard, came to utterance), 2792; acc. sg. ord (sword-point), 1550; dat. instr. orde (id.), 556; on orde (at the head of, in front [of a troop]), 2499, 3126.

ord-fruma, w. m., head lord, high prince : nom. sg., 263.

oret-mecg, st. m., champion, warrior, military retainer : nom. pl. oret-mecgas, 363, 481; acc. pl. oret-mecgas, 332.

oretta, w. m., champion, fighter, hero : nom. sg., 1533, 2539.

or-leg, st. n., war, battle : dat. sg. on orlege, 1327; gen. sg. or-leges, 2408.

or-leg-hwîl, st. f., time of battle, war-time : nom. sg. [or-leg]-hwîl, 2003; gen. sg. orleg-hwîle, 2912; gen. pl orleg-hwîla, 2428.

or-leahtre, adj., blameless : nom. sg 1887.

or-þanc (cf. Gloss. Aldhelm. mid or-þance = argumento in Haupt XI., 436; orþancum = machinamentis, ibid. 477; or-þanc-scipe = mechanica, 479), st. m., mechanical art, skill : instr. pl. or-þoncum, 2088; smiðes or-þancum, 406.

or-wêna, adj. (weak form), hopeless, despairing , w. gen.: aldres or-wêna (hopeless of life), 1003, 1566.

or-wearde, adj., unguarded, without watch or guard : adv., 3128.

oruð, st. n., breath, snorting : nom. sg., 2558; dat. oreðe, 2840.

Ô

ôð (Goth. und, O.H.G. unt, unz): 1) prep. w. acc., to, till, up to , only temporal: ôð þone ânne däg, 2400; ôð dômes däg, 3070; ô woruld-ende, 3084.--2) ôð þät, conj. w. depend, indicative clause, till, until , 9, 56, 66, 100, 145. 219, 296, 307, etc.

ôðer (Goth. anþar), num.: 1) one or other of two, a second , = alter: nom. sg. subs.: se ôðer, 2062; ôðer(one i.e. of my blood-relations, Hæðcyn and Hygelâc), 2482; ôðer ... ôðer (the one ... the other), 1350-1352. Adj.: ôðer ... mihtig mân-sceaða (the second mighty, fell foe , referring to 1350), 1339; se ôðer ... häle, 1816; fem. niht ôðer, 2118; neut. ôðer gear (the next, second, year), 1134; acc. sg. m. ôðerne, 653, 1861, 2441, 2485; þenden reáfode rinc ôðerne(whilst one warrior robbed the other , i.e. Eofor robbed Ongenþeów), 2986; neut. ôðer swylc(another such, an equal number), 1584; instr. sg. ôðre sîðe (for the second time, again), 2671, 3102; dat. sg. ôðrum, 815, 1030, 1166, 1229, 1472, 2168, 2172, etc.; gen. sg. m. ôðres dôgores, 219, 606; neut. ôðres, 1875.--2) another, a different one , = alius: nom. sg., subs. ôðer, 1756; ôðer nænig (no other), 860. Adj.: ænig ôðer man, 503, 534; so, 1561; ôðer in (a different house or room), 1301; acc. sg. ôðer flet, 1087; gen. sg. ôðres ... yrfe-weardes, 2452; acc. pl. ealo drincende ôðer sædan (ale drinkers said other things), 1946; acc. pl. neut. word ôðer, 871.

ôfer, st. m., shore : dat. sg. on ôfre, 1372.

ôfost, st. f., haste : nom. sg. ôfost is sêlest tô gecýðanne (haste is best to make known, best to say at once), 256; so, 3008; dat. sg. beó þu on ôfeste (ôfoste) (be in haste, hasten), 386, 2748; on ôfste, 1293; on ôfoste, 2784, 3091.

ôfost-lîce, adv., in haste, speedily , 3131.

ô-hwær, adv., anywhere , 1738, 2871.

ômig, adj., rusty : nom. sg., 2764; nom. pl. ômige, 3050.

ôr, st. n., beginning, origin; front : nom. sg., 1689; acc. sg., 2408; dat. sg. on ôre, 1042.

ô-wiht, anything, aught : instr. sg. ô-wihte (in any way), 1823, 2433.

P

pâd, st. f., dress ; in comp. here-pâd.

päð, st. m., path, road, way ; in comp. ân-päð.

plega, w. m., play, emulous contest ; lind-plega, 1074.

R

raðe, adv., quickly, immediately , 725, Cf. hrâðe.

rand, rond, st. m., shield : acc. sg, rand, 683; rond, 657, 2567, 2610; dat. ronde (rond, MS.), 2674; under rande, 1210; bî ronde, 2539; acc. pl. randas, 231; rondas, 326, 2654.--Comp.: bord-, hilde-, sîd-rand.

rand-häbbend, pres. part., shield-bearer , i.e. man at arms, warrior : gen. pl. rond-häbbendra, 862.

rand-wîga, w. m., shield-warrior, shield-bearing warrior : nom. sg., 1299; acc. sg. rand-wîgan, 1794.

râd, st. f., road, street ; in comp. hran-, segl-, swan-râd.

ge-râd, adj., clever, skilful, ready : acc. pl. neut. ge-râde, 874.

râp, st. m., rope, bond, fetter : in comp. wäl-râp.

râsian, w. v., to find, discover : pret. part. þâ wäs hord râsod, 2284.

räst. See rest.

rǽcan, w. v., to reach, reach after : pret. sg. rǽhte ongeán feónd mid folme (reached out his hand toward the foe), 748.

ge-rǽcan, to attain, strike, attack : pret. sg. hyne ... wǽpne ge-rǽhte (struck him with his sword), 2966; so, 556.

rǽd, st. m.: 1) advice, counsel, resolution; good counsel, help : nom. sg. nu is rǽd gelong eft ät þe ânum (now is help to be found with thee alone), 1377; acc. sg. rǽd, 172, 278, 3081.--2) advantage, gain, use : acc. sg. þät rǽd talað (counts that a gain), 2028; êcne rǽd (the eternal gain, everlasting life), 1202; acc. pl. êce rǽdas, 1761.--Comp.: folc-rǽd, and adj., ân-, fäst-rǽd.

rǽdan, st. v., to rule; reign; to possess : pres. part. rodera rǽdend (the ruler of the heavens), 1556; inf. þone þe þu mid rihte rǽdan sceoldest (that thou shouldst possess by rights), 2057; wolde dôm godes dǽdum rǽdan gumena gehwylcum (God's doom would rule over, dispose of, every man in deeds), 2859. See sele-rǽdend.

rǽd-bora, w. m. counsellor, adviser : nom. sg., 1326.

rǽden, st. f., order, arrangement, law : see Note on 1143; comp. worold-rǽden(?).

â-rǽran, w. v.: 1) to raise, lift up : pret. pl. þâ wǽron monige þe his mǽg ... ricone â-rǽrdon (there were many that lifted up his brother quickly), 2984.--2) figuratively, to spread, disseminate : pret. part. blǽd is â-rǽred (thy renown is far-spread), 1704.

rǽs, st. m., on-rush, attack, storm : acc. sg. gûðe rǽs (the storm of battle, attack), 2627; instr. pl. gûðe rǽsum, 2357.--Comp.: gûð-, hand-, heaðo-, mägen-, wäl-rǽs.

(ge-)rǽsan, w. v., to rush (upon) : pret. sg. rǽsde on þone rôfan, 2691, 2840.

rǽswa, w. m., prince, ruler : dat. sg. weoroda rǽswan, 60.

reccan, w. v., to explicate, recount, narrate : inf. frum-sceaft fira feorran reccan (recount the origin of man from ancient times), 91; gerund, tô lang is tô reccenne, hû ic ... (too long to tell how I ...), 2094; pret. sg. syllîc spell rehte (told a wondrous tale), 2111; so intrans. feorran rehte (told of olden times), 2107.

reced, st. n., building, house; hall (complete in itself): nom. sg., 412, 771, 1800; acc. sg., 1238; dat. sg. recede, 721, 729, 1573; gen. sg. recedes, 326, 725, 3089; gen. pl. receda, 310.--Comp.: eorð-, heal-, horn-, win-reced.

regn-heard, adj., immensely strong, firm : acc. pl. rondas regn-hearde, 326.

regnian, rênian, w. v., to prepare, bring on or about : inf. deáð rên[ian] hond-gesteallan (prepare death for his comrade), 2169.

ge-regnian, to prepare, deck out, adorn : pret. part. medu-benc monig ... golde ge-regnad, 778.

regn-, rên-weard, st. m., mighty guardian : nom. pl. rên-weardas (of Beówulf and Grendel contending for the possession of the hall), 771.

rest, räst, st. f.: 1) bed, resting-place : acc. sg. räste, 139; dat. sg. on räste (genam) (from his resting-place), 1299, 1586; tô räste (to bed), 1238. Comp.: flet-räst, sele-rest, wäl-rest.--2) repose, rest ; in comp. æfen-räst.

ge-reste (M.H.G. reste), f., resting-place : in comp. wind-gereste.

restan, w. v.: 1) to rest : inf. restan, 1794; pret. sg. reflex. reste hine þâ rûm-heort, 1800.--2) to rest, cease : inf., 1858.

rêc (O.H.G. rouh), st. m., reek, smoke : instr. sg. rêce, 3157.--Comp.: wäl-, wudu-rêc.

rêcan (O.H.G. ruohjan), w. v. w. gen., to reck, care about something, be anxious : pres. sg. III. wæpna ne rêceð (recketh not for weapons, weapons cannot hurt him), 434.

rêðe, adj., wroth, furious : nom. sg., 122, 1586; nom. pl. rêðe, 771. Also, of things, wild, rough, fierce : gen. sg. rêðes and-hâttres (fierce, penetrating heat), 2524.

reáf, st. n., booty, plunder in war; clothing, garments (as taken by the victor from the vanquished): in comp. heaðo-, wäl-reáf.

reáfian, w. v., to plunder, rob , w. acc.: inf. hord reáfian, 2774; pret. sg. þenden reáfode rinc ôðerne, 2986; wäl reáfode, 3028; pret. pl. wäl reáfedon, 1213.

be-reáfian, w. instr., to bereave, rob of : pret. part. since be-reáfod, 2747; golde be-reáfod, 3019.

reord, st. f., speech, language; tone of voice : acc. sg. on-cniów mannes reorde (knew, heard, a human voice), 2556.

reordian, w. v., to speak, talk : inf. fela reordian (speak much), 3026.

ge-reordian, to entertain, to prepare for : pret. part. þâ wäs eft swâ ær ... flet-sittendum fägere ge-reorded (again, as before, the guests were hospitably entertained), 1789

reót, st. m.?, f.?, noise, tumult ? (grave ?): instr. sg. reóte, 2458. Bugge, in Zachers Zeits. 4, 215, takes reóte as dat. from reót (rest, repose).

reóc, adj., savage, furious : nom. sg., 122.

be-reófan, st. v., to rob of, bereave : pret. part. w. instr. acc. sg. fem. golde berofene, 2932; instr. sg. reóte berofene, 2458.

reón. See rôwan.

reótan, st. v., to weep : pres. pl. ôð þät ... roderas reótað, 1377.

reów, adj., excited, fierce, wild : in comp. blôd-, gûð-, wäl-reów. See hreów.

ricone, hastily, quickly, immediately , 2984.

riht, st. n., right or privilege; the (abstract) right : acc. sg. on ryht (according to right), 1556; sôð and riht (truth and right), 1701; dat. sg. wið rihte, 144; äfter rihte (in accordance with right), 1050; syllîc spell rehte äfter rihte (told a wondrous tale truthfully), 2111; mid rihte, 2057; acc. pl. ealde riht (the ten commandments), 2331; --Comp. in êðel-, folc-, land-, un-, word-riht.

riht, adj., straight, right : in comp. up-riht.

rihte, adv., rightly, correctly , 1696. See ät-rihte.

rinc, st. m., man, warrior, hero : nom. sg., 399, 2986; also of Grendel, 721; acc. sg. rinc, 742, 748; dat. sg. rince, 953; of Hrôðgâr, 1678; gen. pl. rinca, 412, 729.-- Comp. in beado-, gûð-, here-, heaðo-, hilde-, mago-, sæ-rinc.

ge-risne, ge-rysne, adj., appropriate, proper : nom. sg. n. ge-rysne, 2654.

rîce, st. n.: 1) realm, land ruled over : nom. sg., 2200, 2208; acc. sg. rîce, 913, 1734, 1854, 3005; gen. sg. rîces, 862, 1391, 1860, 2028, 3081. Comp. Swió-rîce.-- 2) council of chiefs, the king with his chosen advisers (?): nom. sg. oft gesät rîce tô rûne, 172.

rîce, adj., mighty, powerful : nom. sg. (of Hrôðgâr), 1238; (of Hygelâc), 1210; (of Äsc-here), 1299; weak form, se rîca (Hrôðgâr), 310; (Beówulf), 399; (Hygelâc), 1976.--Comp. gimme-rîce.

rîcsian, rîxian, w. v. intrans., to rule, reign : inf. rîcsian, 2212; pret. sg. rîxode, 144.

rîdan, st. v., to ride : subj. pres. þät his byre rîde giong on galgan, 2446; pres. part. nom. pl. rîdend, 2458; inf. wicge rîdan, 234; mearum rîdan, 856; pret. sg. sægenga ... se þe on ancre râd, 1884; him tô-geánes râd (rode to meet them), 1894; pret. pl. ymbe hlæw riodan (rode round the grave-mound), 3171.

ge-rîdan, w. acc., to ride over : pret. sg. se þe näs ge-râd (who rode over the promontory), 2899.

rîm, st. n., series, number : in comp. däg-, un-rîm.

ge-rîm, st. n., series, number : in comp. dôgor-ge-rim.

ge-rîman, w. v., to count together, enumerate in all : pret. part. in comp. forð-gerîmed.

â-rîsan, st. v., to arise, rise : imper. sg. â-rîs, 1391; pret. sg. â-râs þâ se rîca, 399; so, 652, 1791, 3031; â-râs þâ bî ronde (arose by his shield), 2539; hwanan sió fæhð â-râs (whence the feud arose), 2404.

rodor, st. m., ether, firmament, sky (from radius ?, Bugge): gen. sg. rodores candel, 1573; nom. pl. roderas, 1377; dat. pl. under roderum, 310; gen. pl. rodera, 1556.

rôf, adj., fierce, of fierce, heroic, strength, strong : nom. sg., 2539; also with gen. mägenes rôf (strong in might), 2085; so, þeáh þe he rôf sîe nîð-geweorca, 683; acc. sg. rôfne, 1794; on þone rôfan, 2691.--Comp.: beadu-, brego-, ellen-, heaðo-, hyge-, sige-rôf.

rôt, adj., glad, joyous : in comp. un-rôt.

rôwan, st. v., to row (with the arms), swim : pret. pl. reón (for reówon), 512, 539.

rûm, st. m., space, room : nom. sg., 2691.

rûm, adj.: 1) roomy, spacious : nom. sg. þûhte him eall tô rûm, wongas and wîc-stede (fields and dwelling seemed to him all too broad , i.e. could not hide his shame at the unavenged death of his murdered son), 2462.--2) in moral sense, great, magnanimous, noble-hearted : acc. sg. þurh rûmne sefan, 278.

rûm-heort, adj., big-hearted, noble-spirited : nom. sg., 1800, 2111.

ge-rûm-lîc, adj., commodious, comfortable : compar. ge-rûm-lîcor, 139.

rûn, st. f., secrecy, secret discussion, deliberation or council : dat. sg. ge-sät rîce tô rûne, 172.--Comp. beado-rûn.

rûn-stäf, st. m., rune-stave, runic letter : acc. pl. þurh rûn-stafas, 1696.

rûn-wita, w. m., rune-wit, privy councillor, trusted adviser : nom. sg., 1326.

ge-rysne. See ge-risne.

ge-rýman, w. v.: 1) to make room for, prepare, provide room : pret. pl. þät hie him ôðer flet eal ge-rýmdon, 1087; pret. part. þâ wäs Geát-mäcgum ... benc gerýmed, 492; so, 1976.--2) to allow, grant, admit : pret. part. þâ me ge-rýmed wäs (sîð) (as access was permitted me), 3089; þâ him gerýmed wearð, þät hie wäl-stôwe wealdan môston, 2984.

S

ge-saca, w. m., opponent, antagonist, foe : acc. sg. ge-sacan, 1774.

sacan, st. v., to strive, contend : inf. ymb feorh sacan, 439.

ge-sacan, to attain, gain by contending (Grein): inf. gesacan sceal sâwl-berendra ... gearwe stôwe (gain the place prepared , i.e. the death-bed), 1005.

on-sacan: 1) (originally in a lawsuit), to withdraw, take away, deprive of : pres. subj. þätte freoðuwebbe feores on-säce ... leófne mannan, 1943.--2) to contest, dispute, withstand : inf. þät he sæmannum on-sacan mihte (i.e. hord, bearn, and brýde), 2955.

sacu, st. f., strife, hostility, feud : nom. sg., 1858, 2473; acc. sg. säce, 154; säcce, 1978, 1990, 2348, 2500, 2563; dat. sg. ät (tô) säcce, 954, 1619, 1666, 2613, 2660, 2682, 2687; gen. sg. secce, 601; gen. pl. säcca, 2030.

ge-sacu, st. f., strife, enmity : nom. sg., 1738.

sadol, st. m., saddle : nom. sg., 1039.

sadol-beorht, adj., with bright saddles (?): acc. pl. sadol-beorht, 2176.

ge-saga. See secgan.

samne, somne, adv., together, united ; in ät-somne, together, united , 307, 402, 491, 544, 2848.

tô-somne (together), 3123; þâ se wyrm ge-beáh snûde tô-somne (when the dragon quickly coiled together), 2569.

samod, somod: I. adv., simultaneously, at the same time : somod, 1212, 1615, 2175, 2988; samod, 2197; samod ät-gädere, 387, 730, 1064.--II. prep. w. dat., with, at the same time with : samod ær-däge (with the break of day), 1312; somod ær-däge, 2943.

sand, st. n., sand, sandy shore : dat. sg. on sande, 295, 1897, 3043(?); äfter sande (along the shore), 1965; wið sande, 213.

sang, st. m., song, cry, noise : nom. sg. sang, 1064; swutol sang scôpes, 90; acc. sg. sige-leásne sang (Grendel's cry of woe), 788; sârigne sang (Hrêðel's dirge for Herebeald), 2448.

sâl, st. m., rope : dat. sg. sâle, 1907; on sâle (sole, MS.), 302.

sâl. See sæl.

sâr, st. n., wound, pain (physical or spiritual): nom. sg. sâr, 976; sió sâr, 2469; acc. sg. sâr, 788; sâre, 2296; dat. (instr.) sg. sâre, 1252, 2312, 2747.--Comp. lîc-sâr.

sâr, adj., sore, painful : instr. pl. sârum wordum, 2059.

sâre, adv., sorely, heavily, ill , graviter: se þe him [sâ]re gesceôd (who injured him sorely), 2224.

sârig, adj., painful, woeful : acc. sg. sârigne sang, 2448.

sârig-ferð, adj., sore-hearted, grieved : nom. sg. sârig-ferð (Wîglâf), 2864.

sârig-môd, adj., sorrowful-minded, saddened : dat. pl. sârig-môdum, 2943.

sâr-lîc, adj., painful : nom. sg., 843; acc. sg. neut., 2110.

sâwol, sâwl, st. f., soul (the immortal principle as contrasted with lîf, the physical life): nom. sg. sâwol, 2821; acc. sg. sâwle, 184, 802; hæðene sâwle, 853; gen. sg. sâwele, 1743; sâwle, 2423.

sâwl-berend, pres. part., endowed with a soul, human being : gen. pl. sâwl-berendra, 1005.

sâwul-dreór, st. n., (blood gushing from the seat of the soul), soul-gore, heart's blood, life's blood : instr. sg. sâwul-drióre, 2694.

sâwul-leás, adj., soulless, lifeless : acc. sg. sâwol-leásne, 1407; sâwul-leásne, 3034.

sǽce, sǽcce. See sacu.

sǽd, adj., satiated, wearied : in comp. hilde-sǽd.

sǽl, st. n., habitable space, house , hall : dat. sg. sel, 167; sǽl, 307, 2076, 2265.

sǽld, st. n., hall, king's hall or palace : acc. sg. geond þät sǽld (Heorot), 1281.

sǽ, st. m. and f., sea, ocean : nom. sg., 579, 1224; acc. sg. on sîdne sǽ, 507; ofer sǽ, 2381; ofer sǽ sîde, 2395; dat. sg. tô sǽ, 318; on sǽ, 544; dat. pl. be sǽm tweonum, 859, 1298, 1686, 1957.

sǽ-bât, st. m., sea-boat : acc. sg., 634, 896.

sǽ-cyning, st. m., sea-king, king ruling the sea : gen. pl. sǽ-cyninga, 2383.

sǽ-deór, st. n., sea-beast, sea-monster : nom. sg., 1511.

sǽ-draca, w. m., sea-dragon : acc. pl. sǽ-dracan, 1427.

ge-sǽgan, w. v., to fell, slay : pret. part. häfdon eal-fela eotena cynnes sweordum ge-sǽged (felled with the sword), 885.

sǽge. See on-sǽge.

sǽ-genga, w. m., sea-goer , i.e. sea-going ship: nom. sg., 1883, 1909.

sǽ-geáp, adj., spacious (broad enough for the sea): nom. sg. sǽ-geáp naca, 1897.

sǽ-grund, st. m., sea-bottom, ocean-bottom : dat. sg. sǽ-grunde, 564.

sǽl, sâl, sêl, st. f.: 1) favorable opportunity, good or fit time : nom. sg. sǽl, 623, 1666, 2059; sǽl and mǽl, 1009; acc. sg. sêle, 1136; gen. pl. sǽla and mǽla, 1612.--2) Fate (?): see Note on l. 51.--3) happiness, joy : dat. pl. on sâlum, 608; sǽlum, 644, 1171, 1323. See sêl, adj.

ge-sǽlan, w. v., to turn out favorably, succeed : pret. sg. him ge-sǽlde þät ...(he was fortunate enough to , etc.), 891; so, 574; efne swylce mǽla, swylce hira man-dryhtne þearf ge-sǽlde (at such times as need disposed it for their lord), 1251.

sǽlan (see sâl), w. v., to tie, bind : pret. sg. sǽlde ... sîð-fäðme scip, 1918; pl. sǽ-wudu sǽldon, 226.

ge-sǽlan, to bind together, weave, interweave : pret. part. earm-beága fela searwum ge-sǽled (many curiously interwoven armlets , i.e. made of metal wire: see Guide to Scandinavian Antiquities, p. 48), 2765.

on-sǽlan, with acc., to unbind, unloose, open : on-sǽl meoto, sige-hrêð secgum (disclose thy views to the men, thy victor's courage ; or, thy presage of victory ?), 489.

sǽ-lâc, st. n., sea-gift, sea-booty : instr. sg. sǽ-lâce, 1625; acc. pl. þâs sǽ-lâc, 1653.

sǽ-lâd, st. f., sea-way, sea-journey : dat. sg. sǽ-lâde, 1140, 1158.

sǽ-lîðend, pres. part., seafarer : nom. pl. sǽ-lîðend, 411, 1819, 2807; sǽ-lîðende, 377.

sæ-man, m., sea-man, sea-warrior : dat. pl. sæ-mannum, 2955; gen. pl. sæ-manna, 329 (both times said of the Geátas).

sæmra, weak adj. compar., the worse, the weaker : nom. sg. sæmra, 2881; dat. sg. sæmran, 954.

sæ-mêðe, adj., sea-weary, exhausted by sea-travel : nom. pl. sæ-mêðe, 325.

sæ-näs, st. m., sea-promontory, cape, naze : acc. pl. sæ-nässas, 223, 571.

sæne, adj., careless, slow : compar. sg. nom. he on holme wäs sundes þê sænra, þe hyne swylt fornam (was the slower in swimming in the sea, whom death took away), 1437.

sæ-rinc, st. m., sea-warrior or hero : nom. sg., 691.

sæ-sîð, st. m., sea-way, path, journey : dat. sg. äfter sæ-sîðe, 1150.

sæ-wang, st. m., sea-shore or beach : acc. sg. sæ-wong, 1965.

sæ-weal, st. m., (sea-wall), seashore : dat. sg. sæ-wealle, 1925.

sæ-wudu, st. m., (sea-wood), vessel, ship : acc. sg. sæ-wudu, 226.

sæ-wylm, st. m., sea-surf, billow : acc. pl. ofer sæ-wylmas, 393.

scacan, sceacan, st. v., properly, to shake one's self ; hence, to go, glide, pass along or away : pres. sg. þonne mîn sceaceð lîf of lîce, 2743; inf. þâ com beorht [sunne] scacan [ofer grundas], (the bright sun came gliding over the fields), 1804; pret. sg. duguð ellor scôc (the chiefs are gone elsewhither , i.e. have died), 2255; þonne strǣla storm ... scôc ofer scild-weall (when the storm of arrows leapt over the wall of shields), 3119; pret. part. wäs hira blæd scacen (their bravest men had passed away), 1125; þâ wäs winter scacen (the winter was past), 1137; so, sceacen, 2307, 2728.

scadu, sceadu, st. f., shadow, concealing veil of night : acc. sg. under sceadu bregdan (i.e. kill), 708.

scadu-genga, w. m., shadow-goer, twilight-stalker (of Grendel): nom. sg. sceadu-genga, 704.

scadu-helm, st. m., shadow-helm, veil of darkness : gen. pl. scadu-helma ge-sceapu (shapes of the shadow, evil spirits wandering by night), 651.

scalu, st. f., retinue, band (part of an armed force); in comp. hand-scalu: mid his hand-scale (hond-scole), 1318, 1964.

scamian, w. v., to be ashamed : pres. part. nom. pl. scamiende, 2851; nô he þǣre feoh-gyfte ... scamigan þorfte (needed not be ashamed of his treasure-giving), 1027.

scawa (see sceáwlan), w. m., observer, visitor : nom. pl. scawan, 1896.

ge-scâd, st. n., difference, distinction : acc. sg. æg-hwäðres gescâd, worda and worca (difference between, of, both words and deeds), 288.

ge-scâdan, st. v., to decide, adjudge : pret. sg. rodera rædend hit on ryht gescêd (decided it in accordance with right), 1556.

scânan? See scînan, pret. pl. scionon, 303; the imaginary scânan having been abandoned.

ge-scäp-hwîle, st. f., fated hour, hour of death (appointed rest?) : dat. sg. tô gescäp-hwîle (at the fated hour), 26.

sceððan, w. v., to scathe, injure : inf. w. dat. pers., 1034; alder sceððan (hurt her life), 1525; þät on land Dena lâðra nænig mid scipherge sceððan ne meahte (injure through robber incursions), 243; pret. sg. þær him nænig wäter wihte ne sceðede, 1515.

ge-sceððan, the same: inf. þät him ... ne mihte eorres inwit-feng alder gesceððan, 1448.

scenc, st. m., vessel, can : in comp. medu-scenc.

scencan, w. v., to hand drink, pour out : pret. sg. scencte scîr wered, 496 (cf. skinker = cup-bearer).

scenne, w. f.?, sword-guard? : dat. pl. on þæm scennum scîran goldes, 1695.

sceran, st. v., to shear off, cleave, hew to pieces : pres. sg. þonne heoru bunden ... swîn ofer helme andweard scireð (hews off the boar-head on the helm), 1288.

ge-sceran, to divide, hew in two : pret. sg. helm oft ge-scär (often clove the helm in two), 1527; so, gescer, 2974.

scerwen, st. f.?, in comp. ealu-scerwen (ale-scare or panic ?), 770.

scêt. See sceótan.

sceadu. See scadu.

sceaða, w. m.: 1) scather, foe : gen. pl. sceaðena, 4.--2) fighter, warrior : nom. pl. scaðan, 1804.--Comp.: âttor-, dol-, feónd-, gûð-, hearm-, leód-, mân-, sin-, þeód-, uht-sceaða.

sceaðan, st. v. w. dat., to scathe, injure, crush : pret. sg. se þe oft manegum scôd (which has oft oppressed many), 1888.

ge-sceaðan, w. dat., the same: pret. sg. swâ him ær gescôd hild ät Heorote, 1588; se þe him sâre ge-sceôd (who injured him sorely), 2224; nô þý ær in gescôd hâlan lîce, 1503; bill ær gescôd eald-hlâfordes þam þâra mâðma mund-bora wäs (the weapon of the ancient chieftain had before laid low the dragon, the guardian of the treasure), 2778 (or, sheathed in brass ?, if ær and gescôd form compound).

sceaðen-mæl, st. n., deadly weapon, hostile sword : nom. sg., 1940.

sceaft, st. m., shaft, spear, missile : nom. sg. sceft, 3119.--Comp.: here-, wäl-sceaft.

ge-sceaft, st. f.: 1) creation, earth, earthly existence : acc. sg. þâs lænan ge-sceaft, 1623.--2) fate, destiny : in comp. forð-, lîf-, mæl-gesceaft.

scealc, st. m., servant, military retainer : nom. sg., 919; (of Beówulf), 940.--Comp beór-scealc.

ge-sceap, st. n.: 1) shape, creature : nom. pl. scadu-helma ge-sceapu, 651.--2) fate, providence : acc. sg. heáh ge-sceap (heavy fate), 3085.

sceapan, sceppan, scyppan, st. v., to shape, create, order, arrange, establish : pres. part. scyppend (the Creator), 106; pret. sg. scôp him Heort naman (shaped, gave, it the name Heorot), 78; pres. part. wäs sió wrôht scepen heard wið Hûgas, syððan Hygelâc cwom (the contest with the Hûgas became sharp after H. had come), 2915.

ge-sceapan, to shape, create : pret. sg. lîf ge-sceôp cynna gehwylcum, 97.

scear, st. m., massacre : in comp. gûð-, inwit-scear, 2429, etc.

scearp, adj., sharp, able, brave : nom. sg. scearp scyld-wîga, 288.--Comp.: beadu-, heaðo-scearp.

scearu, st. f., division, body, troop : in comp. folc-scearu; that is decided or determined, in gûð-scearu (overthrow ?), 1214.

sceat, st. m., money ; also unit of value in appraising (cf. Rieger in Zacher's Zeits. 3, 415): acc. pl. sceattas, 1687. When numbers are given, sceat appears to be left out, cf. 2196, 2995 (see þûsend).--Comp. gif-sceat.

sceát, st. m., region, field : acc. pl. gefrätwade foldan sceátas leomum and leáfum, 96;-- top, surface, part : gen. pl. eorðan sceáta, 753.

sceáwere, st. m., observer, spy : nom. pl. sceáweras, 253.

sceáwian, w. v. w. acc., to see, look at, observe : inf. sceáwian, 841, 1414, 2403, 2745, 3009, 3033; sceáwigan, 1392; pres. sg. II. þät ge genôge neán sceáwiað beágas and brâd gold, 3105; subj. pres. þät ic ... sceáwige swegle searo-gimmas, 2749; pret. sg. sceáwode, 1688, 2286, 2794; sg. for pl., 844; pret. pl. sceáwedon, 132, 204, 984, 1441.

ge-sceáwian, to see, behold, observe : pret. part. ge-sceáwod, 3076, 3085.

sceorp, st. n., garment : in comp. hilde-sceorp.

sceótan, st. v., to shoot, hurl missiles : pres. sg. se þe of flân-bogan fyrenum sceóteð, 1745; pres. part. nom. pl. sceótend (the warriors, bowmen), 704, 1155; dat. pl. for sceótendum (MS. scotenum), 1027.

ge-sceótan, w. acc., to shoot off, hurry : pret. sg. hord eft gesceát (the dragon darted again back to the treasure), 2320.

of-sceótan, to kill by shooting : pret. sg. his mæg of-scêt ... blôdigan gâre (killed his brother with bloody dart), 2440.

scild, scyld, st. m., shield : nom. sg. scyld, 2571; acc. sg. scyld, 437, 2076; acc. pl. scyldas, 325, 333, 2851.

scildan, scyldan, w. v., to shield, protect : pret. subj. nymðe mec god scylde (if God had not shielded me), 1659.

scild-freca, w. m., shield-warrior (warrior armed with a shield): nom. sg. scyld-freca, 1034.

scild-weall, st. m., wall of shields : acc. sg. scild-weall, 3119.

scild-wîga, w. m., shield-warrior : nom. sg. scyld-wîga, 288.

scinna, w. m., apparition, evil spirit : dat. pl. scynnum, 940.

scip, st. n., vessel, ship : nom. sg., 302; acc. sg., 1918; dat. sg. tô scipe, 1896; gen. sg. scipes, 35, 897; dat pl. tô scypum (scypon, MS.), 1155.

scip-here, st. m., (exercitus navalis) armada, fleet : dat. sg. mid scip-herge, 243.

ge-scîfe (for ge-scýfe), adj., advancing (of the dragon's movement), 2571; = G. schief ?

scînan, st. v., to shine, flash : pres. sg. sunne ... sûðan scîneð, 607; so, 1572; inf. geseah blâcne leóman beorhte scînan, 1518; pret. sg. (gûð-byrne, woruld--candel) scân, 321, 1966; on him byrne scân, 405; pret. pl. gold-fâg scinon web æfter wagum, 995; scionon, 303.

scîr, adj., sheer, pure, shining : nom. sg. hring-îren scîr, 322; scîr metod, 980; acc. sg. n. scîr wered, 496; gen. sg. scîran goldes, 1695.

scîr-ham, adj., bright-armored, clad in bright mail : nom. pl. scîr-hame, 1896.

scoten. See sceóten.

ge-scôd, pret. part., shod (calceatus), covered : in comp. ær-ge-scôd(?). See ge-sceaðan, and Note.

scôp, st. m., singer, shaper, poet : nom. sg., 496, 1067; gen. sg. scôpes, 90.

scræf, st. n., hole in the earth, cavern : in comp. eorð-scræf.

scrîðan, st. v., to stride, go : pres. pl. scrîðað, 163; inf. scrîðan, 651, 704; scrîðan tô, 2570.

scrîfan, st. v., to prescribe, impose (punishment): inf. hû him (Grendel) scîr metod scrîfan wille, 980.

for-scrîfan, w. dat. pers., to proscribe, condemn : pret. part. siððan him scyppend for-scrifen häfde, 106.

ge-scrîfan, to permit, prescribe : pret. sg. swâ him Wyrd ne ge-scrâf (as Weird did not permit him), 2575.

scrûd, st. m., clothing, covering; ornament : in comp. beadu-, byrdu-scrûd.

scucca, w. m., shadowy sprite, demon : dat. pl. scuccum, 940.

sculan, aux. v. w. inf.: 1) shall, must (obligation): pres. sg. I., III. sceal, 20, 24, 183, 251, 271, 287, 440, 978, 1005, 1173, 1387, 1535, etc.; scel, 455, 2805, 3011;

II. scealt, 589, 2667; subj. pres. scyle, 2658; scile, 3178; pret. ind. sg. I., III. scolde, 10, 806, 820, 966, 1071, 1444, 1450, etc.; sceolde, 2342, 2409, 2443, 2590, 2964; II. sceoldest, 2057; pl. scoldon, 41, 833, 1306, 1638; subj. pret. scolde, 1329, 1478; sceolde, 2709.--2) w. inf. following it expresses futurity, = shall, will : pres. sg. I., III. sceal beódan (shall offer), 384; so, 424, 438, 602, 637, 1061, 1707, 1856, 1863, 2070; sceall, 2499, 2509, etc.; II. scealt, 1708; pl. wit sculon, 684; subj. pret. scolde, 280, 692, 911; sceolde, 3069.--3) sculan sometimes forms a periphrastic phrase or circumlocution for a simple tense, usually with a slight feeling of obligation or necessity: pres. sg. he ge-wunian sceall (he inhabits; is said to inhabit?), 2276; pret. sg. se þe wäter-egesan wunian scolde, 1261; wäcnan scolde (was to awake), 85; se þone gomelan grêtan sceolde (was to, should, approach), 2422; þät se byrn-wîga bûgan sceolde (the corseleted warrior had to bow, fell), 2919; pl. þâ þe beado-grîman býwan sceoldon (they that had to polish or deck the battle-masks), 2258; so, 230, 705, 1068.--4) w. omitted inf., such as wesan, gangan: unc sceal worn fela mâðma ge-mænra (i.e. wesan). 1784; so, 2660; sceal se hearda helm ... fätum befeallen (i.e. wesan), 2256; ic him äfter sceal (i.e. gangan), 2817; subj. þonne þu forð scyle (i.e. gangan), 1180. A verb or inf. expressed in an antecedent clause is not again expressed with a subsequent sceal: gæð â Wyrd swâ hió scel (Weird goeth ever as it shall [go]), 455; gûð-bill ge-swâc swâ hit nô sceolde (i.e. ge-swîcan), 2586.

scûa, w. m., shadowy demon : in comp. deáð-scûa.

scûfan, st. v.: 1) intrans., to move forward, hasten : pret. part. þâ wäs morgen-leóht scofen and scynded, 919.--2) w. acc., to shove, push : pret. pl. guman ût scufon ... wudu bundenne (pushed the vessel from the land), 215; dracan scufun ... ofer weall-clif (pushed the dragon over the wall-like cliff), 3132. See wîd-scofen(?).

be-scûfan, w. acc., to push, thrust down, in : inf. wâ bið þäm þe sceal ... sâwle be-scûfan in fýres fäðm (woe to him that shall thrust his soul into fire's embrace), 184.

scûr, st. m., shower, battle-shower : in comp. îsern-scûr.

scûr-heard, adj., fight-hardened? (file-hardened?): nom. pl. scûr-heard, 1034.

scyld, scyldan. See scild, scildan.

scyldig, adj., under obligations or bound for; guilty of, w. gen. and instr.: ealdres (morðres) scyldig, 1339, 1684, 2062; synnum scyldig (guilty of evil deeds), 3072.

scyndan, w. v., to hasten : inf. scyndan, 2571; pret. part, scynded, 919

scynna. See scinna.

scyppend. See sceapan.

scyran, w. v., to arrange, decide : inf. þät hit sceaðen-mæl scyran môste (that the sword must decide it), 1940. O.N. skora, to score, decide .

scýne, adj., sheen, well-formed, beautiful : nom. sg. mägð scýne, 3017.

se, pron. dem. and article, the : m. nom., 79, 84, 86, 87, 90, 92, 102, etc.; fem, seó, 66, 146, etc.; neut. þät;--relative: se (who), 1611, 2866; se þe (he who), 2293; seó þe (she who), 1446; se þe (for seó þe), 1345, 1888, 2686; cf. 1261, 1498; (Grendel's mother, as a wild, demonic creature, is conceived now as man, now as woman: woman, as having borne a son; man, as the incarnation of savage cunning and power); se for seó, 2422; dat. sg. þam (for þam þe), 2780.

secce. See sacu.

secg, st. m., man, warrior, hero, spokesman (secgan?): nom. sg., 208, 872, 2228, 2407, etc.; (Beówulf) 249, 948, 1312, 1570, 1760, etc.; (Wulfgâr), 402; (Hûnferð), 981; (Wîglâf), 2864; acc. sg. sinnigne secg (Grendel's mother, cf. se), 1380; dat. sg. secge, 2020; nom. pl. secgas, 213, 2531, 3129; dat. pl. secgum, 490; gen. pl. secga, 634, 843, 997, 1673.

secg, st. f., sword (sedge?): acc. sg. secge, 685.

secgan, w. v., to say, speak : 1) w. acc.: pres. sg. gode ic þanc secge, 1998; so, 2796; pres. part. swâ se secg hwata secgende wäs lâðra spella (partitive gen.), 3029; inf. secgan, 582, 876, 881, 1050; pret. sg. sägde him þäs leánes þanc, 1810; pret. sg. II. hwät þu worn fela ... sägdest from his sîðe, 532.--2) without acc inf. swâ we sôðlîce secgan hýrdon, 273; pret. sg. sägde, 2633, 2900--3) w. depend. clause: pres. sg. ic secge, 591; pl. III. secgað, 411; inf. secgan, 51, 391, 943, 1347, 1701, 1819, 2865, 3027; gerund. tô secganne, 473, 1725; pret. sg. sägde, 90, 1176; pl. sägdon, 377, 2188; sædan, 1946.

â-secgan (edicere), to say out, deliver : inf. wille ic â-secgan suna Healfdenes ... mîn ærende, 344.

ge-secgan, to say, relate : imper. sg. II. ge-saga, 388; þät ic his ærest þe eft ge-sägde (that I should, after, tell thee its origin), 2158; pret. part. gesägd, 141; gesæd, 1697.

sefa, w. m., heart, mind, soul, spirit : nom. sg., 49, 490, 595, 2044, 2181, 2420, 2601, 2633; acc. sg. sefan, 278, 1727, 1843; dat. sg. sefan, 473, 1343, 1738.-- Comp. môd-sefa.

ge-segen, st. f., legend, tale : in comp. eald-ge-segen.

segl, st. n., sail : nom. sg., 1907.

segl-râd, st. f., sail-road , i.e. sea: dat. sg. on segl-râde, 1430.

segn, st. n., banner , vexillum: nom. sg., 2768, 2959; acc. sg. segen, 47, 1022; segn, 2777; dat. sg. under segne, 1205.--Comp. heáfod-segn.

sel, st. n., hall, palace . See säl.

seld, st. n., dwelling, house : in comp. medu-seld.

ge-selda, w. m., contubernalis, companion : acc. sg. geseldan, 1985.

seldan, adv., seldom : oft [nô] seldan, 2030.

seld-guma, w. m., house-man, home-stayer(?); common man?, house-carl? : nom. sg., 249.

sele, st. m. and n., building consisting of one apartment; apartment, room : nom. sg., 81, 411; acc. sg. sele, 827, 2353; dat. sg. tô sele, 323, 1641; in (on, tô) sele þam heán, 714, 920, 1017, 1985; on sele (in the den of the dragon), 3129.-- Comp.: beáh-, beór-, dryht-, eorð-, gest-, gold-, grund-, gûð-, heáh-, hring-, hrôf-, nið-, win-sele.

sele-dreám, st. m., hall-glee, joy in the hall : acc. sg. þâra þe þis lîf ofgeaf, gesâwon sele-dreám (referring to the joy of heaven?), 2253.

sele-ful, st. n., hall-goblet : acc. sg., 620.

sele-gyst, st. m., hall-guest, stranger in hall or house : acc. sg. þone sele-gyst, 1546.

sele-rædend, pres. part., hall-ruler, possessor of the hall : nom. pl., 51; acc. leóde mîne sele-rædende, 1347.

sele-rest, st. f., bed in the hall : acc. sg. sele-reste, 691.

sele-þegn, st. m., retainer, hall-thane, chamberlain : nom. sg., 1795.

sele-weard, st. m., hall-ward, guardian of the hall : acc. sg., 668.

self, sylf, pron., self : nom. sg. strong form, self, 1314, 1925 (? selfa); þu self, 595; þu þe self, 954; self cyning (the king himself, the king too), 921, 1011; sylf,

1965; in weak form, selfa, 1469; he selfa, 29, 1734; þäm þe him selfa deáh (that can rely upon, trust to, himself), 1840; seolfa, 3068; he sylfa, 505; god sylfa, 3055; acc. sg. m. selfne, 1606; hine selfne (himself), 962; hyne selfne (himself, reflex.), 2876; wið sylfne (beside), 1978; gen. sg. m. selfes, 701, 896; his selfes, 1148; on sînne sylfes dôm (at his own will), 2148; sylfes, 2224, 2361, 2640, 2711, 2777, 3014; his sylfes, 2014, 2326; fem. hire selfre, 1116; nom. pl. selfe, 419; Sûð-Dene sylfe, 1997.

ge-sella, w. m., house-companion, comrade : in comp. hand-gesella.

sellan, syllan, w. v.: 1) w. acc. of thing, dat. of pers., to give, deliver; permit, grant, present : pres. sg. III. seleð him on êðle eorðan wynne, 1731; inf. syllan, 2161, 2730; pret. sg. sealde, 72, 673, 1272, 1694, 1752, 2025, 2156, 2183, 2491, 2995; nefne god sylfa sealde þam þe he wolde hord openian (unless God himself gave to whom he would to open the hoard), 3056; pret. sg. II. sealdest, 1483.-- 2) to give, give up (only w. acc. of thing): ær he feorh seleð (he prefers to give up his life), 1371; nallas on gylp seleð fætte beágas (giveth out gold-wrought rings, etc.), 1750; pret. sg. sinc-fato sealde, 623; pl. byrelas sealdon wîn of wunder-fatum, 1162.

ge-sellan, w. acc. and dat. of pers., to give, deliver; grant, present : inf. ge-sellan, 1030; pret. sg. ge-sealde, 616, 1053, 1867, 1902, 2143, etc.

sel-lîc, syl-lîc (from seld-lîc), adj., strange, wondrous : nom. sg. glôf ... syllîc, 2087; acc. sg. n. syllîc spell, 2110; acc. pl. sellîce sæ-dracan, 1427. Compar. acc. sg. syllîcran wiht (the dragon), 3039.

semninga, adv., straightway, at once 645, 1641, 1768.

sendan, w. v. w. acc. of thing and dat. of pers., to send : pret. sg. þone god sende folce tô frôfre (whom God sent as a comfort to the people), 13; so, 471, 1843.

for-sendan, to send away, drive off pret. part. he wearð on feónda geweald ... snûde for-sended, 905.

on-sendan, to send forth, away , w. acc. of thing and dat. of pers.: imper. sg. on-scnd, 452, 1484; pret. sg. on-sende, 382; pl. þe hine ... forð on-sendon ænne ofer ýðe (who sent him forth alone over the sea), 45; pret. part. bealo-cwealm hafað fela feorh-cynna feorr on-sended, 2267.

sendan (cf. Gl. Aldhelm, sanda = ferculorum, epularum, in Haupt IX. 444), w. v., to feast, banquet : pres. sg. III. sendeð, 601.--Leo.

serce, syrce, w. f., sark, shirt of mail : nom. sg. syrce, 1112; nom. pl. syrcan, 226; acc. pl. græge syrcan, 334.--Comp.: beadu-, heoro-serce; here-, leoðo-, lîc-syrce.

sess, st. m., seat, place for sitting : dat. sg. sesse, 2718; þâ he bî sesse geóng (by the seat , i.e. before the dragon's lair), 2757.

setl, st. n., seat, settle : acc. sg., 2014; dat. sg. setle, 1233, 1783, 2020; gen. sg. setles, 1787; dat. pl. setlum, 1290.--Comp.: heáh-, hilde-, meodu-setl.

settan, w. v., to set : pret. sg. setton sæ-mêðe sîde scyldas ... wið þæs recedes weall (the sea-wearied ones set their broad shields against the wall of the hall), 325; so, 1243.

â-settan, to set, place, appoint : pret. pl. hie him â-setton segen [gyl]-denne heáh ofer heáfod, 47; pret. part. häfde kyninga wuldor Grendle tô-geánes ... sele-weard â-seted, 668.

be-settan, to set with, surround : pret. sg. (helm) besette swîn-lîcum (set the helm with swine-bodies), 1454.

ge-settan: 1) to set, set down : pret. part. swâ wäs ...þurh rûn-stafas rihte ge-mearcod, ge-seted and ge-sæd (thus was ... in rune-staves rightly marked, set down and said), 1697.--2) to set, ordain, create : pret. sg. ge-sette ... sunnan and mônan leóman tô leóhte land-bûendum, 94.--3) = componere, to lay aside, smooth over, appease : pret. sg. þät he mid þý wîfe wäl-fæhða ... dæl ... ge-sette, 2030.

sêcan, w. v., to follow after , hence: 1) to seek, strive for , w. acc.: pret. sg. sinc-fät sôhte (sought the costly cup), 2301; ne sôhte searo-nîðas, 2739; so, 3068. Without acc.: þonne his myne sôhte (than his wish demanded), 2573; hord-weard sôhte georne äfter grunde (the hoard-warden sought eagerly along the ground), 2294.--2) to look for, come or go some whither, attain something , w. acc.: pres. sg. III. se þe ... biorgas sêceð, 2273; subj. þeáh þe hæð-stapa holt-wudu sêce, 1370; imper. sêc gif þu dyrre (look for her , i.e. Grendel's mother, if thou dare), 1380; inf. sêcean, 200, 268, 646, 1598, 1870, 1990, 2514(?), 3103, etc.; sêcan, 665, 1451; drihten sêcean (seek, go to, the Lord), 187; sêcean wyn-leás wîc (Grendel was to seek a joyless place , i.e. Hell), 822; so, sêcan deófla gedräg, 757; sâwle sêcan (seek the life, kill), 802; so, sêcean sâwle hord, 2423; gerund. sächte tô sêceanne, 2563; pret. sg. I., III. sôhte, 139, 208, 376, 417, 2224; II. sôhtest, 458; pl. sôhton, 339.--3) to seek, attack : þe ûs sêceað tô Sweóna leóde, 3002; pret. pl. hine wräc-mäcgas ofer sæ sôhtan, 2381.

ge-sêcan: 1) to seek , w. acc.: inf. gif he gesêcean dear wîg ofer wæpen, 685.--2) to look for, come or go to attain , w. acc.: inf. ge-sêcean, 693; gerund, tô ge-sêcanne, 1923; pret. sg. ge-sôhte, 463, 520, 718, 1952; pret. part. nom. pl. feor-cýððe beóð sêlran ge-sôhte þam þe hine selfa deáh, 1840.--3) to seek with hostile intent, to attack : pres. sg. ge-sêceð 2516; pret. sg. ge-sôhte, 2347; pl. ge-sôhton, 2927; ge-sôhtan, 2205.

ofer-sêcan, w. acc., to surpass, outdo (in an attack): pres. sg. wäs sió hond tô strong, se þe mêca gehwane ... swenge ofer-sôhte, þonne he tô sächte bär wæpen wundrum heard (too strong was the hand, that surpassed every sword in stroke, when he [Beówulf] bore the wondrous weapon to battle , i.e. the hand was too strong for any sword; its strength made it useless in battle), 2687.

sêl, st. f. See sæl.

sêl, sæl, adj., good, excellent, fit , only in compar.: nom. sg. m. sêlra, 861, 2194; þæm þær sêlra wäs (to the one that was the better , i.e. Hygelâc), 2200; deáð bið sêlla þonne edwît-lîf, 2891; neut. sêlre, 1385; acc. sg. m. sêlran þe (a better than thee), 1851; sêlran, 1198; neut. þät sêlre, 1760; dat. sg. m. sêlran sweord-frecan, 1469; nom. pl. fem. sêlran, 1840. Superl., strong form: nom. sg. neut. sêlest, 173, 1060; hûsa sêlest, 146, 285, 936; ôfost is sêlest, 256; bolda sêlest, 2327; acc. sg. neut. hrägla sêlest, 454; hûsa sêlest, 659; billa sêlest, 1145;--weak form: nom. sg. m. reced sêlesta, 412; acc. sg. m. þone sêlestan, 1407, 2383; (þäs, MS.), 1957; dat. sg. m. þäm sêlestan, 1686; nom. pl. sêlestan, 416; acc. pl. þâ sêlestan, 3123.

sêl, compar. adv., better, fitter, more excellent , 1013, 2531; ne byð him wihte þê sêl (he shall be nought the better for it), 2278; so, 2688.

sealma (Frisian selma, in bed-selma), w. m., bed-chamber, sleeping-place : acc. sg. on sealman, 2461.

sealt, adj., salty : acc. sg. neut. ofer sealt wäter (the sea), 1990.

searo (G. sarwa, pl.), st. n.: 1) armor, accoutrements, war-gear : nom. pl. sæ-manna searo, 329; dat. pl. secg on searwum (a man, warrior, in panoply), 249, 2701; in (on) searwum, 323, 1558; 2531, 2569; instr. pl. searwum, 1814.--2) insidiae, ambuscade, waylaying, deception, battle : þâ ic of searwum cwom, fâh from feóndum, 419.--3) cunning, art, skill : instr. pl. sadol searwum fâh (saddle cunningly ornamented), 1039; earmbeága fela, searwum ge-sæled (many cunningly-linked armlets), 2765.--Comp. fyrd-, gûð-, inwit-searo.

searo-bend, st. f., band, bond, of curious workmanship : instr. pl. searo-bendum fäst, 2087.

searo-fâh, adj., cunningly inlaid, ornamented, with gold : nom. sg. here-byrne hondum ge-broden, sîd and searo-fâh, 1445.

searo-ge-þräc, st. n., heap of treasure-objects : acc. sg., 3103.

searo-gim, st. m., cunningly set gem, rich jewel : acc. pl. searo-gimmas, 2750; gen. pl. searo-gimma, 1158.

searo-grim, adj., cunning and fierce : nom. sg., 595.

searo-häbbend, pres. part. as subst., arms-bearing, warrior with his trappings : gen. pl. searo-häbbendra, 237.

searo-net, st. n., armor-net, shirt of mail, corselet : nom. sg., 406.

searo-nîð, st. m.: 1) cunning hostility, plot, wiles : acc. pl. searo-nîðas, 1201, 2739.--2) also, only hostility, feud, contest : acc. pl. searo-nîðas, 3068; gen. pl. searo-nîða, 582.

searo-þanc, st. m., ingenuity : instr. pl. searo-þoncum, 776.

searo-wundor, st. n., rare wonder : acc. sg., 921.

seax, st. n., shortsword, hip-knife; dagger : instr. sg. seaxe, 1546.--Comp. wäl-seax.

seax-ben, st. f., dagger-wound : instr. pl. siex-bennum, 2905.

seofon, num., seven , 517; seofan, 2196; decl. acc. syfone, 3123.

seomian, w. v.: 1) intrans., to be tied; lie at rest : inf. siomian, 2768; pret. sg. seomode, 302.--2) w. acc., to put in bonds, entrap, catch : pret. sg. duguðe and geogoðe seomade (cf. 2086-2092), 161.

seonu, st. f., sinew : nom. pl. seonowe, 818.

seóc, adj., feeble, weak; fatally ill : nom. sg. feorh-bennum seóc (of Beówulf, sick unto death), 2741; siex-bennum seóc (of the dead dragon), 2905; nom. pl. môdes seóce (sick of soul), 1604.--Comp.: ellen-, feorh-, heaðo-seóc.

seóðan, st. v. w. acc., to seethe, boil ; figuratively, be excited over, brood : pret. sg. ic þäs môd-ceare sorh-wylmum seáð (I pined in heart-grief for that), 1994; so, 190.

seóloð, st. m.?, bight, bay (cf. Dietrich in Haupt XI. 416): gen. pl. sióleða bigong (the realm of bights = the [surface of the] sea?), 2368.

seón, sýn, st. f., aspect, sight : in comp. wlite-, wundor-seón, an-sýn.

seón, st. v., to see : a) w. acc.: inf. searo-wunder seón, 921; so, 387, 1181, 1276, 3103; þær mäg nihta ge-hwæm nîð-wundor seón (there may every night be seen a repulsive marvel), 1366; pret. sg. ne seah ic ... heal-sittendra medudreám mâran, 2015.--b) w. acc. and predicate adj.: ne seah ic elþeódige þus manige men môdiglîcran, 336.--c) w. prep. or adv.: pret. sg. seah on enta ge-weorc, 2718; seah on un-leófe, 2864; pl. folc tô sægon (looked on), 1423.

ge-seón, to see, behold : a) w. acc.: pres. sg. III. se þe beáh ge-syhð, 2042; inf. ge-seón, 396, 571, 649, 962, 1079, etc.; pret. sg. geseah, 247, 927, 1558, 1614; pl. ge-sâwon, 1606, 2253.--b) w. acc. and predicate adj., pres. sg. III. ge-syhð ... on his suna bûre win-sele wêstne (sees in his son's house the wine-hall empty ; or, hall of friends ?), 2456.--c) w. inf.: pret. sg. ge-seah ... beran ofer bolcan beorhte randas (saw shining shields borne over the gang-plank), 229; pret. pl. mære mâððum-sweord monige ge-sâwon beforan beorn beran, 1024.--d) w. acc. and inf.: pret. sg. ge-seah, 729, 1517, 1586, 1663, 2543, 2605, etc.; pl. ge-sâwon, 221, 1348, 1426;

ge-sêgan, 3039; ge-sêgon, 3129.--e) w. depend. clause: inf. mäg þonne ... geseón sunu Hrêðles, þät ic (may the son of H. see that I...), 1486; pret. pl. ge-sâwon, 1592.

geond-seón, to see, look through, over , w. acc.: pret. sg. (ic) þät eall geond-seh, 3088.

ofer-seón, to see clearly, plainly : pret. pl. ofer-sâwon, 419.

on-seón, to look on, at , w. acc.: pret. pl. on-sâwon, 1651.

seówian, w. v., to sew, put together, link : pret. part. searo-net seówed smiðes or-þancum (the corselet woven by the smith's craft), 406.

sib, st. f., peace, friendship, relationship : nom. sg., 1165, 1858; sibb, 2601; acc. sibbe, 950, 2432, 2923; instr. sg. sibbe (in peace ?), 154.--Comp.: dryht-, friðo-sib.

sib-äðeling, st. m., nobilis consanguineus, kindred prince or nobleman : nom. pl. -äðelingas, 2709.

sibbe-gedryht, st. f., body of allied or related warriors : acc. sg. sibbe-gedriht (the Danes), 387; (the Geátas), 730.

siððan, syððan: 1) adv.: a) since, after, from now on, further , 142, 149, 283, 567, 1903, 2052, 2065, 2176, 2703, 2807, 2921; seoððan, 1876.--b) then, thereupon, after , 470, 686, 1454, 1557, 1690, 2208; seoððan, 1938; ær ne siððan (neither before nor after), 719.

2) Conj.: a) w. ind. pres., as soon as, when , 413, 605, 1785, 2889, 2912.--b) w. ind. pret., when, whilst , 835, 851, 1205, 1207, 1421, 1590, 2357, 2961, 2971, 3128; seoððan, 1776;-- since , 649, 657, 983, 1199, 1254, 1309, 2202;-- after , either with pluperf.: siððan him scyppend forscrifen häfde (after the Creator had proscribed him), 106; so, 1473; or with pret. = pluperf.: syððan niht becom (after night had come on), 115; so, 6, 132, 723, 887, 1078, 1149, 1236, 1262, 1282, 1979, 2013, 2125; or pret. and pluperf. together, 2104-2105.

siex. See seax.

sige-dryhten, st. m., lord of victory, victorious lord : nom. sg. sige-drihten, 391.

sige-eádig, adj., blest with victory, victorious : acc. sg. neut. sige-eádig bil, 1558.

sige-folc, st. n., victorious people, troop : gen. pl. sige-folca, 645.

sige-hrêð, st. f., confidence of victory (?): acc. sg., 490. See Note.

sige-hrêðig, adj., victorious : nom. sg., 94, 1598, 2757.

sige-hwîl, st. f., hour or day of victory : gen. sg. sige-hwîle, 2711.

sige-leás, adj., devoid of victory, defeated : acc. sg. sige-leásne sang, 788.

sige-rôf, adj., victorious : nom. sg., 620.

sige-þeód, st. f., victorious warrior troop : dat. sg. on sige-þeóde, 2205.

sige-wæpen, st. n., victor-weapon, sword : dat. pl. sige-wæpnum, 805.

sigl, st. n.: 1) sun : nom. sg. sigel, 1967.--2) sun-shaped ornament : acc. pl. siglu, 3165; sigle (bracteates of a necklace), 1201; gen. pl. sigla, 1158.--Comp. mâððum-sigl.

sigor, st. m., victory : gen. sg. sigores, 1022; gen. pl. sigora, 2876, 3056.--Comp.: hrêð-, wîg-sigor.

sigor-eádig, adj., victorious : nom. sg. sigor-eádig secg (of Beówulf), 1312, 2353.

sin. See syn.

sinc, st. n., treasure, jewel, property : nom. sg., 2765; acc. sg. sinc, 81, 1205, 1486, 2384, 2432; instr. sg. since, 1039, 1451, 1616, 1883, 2218, 2747; gen. sg. sinces, 608, 1171, 1923, 2072; gen. pl. sinca, 2429.

sinc-fâh, adj., treasure-decked : acc. sg. neut. weak form, sinc-fâge sel, 167.

sinc-fät, st. n., costly vessel : acc. sg., 2232, 2301;-- a costly object : acc. sg., 1201 (i.e. mene); acc. pl. sinc-fato, 623.

sinc-ge-streón, st. n., precious treasure, jewel of value : instr. pl. -gestreónum, 1093; gen. pl. -gestreóna, 1227.

sinc-gifa, w. m., jewel-giver, treasure-giver = prince, ruler : acc. sg. sinc-gyfan, 1013; dat. sg. sinc-gifan (of Beówulf), 2312; (of Äschere), 1343.

sinc-mâððum, st. m., treasure : nom. sg., 2194.

sinc-þego, f., acceptance, taking, of jewels : nom. sg., 2885.

sin-dolh, st. n., perpetual , i.e. incurable, wound : nom. sg. syn-dolh, 818.

sin-freá, w. m., wedded lord, husband : nom. sg., 1935.

sin-gal, adj., continual, lasting : acc. sg. fem, sin-gale säce, 154.

sin-gales, adv. gen. sg., continually, ever , 1778; syngales, 1136.

singala, adv. gen. pl., the same, 190.

singan, st. v., to sound, ring, sing : pret. sg. hring-îren scîr song in searwum (the ringed iron rang in the armor), 323; horn stundum song fûs-lîc f[yrd]-leóð (at times the horn rang forth a ready battle-song), 1424; scôp hwîlum sang (the singer sang at whiles), 496.

â-singan, to sing out, sing to an end : pret. part. leóð wäs â-sungen, 1160.

sin-here, st. m., (army without end ?), strong army, host : instr. sg. sin-herge, 2937.

sin-niht, st. f., perpetual night, night after night : acc. pl. sin-nihte (night after night), 161.

sin-sceaða, w. m., irreconcilable foe : nom. sg. syn-scaða, 708; acc. sg. syn-scaðan, 802.

sin-snæd, st. f., (continuous biting) bite after bite : dat. pl. syn-snædum swealh (swallowed bite after bite, in great bites), 744.

sittan, st. v.: 1) to sit : pres. sg. Wîglâf siteð ofer Biówulfe, 2907; imper. sg. site nu tô symle, 489; inf. þær swîð-ferhðe sittan eodon (whither the strong-minded went and sat), 493; eode ... tô hire freán sittan (went to sit by her lord), 642; pret. sg. on wicge sät (sat on the horse), 286; ät fôtum sät (sat at the feet), 500, 1167; þær Hrôðgâr sät (where H. sat), 356; so, 1191, 2895; he gewêrgad sät ... freán eaxlum neáh, 2854; pret. pl. sæton, 1165; gistas sêtan (MS. sêcan) ... and on mere staredon (the strangers sat and stared on the sea), 1603.--2) to be in a certain state or condition (quasi copula): pret. sg. mære þeóden ... unblîðe sät, 130.--Comp.: flet-, heal-sittend.

be-sittan, obsidere, to surround, besiege , w. acc.: besät þâ sin-herge sweorda lâfe wundum wêrge (then besieged he with a host the leavings of the sword, wound-weary), 2937.

for-sittan, obstrui, to pass away, fail : pres. sg. eágena bearhtm for-siteð (the light of the eyes passeth away), 1768.

ge-sittan: 1) to sit, sit together : pret. sg. monig-oft ge-sät rîce to rûne (very often sat the king deliberating with his council (see rîce), 171; wið earm ge-sät (supported himself upon his arm, sat on his arm ?), 750; fêða eal ge-sät (the whole troop sat down), 1425; ge-sät þâ wið sylfne (sat there beside, near to, him , i.e. Hygelâc), 1978;

ge-sät þâ on nässe, 2418; so, 2718; pret. part. (syððan) ... we tô symble ge-seten häfdon, 2105.--2) w. acc., to seat one's self upon or in something, to board : pret. sg. þâ ic ... sæ-bât ge-sät, 634.

of-sittan, w. acc., to sit over or upon : pret. sg. of-sät þâ þone sele-gyst, 1546.

ofer-sittan, w. acc., to dispense with, refrain from (cf. ofer, 2 [c]): pres. sg. I. þät ic wið þone gûð-flogan gylp ofer-sitte, 2529; inf. secge ofer-sittan, 685.

on-sittan (O.H.G. int-sizzan, to start from one's seat, to be startled), w. acc., to fear : inf. þâ fæhðe, atole ecg-þräce eówer leóde sîwðe onsittan to dread the hostility, the fierce contest, of your people , 598.

ymb-sittan, to sit around , w. acc.: pret. pl. (þät hie) ... symbel ymb-sæton (sat round the feast), 564. See ymb-sittend.

sîd, adj.: 1) wide, broad, spacious, large : nom. sg. (here-byrne, glôf) sîd, 1445, 2087; acc. sg. m. sîdne scyld, 437; on sîdne sæ, 507; fem. byrnan sîde (of a corselet extending over the legs), 1292; ofer sæ sîde, 2395; neut. sîde rîce, 1734, 2200; instr. sg. sîdan herge, 2348; acc. pl. sîde sæ-nässas, 223; sîde scyldas, 325; gen. pl. sîdra sorga (of great sorrows), 149.--2) in moral sense, great, noble : acc. sg. þurh sîdne sefan, 1727.

side, adv., far and wide, afar , 1224.

sîd-fäðme, adj., broad-bosomed : acc. sg. sîd-fäðme scip, 1918.

sîd-fäðmed, quasi pret. part., the same: nom. sg. sîd-fäðmed scip, 302.

sîd-rand, st. m., broad shield : nom. sg., 1290.

sîð (G. seþu-s), adj., late : superl. nom. sg. sîðast sige-hwîle (the last hour, day, of victory), 2711; dat. sg. ät sîðestan (in the end, at last), 3014.

sîð, adv. compar., later : ær and sîð (sooner and later, early and late), 2501.

sîð (G. sinþ-s), st. m.: 1) road, way, journey, expedition ; esp., road to battle : nom. sg., 501, 3059, 3090; näs þät êðe sîð (that was no easy road, task), 2587; so, þät wäs geócor sîð, 766; acc. sg. sîð, 353, 512, 909, 1279, 1430, 1967; instr. dat. sîðe, 532, 1952, 1994; gen. sg. sîðes, 579, 1476, 1795, 1909. Also, return : nom. sg., 1972.--2) undertaking, enterprise ; esp., battle-work : nom. sg. nis þät eówer sîð, 2533; ne bið swylc earges sîð (such is no coward's enterprise), 2542; acc. sg. sîð, 873. In pl.= adventures : nom. sîðas, 1987; acc. sîðas, 878; gen. sîða, 318.--3) time (as iterative): nom. sg. näs þät forma sîð (that was not the first time), 717, 1464; so, 1528, 2626; acc. sg. oftor micle þonne on ænne sîð, 1580; instr. sg. (forman, ôðre, þriddan) sîðe, 741, 1204, 2050, 2287, 2512, 2518, 2671, 2689, 3102.--Comp.: cear-, eft-, ellor-, gryre-, sæ-, wil-, wræc-sîð.

ge-sîð, st. m., comrade, follower : gen. sg. ge-sîðes, 1298; nom. pl. ge-sîðas, 29; acc. pl. ge-sîðas, 2041, 2519; dat. pl. ge-sîðum, 1314, 1925, 2633; gen. pl. ge-sîða, 1935.--Comp.: eald-, wil-gesîð.

sîð-fät, st. m., way, journey : acc. sg. þone sîð-fät, 202; dat. sg. sîð-fate, 2640.

sîð-fram, -from, adj., ready for the journey : nom. pl. sîð-frome, 1814.

sîðian, w. v., to journey, march : inf., 721, 809; pret. sg. sîðode, 2120.

for-sîðian, iter fatale inire (Grein): pret. sg. häfde þâ for-sîðod sunu Ecg-þeówes under gynne grund (would have found his death , etc.), 1551.

sîe, sý. See wesan.

sîgan, st. v., to descend, sink, incline : pret. pl. sigon ät-somne (descended together), 307; sigon þâ tô slæpe (they sank to sleep), 1252.

ge-sîgan, to sink, fall : inf. ge-sîgan ät sâcce (fall in battle), 2660.

sîn, poss. pron., his : acc. sg. m. sînne, 1961, 1985, 2284, 2790; dat. sg. sînum, 1508.

slæp, st. m., sleep : nom. sg., 1743; dat. sg. tô slæpe, 1252.

slæpan, st. v., to sleep : pres. part. nom. sg. slæpende, 2220; acc. sg. he gefêng ... slæpendne rinc (seized a sleeping warrior] , 742; acc. pl. slæpende frät folces Denigea fîftyne men (devoured, sleeping, fifteen of the people of the Danes), 1582.

sleac, adj., slack, lazy : nom. sg., 2188.

sleahan, sleán: 1) to strike, strike at : a) intrans.: pres. subj. sg. þät he me ongeán sleá (that he should strike at me), 682; pret. sg. yrringa slôh (struck angrily), 1566; so, slôh hilde-bille, 2680. b) trans.: pret. sg. þät he þone nîð-gäst nioðor hwêne slôh (that he struck the dragon somewhat lower , etc.), 2700.--2) w. acc.: to slay, kill : pret. sg. þäs þe he Abel slôg (because he slew A.), 108; so, slôg, 421, 2180; slôh, 1582, 2356; pl. slôgon, 2051; pret. part. þâ wäs Fin slägen, 1153.

ge-sleán, w. acc.: 1) to fight a battle : pret. sg. ge-slôh þîn fader fæhðe mæste, 459.--2) to gain by fighting : syððan hie þâ mærða ge-slôgon, 2997.

of-sleán, to ofslay, kill , w. acc.: pret. sg. of-slôh, 574, 1666, 3061.

slîðe (G. sleiþ-s), adj., savage, fierce, dangerous : acc. sg. þurh slîðne nîð, 184; gen. pl. slîðra ge-slyhta, 2399.

slîðen, adj., furious, savage, deadly nom. sg. sweord-bealo slîðen, 1148.

slîtan, st. v., to slit, tear to pieces , w. acc.: pret. sg. slât (slæpendne rinc), 742.

slyht, st. m., blow : in comp. and-slyht.

ge-slyht, st. n. (collective), battle, conflict : gen. pl. slîðra ge-slyhta, 2399.

smið, st. m., smith, armorer : nom. sg. wæpna smið, 1453; gen. sg. smiðes, 406.--Comp. wundor-smið.

be-smiðian, w. v., to surround with iron-work, bands , etc.: pret. part. he (the hall Heorot) þäs fäste wäs innan and ûtan îren-bendum searo-þoncum besmiðod (i.e. the beams out of which the hall was built were held together skilfully, within and without, by iron clamps), 776.

snell, adj., fresh, vigorous, lively; of martial temper : nom. sg. se snella, 2972.

snellîc, adj., the same: nom. sg., 691.

snotor, snottor, adj., clever, wise, intelligent : nom. sg. snotor, 190, 827, 909, 1385; in weak form, (se) snottra, 1314, 1476, 1787; snotra, 2157, 3121; nom. pl. snotere, 202, 416; snottre, 1592.--Comp. fore-snotor.

snotor-lîce, adv., intelligently, wisely : compar. snotor-lîcor, 1483.

snûde, adv., hastily, quickly, soon , 905, 1870, 1972, 2326, 2569, 2753.

be-snyðian, w. v., to rob, deprive of : pret. sg. þätte Ongenþió ealdre be-snyðede Hæðcyn, 2925.

snyrian, w. v., to hasten, hurry : pret. pl. snyredon ät-somne (hurried forward together), 402.

snyttru, f., intelligence, wisdom : acc. sg. snyttru, 1727; dat. pl. mid môdes snyttrum, 1707; þe we ealle ær ne meahton snyttrum be-syrwan (a deed which all of us together could not accomplish before with all our wisdom), 943. Adv., wisely , 873.

somne. See samne.

sorgian, w. v.: 1) to be grieved, sorrow : imper. sg. II. ne sorga! 1385.--2) to care for, trouble one's self about : inf. nô þu ymb mînes ne þearft lîces feorme leng sorgian (thou needst not care longer about my life's [body's] sustenance), 451.

sorh, st. f., grief, pain, sorrow : nom. sg., 1323; sorh is me tô secganne (pains me to say), 473; acc. sg. sorge, 119, 2464; dat. instr. sg. mid þære sorge, 2469;

sorge (in sorrow, grieved), 1150; gen. sg. worna fela ... sorge, 2005; dat. pl. sorgum, 2601; gen. pl. sorga, 149.--Comp.: hyge-, inwit-, þegn-sorh.

sorh-cearig, adj., curis sollicitus, heart-broken : nom. sg., 2456.

sorh-ful, adj., sorrowful, troublesome, difficult : nom. sg., 2120; acc. sg. sorh-fullne (sorh-fulne) sîð, 512, 1279, 1430.

sorh-leás, adj., free from sorrow or grief : nom. sg., 1673.

sorh-leoð, st. n., dirge, song of sorrow : acc. sg., 2461.

sorh-wylm, st. m., wave of sorrow nom. pl. sorh-wylmas, 905.

sôcn, st. f., persecution, hostile pursuit or attack (see sêcan): dat, (instr.) þære sôcne (by reason of Grendel's persecution), 1778.

sôð, st. n., sooth, truth :: acc. sg. sôð, 532, 701, 1050, 1701, 2865; dat. sg. tô sôðe (in truth), 51, 591, 2326.

sôð, adj., true, genuine : nom. sg, þät is sôð metod, 1612; acc. sg. n. gyd âwräc sôð and sâr-lîc, 2110.

sôðe, adv., truly, correctly, accurately , 524; sôðe gebunden (of alliterative verse: accurately put together), 872.

sôð-cyning, st. m., true king : nom. sg. sigora sôð-cyning (God), 3056.

sôð-fäst, adj., soothfast, established in truth, orthodox (here used of the Christian martyrs): gen. pl. sôð-fästra dôm (glory, realm, of the saints), 2821.

sôð-lîce, adv., in truth, truly, truthfully , 141, 273, 2900.

sôfte, adv., gently, softly : compar. þý sêft (the more easily), 2750.--Comp. un-sôfte.

sôna, adv., soon, immediately , 121, 722, 744, 751, 1281, 1498, 1592, 1619, 1763, etc.

on-spannan, st. v., to un-span, unloose : pret. sg. his helm on-speón (loosed his helm), 2724.

spel, st. n., narrative, speech : acc. sg. spell, 2110; acc. pl. spel, 874; gen. pl. spella, 2899, 3030.--Comp. weá-spel.

spêd, st. f.: 1) luck, success : in comp. here-, wîg-spêd.--2) skill, facility : acc. sg. on spêd (skilfully), 874.

spîwan, st. v., to spit, spew , w. instr.: inf. glêdum spîwan (spit fire), 2313

spor, st. n., spur : in comp. hand-spor.

spôwan, st. v., to speed well, help, avail : pret. sg. him wiht ne speów (availed him naught), 2855; hû him ät æte speów (how he sped in the eating), 3027.

spræc, st. f., speech, language : instr. sg. frêcnan spræce (through bold, challenging, discourse), 1105.--Comp.: æfen-, gylp-spræc.

sprecan, st. v., to speak : inf. ic sceal forð sprecan gen ymbe Grendel (I shall go on speaking about G.), 2070; w. acc. se þe wyle sôð sprecan (he who will speak the truth), 2865; imper. tô Geátum sprec (spræc, MS.), 1172; pret. sg. III. spräc, 1169, 1699, 2511, 2725; word äfter spräc, 341; nô ymbe þâ fæhðe spräc, 2619; II. hwät þu worn fela ... ymb Brecan spræce (how much thou hast spoken of Breca!), 531; pl. hwät wit geó spræcon (what we two spoke of before), 1477; gomele ymb gôdne on-geador spræcon, þät big ... (the graybeards spoke together about the valiant one, that they ...), 1596; swâ wit furðum spræcon (as we two spoke, engaged, before), 1708; pret. part. þâ wäs ... þryð-word sprecen, 644.

ge-sprecan, w. acc., to speak : pret. sg. ge-spräc, 676, 1399, 1467, 3095.

spreót, st. m., pole; spear, pike : in comp. eofor-spreót.

springan, st. v., to jump, leap; flash : pret. sg. hrâ wîde sprong (the body bounded far), 1589; swât ædrum sprong forð under fexe (the blood burst out in streams from under his hair), 2967; pl. wîde sprungon hilde-leóman (flashed afar), 2583. Also figuratively: blæd wîde sprang (his repute spread afar), 18.

ge-springan, to spring forth : pret. sg. swâ þät blôd ge-sprang (as the blood burst forth), 1668. Figuratively, to arise, originate : pret. sg. Sigemunde gesprong äfter deáð-däge dôm un-lytel, 885.

on-springan, to burst in two, spring asunder : pret. pl. seonowe onsprungon, burston bânlocan 818.

standan, st. v.: 1) absolutely or with prep., to stand : pres. III. pl. eóred-geatwe þe ge þær on standað (the warlike accoutrements wherein ye there stand), 2867; inf. ge-seah ... orcas stondan (saw vessels standing), 2761; pret. sg. ät hýðe stôd hringed-stefna (in the harbor stood the curved-prowed?, metal-covered?, ship), 32; stôd on stapole (stood near the [middle] column), 927; so, 1914, 2546; þät him on alder stôd here-stræl hearda (that the sharp war-arrow stood in his vitals), 1435; so, 2680; pl. gâras stôdon ... samod ät-gädere (the spears stood together), 328; him big stôdan bunan and orcas (by him stood cans and pots), 3048. Also of still water: pres. sg. III. nis þät feor heonon ... þät se mere standeð, 1363.--2) with predicate adj., to stand, continue in a certain state : subj. pres. þät þes sele stande ... rinca ge-hwylcum îdel and unnyt (that this hall stands empty and useless for every warrior), 411; inf. hord-wynne fand eald uht-sceaða opene standan, 2272; pret. sg. ôð þät îdel stôd hûsa sêlest, 145; so, 936; wäter under stôd dreórig and ge-drêfed, 1418--3) to belong or attach to; issue : pret. sg. Norð-Denum stôd atelîc egesa (great terror clung to, overcame, the North Danes), 784; þâra ânum stôd sadol searwum fâh (on one of the steeds lay an ingeniously-inlaid saddle), 1038; byrne-leóma eldum on andan (burning light stood forth, a horror to men), 2314; leóht inne stôd (a light stood in it , i.e. the sword), 1571; him of eágum stôd ... leóht unfäger (an uncanny light issued from his eyes), 727; so, þät [fram] þam gyste [gryre-] brôga stôd, 2229.

â-standan, to stand up, arise : pret. sg. â-stôd, 760, 1557, 2093.

ät-standan, to stand at, near , or in : pret. sg. þät hit (i.e. þät swurd) on wealle ät-stôd, 892.

for-standan, to stand against or before , hence: 1) to hinder, prevent : pret. sg. (breóst-net) wið ord and wið ecge in-gang for-stôd (the shirt of mail prevented point or edge from entering), 1550; subj. nefne him witig god wyrd for-stôde (if the wise God had not warded off such a fate from them , i.e. the men threatened by Grendel), 1057.--2) defend , w. dat. of person against whom: inf. þät he ... mihte heáðo-lîðendum hord for-standan, bearn and brýde (that he might protect his treasure, his children, and his spouse from the sea-farers), 2956.

ge-standan, intrans., to stand : pret. sg. ge-stôd, 358, 404, 2567; pl. nealles him on heápe hand-gesteallan ... ymbe gestôdon (not at all did his boon-companions stand serried around him), 2597.

stapa, w. m., stepper, strider : in comp. hæð-, mearc-stapa.

stapan, st. v., to step, stride, go forward : pret. sg. eorl furður stôp, 762; gum-fêða stop lind-häbbendra (the troop of shield-warriors strode on), 1402.

ät-stapan, to stride up or to : pret. sg. forð neár ät-stôp (strode up nearer), 746.

ge-stapan, to walk, stride : pret. sg. he to forð gestôp dyrnan cräfte, dracan heáfde neáh (he , i.e. the man that robbed the dragon of the vessel, had through hidden craft come too near the dragon's head), 2290.

stapol, st. m., (=[Greek: básis]), trunk of a tree ; hence, support, pillar, column : dat. sg. stôd on stapole (stood by or near the wooden middle column of Heorot), 927; instr. pl. þâ stân-bogan stapulum fäste (the arches of stone upheld by pillars), 2719. See Note.

starian, w. v., to stare, look intently at : pres. sg. I. þät ic on þone hafelan ... eágum starige (that I see the head with my eyes), 1782; þâra frätwa ... þe ic her on starie (for the treasures ... that I here look upon), 2797; III. þonne he on þät sine starað, 1486; sg. for pl. þâra þe on swylc starað, 997; pret. sg. þät (sin-freá) hire an däges eágum starede, 1936; pl. on mere staredon, 1604.

stân, st. m., 1) stone : in comp. eorclan-stân.--2) rock : acc. sg. under (ofer) hârne stân, 888, 1416, 2554, 2745; dat. sg. stâne, 2289, 2558.

stân-beorh, st. m., rocky elevation, stony mountain : acc. sg. stân-beorh steápne, 2214.

stân-boga, w. m., stone arch, arch hewn out of the rock : dat. sg. stân-bogan, 2546; nom. pl. stân-bogan, 2719.

stân-clif, st. n., rocky cliff : acc. pl. stân-cleofu, 2541.

stân-fâh, adj., stone-laid, paved with stones of different colors : nom. sg. stræt wäs stân-fâh (the street was of different colored stones), 320.

stân-hlið, st. n., rocky slope : acc. pl. stân-hliðo, 1410.

stäf, st. m.: 1) staff : in comp. rûn-staf.--2) elementum : in comp. âr-, ende-, fâcen-stäf.

stäl, st. m., place, stead : dat. sg. þät þu me â wære forð-gewitenum on fäder stäle (that thou, if I died, wouldst represent a father's place to me), 1480.

stælan, w. v., to place; allure or instigate : inf. þâ ic on morgen ge-frägn mæg ôðerne billes ecgum on bonan stælan (then I learned that on the morrow one brother instigated the other to murder with the sword's edge ; or, one avenged the other on the murderer ?, cf. 2962 seqq.), 2486.

ge-stælan, to place, impose, institute : pret. part. ge feor hafað fæhðe ge-stæled (Grendel's mother has further begun hostilities against us), 1341.

stede, st. m., place, -stead : in comp. bæl-, burh-, folc-, heáh-, meðel-, wang-, wîc-stede.

stefn, st. f., voice : nom. sg., 2553; instr. sg. niwan (niówan) stefne (properly novâ voce) = denuo, anew, again , 2595, 1790.

stefn, st. m., prow of a ship : acc. sg., 213; see bunden-, hringed-, wunden-stefna.

on-stellan, w. v., constituere, to cause, bring about : pret. sg. se þäs or-leges ôr on-stealde, 2408.

steng, st. m., pole, pike : in comp wäl-steng.

ge-steppan, w. v., to stride, go : pret. sg. folce ge-stepte ofer sæ side sunu Ôhtheres (O.'s son , i.e. Eádgils, went with warriors over the broad sea), 2394.

stede (O.H.G. stâti, M.H.G. stæte), adj., firm, steady : nom. sg. wäs stêde nägla ge-hwylc stýle ge-lîcost (each nail-place was firm as steel), 986.

stêpan, w. v. w. acc., to exalt, honor : pret. sg. þeáh þe hine mihtig god ... eafeðum stêpte, 1718.

ge-steald, st. n., possessions, property : in comp. in-gesteald, 1156.

ge-stealla, w. m., (contubernalis), companion, comrade : in comp. eaxl-, fyrd-, hand-, lind-, nýd-ge-stealla.

stearc-heort, adj., (fortis animo), stout-hearted, courageous : nom. sg. (of the dragon), 2289; (of Beówulf), 2553.

steáp, adj., steep, projecting, towering : acc. sg. steápne hrôf, 927; stân-beorh steápne, 2214; wið steápne rond, 2567; acc. pl. m. beorgas steápe, 222; neut. steáp stân-hlið, 1410.--Comp. heaðo-steáp.

stille, adj., still, quiet : nom. sg. wîd-floga wundum stille, 2831.

stille, adv., quietly, 301.

stincan, st. v., to smell; snuff : pret. sg. stonc þâ äfter stâne (snuffed along the stone), 2289.

stîð, adj., hard, stiff : nom. sg. wunden-mæl (swurd) ... stîð and stýlecg, 1534.

stîð-môd, adj., stout-hearted, unflinching : nom. sg., 2567.

stîg, st. m., way, path : nom. sg., 320, 2214; acc. pl. stîge nearwe, 1410--Comp. medu-stîg.

stîgan, st. v., to go, ascend : pret. sg. þâ he tô holme [st]âg (when he plunged forward into the sea), 2363; pl. beornas ... on stefn stigon, 212; Wedera leóde on wang stigon, 225; subj. pret. ær he on bed stige, 677.

â-stîgan, to ascend : pres. sg. þonon ýð-geblond up â-stîgeð won tô wolcnum, 1374; gûð-rinc â-stâh (the fierce hero ascended, i.e. was laid on the pyre? or, the fierce smoke [rêc] ascended?), 1119; gamen eft â-stâh (joy again went up, resounded), 1161; wudu-rêc â-stâh sweart of swioðole, 3145; swêg up â-stâg, 783.

ge-stîgan, to ascend, go up : pret. sg. þâ ic on holm ge-stâh, 633.

storm, st. m., storm : nom. sg. stræla storm (storm of missiles), 3118; instr. sg. holm storme weól (the sea billowed stormily), 1132.

stôl, st. m., chair, throne, seat : in comp. brego-, êðel-, gif-, gum-stôl.

stôw, st. f., place, -stow : nom. sg. nis þät heóru stôw (a haunted spot), 1373; acc. sg. frêcne stôwe, 1379; grund-bûendra gearwe stôwe (the place prepared for men, i.e. death-bed; see gesacan and ge-nýdan), 1007: comp. wäl-stow.

strang, strong, adj., strong; valiant; mighty : nom. sg. wäs þät ge-win tô strang (that sorrow was too great), 133; þu eart mägenes strang (strong of body), 1845; wäs sió hond tô strong (the hand was too powerful), 2685; superl. wîgena strengest (strongest of warriors), 1544; mägenes strengest (strongest in might), 196; mägene strengest, 790.

strâdan? (cf. stræde = passus, gressus), to tread, (be)- stride, stride over (Grein): subj. pres. se þone wong strâde, 3074. See Note.

stræl, st. m., arrow, missile : instr. sg. biteran stræle, 1747; gen. pl. stræla storm, 3118.

stræt, st. f., street, highway : nom. sg., 320; acc. sg. stræte, 1635; fealwe stræte, 917.--Comp.: lagu-, mere-stræt.

strengel, st. m., (endowed with strength), ruler, chief : acc. sg. wîgena strengel, 3116.

strengo, st. f., strength, power, violence : acc. sg. mägenes strenge, 1271; dat. sg. strenge, 1534, strengo, 2541;--dat. pl. strengum = violently, powerfully [loosed from the strings ?], 3118: in comp. hilde-, mägen-, mere-strengo.

strêgan (O.S. strôwian), w. v., to strew, spread : pret. part, wäs þäm yldestan ... morðorbed strêd (the death-bed was spread for the eldest one), 2437.

streám, st. m., stream, flood, sea : acc. sg. streám, 2546; nom. pl. streámas, 212; acc. pl. streámas, 1262: comp. brim-, eágor-, firgen-, lagu-streám.

ge-streón (cf. streón = robur, vis), st. n., property, possessions ; hence, valuables, treasure, jewels : nom. pl. Heaðo-beardna ge-streón (the costly treasure of the Heathobeardas, i.e. the accoutrements belonging to the slain H.),

2038; acc. pl. äðelinga, eorla ge-streón, 1921, 3168.--Comp.: ær-, eald-, eorl-, heáh-, hord-, long-, mâðm-, sinc-, þeód-ge-streón.

strûdan, st. v., to plunder, carry off : subj. pres. näs þâ on hlytme hwâ þät hord strude, 3127.

ge-strýnan, w. v. w. acc., to acquire, gain : inf. þäs þe (because) ic môste mînum leódum ... swylc ge-strýnan, 2799.

stund, st. f., time, space of time, while : adv. dat. pl. stundum (at times), 1424.

styrian, w. v. w. acc.: 1) to arrange, put in order, tell : inf. secg eft on-gan sîð Beówulfes snyttrum styrian (the poet then began to tell B.'s feat skilfully , i.e. put in poetic form), 873.--2) to rouse, stir up : pres. sg. III. þonne wind styreð lâð ge-widru (when the wind stirreth up the loathly weather), 1375.--3) to move against, attack, disturb : subj. pres. þät he ... hring-sele hondum styrede (that he should attack the ring-hall with his hands), 2841.

styrman, w. v., to rage, cry out : pret. sg. styrmde, 2553.

stýle, st. n., steel : dat. sg. stýle, 986.

stýl-ecg, adj., steel-edged : nom. sg., 1534.

be-stýman, w. v., to inundate, wet, flood : pret. part. (wæron) eal benc-þelu blôde be-stýmed, 486.

suhtor-ge-fäderan (collective), w. m. pl., uncle and nephew, father's brother and brother's son : nom. pl., 1165.

sum, pron.: 1) indef., one, a, any, a certain ; neut. something : a) without part. gen.: nom. sg. sum, 1252; hilde-rinc sum, 3125; neut. ne sceal þær dyrne sum wesan (naught there shall be hidden), 271; acc. sg. m. sumne, 1433; instr. sg. sume worde (by a word, expressly), 2157; nom. pl. sume, 400, 1114; acc. pl. sume, 2941. b) with part. gen.: nom. sg. gumena sum (one of men, a man), 1500, 2302; mere-hrägla sum, 1906; þät wäs wundra sum, 1608; acc. sg. gylp-worda sum, 676. c) with gen. of cardinals or notions of multitude: nom. sg. fîftena sum (one of fifteen, with fourteen companions), 207; so, eahta sum, 3124; feára sum (one of few, with a few), 1413; acc. sg. manigra sumne (one of many, with many), 2092; manna cynnes sumne (one of the men), i.e. one of the watchmen in Heorot), 714; feára sumne (some few, one of few ; or, one of the foes ?), 3062.-- 2) with part. gen. sum sometimes = this, that, the afore-mentioned : nom. sg. eówer sum (a certain one, that one, of you , i.e. Beówulf), 248; gûð-beorna sum (the afore-mentioned warrior , i.e. who had shown the way to Hrôðgâr's palace), 314; eorla sum (the said knight , i.e. Beówulf), 1313; acc. sg. hord-ärna sum (a certain hoard-hall), 2280.

sund, st. m.: 1) swimming : acc. sg. ymb sund, 507; dat. sg. ät sunde (in swimming), 517; on sunde (a-swimming), 1619; gen. sg. sundes, 1437.--2) sea, ocean, sound : nom. sg., 223; acc. sg. sund, 213, 512, 539, 1427, 1445.

ge-sund, adj., sound, healthy, unimpaired : acc. sg. m. ge-sundne, 1629, 1999; nom. pl. ge-sunde, 2076; acc. pl. w. gen. fäder alwalda ... eówic ge-healde sîða ge-sunde (the almighty Father keep you safe and sound on your journey!), 318.-- Comp. an-sund.

sund-ge-bland, st. n., (the commingled sea), sea-surge, sea-wave : acc. sg., 1451.

sund-nyt, st. f., swimming-power or employment, swimming : acc. sg. sund-nytte dreáh (swam through the sea), 2361.

sundur, sundor, adv., asunder, in twain : sundur gedælan (to separate, sunder), 2423.

sundor-nyt, st. f., special service (service in a special case): acc. sg. sundor-nytte, 668.

sund-wudu, st. m., (sea-wood), ship : nom. acc. sg. sund-wudu, 208, 1907.

sunne, w. f., sun : nom. sg., 607; gen. sg. sunnan, 94, 649.

sunu, st. m., son : nom. sg., 524, 591, 646, 981, 1090, 1486, etc.; acc. sg. sunu, 268, 948, 1116, 1176, 1809, 2014, 2120; dat. sg. suna, 344, 1227, 2026, 2161, 2730; gen. sg. suna, 2456, 2613, (1279); nom. pl. suna, 2381.

sûð, adv., south, southward , 859.

sûðan, adv., from the south , 607; sigel sûðan fûs (the sun inclined from the south), 1967.

swaðrian, w. v., to sink to rest, grow calm : brimu swaðredon (the waves became calm), 570. See sweðrian.

swaðu, st. f., trace, track, pathway : acc. sg. swaðe, 2099.--Comp.: swât-, wald-swaðu.

swaðul, st. m.? n.?, smoke, mist (Dietrich in Haupt V. 215): dat. sg. on swaðule, 783. See sweoðol.

swancor, adj., slender, trim : acc. pl. þrió wicg swancor, 2176.

swan-râd, st. f., swan-road, sea : acc. sg. ofer swan-râde, 200.

and-swarian, w. v., to answer : pret. sg. him se yldesta and-swarode, 258; so, 340.

swâ: 1) demons, adv., so, in such a manner, thus : swâ sceal man dôn, 1173, 1535; swâ þâ driht-guman dreámum lifdon, 99; þät ge-äfndon swâ (that we thus accomplished), 538; þær hie meahton (i.e. feorh ealgian), 798; so, 20, 144, 189, 559, 763, 1104, 1472, 1770, 2058, 2145, 2178, 2991; swâ manlîce (so like a man), 1047; swâ fela (so many), 164, 592; swâ deórlîce dæd (so valiant a deed), 585; hine swâ gôdne (him so good), 347; on swâ geongum feore (in so youthful age), 1844; ge-dêð him swâ ge-wealdene worolde dælas þät ... (makes parts of the world so subject to him that ...), 1733. In comparisons = ever, the (adv.): me þîn môd-sefa lîcað leng swâ wel (thy mind pleases me ever so well, the longer the better), 1855. As an asseverative − so : swâ me Higelâc sîe ... môdes blîðe (so be Higelac gracious-minded to me!), 435; swâ þeáh (nevertheless, however), 973, 1930, 2879; swâ þêh, 2968; hwäðre swâ þeáh (yet however), 2443.--2): a) conj., as, so as : ôð þät his byre mihte eorlscipe efnan swâ his ærfäder (until his son might do noble deeds, as his old father did), 2623; eft swâ ær (again as before), 643;--with indic.: swâ he selfa bäd (as he himself requested), 29; swâ he oft dyde (as he often did), 444; gæð â Wyrd swâ hió sceal, 455; swâ guman gefrungon, 667; so, 273, 352, 401, 561, 1049, 1056, 1059, 1135, 1232, 1235, 1239, 1253, 1382, etc.;--with subj.: swâ þîn sefa hwette (as pleases thy mind , i.e. any way thou pleasest), 490. b) as, as then, how , 1143; swâ hie â wæron ... nýd-gesteallan (as they were ever comrades in need), 882; swâ hit diópe ... be-nemdon þeódnas mære (as, [how?] the mighty princes had deeply cursed it), 3070; swâ he manna wäs wîgend weorðfullost (as he of men the worthiest warrior was), 3099. c) just as, the moment when : swâ þät blôd gesprang, 1668. d) so that : swâ he ne mihte nô (so that he might not...), 1509; so, 2185, 2007.--3) = qui, quae, quod, German so: worhte wlite-beorhtne wang swâ wäter bebûgeð (wrought the beauteous plain which (acc.) water surrounds), 93.--4) swâ ... swâ = so ... as , 595, 687-8, 3170; efne swâ ... swâ (even so ... as), 1093-4, 1224, 1284; efne swâ hwylc mägða swâ (such a woman as, whatsoever woman), 944; efne swâ hwylcum manna swâ (even so to each man as), 3058.

for-swâfan, st. v., to carry away, sweep off : pret. sg. ealle Wyrd for-sweóf mîne mâgas tô metod-sceafte, 2815.

for-swâpan, st. v., to sweep off, force : pret. sg. hie Wyrd forsweóp on Grendles gryre, 477.

swât, st. m., (sweat), wound-blood : nom. sg., 2694, 2967; instr. sg. swâte, 1287.--Comp. heaðo-, hilde-swât.

swât-fâh, adj., blood-stained : nom. sg., 1112.

swâtig, adj., gory : nom. sg., 1570.

swât-swaðu, st. f., blood-trace : nom. sg., 2947.

be-swælan, w. v., to scorch : pret. part. wäs se lêg-draca ... glêdum beswæled, 3042.

swæs, adj., intimate, special, dear : acc. sg. swæsne êðel, 520; nom. pl. swæse ge-sîðas, 29; acc. pl. leóde swæse, 1869; swæse ge-sîðas, 2041; gen. pl. swæsra ge-sîða, 1935.

swæs-lîce, adv., pleasantly, in a friendly manner , 3090.

swebban, w. v., (to put to sleep), to kill : inf. ic hine sweorde swebban nelle, 680; pres. sg. III. (absolutely) swefeð, 601.

â-swebban, to kill, slay : pret. part. nom. pl. sweordum â-swefede, 567.

sweðrian, w. v., to lessen, diminish : inf. þät þät fyr ongan sweðrian, 2703; pret. siððan Heremôdes hild sweðrode, 902.

swefan, st. v.: 1) to sleep : pres. sg. III. swefeð, 1742; inf. swefan, 119, 730, 1673; pret. sg. swäf, 1801; pl. swæfon, 704; swæfun, 1281.--2) to sleep the death-sleep, die : pres. sg. III. swefeð, 1009, 2061, 2747; pl. swefað, 2257, 2458.

swegel, st. n., ether, clear sky : dat. sg. under swegle, 1079, 1198; gen. sg. under swegles begong, 861, 1774.

swegle, adj., bright, etherlike, clear : acc. pl. swegle searo-gimmas, 2750.

swegel-wered, quasi pret. part., ether-clad : nom. sg. sunne swegl-wered, 607.

swelgan, st. v., to swallow : pret. sg. w. instr. syn-snædum swealh (swallowed in great bites), 744; object omitted, subj. pres. nymðe lîges fäðm swulge on swaðule, 783.

for-swelgan, w. acc., to swallow, consume : pret. sg. for-swealg, 1123, 2081.

swellan, st. v., to swell : inf. þâ sió wund on-gan ... swêlan and swellan, 2714.

sweltan, st. v., to die, perish : pret. sg. swealt, 1618, 2475; draca morðre swealt (died a violent death), 893, 2783; wundor-deáðe swealt, 3038; hioro-dryncum swealt, 2359.

swencan, w. v., to swink, oppress, strike : pret. sg. hine wundra þäs fela swencte (MS. swecte) on sunde, 1511.

ge-swencan, to oppress, strike, injure : pret. sg. syððan hine Hæðcyn ... flâne geswencte, 2439; pret. part. synnum ge-swenced, 976; hæðstapa hundum ge-swenced, 1369.--Comp. lyft-ge-swenced.

sweng, st. m., blow, stroke : dat. sg. swenge, 1521, 2967; swenge (with its stroke), 2687; instr. pl. sweordes swengum, 2387.--Comp.: feorh-, hete-, heaðo-, heoro-sweng.

swerian, st. v., to swear : pret. w. acc. I. ne me swôr fela âða on unriht (swore no false oaths), 2739; he me âðas swôr, 472.

for-swerian, w. instr., to forswear, renounce (protect with magic formulæ?) : pret. part. he sige-wæpnum for-sworen häfde, 805.

swêg, st. m., sound, noise, uproar : nom. sg. swêg, 783; hearpan swêg, 89, 2459, 3024; sige-folca swêg, 645; sang and swêg, 1064; dat. sg. swêge, 1215.--Comp.: benc-, morgen-swêg.

swêlan, w. v., to burn (here of wounds): inf. swêlan, 2714. See swælan.

sweart, adj., swart, black, dark : nom. sg. wudu-rêc sweart, 3146; dat. pl. sweartum nihtum, 167.

sweoðol (cf. O.H.G. suedan, suethan = cremare; M.H.G. swadem = vapor; and Dietrich in Haupt V., 215), st. m.? n.?, vapor, smoke, smoking flame : dat. sg. ofer swioðole (MS. swic ðole), 3146. See swaðul.

sweofot, st. m., sleep : dat. sg. on sweofote, 1582, 2296.

sweoloð, st. m., heat, fire, flame : dat. sg. sweoloðe, 1116. Cf. O.H.G. suilizo, suilizunga = ardor, cauma.

sweorcan, st. v., to trouble, darken . pres. sg. III. ne him inwit-sorh on sefan sweorceð (darkens his soul), 1738.

for-sweorcan, to grow dark or dim : pres. sg. III. eágena bearhtm for-siteð and for-sworceð, 1768.

ge-sweorcan (intrans.), to darken : pret. sg. niht-helm ge-swearc, 1790.

sweord, swurd, swyrd, st. n., sword : nom. sg. sweord, 1287, 1290, 1570, 1606, 1616, 1697; swurd, 891; acc. sg. sweord, 437, 673, 1559, 1664, 1809, 2253, 2500, etc.; swurd, 539, 1902; swyrd, 2611, 2988; instr. sg. sweorde, 561, 574, 680, 2493, 2881; gen. sg. sweordes, 1107, 2194, 2387; acc. pl. sweord, 2639; nom. pl., 3049; instr. pl. sweordum, 567, 586, 885; gen. pl. sweorda, 1041, 2937, 2962.--Comp.: gûð-, mâððum-, wæg-sweord.

sweord, st. f., oath : in comp. âð-sweord (sword-oath ?), 2065.

sweord-bealo, st. n., sword-bale, death by the sword : nom. sg., 1148.

sweord-freca, w. m., sword-warrior : dat. sg. sweord-frecan, 1469.

sweord-gifu, st. f., sword-gift, giving of swords : nom. sg. swyrd-gifu, 2885.

sweotol, swutol, adj.: 1) clear, bright : nom. sg. swutol sang scôpes, 90.-- 2) plain, manifest : nom. sg. syndolh sweotol, 818; tâcen sweotol, 834; instr. sg. sweotolan tâcne, 141.

sweóf, sweóp. See swâfan, swâpan.

swið, st. n.? (O.N. swiði), burning pain : in comp. þryð-swið(?).

swift, adj., swift : nom. sg. se swifta mearh, 2265.

swimman, swymman, st. v., to swim : inf. swymman, 1625.

ofer-swimman, w. acc., to swim over or through : pret. sg. ofer-swam sioleða bigong (swam over the sea), 2368.

swincan, st. v., to struggle, labor, contend : pret. pl. git on wäteres æht seofon niht swuncon, 517.

ge-swing, st. n., surge, eddy : nom. sg. atol ýða geswing, 849.

swingan, st. v., to swing one's self, fly : pres. sg. III. ne gôd hafoc geond säl swingeð, 2265.

swîcan, st. v.: 1) to deceive, leave in the lurch, abandon : pret. sg. næfre hit (the sword) ät hilde ne swâc manna ængum, 1461.--2) to escape : subj. pret. bûtan his lîc swice, 967.

ge-swîcan, to deceive, leave in the lurch : pret. sg. gûð-bill ge-swâc nacod ät nîðe, 2585, 2682; w. dat. seó ecg ge-swâc þeódne ät þearfe (the sword failed the prince in need), 1525.

swîð, swýð (Goth, swinþ-s), adj., strong, mighty : nom. sg. wäs þät ge-win tô swýð, 191.--Comp. nom. sg. sió swîðre hand (the right hand), 2099; harsh , 3086.

swîðe, adv., strongly, very, much , 598, 998, 1093, 1744, 1927; swýðe, 2171, 2188. Compar. swîðor, more, rather, more strongly , 961, 1140, 1875, 2199-- Comp. un-swîðe.

ofer-swîðian, w. v., to overcome, vanquish, w. acc. of person: pres. sg. III. oferswýðeð, 279, 1769.

swîð-ferhð, adj., (fortis animo), strong-minded, bold, brave : nom. sg. swýð-ferhð, 827; gen. sg. swîð-ferhðes, 909; nom. pl. swîð-ferhðe, 493; dat. pl. swîð-ferhðum, 173.

swîð-hycgend, pres. part. (strenue cogitans), bold-minded, brave in spirit : nom. sg. swîð-hycgende, 920; nom. pl. swîð-hycgende, 1017.

swîð-môd, adj., strong-minded : nom. sg., 1625.

on-swîfan, st. v. w. acc., to swing, turn, at or against, elevate : pret. sg. biorn (Beówulf) bord-rand on-swâf wið þam gryre-gieste, 2560.

swîgian, w. v., to be silent, keep silent : pret. sg. lyt swîgode niwra spella (kept little of the new tidings silent), 2898; pl. swîgedon ealle, 1700.

swîgor, adj., silent, taciturn : nom. sg. weak, þâ wäs swîgra secg ... on gylp-spræce gûð-ge-weorca, 981.

swîn, swýn, st. n., swine, boar (image on the helm): nom. sg. swýn, 1112; acc. sg. swîn, 1287.

swîn-lîc, st. n., swine-image or body : instr. pl. swîn-lîcum, 1454.

swôgan, st. v., to whistle, roar : pres. part. swôgende lêg, 3146.

swutol. See sweotol.

swylc, swilc (Goth, swa-leik-s), demons, adj. = talis, such, such a ; relative = qualis, as, which : nom. sg. swylc, 178, 1941, 2542, 2709; swylc ... swylc=talis ... qualis, 1329; acc. sg. swylc, 2799; eall ... swylc (all ... which, as), 72; ôðer swylc (such another , i.e. hand), 1584; on swylc (on such things), 997; dat. sg. gûð-fremmendra swylcum (to such a battle-worker , i.e. Beówulf), 299; gen. sg. swylces hwät (some such), 881; acc. pl. swylce, 2870; call swylce ... swylce, 3166; swylce twegen (two such), 1348; ealle þearfe swylce (all needs that), 1798; swylce hie ... findan meahton sigla searo-gimma (such as they might find of jewels and cunning gems), 1157; efne swylce mæla swylce (at just such times as), 1250; gen. pl. swylcra searo-nîða, 582; swylcra fela ... ær-gestreóna, 2232.

swylce, adv., as, as also, likewise, similarly , 113, 293, 758, 831, 855, 908, 921, 1147, 1166, 1428, 1483, 2460, 2825; ge swylce (and likewise), 2259; swilce, 1153.

swylt, st. m., death : nom. sg., 1256, 1437.

swylt-däg, st. m., death-day : dat. sg. ær swylt-däge, 2799.

swynsian, w. v., to sound : pret. sg. hlyn swynsode, 612.

swyrd. See sweord.

swýðl. See swîð.

swýn. See swîn.

syððan (seðian, Gen. 1525), w. v., to punish, avenge , w. acc.: inf. þonne hit sweordes ecg syððan scolde (then the edge of the sword should avenge it), 1107.

syððan. See siððan.

syfan-wintre, adj., seven-winters-old : nom. sg., 2429.

syhð. See seón.

syl (O.H.G. swella), st. f., sill, bench-support : dat. sg. fram sylle, 776.

sylfa. See selfa.

syllan. See sellan.

syllîc. See sellîc.

symbol, syml, st. n., banquet, entertainment : acc. sg. symbel, 620, 1011; geaf me sinc and symbel (gave me treasure and feasting , i.e. made me his friend and table-companion), 2432; þät hie ... symbel ymbsæton (that they might sit round their banquet), 564; dat. sg. symle, 81, 489, 1009; symble, 119, 2105; gen. pl. symbla, 1233.

symble, symle, adv., continually, ever : symble, 2451; symle, 2498; symle wäs þý sæmra (he was ever the worse, the weaker , i.e. the dragon), 2881.

symbel-wyn, st. f., banqueting-pleasure, joy at feasting : acc. sg. symbel-wynne dreóh, 1783.

syn, st. f., sin, crime : nom. synn and sacu, 2473; dat. instr. pl. synnum, 976, 1256, 3072.

syn. See sin.

syn-bysig, adj., (culpa laborans), persecuted on account of guilt? (Rieger), guilt-haunted? : nom. sg. secg syn-[by]sig, 2228.

ge-syngian, w. v., to sin, commit a crime : pret. part. þät wäs feohleás ge-feoht, fyrenum ge-syngad, 2442.

synnig, adj., sin-laden, sinful : acc. sg. m. sinnigne secg, 1380.--Comp.: fela-, un-synnig.

ge-synto, f., health : dat. pl. on gesyntum, 1870.

syrce. See serce.

syrwan, w. v. w. acc., to entrap, catch unawares : pret. sg. duguðe and geogoðe seomade and syrede, 161.

be-syrwan: 1) to compass or accomplish by finesse; effect : inf. dæd þe we ealle ær ne meahton snyttrum be-syrwan (a deed that all of us could not accomplish before with all our wisdom), 943.--2) to entrap by guile and destroy : inf. mynte se mânscaða manna cynnes sumne be-syrwan (the fell foe thought to entrap some one (all? , see sum) of the men), 714.

sýn, f., seeing, sight, scene : comp., an-sýn.

ge-sýne, adj., visible, to be seen : nom. sg. 1256, 1404, 2948, 3059, 3160.--Comp.: êð-ge-sýne, ýð-ge-sêne.

T

taligean, w. v.: 1) to count, reckon, number; esteem, think : pres. sg. I. nô ic me ... hnâgran gûð-geweorca þonne Grendel hine (count myself no worse than G. in battle-works), 678; wên ic talige ...þät (I count on the hope ... that), 1846; telge, 2068; sg. III. þät ræd talað þät (counts it gain that), 2028.--2) to tell, relate : sôð ic talige (I tell facts), 532; swâ þu self talast (as thou thyself sayst), 595.

tâcen, st. n., token, sign, evidence : nom. sg. tâcen sweotol, 834; dat. instr. sg. sweotolan tâcne, 141; tîres tô tâcne, 1655.--Comp. luf-tâcen.

tân, st. m., twig : in comp. âter-tân. [emended to âter-teárum in text--KTH]

ge-tæcan, w. v., to show, point out : pret. sg. him þâ hilde-deór hof môdigra torht ge-tæhte (the warrior pointed out to them the bright dwelling of the bold ones , i.e. Danes), 313. Hence, to indicate, assign : pret. sôna me se mæra mago Healfdenes ... wið his sylfes sunu setl getæhte (assigned me a seat by his own son), 2014.

tæle, adj., blameworthy : in comp. un-tæle.

ge-tæse, adj., quiet, still : nom. sg. gif him wære ... niht ge-tæse (whether he had a pleasant, quiet, night), 1321.

tela, adv., fittingly, well , 949, 1219, 1226, 1821, 2209, 2738.

telge. See talian.

tellan, w. v., to tell, consider, deem : pret. sg. ne his lîf-dagas leóda ænigum nytte tealde (nor did he count his life useful to any man), 795; þät ic me ænigne under swegles begong ge-sacan ne tealde (I believed not that I had any foe under heaven), 1774; cwäð he þone gûð-wine gôdne tealde (said he counted the war-friend good), 1811; he ûsic gâr-wîgend gôde tealde (deemed us good spear-warriors), 2642; pl. swâ (so that) hine Geáta beam gôdne ne tealdon, 2185.--2) to ascribe, count against, impose : pret. sg. (Þryðo) him wälbende weotode tealde hand-gewriðene, 1937.

ge-tenge, adj., attached to, lying on : w. dat. gold ... grunde ge-tenge, 2759.

teár, st. m., tear : nom. pl. teáras, 1873.

teoh, st. f., troop, band : dat. sg. earmre teohhe, 2939.

(ge?)-teohhian, w. v., to fix, determine, assign : pret. sg. ic for lässan leán teohhode ... hnâhran rince, 952; pres. part. wäs ôðer in ær geteohhod (assigned)... mærum Geáte, 1301.

teón, st. v., to draw, lead : inf. hêht ... eahta mearas ... on flet teón (bade eight horses be led into the hall), 1037; pret. sg. me tô grunde teáh fâh feónd-sceaða (the many-hued fiend-foe drew me to the bottom), 553; eft-sîðas teáh (withdrew, returned), 1333; sg. for pl. æg-hwylcum ...þâra þe mid Beówulfe brim-lâde teáh (to each of those that crossed the sea with B.) 1052; pret. part. þâ wäs ... heard ecg togen (then was the hard edge drawn), 1289; wearð ... on näs togen (was drawn to the promontory), 1440.

â-teón, to wander, go , intrans.: pret. sg. tô Heorute â-teáh (drew to Heorot), 767.

ge-teón: 1) to draw : pret. sg. gomel swyrd ge-teáh, 2611; w. instr. and acc. hyre seaxe ge-teáh, brad brûn-ecg, 1546.--2) to grant, give, lend : imp. nô þu him wearne geteóh þînra gegn-cwida glädnian (refuse not to gladden them with thy answer), 366; pret. sg. and þâ Beówulfe bega gehwäðres eodor Ingwina onweald ge-teáh (and the prince of the Ingwins gave B. power over both), 1045; so, he him êst geteáh (gave possession of), 2166.

of-teón, to deprive, withdraw , w. gen. of thing and dat. pers.: pret. sg. Scyld Scêfing ... monegum mægðum meodo-setla of-teáh, 5; w. acc. of thing, hond ... feorh-sweng ne of-teáh, 2490; w. dat. hond (hord, MS.) swenge ne of-teáh, 1521.

þurh-teón, to effect : inf. gif he torn-gemôt þurh-teón mihte, 1141.

teón (cf. teóh, materia , O.H.G. ziuc), w. v. w. acc., to make, work : pret. sg. teóde, 1453;-- to furnish out, deck : pret. pl. nalas hi hine lässan lâcum teódan (provided him with no less gifts), 43.

ge-teón, to provide, do, bring on : pres. sg. unc sceal weorðan ... swâ unc Wyrd ge-teóð, 2527; pret. sg. þe him ... sâre ge-teóde (who had done him this harm), 2296.

ge-teóna, w. m., injurer, harmer : in comp. lâð-ge-teóna.

til, adj., good, apt, fit : nom. sg. m. Hâlga til, 61; þegn ungemete till (of Wîglâf), 2722; fem. wäs seó þeód tilu, 1251; neut. ne wäs þät ge-wrixle til, 1305.

tilian, w. v. w. gen., to gain, win : inf. gif ic ... ôwihte mäg þînre môd-lufan mâran tilian (if I ... gain), 1824.

timbrian, w. v., to build : pret. part. acc. sg. säl timbred (the well-built hall), 307.

be-timbrian, (construere), to finish building, complete : pret. pl. betimbredon on tyn dagum beadu-rôfes bêcn, 3161.

tîd, st. f., -tide, time : acc. sg. twelf wintra tîd, 147; lange tîd, 1916; in þâ tîde, 2228.--Comp.: ân-, morgen-tîd.

ge-tîðian (from tigðian), w. v., to grant : pret. part. impers. wäs ... bêne (gen.) ge-tîðad feásceaftum men, 2285.

tîr, st. m., glory, repute in war . gen. sg. tîres, 1655.

tîr-eádig, adj., glorious, famous : dat. sg. tîr-eádigum menn (of Beówulf), 2190.

tîr-fäst, adj., famous, rich in glory . nom. sg. (of Hrôðgâr), 923.

tîr-leás, adj., without glory, infamous : gen. sg. (of Grendel), 844.

toga, w. m., leader : in comp. folc-toga.

torht, adj., bright, brilliant : acc. sg. neut. hof ... torht, 313.--Comp.: wuldor-torht, heaðo-torht (loud in battle).

torn, st. n.: 1) wrath, insult, distress : acc. sg. torn, 147, 834; gen. pl. torna, 2190.--2) anger : instr. sg. torne ge-bolgen, 2402.--Comp. lîge-torn.

torn, adj., bitter, cruel : nom. sg, hreówa tornost, 2130.

torn-ge-môt, st. n., (wrathful meeting), angry engagement, battle : acc. sg., 1141.

tô, I. prep. w. dat. indicating direction or tending to, hence: 1) local = whither after verbs of motion, to, up to, at : com tô recede (to the hall), 721; eode tô sele, 920; eode tô hire freán sittan, 642; gæð eft ... tô medo (goeth again to mead), 605; wand tô wolcnum (wound to the welkin), 1120; sigon tô slæpe (sank to sleep), 1252; 28, 158, 234, 438, 553, 926, 1010, 1014, 1155, 1159, 1233, etc.; lîð-wæge bär hælum tô handa (bore the ale-cup to the hands of the men? at hand?), 1984; ôð þät niht becom ôðer tô yldum, 2118; him tô bearme cwom mâððum-fät mære (came to his hands, into his possession), 2405; sælde tô sande sîd-fäðme scip (fastened the broad-bosomed ship to the shore), 1918; þat se harm-scaða tô Heorute â-teáh (went forth to Heorot), 767. After verb sittan: site nu tô symble (sit now to the meal), 489; siððan ... we tô symble geseten häfdon, 2105; tô ham (home, at home), 124, 374, 2993. With verbs of speaking: maðelode tô his wine-drihtne (spake to his friendly lord), 360; tô Geátum sprec, 1172; so, hêht þät heaðo-weorc tô hagan biódan (bade the battle-work be told at the hedge), 2893.--2) with verbs of bringing and taking (cf. under on, I., d): hraðe wäs tô bûre Beówulf fetod (B. was hastily brought from a room), 1311; siððan Hâma ät-wäg tô þære byrhtan byrig Brôsinga mene (since H. carried the Brosing-necklace off from the bright city), 1200; weán âhsode. fæhðo to Frysum (suffered woe, feud as to, from, the Frisians), 1208.--3) =end of motion, hence: a) to, for, as, in : þone god sende folce tô frôfre (for, as, a help to the folk), 14; gesette ... sunnan and mônan leóman to leóhte (as a light), 95; ge-sät ... tô rune (sat in counsel), 172; wearð he Heaðo-lâfe tô hand-bonan, 460; bringe ... tô helpe (bring to, for, help), 1831; Jofore forgeaf ângan dôhtor ... hyldo tô wedde (as a pledge of his favor), 2999; so, 508(?), 666, 907, 972, 1022, 1187, 1263, 1331, 1708, 1712, 2080, etc.; secgan tô sôðe (to say in sooth), 51; so, 591, 2326. b) with verbs of thinking, hoping, etc., on, for, at, against : he tô gyrn-wräce swîðor þôhte þonne tô sæ-lâde (thought more on vengeance than on the sea-voyage), 1139; säcce ne wêneð tô Gâr-Denum (nor weeneth of conflict with the Spear-Danes), 602; þonne wêne ic tô þe wyrsan geþinges (then I expect for thee a worse result), 525; ne ic to Sweóþeóde sibbe oððe treówe wihte ne wêne (nor expect at all of, from, the Swedes ...), 2923; wiste þäm ahlæcan tô þäm heáh-sele hilde ge-þinged (battle prepared for the monster in the high hall), 648; wel bið þäm þe mot tô fäder fäðmum freoðo wilnian (well for him that can find peace in the Father's arms), 188; þâra þe he ge-worhte tô West-Denum (of those that he wrought against the West-Danes), 1579.--4) with the gerund, inf.: tô gefremmanne (to do), 174; tô ge-cýðanne (to make known), 257; tô secganne (to say), 473; to befleónne (to avoid, escape), 1004; so, 1420, 1725, 1732, 1806, 1852, 1923, 1942, etc. With inf.: tô fêran, 316; tô friclan, 2557.--5) temporal: gewât him tô gescäp-hwîle (went at(?) the hour of fate ; or, to his fated rest?), 26; tô wîdan feore (ever, in their lives), 934; âwa tô alder (for life, forever), 956; so, tô aldre, 2006, 2499; tô life (during life, ever), 2433.--6) with particles: wôd under wolcnum tô þäs þe ... (went under the welkin to the point where ...), 715; so, elne ge-eodon tô þäs þe, 1968; so, 2411; he him þäs leán for-geald ... tô þäs þe he on reste geseah Grendel licgan (he paid him for that to the point that he saw G. lying dead), 1586; wäs þät blôd tô þäs hât (the blood was hot to that degree), 1617; näs þâ long tô þon þät ('twas not long till), 2592, 2846; wäs him se man tô þon leóf þät (the man was dear to him to that degree), 1877; tô hwan siððan wearð hond-räs häleða (up to what point, how, the hand-contest turned out), 2072; tô middes (in the midst), 3142.

II. Adverbial modifier, quasi preposition [better explained in many cases as prep. postponed]: l) to, towards, up to, at : geóng sôna tô, 1786; so, 2649; fêhð ôðer tô, 1756; sä-lâc ... þe þu her tô lôcast (upon which thou here lookest), 1655; folc tô sägon (the folk looked on), 1423; þät hî him tô mihton gegnum gangan (might proceed thereto), 313; se þe him bealwa tô bôte gelýfde (who believed in help out of evils from him , i.e. Beówulf), 910; him tô anwaldan âre ge-lyfde (trusted for himself to the Almighty's help), 1273; þe ûs sêceað tô Sweóna leóde (that the Swedes will come against us), 3002.--2) before adj. and adv., too : tô strang (too mighty), 133; tô fäst, 137; tô swýð, 191; so, 789, 970, 1337, 1743, 1749, etc.; tô fela micles (far too much), 695; he tô forð ge-stôp (he had gone too far), 2290.

tôð (G. tunþu-s), st. m., tooth : in comp. blôdig-tôð (adj.).

tredan, st. v. w. acc., to tread : inf. sä-wong tredan, 1965; el-land tredan, 3020; pret. sg. wräc-lâstas träd, 1353; medo-wongas träd, 1644; gräs-moldan träd, 1882.

treddian, tryddian (see trod), w. v., to stride, tread, go : pret. sg. treddode, 726; tryddode getrume micle (strode about with a strong troop), 923.

trem, st. n., piece, part : acc. sg. ne ... fôtes trem (not a foot's breadth), 2526.

treów, st. f., fidelity, good faith : acc. sg. treówe, 1073; sibbe oððe treówe, 2923.

treów, st. n., tree : in comp. galg-treów.

treówian. See trûwian.

treów-loga, w. m., troth-breaker, pledge-breaker : nom. pl. treów-logan, 2848.

trodu, st. f., track, step : acc. sg. or pl. trode, 844.

ge-trum, st. n., troop, band : instr. sg. ge-trume micle, 923.

trum, adj., strong, endowed with : nom. sg. heorot hornum trum, 1370.

ge-trûwan, w. v. w. acc., to confirm, pledge solemnly : pret. sg. þâ hie getrûwedon on twâ healfe fäste frioðu-wäre, 1096.

trûwian, treówan, w. v., to trust in, rely on, believe in : 1) w. dat.: pret. sg. sîðe ne trûwode leófes mannes (I trusted not in the dear man's enterprise), 1994; bearne ne trûwode þät he ... (she trusted not in the child that ...), 2371; gehwylc hiora his ferhðe treówde þät he ... (each trusted his heart that ...), 1167.--2) w. gen.: pret. sg. Geáta leód georne trûwode môdgan mägnes, 670; wiðres ne trûwode, 2954.

ge-trûwian, to rely on, trust in , w. dat.: pret. sg. strenge ge-trûwode, mund-gripe mägenes, 1534;--w. gen. pret. sg. beorges ge-trûwode, wîges and wealles, 2323; strenge ge-trûwode ânes mannes, 2541.

tryddian. See treddian.

trýwe, adj., true, faithful : nom. sg. þâ gyt wäs ... äghwylc ôðrum trýwe, 1166.

ge-trýwe, adj., faithful : nom. sg. her is æghwylc eorl ôðrum ge-trýwe, 1229.

turf, st. f., sod, soil, seat : in comp. êðel-turf.

tux, st. m., tooth, tusk : in comp. hilde-tux.

ge-twæfan, w. v. w. acc. of person and gen. thing, to separate, divide, deprive of, hinder : pres. sg. III. þät þec âdl oððe ecg eafoðes ge-twæfeð (robs of strength), 1764; inf. god eáðe mäg þone dol-scaðan dæda ge-twæfan (God may easily restrain the fierce foe from his deeds), 479; pret. sg. sumne Geáta leód ... feores getwæfde (cut him off from life), 1434; nô þær wæg-flotan wind ofer ýðum sîðes ge-twæfde (the wind hindered not the wave-floater in her course over the water), 1909; pret. part. ät rihte wäs gûð ge-twæfed (almost had the struggle been ended), 1659.

ge-twæman, w. v. acc. pers. and gen. thing, to hinder, render incapable of, restrain : inf. ic hine ne mihte ... ganges getwæman, 969.

twegen, m. f. n. twâ, num., twain, two : nom. m. twegen, 1164; acc. m. twegen, 1348; dat. twæm, 1192 gen. twega, 2533; acc. f. twâ, 1096, 1195.

twelf, num., twelve , gen. twelfa, 3172.

tweone (Frisian twine), num. = bini, two : dat. pl. be sæm tweonum, 859, 1298; 1686.

twidig, adj., in comp. lang-twidig (long-assured), 1709.

tyder, st. m., race, descendant : in comp. un-tyder, 111.

tydre (Frisian teddre), adj., weak, unwarlike, cowardly : nom. pl. tydre, 2848.

tyn, num., ten : uninflect. dat. on tyn dagum, 3161; inflect. nom. tyne, 2848.

tyrwian, w. v., to tar : pret. part. tyrwed in comp.: niw-tyrwed.

on-tyhtan, w. v., to urge on, incite, entice : pret. sg. on-tyhte, 3087.

þ

þafian, w. v. w. acc., to submit to, endure : inf. þät se þeód-cyning þafian sceolde Eofores ânne dôm, 2964.

þanc, st. m.: 1) thought : in comp. fore-, hete-, or-, searo-þanc; inwit-þanc (adj.).--2) thanks (w. gen. of thing): nom. sg., 929, 1779; acc. sg. þanc, 1998, 2795.--3) content, favor, pleasure : dat. sg. þâ þe gif-sceattas Geáta fyredon þyder tô þance (those that tribute for the Geâtas carried thither for favor). 379.

ge-þanc, st. m., thought : instr. pl. þeóstrum ge-þoncum, 2333.--Comp. môd-ge-þanc.

þanc-hycgende, pres. part., thoughtful , 2236.

þancian, w. v., to thank : pret. sg. gode þancode ... þäs þe hire se willa ge-lamp (thanked God that her wish was granted), 626; so, 1398; pl. þancedon, 627(?).

þanon, þonon, þonan, adv., thence : 1) local: þanon eft gêwât (he went thence back), 123; þanon up ... stigon (went up thence), 224; so, þanon, 463, 692, 764, 845, 854, 1293; þanan, 1881; þonon, 520, 1374, 2409; þonan, 820, 2360, 2957.--2) personal: þanon untydras ealle on-wôcon (from him , i.e. Cain, etc.), 111; so, þanan, 1266; þonon, 1961; unsôfte þonon feorh ôð-ferede (i.e. from Grendel's mother), 2141.

þâ, adv.: 1) there, then , 3, 26, 28, 34, 47, 53, etc. With þær: þâ þær, 331. With nu: nu þâ (now then), 658.--2) conjunction, when, as, since , w. indic., 461, 539, 633, etc.;-- because, whilst, during, since , 402, 465, 724, 2551, etc.

þät, I. demons, pron. acc. neut. of se: demons, nom. þät (that), 735, 766, etc.; instr. sg. þý, 1798, 2029; þät ic þý wæpne ge-bräd (that I brandished as(?) a weapon; that I brandished the weapon?), 1665; þý weorðra (the more honored),

521

1903; þý sêft (the more easily), 2750; þý läs hym ýðe þrym wudu wynsuman for-wrecan meahte (lest the force of the waves the winsome boat might carry away), 1919; nô þý ær (not sooner), 755, 1503, 2082, 2374, 2467; nô þý leng (no longer, none the longer), 975. þý =adv., therefore, hence , 1274, 2068; þê ... þê = on this account; for this reason ... that, because , 2639-2642; wiste þê geornor (knew but too well), 822; he ... wäs sundes þê sænra þe hine swylt fornam (he was the slower in swimming as [whom?] death carried him off), 1437; näs him wihte þê sêl (it was none the better for him), 2688; so, 2278. Gen. sg. þäs = adv., for this reason, therefore , 7, 16, 114, 350, 589, 901, 1993, 2027, 2033, etc. þäs þe, especially after verbs of thanking, = because , 108, 228, 627, 1780, 2798;--also = secundum quod: þäs þe hie gewislîcost ge-witan meahton, 1351;-- therefore, accordingly , 1342, 3001; tô þäs (to that point; to that degree), 715, 1586, 1617, 1968, 2411; þäs georne (so firmly), 969; ac he þäs fäste wäs ... besmiðod (it was too firmly set), 774; nô þäs frôd leofað gumena bearna þät þone grund wite (none liveth among men so wise that he should know its bottom), 1368; he þäs (þäm, MS.) môdig wäs (had the courage for it), 1509.

II. conj. (relative), that, so that , 15, 62, 84, 221, 347, 358, 392, 571, etc.; ôð þät (up to that, until); see ôð.

þätte (from þät þe, see þe), that , 151, 859, 1257, 2925, etc.; þät þe (that), 1847.

þær: 1) demons. adv., there (where) , 32, 36, 89, 400, 757, etc.; morðor-bealo mâga, þær heó ær mæste heóld worolde wynne (the death-bale of kinsmen where before she had most worldly joy), 1080. With þâ: þâ þær, 331; þær on innan (therein), 71. Almost like Eng. expletive there , 271, 550, 978, etc.;-- then, at that time , 440;-- thither : þær swîð-ferhðe sittan eodon (thither went the bold ones to sit , i.e. to the bench), 493, etc.--2) relative, where , 356, 420, 508, 513, 522, 694, 867, etc.; eode ... þær se snottra bâd (went where the wise one tarried), 1314; so, 1816;-- if , 763, 798, 1836, 2731, etc.;-- whither : gâ þær he wille, 1395.

þe, I. relative particle, indecl., partly standing alone, partly associated with se, seó, þät: Hunferð maðelode, þe ät fôtum sät (H., who sat at his feet, spake), 500; so, 138, etc.; wäs þät gewin tô swýð þe on þâ leóde be-com (the misery that had come on the people was too great), 192, etc.; ic wille ... þe þâ and-sware ädre ge-cýðan þe me se gôda â-gifan þenceð (I will straightway tell thee the answer that the good one shall give), 355; ôð þone ânne däg þe he ... (till that very day that he ...), 2401; heó þâ fæhðe wräc þe þu ... Grendel cwealdest (the fight in which thou slowest G.), 1335; mid þære sorge þe him sió sâr belamp (with the sorrow wherewith the pain had visited him), 2469; pl. þonne þâ dydon þe ... (than they did that ...), 45; so, 378, 1136; þâ mâðmas þe he me sealde (the treasures that he gave me), 2491; so, ginfästan gife þe him god sealde (the great gifts that God had given him), 2183. After þâra þe (of those that), the depend. verb often takes sg. instead of pl. (Dietrich, Haupt XI., 444 seqq.): wundor-sióna fela secga ge-hwylcum þâra þe on swylc staræð (to each of those that look on such), 997; so, 844, 1462, 2384, 2736. Strengthened by se, seó, þät: sägde se þe cûðe (said he that knew), 90; wäs se grimma gäst Grendel hâten, se þe môras heóld (the grim stranger hight Grendel, he that held the moors), 103; here-byrne ... seó þe bân-cofan beorgan cûðe (the corselet that could protect the body), 1446, etc.; þær ge-lýfan sceal dryhtnes dôme se þe hine deáð nimeð (he shall believe in God's judgment whom death carrieth off), 441; so, 1437, 1292 (cf. Heliand I., 1308).

þäs þe. See þät.
þeáh þe. See þeáh.

for þam þe. See for-þam.

þý, þê, the, by that, instr. of se: âhte ic holdra þý läs ... þe deáð for-nam (I had the less friends whom death snatched away), 488; so, 1437.

þeccan, w. v., to cover (thatch), cover over : inf. þâ sceal brond fretan, äled þeccean (fire shall eat, flame shall cover, the treasures), 3016; pret. pl. þær git eágor-streám earmum þehton (in swimming), 513.

þegn, st. m., thane, liegeman, king's higher vassal; knight : nom. sg., 235, 494, 868, 2060, 2710; (Beówulf), 194; (Wîglâf), 2722; acc. sg. þegen (Beówulf, MS. þegn), 1872; dat. sg. þegne, 1342, 1420; (Hengest), 1086; (Wîglâf), 2811; gen. sg. þegnes, 1798; nom. pl. þegnas, 1231; acc. pl. þegnas, 1082, 3122; dat. pl. þegnum, 2870; gen. pl. þegna, 123, 400, 1628, 1674, 1830, 2034, etc.--Comp.: ambiht-, ealdor-, heal-, magu-, sele-þegn.

þegnian, þênian, w. v., to serve, do liege service : pret. sg. ic him þênode deóran sweorde (I served them with my good sword , i.e. slew them with it), 560.

þegn-sorh, st. f., thane-sorrow, grief for a liegeman : acc. sg. þegn-sorge, 131.

þegu, st. f., taking : in comp.: beáh-, beór-, sinc-þegu.

þel, st. n., deal-board, board for benches : in comp. benc-þel, 486, 1240.

þencan, w. v.: 1) to think : absolutely: pres. sg. III. se þe wel þenceð, 289; so, 2602. With depend. clause: pres. sg. nænig heora þôhte þät he ... (none of them thought that he), 692.--2) w. inf., to intend : pres. sg. III. þâ and-sware ... þe me se gôda â-gifan þenceð (the answer that the good one intendeth to give me), 355; (blôdig wäl) byrgean þenceð, 448; þonne he ... gegân þenceð longsumne lof (if he will win eternal fame), 1536; pret. sg. ne þät aglæca yldan þôhte (the monster did not mean to delay that), 740; pret. pl. wit unc wið hronfixas werian þôhton, 541; (hine) on healfa ge-hwone heáwan þôhton, 801.

â-þencan, to intend, think out : pret. sg. (he) þis ellen-weorc âna â-þôhte tô ge-fremmanne, 2644.

ge-þencan, w. acc.: 1) to think of : þät he his selfa ne mäg ... ende ge-þencean (so that he himself may not think of, know, its limit), 1735.--2) to be mindful : imper. sg. ge-þenc nu ... hwät wit geó spræcon, 1475.

þenden: 1) adv., at this time, then, whilst : nalles fâcen-stafas Þeód-Scyldingas þenden fremedon (not at all at this time had the Scyldings done foul deeds), 1020 (referring to 1165; cf. Wîdsîð, 45 seqq.); þenden reáfode rinc ôðerne (whilst one warrior robbed another , i.e. Eofor robbed Ongenþeów), 2986.--2) conj., so long as, whilst , 30, 57, 284, 1860, 2039, 2500, 3028;-- whilst , 2419. With subj., whilst, as long as : þenden þu môte, 1178; þenden þu lifige, 1255; þenden hyt sý (whilst the heat lasts), 2650.

þengel, st. m., prince, lord, ruler : acc. sg. hringa þengel (Beówulf), 1508.

þes (m.), þeós (f.), þis (n.), demons. pron., this : nom. sg. 411, 432, 1703; f., 484; nom. acc. neut., 2156, 2252, 2644; þys, 1396; acc. sg. m. þisne, 75; f. þâs, 1682; dat. sg. neut. þissum, 1170; þyssum, 2640; f. þisse, 639; gen. m. þisses, 1217; f. þisse, 929; neut. þysses, 791, 807; nom. pl. and acc. þâs, 1623, 1653, 2636, 2641; dat. þyssum, 1063, 1220.

þê. See þät.

þêh. See þeáh.

þearf, st. f., need : nom. sg. þearf, 1251, 2494, 2638; þâ him wäs manna þearf (as he was in need of men), 201; acc. sg. þearfe, 1457, 2580, 2850; fremmað ge nu leóda þearfe (do ye now what is needful for the folk), 2802; dat. sg. ät þearfe, 1478, 1526, 2695, 2710; acc. pl. se for andrysnum ealle beweotede þegnes þearfe

(who would supply in courtesy all the thane's needs), 1798 (cf. sele-þegn, 1795).--Comp.: firen-, nearo-, ofer-þearf.

þearf. See þurfan.

ge-þearfian, w. v., = necessitatem imponere : pret. part. þâ him swâ ge-þearfod wäs (since so they found it necessary), 1104.

þearle, adv., very, exceedingly , 560.

þeáh, þêh, conj., though, even though or if : 1) with subj. þeáh, 203, 526, 588, 590, 1168, 1661, 2032, 2162. Strengthened by þe: þeáh þe, 683, 1369, 1832, 1928, 1942, 2345, 2620; þeáh ... eal (although), 681.--2) with indic.: þeáh, 1103; þêh, 1614.--3) doubtful: þeáh he ûðe wel, 2856; swâ þeáh (nevertheless), 2879; nô ... swâ þeáh (not then however), 973; näs þe forht swâ þêh (he was not, though, afraid), 2968; hwäðre swâ þeáh (yet however), 2443.

þeáw, st. m., custom, usage : nom. sg., 178, 1247; acc. sg. þeáw, 359; instr. pl. þeáwum (in accordance with custom), 2145.

þeód, st. f.: 1) war-troop, retainers : nom. sg., 644, 1231, 1251.--2) nation, folk : nom. sg., 1692; gen. pl. þeóda, 1706.--Comp.: sige-, wer-þeód.

þeód-cyning, st. m., (=folc-cyning), warrior-king, king of the people : nom. sg. (Hrôðgâr), 2145; (Ongenþeów), 2964, 2971; þiód-cyning (Beówulf), 2580; acc. sg. þeód-cyning (Beówulf), 3009; gen. sg. þeód-cyninges (Beówulf), 2695; gen. pl. þeód-cyninga, 2.

þeóden, st. m., lord of a troop, war-chief, king; ruler : nom. sg., 129, 365, 417, 1047, 1210, 1676, etc.; þióden, 2337, 2811; acc. sg. þeóden, 34, 201, 353, 1599, 2385, 2722, 2884, 3080; þióden, 2789; dat. sg. þeódne, 345, 1526, 1993, 2573, 2710, etc.; þeóden, 2033; gen. sg. þeódnes 798, 911, 1086, 1628, 1838, 2175; þiódnes, 2657; nom. pl. þeódnas, 3071.

þeóden-leás, adj., without chief or king : nom. pl. þeóden-leáse, 1104.

þeód-gestreón, st. n., people's-jewel, precious treasure : instr. pl. þeód-ge-streónum, 44; gen. pl. þeód-ge-streóna, 1219.

þeódig, adj., appertaining to a þeód: in comp. el-þeódig.

þeód-scaða, w. m., foe of the people, general foe : nom. sg. þeód-sceaða (the dragon), 2279, 2689.

þeód-þreá, st. f. m., popular misery, general distress : dat. pl. wið þeód-þreáum, 178.

þeóf, st. m., thief : gen. sg. þeófes cräfte, 2221.

þeón, st. v.: 1) to grow, ripen, thrive : pret. sg. weorðmyndum þâh (grew in glory), 8.--2) to thrive in, succeed : pret. sg. hûru þät on lande lyt manna þâh (that throve to few), 2837. See Note, l. 901.

ge-þeón, to grow, thrive; increase in power and influence : imper. ge-þeóh tela, 1219; inf. lof-dædum sceal ... man geþeón, 25; þät þät þeódnes bearn ge-þeón scolde, 911.

on-þeón? to begin, undertake , w. gen.: pret. he þäs ær onþâh, 901. [In MS. Emended in text.--KTH] See Note, l. 901.

þeon (for þeówan), w. v., to oppress, restrain : inf. näs se folc-cyning ymb-sittendra ænig þâra þe mec ... dorste egesan þeón (that durst oppress me with terror), 2737.

þeóstor, adj., dark, gloomy : instr. pl. þeóstrum ge-þoncum, 2333.

þicgan, st. v. w. acc., to seize, attain, eat, appropriate : inf. þät he (Grendel) mâ môste manna cynnes þicgean ofer þâ niht, 737; symbol þicgan (take the meal, enjoy the feast), 1011; pret. pl. þät hie me þêgon, 563; þær we medu þêgun, 2634.

ge-þicgan, w. acc., to grasp, take : pret. sg. (symbel and sele-ful, ful) ge-þeah, 619, 629; Beówulf ge-þah ful on flette, 1025; pret. pl. (medo-ful manig) ge-þægon, 1015.

þider, þyder, adv., thither : þyder, 3087, 379, 2971.

þihtig, þyhtig, adj., doughty, vigorous, firm : acc. sg. neut. sweord ... ecgum þyhtig, 1559.--Comp. hyge-þihtig.

þincan. See þyncan.

þing, st. n.: 1) thing : gen. pl. ænige þinga (ullo modo), 792, 2375, 2906.--2) affair, contest, controversy : nom. sg. me wearð Grendles þing ... undyrne cûð (Grendel's doings became known to me), 409.--3) judgment, issue, judicial assembly (?): acc. sg. sceal ... âna gehegan þing wið þyrse (shall bring the matter alone to an issue against the giant : see hegan), 426.

ge-þing, st. n.: 1) terms, covenant : acc. pl. ge-þingo, 1086.--2) fate, providence, issue : gen. sg. ge-þinges, 398, 710; (ge-þingea, MS.), 525.

ge-þingan, st. v., to grow, mature, thrive (Dietrich, Haupt IX., 430): pret. part. cwên môde ge-þungen (mature-minded, high-spirited, queen), 625. See wel-þungen.

ge-þingan (see ge-þing), w. v.: 1) to conclude a treaty : w. refl. dat, enter into a treaty : pres. sg. III. gif him þonne Hrêðrîc tô hofum Geáta ge-þingeð (if H. enters into a treaty (seeks aid at?) with the court of the Geátas , referring to the old German custom of princes entering the service or suite of a foreign king), 1838. Leo.--2) to prepare, appoint : pret. part. wiste [ät] þäm ahlæcan ... hilde ge-þinged, 648; hraðe wäs ... mêce ge-þinged, 1939.

þingian, w. v.: 1) to speak in an assembly, make an address : inf. ne hýrde ic snotor-lîcor on swâ geongum feore guman þingian (I never heard a man so young speak so wisely), 1844.--2) to compound, settle, lay aside : inf. ne wolde feorh-bealo ... feó þingian (would not compound the life-bale for money), 156; so, pret. sg. þâ fæhðe feó þingode, 470.

þîhan. See þeón.

þin, possess, pron., thy, thine , 267, 346, 353, 367, 459, etc.

ge-þôht, st. m., thought, plan : acc. sg. ân-fealdne ge-þôht, 256; fäst-rædne ge-þôht, 611.

þolian, w. v. w. acc.: 1) to endure, bear : inf. (inwid-sorge) þolian, 833; pres. sg. III. þreá-nýd þolað, 284; pret. sg. þolode þryðswyð, 131.--2) to hold out, stand, survive : pres. sg. (intrans.) þenden þis sweord þolað (as long as this sword holds out), 2500; pret. sg. (seó ecg) þolode ær fela hand-gemôta, 1526.

ge-þolian: 1) to suffer, bear, endure : gerund. tô ge-þolianne, 1420; pret. sg. earfoð-lice þrage ge-þolode..., þät he ... dreám gehýrde (bore ill that he heard the sound of joy), 87; torn ge-þolode (bore the misery), 147.--2) to have patience, wait : inf. þær he longe sceal on þäs waldendes wære ge-þolian, 3110.

þon (Goth, þan) = tum, then, now , 504; äfter þon (after that), 725; ær þon däg cwôme (ere day came), 732; nô þon lange (it was not long till then), 2424; näs þâ long tô þon (it was not long till then), 2592, 2846; wäs him se man tô þon leóf þät ... (the man was to that degree dear to him that ...), 1877.

þonne: 1) adv., there, then, now , 377, 435, 525, 1105, 1456, 1485, 1672, 1823, 3052, 3098(?).--2) conj., if, when, while : a) w. indic., 573, 881, 935, 1034, 1041, 1043, 1144, 1286, 1327, 1328, 1375, etc.; þät ic gum-cystum gôdne funde beága bryttan, breác þonne môste (that I found a good ring-giver and enjoyed him whilst I could), 1488. b) w. subj., 23, 1180, 3065; þonne ...þonne (then ... when), 484-

85, 2447-48; gif þonne ...þonne (if then ... then), 1105-1107. c) than after comparatives, 44, 248, 469, 505, 534, 679, 1140, 1183, etc.; a comparative must be supplied, l. 70, before þone: þät he ... hâtan wolde medo-ärn micel men ge-wyrcean þone yldo bearn æfre ge-frunon (a great mead-house (greater) than men had ever known).

þracu, st. f., strength, boldness : in comp. môd-þracu; = impetus in ecg-þracu.

þrag, st. f., period of time, time : nom. sg. þâ hine sió þrag be-cwom (when the [battle]- hour befell him), 2884; acc. sg. þrage (for a time), 87; longe (lange) þrage, 54, 114.--Comp. earfoð-þrag.

ge-þräc, st. n., multitude, crowd : in comp. searo-ge-þräc.

þrec-wudu, st. m., (might-wood), spear (cf. mägen-wudu): acc. sg., 1247.

þreá, st. m. f., misery, distress : in comp. þeód-þreá, þreá-nêdla, -nýd.

þreá-nêdla, w. m., crushing distress, misery : dat. sg. for þreá-nêdlan, 2225.

þrea-nýd, st. f., oppression, distress : acc. sg. þreá-nýd, 284; dat. pl. þreá-nýdum, 833.

þreát, st. m., troop, band : dat. sg. on þam þreáte, 2407; dat. pl. sceaðena þreátum, 4.--Comp. îren-þreát.

þreátian, w. v. w. acc., to press, oppress : pret. pl. mec ...þreátedon, 560.

þreot-teoða, num. adj. w. m., thirteenth : nom. sg. þreot-teoða secg, 2407.

þreó, num. (neut.), three : acc. þrió wicg, 2175; þreó hund wintra, 2279.

þridda, num. adj. w. m., third : instr. þriddan sîðe, 2689.

ge-þring, st. n., eddy, whirlpool, crush : acc. on holma ge-þring, 2133.

þringan, st. v., to press : pret. sg. wergendra tô lyt þrong ymbe þeóden (too few defenders pressed round the prince), 2884; pret. pl. syððan Hrêðlingas tô hagan þrungon (after the Hrethlingas had pressed into the hedge), 2961.

for-þringan, to press out; rescue, protect : inf. þät he ne mehte ...þâ weá-lâfe wîge for-þringan þeódnes þegne (that he could not rescue the wretched remnant from the king's thane by war), 1085.

ge-þringan, to press : pret. sg. ceól up geþrang (the ship shot up), i.e. on the shore in landing), 1913.

þritig, num., thirty (neut. subst.): acc. sg. w. partitive gen.: þritig þegna, 123; gen. þrittiges (XXXtiges MS.) manna, 379.

þrîst-hydig, adj., bold-minded, valorous : nom. sg. þióden þrîst-hydig (Beówulf), 2811.

þrowian, w. v. w. acc., to suffer, endure : inf. (hât, gnorn) þrowian, 2606, 2659; pret. sg. þrowade, 1590, 1722; þrowode, 2595.

þryð, st. f., abundance, multitude , excellence, power : instr. pl. þryðum (excellently, extremely; excellent in strength?), 494.

þryð-ärn, st. n., excellent house, royal hall : acc. sg. (of Heorot), 658.

þryðlîc, adj., excellent, chosen : nom. sg. þryð-lîc þegna heáp, 400, 1628; superl. acc. pl. þryð-lîcost, 2870.

þrýð-swýð, st. n.?, great pain (?): acc., 131, 737 [? adj., very powerful, exceeding strong].

þryð-word, st. n., bold speech, choice discourse : nom. sg., 644. (Great store was set by good table-talk: cf. Lachmann's Nibelunge, 1612; Rîgsmâl, 29, 7, in Möbius, p. 79b, 22.)

þrym, st. m.: 1) power, might, force : nom. sg. ýða þrym, 1919; instr. pl. = adv. þrymmum (powerfully), 235.--2) glory, renown : acc. sg. þrym, 2.--Comp. hyge-þrym.

þrym-lîc, adj., powerful, mighty : nom. sg. þrec-wudu þrym-lîc (the mighty spear), 1247.

þu, pron., thou , 366, 407, 445, etc.; acc. sg. þec (poetic), 948, 2152, etc.; þe, 417, 426, 517, etc.; after compar. sêlran þe (a better one than thee), 1851. See ge.

þunca, w. m. See äf-þunca.

ge-þungen. See ge-þingan, st. v.

þurfan, pret.-pres. v., to need : pres. sg. II. nô þu ne þearft ... sorgian (needest not care), 450; so, 445, 1675; III. ne þearf ... onsittan (need not fear), 596; so, 2007, 2742; pres. subj. þät he ... sêcean þurfe, 2496; pret. sg. þorfte, 157, 1027, 1072, 2875, 2996; pl. nealles Hetware hrêmge þorfton (i.e. wesan) fêðe-wîges (needed not boast of their foot-fight), 2365.

ge-þuren. See þweran.

þurh, prep. w. acc. signifying motion through, hence: I. local, through, throughout : wôd þâ þurh þone wäl-rêc (went then through the battle-reek), 2662.--II. causal: 1) on account of, for the sake of, owing to : þurh slîðne nîð (through fierce hostility, heathenism), 184; þurh holdne hige (from friendliness), 267; so, þurh rûmne sefan, 278; þurh sîdne sefan, 1727; eóweð þurh egsan uncûðne nîð (shows unheard-of hostility by the terror he causes), 276; so, 1102, 1336, 2046. 2) by means of, through : heaðo-ræs for-nam mihtig mere-deór þurh mîne hand, 558; þurh ânes cräft, 700; so, 941, 1694, 1696, 1980, 2406, 3069.

þus, adv., so, thus , 238, 337, 430.

þunian, w. v., to din, sound forth : pret. sg. sund-wudu þunede, 1907.

þûsend, num., thousand : 1) fem. acc. ic þe þûsenda þegna bringe tô helpe, 1830.--2) neut. with measure of value (sceat) omitted: acc. seofan þûsendo, 2196; gen. hund-þûsenda landes and locenra beága (100,000 sceattas' worth of land and rings), 2995.--3) uninflected: acc. þûsend wintra, 3051.

þwære, adj., affable, mild : in comp. man-þwære.

ge-þwære, adj., gentle, mild : nom. pl. ge-þwære, 1231.

ge-þweran, st. v., to forge, strike : pret. part. heoru ... hamere ge-þuren (for ge-þworen) (hammer-forged sword), 1286.

þyhtig. See þihtig.

ge-þyld (see þolian), st. f.: 1) patience, endurance : acc. sg. ge-þyld, 1396.--2) steadfastness : instr. pl. = adv.: ge-þyldum (steadfastly, patiently), 1706.

þyle, st. m., spokesman, leader of the conversation at court : nom. sg., 1166, 1457.

þyncan, þincean, w. v. w. dat. of pers., to seem, appear : pres. sg. III. þinceð him tô lytel (it seems to him too little), 1749; ne þynceð me gerysne, þät we (it seemeth to me not fit that we ...), 2654; pres. pl. hy ... wyrðe þinceað eorla ge-æhtlan (they seem worthy contenders with (?) earls ; or, worthy warriors), 368; pres. subj. swâ him ge-met þince, 688; inf. þincean, 1342; pret. sg. þûhte, 2462, 3058; nô his lîf-gedâl sâr-lîc þûhte secga ænigum (his death seemed painful to none of men), 843; pret. pl. þær him fold-wegas fägere þûhton, 867.

of-þincan, to displease, offend : inf. mäg þäs þonne of-þyncan þeóden (dat.) Heaðo-beardna and þegna gehwâm þâra leóda, 2033.

þyrs, st. m., giant : dat. sg. wið þyrse (Grendel), 426.

þys-lîc, adj., such, of such a nature : nom. sg. fem. þys-lîcu þearf, 2638.

þý. See þät.

þýwan (M.H.G. diuhen, O.H.G. duhan), w. v., to crush, oppress : inf. gif þec ymb-sittend egesan þýwað (if thy neighbors oppress thee with dread), 1828.

þýstru, st. f., darkness : dat. pl. in þýstrum, 87.

ge-þýwe, adj., customary, usual : nom. sg. swâ him ge-þýwe ne wäs (as was not his custom), 2333.

U

ufan, adv., from above , 1501; above , 330.

ufera (prop. higher), adj., later : dat. pl. ufaran dôgrum, 2201, 2393.

ufor, adv., higher , 2952.

uhte, w. f., twilight or dawn : dat. or acc. on uhtan, 126.

uht-floga, w. m., twilight-flier, dawn-flier (epithet of the dragon): gen. sg. uht-flogan, 2761.

uht-hlem, st. m., twilight-cry, dawn-cry : acc. sg., 2008.

uht-sceaða, w. m., twilight- or dawn-foe : nom. sg., 2272.

umbor, st. n., child, infant : acc. sg., 46; dat. sg., 1188.

un-blîðe, adv.(?), unblithely, sorrowfully , 130, 2269; (adj., nom. pl.?), 3032.

un-byrnende, pres. part., unburning, without burning , 2549.

unc, dat. and acc. of the dual wit, us two, to us two , 1784, 2138, 2527; gen. hwäðer ... uncer twega (which of us two), 2533; uncer Grendles (of us two, G. and me), 2003.

uncer, poss. pron., of us two : nom. sg. [uncer], 2002(?); dat. pl. uncran eaferan, 1186.

un-cûð, adj.: 1) unknown : nom. sg. stîg ... eldum uncûð, 2215; acc. sg. neut. uncûð ge-lâd (unknown ways), 1411.--2) unheard-of, barbarous, evil : acc. sg. un-cûðne nîð, 276; gen. sg. un-cûðes (of the foe , Grendel), 961.

under, I. prep. w. dat. and acc.: 1) w. dat., answering question where? = under (of rest), contrasted with over : bât (wäs) under beorge, 211; þâ cwom Wealhþeó forð gân under gyldnum beáge (W. walked forth under a golden circlet , i.e. decked with), 1164; siððan he under segne sine ealgode (under his banner), 1205; he under rande ge-cranc (sank under his shield), 1210; under wolcnum, 8, 1632; under heofenum, 52, 505; under roderum, 310; under helme, 342, 404; under here-grîman, 396, 2050, 2606; so, 711, 1198, 1303, 1929, 2204, 2416, 3061, 3104.--2) w. acc.: a) answering question whither? = under (of motion): þâ secg wîsode under Heorotes hrôf, 403; siððan æfen-leóht under heofenes hâdor be-holen weorðeð, 414; under sceadu bregdan, 708; fleón under fen-hleoðu, 821; hond âlegde ... under geápne hrôf, 837; teón in under eoderas, 1038; so, 1361, 1746, 2129, 2541, 2554, 2676, 2745; so, häfde þâ for-sîðod sunu Ecg-þeówes under gynne grund, 1552 (for-sîðian requires acc.). b) after verbs of venturing and fighting, with acc. of object had in view: he under hârne stân ...âna ge-nêðde frêcne dæde, 888; ne dorste under ýða ge-win alder ge-nêðan, 1470. c) indicating extent, with acc. after expressions of limit, etc.: under swegles begong (as far as the sky extends), 861, 1774; under heofenes hwealf (as far as heaven's vault reaches), 2016.

II. Adv., beneath, below : stîg under läg (a path lay beneath , i.e. the rock), 2214.

undern-mæl, st. n., midday : acc. sg., 1429.

un-dyrne, un-derne, adj., without concealment, plain, clear : nom. sg., 127, 2001; un-derne, 2912.

un-dyrne, adv., plainly, evidently ; un-dyrne cûð, 150, 410.

un-fäger, adj., unlovely, hideous : nom. sg. leóht un-fäger, 728.

un-fæcne, adj., without malice, sincere : nom. sg., 2069.

un-fæge, adj., not death-doomed or "fey": nom. sg., 2292; acc. sg. un-fægne eorl, 573.

un-flitme, adv., solemnly, incontestably : Finn Hengeste elne unflitme âðum benemde (F. swore solemnly to H. with oaths) [if an adj., elne un-f. = unconquerable in valor], 1098.

un-forht, adj., fearless, bold : nom. sg., 287; acc. pl. unforhte (adv.?), 444. See Note.

un-from, adj., unfit, unwarlike : nom. sg., 2189.

un-frôd, adj., not aged, young : dat sg. guman un-frôdum, 2822.

un-gedêfelîce, adv., unjustly, contrary to right and custom , 2436.

un-gemete, adv., immeasurably, exceedingly , 2421, 2722, 2729.

un-gemetes, adv. gen. sg., the same, 1793.

un-geâra, adv., (not old), recently, lately , 933; soon , 603.

un-gifeðe, adj., not to be granted; refused : nom. sg., 2922.

un-gleáw, adj., regardless, reckless : acc. sg. sweord ... ecgum ungleáw (of a sharp-edged sword), 2565.

un-hâr, adj., very gray : nom. sg., 357; (bald ?).

un-hælo, st. f., mischief, destruction : gen. sg. wiht un-hælo (the demon of destruction , Grendel), 120.

un-heóre, un-hýre, adj., monstrous, horrible : nom. sg. m., weard un-hióre (the dragon), 2414; neut. wîf un-hýre (Grendel's mother), 2121; nom. pl. neut. hand-sporu ... unheóru (of Grendel's claws), 988.

un-hlytme, un-hlitme, adv. (cf. A.S. hlytm = lot ; O.N. hluti = part division), undivided, unseparated , united , 1130 [unless = un-flitme, 1098]. See Note.

un-leóf, adj., hated : acc. pl. seah on un-leófe, 2864.

un-lifigende, pres. part., unliving, lifeless : nom. sg. un-lifigende, 468; acc. sg. un-lyfigendne, 1309; dat. sg. un-lifgendum, 1390; gen. sg. un-lyfigendes, 745.

un-lytel, adj., not little, very large : nom. sg. duguð un-lytel (a great band of warriors ? or great joy ?), 498; dôm un-lytel (no little glory), 886; acc. sg. torn un-lytel (very great shame, misery), 834.

un-murnlîce, adv., unpityingly, without sorrowing , 449, 1757.

unnan, pret.-pres. v., to grant, give; wish, will : pret.-pres. sg. I. ic þe an tela sinc-gestreóna, 1226; weak pret. sg. I. ûðe ic swîðor þät þu hine selfne ge-seón môste, 961; III. he ne ûðe þät ...(he granted not that ...), 503; him god ûðe þät ... he hyne sylfne ge-wräc (God granted to him that he avenged himself), 2875; þeáh he ûðe wel (though he well would), 2856.

ge-unnan, to grant, permit : inf. gif he ûs ge-unnan wile þät we hine ... grêtan môton, 346; me ge-ûðe ylda waldend, þät ic ... ge-seah hangian (the Ruler of men permitted me to see hanging ...), 1662.

un-nyt, adj., useless : nom. sg., 413, 3170.

un-riht, st. n., unright, injustice, wrong : acc. sg. unriht, 1255, 2740; instr. sg. un-rihte (unjustly, wrongly), 3060.

un-rîm, st. n., immense number : nom. sg., 1239, 3136; acc. sg., 2625.

un-rîme, adj., countless, measureless : nom. sg. gold un-rîme, 3013.

un-rôt, adj., sorrowing : nom. pl. un-rôte, 3149.

un-snyttru, st. f., lack of wisdom : dat. pl. for his un-snyttrum (for his unwisdom), 1735.

un-softe, adv., unsoftly, with violence (hardly ?), 2141; scarcely , 1656.

un-swýðe, adv., not strongly or powerfully : compar. (ecg) bât unswîðor þonne his þiód-cyning þearfe häfde (the sword bit less sharply than the prince of the people needed), 2579; fýr unswîðor weóll, 2882.

un-synnig, adj., guiltless, sinless : acc. sg. un-synnigne, 2090.

un-synnum, adv. instr. pl., guiltlessly , 1073.

un-tæle, adj., blameless : acc. pl. un-tæle, 1866.

un-tyder, st. m., evil race, monster : nom. pl. un-tydras, 111. [Cf. Ger. un-mensch.]

un-wâclîc, adj., that cannot be shaken; firm, strong : acc. sg. âd ... un-wâclîcne, 3139.

un-wearnum, adv. instr. pl., unawares, suddenly ; (unresistingly ?), 742.

un-wrecen, pret. part., unavenged , 2444.

up, adv., up, upward , 224, 519, 1374, 1620, 1913, 1921, 2894; (of the voice), þâ wäs ... wôp up âhafen, 128; so, 783.

up-lang, adj., upright, erect : nom. sg., 760.

uppe (adj., ûfe, ûffe), adv., above , 566.

up-riht, adj., upright, erect : nom. sg., 2093.

uton. See wuton.

Û

ûð-genge, adj., transitory, evanescent, ready to depart , (fled ?): þær wäs Äschere ... feorh ûð-genge, 2124.

ûs, pers. pron. dat. and acc. of we (see we), us, to us , 1822, 2636, 2643, 2921, 3002, 3079; acc. (poetic), ûsic, 2639, 2641, 2642;--gen. ûre: ûre æg-hwylc (each of us), 1387; ûser, 2075.

ûser, possess, pron.: nom. sg. ûre man-drihten, 2648; dat. sg. ûssum hlâforde, 2635; gen. sg. neut. ûsses cynnes, 2814; dat. pl. ûrum ... bâm (to us both, two) (for unc bâm), 2660.

ût, adv., out , 215, 537, 664, 1293, 1584, 2082, 2558, 3131.

ûtan, adv., from without, without , 775, 1032, 1504, 2335.

ût-fûs, adj., ready to go : nom. sg. hringed-stefna îsig and ût-fûs, 33.

ût-weard, adj., outward, outside, free : nom. sg. eoten (Grendel) wäs ût-weard, 762.

ûtan-weard, adj., without, outward, from without : acc. sg. hlæw ... ealne ûtan-weardne, 2298.

W

*wacan, st. v., to awake, arise, originate : pret. sg. þanon (from Cain) wôc fela geó-sceaft-gâsta, 1266; so, 1961; pl. þâm feówer bearn ... in worold wôcun, 60.

*on-wacan: 1) to awake (intrans.): pret. sg. þâ se wyrm on-wôc (when the drake awoke), 2288.--2) to be born : pret. sg. him on-wôc heáh Healfdene, 56; pl. on-wôcon, 111.

wacian, w. v., to watch : imper. sg. waca wið wrâðum! 661.

wadan, st. v., (cf. wade, waddle) to traverse; stride, go : pret. sg. wôd þurh þone wäl-rêc, 2662; wôd under wolcnum (stalked beneath the clouds), 715.

ge-wadan, to attain by moving, come to, reach : pret. part. ôð þät ... wunden-stefna ge-waden häfde, þät þâ lîðende land ge-sâwon (till the ship had gone so far that the sailors saw land), 220.

on-wadan, w. acc., to invade, befall : pret. sg. hine fyren on-wôd(?), 916.

þurh-wadan, to penetrate, pierce : pret. sg. þät swurd þurh-wôd wrät-lîcne wyrm, 891; so, 1568.

wag, st. m., wall : dat. sg. on wage, 1663; dat. pl. äfter wagum (along the walls), 996.

wala, w. m., boss : nom. pl. walan, 1032 (cf. Bouterwek in Haupt XI., 85 seqq.).

walda, w. m., wielder, ruler : in comp. an-, eal-walda.

wald-swaðu, st. f., forest-path : dat. pl. äfter wald-swaðum (along the wood-paths), 1404.

wam, wom, st. m., spot, blot, sin : acc. sg. him be-beorgan ne con wom (cannot protect himself from evil or from the evil strange orders , etc.; wom = wogum? = crooked ?), 1748; instr. pl. wommum, 3074.

wan, won, adj., wan, lurid, dark : nom. sg, ýð-geblond ... won (the dark waves), 1375; se wonna hrefn (the black raven), 3025; wonna lêg (lurid flame), 3116; dat. sg. f. on wanre niht, 703; nom. pl. neut. scadu-helma ge-sceapu ... wan, 652.

wang, st. m., mead, field; place : acc. sg. wang, 93, 225; wong, 1414, 2410, 3074; dat. sg. wange, 2004; wonge, 2243, 3040; acc. pl. wongas, 2463.--Comp.: freoðo-, grund-, medo-, sæ-wang.

wang-stede, st. m., (locus campestris), spot, place : dat. sg. wong-stede, 2787.

wan-hýd (for hygd), st. f., heedlessness, recklessness : dat. pl. for his won-hýdum, 434.

wanian, w. v.: 1) intrans., to decrease, wane : inf. þâ þät sweord ongan ... wanian, 1608.--2) w. acc., to cause to wane or lessen : pret. sg. he tô lange leóde mîne wanode, 1338.

ge-wanian, to decrease, diminish : pret. part. is mîn flet-werod ... ge-wanod, 477.

wan-sælig, adj., unhappy, wretched : nom. sg. won-sælig wer (Grendel), 105.

wan-sceaft, st. f., misery, want : acc. sg. won-sceaft, 120.

warian, w. v. w. acc., to occupy, guard, possess : pres. sg. III. þær he hæðen gold waráð (where he guards heathen gold), 2278; pl. III. hie (Grendel and his mother) dýgel land warigeað, 1359; pret. sg. (Grendel) goldsele warode, 1254; (Cain) wêsten warode, 1266.

waroð, st. m., shore : dat. sg. tô waroðe, 234; acc. pl. wide waroðas, 1966.

waru, st. f., inhabitants , (collective) population : in comp. land-waru.

wâ, interj., woe! wâ bið þäm þe... (woe to him that...), 183.

wâðu, st. f., way, journey : in comp. gamen-wâðu.

wânian, w. v., to weep, whine, howl , w. acc.: inf. gehýrdon ... sâr wânigean helle häftan (they heard the hell-fastened one lamenting his pain), 788; pret. sg. [wânode], 3152(?).

wât. See witan.

wäcean, w. v., to watch : pret. part wäccende, 709, 2842; acc. sg. m. wäccendne wer, 1269. See wacian.

wäcnan, w. v., to be awake, come forth : inf., 85.

wäd, st. n., (the moving) sea, ocean : nom. wado weallende, 546; wadu weallendu, 581; gen. pl. wada 508.

wäfre, adj., wavering (like flame), ghostlike, without distinct bodily form : nom. sg. wäl-gæst wäfre (of Grendel's mother), 1332;-- flickering, expiring : nom. sg. wäfre môd, 1151; him wäs geômor sefa, wäfre and wäl-fûs, 2421.

be-wägnan, w. v., to offer : pret part, him wäs ... freónd-laðu wordum be-wägned, 1194.

wäl, st. n., battle, slaughter, the slain in battle : acc. sg. wäl, 1213, 3028, blôdig wäl, 448; oððe on wäl crunge (or in battle, among the slain, fall), 636; dat. sg. sume on wäle crungon (some fell in the slaughter), 1114; dat. sg. in Fr...es wäle (proper name in MS. destroyed), 1071; nom. pl. walu, 1043.

wäl-bed, st. n., slaughter-bed, deathbed : dat. sg. on wäl-bedde, 965.

wäl-bend, st. f., death-bond : acc. sg. or pl. wäl-bende ... hand-gewriðene, 1937.

wäl-bleát, adj., deadly, mortal, cruel : acc. sg. wunde wäl-bleáte, 2726.

wäl-deáð, st. m., death in battle : nom. sg., 696.

wäl-dreór, st. m., battle-gore : instr. sg. wäl-dreóre, 1632.

wäl-fâh, adj., slaughter-stained, blood-stained : acc. sg. wäl-fâgne winter, 1129.

wäl-fähð, st. f., deadly feud : gen. pl. wäl-fæhða, 2029.

wäl-feall, st. m., (fall of the slain), death, destruction : dat. sg. tô wäl-fealle, 1712.

wäl-fûs, adj., ready for death, foreboding death : nom. sg., 2421.

wäl-fyllo, st. f., fill of slaughter : dat. sg. mid þære wäl-fulle (i.e. the thirty men nightly slaughtered at Heorot by Grendel), 125; wäl-fylla? 3155.

wäl-fýr, st. n.: 1) deadly fire : instr. sg. wäl-fýre (of the fire-spewing dragon), 2583.--2) corpse-consuming fire, funeral pyre : gen. pl. wäl-fýra mæst, 1120.

wäl-gæst, st. m., deadly sprite (of Grendel and his mother): nom. sg. wäl-gæst, 1332; acc. sg. þone wäl-gæst, 1996.

wäl-hlem, st. m., death-stroke : acc. sg. wäl-hlem þone, 1996.

wälm, st. m., flood, whelming water : nom. sg. þære burnan wälm, 2547; gen. sg. þäs wälmes (of the surf), 2136.--Comp. cear-wälm.

wäl-nîð, st. m., deadly hostility : nom. sg., 3001; dat. sg. äfter wäl-nîðe, 85; nom. pl. wäl-nîðas, 2066.

wäl-râp, st. m., flood-fetter, i.e. ice : acc. pl. wäl-râpas, 1611; (cf. wäll, wel, wyll = well, flood : leax sceal on wäle mid sceóte scrîðan, Gnom. Cott. 39).

wäl-ræs, st. m., deadly onslaught : nom. sg., 2948; dat. sg. wäl-ræse, 825, 2532.

wäl-rest, st. f., death-bed , acc. sg. wäl-reste, 2903.

wäl-rêc, st. m., deadly reek or smoke : acc. sg. wôd þâ þurh þone wäl-rêc, 2662.

wäl-reáf, st, n., booty of the slain, battle-plunder : acc. sg., 1206.

wäl-reów, adj., bold in battle : nom. sg., 630.

wäl-sceaft, st. m., deadly shaft, spear : acc. pl. wäl-sceaftas, 398.

wäl-seax, st. n., deadly knife, war-knife : instr. sg. wäll-seaxe, 2704.

wäl-stenge, st. m., battle-spear : dat. sg. on þam wäl-stenge, 1639.

wäl-stôw, st. f., battle-field : dat. sg. wäl-stôwe, 2052, 2985.

wästm, st. m., growth, form, figure : dat. sg. on weres wästmum (in man's form), 1353.

wäter, st. n., water : nom. sg., 93, 1417, 1515, 1632; acc. sg. wäter, 1365, 1620; deóp wäter (the deep), 509, 1905; ofer wîd wäter (over the high sea] , 2474; dat. sg. äfter wätere (along the Grendel-sea), 1426; under wätere (at the bottom of the sea), 1657; instr. wätere, 2723; wätre, 2855; gen. sg. ofer wäteres hrycg (over the surface of the sea), 471; on wäteres äht, 516; þurh wäteres wylm

(through the sea-wave), 1694; gen. = instr. wäteres weorpan (to sprinkle with water), 2792.

wäter-egesa, st. m., water-terror , i.e. the fearful sea : acc. sg., 1261

wäter-ýð, st. f., water-wave, billow : dat. pl. wäter-ýðum, 2243.

wæd, st. f., (weeds), garment : in comp. here-, hilde-wæd.

ge-wæde, st. n., clothing , especially battle-equipments : acc. pl. gewædu, 292.--Comp. eorl-gewæde.

wæg, st. m., wave : acc. sg. wæg, 3133.

wæg-bora, w. m., wave-bearer, swimmer (bearing or propelling the waves before him): nom. sg. wundorlîc wæg-bora (of a sea-monster), 1441.

wæg-flota, w. m., sea-sailer, ship : acc. sg. wêg-flotan, 1908.

wæg-holm, st. m., the wave-filled sea : acc. sg. ofer wæg-holm, 217.

wæge, st. n., cup, can : acc. sg. fäted wæge, 2254, 2283.--Comp.: ealo-, lîð-wæge.

wæg-lîðend, pres. part., sea-farer : dat. pl. wæg-lîðendum (et lîðendum, MS.), 3160.

wæg-sweord, st. n., heavy sword : acc. sg., 1490.

wæn, st. m., wain, wagon : acc. sg. on wæn, 3135.

wæpen, st. n., weapon; sword : nom. sg., 1661; acc. sg. wæpen, 686, 1574, 2520, 2688; instr. wæpne, 1665, 2966; gen. wæpnes, 1468; acc. pl. wæpen, 292; dat. pl. wæpnum, 250, 331, 2039, 2396. --Comp.: hilde-, sige-wæpen.

wæpned-man, st. m., warrior, man : dat. sg. wæpned-men, 1285.

wær, st. f., covenant, treaty : acc. sg. wære, 1101;-- protection, care : dat. sg. on freán (on þäs waldendes) wære (into God's protection), 27, 3110.--Comp.: frioðo-wær.

wæsma, w. m., fierce strength, war-strength : in comp. here-wæsma, 678.

we, pers. pron., we , 942, 959, 1327, 1653, 1819, 1820, etc.

web, st. n., woven work, tapestry :, nom. pl. web, 996.

webbe, w. f., webster, female weaver : in comp. freoðu-webbe.

weccan, weccean, w. v. w. acc., to wake, rouse; recall : inf. wîg-bealu weccan (to stir up strife), 2047; nalles hearpan swêg (sceal) wîgend weccean (the sound of the harp shall not wake up the warriors), 3025; ongunnon þâ ... bæl-fýra mæst wîgend weccan (the warriors then began to start the mightiest of funeral pyres), 3145; pret. sg. wehte hine wätre (roused him with water , i.e. Wîglâf recalled Beówulf to consciousness), 2855.

tô-weccan, to stir up, rouse : pret, pl. hû þâ folc mid him (with one another), fæhðe tô-wehton, 2949.

wed, st. n., (cf. wed-ding), pledge : dat. sg. hyldo tô wedde (as a pledge of his favor), 2999.

weder, st. n., weather : acc. pl. wuldor-torhtan weder, 1137; gen. pl. wedera cealdost, 546.

ge-wef, st. n., woof, weaving : acc. pl. wîg-spêda ge-wiofu (the woof of war-speed : the battle-woof woven for weal or woe by the Walkyries; cf. Njals-saga, 158), 698.

weg, st. m., way : acc. sg. on weg (away, off), 264, 764, 845, 1431, 2097; gyf þu on weg cymest (if thou comest off safe , i.e. from the battle with Grendel's mother), 1383.--Comp.: feor-, fold-, forð-, wîd-weg.

wegan, st. v. w. acc., to bear, wear, bring, possess : subj. pres. nâh hwâ sweord wege (I have none that may bear the sword), 2253; inf. nalles (sceal) eorl wegan mâððum tô ge-myndum (no earl shall wear a memorial jewel), 3016; pret. ind. he þâ frätwe wäg ... ofer ýða ful (bore the jewels over the goblet of the waves), 1208; wäl-seaxe ... þät he on byrnan wäg, 2705; heortan sorge wäg (bore heart's sorrow); so, 152, 1778, 1932, 2781.

ät-wegan = auferre, to carry off : syððan Hâma ät-wäg tô þære byrhtan byrig Brosinga mene (since H. bore from the bright city the Brosing-collar), 1199.

ge-wegan (O.N. wega), to fight : inf. þe he wið þam wyrme ge-wegan sceolde, 2401.

wel, adv.: 1) well : wel bið þäm þe ... (well for him that ...!), 186; se þe wel þenceð (he that well thinketh, judgeth), 289; so, 640, 1046, 1822, 1834, 1952, 2602; well, 2163, 2813.--2) very, very much : Geát ungemetes wel ... restan lyste (the Geat longed sorely to rest), 1793.--3) indeed, to be sure , 2571, 2856.

wela, w. m., wealth, goods, possessions : in comp. ær-, burg-, hord-, mâððum-wela.

wel-hwylc, indef. pron., = quivis, any you please, any (each, all): gen. pl. wel-hwylcra wilna, 1345; w. partitive gen.: nom. sg. witena wel-hwylc, 266;-- substantively: acc. neut. wel-hwylc, 875.

welig, adj., wealthy, rich : acc. sg. wîc-stede weligne Wægmundinga, 2608.

wel-þungen, pres. part., well-thriven (in mind), mature, high-minded : nom. sg. Hygd (wäs) swîðe geong, wîs, wel-þungen, 1928.

wenian, w. v., to accustom, attract, honor : subj. pret. þät ... Folcwaldan sunu ... Hengestes heáp hringum wenede (sh. honor), 1092.

be-(bi-)wenian, entertain, care for, attend : pret. sg. mäg þäs þonne of-þyncan þeóden Heaðo-beardna ... þonne he mid fæmnan on flet gæð, dryht-bearn Dena duguða bi-wenede (may well displease the prince of the H.... when he with the woman goes into the hall, that a noble scion of the Danes should entertain, bear wine to, the knights , cf. 494 seqq.; or, a noble scion of the Danes should attend on her?), 2036; pret. part. nom. pl. wæron her tela willum be-wenede, 1822.

wendan, w. v., to turn : pres. sg. III. him eal worold wendeð on willan (all the world turns at his will), 1740.

ge-wendan, w. acc.: l) to turn, turn round : pret. sg. wicg gewende (turned his horse), 315.--2) to turn (intrans.), change : inf. wâ bið þäm þe sceal ... frôfre ne wênan, wihte ge-wendan (woe to him that shall have no hope, shall not change at all), 186.

on-wendan, to avert, set aside : 1) w. acc.: inf. ne mihte snotor häleð weán on-wendan, 191.--2) intrans.: sibb æfre ne mäg wiht on-wendan þam þe wel þenceð (in, to, him that is well thinking friendship can not be set aside), 2602.

wer, st. m., man, hero : nom. sg. (Grendel), 105; acc. sg. wer (Beówulf), 1269, 3174; gen. sg. on weres wästmum (in man's form), 1353; nom. pl. weras, 216, 1223, 1234, 1441, 1651; dat. pl. werum, 1257; gen. pl. wera, 120, 994, 1732, 3001; (MS. weora), 2948.

wered, st. n., (as adj. = sweet), a sort of beer (probably without hops or such ingredients): acc. sg. scîr wered, 496.

were-feohte, f., defensive fight, fight in self-defence : dat. pl. for were-fyhtum (fere fyhtum, MS.), 457.

werhðo, st. f., curse, outlawry, condemnation : acc. sg. þu in helle scealt werhðo dreógan, 590.

werian, to defend, protect : w. vb., pres. sg. III. beaduscrûda ... þät mîne breóst wereð, 453; inf. wit unc wið hron-fixas werian þôhton, 541; pres. part. w. gen. pl. wergendra tô lyt (too few defenders), 2883; pret. ind. wäl-reáf werede (guarded the battle-spoil), 1206; se hwîta helm hafelan werede (the shining helm protected his head), 1449; pl. hafelan weredon, 1328; pret. part. nom. pl. ge ... byrnum werede (ye ... corselet-clad), 238, 2530.

be-werian, to protect, defend : pret. pl. þät hie ... leóda land-geweorc lâðum be-weredon scuccum and scinnum (that they the people's land-work from foes, from monsters and demons, might defend), 939

werig, adj., accursed, outlawed : gen. sg. wergan gâstes (Grendel), 133; (of the devil), 1748.

werod, weorod, st. n., band of men, warrior-troop : nom. sg. werod, 652; weorod, 290, 2015, 3031; acc. sg. werod, 319; dat. instr. sg. weorode, 1012, 2347; werede, 1216; gen. sg. werodes, 259; gen. pl. wereda, 2187; weoroda, 60.--Comp.: eorl-, flet-werod.

wer-þeód, st. f., people, humanity : dat. sg. ofer wer-þeóde, 900.

wesan, v., to be : pres. sg. I. ic eom, 335, 407; II. þu eart, 352, 506; III. is, 256, 272, 316, 343, 375, 473, etc.; nu is þînes mägenes blæd âne hwîle (the prime [fame?] of thy powers lasteth now for a while), 1762; ys, 2911, 3000, 3085; pl. I. we synt, 260, 342; II. syndon, 237, 393; III. syndon, 257, 361, 1231; synt, 364; sint, 388; subj. pres. sîe, 435, 683, etc.; sý, 1832, etc.; sig, 1779, etc.; imper. sg. II. wes, 269 (cf. wassail, wes hæl), 407, 1171, 1220, 1225, etc.; inf. wesan, 272, 1329, 1860, 2709, etc. The inf. wesan must sometimes be supplied: nealles Hetware hrêmge þorfton (i.e. wesan) feðe-wîges, 2364; so, 2498, 2660, 618, 1858; pres. part. wesende, 46; dat. sg. wesendum, 1188; pret. sg. I., III. wäs, 11, 12, 18, 36, 49, 53, etc.; wäs on sunde (was a-swimming), 1619; so, 848, 850(?), 970, 981, 1293; progressive, wäs secgende (for säde), 3029; II. wære, 1479, etc.; pl. wæron, 233, 536, 544, etc.; wæran (w. reflex, him), 2476; pret. subj. wære, 173, 203, 594, 946, etc.; progressive, myndgiend wære (for myndgie), 1106.--Contracted neg. forms: , nis = ne + is, 249, 1373, etc.; näs = ne + wäs, 134, 1300, 1922, 2193, etc. (cf. uncontracted: ne wäs, 890, 1472); næron = ne + wæron, 2658; nære = ne + wære, 861, 1168. See cniht-wesende.

wêg. See wæg.

wên, st. f., expectation, hope : nom. sg., 735, 1874, 2324; nu is leódum wên orleg-hwîle (gen.) (now the people have weening of a time of strife), 2911; acc. sg. þäs ic wên häbbe (as I hope, expect), 383; so, þäs þe ic [wên] hafo, 3001; wên ic talige, 1846; dat. pl. bega on wênum (in expectation of both , i.e. the death and the return of Beówulf), 2896. See or-wêna.

wênan, w. v., to ween, expect, hope : 1) absolutely; pres. sg. I. þäs ic wêne (as I hope), 272; swâ ic þe wêne tô (as I hope thou wilt : Beówulf hopes Hrôðgâr will now suffer no more pain), 1397.--2) w. gen. or acc. pres. sg. I. þonne wêne ic tô þe wyrsan ge-þinges, 525; ic þær heaðu-fýres hâtes wêne, 2523; III. secce ne wêneð to Gâr Denum (weeneth not of contest with the Gar-Danes), 601; inf. (beorhtre bôte) wênan (to expect, count on, a brilliant [? a lighter penalty] atonement), 157; pret. pl. þäs ne wêndon ær witan Scyldinga þät ... the wise men of the Scyldings weened not of this before, that ...), 779; þät hig þäs äðelinges eft ne wêndon þät he ... sêcean côme (that they looked not for the atheling again that he ... would come to seek ...), 1598.--3) w. acc. inf.: pret. sg. wênde, 934.--4) w. depend. clause: pres. sg. I. wêne ic þät..., 1185; wên' ic þät..., 338, 442; pret. sg. wênde, 2330; pl. wêndon, 938, 1605.

wêpan, st. v., to weep : pret. sg. [weóp], 3152 (?).

werig, adj., weary, exhausted , w. gen.: nom. sg. siðes wêrig (weary from the journey, way-weary), 579; dat. sg. siðes wêrgum, 1795;--w. instr.: acc. pl. wundum wêrge (wound-weary), 2938.--Comp.: deáð-, fyl-, gûð-wêrig.

ge-werigean, w. v., to weary, exhaust : pret. part. ge-wêrgad, 2853.

wêrig-môd, adj., weary-minded (animo defessus) : nom. sg., 845, 1544.

wêste, adj., waste, uninhabited : acc. sg. win-sele wêstne, 2457.

wêsten, st. n., waste, wilderness : acc. sg. wêsten, 1266.

wêsten, st. f., waste, wilderness : dat. sg. on þære wêstenne, 2299.

weal, st. m.: 1 wall, rampart : dat. instr. sg. wealle, 786, 892, 3163; gen. sg. wealles, 2308.--2) elevated sea-shore : dat. sg. of wealle, 229; acc. pl. windige weallas, 572, 1225.--3) wall of a building : acc, sg. wið þäs recedes weal, 326; dat. sg. be wealle, 1574; hence, the inner and outer rock-walls of the dragon's lair (cf. Heyne's essay: Halle Heorot, p. 59): dat. sg., 2308, 2527, 2717, 2760, 3061, 3104; gen. sg. wealles, 2324.--Comp.: bord-, eorð-, sæ-, scyld-weal.

ge-wealc, st. n., rolling : acc. sg. ofer ýða ge-wealc, 464.

ge-weald, st. n., power, might : acc. sg. on feónda ge-weald (into the power of his foes), 809, 904; so, 1685; geweald âgan, häbban, â-beódan (w. gen. of object = to present) = to have power over , 79, 655, 765, 951, 1088, 1611, 1728. See on-weald.

wealdan, st. v., to wield, govern, rule over, prevail : 1) absolutely or with depend. clause: inf. gif he wealdan môt (if he may prevail), 442; þær he ... wealdan môste swâ him Wyrd ne ge-scrâf (if [where?] he was to prevail, as Weird had not destined for him), 2575; pres. part. waldend (God), 1694; dat. wealdende, 2330; gen. waldendes, 2293, 2858, 3110.--2) with instr. or dat.: inf. þâm wæpnum wealdan (to wield, prevail with, the weapons), 2039; Geátum wealdan (to rule the Geátas), 2391; þeáh-hordum wealdan (to rule over, control, the treasure of rings), 2828; wäl-stôwe wealdan (to hold the field of battle), 2985; pret. sg. weóld, 465, 1058, 2380, 2596; þenden wordum weóld wine Scyldinga (while the friend of the S. ruled the G.), 30; pl. weóldon, 2052.--3) with gen.: pres. sg. I. þenden ic wealde wîdan rîces, 1860; pres. part. wuldres wealdend(waldend), 17, 183, 1753; weard, 2514; the 'dragon is called ylda waldend, 1662; waldend fira, 2742; sigora waldend, 2876 (designations of God); pret. sg. weóld, 703, 1771.

ge-wealdan, to wield, have power over, arrange : 1) w. acc.: pret. sg. hâlig god ge-weóld wîg-sigor, 1555.--2) w. dat.: pret. cyning ge-weóld his ge-witte (the king possessed his senses), 2704.--3) w. gen.: inf. he ne mihte nô ... wæpna ge-wealdan, 1510.

ge-wealden, pret. part., subject, subjected : acc. pl. gedêð him swâ gewealdene worolde dælas, 1733.

weallan, st. v.: 1) to toss, be agitated (of the sea): pres. part. nom. pl. wadu weallende (weallendu), 546, 581; nom. sg. brim weallende, 848; pret. ind. weól, 515, 850, 1132; weóll, 2139.--2) figuratively (of emotions), to be agitated : pres. pl. III. syððan Ingelde weallað wäl-nîðas (deadly hate thus agitates Ingeld), 2066; pres. part. weallende, 2465; pret. sg. hreðer inne weóll (his heart was moved within him), 2114; hreðer æðme weóll (his breast [the dragon's] swelled from breathing, snorting), 2594; breóst innan weóll þeóstrum ge-þoncum, 2332; so, weóll, 2600, 2715, 2883.

weall-clif, st. n., sea-cliff : acc. sg. ofer weall-clif, 3133.

weallian, w. v., to wander, rove about : pres. part. in comp. heoro-weallende, 2782.

weard, st. m., warden, guardian; owner : nom. sg. weard Scyldinga (the Scyldings' warden of the march), 229; weard, 286, 2240; se weard, sâwele hyrde, 1742; the king is called beáh-horda weard, 922; rîces weard, 1391; folces weard, 2514; the dragon is called weard, 3061; weard un-hióre, 2414; beorges weard, 2581; acc. sg, weard, 669; (dragon), 2842; beorges weard (dragon), 2525, 3067.-- Comp.: bât-, êðel-, gold-, heáfod-, hord-, hýð-, land-, rên-, sele-, yrfe-weard.

weard, st. m., possession (Dietrich in Haupt XI., 415): in comp. eorð-weard, 2335.

weard, st. f., watch, ward : acc. sg. wearde healdan, 319; wearde heóld, 305.-- Comp. æg-weard.

weard, adj., -ward : in comp. and-, innan-, ût-weard, 1288, etc.

weardian, w. v. w. acc.: 1) to watch, guard, keep : inf. he his folme forlêt tô lîf-wraðe, lâst weardian (Grendel left his hand behind as a life-saver, to guard his track [Kemble]), 972; pret. sg. him sió swîðre swaðe weardade hand on Hiorte (his right hand kept guard for him in H. , i.e. showed that he had been there), 2099; sg. for pl. hýrde ic þät þâm frätwum feówer mearas lungre gelîce last weardode (I heard that four horses, quite alike, followed in the traces of the armor), 2165.-- 2) to hold, possess, inhabit : pret. sg. fîfel-cynnes eard ... weardode (dwelt in the abode of the sea-fiends), 105; reced weardode un-rîm eorla (an immense number of earls held the hall), 1238; pl. þær we gesunde säl weardodon, 2076.

wearh, st. m., the accursed one; wolf : in comp. heoro-wearg, 1268.

wearn, st. f.: 1) resistance, refusal , 366.--2) warning?, resistance? See un-wearnum, 742.

weaxan, st. v., to wax, grow : pres. sg. III. ôð þät him on innan ofer-hygda dæl weaxeð (till within him pride waxeth), 1742; inf. weaxan, 3116; pret. sg. weôx, 8.

ge-weaxan, to grow up : pret. sg. oft þät seó geogoð ge-weôx, 66.

ge-weaxan to, to grow to or for something : pret. sg. ne ge-weôx he him to willan (grew not for their benefit), 1712.

weá, w. m., woe, evil, misfortune : nom. sg., 937; acc. sg. wean, 191, 423, 1207, 1992, 2293, 2938; gen. pl. weána, 148, 934, 1151, 1397.

weá-lâf, st. f., wretched remnant : acc. pl. þâ weá-lâfe (the wretched remnant , i.e. Finn's almost annihilated band), 1085, 1099.

weá-spel, st. n., woe-spell, evil tidings : dat. sg. weá-spelle, 1316.

ge-weoldum. See ge-wild.

weorc, st. n.: 1) work, labor, deed : acc. sg., 74; (war-deed), 1657; instr. sg. weorce, 1570; dat. pl. weorcum, 2097; wordum ne (and) worcum, 1101, 1834; gen. pl. worda and worca, 289.--2) work, trouble, suffering : acc. sg. þäs gewinnes weorc (misery on account of this strife), 1722; dat. pl. adv. weorcum (with labor), 1639.--Comp.: bædo-, ellen-, heaðo-, niht-weorc.

ge-weorc, st. n.: 1) work, deed, labor : nom. acc. sg., 455, 1563, 1682, 2718, 2775; gen. sg. ge-weorces, 2712. Comp.: ær-, fyrn-, gûð-, hond-, nîð-ge-weorc.-- 2) fortification, rampart : in comp. land-geweorc, 939.

weorce, adj., painful, bitter : nom. sg., 1419.

weorð, st. n., precious object, valuable : dat. sg. weorðe, 2497.

weorð, adj., dear, precious : nom. sg. weorð Denum äðeling (the atheling dear to the Danes , Beówulf), 1815; compar. nom. sg. þät he syððan wäs ... mâðme þý weorðra (more honored from the jewel), 1903; cf. wyrðe.

weorðan, st. v.: 1) to become : pres. sg. III. beholen weorðeð (is concealed), 414; underne weorðeð (becomes known), 2914; so, pl. III. weorðað, 2067;

wurðað, 282; inf. weorðan, 3179; wurðan, 808; pret. sg. I., III. wearð, 6, 77, 149, 409, 555, 754, 768, 819, 824, etc.; pl. wurdon, 228; subj. pret. wurde, 2732.--2) inf. to frôfre weorðan (to become a help), 1708; pret. sg. wearð he Heaðolâfe tô handbonan, 460; so, wearð, 906, 1262; ne wearð Heremôd swâ (i.e. to frôfre) eaforum Ecgwelan, 1710; pl. wurdon, 2204; subj. pret. sg. II. wurde, 588.--3) pret. sg. þät he on fylle wearð (that he came to a fall), 1545.--4) to happen, befall : inf. unc sceal weorðan ... swâ unc Wyrd ge-teóð (it shall befall us two as Fate decrees), 2527; þurh hwät his worulde gedâl weorðan sceolde, 3069; pret. sg. þâ þær sôna wearð ed-hwyrft eorlum (there was soon a renewal to the earls , i.e. of the former perils), 1281.

ge-weorðan: 1) to become : pret. sg. ge-wearð, 3062; pret. part. cearu wäs geniwod ge-worden (care was renewed), 1305; swâ us ge-worden is, 3079.--2) to finish; complete? : inf. þät þu ... lête Sûð-Dene sylfe ge-weorðan gûðe wið Grendel (that thou wouldst let the S. D. put an end to their war with Grendel), 1997.--3) impersonally with acc., to agree, decide : pret. sg. þâ þäs monige ge-wearð þät ... (since many agreed that ...), 1599; pret. part. hafað þäs ge-worden wine Scyldinga, rîces hyrde, and þät ræd talað þät he ... (therefore hath it so appeared(?) advisable to the friend of the S., the guardian of the realm, and he counts it a gain that ...), 2027.

weorð-ful, adj., glorious, full of worth : nom. sg. weorð-fullost, 3100.

weorðian, w. v., to honor, adorn : pret. sg. þær ic ... þîne leóde weorðode weorcum (there honored I thy people by my deeds), 2097; subj. pret. (þät he) ät feoh-gyftum ... Dene weorðode (that he would honor the Danes at, by, treasure-giving), 1091.

ge-weorðian, ge-wurðian, to deck, ornament : pret. part. hire syððan wäs äfter beáh-þege breóst ge-weorðod, 2177; wæpnum ge-weorðad, 250; since ge-weorðad, 1451; so, ge-wurðad, 331, 1039, 1646; wide ge-weorðad (known, honored, afar), 1960.

weorð-lîce, adv., worthily, nobly : superl. weorð-lîcost, 3163.

weorð-mynd, st. f. n., dignity, honor, glory : nom. sg., 65; acc. sg. geseah þâ eald sweord ..., wîgena weorðmynd (saw an ancient sword there, the glory of warriors), 1560; dat. instr. pl. weorð-myndum, 8; tô worð-myndum, 1187; gen. pl. weorð-mynda dæl, 1753.

weorðung, st. f., ornament : in comp. breóst-, hâm-, heorft-, hring-, wîg-weorðung.

weorod. See werod.

weorpan, st. v.: 1) to throw, cast away , w. acc.: pret. sg. wearp þâ wunden-mæl wrättum gebunden yrre oretta, þät hit on eorðan läg (the wrathful warrior threw the ornamented sword, that it lay on the earth), 1532.--2) to throw around or about , w. instr.: pret. sg. beorges weard ... wearp wäl-fýre (threw death-fire around), 2583.--3) to throw upon : inf. he hine eft ongan wäteres (instr. gen.) weorpan (began to cast water upon him again), 2792.

for-weorpan, w. acc., to cast away, squander : subj. pret. þät he genunga gûð-géwædu wrâðe for-wurpe (that he squandered uselessly the battle-weeds , i.e. gave them to the unworthy), 2873.

ofer-weorpan, to stumble : pret. sg. ofer-wearp þâ ... wîgena strongest, 1544.

weotian, w. v., to provide with, adjust (?): pret. part. acc. pl. wäl-bende weotode, 1937.

be-weotian, be-witian, w. v. w. acc., to regard, observe, care for : pres. pl. III. be-witiað, 1136; pret. sg. þegn ... se þe ... ealle be-weotede þegnes þearfe (who would attend to all the needs of a thane), 1797; draca se þe ... hord be-weotode (the drake that guarded a treasure), 2213;-- to carry out, undertake : pres. pl. III. þâ ... oft be-witigað sorh-fulne sîð on segl-râde, 1429.

    wicg, st. n., steed, riding-horse : nom. sg., 1401; acc. sg. wicg, 315; dat. instr. sg. wicge, 234; on wicge, 286; acc. pl. wicg, 2175; gen. pl. wicga, 1046.

    ge-widor, st. n., storm, tempest : acc. pl. lâð ge-widru (loathly weather), 1376.

    wið prep. w. dat. and acc., with fundamental meanings of division and opposition: 1) w. dat., against, with (in hostile sense), from : þâ wið gode wunnon, 113; âna (wan) wið eallum, 145; ymb feorh sacan, lâð wið lâðum, 440; so, 426, 439, 550, 2372, 2521, 2522, 2561, 2840, 3005; þæt him holt-wudu ... helpan ne meahte, lind wið lîge, 2342; hwät ... sêlest wære wið fær-gryrum tô ge-fremmanne, 174; þæt him gâst-bona geóce gefremede wið þeód-þreáum, 178; wið rihte wan (strove against right), 144; häfde ... sele Hrôðgâres ge-nered wið nîðe (had saved H.'s hall from strife), 828; (him dyrne langað ...) beorn wið blôde (the hero longeth secretly contrary to his blood , i.e. H. feels a secret longing for the non-related Beówulf), 1881; sundur ge-dælan lîf wið lîce (to sunder soul from body), 2424; streámas wundon sund wið sande (the currents rolled the sea against the sand), 213; lîg-ýðum forborn bord wið ronde (rond, MS.) (with waves of flame burnt the shield against, as far as, the rim), 2674; holm storme weól, won wið winde (the sea surged, wrestled with the wind), 1133; so, hiora in ânum weóll sefa wið sorgum (in one of them surged the soul with sorrow [against ?, Heyne]), 2601; þæt hire wið healse heard grâpode (that the sharp sword bit against her neck), 1567.--2) w. acc.: a) against, towards : wan wið Hrôðgâr (fought against H.), 152; wið feónda gehwone, 294; wið wrâð werod, 319; so, 540, 1998, 2535; hine hâlig god ûs on-sende wið Grendles gryre, 384; þæt ic wið þone gûð-flogan gylp ofer-sitte (that I refrain from boastful speech against the battle-flier), 2529; ne wolde wið manna ge-hwone ... feorh-bealo feorran (would not cease his life-plotting against any of the men ; or, withdraw life-bale from , etc.? or, peace would not have with any man..., mortal bale withdraw ?, Kemble), 155; ic þâ leóde wât ge wið feónd ge wið freónd fäste geworhte (towards foe and friend), 1865; hcóld heáh-lufan wið häleða brego (cherished high love towards the prince of heroes), 1955; wið ord and wið ecge ingang forstôd (prevented entrance to spear-point and sword-edge), 1550. b) against, on, upon, in : setton sîde scyldas ... wið þäs recedes weal (against the wall of the hall), 326; wið eorðan fäðm (eardodon) (in the bosom of the earth), 3050; wið earm ge-sät (sat on, against, his arm), 750; so, stîð-môd ge-stôd wið steápne rond, 2567; [wið duru healle eode] (went to the door of the hall), 389; wið Hrefna-wudu (over against, near, H.), 2926; wið his sylfes sunu setl ge-tæhte (showed me to a seat with, near, beside, his own son), 2014. c) towards, with (of contracting parties): þæt hie healfre ge-weald wið Eotena bearn âgan môston (that they power over half the hall with the Eotens' sons were to possess), 1089; þenden he wið wulf wäl reáfode (whilst with the wolf he was robbing the slain), 3028.--3) Alternately with dat. and acc., against : nu wið Grendel sceal, wið þam aglæcan, âna gehegan þing wið þyrse, 424-426;-- with, beside : ge-sät þâ wið sylfne..., mæg wið mæge, 1978-79.

    wiðer-gyld, st. n., compensation : nom. sg., 2052, [proper name?].

    wiðer-rähtes, adv., opposite, in front of , 3040.

    wiðre, st. n., resistance : gen. sg. wiðres ne trûwode, 2954.

    wig-weorðung, st. f., idol-worship, idolatry, sacrifice to idols : acc. pl. -weorðunga, 176.

wiht, st. f.: 1) wight, creature, demon : nom. sg. wiht unhælo (the demon of destruction , Grendel), 120; acc. sg. syllîcran wiht (the dragon), 3039.--2) thing, something, aught : nom. sg. w. negative, ne hine with dweleð (nor does aught check him), 1736; him wiht ne speów (it helped him naught), 2855; acc. sg. ne him þäs wyrmes wîg for wiht dyde (nor did he count the worm's warring for aught), 2349; ne meahte ic ... wiht gewyrcan (I could not do aught ...), 1661;--w. partitive gen.: nô ... wiht swylcra searo-niða, 581;--the acc. sg. = adv. like Germ. nicht : ne hie hûru wine-drihten wiht ne lôgon (did not blame their friendly lord aught), 863; so, ne wiht = naught, in no wise , 1084, 2602, 2858; nô wiht, 541; instr. sg. wihte (in aught, in any way), 1992; ne ... wihte (by no means), 186, 2278, 2688; wihte ne, 1515, 1996, 2465, 2924.--Comp.: â-wiht (âht = aught), äl-wiht, ô-wiht.

wil-cuma, w. m., one welcome (qui gratus advenit): nom. pl. wil-cuman Denigea leódum (welcome to the people of the Danes), 388; so, him (the lord of the Danes) wil-cuman, 394; wil-cuman Wedera leódum (welcome to the Geátas), 1895.

ge-wild, st. f., free-will ? dat. pl. nealles mid ge-weoldum (sponte, voluntarily , Bugge), 2223.

wil-deór (for wild-deór), st. n., wild beast : acc. pl. wil-deór, 1431.

wil-gesîð, st. m., chosen or willing companion : nom. pl. -ge-sîðas, 23.

wil-geofa, w. m., ready giver (= voti largitor: princely designation), joy-giver ?: nom. sg. wil-geofa Wedra leóda, 2901.

willa, w. m.: 1) will, wish, desire, sake : nom. sg. 627, 825; acc. sg. willan, 636, 1740, 2308, 2410; instr. sg. ânes willan (for the sake of one), 3078; so, 2590; dat. sg. tô willan, 1187, 1712; instr. pl. Willum (according to wish), 1822; sylfes willum, 2224, 2640; gen. pl. wilna, 1345.--2) desirable thing, valuable : gen. pl. wilna, 661, 951.

willan, aux. v., will : in pres. also shall (when the future action is depend. on one's free will): pres. sg. I. wille ic â-secgan (I will set forth, tell out), 344; so, 351, 427; ic tô sæ wille (I will to sea), 318; wylle, 948, 2149, 2513; sg. II. þu wylt, 1853; sg. III. he wile, 346, 446, 1050, 1182, 1833; wyle, 2865; wille, 442, 1004, 1185, 1395; ær he in wille (ere he will in , i.e. go or flee into the fearful sea), 1372; wylle, 2767; pl. I. we ... wyllað, 1819; pret. sg. I., III. wolde, 68, 154, 200, 646, 665, 739, 756, 797, 881, etc.; nô ic fram him wolde (i.e. fleótan), 543; so, swâ he hira mâ wolde (i.e. â-cwellan), 1056; pret. pl. woldon, 482, 2637, 3173; subj. pret., 2730.--Forms contracted w. negative: pres. sg. I. nelle (= ne + wille, I will not , nolo), 680, 2525(?); pret. sg. III. nolde (= ne + wolde), 792, 804, 813, 1524; w. omitted inf. þâ metod nolde, 707, 968; pret. subj. nolde, 2519.

wilnian, w. v., to long for, beseech : inf. wel bið þäm þe môt ... tô fäder fäðmum freoðo wilnian (well for him that may beseech protection in the Father's arms), 188.

wil-sîð, st. m., chosen journey : acc. sg. wil-sîð, 216.

ge-win, st. n.: 1) strife, struggle, enmity, conflict : acc. sg., 878; þâ hie ge-win drugon (endured strife), 799; under ýða ge-win (under the tumult of the waves), 1470; gen. sg. þäs ge-winnes weorc (misery for this strife), 1722.--2) suffering, oppression : nom. sg., 133, 191; acc. sg. eald ge-win, 1782.--Comp.: fyrn-, ýð-ge-win.

wîn-ärn, st. n., hall of hospitality, hall, wine-hall : gen. sg. wîn-ärnes, 655.

wind, st. m., wind, storm : nom. sg., 547, 1375, 1908; dat. instr. sg. winde, 217; wið winde, 1133.

windan, st. v.: 1) intrans., to wind, whirl : pret. sg. wand tô wolcnum wäl-fýra mæst, 1120.--2) w. acc., to twist, wind, curl : pret. pl. streámas wundon sund wið sande, 212; pret. part. wunden gold (twisted, spirally-twined, gold), 1194, 3135; instr. pl. wundnum (wundum, MS.) golde, 1383.

ät-windan, to wrest one's self from, escape : pret. sg. se þäm feónde ät-wand, 143.

be-windan, to wind with or round, clasp, surround, envelop (involvere): pret. sg. þe hit (the sword) mundum be-wand, 1462; pret. part. wîrum be-wunden (wound with wires) 1032; feorh ... flæsce be-wunden (flesh-enclosed), 2425; gâr ... mundum be-wunden (a spear grasped with the hands), 3023; iû-manna gold galdre be-wunden (spell-encircled gold), 3053; (âstâh ...) lêg wôpe be-wunden (uprose the flame mingled with a lament), 3147.

ge-windan, to writhe, get loose, escape : inf. wîdre ge-windan (to flee further), 764; pret. sg. on fleám ge-wand, 1002.

on-windan, to unwind, loosen : pres. sg. (þonne fäder) on-windeð wäl-râpas, 1611.

win-däg, st. m., day of struggle or suffering : dat. pl. on þyssum win-dagum (in these days of sorrow , i.e. of earthly existence), 1063.

wind-bland (blond), st. n., wind-roar : nom. sg., 3147.

wind-gereste, f., resting-place of the winds : acc. sg., 2457.

windig, adj., windy : acc. pl. windige (weallas, nässas), 572, 1359; windige weallas (wind geard weallas, MS.), 1225.

wine, st. m., friend, protector , especially the beloved ruler : nom. sg. wine Scyldinga, leóf land-fruma (Scyld), 30; wine Scyldinga (Hrôðgâr), 148, 1184. As vocative: mîn wine, 2048; wine mîn, Beówulf (Hunferð), 457, 530, 1705; acc. sg. holdne wine (Hrôðgâr), 376; wine Deniga, Scyldinga, 350, 2027; dat. sg. wine Scyldinga, 170; gen. sg. wines (Beówulf), 3097; acc. pl. wine, 21; dat. pl. Denum eallum, winum Scyldinga, 1419; gen. pl. winigea leásum, 1665; winia bealdor, 2568.--Comp.: freá-, freó-, gold-, gûð-, mæg-wine.

wine-dryhten, st. m., (dominus amicus), friendly lord, lord and friend : acc. sg. wine-drihten, 863, 1605; wine-dryhten, 2723, 3177; dat. sg. wine-drihtne, 360.

wine-geômor, adj., friend-mourning : nom. sg., 2240.

wine-leás, adj., friendless : dat. sg. wine-leásum, 2614.

wine-mæg, st. m., dear kinsman : nom. pl. wine-mâgas, 65.

ge-winna, w. m., striver, struggler, foe : comp. eald-, ealdor-gewinna.

winnan, st. v., to struggle, fight : pret. sg. III. wan âna wið eallum, 144; Grendel wan ... wið Hrôðgâr, 151; holm ... won wið winde (the sea fought with the wind : cf. wan wind endi water, Heliand, 2244), 1133; II. eart þu se Beówulf, se þe wið Brecan wunne, 506; pl. wið gode wunnon, 113; þær þâ graman wunnon (where the foes fought), 778.

wîn-reced, st. n., wine-hall, guest-hall, house for entertaining guests : acc. sg., 715, 994.

wîn-sele, st. m., the same, wine-hall : nom. sg., 772; dat. sg. wîn-sele, 696 (cf. Heliand Glossary, 369 [364]).

winter, st. m. n.: 1) winter : nom. sg., 1133, 1137; acc. sg. winter, 1129; gen. sg. wintres, 516.--2) year (counted by winters): acc. pl. fîftig wintru (neut.), 2210; instr. pl. wintrum, 1725, 2115, 2278; gen. pl. wintra, 147, 264, 1928, 2279, 2734, 3051.

wintre, adj., so many winters (old): in comp. syfan-wintre.

ge-wislîce, adv., certainly, undoubtedly : superl. gewislîcost, 1351.

wist, st. f., fundamental meaning = existentia , hence: 1) good condition, happiness, abundance : dat. sg. wunað he on wiste, 1736.--2) food, subsistence, booty : dat. sg. þâ wäs äfter wiste wôp up â-hafen (a cry was then uplifted after the meal , i.e. Grendel's meal of thirty men), 128.

wist-fyllo, st. f., fulness or fill of food, rich meal : gen. sg. wist-fylle, 735.

wit, st. n., (wit), understanding : nom. sg., 590.--Comp.: fyr-, in-wit.

ge-wit, st. n.: 1) consciousness . dat. sg. ge-weóld his ge-witte, 2704.--2) heart, breast : dat. sg. fýr unswîðor weóll (the fire surged less strongly from the dragon's breast), 2883.

wit, pers. pron. dual of we, we two , 535, 537, 539, 540, 544, 1187, etc. See unc, uncer.

wita, weota, w. m., counsellor, royal adviser ; pl., the king's council of nobles : nom. pl. witan, 779: gen. pl. witena, 157, 266, 937 weotena, 1099.-- Comp.: fyrn-, rûn-wita.

witan, pret.-pres. v., to wot, know . 1) w. depend. clause: pres. sg. I., III. wât, 1332, 2657; ic on Higelâce wât þät he ... (I know as to H., that he ...), 1831; so, god wât on mec þät ...(God knows of me, that ...), 2651; sg. II. þu wâst, 272; weak pret. sg. I., III. wiste, 822; wisse, 2340, 2726; pl. wiston, 799, 1605; subj. pres. I. gif ic wiste, 2520.--2) w. acc. and inf.: pres. sg. I. ic wât, 1864.--3) w. object, predicative part, or adj.: pret. sg. III. tô þäs he win-reced ... gearwost wisse, fättum fâhne, 716; so, 1310; wiste þäm ahlæcan hilde ge-binged, 647.--4) w. acc., to know : inf. witan, 252, 288; pret. sg. wisse, 169; wiste his fingra ge-weald on grames grâpum, 765; pl. II. wisson, 246; wiston, 181.

nât = ne + wât, I know not : 1) elliptically with hwylc, indef. pronoun = some or other : sceaða ic nât hwylc.--2) w. gen. and depend. clause: nât he þâra gôda, þät he me on-geán sleá, 682.

ge-witan, to know, perceive : inf. þäs þe hie gewis-lîcost ge-witan meahton, 1351.

be-witian. See be-weotian.

witig, adj., wise, sagacious : nom. sg. witig god, 686, 1057; witig drihten (God), 1555; wittig drihten, 1842.

ge-wittig, adj., conscious : nom. sg. 3095.

ge-witnian, w. v., to chastise, punish : wommum gewitnad (punished with plagues), 3074.

wîc, st. n., dwelling, house : acc. sg. wîc, 822, 2590;--often in pl. because houses of nobles were complex: dat. wîcum, 1305, 1613, 3084; gen. wîca, 125, 1126.

ge-wîcan, st. v., to soften, give way, yield (here chiefly of swords): pret. sg. ge-wâc, 2578, 2630.

wîc-stede, st. m., dwelling-place : nom. sg. 2463; acc. sg. wîc-stede, 2608.

wîd, adj., wide, extended : 1) space: acc. sg. neut. ofer wîd wäter, 2474; gen. sg. wîdan rîces, 1860; acc. pl. wîde sîðas, waroðas, 878, 1966.--2) temporal: acc. sg. wîdan feorh (acc. of time), 2015; dat. sg. tô wîdan feore, 934.

wîde, adv., widely, afar , 18, 74, 79, 266, 1404, 1589, 1960, etc.; wide cûð (widely, universally, known), 2136, 2924; so, underne wîde, 2914; wîde geond eorðan (over the whole earth, widely), 3100;--modifier of superl.: wreccena wîde mærost (the most famous of wanderers, exiles), 899.--Compar. wîdre, 764.

wîd-cûð, adj., widely known, very celebrated : nom. sg. neut., 1257; acc. sg. m. wîd-cûðne man (Beówulf), 1490; wîd-cûðne weán, 1992; wîd-cûðes (Hrôðgâr), 1043.

wîde-ferhð, st. m. n., (long life), great length of time : acc. sg. as acc. of time: wîde-ferhð (down to distant times, always), 703, 938; ealne wîde-ferhð, 1223.

wîd-floga, w. m., wide-flier (of the dragon): nom. sg., 2831; acc. sg. wîd-flogan, 2347.

wîd-scofen, pret. part., wide-spread ? causing fear far and wide ? 937.

wîd-weg, st. m., wide way, long journey : acc. pl. wîd-wegas, 841, 1705.

wîf, st. n., woman, lady, wife : nom. sg. freó-lîc wîf (Queen Wealhþeów), 616; wîf un-hýre (Grendel's mother), 2121; acc. sg. drihtlîce wîf (Finn's wife), 1159; instr. sg. mid þý wîfe (Hrôðgâr's daughter, Freáwaru), 2029; dat. sg. þam wîfe (Wealhþeów), 640; gen. sg. wîfes (as opposed to man), 1285; gen. pl. wera and wîfa, 994.--Comp.: aglæc-, mere-wîf.

wîf-lufe, w. f., wife-love, love for a wife, woman's love : nom. pl. wîf-lufan, 2066.

wîg, st. m.: 1) war, battle : nom. sg., 23, 1081, 2317, 2873; acc. sg., 686, 1084, 1248; dat. sg. wîge, 1338, 2630; as instr., 1085; (wigge, MS.), 1657, 1771; gen. sg. wîges, 65, 887, 1269.--2) valor, warlike prowess : nom. sg. wäs his môd-sefa manegum ge-cýðed, wîg and wîsdôm, 350; wîg, 1043; wîg ... eafoð and ellen, 2349; gen. sg. wîges, 2324.--Comp. fêðe-wîg.

wîga, w. m., warrior, fighter : nom. sg., 630; dat. pl. wîgum, 2396; gen. pl. wîgena, 1544, 1560, 3116.--Comp.: äsc-, byrn-, gâr-, gûð-, lind-, rand-, scyld-wîga.

wîgan, st. v., to fight : pres. sg. III. wîgeð, 600; inf., 2510.

wîgend, pres. part., fighter, warrior : nom. sg., 3100; nom. pl. wîgend, 1126, 1815, 3145; acc. pl. wîgend, 3025; gen. pl. wîgendra, 429, 900, 1973, 2338.--Comp. gârwîgend.

wîg-bealu, st. n., war-bale, evil contest : acc. sg., 2047.

wîg-bil, st. n., war-bill, battle-sword : nom. sg., 1608.

wîg-bord, st. n., war-board or shield : acc. sg., 2340.

wîg-cräft, st. m., war-power : acc. sg., 2954.

wîg-cräftig, adj., vigorous in fight, strong in war : acc. sg. wîg-cräftigne (of the sword Hrunting), 1812.

wîg-freca, w. m., war-wolf, war-hero : acc. sg. wîg-frecan, 2497; nom. pl. wîg-frecan, 1213.

wîg-fruma, w. m., war-chief or king : nom. sg., 665; acc. sg. wîg-fruman, 2262.

wîg-geatwe, st. f. pl., war-ornaments, war-gear : dat. pl. on wîg-geatwum (-getawum, MS.), 368.

wîg-ge-weorðad, pret. part., war-honored, distinguished in war , 1784? See Note.

wîg-gryre, st. m., war-horror or terror : nom. sg., 1285.

wîg-hete, st. m., war-hate, hostility : nom. sg., 2121.

wîg-heafola, w. m., war head-piece, helmet : acc. sg. wîg-heafolan, 2662.--Leo.

wîg-heáp, st. m., war-band : nom sg., 447.

wîg-hryre, st. m., war-ruin, slaughter, carnage : acc. sg., 1620.

wîg-sigor, st. m., war-victory : acc. sg., 1555.

wîg-sped, st. f.?, war-speed, success in war : gen. pl. wîg-spêda, 698.

wîn, st. n., wine : acc. sg., 1163, 1234; instr. wîne, 1468.

wîr, st. n., wire, spiral ornament of wire : instr. pl. wîrum, 1032; gen. pl. wîra, 2414.

wîs, adj., wise, experienced, discreet : nom. sg. m. wîs (in his mind, conscious), 3095; f. wîs, 1928; in w. form, se wîsa, 1401, 1699, 2330; acc. sg. þone wîsan, 1319; gen. pl. wîsra, 1414; w. gen. nom. sg. wîs wordcwida (wise of speech), 1846.

wîsa, w. m., guide, leader : nom. sg. werodes wîsa, 259.--Comp.: brim-, here-, hilde-wîsa.

wîscte. See wýscan.

wîs-dôm, st. m., wisdom, experience : nom. sg., 350; instr. sg. wîs-dôme, 1960.

wîse, w. f., fashion, wise, custom : acc. sg. (instr.) ealde wîsan (after ancient custom), 1866.

wîs-fäst, adj., wise, sagacious (sapientiâ firmus): nom. sg. f., 627.

wîs-hycgende, pres. part. wise-thinking, wise , 2717.

wîsian, w. v., to guide or lead to, direct, point out : 1) w. acc.: inf. heán wong wîsian, 2410; pret. sg. secg wîsade land-gemyrcu, 208.--2) w. dat.: pres. sg. I. ic eów wîsige (I shall guide you), 292, 3104; pret. sg. se þæm heaðo-rincum hider wîsade, 370; sôna him sele-þegn ... forð wîsade (the hall-thane led him thither forthwith , i.e. to his couch), 1796; stîg wîsode gumum ät-gädere, 320; so, 1664.--3) w. prep.?: pret. sg. þâ secg wîsode under Heorotes hrôf (when the warrior showed them the way under Heorot's roof , [but under H.'s hrôf depends rather on snyredon ätsomne]), 402.

wîtan, st. v., properly to look at; to look at with censure, to blame, reproach, accuse , w. dat. of pers. and acc. of thing: inf. for-þam me wîtan ne þearf waldend fira morðor-bealo mâga, 2742.

ät-wîtan, to blame, censure (cf. 'twit), w. acc. of thing: pret. pl. ät-witon weána dæl, 1151.

ge-wîtan, properly spectare aliquo; to go (most general verb of motion): 1) with inf. after verbs of motion: pret. sg. þanon eft ge-wât ... tô hâm faran, 123; so, 2570; pl. þanon eft gewiton ... mearum rîdan, 854. Sometimes with reflex, dat.: pres. sg. him þâ Scyld ge-wât ... fêran on freán wære, 26; gewât him ... rîdan, 234; so, 1964; pl. ge-witon, 301.--2) associated with general infinitives of motion and aim: imper. pl. ge-wîtað forð beran wæpen and gewædu, 291; pret. sg. ge-wât þâ neósian heán hûses, 115; he þâ fâg ge-wât ... man-dreám fleón, 1264; nyðer eft gewât dennes niósian, 3045; so, 1275, 2402, 2820. So, with reflex, dat.: him eft gewât ... hâmes niósan, 2388; so, 2950; pl. ge-witon, 1126.--3) without inf. and with prep, or adv.: pres. sg. III. þær firgen-streám under nässa genipu niðer ge-wîteð, 1361; ge-wîteð on sealman, 2461; inf. on flôdes æht feor ge-wîtan, 42; pret. sg. ge-wât, 217; him ge-wât, 1237, 1904; of lîfe, ealdre ge-wât (died), 2472, 2625; fyrst forð ge-wât (time went on), 210; him ge-wât ût of healle, 663; ge-wât him hâm, 1602; pret. part. dat. sg. me forð-ge-witenum (me defuncto, I dead), 1480.

ôð-wîtan, to blame, censure, reproach : inf. ne þorfte him þâ lean ôð-wîtan mon on middan-gearde, 2997.

wlanc, wlonc, adj., proud, exulting : nom. sg. wlanc, 341; w. instr. æse wlanc (proud of, exulting in, her prey, meal), 1333; wlonc, 331; w. gen. mâðm-æhta wlonc (proud of the treasures), 2834; gen. sg. wlonces, 2954.--Comp. gold-wlanc.

wlâtian, w. v., to look or gaze out, forth : pret. sg. se þe ær ... feor wlâtode, 1917.

wlenco, st. f., pride, heroism : dat. sg. wlenco, 338, 1207; wlence, 508.

wlite, st. m. form, noble form, look, beauty : nom. sg., 250.

wlite-beorht, adj., beauteous, brilliant in aspect : acc. sg. wlite-beorhtne wang, 93.

wlite-seón, st. n. f., sight, spectacle : acc. sg., 1651.

wlitig, adj., beautiful, glorious, fair in form : acc. sg. wlitig (sweord), 1663.

wlîtan, st. v., to see, look, gaze : pret. sg. he äfter recede wlât (looked along the hall), 1573; pret. pl. on holm wliton (looked on the sea), 1593; wlitan on Wîglâf, 2853.

geond-wlîtan, w. acc., to examine, look through, scan : inf. wräte giond-wlîtan, 2772.

woh-bogen, pret. part., (bent crooked), crooked, twisted : nom. sg. wyrm woh-bogen, 2828.

wolcen, st. n. m., cloud (cf. welkin): dat. pl. under wolcnum (under the clouds, on earth), 8, 652, 715, 1771; tô wolcnum, 1120, 1375.

wollen-teár, adj., tear-flowing, with flowing tears : nom. pl. wollen-teáre, 3033.

wom. See wam.

won. See wan.

worc. See weorc.

word, st. n.: 1) word, speech : nom. sg., 2818; acc. sg. þät word, 655, 2047; word, 315, 341, 390, 871, 2552; instr. sg. worde, 2157; gen. sg. wordes, 2792; nom. pl. þâ word, 640; word, 613; acc. pl. word (of an alliterative song), 871; instr. pl, wordum, 176, 366, 627, 875, 1101, 1173, 1194, 1319, 1812, etc.; ge-saga him wordum (tell them in words, expressly), 388. The instr. wordum accompanies biddan, þancian, be-wägnan, secgan, hêrgan, to emphasize the verb, 176, 627, 1194, 2796, 3177; gen. pl. worda, 289, 398, 2247, 2263(?), 3031.--2) command, order : gen. sg. his wordes geweald habban (to rule, reign), 79; so, instr. pl. wordum weóld, 30.--Comp.: beót-, gylp-, meðel-, þryð-word.

word-cwide, st. m., (word-utterance), speech : acc. pl. word-cwydas, 1842; dat. pl. word-cwydum, 2754; gen. pl. word-cwida, 1846.

word-gid, st. m, speech, saying : acc. sg. word-gyd, 3174.

word-hord, st. n., word-hoard, treasury of speech, mouth : acc. sg. word-hord on-leác (unlocked his word-hoard , opened his mouth, spoke), 259.

word-riht, st. n., right speech, suitable word : gen. pl. Wîglâf maðelode word-rihta fela, 2632.

worð-mynd. See weorð-mynd.

worðig (for weorðig), st. m., palace, estate, court : acc. sg. on worðig (into the palace), 1973.

worn, st. n., multitude, number : acc. sg. worn eall (very many), 3095; wintra worn (many years), 264; þonne he wintrum frôd worn ge-munde (when he old in years thought of their number), 2115. Used with fela to strengthen the meaning: nom. acc. sg. worn fela, 1784; hwät þu worn fela ... spræce (how very much thou hast spoken!), 530; so, eal-fela eald-gesegena worn, 871; gen. pl. worna fela, 2004, 2543.

woruld, worold, st. f., humanity, world, earth : nom. sg. eal worold, 1739; acc. sg. in worold (wacan) (to be born, come into the world), 60; worold oflætan, of-gifan (die), 1184, 1682; gen. sg. worolde, 951, 1081, 1388, 1733; worulde, 2344; his worulde ge-dâl (his separation from the world, death), 3069; worolde brûcan (to enjoy life, live), 1063; worlde, 2712.

worold-âr, st. f., worldly honor or dignity : acc. sg. worold-âre, 17.

woruld-candel, st. f., world-candle, sun : nom. sg., 1966.

worold-cyning, st. m., world king, mighty king : nom. sg., 3182; gen. pl. worold-cyninga, 1685.

woruld-ende, st. m., world's end : acc. sg., 3084.

worold-ræden, st. f., usual course, fate of the world, customary fate : dat. sg. worold-rædenne, 1143?

wôp, st. m., (whoop), cry of grief, lament : nom. sg., 128; acc. sg. wôp, 786; instr. sg. wôpe, 3147.

wracu, st. f., persecution, vengeance, revenge : nom. sg. wracu (MS, uncertain), 2614; acc. sg. wräce, 2337.--Comp.: gyrn-, nýd-wracu.

wraðu, st. f., protection, safety : in comp. lîf-wraðu.

wrâð, adj., wroth, furious, hostile : acc. sg. neut. wrâð, 319; dat. sg. wrâðum, 661, 709; gen. pl. wrâðra, 1620.

wrâðe, adv., contemptibly, disgracefully , 2873.

wrâð-lîce, adv., wrathfully, hostilely (in battle), 3063.

wrâsn, st. f., circlet of gold for the head, diadem, crown : in comp. freá-wrâsn.

wräc-lâst, st. m., exile-step, exile, banishment : acc. sg. wräc-lâstas träd (trod exile-steps, wandered in exile), 1353.

wräc-mäcg, st. m., exile, outcast : nom. pl. wräc-mäcgas, 2380.

wräc-sîð, st. m., exile-journey, banishment, exile, persecution : acc. sg., 2293; dat. sg. -sîðum, 338.

wrät, st. f., ornament, jewel : acc. pl. wräte (wræce, MS.), 2772, 3061; instr. pl. wrättum, 1532; gen. pl. wrätta, 2414.

wrät-lîc, adj.: 1) artistic, ornamental; valuable : acc. sg. wrät-lîcne wundur-mâððum, 2174; wrät-lîc wæg-sweord, 1490; wîg-bord wrät-lîc, 2340.--
2) wondrous, strange : acc. sg. wrät-lîcne wyrm [from its rings or spots?], 892; wlite-seón wrät-lîc, 1651.

wræc, st. f., persecution ; hence, wretchedness, misery : nom. sg., 170; acc. sg. wræc, 3079.

wrecan, st. v. w. acc.: 1) to press, force : pret. part. þær wäs Ongenþeó ... on bîd wrecen, 2963.--2) to drive out, expel : pret. sg. ferh ellen wräc, 2707.--3) to wreak or utter : gid, spel wrecan (to utter words or songs); subj. pres. sg. III. he gyd wrece, 2447; inf. wrecan spel ge-râde, 874; word-gyd wrecan, 3174; pret. sg. gyd äfter wräc, 2155; pres. part. þær wäs ... gid wrecen, 1066.--4) to avenge, punish : subj. pres. þät he his freónd wrece, 1386; inf. wolde hire mæg wrecan, 1340; so, 1279, 1547; pres. part. wrecend (an avenger), 1257; pret. sg. wräc Wedera nîð, 423; so, 1334, 1670.

â-wrecan, to tell, recount : pret. sg. ic þis gid be þe â-wräc (I have told this tale for thee), 1725; so, 2109.

for-wrecan, w. acc., to drive away, expel; carry away : inf. þý läs him ýða þrym wudu wyn-suman for-wrecan meahte (lest the force of the waves might carry away the winsome ship), 1920; pret. sg. he hine feor for-wräc ... man-cynne fram, 109.

ge-wrecan, w. acc., to avenge, wreak vengeance upon, punish : pret. sg. ge-wräc, 107, 2006; he ge-wräc (i.e. hit, this) cealdum cear-sîðum, 2396; he hine sylfne ge-wräc (avenged himself), 2876; pl. ge-wræcan, 2480; pret. part. ge-wrecen, 3063.

wrecca, w. m., (wretch), exile, adventurer, wandering soldier, hero : nom. sg. wrecca (Hengest), 1138; gen. pl. wreccena wîde mærost (Sigemund), 899.

wreoðen-hilt, adj., wreathen-hilted, with twisted hilt : nom. sg., 1699.

wridian, w. v., to flourish, spring up : pret. sg. III. wridað, 1742.

wriða, w. m., band : in comp. beág-wriða (bracelet), 2019.

wrixl, st. n., exchange, change : instr. sg. wyrsan wrixle (in a worse way, with a worse exchange), 2970.

ge-wrixle, st. n., exchange, arrangement, bargain : nom. sg. ne wäs þät ge-wrixle til (it was not a good arrangement, trade), 1305.

wrixlan, w. v., to exchange : inf. wordum wrixlan (to exchange words, converse), 366; 875 (tell).

wrîðan, st. v. w. acc.: 1) to bind, fasten, wreathe together : inf. ic hine (him, MS.) ... on wäl-bedde wrîðan þôhte, 965.--2) to bind up (a wounded person, a wound): pret. pl. þâ wæron monige þe his mæg wriðon, 2983. See hand-gewriðen.

wrîtan, st. v., to incise, engrave : pret. part. on þäm (hilte) wäs ôr writen fyrn-gewinnes (on which was engraved the origin of an ancient struggle), 1689.

for-wrîtan, to cut to pieces or in two : pret. sg. for-wrât Wedra helm wyrm on middan, 2706.

wrôht, st. m. f., blame, accusation, crime ; here strife, contest, hostility : nom. sg., 2288, 2474, 2914.

wudu, st. m., wood : 1) material, timber : nom. pl. wudu, 1365; hence, the wooden spear : acc. pl. wudu, 398.--2) forest, wood : acc. sg. wudu, 1417.-- 3) wooden ship : nom. sg. 298; acc. sg. wudu, 216, 1920.--Comp.: bæl-, bord-, gamen-, heal-, holt-, mägen-, sæ-, sund-, þrec-wudu.

wudu-rêc, st. m., wood-reek or smoke : nom. sg., 3145.

wuldor, st. n., glory : nom. sg. kyninga wuldor (God), 666; gen. sg. wuldres wealdend, 17, 183, 1753; wuldres hyrde, 932, (designations of God).

wuldor-cyning, st. m., king of glory, God . dat. sg. wuldur-cyninge, 2796

wuldor-torht, adj., glory-bright, brilliant, clear : acc. pl. wuldor-torhtan weder, 1137.

wulf, st. m., wolf : acc. sg., 3028.

wulf-hlið, st. n., wolf-slope, wolf's retreat, slope whereunder wolves house : acc. pl. wulf-hleoðu, 1359.

wund, st. f., wound : nom. sg., 2712, 2977; acc. sg. wunde, 2532, 2907; acc. sg. wunde, 2726; instr. pl. wundum, 1114, 2831, 2938.--Comp. feorh-wund.

wund, adj., wounded, sore : nom. sg., 2747; dat. sg. wundum, 2754; nom. pl. wunde, 565, 1076.

wunden-feax, adj., curly-haired (of a horse's mane): nom. sg., 1401.

wunden-heals, adj., with twisted or curved neck or prow : nom. sg. wudu wunden-hals (the ship), 298.

wunden-heorde?, curly-haired ?: nom. sg. f., 3153.

wunden-mæl, adj., damascened, etched, with wavy ornaments (?): nom. sg. neut., 1532 (of a sword).

wunden-stefna, w. m. curved prow, ship : nom. sg., 220.

wundor, st. n.: 1) wonder, wonderwork : nom. sg., 772, 1725; wundur, 3063; acc. sg. wundor, 841; wunder, 932; wundur, 2760, 3033, 3104; dat. sg. wundre, 932; instr. pl. wundrum (wondrously), 1453, 2688; gen. pl. wundra, 1608.-- 2) portent, monster : gen. pl. wundra, 1510.--Comp.: hand-, nîð-, searo-wundor.

wundor-bebod, st. n., wondrous command, strange order : instr. pl. -bebodum, 1748.

wundor-deáð, st. m., wonder-death, strange death : instr. sg. wundor deáðe, 3038.

wundor-fät, st. n., wonder-vat, strange vessel : dat. pl. of wundor-fatum (from wondrous vessels), 1163.

wundor-lîc, adj., wonder like, remarkable : nom. sg., 1441.

wundor-mâðöum, st. m., wonder-jewel, wonderful treasure : acc. sg., 2174.

wundor-smið, st. m., wonder-smith, skilled smith, worker of marvellous things : gen. pl. wundor-smiða geweorc (the ancient giant's sword), 1682.

wundor-seón, st. f., wondrous sight : gen. pl. wunder-sióna, 996.

wunian, w. v.: 1) to stand, exist, remain : pres. sg. III. þenden þær wunað on heáh-stede hûsa sêlest (as long as the best of houses stands there on the high place), 284; wunað he on wiste (lives in plenty), 1736; inf. on sele wunian (to remain in the hall), 3129; pret. sg. wunode mid Finne (remained with F.), 1129.-- 2) w. acc. or dat., to dwell in, to inhabit, to possess : pres. sg. III. wunað wäl-reste (holds his death-bed), 2903; inf. wäter-egesan wunian scolde..., streámas, 1261; wîcum wunian, 3084; w. prep.: pres. sg. Higelâc þær ät hâm wunað, 1924.

ge-wunian, w. acc.: 1) to inhabit : inf. ge-[wunian], 2276.--2) to remain with, stand by : subj. pres. þät hine on ylde eft ge-wunigen wil-ge-sîðas, 22.

wurðan. See weorðan.

wuton, v. from wîtan, used as interj., let us go! up! w. inf.: wutun gangan tô (let us go to him!), 2649; uton hraðe fêran! 1391; uton nu êfstan, 3102.

wylf, st. f., she-wolf : in comp. brim-wylf.

wylm, st. m., surge, surf, billow : num. sg. flôdes wylm, 1765; dat. wintres wylme (with winter's flood), 516; acc. sg. þurh wäteres wylm, 1694; acc. pl. heortan wylmas, 2508.--Comp.: breóst-, brim-, byrne-, cear-, fýr-, heaðo-, holm-, sæ-, sorh-wylm. See wälm.

wyn, st. f., pleasantness, pleasure, joy, enjoyment : acc. sg. mæste ... worolde wynne (the highest earthly joy), 1081; eorðan wynne (earth-joy, the delightful earth), 1731; heofenes wynne (heaven's joy , the rising sun), 1802; hearpan wynne (harp-joy, the pleasant harp), 2108; þät he ... ge-drogen häfde eorðan wynne (that he had had his earthly joy), 2728; dat. sg. weorod wäs on wynne, 2015; instr. pl. mägenes wynnum (in joy of strength), 1717; so, 1888.--Comp.: êðel-, hord-, lîf-, lyft-, symbel-wyn.

wyn-leás, adj., joyless : acc. sg. wyn-leásne wudu, 1417; wyn-leás wîc, 822.

wyn-sum, adj., winsome, pleasant : acc. sg. wudu wyn-suman (the ship), 1920; nom. pl. word wæron wyn-sume, 613.

wyrcan, v. irreg.: 1) to do, effect , w. acc.: inf. (wundor) wyrcan, 931.--2) to make, create , w. acc.: pret. sg. þät se äl-mihtiga eorðan worh[te], 92; swâ hine (the helmet) worhte wæpna smið, 1453.--3) to gain, win, acquire , w. gen.: subj. pres. wyrce, se þe môte, dômes ær deáðe, 1388.

be-wyrcan, to gird, surround : pret. pl. bronda betost wealle be-worhton, 3163.

ge-wyrcan: 1) intrans., to act, behave : inf. swâ sceal geong guma gôde gewyrcean ... on fäder wine þät ... (a young man shall so act with benefits towards his father's friends that ...), 20.--2) w. acc., to do, make, effect, perform : inf. ne meahte ic ät hilde mid Hruntinge wiht ge-wyrcan, 1661; sweorde ne meahte on þam aglæcan ... wunde ge-wyrcean, 2907; pret. sg. ge-worhte, 636, 1579, 2713; pret. part. acc. ic þâ leóde wât ... fäste ge-worhte. 1865.--3) to make, construct : inf. (medo-ärn) ge-wyrcean, 69; (wîg-bord) ge-wyrcean, 2338; (hlæw) ge-wyrcean, 2803; pret. pl. II. ge-worhton, 3097; III. ge-worhton, 3158; pret. part. ge-worht, 1697.--4) to win, acquire : pres. sg. ic me mid Hruntinge dôm ge-wyrce, 1492.

Wyrd, st. f., Weird (one of the Norns, guide of human destiny; mostly weakened down = fate, providence): nom. sg., 455, 477, 572, 735, 1206, 2421, 2527, 2575, 2815; acc. sg. wyrd, 1057, 1234; gen. pl. wyrda, 3031. (Cf. Weird Sisters of Macbeth.)

wyrdan, w. v., to ruin, kill, destroy : pret. sg. he tô lange leóde mine wanode and wyrde, 1338.

â-wyrdan, w. v., to destroy, kill : pret. part.: äðeling monig wundum â-wyrded, 1114.

wyrðe, adj., noble; worthy, honored, valued : acc. sg. m. wyrðne (ge-dôn) (to esteem worthy), 2186; nom. pl. wyrðe, 368; compar. nom. sg. rîces wyrðra (worthier of rule), 862.--Comp. fyrd-wyrðe. See weorð.

wyrgen, st, f., throttler [cf. sphinx], she-wolf ; in comp. grund-wyrgen.

ge-wyrht, st. n., work; desert ; in comp. eald-gewyrht, 2658.

wyrm, st. m., worm, dragon, drake : nom. sg., 898, 2288, 2344, 2568, 2630, 2670, 2746, 2828; acc. sg. wyrm, 887, 892, 2706, 3040, 3133; dat. sg. wyrme, 2308, 2520; gen. wyrmes, 2317, 2349, 2760, 2772, 2903; acc. pl. wyrmas, 1431.

wyrm-cyn, st. m., worm-kin, race of reptiles, dragons : gen. sg. wyrm-cynnes fela, 1426.

wyrm-fâh, adj., dragon-ornamented, snake-adorned (ornamented with figures of dragons, snakes, etc.: cf. Dietrich in Germania X., 278): nom. sg. sweord ... wreoðen-hilt and wyrm-fâh, 1699.

wyrm-hord, st. n., dragon-hoard : gen. pl. wyrm-horda, 2223.

for-wyrnan, w. v., to refuse, reject : subj. pres. II. þät þu me nô for-wyrne, þät... (that thou refuse me not that ...), 429; pret. sg. he ne for-wyrnde woroldrædenne, 1143.

ge-wyrpan, w. v. reflex., to refresh one's self, recover : pret. sg. he hyne ge-wyrpte, 2977.

wyrpe, st. m., change : acc. sg. äfter weá-spelle wyrpe ge-fremman (after the woe-spell to bring about a change of things), 1316.

wyrsa, compar. adj., worse : acc. sg. neut. þät wyrse, 1740; instr. sg. wyrsan wrixle, 2970; gen. sg. wyrsan geþinges, 525; nom. acc. pl. wyrsan wîg-frecan, 1213, 2497.

wyrt, st. f., [-wort], root : instr. pl. wudu wyrtum fäst, 1365.

wýscan, w. v., to wish, desire : pret. sg. wîscte (rihde, MS.) þäs yldan (wished to delay that or for this reason , 2440, 1605(?). See Note.

Y

yfel, st n., evil : gen. pl. yfla, 2095.

yldan, w. v., to delay, put off : inf. ne þät se aglæca yldan þôhte, 740; weard wine-geômor wîscte þäs yldan, þät he lytel fäc long-gestreóna brûcan môste, 2240.

ylde, st. m. pl., men : dat. pl. yldum, 77, 706, 2118; gen. pl. ylda, 150, 606, 1662. See elde.

yldest. See eald.

yldo, st. f., age (senectus), old age : nom. sg., 1737, 1887; atol yldo, 1767; dat. sg. on ylde, 22.--2) age (ætas), time, era : gen. sg. yldo bearn, 70. See eldo.

yldra. See eald.

ylf, st. f., elf (incubus, alp): nom. pl. ylfe, 112.

ymb, prep. w. acc.: 1) local, around, about, at, upon : ymb hine (around, with, him), 399. With prep, postponed: hine ymb, 690; ymb brontne ford (around the seas, on the high sea), 568; ymb þâ gif-healle (around the gift-hall, throne-hall), 839; ymb þäs helmes hrôf (around the helm's roof, crown), 1031.--2) temporal, about, after : ymb ân-tîd ôðres dôgores (about the same time the next day), 219; ymb âne niht (after a night), 135.--3) causal, about, on account of, for, owing to : (frînan) ymb þînne sîð (on account of, concerning?, thy journey), 353; hwät þu ... ymb Brecan spræce (hast spoken about B.), 531; so, 1596, 3174; nâ ymb his lîf cearað (careth not for his life), 1537; so, 450; ymb feorh sacan, 439; sundor-nytte beheóld ymb aldor Dena, 669; ymb sund (about the swimming, the prize for swimming), 507.

ymbe, I. prep. w. acc. = ymb: 1) local, 2884, 3171; hlæw oft ymbe hwearf (prep. postponed), 2297. 2) causal, 2071, 2619.--II. adv., around : him ... ymbe, 2598.

ymb-sittend, pres. part., neighbor gen. pl. ymb-sittendra, 9.

ymbe-sittend, the same: nom. pl. ymbe-sittend, 1828; gen. pl. ymbe-sittendra, 2735.

yppe, w. f., high seat, dais, throne : dat. sg. eode ... tô yppan, 1816.

yrfe, st. n., bequest, legacy : nom. sg., 3052.

yrfe-lâf, st. f., sword left as a bequest : acc. sg. yrfe-lâfe, 1054; instr. sg. yrfe-lâfe, 1904.

yrfe-weard, st. m., heir, son : nom. sg., 2732; gen. sg. yrfe-weardes, 2454. (-as, MS.)

yrmðo, st. f., misery, shame, wretchedness : acc. sg. yrmðe, 1260, 2006.

yrre, st. n., anger, ire, excitement : acc. sg. godes yrre, 712; dat. sg, on yrre, 2093.

yrre, adj., angry, irate, furious : nom. sg. yrre oretta (Beówulf), 1533; þegn yrre (the same), 1576; gäst yrre (Grendel), 2074; nom. pl. yrre, 770. See eorre.

yrringa, adv., angrily, fiercely , 1566, 2965.

yrre-môd, adj., wrathful-minded, wild : nom. sg., 727.

ys, he is . See wesan.

Ý

ýð (O.H.G. unda), st. f., wave; sea : nom. pl. ýða, 548; acc. pl. ýðe, 46, 1133, 1910; dat. pl. ýðum, 210, 421, 534, 1438, 1908; ýðum weallan (to surge with waves), 515, 2694; gen. pl. ýða, 464, 849, 1209, 1470, 1919.--Comp: flôd-, lîg-, wäter-ýð.

ýðan, w. v., to ravage, devastate, destroy : pret. sg. ýðde eotena cyn, 421 (cf. îðende = depopulating , Bosworth, from Ælfric's Glossary; pret. ýðde, Wanderer, 85).

ýðe. See eáðe.

ýðe-lîce, adv., easily : ýðe-lîce he eft â-stôd (he easily arose afterwards), 1557.

ýð-gebland, st. n., mingling or surging waters, water-tumult : nom. sg. -geblond, 1374, 1594; nom. pl. -gebland, 1621.

ýð-gewin, st. n., strife with the sea, wave-struggle, rushing of water : dat. sg. ýð-gewinne, 2413; gen. sg. -gewinnes, 1435.

ýð-lâd, st. f., water-journey, sea-voyage : nom. pl. ýð-lâde, 228.

ýð-lâf, st. f., water-leaving, what is left by the water (undarum reliquiae), shore : dat. sg. be ýð-lâfe, 566.

ýð-lida, w. m., wave-traverser, ship : acc. sg. ýð-lidan, 198.

ýð-naca, w. m., sea-boat : acc. sg. [ýð-]nacan, 1904.

ýð-gesêne. See êð-gesýne.

ýwan, w. v. w. acc., to show : pret. sg. an-sýn ýwde (showed itself, appeared), 2835. See eáwan, eówan.

ge-ýwan, w. acc. of thing, dat. of pers., to lay before, offer : inf., 2150.

GLOSSARY TO FINNSBURH

âbrecan, st. v., to shatter : part. his byrne âbrocen wære (his byrnie was shattered).

ânyman, st. v., to take, take away .

bân-helm, st. m., bone-helmet; skull , [shield , Bosw.].

buruh-þelu, st. f., castle-floor .

cêlod, part, (adj.?), keeled , i.e. boat-shaped or hollow.

dagian, w. v., to dawn : ne þis ne dagiað eástan (this is not dawning from the east).

deór-môd, adj., brave in mood : deór-môd häleð.

driht-gesîð, st m., companion, associate .

eástan, adv., from the east .

eorð-bûend, st. m., earth-dweller, man .

fêr, st. m. fear, terror .

fýren, adj., flaming, afire : nom. f. swylce eal Finns-buruh fýrenu wære (as if all Finnsburh were afire).

gehlyn, st. n., noise, tumult .

gellan, st. v., to sing (i.e. ring or resound): pres. sg. gylleð græg-hama (the gray garment [byrnie] rings); (the gray wolf yelleth ?).

genesan, st. v., to survive, recover from : pret. pl. þâ wîgend hyra wunda genæson (the warriors were recovering from their wounds).

gold-hladen, adj., laden with gold (wearing heavy gold ornaments).

græg-hama, w. m., gray garment, mail-coat ; (wolf ?--Brooke).

gûð-wudu, st. m., war-wood, spear .

häg-steald, st. m., one who lives in his lord's house, a house-carl.

heaðo-geong, adj., young in war.

here-sceorp, st. n., war-dress, coat of mail .

hleoðrian, w. v., to speak, exclaim : pret. sg. hleoðrode ... cyning (the prince exclaimed).

hræw, st. n., corpse .

hrôr, adj., strong : here-sceorpum hrôr (strong [though it was] as armor , Bosw.).

lac (lað?)? for flacor, fluttering?

oncweðan, st. v., to answer : pres. sg. scyld scefte oncwyð (the shield answers the spear).

onwacnian, w. v., to awake, arouse one's self : imper. pl. onwacnigeað..., wîgend mine (awake, my warriors!).

sceft (sceaft), st. m., spear, shaft .

sealo-brûn, adj., dusky-brown .

sige-beorn, st. m., victorious hero, valiant warrior .

swäðer (swâ hwäðer), pron., which of two, which .

swân, st. m., swain, youth; warrior .

sweart, adj., swart, black .

Beowulf: Scholar's Edition

swêt, adj., sweet : acc. m. swêtne medo ... forgyldan (requite the sweet mead, i.e. repay, by prowess in battle, the bounty of their chief).

swurd-leóma, w. m., sword-flame, flashing of swords .

þyrl, adj., pierced, cloven .

undearninga, adv., without concealment, openly .

wandrian, w. v., to fly about, hover : pret. sg. hräfn wandrode (the raven hovered).

waðol, st. m., the full moon [Grein]; [adj., wandering , Bosw.].

wäl-sliht (-sleaht), st. m., combat, deadly struggle : gen. pl. wäl-slihta gehlyn (the din of combats)

weâ-dæd, st. f., deed of woe : nom. pl. ârisað weâ-dæda.

witian (weotian), w. v., to appoint, determine : part. þe is ... witod.

wurðlîce (weorðlîce), adv., worthily, gallantly : compar. wurð-lîcor.

wäg, weg, st. m., way .

CORRECTIONS MADE TO THE SOURCE TEXT:

ARGUMENT, recals = recalls

POEM:
    ll. 131, 737 þryð-swyð = þrýð-swýð
    l. 256 ôfest = ôfost
    l. 303 sciónon = scionon
    l. 706 buton = bûton
    l. 1115 ât = ät
    l. 1133 wîð = wið
    ll. 1304, 1560, 1616 missing caesuras supplied
    l. 1436 here-sträl = here-stræl
    l. 1642 feôwer- = feówer
    l. 1747 sträle = stræle
    l. 1828 þywað = þýwað
    l. 1926 betlic = betlîc
    l. 2224 gesceód = gesceôd
    ll. 2288, 3036 wâs = wäs
    l. 2453 to = tô
    l. 2503 Huga = Hûga
    l. 2586 niðe = nîðe
    l. 2587 sið = sîð
    l. 2684 irenna = îrenna
    l. 2915 Hugas = Hûgas
    l. 2956 heáðo-liðendum = heaðo-lîðendum
    l. 3000 Þât = Þät; feônd- = feónd-
    l. 3056 sóð = sôð
    l. 3137 Hrônes = Hrones
    list of names, under:
     Dene, Scedenîgge = Scedenigge
     Eádgils, Ohthere = Ôhthere
     Freáwaru, Freawaru = Freáwaru
     Hrôðgâr, Hrôð-gâre = Hrôðgâre
     Hygelac, Hæreð = Häreð
    NOTES for
    l. 31, of l. 31 = of l. 30
    l. 1441, wôð- = wæg-
    l. 1916, leôfra = leófra

GLOSSARY, under headword
    äðele, Beowulf's = Beówulf's
    ân, gehwilces = gehwylces
    æg-hwâ, ægh-wäs = æghwäs

ät-beran, beadolâce = beadulâce
beadu-lâc, beado- = beadu- (twice)
beág, beages = beáges
beorh, heáford- = heáfod
beódan, leodum = leódum
beón, cwênlic = cwênlîc
biddan, bliðne = blîðne
bitter, sträle = stræle
ge-bîdan, therefor = therefore
on-bîdan, earfôðlîce = earfoðlîce
brecan, lêtdse = lêt se
burne, of of = of
bûtan, swîce = swice
cempa, Huga = Hûga
ge-ceósan, usic = ûsic
on-cirran, wealdendas = wealdendes
corðer, þä = þâ
cunnan, þeáwe = þeáw
cûð, wîð- = wîd-
dôgor, gehwam = gehwâm
dôn, ymbsittend = ymbesittend; hettend = hetend; þywað = þýwað
drîfan, feoran = feorran
dryhten, freáh- = freá-
dryht-scipe, drihtscipe = drihtscype
ge-dýgan, wräcsið = wræcsîð
eal, oncyððe = oncýððe
ealdor, heresträl = herestræl
eácen-cräftig, iúmanna = iúmonna
eofor-spreót, hocyhtum = hôcyhtum
eorlîc, eorlic [ellen] = eorlîc
fâh, wâldreóre = wäldreóre
ôð-ferian, panon = þonan
fela, maððum- = mâððum
fêran, wäre = wære
feónd, feonda = feónda
fleón, fenhôpu = fenhopu
floga, wîð- = wîd-
folc-toga, Hrôðgar = Hrôðgâr
for, wonhydum = wonhýdum; handgeweorc = hondgeweorc
fôt-gemearc, long = lang
ge-frignan, þeodcyninga = þeódcyninga
ge-fyrðran, fratwum = frätwum
ge-fýsan, to sêcanne = tô sêceanne
gân, swa = swâ; [or] giong = gióng; flore = flôre; sîttan = sittan
ge-gan, Wîglaf = Wîglâf
gâr-wîga, Wîglaf = Wîglâf
gäst, fêde- = fêðe-
gegn-cwide, þinra = þînra
ge-gyrwan, yðlidan = ýðlidan
geóc, gást = gâst

geômore-lîc, [bið] geômorlic = geômorlîc
for-gildan, therefor = therefore
gold-wlanc, guðrinc = gûðrinc
grêtan, walgæst = wälgæst
grim, searo-grimm = searo-grim
habban, gecorene = gecorone
wið-habban, winsele = wînsele
hatan, sæliðend = sælîðend
hatian, guð-sceaða = gûð-sceaða
hâr, heâre = heáre
here-stræl, -sträl = stræl
heard, -sträl = -stræl; regen- = regn-
heorte, starc- = stearc
heoro-dreór, heoro-dreore (citation) = heoro-dreóre
hlið, hliðu = hliðo (twice)
hôp, hôp = hop (twice)
hreow, þât = þät
hrôf, geseáh = geseah
hwîl, seo = seó
hýran, æghwilc = æghwylc
inne, abeád = âbeád
îren, drihtlîc = dryhtlîc
lâð, gewiðru = gewidru; scynnum = scinnum
be-leán, beleân = beleán
mêtan, Aescheres = Äscheres
mearcian, môrhôpu = môrhopu
ge-mearian, hwam = hwâm
morðor-bed, stred = strêd
môd, stið- = stîð-
nænig, horð-mâðum – hord-mâððum
on, heáðe = heoðe; willen = willan
ræd, fæst- = fäst
reccan, hu = hû
rîdan, gealgan = galgan
sang, -leasne = leásne
sceapan, Hugas = Hûgas (twice)
scânan, sciónon = scionon
scînan, scînon = scinon
secg, synnigne = sinnigne
ge-sêcan, -cyððe = cýððe
ge-sîgan, ätsäcce = ät säcce
ge-sleán, ge-slôgan = ge-slôgon
standan, sträl = stræl
stapan, furðor = furður
ge-steppan, Ohtheres = Ôhteres
stincan, þä = þâ
styrian, ge-wiðru = ge-widru
sweord, maððum- = mâððum
ge-swîcan, þeodne = þeódne

Beowulf: Scholar's Edition

    teón (w. v.), naläs = nalas; teodan = teódan
    tô, hälum = hælum; sitte = site; Eofore = Jofore
    ge-trûwan, -wäre = wære
    ge-twæfan, ôðð e = oðð e
    þær, snotera = snottra
    þe, gimfästan = ginfästan
    of-þincan, gehwam = gehwâm
    ge-þolian, þât = þät
    þu, sælran = selran
    þûsend, seófon = seofan
    un-heóre, -speru = -sporu
    ûs, æg-hwilc = æg-hwylc
    wacan, wôcon = wôcun
    werian, beaduscrûd = beaduscrûda
    be-werian, scynnum = scinnum
    wên, orlêg = orleg; ôr-wena = or-wêna
    weorðian, leôde = leóde
    willa, wyllum = willum
    wilnian, fäðer = fäder
    nât, hwilc = hwylc (twice)
    ge-wîtan, wäre = wære

www.ingramcontent.com/pod-product-compliance
Lightning Source LLC
Chambersburg PA
CBHW071947070526
44583CB00015B/1093